Lecture Notes in Computer Sci

T0238171

Commenced Publication in 1973
Founding and Former Series Editors:
Gerhard Goos, Juris Hartmanis, and Jan van Leeuwe..

Holger Hermanns   Jens Palsberg (Eds.)

Tools and Algorithms for the Construction and Analysis of Systems

12th International Conference, TACAS 2006
Held as Part of the Joint European Conferences
on Theory and Practice of Software, ETAPS 2006
Vienna, Austria, March 25 – April 2, 2006
Proceedings

 Springer

Volume Editors

Holger Hermanns
Saarland University
Department of Computer Science, Dependable Systems and Software
Stuhlsatzenhausweg 45, 66123 Saarbrücken, Germany
E-mail: hermanns@cs.uni-sb.de

Jens Palsberg
University of California at Los Angeles, Computer Science Department
4531K Boelter Hall, Los Angeles, CA 90095-1596, USA
E-mail: palsberg@ucla.edu

Library of Congress Control Number: 2006922189

CR Subject Classification (1998): F.3, D.2.4, D.2.2, C.2.4, F.2.2

LNCS Sublibrary: SL 1 – Theoretical Computer Science and General Issues

ISSN   0302-9743
ISBN-10   3-540-33056-9 Springer Berlin Heidelberg New York
ISBN-13   978-3-540-33056-1 Springer Berlin Heidelberg New York

Springer is a part of Springer Science+Business Media

springer.com

© Springer-Verlag Berlin Heidelberg 2006
Printed in Germany

Typesetting: Camera-ready by author, data conversion by Scientific Publishing Services, Chennai, India
Printed on acid-free paper   SPIN: 11691372   06/3142   5 4 3 2 1 0

Foreword

ETAPS 2006 was the ninth instance of the European Joint Conferences on Theory and Practice of Software. ETAPS is an annual federated conference that was established in 1998 by combining a number of existing and new conferences. This year it comprised five conferences (CC, ESOP, FASE, FOSSACS, TACAS), 18 satellite workshops (AC-CAT, AVIS, CMCS, COCV, DCC, EAAI, FESCA, FRCSS, GT-VMT, LDTA, MBT, QAPL, SC, SLAP, SPIN, TERMGRAPH, WITS and WRLA), two tutorials, and seven invited lectures (not including those that were specific to the satellite events). We received over 550 submissions to the five conferences this year, giving an overall acceptance rate of 23%, with acceptance rates below 30% for each conference. Congratulations to all the authors who made it to the final programme! I hope that most of the other authors still found a way of participating in this exciting event and I hope you will continue submitting.

The events that comprise ETAPS address various aspects of the system development process, including specification, design, implementation, analysis and improvement. The languages, methodologies and tools which support these activities are all well within its scope. Different blends of theory and practice are represented, with an inclination towards theory with a practical motivation on the one hand and soundly based practice on the other. Many of the issues involved in software design apply to systems in general, including hardware systems, and the emphasis on software is not intended to be exclusive.

ETAPS is a loose confederation in which each event retains its own identity, with a separate Program Committee and proceedings. Its format is open-ended, allowing it to grow and evolve as time goes by. Contributed talks and system demonstrations are in synchronized parallel sessions, with invited lectures in plenary sessions. Two of the invited lectures are reserved for "unifying" talks on topics of interest to the whole range of ETAPS attendees. The aim of cramming all this activity into a single one-week meeting is to create a strong magnet for academic and industrial researchers working on topics within its scope, giving them the opportunity to learn about research in related areas, and thereby to foster new and existing links between work in areas that were formerly addressed in separate meetings.

ETAPS 2006 was organized by the Vienna University of Technology, in cooperation with:

- European Association for Theoretical Computer Science (EATCS);
- European Association for Programming Languages and Systems (EAPLS);
- European Association of Software Science and Technology (EASST);
- Institute for Computer Languages, Vienna;
- Austrian Computing Society;
- The *Bürgermeister der Bundeshauptstadt Wien*;
- Vienna Convention Bureau;
- Intel.

The organizing team comprised:

Chair:	Jens Knoop
Local Arrangements:	Anton Ertl
Publicity:	Joost-Pieter Katoen
Satellite Events:	Andreas Krall
Industrial Liaison:	Eva Kühn
Liaison with City of Vienna:	Ulrich Neumerkel
Tutorials Chair, Website:	Franz Puntigam
Website:	Fabian Schmied
Local Organization, Workshops Proceedings:	Markus Schordan

Overall planning for ETAPS conferences is the responsibility of its Steering Committee, whose current membership is:

Perdita Stevens (Edinburgh, Chair), Luca Aceto (Aalborg and Reykjavík), Rastislav Bodík (Berkeley), Maura Cerioli (Genova), Matt Dwyer (Nebraska), Hartmut Ehrig (Berlin), José Fiadeiro (Leicester), Marie-Claude Gaudel (Paris), Roberto Gorrieri (Bologna), Reiko Heckel (Leicester), Michael Huth (London), Joost-Pieter Katoen (Aachen), Paul Klint (Amsterdam), Jens Knoop (Vienna), Shriram Krishnamurthi (Brown), Kim Larsen (Aalborg), Tiziana Margaria (Göttingen), Ugo Montanari (Pisa), Rocco de Nicola (Florence), Hanne Riis Nielson (Copenhagen), Jens Palsberg (UCLA), Mooly Sagiv (Tel-Aviv), João Saraiva (Minho), Don Sannella (Edinburgh), Vladimiro Sassone (Southampton), Helmut Seidl (Munich), Peter Sestoft (Copenhagen), Andreas Zeller (Saarbrücken).

I would like to express my sincere gratitude to all of these people and organizations, the Program Committee chairs and PC members of the ETAPS conferences, the organizers of the satellite events, the speakers themselves, the many reviewers, and Springer for agreeing to publish the ETAPS proceedings. Finally, I would like to thank the Organizing Chair of ETAPS 2006, Jens Knoop, for arranging for us to have ETAPS in the beautiful city of Vienna.

Edinburgh   Perdita Stevens
January 2006   ETAPS Steering Committee Chair

Preface

This volume contains the proceedings of the 12th TACAS, International Conference on Tools and Algorithms for the Construction and Analysis of Systems. TACAS 2006 took place in Vienna, Austria, March 27–31, 2006. TACAS is a forum for researchers, developers, and users interested in rigorously based tools for the construction and analysis of systems. The conference serves to bridge the gaps among communities that are devoted to formal methods, software and hardware verification, static analysis, programming languages, software engineering, real-time systems, and communication protocols. By providing a venue for the discussion of common problems, heuristics, algorithms, data structures, and methodologies, TACAS aims to support researchers in their quest to improve the utility, reliability, flexibility, and efficiency of tools for building systems.

Topics covered by TACAS include specification and verification techniques for finite and infinite state systems, software and hardware verification, theorem-proving and model-checking, system construction and transformation techniques, static and run-time analysis, abstract interpretation, refinement-based and compositional methodologies, testing and test-case generation, analytical techniques for security protocols, real-time, hybrid, and safety-critical systems, integration of formal methods and static analysis in high-level hardware design, tool environments and tool architectures, and applications and case studies.

TACAS traditionally considers two types of papers: full-length research papers, including those describing tools, and short tool-demonstration papers that give an overview of a particular tool and its applications. TACAS 2006 received 118 research and 9 tool-demonstration submissions, and accepted 30 research papers and 4 tool-demonstration papers. Each submission was evaluated by at least three reviewers and each submission co-authored by a PC member was evaluated by at least four reviewers. After a five-week reviewing process, the program selection was carried out in a two-week electronic Program Committee meeting. We believe that the result of the committee deliberations is a strong technical program. As this year's invited speaker, the Program Committee selected Somesh Jha, who presented work on weighted pushdown systems and trust-management systems. We thank the authors of the submitted papers, the Program Committee members, the referees, and especially the Tool Chair Thierry Jeron and the TACAS Steering Committee. Martin Karusseit gave us prompt support in dealing with the online conference management service. The help of Reza Pulungan in the general organization and the production of the proceedings is much appreciated.

TACAS 2006 was part of the 9th European Joint Conference on Theory and Practice of Software (ETAPS), whose aims, organization, and history are detailed in the separate foreword by the ETAPS Steering Committee Chair, Perdita Stevens. We would like to express our appreciation to the ETAPS Steering Committee, particularly Perdita Stevens, and the Organizing Committee for their efforts in making ETAPS 2006 a successful event.

January 2006   Holger Hermanns and Jens Palsberg
Program Committee Co-chairs

Organization

Steering Committee

Ed Brinksma   ESI and University of Twente, The Netherlands
Rance Cleaveland   SUNY, Stony Brook, USA
Kim Larsen   Aalborg University, Aalborg, Denmark
Bernhard Steffen   University of Dortmund, Dortmund, Germany
Lenore Zuck   University of Illinois, Chicago, USA

Programme Committee

Armin Biere   Johannes Kepler University, Linz, Austria
Ed Brinksma   ESI and University of Twente, The Netherlands
Gianfranco Ciardo University of California, Riverside, USA
Alessandro Cimatti ITC-IRST, Trento, Italy
Rance Cleaveland SUNY, Stony Brook, USA
Hubert Garavel   INRIA Rhones-Alpes, Grenoble, France
Andy Gordon   Microsoft Research, Cambridge, UK
Orna Grumberg   Technion, Haifa, Israel
Klaus Havelund   Kestrel Technology, Palo Alto, California, USA
Holger Hermanns Saarland University, Saarbrücken, Germany
Michael Huth   Imperial College, London, UK
Thierry Jeron   IRISA, Rennes, France
Kim Larsen   Aalborg University, Aalborg, Denmark
Ken McMillan   Cadence, Berkely, USA
Peter Niebert   University of Provence, Marseille, France
Jens Palsberg,   UCLA, Los Angeles, USA
Anna Phillipou   University of Cyprus, Nicosia, Cyprus
Jaco van de Pol   CWI, Amsterdam, The Netherlands
John Rushby   SRI, Menlo Park, USA
David Sands   Chalmers University of Technology, Goeteborg, Sweden
Helmut Seidl   Technical University of Munich, Munich, Germany
Bernhard Steffen   University of Dortmund, Dortmund, Germany
Martin Steffen   University of Kiel, Kiel, Germany
Zhendong Su   University of California, Davis, USA
Wang Yi   Uppsala University, Uppsala, Sweden
Lenore Zuck   University of Illinois, Chicago, USA

Referees

Parosh Abdulla
Erika Ábrahám
Wolfgang Ahrendt
Rajeev Alur
Cyrille Artho
Howard Barringer
Nicolas Baudru
Gerd Behrmann
Saddek Bensalem
Josh Berdine
Alexandru Berlea
Piergiorgio Bertoli
Ritwik Bhattacharya
Roderick Bloem
Stefan Blom
Patricia Bouyer
Marco Bozzano
Laura Brandán Briones
Sebastien Briais
Roberto Bruttomesso
Jens Calamé
Jan Cederquist
Swarat Chaudhuri
Taolue Chen
Hana Chockler
Ming Chung
Koen Claessen
Ricardo Corin
Mohammad Dashti
Alexandre David
Lugiez Denis
Aleksandar Dimovski
Martí
n Domí
nguez
Bruno Dutertre
Cindy Eisner
Harald Fecher
Jose Fiadeiro
Bernd Finkbeiner
Emmanuel Fleury
Anders Franzen
Olga Grinchtein

Andreas Grüner
Dilian Gurov
Jörgen Gustavsson
John Håkansson
Klaus Havelund
Natalia Ioustinova
Radha Jagadeesan
David Jansen
Bertrand Jeannet
Ole Jensen
Lingxiao Jiang
Sara Kalvala
Raimund Kirner
Felix Klaedtke
Peter Koppensteiner
Pavel Krcal
Daniel Kröning
Ruurd Kuiper
Orna Kupferman
Marcos Kurban
Marcel Kyas
Rom Langerak
Frédéric Lang
Ranko Lazic
Rustan Leino
Flavio Lerda
Stephen Magil
Roman Manevich
Radu Mateescu
Teddy Matinde
Marius Mikucionis
Ghassan Misherghi
Leonid Mokrushin
Remi Morin
Wojciech Mostowski
Markus Müller-Olm
Brian Nielsen
Ulrik Nyman
Peter Csaba Ölveczky
Julien d'Orso
Simona Orzan
Karol Ostrovsky
Corina Pasareanu

Doron Peled
Michael Petter
Paul Pettersson
Alessandra di Pierro
Henrik Pilegaard
HongYang Qu
Harald Raffelt
A. Ramanujam
Jakob Rehof
Arend Rensink
Jan-Willem Roorda
Marco Roveri
Oliver Rüthing
Theo Ruys
Hassen Saidi
Gwen Salaün
Luigi Santocanale
Roberto Sebastiani
Roberto Segala
Simone Semprini
Wendelin Serwe
Sanjit Seshia
Natarajan Shankar
Sharon Shoham
João Marques Silva
Radu Siminiceanu
Carsten Sinz
Doug Smith
Oleg Sokolsky
Rafal Somla
Jeremy Sproston
Martin Steffen
Mariëlle Stoelinga
Ofer Strichman
Stephan Thesing
Tayssir Touili
Stavros Tripakis
Rachel Tzoref
Frits Vaandrager
Helmut Veith
Arnaud Venet
Björn Victor
Tomas Vojnar

Table of Contents

Abstraction

Model Checking Algorithms

Program Verification

Runtime Diagnostics

Quantitative Techniques

Tool Demonstrations

Weighted Pushdown Systems and Trust-Management Systems

Somesh Jha[1], Stefan Schwoon[2], Hao Wang[1], and Thomas Reps[1]

[1] Computer Science Department, University of Wisconsin, Madison, WI 53706
{hbwang, jha, reps}@cs.wisc.edu
[2] Institut für Formale Methoden der Informatik, Universität Stuttgart,
Universitätsstr. 38, 70569 Stuttgart, Germany
schwoosn@fmi.uni-stuttgart.de

Abstract. The authorization problem is to decide whether, according to a security policy, some principal should be allowed access to a resource. In the trust-management system SPKI/SDSI, the security policy is given by a set of certificates, and proofs of authorization take the form of certificate chains. The certificate-chain-discovery problem is to discover a proof of authorization for a given request. Certificate-chain-discovery algorithms for SPKI/SDSI have been investigated by several researchers. We consider a variant of the certificate-chain discovery problem where the certificates are distributed over a number of servers, which then have to cooperate to identify the proof of authorization for a given request. We propose two protocols for this purpose. These protocols are based on distributed model-checking algorithms for weighted pushdown systems (WPDSs). These protocols can also handle cases where certificates are labeled with weights and where multiple certificate chains must be combined to form a proof of authorization. We have implemented these protocols in a prototype and report preliminary results of our evaluation.

1 Introduction

In access control of shared computing resources, the *authorization problem* addresses the following question: "Given a security policy, should a principal be allowed access to a specific resource?" In trust-management systems [4, 5, 25], such as SPKI/SDSI [9], the security policy is given by a set of signed certificates, and a proof of authorization consists of a set of certificate chains. In SPKI/SDSI, the *principals are the public keys*, i.e., the identity of a principal is established by checking the validity of the corresponding public key. In SPKI/SDSI, *name certificates* define the names available in an issuer's local name space; *authorization certificates* grant authorizations, or delegate the ability to grant authorizations. The *certificate-chain-discovery problem* is to discover a set of certificate chains that provides a proof of authorization for a request by a principal to access a resource.

An efficient certificate-chain-discovery algorithm for SPKI/SDSI was presented by Clarke et al. [8]. An improved algorithm was presented by Jha and Reps [14]. The latter algorithm is based on translating SPKI/SDSI certificates

H. Hermanns and J. Palsberg (Eds.): TACAS 2006, LNCS 3920, pp. 1–26, 2006.

to rules in a pushdown system [10, 11]. In [14] it was also demonstrated how this translation enables many other questions to be answered about a security policy expressed as a set of certificates. Algorithms presented in [8] and [14] assume that the proof of authorization consists of a *single* certificate chain. In general, however, a proof of authorization in SPKI/SDSI requires a *set* of certificate chains, each of which proves some *part* of the required authorization. Hence, the certificate-chain-discovery algorithms presented in [8, 14] are incomplete. This observation is also the basis for the observation by Li and Mitchell [19] that the "5-tuple reduction rule" of [9] is incomplete.

Schwoon et al. [24] introduced a new algorithm for certificate-chain discovery that translates SPKI/SDSI certificates to rules in a weighted pushdown system (WPDS) [22]. The algorithm presented by Schwoon et al. [24] can discover proofs of authorization that consist of multiple certificate chains. Moreover, the algorithm presented in [24] addresses such issues as trust, privacy, and recency in the context of authorization in SPKI/SDSI. As in [24], in this paper we translate SPKI/SDSI certificates into rules in a WPDS, where the authorization specifications of the certificates are translated to weights on rules. This translation to a WPDS yields a complete certificate-chain-discovery algorithm and is described in Section 5.

The algorithms of [8, 14, 24] assume that the set of all certificates relevant to a given request are known to a single site, which can then compute the answer to the authorization problem for a given principal and a given resource. In practice, however, there may be no such central authority. Certificates may be held by a number of different sites, each of which knows only a subset of the certificates. If a principal K from site S_1 wants to access a resource at site S_2, the certificate chain authorizing K to do so may involve certificates from both S_1 and S_2 (and possibly a number of other sites in between). For instance, consider the following example: The Computer Sciences department (CS) at the University of Wisconsin (UW) is part of the College of Letters and Sciences (LS). The department, the college, and the university could be different sites in the sense above. UW might grant access to some resource R to all of its faculty members by issuing a corresponding authorization certificate. The actual principals authorized to access R would be specified by name certificates, e.g., UW would declare that its faculty members are (among others) those of LS, LS would declare that its faculty members are (among others) those of CS, and CS would have a list of its faculty members. If members of CS want to access R, they need a chain of certificates from UW, LS, and CS, and none of these sites may know all of the certificates involved.

This paper makes two major contributions. First, we present a distributed model-checking algorithm for WPDSs. Second, using this algorithm we develop a distributed certificate-chain-discovery algorithm for SPKI/SDSI where the certificates are distributed across various sites. Background on the trust-management system SPKI/SDSI is given in Section 4. A distributed certificate-chain-discovery algorithm for SPKI/SDSI is described in Section 6. We have implemented a prototype of our algorithm. Our experimental results, presented in Section 7, demonstrate that the algorithm incurs a moderate overhead.

2   Related Work

A certificate-chain-discovery algorithm for SPKI/SDSI was first proposed by Clarke et al. [8]. An improved certificate-chain-discovery based on the theory of pushdown systems was presented by Jha and Reps [14]. As indicated earlier, both of these algorithms are centralized and assume that the proof of authorization consists of a single certificate chain. In the proof-carrying-authorization (PCA) framework of Appel and Felten [2], a client uses the theorem prover *Twelf* [21] to construct a proof of authorization, which the client presents to the server. However, they too assume that all logical facts used by the theorem prover reside at a single server. Li et al. [20] presented a distributed certificate-chain-discovery algorithm for the trust-management system RT_0. Their algorithm allows certificates to be distributed, but the proof of authorization is maintained at one site. SPKI/SDSI is a subset of RT_0 (SPKI/SDSI is equivalent to RT_0 without role intersection). In our distributed certificate-chain-discovery algorithm, various sites summarize their part of the proof of authorization before sending it to other sites; thus, the proof of authorization is distributed. Moreover, summarizing intermediate results also provides some privacy. We also implemented our algorithm in a trust-management server. To the best of our knowledge, Li et al. did not implement their algorithm. Bauer et al. [3] present an algorithm for assembling a proof that a request satisfies an access-control policy expressed in formal logic [18]. Bauer et al. advocate a lazy strategy, in which a party enlists help of others to prove particular subgoals. The precise relationship between the distributed algorithm of Bauer et al. and the algorithm presented in this paper will be explored in the future. The semantics of SPKI/SDSI has been widely studied [13, 1, 12]. In this context, the work that is most relevant is by Li and Mitchell [19], who pointed out that the "5-tuple reduction rule" of [9] is incomplete because, in general, a proof of authorization can require multiple certificate chains. Our algorithm does not suffer from this problem, due to the translation into a WPDS.

The work by Jim and Suciu on SD3 [16, 17], the successor of QCM, is also related to ours. SD3 is a trust-management system based on Datalog that, like our algorithms, allows for distributed evaluation of authorization queries. In [16], the author claims that SD3 can express "roughly the same policies as SDSI 2". While this claim is not further substantiated in [16], we believe it to be true. However, there are several differences that set our work apart from SD3:

- SD3 describes a generic evaluation algorithm where each instantiation corresponds to a particular strategy for distributing the computation. We propose several concrete evaluation strategies and argue that these strategies have certain advantages with respect to efficiency and privacy.
- Since [16] does not provide a concrete encoding of SPKI/SDSI in SD3, any comparison of the relative merits of our encoding vs SD3's is bound to be speculative. However, we believe that SD3's *site-safety* requirement would limit their evaluation to "forward" mode, whereas our algorithms can search both forward and backward (the latter is explained in Section 6).

- Unlike SD3, our framework allows certificates to have weights. As pointed out in [15], this provides a solution for situations in which proofs of authorization require multiple certificate chains, each of which prove *part* of the authorization. This solves the problem of semantic incompleteness pointed out by Li and Mitchell [19]. Moreover, in [24], we pointed out that weights allow to address such issues as privacy, recency, validity, and trust.

3 Weighted Pushdown Systems

Weighted pushdown systems were introduced in [7, 22, 23, 24]. In short, a pushdown system defines an infinite-state transition system whose states involve a stack of unbounded length. In a weighted pushdown system, the rules are given values from some domain of weights. Our weight domains of interest are the bounded idempotent semirings defined in Defn. 1.

Definition 1. *A* **bounded idempotent semiring** *is a quintuple* $(D, \oplus, \otimes, 0, 1)$, *where D is a set, 0 and 1 are elements of D, and $\oplus$ (the combine operation) and $\otimes$ (the extend operation) are binary operators on D such that*

1. $(D, \oplus)$ *is a commutative monoid whose neutral element is 0, and where $\oplus$ is idempotent.*
2. $(D, \otimes)$ *is a monoid with the neutral element 1.*
3. $\otimes$ *distributes over $\oplus$, i.e., for all $a, b, c \in D$ we have $a \otimes (b \oplus c) = (a \otimes b) \oplus (a \otimes c)$ and $(a \oplus b) \otimes c = (a \otimes c) \oplus (b \otimes c)$.*
4. 0 *is an annihilator with respect to $\otimes$, i.e., for all $a \in D$, $a \otimes 0 = 0 = 0 \otimes a$.*
5. *In the partial order $\sqsubseteq$ defined by: $\forall a, b \in D$, $a \sqsubseteq b$ iff $a \oplus b = a$, there are no infinite descending chains.*

Definition 2. *A* **pushdown system** *is a triple $\mathcal{P} = (P, \Gamma, \Delta)$, where P and Γ are finite sets called the* **control locations** *and the* **stack alphabet***, respectively. The elements of $Conf(\mathcal{P}) := P \times \Gamma^*$ are called the* **configurations** *of $\mathcal{P}$. Δ contains a finite number of* **rules** *of the form $\langle p, \gamma \rangle \hookrightarrow_{\mathcal{P}} \langle p', w \rangle$, where $p, p' \in P$, $\gamma \in \Gamma$, and $w \in \Gamma^*$, which define a transition relation $\Rightarrow_{\mathcal{P}}$ between configurations of $\mathcal{P}$ as follows:*

$$\text{If } r = \langle p, \gamma \rangle \hookrightarrow_{\mathcal{P}} \langle p', w \rangle, \text{ then } \langle p, \gamma w' \rangle \xLongrightarrow{\langle r \rangle}_{\mathcal{P}} \langle p', ww' \rangle \text{ for all } w' \in \Gamma^*.$$

We write $c \Rightarrow_{\mathcal{P}} c'$ to express that there exists some rule r such that $c \xLongrightarrow{\langle r \rangle}_{\mathcal{P}} c'$; we omit the subscript $\mathcal{P}$ if $\mathcal{P}$ is understood. The reflexive transitive closure of $\Rightarrow$ is denoted by $\Rightarrow^*$.

Given a set of configurations C, we define $pre(C) \overset{\text{def}}{=} \{ c' \mid \exists c \in C : c' \Rightarrow c \}$ and $post(C) \overset{\text{def}}{=} \{ c' \mid \exists c \in C : c \Rightarrow c' \}$ as the sets of configurations that are reachable—backwards and forwards, respectively—from elements of C in a single step. Moreover, $pre^*(C) \overset{\text{def}}{=} \{ c' \mid \exists c \in C : c' \Rightarrow^* c \}$ and $post^*(C) \overset{\text{def}}{=} \{ c' \mid \exists c \in C : c \Rightarrow^* c' \}$ are the configuration reachable—backwards and forwards— in arbitrarily many steps. C is called **regular** *if for all $p \in P$ the language $\{ w \mid \langle p, w \rangle \in C \}$ is regular.*

Definition 3. *A **weighted pushdown system** is a triple $\mathcal{W} = (\mathcal{P}, \mathcal{S}, f)$ such that $\mathcal{P} = (P, \Gamma, \Delta)$ is a pushdown system, $\mathcal{S} = (D, \oplus, \otimes, 0, 1)$ is a bounded idempotent semiring, and $f \colon \Delta \to D$ is a function that assigns a value from D to each rule of $\mathcal{P}$.*

Let $\sigma \in \Delta^*$ be a sequence of rules. Using f, we can associate a value to σ, i.e., if $\sigma = [r_1, \ldots, r_k]$, then we define $v(\sigma) \stackrel{\text{def}}{=} f(r_1) \otimes \ldots \otimes f(r_k)$. Moreover, for any two configurations c and c' of $\mathcal{P}$, we let $path(c, c')$ denote the set of all rule sequences $[r_1, \ldots, r_k]$ that transform c into c', i.e., $c \xrightarrow{\langle r_1 \rangle} \cdots \xrightarrow{\langle r_k \rangle} c'$.

Definition 4. *Let $\mathcal{W} = (\mathcal{P}, \mathcal{S}, f)$, where $\mathcal{P} = (P, \Gamma, \Delta)$ and $\mathcal{S} = (D, \oplus, \otimes, 0, 1)$, and let C be a set of configurations. A **forwards** (resp. **backwards**) $(\mathcal{W}, C)$-**dag** is an edge-labeled directed acyclic graph (V, E) where $V \subseteq Conf(\mathcal{P}) \times D$ and $E \subseteq V \times \Delta \times V$ such that*

- *if a vertex (c, d) has no incoming edges, then $c \in C$ and $d = 1$;*
- *if $((c_1, d_1), r_1, (c, d)), \ldots, ((c_k, d_k), r_k, (c, d)),\ \ k \geq 1$ are the incoming edges of (c, d), then*
  - *$d = \bigoplus_{i=1}^{k} (d_i \otimes f(r_i))$ and $c_i \xrightarrow{\langle r_i \rangle}_{\mathcal{P}} c$ for all $1 \leq i \leq k$ (in a forwards $(\mathcal{W}, C)$-dag);*
  - *$d = \bigoplus_{i=1}^{k} (f(r_i) \otimes d_i)$ and $c \xrightarrow{\langle r_i \rangle}_{\mathcal{P}} c_i$ for all $1 \leq i \leq k$ (in a backwards $(\mathcal{W}, C)$-dag).*

*We call a (forwards/backwards) $(\mathcal{W}, C)$-dag $\mathcal{D}$ a **witness dag** for (c, d) if $\mathcal{D}$ is finite and (c, d) is the only vertex with no outgoing edges in $\mathcal{D}$.*

Notice that the extender operation $\otimes$ is used to calculate the value of a path. The value of a set of paths is computed using the combiner operation $\oplus$. The existence of a witness dag for (c, d) can be considered a proof that there exists a set of paths from C to c (or vice versa) whose combined value is d. Because of Defn. 1(5), it is always possible to identify a finite witness dag if such a set of paths exists.

3.1 Known Results

We briefly review some known results about (weighted) pushdown systems.

Let $\mathcal{P} = (P, \Gamma, \Delta)$ be a pushdown system, and let C be a *regular* subset of $Conf(\mathcal{P})$. Then, according to [10], the sets $pre^*(C)$ and $post^*(C)$ are also regular and effectively computable (in the form of a finite automaton).

The results from [23, 24] show that the result can be extended to **generalized pushdown reachability (GPR) problems** on weighted pushdown systems:

Definition 5. *Let $\mathcal{W} = (\mathcal{P}, \mathcal{S}, f)$ be a weighted pushdown system, where $\mathcal{P} = (P, \Gamma, \Delta)$, and let $C \subseteq P \times \Gamma^*$ be a regular set of configurations. The **generalized pushdown predecessor (GPP) problem** is to find for each $c \in pre^*(C)$:*

- *$\delta(c) \stackrel{\text{def}}{=} \bigoplus \{ v(\sigma) \mid \sigma \in path(c, c'), c' \in C \}$;*
- *a backwards witness dag for $(c, \delta(c))$.*

The **generalized pushdown successor (GPS) problem** *is to find for each*
$c \in post^*(C)$*:*

- $\delta(c) \overset{\text{def}}{=} \bigoplus \{ v(\sigma) \mid \sigma \in path(c', c), c' \in C \}$;
- *a forwards witness dag for* $(c, \delta(c))$.

In [23, 24], the solutions for GPS and GPP are computed in the form of annotated finite automata. We describe the GPP case here; the GPS case is analogous, modulo certain details. Moreover, for the sake of keeping the presentation simple, we concentrate on the computation of the $\delta(c)$ values. A method for computing the witness dags is given in [23], and it is straightforward to transfer it to the distributed case.

Our input is a weighted pushdown system $\mathcal{W} = (\mathcal{P}, \mathcal{S}, f)$, where $\mathcal{P} = (P, \Gamma, \Delta)$ and $\mathcal{S} = (D, \oplus, \otimes, 0, 1)$, together with a regular set of configurations C. The output is $\delta(c)$ for each $c \in pre^*(C)$. In general, there are infinitely many configurations in $pre^*(C)$ even if C itself is finite, so we can only hope to compute the solution symbolically. We use (annotated) finite automata for this purpose:

Definition 6. *A $\mathcal{P}$-automaton is a quintuple $\mathcal{A} = (Q, \Gamma, \eta, P, F)$ where $Q \supseteq P$ is a finite set of* **states***, $\eta \subseteq Q \times \Gamma \times Q$ is the set of* **transitions***, and $F \subseteq Q$ are the* **final states***. The* **initial states** *of $\mathcal{A}$ are the control locations P. We say that a sequence of transitions $(p, \gamma_1, p_1), \ldots, (p_{n-1}, \gamma_n, q) \in \eta$* **reads** *configuration $\langle p, \gamma_1 \ldots \gamma_n \rangle$ if $p_1, \ldots, p_{n_1}, q$ are arbitrary states. The sequence is* **accepting** *iff q is a final state. If c is a configuration of $\mathcal{A}$, we denote by $acc_{\mathcal{A}}(c)$ the set of all accepting transition sequences in $\mathcal{A}$ for c; we say that c is accepted by $\mathcal{A}$ if $acc_{\mathcal{A}}(c)$ is non-empty.*

Note that a set of configurations of $\mathcal{P}$ is **regular** if and only if it is accepted by some $\mathcal{P}$-automaton. In what follows, $\mathcal{P}$ is fixed; hence, we usually omit the prefix $\mathcal{P}$ and speak simply of "automata".

A convenient property of regular sets of configurations is that they are closed under forwards and backwards reachability [6]. In other words, given an automaton $\mathcal{A}$ that accepts the set C, one can construct automata that accept the sets of all configurations that are forward or backwards reachable from C. Following [23, 24], two additional labelings for the transitions of $\mathcal{A}$ are computed to solve the GPP and GPS problems. The first, $l \colon \eta \to D$ assigns a weight from D to each automaton transition and allows to compute δ (see below). The second allows to compute the ω function. As mentioned earlier, we omit the second labeling for the sake of simplicity.

Without loss of generality, we assume henceforth that for every rule $\langle p, \gamma \rangle \hookrightarrow \langle p', w \rangle$ we have $|w| \leq 2$; this is not restrictive because every pushdown system can be simulated by another one that obeys this restriction and is larger by only a constant factor (e.g., [14]).

In the following, we first present an abstract version of the procedure given in [23, 24], which is designed for centralized computation. We then proceed to give an implementation for the distributed case.

Abstract Algorithm. Let $\mathcal{A} = (Q, \Gamma, \eta, P, F)$ be a $\mathcal{P}$-automaton that accepts a set of configurations C. Without loss of generality, we assume that $\mathcal{A}$ has no transition leading to an initial state.

Initially, we set $l(t) := 1$ for all $t \in \eta$. When we say that transition t should be updated with value d, we mean the following action: if t is not yet in η, add t to η and set $l(t) := d$; otherwise, update $l(t)$ to $l(t) \oplus d$.

For GPP, we add new transitions to $\mathcal{A}$ according to the following saturation rule:

> If $r := \langle p, \gamma \rangle \hookrightarrow \langle p', w \rangle$ is a rule, $t_1 \ldots t_{|w|}$ a sequence that reads $\langle p, w \rangle$ and ends in state q, then let d be $l(t_1) \otimes \ldots \otimes l(t_{|w|})$ and update (p, γ, q) with the value $f(r) \otimes d$.

The procedure terminates when the saturation rule can no longer be applied (i.e., a fixed point has been reached).

Concrete Algorithm. A concrete implementation is given in [23] and reproduced in Figure 1. Each iteration of the loop starting at line 14 executes one or more applications of the saturation rule. After the computation has finished, the resulting automaton accepts all configurations $c \in pre^*(C)$. Then, we have $\delta(c) = \bigoplus_{t_1 \cdots t_n \in acc_{\mathcal{A}'}(c)} l(t_1) \otimes \cdots \otimes l(t_n)$.

In [23] the time complexity of the GPP algorithm from Figure 1 was stated as $\mathcal{O}(|Q|^2 \cdot |\Delta| \cdot \ell)$, where ℓ is the length of the longest descending chain in $\mathcal{S}$, and the space complexity (determined by the number of transitions in the final automaton) as $\mathcal{O}(|Q| \cdot |\Delta| + |\eta|)$.

3.2   A Distributed Algorithm

We now discuss how the computation can be distributed when the rules in Δ are distributed over a set *Sites* of servers. As in Section 3.1, we discuss both the GPP and the GPS case, and give a concrete implementation for GPP, as the one for GPS is very similar.

We fix a weighted pushdown system $\mathcal{W} = (\mathcal{P}, \mathcal{S}, f)$, where $\mathcal{P} = (P, \Gamma, \Delta)$ and $\mathcal{S} = (D, \oplus, \otimes, 0, 1)$, and a regular set C of configurations. The solution we discuss here distributes the workload among the servers according to control locations, i.e., for every control location there is a server that is 'responsible' for it. More precisely, we make the following assumptions:

1. There exists a mapping $f_S \colon P \to Sites$ that assigns control locations to sites.
2. Every rule $\langle p, \gamma \rangle \hookrightarrow \langle p', w \rangle$ is stored at the site $f_S(p)$ (for the GPS problem), or at $f_S(p')$ (for the GPP problem).

Stating assumption 2 differently, we are working with a collection $(\mathcal{W}_s)_{s \in Sites}$ of weighted pushdown systems that differ only in their rules, i.e., $\mathcal{W}_s = (\mathcal{P}_s, \mathcal{S}, f_{|\Delta_s})$ and $\mathcal{P}_s = (P, \Gamma, \Delta_s)$, where the set Δ_s satisfies assumption 2.

We say that a rule $\langle p, \gamma \rangle \hookrightarrow \langle p', w \rangle$ is a **boundary rule** if p and p' are assigned to different sites. If such a boundary rule exists, we call the sites responsible for p and p' **neighboring sites**.

Algorithm 1
Input: a weighted pushdown system $\mathcal{W} = (\mathcal{P}, \mathcal{S}, f)$, where $\mathcal{P} = (P, \Gamma, \Delta)$ and
$\mathcal{S} = (D, \oplus, \otimes, 0, 1)$, and an automaton $\mathcal{A} = (Q, \Gamma, \eta_0, P, F)$ that accepts C,
such that $\mathcal{A}$ has no transitions into states from P.

Output: an automaton $\mathcal{A}' = (Q, \Gamma, \eta, P, F)$ that accepts $pre^*(C)$,
with annotation function $l : \eta \to D$

```
1   procedure update(t, v)
2   begin
3       η := η ∪ {t}
4       newValue := l(t) ⊕ v
5       if newValue ≠ l(t) then
6           workset := workset ∪ {t}
7           l(t) := newValue
8   end
9
10  η := η₀;  workset := η₀;  l := λt.0
11  for all t ∈ η₀ do l(t) := 1
12  for all r = ⟨p,γ⟩ ↪ ⟨p′,ε⟩ ∈ Δ do
13      update((p,γ,p′), f(r))
14  while workset ≠ ∅ do
15      remove some transition t = (q,γ,q′) from workset;
16      for all r = ⟨p₁,γ₁⟩ ↪ ⟨q,γ⟩ ∈ Δ do
17          update((p₁,γ₁,q′), f(r) ⊗ l(t))
18      for all r = ⟨p₁,γ₁⟩ ↪ ⟨q,γγ₂⟩ ∈ Δ do
19          for all t′ = (q′,γ₂,q″) ∈ η do
20              update((p₁,γ₁,q″), f(r) ⊗ l(t) ⊗ l(t′))
21      for all r = ⟨p₁,γ₁⟩ ↪ ⟨p′,γ₂γ⟩ ∈ Δ do
22          if t′ = (p′,γ₂,q) ∈ η then
23              update((p₁,γ₁,q′), f(r) ⊗ l(t′) ⊗ l(t))
24  return ((Q,Γ,η,P,F), l)
```

Fig. 1. An algorithm for creating a weighted automaton for the GPP problem

Definition 7. *Let $\mathcal{D} = (V, E)$ be a $(\mathcal{W}, C)$-dag and $s \in$ Sites. An edge (v, r, v') of $\mathcal{D}$, where $v = (\langle p, w \rangle, d)$, is called a **boundary edge** if r is a boundary rule. Moreover, v' is called a **boundary node** of the site $f_S(p)$. We denote by $\mathcal{T}(s) = \{ \langle p, w \rangle \mid f_S(p) = s, \ w \in \Gamma^* \}$ the configurations that begin with the control locations for which site s is responsible. Moreover, the s-**region of** $\mathcal{D}$ is the subgraph (V_s, E_s) of $\mathcal{D}$, where $V_s = \{ (c, d) \in V \mid c \in \mathcal{T}(s) \}$ and $E_s = \{ (v, r, v') \in E \mid v \in V_s \}$.*

Informally, the s-region contains the subgraph of $\mathcal{D}$ induced by V_s, i.e., the nodes for whose configurations s is responsible, plus the "fringe" of this subgraph, i.e., the boundary edges originating in V_s and their target nodes.

Abstract Algorithm. We can now give an abstract description of the GPP and GPS algorithms. Given $\mathcal{W}$ and C, every site s computes the set $\mathcal{T}_{pre}^{C}(s) \overset{\text{def}}{=} (pre \cup id)(pre^*(C) \cap \mathcal{T}(s))$ (in the GPP case) or $\mathcal{T}_{post}^{C}(s) \overset{\text{def}}{=} (post \cup id)(post^*(C) \cap \mathcal{T}(s))$

(in the GPS case). In the following, we write $\bar{T}(s)$ to mean $T_{pre}^C(s)$ or $T_{post}^C(s)$, depending on the context.

Intuitively speaking, every site s computes a partition of $pre^*(C)$ or $post^*(C)$, namely, the set of configurations that have control locations for which s is responsible, extended with the configurations reached by boundary rules. Note that the set $\bar{T}(s)$ contains all the configurations that can be generated using rules stored at s.

The idea is that site s becomes involved in a GPP/GPS computation if it is discovered that $\bar{T}(s) \neq \emptyset$. Initially, each site s starts with the set $C \cap T(s)$. If a boundary rule causes a site s to discover configurations that belongs to $T(s')$ (for some site $s' \neq s$), then s will send those configurations to s', and s' continues its GPP/GPS computation using those configuration.

Concrete Algorithm. At a more concrete level of description, every site s computes an automaton $\mathcal{A}_s$ that accepts $\bar{T}(s)$, and appropriate labeling functions for δ and for the witness dags. Basically, the distributed algorithm is a straightforward extension of the non-distributed case: every site s runs a GPP/GPS algorithm similar to the one in Figure 1 with $\mathcal{W}_s$. The main complication is that some parts of the automata need to be shared between sites.

To be more precise, let $\mathcal{A}$ be an automaton that accepts C. Initially, $\mathcal{A}_s$ is an automaton that accepts $C \cap T(s)$, which can be constructed by merely taking the states and transitions of $\mathcal{A}$ that are reachable from initial states p such that $f_S(p) = s$.

Each site s then carries out the algorithm from Figure 1 using $\mathcal{W}_s$. If s and s' are neighboring sites, then, at some stage of the computation at s, the automaton $\mathcal{A}_s$ may accept configurations from $T(s') \cap \bar{T}(s)$, i.e., configurations that ought to be maintained by s'. Let $T_{s,s'}$ be the set of transitions in $\bigcup_{c \in T(s')} acc_{\mathcal{A}_s}(c)$, i.e., the transitions in $\mathcal{A}_s$ that form part of an accepting path for such configurations. Whenever s detects a transition t that belongs to $T_{s,s'}$ (or an update in such a transition), then s keeps t in its automaton, but also sends it to s'. Thus, every site s ends up with an automaton that accepts $\bar{T}(s)$.

Along with the configurations, every site also computes information to construct the δ function and witness dags. Notice that the vertices in an s-region of a $(\mathcal{W}, C)$-dag $\mathcal{D}$ are labeled with configurations from $\bar{T}(s)$, and that the edges of the region are labeled with the rules stored at s. Thus, s has all the information needed to construct the s-region of $\mathcal{D}$. More precisely, the information needed to construct an s-region can be generated by an annotation of the automaton maintained by s, in the same way as in [23].

The δ function is computed in the form of another annotation that labels automaton transitions with semiring values. When sending a transition from one site to another, the semiring values are also sent. For a configuration $c = \langle p, w \rangle$, the value of $\delta(c)$ can be obtained by evaluating the automaton $A_{f_S(p)}$, as shown in Section 3.1.

Figure 2 shows the changes that must be made to Algorithm 1 to implement this approach. The figure shows the algorithm from the point of view of site s. The algorithm maintains a mapping $sites: Q \rightarrow 2^{Sites}$. If $s' \in sites(q)$, then

Algorithm 2 (running on site s)

Input: a weighted pushdown system $\mathcal{W}_s = (\mathcal{P}_s, \mathcal{S}, f_{|\Delta_s|})$, where $\mathcal{P}_s = (P, \Gamma, \Delta_s)$, and $\mathcal{S} = (D, \oplus, \otimes, 0, 1)$, and an automaton $\mathcal{A}_s = (Q, \Gamma, \eta_0, P, F)$ that accepts $C \cap \mathcal{T}(s)$, such that $\mathcal{A}$ has no transitions into states from P.

Output: an automaton $\mathcal{A}'_s = (Q, \Gamma, \eta, P, F)$ that accepts $\mathcal{T}^C_{pre}(s))'$ with annotation function $l: \eta \to D$

Replacement for *update* procedure:

```
1  procedure update(t, v)
2  begin
3      η := η ∪ {t}
4      newValue := l(t) ⊕ v
5      if newValue ≠ l(t) then
6          workset := workset ∪ {t}
7          l(t) := newValue
8          // assume t = (p, γ, q)
9          for all s' ∈ sites(p) do
10             update_{s'}(t, l(t));
11             add_recursive(q, s');
12 end
```

New procedure *add_recursive*:

```
1  procedure add_recursive(q, s')
2  begin
3      if s' ∈ sites(q) then return;
4      sites(q) := sites(q) ∪ {s'};
5      for all t' = (q, γ', q') ∈ η do
6          update_{s'}(t', l(t'));
7          add_recursive(q', s');
8  end
```

Additions to main procedure:

```
1  sites := λp.∅;
2  for all r = ⟨p, γ⟩ ↪ ⟨p', w⟩ ∈ Δ do
3      if f_S(p) ≠ s then
4          sites(p) := sites(p) ∪ {f_S(p)}
```

Fig. 2. Modification of Algorithm 1 for distributed GPP

the current automaton contains a path that leads from an initial state p, where $f_S(p) = s'$, to the state q. This means that all transitions of the form (q, y, q') are part of accepting paths for configurations from $\mathcal{T}(s')$. As a consequence, whenever such a transition is first generated or updated, it needs to be sent to s', and q' must be added to $sites(s')$.

The changes to Algorithm 1 consist of three parts:

- The procedure *update* is replaced by a new version;
- there is an additional procedure *add_recursive*;
- a couple of lines are added to the beginning of the main procedure.

The new lines in the main procedure initialize the *sites* function. The *update* function is extended by lines 8–11. These lines send the updated transition to other sites as required. Sending a transition t with value v to site s' is represented by $update_{s'}(t, v)$, which can be thought of as a remote procedure call (of the function *update*) on site s' that adds t to the worklist of s'. Finally, the target state of t must be added to $sites(s')$. This is done by procedure *add_recursive*, which also takes care of sending additional transitions to s', if required.

Complexity. Let us state the complexity of Algorithm 1 when run on site s. The main procedure is unchanged and runs in $\mathcal{O}(|Q|^2 \cdot |\Delta_s| \cdot \ell)$ time, where ℓ is the longest descending chain in $\mathcal{S}$. Additional work is required for sending and receiving transitions to/from neighboring sites. Suppose that s has n neighboring sites, and that these sites send t transitions to s. For every send or receive action, s needs to perform some constant amount of work.

Note that t is bounded by $\mathcal{O}(|Q| \cdot |\Delta|)$, and that every transition can be received at most ℓ times, so the effort for received transitions is at most $\mathcal{O}(|Q| \cdot |\Delta| \cdot \ell)$, although in practice we expect it to be much lower.

In the worst case, s must send all of its transitions to all n neighbors at most ℓ times, i.e., $\mathcal{O}(|Q| \cdot |\Delta| \cdot n \cdot \ell)$. Again, we expect his number to be much lower in practice.

4   Background on SPKI/SDSI

In SPKI/SDSI, all *principals* are represented by their public keys, i.e., the principal *is* its public key. A principal can be an individual, process, host, or any other entity. $\mathcal{K}$ denotes the set of public keys. Specific keys are denoted by K, K_A, K_B, K', etc. An *identifier* is a word over some alphabet Σ. The set of identifiers is denoted by $\mathcal{A}$. Identifiers will be written in typewriter font, e.g., A and Bob. A *term* is a key followed by zero or more identifiers. Terms are either keys, local names, or extended names. A *local name* is of the form K A, where $K \in \mathcal{K}$ and A $\in \mathcal{A}$. For example, K Bob is a local name. Local names are important in SPKI/SDSI because they create a decentralized name space. The local name space of K is the set of local names of the form K A. An *extended name* is of the form K σ, where $K \in \mathcal{K}$ and σ is a sequence of identifiers of length greater than one. For example, K UW CS faculty is an extended name.

4.1   Certificates

SPKI/SDSI has two types of certificates, or "certs":

Name Certificates (or *name certs*): A name cert provides a definition of a local name in the issuer's local name space. Only key K may issue or sign a cert that defines a name in its local name space. A name cert C is a signed four-tuple (K, A, S, V). The issuer K is a public key and the certificate is signed by K. A is an identifier. The subject S is a term. Intuitively, S gives additional meaning for the local name K A. V is the *validity specification* of the certificate. Usually, V takes the form of an interval $[t_1, t_2]$, i.e., the cert is valid from time t_1 to t_2 inclusive.

Authorization Certificates (or *auth certs*): An auth cert grants or delegates a specific authorization from an issuer to a subject. Specifically, an auth cert c is a five-tuple (K, S, D, T, V). The *issuer* K is a public key, which is also used to sign the cert. The *subject* S is a term. If the *delegation bit* D is turned on, then a subject receiving this authorization can delegate this authorization to other keys. The *authorization specification* T specifies the permission being granted; for example, it may specify a permission to read a specific file, or a permission to login to a particular host. The *validity specification* V for an auth cert is the same as in the case of a name cert.

A *labeled rewrite rule* is a pair $(L \longrightarrow R, T)$, where the first component is a rewrite rule and the second component T is an authorization specification. For notational convenience, we will write the labeled rewrite rule $(L \longrightarrow R, T)$ as $L \xrightarrow{T} R$. We will treat certs as labeled rewrite rules:[1]z

- A name cert $(K, \mathtt{A}, S, V)$ will be written as a labeled rewrite rule $K \mathtt{A} \xrightarrow{T} S$, where T is the authorization specification such that for all other authorization specifications t, $T \cap t = t$, and $T \cup t = T$. [2] Sometimes we will write $\xrightarrow{T}$ as simply $\longrightarrow$, i.e., a rewrite rule of the form $L \longrightarrow R$ has an implicit label of T.
- An auth cert (K, S, D, T, V) will be written as $K \square \xrightarrow{T} S \square$ if the delegation bit D is turned on; otherwise, it will be written as $K \square \xrightarrow{T} S \blacksquare$.

4.2   Authorization

Because we only use labeled rewrite rules in this paper, we refer to them as rewrite rules or simply rules. A term S appearing in a rule can be viewed as a string over the alphabet $\mathcal{K} \cup \mathcal{A}$, in which elements of $\mathcal{K}$ appear only in the beginning. For uniformity, we also refer to strings of the form $S \square$ and $S \blacksquare$ as terms. Assume that we are given a labeled rewrite rule $L \xrightarrow{T} R$ that corresponds to a cert. Consider a term $S = LX$. In this case, the labeled rewrite rule $L \xrightarrow{T} R$ applied to the term S (denoted by $(L \xrightarrow{T} R)(S)$) yields the term RX. Therefore, a rule can be viewed as a function from terms to terms that rewrites the left prefix of its argument, for example,

$$(K_A \, \mathtt{Bob} \longrightarrow K_B)(K_A \, \mathtt{Bob \, myFriends}) = K_B \, \mathtt{myFriends}$$

Consider two rules $c_1 = (L_1 \xrightarrow{T} R_1)$ and $c_2 = (L_2 \xrightarrow{T'} R_2)$, and, in addition, assume that L_2 is a prefix of R_1, i.e., there exists an X such that $R_1 = L_2 X$. Then the *composition* $c_2 \circ c_1$ is the rule $L_1 \xrightarrow{T \cap T'} R_2 X$. For example, consider the two rules:

$$c_1 : \quad K_A \, \mathtt{friends} \xrightarrow{T} K_A \, \mathtt{Bob \, myFriends}$$
$$c_2 : \quad K_A \, \mathtt{Bob} \xrightarrow{T'} K_B$$

The composition $c_2 \circ c_1$ is $K_A \, \mathtt{friends} \xrightarrow{T \cap T'} K_B \, \mathtt{myFriends}$. Two rules c_1 and c_2 are called *compatible* if their composition $c_2 \circ c_1$ is well defined.[3]

---

[1] In authorization problems, we only consider valid certificates, so the validity specification V for a certificate is not included in its rule.

[2] The issue of intersection and union of authorization specifications is discussed in detail in [9, 13].

[3] In general, the composition operator $\circ$ is not associative. For example, c_3 can be compatible with $c_2 \circ c_1$, but c_3 might not be compatible with c_2. Therefore, $c_3 \circ (c_2 \circ c_1)$ can exist when $(c_3 \circ c_2) \circ c_1$ does not exist. However, when $(c_3 \circ c_2) \circ c_1$ exists, so does $c_3 \circ (c_2 \circ c_1)$; moreover, the expressions are equal when both are defined. Thus, we allow ourselves to omit parentheses and assume that $\circ$ is right associative.

4.3 The Authorization Problem in SPKI/SDSI

Assume that we are given a set of certs C and that principal K wants access specified by authorization specification T. The authorization question is: "Can K be granted access to the resource specified by T?"

A *certificate chain* $ch = (c_k \circ c_{k-1} \circ \cdots \circ c_1)$ is a sequence such that for C, where $c_1, c_2, \cdots, c_k$ are certificates in C, certificate chain ch defines the transformation $c_k \circ c_{k-1} \circ \cdots \circ c_1$. The label of ch, denoted by $L(ch)$, is the label of $c_k \circ c_{k-1} \circ \cdots \circ c_1$. We assume that the authorization specification T is associated with a unique principal K_r (which could be viewed as the owner of the resource r to which T refers). Given a set of certificates C, an authorization specification T, and a principal K, a *certificate-chain-discovery* algorithm looks for a finite set of certificate chains that "prove" that principal K is allowed to make the access specified by T.

Formally, certificate-chain discovery attempts to find a finite set $\{ch_1, \cdots, ch_m\}$ of certificate chains such that for all $1 \leq i \leq m$

$$ch_i(K_r \,\square) \in \{K \,\square, K \,\blacksquare\}\,.$$

and $T \subseteq \bigcup_{i=1}^{m} L(ch_i)$.

Clarke et al. [8] presented an algorithm for certificate-chain discovery in SPKI/SDSI with time complexity $O(n_K^2 |C|)$, where n_K is the number of keys and $|C|$ is the sum of the lengths of the right-hand sides of all rules in C. However, this algorithm only solved a restricted version of certificate-chain discovery: a solution could only consist of a *single* certificate chain. For instance, consider the following certificate set:

$$c_1 : \quad (K,\ K_A,\ 0,\ ((\text{dir /etc}) \text{ read}),\ [t_1, t_2])$$
$$c_2 : \quad (K,\ K_A,\ 0,\ ((\text{dir /etc}) \text{ write}),\ [t_1, t_2])$$

Suppose that Alice makes the request

$$(K_A, ((\text{dir /etc}) \ (* \ \text{set read write}))).$$

In this case, the chain "(c_1)" authorizes Alice to read from directory /etc, and a separate chain "(c_2)" authorizes her to write to /etc. Together, (c_1) and (c_2) prove that she has both read and write privileges for /etc. However, both of the certificates c_1 and c_2 would be removed from the certificate set prior to running the certificate-chain discovery algorithm of Clarke et al., because read $\not\supseteq$ (* set read write) and write $\not\supseteq$ (* set read write). Consequently, no proof of authorization for Alice's request would be found. Schwoon et al. [24] presented algorithms for the full certificate-chain-discovery problem, based on solving reachability problems in weighted pushdown systems. Their formalization allows a proof of authorization to consist of a set of certificate chains. This paper uses the WPDS-based algorithm for certificate-chain-discovery introduced in [24].

5   Weighted Pushdown Systems and SPKI/SDSI

In the section, we show that WPDSs are a useful tool for solving problems related to certificate-chain discovery in SPKI/SDSI. The following definitions are largely taken from [23].

The following correspondence between SPKI/SDSI and pushdown systems was presented in [24]: let C be a (finite) set of certificates such that $\mathcal{K}_C$ and $\mathcal{I}_C$ are the keys and identifiers, respectively, that appear in C. Moreover, let $\mathcal{T}$ be the set from which the authorization specifications in C are drawn. Then $\mathcal{S}_C = (\mathcal{T}, \cup, \cap, \bot, \top)$, where $\cap, \cup$ are the intersection and union of auth specs as discussed in [9, 13], forms a semiring with domain $\mathcal{T}$. We now associate with C the weighted pushdown system $\mathcal{W}_C = (\mathcal{P}_C, \mathcal{S}_C, f)$, where $\mathcal{P}_C = (\mathcal{K}_C, \mathcal{I}_C \cup \{\Box, \blacksquare\}, \Delta_C)$, i.e., the keys of C are the control locations; the identifiers form the stack alphabet; the rule set Δ_C is defined as the set of labeled rewrite rules derived from the name and auth certs as shown in Section 4.1; and f maps every rule to its corresponding authorization specification.

The usefulness of this correspondence stems from the following simple observation: A configuration $\langle K, \sigma \rangle$ of $\mathcal{P}_C$ can reach another configuration $\langle K', \sigma' \rangle$ if and only if C contains a chain of certificates $(c_1, \ldots, c_k)$ such that $(c_k \circ \cdots \circ c_1)(K \, \sigma) = K' \, \sigma'$. Moreover, the label of the certificate chain is precisely $v(c_1 \cdots c_k)$. Thus, solving the GPP/GPS problem provides a way to find a set of certificate chains to prove that a certain principal K' is allowed to access a resource of principal K. Moreover, the solution of the problem identifies a set of certificate chains such that the union of their labels is maximal (with respect to the semiring ordering $\sqsubseteq$).

In the authorization problem, we are given a set of certs C, a principal K, and resource K_r. In the PDS context, K can access the resource with authorization specification T iff the following statement is true: In the GPP problem for $\mathcal{W}_C$ and $C = \{\langle K, \Box \rangle, \langle K, \blacksquare \rangle\}$, it holds that $\delta(\langle K_r, \Box \rangle) \sqsubseteq T$; equivalently, in the GPS problem for $\mathcal{W}_C$ and $C = \{\langle K_r, \Box \rangle\}$ we have $\delta(\langle K, \Box \rangle) \oplus \delta(\langle K, \blacksquare \rangle) \sqsubseteq T$.

6   Distributed Certificate-Chain Discovery

The algorithms for GPR problems proposed in [23, 24] work under the assumption that all pushdown rules (or certificates, resp.) are stored centrally at the site that carries out the computation. In a real-world setting, certificates may be issued by many principals, and centralized storage at one site may not be desirable or possible. We therefore propose versions of these algorithms that solve the problems in a distributed environment.

Let C be a (finite) set of certificates and $\mathcal{W}_C = (\mathcal{P}_C, \mathcal{S}_C, f)$ be the WPDS associated with C (see Section 5 for details). As in Section 3.2, we assume that the rules/certificates in Δ are distributed over a set of servers, where the f_S function describes the distribution of principals over the sites, and also assume that every certificate/rule is stored at the site responsible for its issuer or subject. In the remainder of this section, we consider distributed solutions for the following distributed certificate-chain-discovery problem, under the aforementioned assumptions:

> Given a principal r (the **resource**) and a principal c (the **client**) with public keys K_r and K_c, is there a set of certificate chains in $\mathcal{W}$ that allows c to access r and, if there is, what is their combined value?

The problem is equivalent to either of the following problems in the WPDS setting:

- As a GPP problem: For $C = \{\langle K_c, \square \rangle, \langle K_c, \blacksquare \rangle\}$ and $c = \langle K_r, \square \rangle$, compute $\delta(c)$ and a backwards witness dag for $(c, \delta(c))$.
- As a GPS problem: For $C = \{\langle K_r, \square \rangle\}$, $c_1 = \langle K_c, \square \rangle$, and $c_2 = \langle K_c, \blacksquare \rangle$, compute $\delta(c_1) \oplus \delta(c_2)$ and forwards witness dags for $(c_1, \delta(c_1))$ and $(c_2, \delta(c_2))$.

Sections 6.1 and 6.2 propose protocols for the communication between the client, the resource, and the servers that co-operate to solve the distributed access problem. We propose two protocols, one based on the GPP formulation of the above problem, the other on the GPS formulation. The protocols assume algorithms for solving GPP and GPS in the distributed setting, and which are provided in Section 3. The relative merits of the protocols, as well as security and privacy-related issues, are discussed in Section 6.3.

6.1   The GPS Protocol for Distributed Certificate-Chain Discovery

In a distributed setting, multiple access requests may happen at the same time. We shall use unique *request ids* to distinguish them. In the GPS variant, the protocol consists of three phases.

Initialization. The initialization consists of the following steps:

1. The client c sends a message to the resource r requesting access. The message contains the public key of the client, K_c.
2. The resource r responds by sending a unique request identifier *reqid*, which will distinguish this request from other requests that may currently be in progress.
3. The client sends a message to the site $f_S(K_c)$ (called the *client site* and denoted s_c from here on). The message contains (i) its key K_c, (ii) the request id *reqid*, (iii) the so-called *client certificate*: the request id signed by the client.
4. The client site checks whether the contents and signature of the client certificate match expectations. If the check is successful, the client site tells the client that certificate discovery may begin.
5. The client asks the resource to initiate the search.
6. The resource sends a message to the site $f_S(K_r)$ (called the *resource site* and written s_r) containing its public key K_r, the request id *reqid*, and a request to initiate certificate discovery.

Search. The resource site initiates a GPS query for the singleton set $C = \{\langle K_r, \square \rangle\}$, where *reqid* is used to distinguish this query from others (so that servers may work on multiple requests at the same time). The query is resolved by all the servers together, and the details of the search algorithm are given in Section 3. Here, the crucial points are that s_r starts a local GPS computation, and if it notices that $post^*(C)$ intersects $\mathcal{T}(s)$ for some other site s (because of some boundary certificate), then s is asked to participate in the search. Site s may, in the course of its computation, contact other sites. Each site s constructs the set $\mathcal{T}_{post}^C(s)$ and maintains information that allows to construct the s-region of the required witness dags.

Verification. Because of its earlier communication with the client, the client site s_c knows that $c_1 := \langle K_c, \square \rangle$ and $c_2 := \langle K_c, \blacksquare \rangle$ are the targets of the search. Moreover, because $c_1, c_2 \in \mathcal{T}(s_c)$, the client site knows whether the finished search has reached c_1, c_2. To complete the algorithm, the result must be reported to the resource. Thus, in the verification phase, the direction of the flow of information is contrary to the search phase.

The client site starts by constructing the s_c-region of the witness dags. It then sends this sub-dag starting at its boundary nodes 'upstream' to the corresponding neighboring sites. The neighboring sites use this information to complete their own sub-dags and send them further upstream until s_r has the full witness dags for c_1 and c_2. The result is then reported by s_r to the resource. Moreover, all communications in this phase are accompanied by the *client certificate* mentioned earlier.

The resource verifies the result, i.e., checks the integrity of the dag, the signatures on all certificates used in the dags, whether the client certificate matches *reqid*, and whether its signature matches the client. Depending on the outcome, access is allowed or denied to the client.

The verification of the complete dag may place a great workload on the resource. An alternative is as follows: Instead of sending complete sub-dags, the sites only report the sum (w.r.t. $\oplus$) of the paths inside the dags. Then, the result given by s_r to the resource consists of certificates issued by the resource and the combined values of the paths below them. This also reduces the amount of network traffic.

6.2   The GPP Protocol for Distributed Certificate-Chain Discovery

In this setting, the search is started at the client site, and, in comparison with Section 6.1, the flow of information between the sites is reversed.

Initialization

1. The client c sends a message to the resource r requesting access.
2. The resource generates *reqid* and sends the pair $(R, reqid)$ to the resource site s_r (to notify it of an 'incoming' search). After s_r has acknowledged receipt of the message, the resource sends *reqid* to the client.

3. The client contacts the client site s_c and asks it to initiate a GPP computation. Along with the request, it sends *reqid* and the client certificate as in Section 6.1.
4. The client site again checks correctness of the client certificate. If correct, s_c begins the search.

Search. The search stage is analogous to the GPS protocol, except that it is started at the client site and from the set $C = \{\langle K_c, \blacksquare \rangle, \langle K_c, \square \rangle\}$. In brief, a site s becomes involved in the search if $pre^*(C)$ intersects $T(s)$. Communications between sites are tagged with *both* *reqid* and the client certificate.

Verification. At the end of the search, the resource site (which knows that the search with id *reqid* has the target $c = \langle K_r, \square \rangle$) can determine whether c was reachable from C and what the value of $\delta(c)$ is.

To generate a complete witness dag, s_r can request from the sites further 'downstream' their regions of the witness dag, and then pass the complete dag along with the client certificate to the resource, which will verify it and (if successful) grant access to the client.

As an alternative solution, s_r may report to the resource just the certificates issued by the resource and the combined values of the paths above them. In that case, no further communication between the sites is necessary.

Example 1. Consider the rules shown below:

$$r_1 := \langle K_r, \square \rangle \hookrightarrow \langle K_{uw}, \texttt{faculty}\,\blacksquare \rangle$$
$$r_2 := \langle K_{uw}, \texttt{faculty} \rangle \hookrightarrow \langle K_{ls}, \texttt{faculty} \rangle$$
$$r_3 := \langle K_{ls}, \texttt{faculty} \rangle \hookrightarrow \langle K_{cs}, \texttt{faculty} \rangle$$
$$r_4 := \langle K_{ls}, \texttt{faculty} \rangle \hookrightarrow \langle K_{bio}, \texttt{faculty} \rangle$$
$$r_5 := \langle K_{cs}, \texttt{faculty} \rangle \hookrightarrow \langle K_{Bob}, \varepsilon \rangle$$

with $f(r_1) := t$ and $f(r_i) := \top$ for $2 \leq i \leq 5$. We assume that there are four sites, *UW*, *LS*, *CS*, and *BIO*. The sitemap f_S is as follows: $f_S(K_r)$ and $f_S(K_{uw})$ are equal to *UW*, $f_S(K_{ls})$ is equal to *LS*, $f_S(K_{bio})$ is equal to *BIO*, and $f_S(K_{cs})$ and $f_S(K_{Bob})$ are equal to *CS*. This example is used as Case 1 in Section 7.1. Suppose that Bob (at site *CS*) wants to access resource R (at site *UW*). Then, the site CS starts the search with $C = \{\langle K_{Bob}, \square \rangle, \langle K_{Bob}, \blacksquare \rangle\}$ and discovers, through r_5 and r_3, that $pre^*(C)$ intersects $T(LS)$, so site LS gets involved and notices that (because of r_2), site *UW* must also take part in the search. The automata computed by *CS*, *LS*, and *UW* are shown in Figure 3; notice that site *Bio* does not become involved. At the end of the computation, site *UW* sees that $\langle K_r, \square \rangle$ is accepted by its automaton $\mathcal{A}_{UW}$ with weight t, and that is the result reported to resource R.

6.3   Discussion

Here, we discuss privacy and security-related topics, compare the two protocols, and discuss possible improvements.

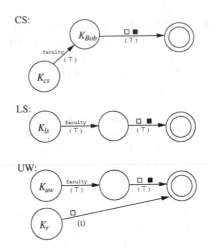

Fig. 3. pre^* automata for $\langle R, \square \rangle$ computed at sites CS, LS, and UW; weights on transitions shown in parentheses

Privacy. During the search, the parties involved learn the following:

- Only the resource and the client know that the client has asked to access the resource.
- The resource site knows that a request has been made to the resource, but not by whom.
- The client site knows only that the client has made a request, but not to whom.
- All other sites know only that a request has been made, but not by whom or to whom. They may surmise something about the nature of the request judging from the identifiers on the transitions, the direction from which the query comes, and the direction from where a confirmation comes, but they can only observe the communication with their neighbor sites.

Thus, the privacy of the access request is ensured during the search. However, when the witness dag is constructed during the construction phase, all sites learn the identity of the client. This can be avoided if the alternative method is used, in which only the values of certain paths in the dag are transmitted among sites. This alternative solution also prevents the unnecessary spread of certificates among sites (which might contain sensitive information).

Security Against Attacks

Spoofing and Eavesdropping. We assume that all parties involved in the search can communicate securely and that no identification spoofing can take place.

Trusting the Sites. Because the main part of the computation is carried out by the sites, the protocols are potentially susceptible to malicious behavior of the sites. A malicious site could either invent or ignore certificates. Ignoring certificates would only be to the detriment of the users for which the site is responsible, and seems unlikely to be a cause for concern.

Inventing certificates is also not a problem if the verification stage constructs the full witness dag because in this case all certificates (which are signed by their issuers) have to be supplied. The alternative solution, in which only values are reported, is more problematic: in essence, reporting the value of the paths in a sub-dag rooted at a node $(\langle K, w \rangle, d)$ amounts to issuing a confirmation (in the name of principal K) that there is a certificate chain from $\langle K, w \rangle$ to the client. Therefore, the alternative solution requires K to trust the site to use K's certificates truthfully. Note that if all boundary certificates have subjects that are under direct control of the respective site operator, this is not a problem.

The Client Certificate. The resource must verify that the reported result is indeed valid for the client who has initiated the request. If the verification stage constructs full witness dags, this becomes straightforward: the maximal nodes of the dags must refer to the client.

If the alternative solution is used in the verification, the client certificate serves this purpose, provided that both resource and client site verify its correctness.

A Comparison of the Two Protocols. In the GPP-based protocol, the search starts at the client site; in the GPS-based protocol it starts at the resource site. If a site is responsible for a 'popular' resource, the GPS-based protocol may put too much workload on it. Moreover, denial-of-service attacks are conceivable in which a malicious client causes a large number of GPS computations (under different identities) that are doomed to fail. In the GPP-based protocol, this is less likely to happen: the workload would fall mostly on the client site, which can be assumed to have a relationship to the client (e.g., the site is the client's company, ISP, etc.), and thus there is some 'social safeguard' against denial-of-service attacks.

Moreover, when the construction of complete witness dags is omitted, the GPP-based solution does not require a separate verification stage. For these reasons, it seems that the GPP-based solution has some advantages over the GPS-based solution. However, we have yet to carry out a more precise investigation of this issue.

Possible Improvements

Caching Results. Notice that the methods we describe do *not* have to be carried out every time that a client tries to access a resource. This would only have to be done for the first contact between a given client and a given resource. If the outcome is successful, the resource may remember this and grant access without a full search the next time.

Caching can also be used by the sites: unless a site is the client site or the resource site for some request, the result of its local search is independent of the request identifier. Therefore, sites may cache recent results and reuse them when an identical request (modulo *reqid*) comes along.

Guided Search. In both protocols, the sets $pre^*(C)/post^*(C)$ may intersect the domains of many sites; therefore, any request could involve many different sites even if only a few of them are 'relevant' for the search. This increases the length of the computation as well as the amount of network traffic. Thus, the protocol could be improved by limiting the scope of the search. It is likely that the client has an idea of *why* he/she should be allowed to access the resource; therefore, one possibility would be to let the client and/or the client site suggest a set of sites that are likely to contain suitable certificates.

Termination. In the distributed GPP/GPS computation, a standard termination-detection algorithm can be applied to determine that the search has terminated, which entails additional time and communication overhead. However, even before the search has terminated, or before all relevant certificate chains have been found, the client site (in the GPS case) or the resource site (in the GPP case) may have discovered *some* paths with a tentative value (which may be 'larger' – with respect to the ordering – than the δ value). If the goal of the search is just to establish that the δ value is no larger than a certain threshold, then this information could be used to terminate the search early. Moreover, the computation could be limited by a timeout.

7   Implementation

We have implemented a prototype of our distributed certificate-chain-discovery algorithm. Figure 4 shows how a site is organized. Each SPKI/SDSI site consists of a SPKI/SDSI server and a WPDS server. The SPKI/SDSI server deals with SPKI/SDSI certificates and provides the interface for clients to perform requests for authorization. The WPDS server implements distributed certificate-chain discovery using an algorithm for solving reachability problems in Weighted Pushdown Systems (WPDS). The clients do not interact directly with the WPDS servers. In a typical authorization-request scenario, a client first initiates the request by contacting the SPKI/SDSI server (1). The SPKI/SDSI server then parses the request and sends it to the WPDS server at the same site (2). At this point, the WPDS server starts the distributed certificate-chain-discovery process and contacts other WPDS servers (3, 4) as necessary. If a proof of authorization is found and verified, the client is granted access to the resource; otherwise the request is denied (5, 6).

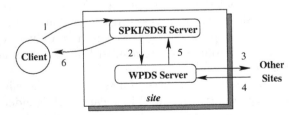

Fig. 4. Architecture Diagram Inside a Site

7.1 Examples

We illustrate how the system works using three examples. A graph is used to illustrate the configuration of sites for each example. In each graph, shaded nodes represents distinct sites of a distributed SPKI/SDSI system, while labels represent the cross-boundary SPKI/SDSI certificates. Nodes with a symbol *(R)* denote the resource from where SPKI/SDSI auth certs are issued. The dashed lines denote the certificate chain discovered by our algorithms when *Bob* requests access to resource *R*.

- **(Case 1):** This case demonstrates the basic idea of distributed certificate-chain discovery. Let us assume that a university has the hierarchical structure shown in Figure 5, where each site represents one level of the university. Site *UW* denotes the top level of the University of Wisconsin; *LS* denotes one of the colleges of *UW*, i.e., the college of Letters and Sciences; while *CS* and *BIO* represent two departments under *LS*. Two sites are linked together if a SPKI/SDSI certificate refers to both sites. For instance, the site *UW* has issued two certificates with respect to site *LS*: the auth cert $K_r \ \square \xrightarrow{t} K_{uw}$ faculty ∎ grants access right t to all K_{uw}'s faculty; the name cert K_{uw} faculty → K_{ls} faculty states that all K_{ls}'s faculty are K_{uw}'s faculty. Let us assume that *Bob*, from *CS*, requests access to a service *R* located at *UW*. The certificate-chain-discovery process starts from *UW* and continues down the hierarchy (*LS*, then *CS*) until it reaches *CS*, where *Bob* is granted access rights. Note that each individual site does not have sufficient knowledge to decide the authorization request. Instead, the certificates along the path must be used together to show that *Bob* has the required permissions.
- **(Case 2):** While Case 1 demonstrates the basic idea behind distributed certificate-chain discovery, Case 2 illustrates the situation where certificates from multiple paths must be combined to obtain the required authorization specifications (i.e., access permission). For instance, continuing with the example from Case 1, we now add a new joint department *BCS*, which is formed from both *CS* and *BIO* departments. The new structure is shown in Figure 6. Furthermore, *LS* issues two authorization certificates with distinct authorization specifications t_1 and t_2, to *CS* and *BIO*, respectively. Suppose

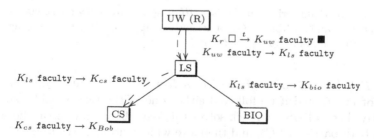

Fig. 5. (Case 1.): *R* grants **read** permission to directory /etc to *UW*'s faculty: t = (tag (dir /etc (read))); *Bob* requests **read** access for directory /etc

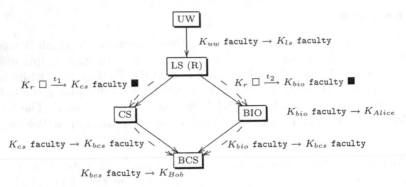

Fig. 6. (Case 2.): Authorization Over Multiple Paths. R grants **read** privilege to directory /etc to CS's faculty: t_1 = (tag (dir /etc (read))), and **write** privilege to BIO's faculty: t_2 = (tag (dir /etc (write))); Bob requests (**read write**) for the directory /etc.

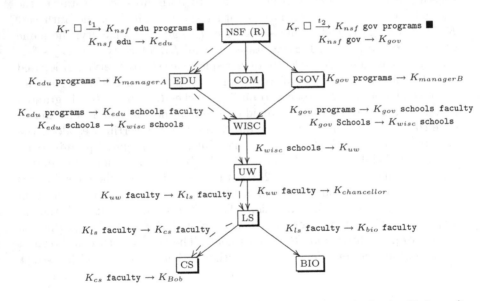

Fig. 7. (Case 3.): R authorizes all NSF's EDU programs to **apply** for fundA: t_1 = (tag (fundA apply)), and all NSF's GOV programs can **apply** for fundB: t_2 = (tag (fundB apply)); Bob attempts to **apply** for fundA

that Bob, from BCS, wants to access R with both t_1 and t_2. This request cannot be granted if we followed either one of the two possible paths separately. The WPDS approach solves this issue by combining authorizations from both paths at BCS, and therefore will grant authorization to Bob.

– **(Case 3):** The third case, shown in Figure 7, builds on top of the first two and demonstrates an even more complex environment. This case is constructed for two purposes. One, we want to demonstrate the scalability of the WPDS algorithm. Two, we want to study the performance with respect to certificate-chain length. We will measure computation time against the length of chains in Section 7.2.

7.2 Performance Analysis

In this section, we report on the performance of our implementation, using the examples discussed before. We use response time from the perspective of clients as the performance metrics. Because we currently do not have the resources to perform a real-world test, all tests are conducted under a simulated environment: each site runs on a separate machine on a local area network. Therefore, the timing results do not reflect network latency in a real distributed environment. All test machines have 800 MHz Pentium III processors, 256 MB of RAM, running TAO Linux version 1.0.

For each experiment, we used three different configurations: *base*, *simple*, and *complex*. For comparison purposes, we also collected performance data for running certificate-chain discovery in centralized mode (i.e., all the certificates are stored at a single site), using the complex configuration.

– **Base configuration:** The base uses only the bare minimum number of certificates required for the tests (exactly as shown in Figures 5 - 7); the number of certificates ranges from 6 to 16 certs in these tests. We use the results from this configuration as the baseline for the other two test cases.
– **Simple configuration:** In a real-world scenario, each site would have more certificates. Each simple configuration adds between 60 and 160 certificates

Table 1. Performance Results

Client (Request)	Time (ms) Distributed			Centralized
	Base	**Simple**	**Complex**	**Complex**
Case 1. See Figure 5				
Bob ((dir /etc (read)))	661	685	713	54
Case 2. See Figure 6				
Bob ((dir /etc (read)))	663	685	716	55
Bob ((dir /etc (write)))	717	730	741	55
Bob ((dir /etc (read write)))	723	736	741	55
Alice ((dir /etc (write)))	668	679	693	53
Case 3. See Figure 7				
ManagerA ((fundA apply))	654	683	664	118
ManagerB ((fundB apply))	793	769	796	116
Chancellor ((fundA apply))	979	960	996	107
Bob ((fundA apply))	1146	1133	1218	110
Bob ((fundB apply))	1132	1150	1232	115

to the base configuration. For each site, we added a number of additional certificates (for students, staff, etc.), such as K_{uw} student $\rightarrow K_{ls}$ student, and K_{cs} faculty $\rightarrow K_{profA}$.

- **Complex configuration:** To measure how the system scales, we also tested each case using between 760 and 1600 certificates.

Table 1 shows the performance results for the three configurations. As one might expect, the more certificates there are in the system, the longer it takes to perform certificate-chain discovery. However, the time it takes to perform certificate-chain discovery increases at a lower rate compared to the increase in the number of certificates. The data shows insignificant changes from the base configuration to the simple configuration; and it shows a very small increase

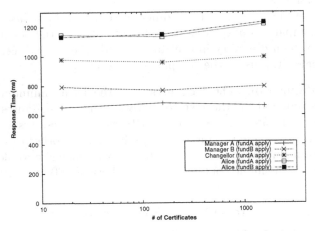

Fig. 8. Response Time vs. # of Certificates (Case 3.)

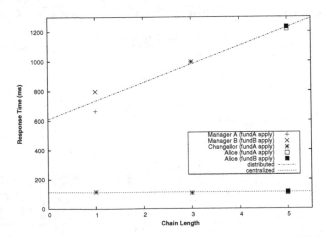

Fig. 9. Response Time vs. Chain Length (Case 3. complex configuration)

(about 4% on average) from simple to complex. Figure 8 illustrates this using data from case 3.[4] In addition, Table 1 shows that the performance difference between running certificate-chain discovery in distributed and in centralized mode is quite significant. For instance, in Case 3, distributed certificate-chain discovery took more than ten times as long as the centralized version. This is because in distributed certificate-chain discovery a significant percentage of time (about 80% to 93%) is spent on network-related operations, such as sending and receiving messages. We expect to be able to reduce some of the network overhead through optimizations. For example, we can reduce the number of messages exchanged during certificate-chain discovery by bundling several messages together and sending the bundle using one packet whenever possible. This is part of planned future work.

Performance data from Case 3 also illustrates an area for future work: *reducing response time for long certificate chains*. Here we define the length of a certificate chain as the number of distinct sites between the request site and the resource site. For example, Manager A is of chain length 1 since her site *EDU* is only one hop away from the resource site *NSF*. As illustrated by the ascending line at the top of Figure 9, the length of the certificate chain has a great impact on performance: the longer the chain, the longer it takes to service the request. For comparison purposes, the flat line shows the response time had we centralized all the certificates at one location. This time reflects the cost of running the GPS algorithm at one site, and therefore does not contain any network overhead. We are currently investigating techniques to improve the average performance for long certificate chains. For instance, in Section 6.3 we have discussed the possibility of using caching to reduce the discovery time.

References

1. M. Abadi. On SDSI's linked local name spaces. *Journal of Computer Security*, 6(1-2):3–21, 1998.
2. A. W. Appel and E. W. Felten. Proof-carrying authentication. In *Conf. on Comp. and Commun. Sec.*, Nov. 1999.
3. L. Bauer, S. Garriss, and M. K. Reiter. Distributed proving in access-control systems. In *In Proceedings of the 2005 IEEE Symposium on Security and Privacy*, pages 81–95, May 2005.
4. M. Blaze, J. Feigenbaum, J. Ioannidis, and A. D. Keromytis. The role of trust management in distributed systems security. In Vitek and Jensen, editors, *Secure Internet Programming: Security Issues for Mobile and Distributed Objects*, pages 185–210, 1999. LNCS 1603.
5. M. Blaze, J. Feigenbaum, J. Ioannidis, and A. D. Keromytis. The KeyNote Trust-Management System Version 2. RFC 2704, Sept. 1999.
6. A. Bouajjani, J. Esparza, and O. Maler. Reachability analysis of pushdown automata: Application to model-checking. In *Proceedings of CONCUR'97*, volume 1243 of *Lecture Notes in Computer Science*, pages 135–150. Springer, 1997.
7. A. Bouajjani, J. Esparza, and T. Touili. A generic approach to the static analysis of concurrent programs with procedures. In *Proceedings of POPL'03*, 2003.

---

[4] Two other cases tested showed similar results and therefore are omitted here.

8. D. Clarke, J.-E. Elien, C. M. Ellison, M. Fredette, A. Morcos, and R. L. Rivest. Certficate chain discovery in SPKI/SDSI. *Journal of Computer Security*, 9(1/2):285–322, 2001.

9. C. M. Ellison, B. Frantz, B. Lampson, R. Rivest, B. Thomas, and T. Ylönen. *RFC 2693: SPKI Certificate Theory*. The Internet Society, September 1999.

10. J. Esparza, D. Hansel, P. Rossmanith, and S. Schwoon. Efficient algorithms for model checking pushdown systems. In E. A. Emerson and A. P. Sistla, editors, *Proceedings of CAV'2000*, volume 1855 of *Lecture Notes in Computer Science*, pages 232–247. Springer, July 2000.

11. A. Finkel, B.Willems, and P. Wolper. A direct symbolic approach to model checking pushdown systems. *Elec. Notes in Theor. Comp. Sci.*, 9, 1997.

12. J. Y. Halpern and R. van der Meyden. A logical reconstruction of SPKI. In *Proceedings of the 14th IEEE Computer Security Foundations Workshop*, pages 59–70. IEEE Computer Society Press, 2001.

13. J. Howell and D. Kotz. A formal semantics for SPKI. Technical Report 2000-363, Department of Computer Science, Dartmouth College, Hanover, NH, Mar. 2000.

14. S. Jha and T. Reps. Analysis of SPKI/SDSI certificates using model checking. In *Proceedings of the 15th IEEE Computer Security Foundations Workshop (CSFW)*, pages 129–146. IEEE Computer Society, June 2002.

15. S. Jha and T. Reps. Model checking SPKI/SDSI. *Journal of Computer Security*, 12(3–4):317–353, 2004.

16. T. Jim. SD3: A trust management system with certified evaluation. In *SP '01: Proceedings of the IEEE Symposium on Security and Privacy*, page 106. IEEE Computer Society, 2001.

17. T. Jim and D. Suciu. Dynamically distributed query evaluation. In *PODS '01: Proceedings of the twentieth ACM SIGMOD-SIGACT-SIGART symposium on Principles of database systems*, pages 28–39. ACM Press, 2001.

18. B. Lampson, M. Abadi, M. Burrows, and E. Wobber. Authentication in distributed systems: Theory and practice. *ACM Transactions on Computer Systems*, 10(4):265–310, November 1992.

19. N. Li and J. C. Mitchell. Understanding SPKI/SDSI using first-order logic. In *Proceedings of the 16th IEEE Computer Security Foundations Workshop (CSFW)*. IEEE Computer Society, 2003.

20. N. Li, W. H. Winsborough, and J. C. Mitchell. Distributed credential chain discovery in trust management. *Journal of Computer Security*, 11(1):35–86, February 2003.

21. F. Pfenning and C. Schürmann. System description: Twelf — a meta-logical framework for deductive systems. In H. Ganzinger, editor, *Int. Conf. on Auto. Deduc.*, pages 202–206. Springer-Verlag, LNAI 1632, July 1999.

22. T. Reps, S. Schwoon, and S. Jha. Weighted pushdown systems and their application to interprocedural dataflow analysis. In *Proceedings of the 10th Internation Static Analysis Symposium (SAS)*, San Diego, CA, June 11-13 2003.

23. T. Reps, S. Schwoon, S. Jha, and D. Melski. Weighted pushdown systems and their application to interprocedural dataflow analysis. *Science of Computer Programming*, 58(1-2):206–263, October 2005.

24. S. Schwoon, S. Jha, T. Reps, and S. Stubblebine. On generalized authorization problems. In *Proceedings of the 16th IEEE Computer Security Foundations Workshop (CSFW)*, pages 202–218. IEEE Computer Society, June 2003.

25. S. Weeks. Understanding trust management systems. In *Proceedings of the IEEE Symposium on Research in Security and Privacy*, Research in Security and Privacy, Oakland, CA, May 2001. IEEE Computer Society,Technical Committee on Security and Privacy, IEEE Computer Society Press.

Automatic Verification of Parameterized Data Structures*

Jyotirmoy V. Deshmukh, E. Allen Emerson, and Prateek Gupta

Department of Computer Sciences and Computer Engineering Research Center,
The University of Texas at Austin, Austin TX 78712, USA
{deshmukh, emerson, prateek}@cs.utexas.edu

Abstract. Verifying correctness of programs operating on data structures has become an integral part of software verification. A method is a program that acts on an input data structure (modeled as a graph) and produces an output data structure. The *parameterized correctness* problem for such methods can be defined as follows: Given a method and a property of the input graphs, we wish to verify that for all input graphs, parameterized by their size, the output graphs also satisfy the property. We present an automated approach to verify that a given method *preserves* a given property for a large class of methods. Examples include reversals of linked lists, insertion, deletion and iterative modification of nodes in directed graphs. Our approach draws on machinery from automata theory and temporal logic. For a useful class of data structures and properties, our solution is polynomial in the size of the method and size of the property specification.

Keywords: Parameterized correctness, Data structures.

1 Introduction

Data structures are the basic building blocks for all large software systems. Such systems typically manipulate arbitrarily large data structures using specialized programs known as *methods*. An incorrect implementation of a method can lead to failure of the entire software system. Consequently, reasoning about methods operating on data structures is a significant part of the software verification effort.

We investigate the problem of automatic verification of methods operating on data structures, *parameterized* by their size. Given a method $\mathcal{M}$, operating on an input data structure modeled as a graph G_i, and a property φ of the graph, we wish to verify that: if φ holds for the input graph G_i, then φ also holds for the graph G_o obtained by the action of $\mathcal{M}$ on G_i, *i.e.*, $\mathcal{M}$ preserves φ. For instance, given a method that adds a node to an acyclic singly linked list, we would like to verify that the output data structure is also a well formed acyclic singly linked list. In contrast to the standard testing approach for validation of such methods,

---

* This research is supported in part by NSF grants CCR-009-8141 & ITR-CCR-020-5483, and SRC Contract No. 2002-TJ-1026.

H. Hermanns and J. Palsberg (Eds.): TACAS 2006, LNCS 3920, pp. 27–41, 2006.

which ensures correctness for a few candidate data structures up to a bounded size, we would like to verify that methods exhibit correct behavior for arbitrarily large input data structures.

We provide an automatic procedure based on machinery from automata theory and temporal logic to establish parameterized correctness. Our approach is applicable to a broad spectrum of methods that perform updates on dynamically created data structures. For example, our technique can establish correctness for methods such as: reversal of singly linked lists; insertion or deletion of nodes in general graphs (such as linked lists, k-ary trees, directed acyclic graphs, etc.); swapping of nodes within a bounded distance in any general graph; and iterative modification of data values at nodes in any general graph.

In our technique the property to be verified is generally specified using a (tree) automaton running on graphs. Alternatively, we can use temporal logic as the specification language for properties. Thus, we can specify a rich class of properties, including, but not limited to:

1. Connectivity properties such as: reachability of a target node from a source node (where the nodes are specified by pointers); reachability of a given data value from a given node; existence of cycles; existence of sharing (two nodes point to a common node); treeness (each non-root node has a unique parent); list-ness; and checking whether two nodes are fully connected (either node is reachable from the other using the *next* pointer fields).
2. Data-dependent properties such as sortedness (*i.e.*, all nodes in a given graph obey a certain sorting discipline on data values).
3. Properties of dynamically allocated storage such as checking null pointer dereferences and absence of dangling pointers.

We refer to the automaton specifying the property as the *property automaton*, denoted by $\mathcal{A}_\varphi$. Similarly, the automaton specifying the negation of the property is specified as $\mathcal{A}_{\neg\varphi}$.

The method ($\mathcal{M}$) to be verified is algorithmically translated into an automaton. We refer to this automaton as the *method automaton*, denoted by $\mathcal{A}_\mathcal{M}$. $\mathcal{A}_\mathcal{M}$ operates on a pair of input-output graphs; it simulates the action of $\mathcal{M}$ on the input graph checking whether the output matches the output graph. It accepts only those pairs of graphs which represent a valid operation of the method. The pair of input-output graphs is represented using a single *composite graph*.

The central step is to use the method automaton and the property automata to obtain a *composite automaton* (denoted by $\mathcal{A}_c$) that accepts counterexamples to the correct operation of the method. On a given composite graph, $\mathcal{A}_c$ accepts iff: the property holds for the input, the output conforms to a valid action of the method on the input, and the property fails for the output. Thus if a graph is accepted by $\mathcal{A}_c$, it represents a witness to the failure of the method. Checking if such a graph exists is equivalent to checking the language accepted by $\mathcal{A}_c$ for nonemptiness.

Formally, we obtain the composite product automaton $\mathcal{A}_c$, by the product of $\mathcal{A}_\varphi$, $\mathcal{A}_\mathcal{M}$ and $\mathcal{A}_{\neg\varphi}$. $\mathcal{A}_c$ accepts a graph G_c representing an input-output pair (G_i, G_o), iff $G_o = \mathcal{M}(G_i)$ and $\varphi(G_i)$ and $\neg\varphi(G_o)$ are true.

In the above approach, correctness properties are specified by the user, using automata as the specification language. In a variant, but closely related approach, we use a suitable temporal logic in lieu of automata to specify the properties of interest. Temporal logics such as CTL often allow an easier specification of properties. The property to be verified is specified as a formula f_φ in the given logic. The method automaton is translated to a formula $f_\mathcal{M}$. The parameterized correctness problem reduces to checking the satisfiability of the conjunction: $f_c = f_{\varphi(G_i)} \wedge f_\mathcal{M} \wedge f_{\neg\varphi(G_o)}$.

In practice, we provide a simple programming language for describing methods. Our programming language is a useful subset of most modern day high level languages. We can efficiently compile any program written in our language into a method automaton. The time complexity of our technique is polynomial in the size of the method and property automata.

The outline of the paper is as follows: In Section 2, we provide the preliminary background, the problem definition and the scope of our technique. Section 3 discusses the syntax and semantics of our programming language. The algorithm for translation of a method into a method automaton is given in Section 4. We briefly examine the specification of properties as automata in Section 5. We present an application in Section 6 and discuss a variant approach using temporal logic in Section 7. The complexity analysis is discussed in Section 8 and finally, a summary of our paper with related work is given in Section 9.

2   Preliminaries

A data structure can be readily modeled as a directed graph $G(V, E)$ by establishing a one to one correspondence between the nodes of the data structure and the vertices (V) of G, and similarly between links of the data structure and the edges (E) of G. Each node of the data structure is a vertex $v \in V$ in G and a pointer from a source node ($\equiv$ vertex v_i) to a destination node ($\equiv$ vertex v_j) represents a directed edge $(v_i, v_j) \in E$. The data content at each node of the data structure is modeled as a labelling function $L : V \to \mathcal{D}$, where $\mathcal{D}$ is the domain of data values. For simplicity, we consider graphs with only a bounded *out-degree*, where the out-degree of a graph is defined as the maximum number of outgoing edges from a vertex in the graph.

A method $\mathcal{M}$ is a program that has one or more data structures as input and produces an output data structure which is a mutation of the input. A property φ of a graph $G(V, E)$ is a predicate on the labeled set of vertices and edges of the graph. The property φ is often referred to as the *shape* of a graph. Conversely, a shape φ is identified with a family of graphs for which the property φ is true. For instance, graphs satisfying the property that every non-root vertex has a unique incident edge and the root vertex has no incident edges, are said to constitute the family of trees. Properties of graphs can be conveniently specified as tree automata (See Section 5). We now revisit some important definitions for tree automata operating on trees with out-degree k (*i.e.*, a k-ary tree).

2.1 Tree Automata

A *finite tree automaton* over an infinite k-ary tree is a tuple $\mathcal{A} = (\Sigma, Q, \delta, q_0, \Phi)$ where:

> Σ is the finite, nonempty input alphabet labeling the nodes of the tree,
> Q is the finite, nonempty set of states of the automaton,
> $\delta : Q \times \Sigma \rightarrow 2^{Q \times \ldots \times Q(k \; times)}$ is the nondeterministic transition function,
> $q_0 \in Q$ is the start state of the automaton, and
> Φ is the acceptance condition.

In our technique, it is convenient to use the parity acceptance condition. The parity acceptance condition $\Phi = (\Phi_0, \Phi_1, \ldots \Phi_m)$ is expressed in terms of sequence of mutually disjoint subsets of Q. If $\pi = q_0, \ldots, q_i, \ldots$ is a finite or infinite sequence of automaton states q_i, then we say that π satisfies the acceptance condition if the following condition is satisfied: there exists an even number r, $0 < r < m$, such that some state in Φ_r appears infinitely often in π and each of the states in the set $\bigcup_{r<j\leq m} \Phi_j$ appears only finitely often in π. The parity condition is often alternately expressed as follows: A sequence of states π satisfies the parity acceptance condition, when the states of the automaton are colored with a set of colors $\{c_0, \ldots, c_m\}$, and the maximal index of the color appearing infinitely often in π is even. For the rest of this paper, we implicitly assume the parity acceptance condition for all tree automata used.

A tree automaton can be meaningfully defined to run on graphs. Essentially a run ρ of a tree automaton on a Σ-labeled input graph is an annotation of the graph with the automaton states compatible with the transition relation of the automaton. Not every automaton has a run on every graph, but if an automaton accepts some tree, it accepts some "small", finite graph, [EJ '88, Em '85]. Note that when $k = 1$, the tree automaton can be specialized to a string automaton.

2.2 Problem Definition

We define a parameterized family of graphs as the set $\mathcal{G} = \{G | \varphi(G) \; is \; true\}$, where the graphs are parameterized by their size. For all input graphs $G \in \mathcal{G}$ and a method $\mathcal{M}$ operating on G, we wish to verify if the resultant graphs $\mathcal{M}(G)$ satisfy the property φ. Formally, we wish to verify the correctness assertion: $\langle \varphi(G_i) \rangle \mathcal{M} \langle \varphi(G_o) \rangle$.

2.3 Scope

Most methods that operate on data structures use a *cursor* or an iterator to traverse the data structure. Methods which have multiple cursors are analogous to multi-head automata. Unfortunately, the parameterized correctness problem for such methods is undecidable, since the nonemptiness problem of a k-head automaton with $k \geq 2$ is undecidable [Rose '65, NSV '04]. Thus, we focus on methods which can be simulated by a single head automaton. Such methods can have multiple cursors, which are constrained to remain within some bounded distance at all times.

Methods can also be characterized by the way they access and mutate the data structure. Some methods perform only a bounded number of *destructive passes* over the data structure. We define a destructive pass as a single traversal of the data structure involving at least one update to some node of the data structure. It is difficult to reason about the parameterized correctness of methods which perform an unbounded number of destructive passes over the data structure, since their operation simulates a linear bounded automaton (LBA). The nonemptiness problem of an LBA is undecidable [HU '79]. Thus, our work focusses on methods which can only perform a bounded number of destructive passes over the data structure.

It is stipulated that the method terminates[1] and performs only a bounded number of destructive passes over the data structure. We also assume that the domain $\mathcal{D}$ of data values is finite.

2.4   Solution Framework

In our approach, we use automata to check if a given method $\mathcal{M}$ preserves a property φ. Our technique involves determining the existence of a pair of input-output graphs (G_i, G_o) such that:

1. the input graph G_i satisfies φ or $\varphi(G_i)$ is true (*i.e.*, the input is well formed),
2. the output graph G_o does not satisfy φ or $\neg\varphi(G_o)$ is true and
3. G_o represents a valid action of $\mathcal{M}$ on G_i or $G_o = \mathcal{M}(G_i)$ is true.

Formally, a property φ to be verified is specified as a tree automaton $\mathcal{A}_\varphi$, which accepts the set of all graphs which satisfy φ. We are given a similar automaton $\mathcal{A}_{\neg\varphi}$, to accept all graphs that satisfy $\neg\varphi$. The method $\mathcal{M}$ is algorithmically translated into a *method automaton* $\mathcal{A}_\mathcal{M}$, which checks whether $G_o = \mathcal{M}(G_i)$. The input-output graph pair is represented using a *composite graph*, denoted by G_c.

The composite graph $G_c(V, E)$ has each vertex $v \in V$ and each edge $e \in E$ annotated with one of three colors *black, green* or *red*. The color *black* represents part of the input graph that remains the same, color *red* represents deleted nodes or edges, and the color *green* represents new nodes or edges. Each vertex of the composite graph is labeled with an ordered pair of labels (d_i, d_o) $(d_i, d_o \in \mathcal{D})$ to model the old and the new data values at the corresponding node in the data structure. The input graph G_i, can be extracted from G_c by considering the subgraph composed of vertices and edges colored *red* or *black* and the labels d_i. Similarly, the output graph G_o can be extracted by considering the set of nodes and edges labeled *black* or *green* and the labels d_o. We define projection operators Γ_i and Γ_o to obtain the graphs G_i and G_o respectively, from the composite graph G_c. The method automaton $\mathcal{A}_\mathcal{M}$ runs on such composite graphs and accepts a composite graph G_c iff $G_i = \Gamma_i(G_c)$ $G_o = \Gamma_o(G_c)$ and $G_o = \mathcal{M}(G_i)$. Similarly, the property automata $\mathcal{A}_\varphi$ and $\mathcal{A}_{\neg\varphi}$ run on composite graphs, and look at the input or output parts of the composite graph.

---

[1] A similar assumption on program termination can be found in techniques such as shape analysis [Lev-Ami *et al.*], PALE [MS '01], and separation logic [ORY '01], which implicitly assume the termination of the program being analyzed.

Remark: Such an annotated graph can be obtained only if the method performs a bounded number of destructive passes over the data structure. For our current discussion, we assume that the method performs a single destructive pass of the data structure, *i.e.*, the method automaton traverses each node of the data structure exactly once. We generalize the assumption to handle multiple, but a bounded number of passes over the data structure, later in Section 4.

Finally, we construct a composite automaton $\mathcal{A}_c$, which is the synchronous product of $\mathcal{A}_{\neg\varphi}$, $\mathcal{A}_M$ and $\mathcal{A}_\varphi$. The product construction for the composite automaton is defined in standard fashion, [Car '94]. The number of states of the composite automaton is proportional to the product of the number of states of the constituent automata. The composite automaton is empty iff the method preserves the property. If the automaton is non-empty, then there exists a graph G which satisfies the property φ, but $\mathcal{M}(G)$ does not satisfy φ. Thus we also obtain a counterexample which illustrates erroneous behavior of the method.

3   Programming Language Description

In this section, we define the syntax and semantics of our programming language. An atomic unit of a data structure is termed as a *node*. Each node has a data field and a set of k pointer fields next_1, ..., next_k. We define **cursor** as a reserved word for an iterator through a given data structure. Since we focus on methods which can be mimicked using a single headed automaton, our programming language supports a single **cursor**[2]. If the node being pointed to by the cursor is n, a bounded window w is defined as a set of all nodes within a fixed distance from n. The size of the window w, denoted by $|w|$, is the cardinality of w. We define **head** or **root** as reserved words to indicate start nodes of the data structure.

We use a C-like syntax for describing methods, and accordingly use the abbreviation **cursor->field** to indicate the corresponding *field* of a node pointed to by the **cursor**. A statement in our programming language can have one of the forms as show in Table 1.

The sequential composition of two more statements with ; as the composition operator is called a *block statement*. For memory related operations, our language allows deletion of nodes being pointed to by any pointer $ptr(\neq \text{cursor})$, using the **delete** statement.

Every update to a **cursor** is preceded by storing the current value of the **cursor** in a special variable called **prev**, which cannot be used on the left hand side of an assignment statement. The addition of **prev** enhances the expressive power of our language by allowing methods to perform operations based on past value of the **cursor**. Destructive updates are allowed only within the bounded window defined by the **cursor**. When a new node is created, the pointer fields of the new node are initialized to any value within the current window. The initialization of the fields of a new node is made before **cursor** or **cursor->next**$_i$ is updated.

---

[2] We can easily extend our approach to handle a fixed number of *virtual* cursors within a bounded window.

Table 1. Programming language syntax

Assignment statement
     cursor->data := *data-constant*;
     cursor->next$_i$:= *ptr*[a]
     cursor := *ptr*;
     cursor := **new node** { data := *data-constant*;
                           next$_1$:= *ptr*;...; next$_k$:= *ptr*;};
     cursor->next$_i$:= **new node** {...};
Conditional statement
     if (*test-expr*) {
        block statement;
     } **else** { *block statement*; }
Loop statement
     while (*loop-cond*) {
        loop-body;
        update statement; }
     Here, the *update statement* is of the form:
     cursor:= ncursor$_1$ **when** *cond$_1$*
             ncursor$_2$ **when** *cond$_2$*
                 ⋮
             ncursor$_k$ **when** *cond$_k$*;
Break statement
     break;
Null statement
     null;

---

[a] *ptr* represents an allowable pointer expression, which can take one of the following forms:
cursor->next$_{i_1}$->next$_{i_2}$->... next$_{i_m}$ or prev or cursor, where m is bounded by the size of the window.

In a conditional statement, a *test-expr* is a boolean expression which either involves a comparison of the data value of the current node with another data value or a comparison of two *ptr* expressions.

A loop statement consists of three parts, a *loop condition*, the *loop body* and an *update statement*. A loop condition *loop-cond*, is a boolean expression involving the comparison of a *ptr* expression with null[3]. A method continues executing the loop as long as the loop condition is true. The loop body is a sequence of two or more non-loop statements. We do not allow nesting of loop statements, since this can in general mimic a k-head automaton. At the beginning of each iteration of the loop the values cursor->next$_i$ are cached in special variables ncursor$_i$ which cannot be used on the left hand side of an assignment statement.

---

[3] Note that any special termination condition required can always be modeled with the help of a **break** statement coupled with a conditional statement inside the loop body.

The `cursor` can be updated inside a loop statement only using an update statement. The value of `cursor` is assigned to `ncursor_i` if `cond_i` evaluates to true and `cond_j` $\forall j < i$ evaluates to false, where $cond_1 \ldots cond_k$ are any boolean valued expressions. A `break` statement breaks out from the `while` loop enclosing the break statement. If the break statement is not inside a loop body, no action is taken.

4   Translation into Automata

We can mechanically compile any given method in our language into corresponding parts of the *method automaton*, $\mathcal{A_M}$. $\mathcal{A_M}$ is a k-ary tree automaton running on graphs. For ease of exposition, we presently assume that each node has a single successor. We assume that all the statements in the method are labeled with a unique line number $\{1, \ldots, |\mathcal{M}|\}$, where $|\mathcal{M}|$ is the length of $\mathcal{M}$.

$\mathcal{A_M}$ is of the form $(\Sigma, Q_\mathcal{M}, \delta_\mathcal{M}, q_{0_\mathcal{M}}, \Phi_\mathcal{M})$, where the notation used is similar to the one described in Section 2.1. The parity acceptance condition $\Phi_\mathcal{M}$ is specified using two colors $\{(red = c_1), (green = c_2)\}$. States colored *green* are accepting states and those colored *red* are rejecting.

The action of a statement of $\mathcal{M}$ is mimicked by a transition of $\mathcal{A_M}$. On a given input graph G_i, the moves of the automaton are completely deterministic and a run of $\mathcal{A_M}$ on G_i is unique and well defined. For two different input graphs, the state of $\mathcal{A_M}$ after executing the same statement of $\mathcal{M}$ may be different. We use Q_j to denote the set of all possible states of $\mathcal{A_M}$ (for all input graphs) after executing the statement s_j.

A state q_j of $\mathcal{A_M}$ is modeled as a tuple $(j, cur_d, cur_p, new_d, new_p)$, where j corresponds to the line number of the statement s_j, cur_d is the current data value of the node being pointed to by the `cursor`, cur_p is the value of `cursor->next`, new_p is 0 if no new node is added at the current `cursor` position, else it is a non-zero value indicating the location of `new_node->next`, and new_d contains the data value of the new node that is added. The initial state of the automaton is denoted by $q_{0_\mathcal{M}} = (0, 0, 0, 0, 0)$.

Let θ be a boolean valued expression over the set of program variables. We say that a state q satisfies θ, denoted by $q \vDash \theta$, if the valuation of θ over the components of q is true. (Note that a state q completely encodes the values of all program variables.). We denote by Q^θ the set $\{q | q \vDash \theta\}$ and $Q^{\neg\theta}$, the set $\{q | q \nvDash \theta\}$.

4.1   Algorithm for Translation

We now give the algorithm used to populate the transition relation of $\mathcal{A_M}$:

1. Let Q be the set of possible states prior to an assignment statement s_j. For every state $q \in Q$, s_j is modeled by adding a transition of the form (q, ϵ, q'), where q' encodes the new data value, the pointer field value or a new node inserted at the `cursor` position by s_j. For instance given a state $q = (k, cur_d, cur_p, new_d, new_p)$, the assignment statement `cursor->data:=` *val* is modeled by adding the transition (q, ϵ, q'), where $q' = (j, val, cur_p, new_d, new_p)$.

2. Let Q be the set of possible states prior to a conditional statement s_j. Let ϕ be the test expression of s_j. Let s_k (s_m, resp.) be the first statement within the **if** (**else**, resp.) block of the conditional statement. For a conditional statement, we add transitions of the form: $\forall q \in Q^\phi, \forall t \in Q_k : \{(q, \epsilon, t)\}$, and $\forall q' \in Q^{\neg\phi}, \forall t' \in Q_m : \{(q', \epsilon, t')\}$.

3. (a) Let Q denote the set of possible states prior to a loop statement s_j. For the loop statement shown in the left hand column of the table below, we add transitions shown in the right hand column.

j: **while** (ψ) {	$\forall q \in Q^\psi, \forall q' \in Q_k : \{(q, \epsilon, q')\}$
k: s_k;	$\forall q \in Q^{\neg\psi}, \forall q' \in Q_m : \{(q, \epsilon, q')\}$
$\vdots$	
	$\forall q \in Q_l^\psi, \forall q' \in Q_k : \{(q, \epsilon, q')\}$
l: *update statement*; }	$\forall q \in Q_l^{\neg\psi}, \forall q' \in Q_m : \{(q, \epsilon, q')\}$
m: s_m;	

(b) Suppose a loop body contains the **break** statement s_b. Let the set of possible states before the **break** statement be Q. We add transitions of the form: $\forall q \in Q, \forall q' \in Q_b : \{(q, \epsilon, q')\}$.

4. A statement s_j that alters the current **cursor** position initializes the window w to a new **cursor** position. The state q of $\mathcal{A}_\mathcal{M}$ before the execution of s_j encodes the action of $\mathcal{M}$ on the current input node n_i. Let τ be a boolean valued expression, which is *true* iff the output node in the composite graph n_o, conforms to $\mathcal{M}(n_i)$ and *false* otherwise. (For details on how the check is performed please refer to the Appendix.). Let the next node that the automaton reads be n', with $n_i' = \Gamma_i(n')$. Let n_i'->**data** $= d'$ and n_i'->**next** $= p'$. The next state q' after execution of s_j is $q' = (k, d', p', 0, 0)$, where k is the line number of the statement following s_j in the control flow graph. The state q_{rej} represents a *reject* state. Let the set of possible states prior to s_j be Q. We add a set of transitions of the form: $\forall q \in Q^\tau : \{(q, n', q')\}$, $\forall q \in Q^{\neg\tau} : \{(q, \epsilon, q_{rej})\}$, and $\forall \sigma \in \Sigma \cup \{\epsilon\} : \{(q_{rej}, \sigma, q_{rej})\}$. Intuitively, if a node is found in a composite graph such that the input and output parts of the node do not conform to the action of the method, the automaton rejects that composite graph.

5. Let Q_{last} be the set of possible states after executing the last statement of $\mathcal{M}$. We add transitions of the form: $\forall q \in Q_{last} : \{(q, \epsilon, q_{acc})\}$, and $\forall \sigma \in \Sigma \cup \{\epsilon\} : \{(q_{acc}, \sigma, q_{acc})\}$.

The transition relation computed by the above algorithm is *partial* and in order to make it complete, we add transitions (q, ϵ, q_{rej}) for all states q which do not have a successor. The number of states of the method automaton is bounded above by $O(|\mathcal{M}|)$, since cur_p, new_p range over $|w|$ values; cur_d, new_d range over $\mathcal{D}$; and $|w|$ and $|\mathcal{D}|$ are fixed constants. In practice, the size of the data domain $|\mathcal{D}|$ can be significantly reduced by techniques such as data abstraction. For instance, for a method that searches for a node with a particular data value d, we can easily abstract the data domain to have just two values, $\mathcal{D}' = \{0, 1\}$, where $\forall x \in \mathcal{D} : x \mapsto 0$ (if $x \neq d$) and $x \mapsto 1$ (if $x = d$). Similarly, we can apply techniques such as reachable state space analysis to further reduce the size of the automaton. Note that, for a method operating on a tree, the automaton deterministically chooses a path in the tree, and trivially accepts along all other branches.

Remark: Our approach can be extended to handle methods that perform a bounded number of passes over the input graph. The basic idea is to encode the changes for each pass in the composite graph. Assuming that we make at most k destructive passes, the composite graph is represented as a k-tuple, $G_c = (G_0, G_1, \ldots, G_k)$ with $G_0 = G_i$ and $G_k = G_o$. Intuitively, the result of the jth traversal is encoded as G_j and the automaton can verify that the graph $G_j = \mathcal{M}(G_{j-1})$. We use colors $\{red_1, \ldots, red_k\}$, $\{green_1, \ldots, green_k\}$ and $\{black\}$ to define the annotation encoding the kth traversal in the composite graph. The color red_i, ($green_i$, resp.) represents nodes or edges deleted (added, resp.) in the ith traversal of the method. Note that these colors are annotations in the composite graph and not related to the coloring of the automaton states.

5   Property Specification

We use automata as the specification language for properties. A property automaton $\mathcal{A}_\varphi$ is a finite tree automaton specified as a tuple $(\Sigma, Q, \delta, q_0, \Phi)$, where all symbols have the usual meanings as described in Section 2.1. We assume that the states of the automaton are colored using a coloring function $c : Q \rightarrow \{c_0, \ldots, c_k\}$.

Existence of a cycle: A rooted directed graph is said to have a cycle if there exists some path in the graph which visits a node infinitely often. The property automaton for checking existence of a cycle in a binary graph (maximum outdegree 2) has the form: $\mathcal{A}_\varphi = (\Sigma, \{q, q_f\}, \delta, q, \{c(q_f) = c_1, c(q) = c_2\})$, where the transition relation is given as: $\delta(q, n) = (q_f, q_f)$ when $n = \texttt{null}$, $\delta(q, n) = (q, q)$ when $n \neq \texttt{null}$ and $\delta(q_f, n) = (q_f, q_f)$ for all n including $\texttt{null}$. Intuitively, the automaton labels every node of the input graph with the state q. The automaton transitions to a final state iff the path is terminating. Thus the automaton accepts a graph iff there exists a non-terminating path along which q is visited infinitely often. Note that the automaton for the complement property, *i.e.* acyclicity is obtained by simply reversing the coloring of the states.

Reachability of a given data value: Suppose, given a binary tree we wish to determine if there exists a node with a given data value (key) reachable from the unique root node of the graph. Intuitively, the automaton non-deterministically guesses a node with the desired value and then checks it. If the desired node is found, then the automaton transits to a final state for each child node. Formally the automaton is given as: $(\Sigma, \{q, q_f\}, \delta, q, \{c(q) = c_1, c(q_f) = c_2\})$. The transition relation is defined as: $\delta(q, n) = \{(q, q_f), (q_f, q)\}$ when $n\texttt{->data} \neq key$ and $n \neq \texttt{null}$; $\delta(q, n) = (q_f, q_f)$ when $n\texttt{->data} = key$ and $\forall n : \delta(q_f, n) = (q_f, q_f)$.

Sortedness: A linked structure satisfies the sortedness property if within each bounded window of size two, the value of the current node is smaller (or greater) than the successor node. An automaton that checks if a list is sorted in ascending order rejects the list iff there exists a window such that the data value of the current node is greater than the data value of the successor node.

6   Application: Insertion in a Singly Linked List

We wish to make sure that the method **InsertNode** that inserts a node in an acyclic singly linked list, preserves *acyclicity*. Since the underlying data structure is a linear list, the method automaton and the property automata are string automata. A representation of the method automaton obtained by the algorithm in Section 4.1 is shown in Figure 1. In the figure, ψ is the loop condition, ϕ is the test expression of the **if** statement ϕ=cursor->data == value, and τ is the boolean expression which is true iff $n_o = \mathcal{M}(n_i)$. Q_is represent sets of states of the automaton. A dotted arrow represents an ϵ-transition and a solid line indicates a normal transition. The states q_{rej} and q_{acc} represent the reject and accept states respectively.

```
method InsertNode (value, newValue){
    1: cursor := head;
    2: while (cursor != null) {
            [ncursor := cursor->next]
    3:        if (cursor->data == value) {
    4:            cursor->next := new node {
                        data := newValue;
                        next := ncursor;};
    5:            break; }
    6:        cursor := ncursor when true; } }
```

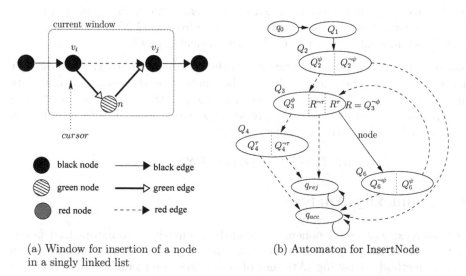

(a) Window for insertion of a node in a singly linked list

(b) Automaton for InsertNode

Fig. 1. Insertion of a node in a linked list

The property automaton for checking acyclicity is given as: $\mathcal{A}_\varphi = (\Sigma, \{q, q_f\},$ $\delta, q, \{c(q) = c_1, c(q_f) = c_2\})$. The complement automaton $\mathcal{A}_{\neg\varphi}$ is given by reversing the coloring of q and q_f. The transition relation for the automaton is given as: $\delta(q, n) = q$ for $n \neq$ null, $\delta(q, n) = q_f$ for $n =$ null and $\delta(q_f, n) = q_f$ for all n, including null. The composite automaton can be constructed in the standard fashion, and calculations show that the resultant automaton is empty, i.e., the method InsertNode preserves acyclicity.

7   Extensions

In a variant approach, we use a suitable temporal logic in lieu of automata to specify the properties of interest. In this approach, method automaton $\mathcal{A}_\mathcal{M}$ is translated to formula $f_\mathcal{M}$ in the given logic. The property φ is specified as a formula $f_{\varphi(G_i)}$. The parameterized correctness problem reduces to checking the satisfiability of the conjunction: $f_c = f_{\varphi(G_i)} \wedge f_\mathcal{M} \wedge f_{\neg\varphi(G_o)}$. The method $\mathcal{M}$ does not preserve property φ, iff f_c is satisfiable. Most temporal logics also have the nice property that the logic is closed under complementation. Thus given a property φ specified as a formula f_φ, the negation of the property is simply the formula $\neg f_\varphi$. We take a look at two example properties that can be specified using temporal logic.

Reachability: A node n_y is said to be reachable from a node n_x if n_y can be reached from n_x by using only the next pointer links. Since particular nodes in the data structure are usually specified as pointers, we are interested in checking reachability of pointer expressions, where x and y are pointers to nodes n_x and n_y respectively. We introduce virtual nodes labeled with v_x and v_y, such that their next pointers point to n_x and n_y respectively and then check whether $\mathbf{AG}(\mathbf{EX}v_x \Rightarrow \mathbf{EFEY}v_y)$. Intuitively, this formula checks that for all nodes being pointed to by v_x->next (alias for x), there exists some node n_y being pointed to by v_y->next (alias for y) which is reachable from x. ($\mathbf{EY}$ (there exists some past) is a temporal operator in CTL with branching past).

Sharing: A node n in a data structure is called *shared* if there exist two distinct nodes, x and y in the graph such that they have n as the common immediate successor. We say that *sharing exists* in a graph if there exists a node in the graph which is *shared*. The above property (*sharing exists*) can be specified in CTL with branching past, as follows:

$$\exists(x, y, n) : (x \equiv \mathbf{EY}(n)) \wedge (y \equiv \mathbf{EY}(n)) \wedge \neg(x \equiv y).$$

8   Complexity Analysis

The complexity of testing nonemptiness of the composite automaton $\mathcal{A}_c$, depends on the sizes of the property automata $\mathcal{A}_\varphi$ and $\mathcal{A}_{\neg\varphi}$, and the method automaton $\mathcal{A}_\mathcal{M}$. A method $\mathcal{M}$ having $|\mathcal{M}|$ lines of code gives rise to an automaton of size $O(|\mathcal{M}|)$ states. The number of states of the composite automaton is proportional to the product of the number of states of its constituent automata. Hence the number of states of $\mathcal{A}_c$ is linear in the number of states of the property automata and the size of the method. Since the number of colors used for the parity condition by the property and method automata is fixed (and typically small), the number of colors used by the composite automaton is also fixed.

The complexity of checking nonemptiness of a parity tree automaton is polynomial in the number of states [EJ '91] (for a fixed number of colors in the parity acceptance condition). Thus, our solution is polynomial in the size of the method as well as the sizes of the property automata. Note that for linear graphs the method automaton and property automata can be specialized to string automata and thus the complexity of our technique is *linear*.

If we use temporal logic to specify properties, satisfiability of a formula in the *CTL* with branching past can be done in time exponential in the size of the formula [Sch '02]. We argue that the exponential cost is incurred in the construction of the tableaux from the formula. If the size of the formula is small, we can easily bear this penalty. The cost of checking emptiness of the tableau is still polynomial in the size of the tableau.

9   Conclusions and Related Work

We present an efficient solution to the parameterized correctness problem for methods operating on linked data structures. In our technique, a method is algorithmically compiled into a method automaton and properties are specified as tree automata. We construct a composite automaton, from the method automaton and the property automata, for checking if the given method preserves the given property. The property is not preserved iff the language accepted by the composite automaton is nonempty. Our technique is polynomial in the size of the method and the sizes of the property automata. In a variant approach an appropriate temporal logic can be used for specifying properties.

A key advantage of our approach is that for a broad, useful class of programs and data structures we provide an efficient algorithmic solution for verifying safety properties. Since reasoning about parameterized data structures is undecidable in general, we present a solution for methods which are known to terminate for all well-formed inputs. Techniques such as shape analysis [SRW '99], pointer assertion logic engine [MS '01] and separation logic [ORY '01] make interesting comparison with our approach, since they address a similar genre of problems.

Shape analysis is a technique for computing shape invariants for programs by providing over-approximations of structure descriptors at each program point using 3-valued logic. In contrast to our technique which provides exact solutions, shape analysis provides imprecise (albeit conservative) results in double exponential time. In [BRS '99] the authors discuss a decidable logic L_r for describing linked data structures. However, their work does not provide a practical algorithm for checking the validity of formulas in this logic and the complexity of the given decision procedure is high.

Pointer Assertion Logic Engine tool [MS '01] encodes programs and partial specifications as formulas of monadic second order logic. Though their approach can handle a large number of data structures and methods, the complexity of the decision procedure is non-elementary. Moreover, the technique works only for loop-free code and loops need to be broken using user specified loop invariants.

Separation logic [ORY '01], which is an extension of Hoare Logic for giving proofs of partial correctness of methods, does not easily lend itself to automation. Furthermore, classical separation logic without arithmetic is not recursively enumerable [Rey '02].

In [Bou et al.] the authors describe a technique to verify safety properties of programs that modify data structures. Initial configurations of a program are encoded as automata and the program is translated into a transducer. The main idea is to check whether action of the transducer on the initial configurations leads to a bad configuration of the program. This problem is undecidable since a transducer could, in general, encode a Turing machine computation. The authors use abstraction-refinement to verify properties. Their technique is restricted to data structures with a single successor, and also limited by the efficiency of abstractions and the refinement process.

References

[BRS '99]   Michael Benedikt, Thomas W. Reps, Shmuel Sagiv, *A Decidable Logic for Describing Linked Data Structures*, In Proceedings of 8th European Symposium on Programming, 1999, (ESOP '99), pp. 2-19

[Bou et al.]   A. Bouajjani, P. Habermehl, P. Moro, T. Vojnar, *Verifying Programs with Dynamic 1-Selector-Linked Structures in Regular Model Checking*, In Proceedings of 12th International Conference on Tools and Algorithms for the Construction and Analysis of Systems, 2005, (TACAS'05), LNCS 3440, April 2005.

[Car '94]   Olivier Carton, *Chain Automata*, In IFIP World Computer Congress 1994, Hamburg, pp. 451-458, Elsevier (North-Holland).

[EJ '88]   E. Allen Emerson, Charanjit S. Jutla, *The Complexity of Tree Automata and Logics of Programs*, In Proceedings of 29th IEEE Foundations of Computer Science, 1988, (FOCS '88), pp. 328-337.

[EK '02]   E. Allen Emerson, Vineet Kahlon, *Model Checking Large-Scale and Parameterized Resource Allocation Systems*, In Proceedings of Tools and Algorithms for the Construction and Analysis of Systems, 8th International Conference, 2002, (TACAS '02), pp. 251-265

[EJ '91]   E. A. Emerson and C. S. Jutla, *Tree Automata, Mu-Calculus and Determinacy*, (Extended Abstract), In Proceedings of Foundations of Computer Science 1991, (FOCS '91), pp. 368-377.

[Em '85]   E. Allen Emerson. *Automata, Tableaux, and Temporal Logics*, Conference on Logics of Programs, New York, NY. LNCS 193, pp. 79-88

[HU '79]   John E. Hopcroft and Jeffrey D. Ullman, *Introduction to Automata Theory, Languages and Computation*, Addison Wesley, (1979).

[Lev-Ami et al.] Tal Lev-Ami, Thomas W. Reps, Shmuel Sagiv, Reinhard Wilhelm, *Putting static analysis to work for verification: A case study* In International Symposium on Software Testing and Analysis, 2000, (ISTA'00), pp. 26-38

[MS '01]   Andres Møller, Michael I. Schwartzbach, *The Pointer Assertion Logic Engine*, In Proceedings of SIGPLAN Conference on Programming Languages Design and Implementation, 2001, (PLDI '01), pp. 221-231.

[NSV '04]   Frank Neven, Thomas Schwentick, Victor Vianu, *Finite state machines for strings over infinite alphabets*, In ACM Transactions on Computational Logic, (TOCL), Volume 15 Number 3, pp. 403-435, July 2004.

[ORY '01]   Peter O'Hearn, John Reynolds, Hongseok Yang, *Local Reasoning about Programs that Alter Data Structures*, Invited Paper, In Proceedings of 15th Annual Conference of the European Association for Computer Science Logic, 2001, (CSL '01), pp. 1-19.

[Rey '02]   John C. Reynolds, *Separation Logic: A Logic for Shared Mutable Data Structures*, In Proceedings of the 17th IEEE Symposium on Logic in Computer Science, 2002, (LICS 2002), pp. 55-74.

[Rose '65]   Arnold L. Rosenberg, *On multi-head finite automata*, FOCS 1965, pp.221-228

[Sch '02]   Ph. Schnoebelen, *The complexity of temporal logic model checking*, In Advances in Modal Logic, papers from 4th International Workshop on Advances in Modal Logic 2002, (AiML'02), Sep.-Oct. 2002, Toulouse, France.

[SRW '99]   M. Sagiv, T. Reps, and R. Wilhelm, *Parametric shape analysis via 3-valued logic*, In Symposium on Principles of Programming Languages, 1999, (POPL '99).

Appendix: Checking Whether $n_o = \mathcal{M}(n_i)$

For simplicity, we discuss only methods operating on linear graphs. Let the state of the automaton before checking the condition $n_o = \mathcal{M}(n_i)$ be $q = (j, cur_d, cur_p, new_d, new_p)$. For a given node, the method can modify either the outgoing edge from the current node, add a new node m at the current position, or delete the current node. Let the old and new successor nodes be n_1 and n_1' respectively. Let l be the coloring function for the nodes and edges. Let the (data, next) fields for the nodes n_i, n_o and m be (d, n_1), (d', n_1') and (d_m, m') respectively. We need to check for the following conditions:

1. $d' = cur_d$
2. If $n_1 \neq n_1'$, *i.e.* the next pointer of the cursor has changed, $(l(n_i, n_1) = red) \wedge (l(n_o, n_1') = green)$,
3. If m exists, $(l(m) = green) \wedge (d_m = new_d) \wedge (l(m, m') = green) \wedge (l(n_o, m) = green) \wedge (l(n_i, n_1) = red)$.

Additionally, the action of a delete statement is checked by checking whether the color of a node is *red*.

Parameterized Verification of π-Calculus Systems[*]

Ping Yang[1], Samik Basu[2], and C.R. Ramakrishnan[1]

[1] Dept. of Computer Science, Stony Brook Univ., Stony Brook, NY, 11794, USA
[2] Dept. of Computer Science, Iowa State Univ., Ames, IA, 50014, USA
{pyang, cram}@cs.sunysb.edu, sbasu@cs.iastate.edu

Abstract. In this paper we present an automatic verification technique for parameterized systems where the subsystem behavior is modeled using the π-calculus. At its core, our technique treats each process instance in a system as a property transformer. Given a property φ that we want to verify of an N-process system, we use a partial model checker to infer the property φ' (stated as a formula in a sufficiently rich logic) that must hold of an $(N-1)$-process system. If the sequence of formulas $\varphi, \varphi', \ldots$ thus constructed converges, and the limit is satisfied by the deadlocked process, we can conclude that the N-process system satisfies φ. To this end, we develop a partial model checker for the π-calculus that uses an expressive value-passing logic as the property language. We also develop a number of optimizations to make the model checker efficient enough for routine use, and a light-weight widening operator to accelerate convergence. We demonstrate the effectiveness of our technique by using it to verify properties of a wide variety of parameterized systems that are beyond the reach of existing techniques.

1 Introduction

A parameterized system consists of a number of instances of a component, the number of such occurrences being the parameter to the system. Many safety-critical systems are naturally parameterized: e.g. resource arbitration protocols, communication protocols, etc. Traditional model checking techniques are limited to verifying properties of a given instance of a parameterized system (i.e. for a specific value of the parameter). Many novel techniques have been developed to verify such systems for all instances of their parameters [12, 15, 16, 10]. These techniques vary in the classes of systems they can handle and the degree of automation they provide. Automatic techniques typically restrict the communication topology (e.g. rings or trees) or, at least, demand that the communication patterns be fixed.

The Driving Problem. In many systems, e.g. mobile systems, the process interconnections can change dynamically. Existing techniques for verifying parameterized systems do not readily extend to such systems. In this paper, we present an automatic technique to address this problem.

The π-calculus [28] is a well-known process calculus where communication channels as well as values transmitted over them belong to the same domain of *names*; names can be dynamically created, communicated to other processes, and can be used as channels. Due to these features, it is widely used as the basis for modeling mobile

---

[*] This research was supported in part by NSF grants CCR-0205376, CCR-0311512, and CCR 0509340.

H. Hermanns and J. Palsberg (Eds.): TACAS 2006, LNCS 3920, pp. 42–57, 2006.

$$p(x) \overset{\text{def}}{=} (\nu y)\overline{x}y.p(x)$$

$$q(x) \overset{\text{def}}{=} x(y).q(x)$$

$$sys(\mathbf{n}) \overset{\text{def}}{=} (\nu x)(p(x) \mid q^{\mathbf{n}}(x))$$

(a)

$$\varphi_0 \equiv X =_\nu \langle \tau \rangle tt \wedge [\tau] X$$

$$\varphi_1 \equiv X_1(x) =_\nu \nu y'(((\langle xy' \rangle tt \vee \langle \tau \rangle tt) \wedge [xy'] X_1(x) \wedge [\tau] X_1(x))$$

$$\varphi_2 \equiv X_2(x) =_\nu \nu y'([xy'] X_2(x) \wedge [\overline{x}\{y\}] X_2(x) \wedge [\tau] X_2(x))$$

$$\varphi_3 \equiv X_3(x) =_\nu \nu y'([xy'] X_3(x) \wedge [\overline{x}\{y\}] X_3(x) \wedge [\tau] X_3(x))$$

(b)

Fig. 1. A simple example of a parameterized system

systems. In a parameterized mobile system, we assume that each component is specified as a finite-control π-calculus process: i.e. specified without using the replication operator of the calculus, and not containing a parallel composition within the scope of a recursive definition. A simple example of a parameterized system based on the π-calculus is shown in Fig. 1(a). In the figure, the parameterized system is represented by process $sys(n)$, which consists of one instance of process $p(x)$ and n instances $q(x)$. The process $p(x)$ creates a new name y and outputs it via channel x, while the process $q(x)$ receives a name via x. The property to be verified, φ_0, is specified in the modal μ-calculus [24, 8] and written in equational form (Fig. 1(b)). The property is a greatest fixed point formula (specified by a $=_\nu$ equation) and states that *a τ action is possible after every τ action*. An example of parameterized verification problem is to determine whether $\forall n. \; sys(n) \models \varphi_0$.

Background. In [6], we developed a compositional model checker for the process algebra CCS [27] and for properties specified in the model μ-calculus [8]. We used the compositional checker for the verification of parameterized CCS processes. The central idea of our approach is to view processes as property transformers: given a μ-calculus formula φ and a system containing a CCS process P, we compute the property φ' that should hold in P's environment (say, Q) if φ holds in $P|Q$. The property transformer of a process P, denoted by $\Pi(P)$, is such that: $\forall Q. \; (P|Q \models \varphi) \Leftrightarrow (Q \models \Pi(P)(\varphi))$.

Consider a parameterized system P^n consisting of n instances of a process P. To verify whether φ holds in P^n for all n, we construct the sequence of properties $\varphi_0, \varphi_1, \ldots$ such that $\varphi_0 = \varphi$ and $\varphi_{i+1} = \Pi(P)(\varphi_i)$ for all $i \geq 0$. Let the sequence converge after k steps: i.e. $\varphi_{k+1} = \varphi_k$. By definition of Π, note that for $n \geq k$, $P^n \models \varphi$ if $P^{n-k} \models \varphi_k$. Let 0 denote the deadlocked process, the unit of the parallel composition operator. Specifically, P^n is equivalent to $P^n|0$. It then follows that $\forall n \geq k, P^n \models \varphi$ if $0 \models \varphi_k$, i.e. the zero process has the property specified by limit of the sequence of formulas.

Our Solution. Following the approach of [6], we develop a compositional model checker for the π-calculus and use that as the basis for verifying parameterized mobile systems. Consider the example in Figure 1. In order to show that $sys(n) \models \varphi_0$ for arbitrary n, we begin by determining a property $\varphi_1 = \Pi(p(x))(\varphi_0)$. By the definition of Π, we know $q^n(x) \models \varphi_1$ whenever $sys(n) \models \varphi_0$.

In order to specify φ_1 correctly, the property language needs to be expressive enough to specify names and their scopes. We extend the modal μ-calculus to a logic called the $C\mu$-calculus. In this logic, formula variables may be parameterized by names. Moreover, formulas may specify local names (denoted by νx) and may contain modalities with new actions such as the *free input* action xy (see Section 2).

In the above example, observe that $p(x)|Q$ (for any process Q) can do a τ-action if (a) Q can do an input action on x to synchronize with $p(x)$'s bound output action $\overline{x}\nu y$, or (b) Q itself can do a τ-action. Thus the term $\langle\tau\rangle\varphi'$ holds in $p(x)|Q$ if $(\langle xy\rangle\varphi'' \vee \langle\tau\rangle\varphi'')$ holds in Q. The other modalities and operations in the formula are derived along the same lines using the property transformer for $p(x)$. The resulting property φ_1, defined in Cμ-calculus using the formula variable X_1, is shown in Figure 1(b). It states that it is always possible to input from x or perform a τ action after any such action. Observe that free name x is the parameter to the formula variable X_1. We now check if φ_1 holds in $q^n(x)$, by checking if $\varphi_2 = \Pi(q(x))(\varphi_1)$ holds in $q^{n-1}(x)$. Observe that φ_2 does not have the conjunct $\langle xy'\rangle tt \vee \langle\tau\rangle tt$ since a single instance of $q(x)$ can satisfy it. Using the terminology of assume-guarantee proof techniques [19], we can say that the obligation of $\langle xy'\rangle tt \vee \langle\tau\rangle tt$ on $q^n(x)$ is satisfied by one instance of $q(x)$ and hence is not passed on to $q^{n-1}(x)$. Continuing further, we can check if φ_2 holds in $q^{n-1}(x)$ by checking if $\varphi_3 = \Pi(q(x))(\varphi_2)$ holds in $q^{n-2}(x)$.

Observe from the figure that φ_3 and φ_2 differ only in the names of formula variables and hence represent the same property. We thus conclude that the sequence φ_i converges to φ_2. Moreover, since 0 satisfies φ_2 we can conclude that the original formula φ_0 is satisfied by $sys(n)$ for sufficiently large n. It should also be noted that since φ_2 is a greatest fixed point formula and involves a conjunction of universal modalities, it is equivalent to tt; hence the last iteration (to compute φ_3) is redundant. Techniques to simplify formulas and to find equivalences will in general enable us to detect convergence earlier. A more careful analysis of the sequence of formulas reveals that it converges after *one* instance of $q(x)$ is considered, and hence we can conclude that $\forall n \geq 1\ sys(n) \models \varphi_0$.

Contributions. The main contributions of this paper are as follows.

- *A compositional model checker for the π-calculus.* The model checker works for finite-control π-calculus processes, as well as value-passing calculus with equality (=) and dis-equality ($\neq$) constraints between names (see Section 3).
- *Operations to efficiently check for convergence of formula sequences, and to accelerate convergence.* The verification technique for parameterized systems is based on computing the limit of a sequence of Cμ-calculus formulas. We describe effective techniques to check if two Cμ-calculus formulas are equivalent. We also describe a widening operator to extrapolate the sequence to estimate (approximately) its limit (Section 4).
- *Optimizations to compositional model checking.* We develop a number of lightweight optimization techniques to reduce the size of formulas generated in the intermediate steps of compositional model checking. We find that such optimizations are necessary and effective. Without these, parameterized system verification based on compositional model checking appears infeasible (see Section 5).

We also demonstrate the utility of our technique by applying it on a variety of parameterized π-calculus systems: ranging from simple ones that can also be expressed as parameterized CCS systems, to those that exhibit π-calculus-specific features of name creation, link passing and scope extrusion (Section 6).

Related work. A number of model checking techniques for the π-calculus have been developed. Examples include the model checking technique for polyadic π-calculus [11]; the Mobility Workbench (MWB) [33], a model checker and bisimulation checker for the π-calculus; a system [32] to translate a subset of π-calculus specifications into Promela for verification using Spin [20]; and MMC [35, 36] model checker for the π-calculus based on logic programming. All these techniques, however, apply only to finite-control π-calculus, and cannot be used for verifying parameterized systems.

Type systems for the verification of π-calculus processes [9, 21] handle the replication operator and appear to be a promising alternative to the verification of parameterized mobile systems. The PIPER system [9] generates CCS processes as "types" for π-calculus processes (based on user-supplied type signatures), and formulates the verification problem in terms of these process types. In [21], a generic type system for the π-calculus is proposed as a framework for analyzing properties such as deadlock- and race-freedom. The replication operator alone is insufficient to model many parameterized systems where the repeated instances may have different free variables.

The area of compositional verification has received considerable attention. Most techniques for compositional verification are based on assume-guarantee reasoning [18, 1, 26, 7, 19], and need user guidance. An approach to learn assumptions using automata learning techniques is proposed in [2]; but the technique is limited to the verification of systems with a fixed number of finite-state components. The technique presented in this paper is broadly based on our earlier technique [6] which is restricted to parameterized CCS systems and does not support dynamic change of communication topology. Other closely-related works include the compositional model checker for synchronous CCS [4] and the partial model checker of [3]. The latter defines property transformers for parallel composition of sequential automata, while we generalize the transformers for arbitrary π-calculus processes. These papers also proposed techniques to reduce the size of formulas, but the optimizations are done after the formulas are generated in the first place; in contrast, we apply our optimizations during the model checking process, thereby reducing the size of formulas generated.

Verification of parameterized systems has been recognized as an important problem and significant progress has been made in the recent years [37, e.g.]. One popular approach to the verification of a parameterized system of the form P^n is to identify a finite cut off k for a property φ such that $\forall n. P^n \models \varphi \Leftrightarrow P^k \models \varphi$, thereby reducing it to a finite-state verification problem. Techniques following this approach range from those that provide cutoffs for particular communication topologies [13, 14, e.g.], to those based on symmetries and annotations in the system specification [22]. Later works, such as [30, 5] have proposed automatic techniques, based on identification of appropriate cut-off of the parameters, for verification of wide range of parameterized systems using rich class of data objects and operations (inequalities, incrementations). Another approach is to identify an appropriate representation technique for a given parameterized system; e.g. counting abstraction with arithmetic constraints [12], covering graphs [15, 16], and context-free grammars [10], and regular languages [31]. The use of abstractions to generate invariants of parameterized systems is explored in [23]. None of these techniques, however, consider dynamically changing communication topologies.

2 A Logic for Compositional Analysis of π-Calculus Processes

In this section, we present the fundamentals of π-calculus (Section 2.1) and property specification logic, which we will refer to as $C\mu$-calculus (Section 2.2), followed by our technique of compositional analysis (Section 3).

2.1 Syntax and Semantics of the π-Calculus

Process algebra π-calculus [28] is used to represent behavior of systems whose interconnection pattern changes dynamically. Let $x, y, z, \ldots$ range over names, $p, q, r, \ldots$ range over process identifiers, and $\vec{x}$ represent comma-separated list of names $x_1, \ldots, x_n$. In the following, we recall the syntax of the calculus.

$$\alpha ::= x(y) \mid \overline{x}y \mid \tau$$

$$\mathcal{P} ::= 0 \mid \alpha.\mathcal{P} \mid (\nu x)\mathcal{P} \mid \mathcal{P} \mid \mathcal{P} \mid \mathcal{P} + \mathcal{P} \mid [x = y]\mathcal{P} \mid p(\vec{y})$$

$$\mathcal{D}_p ::= p(\vec{x}) \stackrel{\text{def}}{=} \mathcal{P} \text{ (where } i \neq j \Rightarrow x_i \neq x_j \text{ and } fn(\mathcal{P}) \subseteq \{\vec{x}\})$$

In the above, α denotes the set of actions where $x(y)$, $\overline{x}y$ and τ represent input, (free) output and internal actions. Input action $x(y)$ has binding occurrence of variable y. All other variables in every action are *free*. The set of process expressions is represented by $\mathcal{P}$. Process 0 represents a deadlocked process. Process $\alpha.P$ can perform an α action and subsequently behave as P. Process $(\nu x)P$ behaves as P with the scope of x initially restricted to P; x is called a local name. Process $[x = y]P$ behaves as P if the names x and y are the same name, and as 0 otherwise. The operators $+$ and $\mid$ represent non-deterministic choice and parallel composition, respectively. The expression $p(\vec{y})$ denotes a *process invocation* where p is a process name (having a corresponding definition) and $\vec{y}$ is the actual parameters of the invocation. Finally, $\mathcal{D}_p$ is the set of process definitions where each definition is of the form $p(\vec{x}) \stackrel{\text{def}}{=} P$. A definition associates a process name p and a list of formal parameters $\vec{x}$ with process expression P.

The operational semantics of the π-calculus is given in terms of *symbolic transition systems* where each state denotes a process expression and each transition is labeled by a boolean guard and action [25]. The operational semantics is standard and is omitted.

2.2 Syntax and Semantics of the $C\mu$-Calculus

For the purpose of compositional analysis, we extend value-passing μ-calculus in two ways: (i) with explicit syntactic structures to specify and manipulate local names, and (ii) with actions that are closed under complementation. We will refer to this logic as $C\mu$-calculus. The set of formula expressions $\mathcal{F}$ in the $C\mu$-calculus is defined as follows:

$$\mathcal{F} ::= tt \mid ff \mid x = y \mid x \neq y \mid loc(x) \mid nloc(x) \mid (\nu x)\mathcal{F} \mid \mathcal{F} \vee \mathcal{F} \mid \mathcal{F} \wedge \mathcal{F}$$
$$\mid \langle \mathcal{A} \rangle \mathcal{F} \mid [\mathcal{A}]\mathcal{F} \mid \langle x(y) \rangle \exists y.\mathcal{F} \mid \langle x(y) \rangle \forall y.\mathcal{F} \mid [x(y)]\forall y.\mathcal{F} \mid [x(y)]\exists y.\mathcal{F}$$
$$\mid X(\vec{e}) \mid (\mu X(\vec{z}).\mathcal{F})(\vec{e}) \mid (\nu X(\vec{z}).\mathcal{F})(\vec{e})$$
$$\mathcal{A} ::= xy \mid \overline{x}y \mid \overline{x}\{y\} \mid \overline{x}\nu y \mid \tau$$

1a: $\llbracket x = y \rrbracket \xi \delta l = \begin{cases} \{s\delta \mid s \in S\} & \text{if } \delta \models x = y \\ \emptyset & \text{otherwise.} \end{cases}$

1b: $\llbracket x \neq y \rrbracket \xi \delta l = \begin{cases} \{s\delta \mid s \in S\} & \text{if } \delta \models x \neq y \\ \emptyset & \text{otherwise.} \end{cases}$

2a: $\llbracket loc(x) \rrbracket \xi \delta l = \begin{cases} \{s\delta \mid s \in S\} & \text{if } x \in l \\ \emptyset & \text{otherwise.} \end{cases}$

2b: $\llbracket nloc(x) \rrbracket \xi \delta l = \begin{cases} \{s\delta \mid s \in S\} & \text{if } x \notin l \\ \emptyset & \text{otherwise.} \end{cases}$

3: $\llbracket \varphi_1 \vee \varphi_2 \rrbracket \xi \delta l = \llbracket \varphi_1 \rrbracket \xi \delta l \cup \llbracket \varphi_2 \rrbracket \xi \delta l$

4: $\llbracket \varphi_1 \wedge \varphi_2 \rrbracket \xi \delta l = \llbracket \varphi_1 \rrbracket \xi \delta l \cap \llbracket \varphi_2 \rrbracket \xi \delta l$

5: $\llbracket (\nu x)\varphi \rrbracket \xi \delta l = \{s \mid s \in \llbracket \varphi\{x'/x\} \rrbracket \xi \delta (l \cup \{x'\}) \text{ where } x' \notin fn(s)\}$

6: $\llbracket \langle \tau \rangle \varphi \rrbracket \xi \delta l = \{s \mid \exists s'.s \xrightarrow{b,\tau} s' \wedge (\delta, l \models b) \wedge s' \in \llbracket \varphi \rrbracket \xi \delta l\}$

7: $\llbracket \langle \overline{x_1} v \rangle \varphi \rrbracket \xi \delta l = \{s \mid \exists s'.s \xrightarrow{b,\overline{x_2}v} s' \wedge (\delta, l \models b \wedge (x_1 = x_2)) \wedge s' \in \llbracket \varphi \rrbracket \xi \delta l\}$

8: $\llbracket \langle \overline{x_1}\{y\} \rangle \varphi \rrbracket \xi \delta l = \{s \mid \exists s'.s \xrightarrow{b,\overline{x_2}v} s' \wedge (\delta, l \models b \wedge (x_1 = x_2)) \wedge s' \in \llbracket \varphi\{v/y\} \rrbracket \xi \delta l\}$

9: $\llbracket \langle \overline{x_1}\nu y \rangle \varphi \rrbracket \xi \delta l = \{s \mid \exists s'.s \xrightarrow{b,\overline{x_2}\nu v} s' \wedge v \notin fn(\varphi) - \{y\} \wedge (\delta, l \models b \wedge (x_1 = x_2))$
$\wedge s' \in \llbracket \varphi\{v/y\} \rrbracket \xi \delta (l \cup \{v\})\}$

10: $\llbracket \langle x_1 y \rangle \varphi \rrbracket \xi \delta l = \{s \mid \exists s'.s \xrightarrow{b,x_2(w)} s' \wedge (\delta, l \models b \wedge (x_1 = x_2)) \wedge s'\{y/w\} \in \llbracket \varphi \rrbracket \xi \delta l\}$

11: $\llbracket \langle x_1(y) \rangle \exists y.\varphi \rrbracket \xi \delta l = \{s \mid \exists s'.s \xrightarrow{b,x_2(w)} s' \wedge (\delta, l \models b \wedge (x_1 = x_2)) \wedge \exists v.s'\{v/w\} \in \llbracket \varphi\{v/y\} \rrbracket \xi \delta l\}$

12: $\llbracket \langle x_1(y) \rangle \forall y.\varphi \rrbracket \xi \delta l = \{s \mid \exists s'.s \xrightarrow{b,x_2(w)} s' \wedge (\delta, l \models b \wedge (x_1 = x_2)) \wedge \forall v.s'\{v/w\} \in \llbracket \varphi\{v/y\} \rrbracket \xi \delta l\}$

13: $\llbracket X(\overrightarrow{e}) \rrbracket \xi \delta l = \xi(X)(\overrightarrow{e}\delta)$

14: $\llbracket (\mu X(\overrightarrow{z}).\varphi)(\overrightarrow{e}) \rrbracket \xi \delta l = (\cap\{f \mid \llbracket \varphi \rrbracket(\xi \circ \{X \mapsto f\}) \subseteq f\})\delta[\overrightarrow{e}/\overrightarrow{z}]l$

15: $\llbracket (\nu X(\overrightarrow{z}).\varphi)(\overrightarrow{e}) \rrbracket \xi \delta l = (\cup\{f \mid f \subseteq \llbracket \varphi \rrbracket(\xi \circ \{X \mapsto f\})\})\delta[\overrightarrow{e}/\overrightarrow{z}]l$

Fig. 2. Semantics of the $C\mu$-calculus

In the above, tt and $f\!f$ stand for propositional constants true and false, respectively. $loc(x)$ is true iff x is a local name, and $nloc(x)$ is true iff x is not a local name. The scope of names can be specified by formulas of the form $(\nu x)\mathcal{F}$ which means that x is a local name in the formula. Formulas can be constructed using conjunction, disjunction, diamond (existential) and box (universal) modalities and quantifiers. The modal actions $x(y)$, xy, and τ represent input, free input and internal actions, respectively. $\overline{x}y$ is a free output action where y is a free name and $\overline{x}\{y\}$ is an output action that has binding occurrence of variable y. In input and output actions $x(y)$ and $\overline{x}\{y\}$, x is free and y is bound; in free input and free output actions, all names are free. $\overline{x}\nu y$ is a bound output action; in such an action x is free and y is bound. Bound names of a formula are either bound names in the modalities or names bound by the ν operator. $\langle x(y) \rangle \exists y.\mathcal{F}$ and $\langle x(y) \rangle \forall y.\mathcal{F}$ represent basic and late diamond modalities for input action $x(y)$, respectively. $[x(y)]\forall y.\mathcal{F}$ and $[x(y)]\exists y.\mathcal{F}$ represent the basic and late box modalities for input action $x(y)$, respectively.

The least and greatest fixed point formulas are specified as $(\mu X(\overrightarrow{z}).\mathcal{F})(\overrightarrow{e})$ and $(\nu X(\overrightarrow{z}).\mathcal{F})(\overrightarrow{e})$, respectively, where $\overrightarrow{z}$ represents formal parameters and $\overrightarrow{e}$ represents actual parameters. For convenience, we often represent a formula as a sequence of fixed point equations [17]. We assume that all formulas are *closed*, i.e., all free names in a formula appear in the parameters of the definition.

Semantics of the $C\mu$-calculus. The semantics of formulas in the $C\mu$-calculus is given using four structures: (i) a symbolic transition system $\mathcal{S} = \langle S, \rightarrow \rangle$ where S represents the set of symbolic states and '$\rightarrow$' is the symbolic transition relation; (ii) a substitution δ over which the equality ($=$) and disequality ($\neq$) constraints between names are interpreted; (iii) a function ξ that maps formula variables to sets of symbolic states of $\mathcal{S}$; and a set of local names l used to assign meaning to loc and $nloc$ predicates. The semantic function is written as $[\![\varphi]\!]\xi\delta l$ and maps each formula to a set of states in S. The symbolic transition system is used as an implicit parameter in the definition: all rules are evaluated w.r.t. the same transition system. The treatment of boolean connectives is straightforward. The set of local names, l, is updated in Rules 5 and 9 to include names bound by ν operator. Similarly, the substitution δ is updated to capture the mapping of formal parameters (free names) to actual arguments in Rules 14 and 15. Constraints of the form $x = y$ and $x \neq y$ are evaluated under this substitution. Rules 6–12 give the semantics for the diamond modality. The semantics of the box modality can be easily obtained by considering it as the dual of the diamond modality. For instance, the semantics for $[\tau]\varphi$ is: $[\![[\tau]\varphi]\!]\xi\delta l = \{s \mid \forall s'. \text{ if } s \xrightarrow{b,\tau} s' \wedge \delta, l \models b \text{ then } s' \in [\![\varphi]\!]\xi\delta l\}$. For brevity, we will henceforth discuss only about the diamond modality. The details related to the box modality are given in [34]. We will use $s \models_{\delta,l} \varphi$ to denote $s \in [\![\varphi]\!]\xi\delta l$.

3 Compositional Model Checker for the π-Calculus

In this section, we define the transformation function $\Pi : \mathcal{P} \to \mathcal{F} \to \mathcal{F}$ which is the core of our technique. Given a process $P \in \mathcal{P}$, a formula $\varphi \in \mathcal{F}$, a set of substitutions δ and a set of local names l, we define Π such that

$$P \mid Q \mid 0 \models_{\delta,l} \varphi \Leftrightarrow Q \mid 0 \models_{\delta,l} \Pi(P)(\varphi) \Leftrightarrow 0 \models_{\delta,l} \Pi(Q)(\Pi(P)(\varphi))$$

In words, the main objective of Π is to generate a $C\mu$-calculus formula which represents the temporal obligation of the environment of the process used for transformation. This process of transforming formula iteratively by each process in the parallel composition is similar to the one proposed in [3, 6], where the transformation operation is defined for labeled transitions system or process algebra CCS and the technique of model checking is referred to as *partial model checking*.

The function Π for each formula expression is presented in Fig. 3. Here, we illustrate only those rules that are not obvious. Rules 3(a) and 3(b) leave the formula expressions $loc(x)$ and $nloc(x)$ unchanged; evaluation of these formulas is performed when all but the 0 processes are used to transform the formula iteratively. Rule 6 transforms a parameterized formula variable $X(\vec{e})$ into new formula variable $X_p(\vec{e_1})$ (the definition is in Rule A) where $\vec{e_1}$ is formed by concatenation of $\vec{e}$ and free names of P. Transformation using a process identifier is equivalent to transformation using its definition (Rule 9).

Rule 10 captures the compositionality of property transformers; the order of transformation using P_1 or P_2 does not matter. Rule 11 presents the property transformer for process $(\nu x)P$ where (νx) is moved from the process side to the transformed formula. In order to avoid name clash, x is renamed to x' ($\{x'/x\}$)that is different from any free names in φ. Note that, x' is a local name in the context of the transformed formula.

Rule 12 deals with the formulas with local name restrictions (possibly generated via Rule 11). Transformation using P results in the extension of the scope of x to the transformed formula. Similar to Rule 11, name x in φ is renamed to a new name x' (not present as a free name in P). Observe that, Rules 11 and 12 have a similar effect

1(a) $\qquad \Pi(P)(tt) = tt$ $\qquad\qquad\qquad$ 1(b) $\Pi(P)(ff) = ff$

2(a) $\qquad \Pi(P)(x = y) = \begin{cases} tt & \text{if } x = y \\ x = y & \text{otherwise} \end{cases}$ $\quad$ 2(b) $\Pi(P)(x \neq y) = \begin{cases} ff & \text{if } x = y \\ x \neq y & \text{otherwise} \end{cases}$

3(a) $\qquad \Pi(P)(loc(x)) = loc(x)$ $\qquad\qquad$ 3(b) $\Pi(P)(nloc(x)) = nloc(x)$

4 $\qquad \Pi(P)(\varphi_1 \vee \varphi_2) = \Pi(P)(\varphi_1) \vee \Pi(P)(\varphi_2)$

5 $\qquad \Pi(P)(\varphi_1 \wedge \varphi_2) = \Pi(P)(\varphi_1) \wedge \Pi(P)(\varphi_2)$

6 $\qquad \Pi(P)(X(\vec{e})) = X_P(\vec{e_1})$ where $\vec{e_1} = \vec{e} + fn(P)$

7 $\qquad \Pi(P)(\exists x.\varphi) = \exists x.\Pi(P)(\varphi) \quad \Pi(P)(\forall x.\varphi) = \forall x.\Pi(P)(\varphi)$

8 $\qquad \Pi(0)(\varphi) = \varphi$

9 $\qquad \Pi(p(\vec{x}))(\varphi) = \Pi(P)(\varphi)$ where $p(\vec{x}) \overset{\text{def}}{=} P$

10 $\quad \Pi(P_1 \mid P_2)(\varphi) = \Pi(P_2)(\Pi(P_1)(\varphi))$

11 $\quad \Pi((\nu x)P)(\varphi) = (\nu x')\Pi(P\{x'/x\})(\varphi)$ where $x' \cap n(\varphi) = \emptyset$

12 $\quad \Pi(P)((\nu x)\varphi) = (\nu x')(\Pi(P)(\varphi\{x'/x\}))$ where $x' \notin fn(P)$

13 $\quad \Pi(a.P)((\langle a \rangle\varphi) = \langle \alpha \rangle\Pi(a.P)(\varphi)$ where $bn(\alpha) \cap fn(a.P) = \emptyset$

$$\vee \left\{ \begin{array}{ll} \Pi(P)(\varphi) & \text{if } a = \tau \wedge \alpha = \tau \\ x_1 = x_2 \wedge nloc(y_1) \wedge \Pi(P)(\varphi) & \text{if } a = \overline{x_1}y_1 \wedge \alpha = \overline{x_2}y_1 \\ x_1 = x_2 \wedge nloc(y_1) \wedge \Pi(P)(\varphi\{y_1/y_2\}) & \text{if } a = \overline{x_1}y_1 \wedge \alpha = \overline{x_2}\{y_2\} \\ x_1 = x_2 \wedge loc(y_1) \wedge \Pi(P)(\varphi\{y_1/y_2\}) & \text{if } a = \overline{x_1}y_1 \wedge \alpha = \overline{x_2}\nu y_2 \\ x_1 = x_2 \wedge \Pi(P)(\varphi\{y_1/y_2\}) & \text{if } a = x_1(y_1) \wedge \alpha = x_2(y_2) \\ x_1 = x_2 \wedge \Pi(P\{y_2/y_1\})(\varphi) & \text{if } a = x_1(y_1) \wedge \alpha = x_2 y_2 \\ ff & \text{otherwise} \end{array} \right\}$$

$$\vee \left\{ \begin{array}{ll} \langle \overline{a} \rangle\Pi(P)(\varphi), \text{ where } bn(a) \cap n(\varphi) = \emptyset & \text{if } \alpha = \tau \\ ff & \text{otherwise} \end{array} \right\}$$

14 $\quad \Pi(P_1 + P_2)((\langle\alpha\rangle\varphi) = \langle\alpha\rangle\Pi(P_1 + P_2)(\varphi) \vee \Pi(P_1)((\langle\alpha\rangle\varphi) \vee \Pi(P_2)((\langle\alpha\rangle\varphi)$

15 $\quad \Pi([x = y]P)(\varphi) = C \wedge \Pi(P)(\varphi)$ where $C = \begin{cases} tt & \text{if } x = y \\ x = y & \text{otherwise} \end{cases}$

A. $\Pi(P)(X(\vec{z}) =_\sigma \varphi \cup E) = \{X_P(\vec{z_1}) =_\sigma \Pi(P)(\varphi)$ where $(n(\varphi) - \vec{z}) \cap fn(P) = \emptyset)$ and $\vec{z_1} = \vec{z} + fn(P)\}$
$\qquad\qquad \cup \Pi(P)(E) \cup \bigcup\{\Pi(P')(X'(\vec{z_2}) =_{\sigma'} \varphi')$ s.t $X'_{p'}(\vec{z_3})$ is a subformula of
$\qquad\qquad \Pi(P)(\varphi), \vec{z_3} = \vec{z_2} + fn(P')$ and $(n(\varphi') - \vec{z_2}) \cap fn(P') = \emptyset)\}$

B. $\qquad \Pi(P)(\{\}) = (\{\})$

Fig. 3. Partial Model Checker for π-Calculus

as pulling the ν out using the *structural congruence* rule: $(\nu x)P \mid Q \equiv (\nu x)(P \mid Q)$ *where x does not appear in Q.* Renamings in these two rules correspond to the side condition of the congruence rule.

Rule 13 presents the transformation $\langle\alpha\rangle\varphi$ using prefix process expression $a.P$. The rule relies on three different possibilities following which $a.P$, when composed with an environment, can satisfy $\langle\alpha\rangle\varphi$.

1. The environment makes a move on α satisfying the modal obligation (1st disjunct).
2. $a.P$ satisfies the modal obligation α (2nd disjunct).
3. $\alpha = \tau$ and the environment synchronizes with $a.P$ (the 3rd disjunct), i.e., performs an $\overline{a}$ action.

In Case 1, the side condition demands that the bindings in modal action α does not bind any free names of prefixed process expression. As such we apply alpha-conversion to satisfy the side condition: alpha-conversion renames all the binding occurrences in formula with new names that are disjoint from the free names of the process. In Case 2 there are multiple possibilities depending on the nature of modal action α. Note that if

α is an output or a free output, then formula expression $nloc(y_1)$ is generated meaning that y_1 must not be a local name to satisfy the modal obligation. This is because at the time of transformation, it is not known whether y_1 is a local name or not. Similarly, when α is a bound output modal action, the formula expression $loc(y_1)$ is generated.

In Rule 14, a diamond modal formula is transformed using choice process expression. The result is a disjunction where (a) the first disjunct corresponds to the case where the environment is left with the obligation to satisfy the modal action and (b) the second and the third disjunct, respectively, corresponds to the case where the first or the second process is selected for subsequent transformation.

Finally, Rules A and B correspond to transformation of formula equations. Observe that, we are using equational syntax of the $C\mu$-calculus. Any property with formula expressions of the form $\sigma X(\vec{z}).\varphi$ can be converted in linear time to set of equations of the form $X(\vec{z}) =_\sigma \varphi$. Specifically, given a $C\mu$-calculus formula φ where each fixed point variable has distinct names, the number of equations in the corresponding equational set is equal to the number of fixed point sub-formulas of φ. Each such sub-formula of the form $\sigma_x X.\varphi_x$ is translated to a equation $X =_{\sigma_x} \psi_x$ where ψ_x is obtained by replacing every occurrences of its sub-formula $\sigma_y Y.\varphi_y$ with Y. For example the formula expression: $\nu X.(\mu Y.([a_1]X \wedge [a_2]Y))$ is translated to $X =_\nu Y$ and $Y =_\mu [a_1]X \wedge [a_2]Y$ where X is the outer-fixed point variable and Y is the inner one. The use of equational form is driven by the fact that transformation can be done in a per-equation basis, instead of keeping track of all the sub-formula expressions of a formula if the transformation was done for non-equational form.

Let $\mathcal{E}$ represent the sets of formula equations. Rules A and B define a function Π : $\mathcal{P} \rightarrow \mathcal{E} \rightarrow \mathcal{E}$ that represents the transformer over a set of $C\mu$-calculus equations. Rule A states that given a formula equation of the form $X(\vec{z}) =_\sigma \varphi$, transformation leads to the generation of a new equation of the form $X_P(\vec{z_1}) =_\sigma \Pi(P)(\varphi)$ where $\vec{z_1}$ is formed by concatenation of $\vec{z}$ and free names of P. Moreover, if there is a formula expression $X'_{P'}(\vec{z_3})$ present in $\Pi(P)(\varphi)$, then the corresponding formula equation for $X'(\vec{z_2})$ is transformed using P', where $\vec{z_2}$ is formed by removing free names of P' from $\vec{z_3}$. Rule A also requires that names in the right-hand side of the equation that do not appear in the parameters should be different from any free names of P.

Theorem 1. *Let P and Q be two process expressions, δ a set of substitutions, and l a set of local names. Then for all formulas φ, the following holds:*

$$Q \mid P \models_{\delta,l} \varphi \Leftrightarrow Q \models_{\delta,l} \Pi(P)(\varphi)$$

The proof is by induction on the size of the process expression and the formula. □

Computing Constraints. Given a process $P|0$ and a formula φ, let $\psi = \Pi(P)(\varphi)$. According to Theorem 1, given a set of constraints δ and a set of local names l, $P \models_{\delta,l} \varphi \Leftrightarrow 0 \models_{\delta,l} \psi$. In Figure 4, we present a function $f^l(\psi)$ that, given a set of local names l, computes a set of constraints δ under which $0 \models_{\delta,l} \psi$.

Rules 1 and 2 in Figure 4 are straightforward. In Rules 3 and 4, if one of x and y is a local name, then since local names are different from any other names in the system, $x = y$ is false. In Rule 7, if x occurs in l, then $loc(x)$ is true, otherwise false. Rule 11 evaluates $\langle \alpha \rangle \varphi$ to $f\!f$ because 0 cannot perform any action. In Rule 12, the local name

1. $f^l(tt) = tt$	2. $f^l(ff) = ff$
3. $f^l(x = y) = \left\{ \begin{array}{ll} tt & \text{if } x = y \\ ff & \text{if } \{x, y\} \cap l \neq \emptyset \\ x = y & \text{otherwise} \end{array} \right\}$	4. $f^l(x \neq y) = \left\{ \begin{array}{ll} ff & \text{if } x = y \\ tt & \text{if } \{x, y\} \cap l \neq \emptyset \\ x \neq y & \text{otherwise} \end{array} \right\}$
5. $f^l(\exists x.\varphi) = \exists x.f^l(\varphi)$	6. $f^l(\forall x.\varphi) = \forall x.f^l(\varphi)$
7. $f^l(loc(x)) = \left\{ \begin{array}{l} ff \text{ if } x \notin l \\ tt \text{ if } x \in l \end{array} \right\}$	8. $f^l(nloc(x)) = \left\{ \begin{array}{l} tt \text{ if } x \notin l \\ ff \text{ if } x \in l \end{array} \right\}$
9. $f^l(\varphi_1 \wedge \varphi_2) = f^l(\varphi_1) \wedge f^l(\varphi_2)$	10. $f^l(\varphi_1 \vee \varphi_2) = f^l(\varphi_1) \vee f^l(\varphi_2)$
11. $f^l((\alpha)\varphi) = ff$	12. $f^l((\nu x)\varphi) = f^{l \cup \{x\}}(\varphi)$
13. $f^l(X(\overrightarrow{e})) = f^l(\varphi\{\overrightarrow{e}/\overrightarrow{z}\})$ where $X(\overrightarrow{z}) =_\sigma \varphi$	

Fig. 4. Computing $f^l(\varphi)$

x is added to l in order to evaluate the $loc(x)$ and $nloc(x)$ predicates. Note that $f^l(\psi)$ generates a formula over equality and disequality expressions and standard constraint solving algorithms are applied to solve the constraints of the form $\exists x.\varphi$ and $\forall x.\varphi$.

Following example illustrates the use of loc and $nloc$ formula expressions.

Example 1. *Given a process $p(x) \stackrel{\text{def}}{=} (\nu y)\overline{x}y.p(x)$ and a formula $\varphi \equiv X(x) =_\nu \langle \overline{x}\nu z \rangle tt$:*

$$\Pi(p(x))(\varphi) \equiv X_1(x) =_\nu \Pi((\nu y)\overline{x}y.p(x))(\langle \overline{x}\nu z \rangle tt)$$
$$=_\nu (\nu y)\Pi(\overline{x}y.p(x))(\langle \overline{x}\nu z \rangle tt) =_\nu (\nu y)loc(y)$$

As $f^\emptyset((\nu y)loc(y)) = f^{\{y\}}(loc(y)) = tt$, therefore, $0 \models_{tt,\emptyset} \Pi(p(x))(\varphi)$ □

In Example 1, when computing $\Pi(\overline{x}y.p(x))(\langle \overline{x}\nu z \rangle tt)$, since (νy) is not in the scope of transformation, the model checker cannot determine if y is a local name. Thus, we generate the constraint $loc(y)$. After the transformation is done, we verify if 0 satisfies the resulting formula $(\nu y)loc(y)$. Since y is a local name, $(\nu y)loc(y)$ is evaluated to tt.

4   Verification of Parameterized π-Calculus Systems

We outline here the compositional analysis based technique for verification of parameterized systems where instances of subsystems are represented by finite control π-calculus processes. Let P^n be a system with n instances of π-calculus process P. Consider verifying that the ith instance of above system satisfies a property φ. The result of transforming φ using the ith instance is $\varphi_i = \Pi(P^i)(\varphi)$. Therefore, from Theorem 1, given a set of substitutions δ and a set of local names l, $0 \models_{\delta,l} \varphi_i \Leftrightarrow P^i \models_{\delta,l} \varphi$.

Now consider verifying whether $\forall i. P^i \models \varphi$. Let φ'_i be defined as:

$$\varphi'_i = \left\{ \begin{array}{ll} \varphi_1 & \text{if } i = 1 \\ \varphi'_{i-1} \wedge \varphi_i & \text{if } i > 1 \end{array} \right.$$

By definition of φ'_i, $(\forall 1 \leq j \leq i.0 \models_{\delta,l} \varphi_j) \Leftrightarrow 0 \models_{\delta,l} \varphi'_i$. Thus, $0 \models_{\delta,l} \varphi'_i$ means that $\forall 1 \leq j \leq i.P^j \models_{\delta,l} \varphi$. If φ'_ω is the limit of sequence $\varphi'_1, \varphi'_2 \ldots$, then, $0 \models_{\delta,l} \varphi'_\omega \Leftrightarrow \forall i \geq 1.P^i \models_{\delta,l} \varphi$.

A dual technique is applied for the verification problem $\exists i.P^i \models \varphi$. Let φ_i'' be defined as:

$$\varphi_i'' = \begin{cases} \varphi_1 & \text{if } i = 1 \\ \varphi_{i-1}'' \vee \varphi_i & \text{if } i > 1 \end{cases}$$

In this case, if φ_ω'', the limit of the sequence $\varphi_1'', \varphi_2'', \ldots$, is satisfied by 0 under the substitution δ, then $\exists n.P^n \models \varphi$. We say that the series of φ_i' is *contracting* since $\varphi_i' \Rightarrow \varphi_{i-1}'$ and the series of φ_i'' is *relaxing* as $\varphi_{i-1}'' \Rightarrow \varphi_i''$.

Before deploying the above technique for solving verification of parameterized systems, we need to solve the following problems:

1. *Entailment*: To detect whether a limit is reached requires developing the equivalence relation between $C\mu$-calculus formulas.
2. *Convergence acceleration*: The limit in the chain of $C\mu$-calculus formulas may not be realized in general. As such, we need to identify a suitable abstraction to the generated formulas to ensure termination of the iterative process.

Entailment. Equivalence checking of formula expressions in logic with explicit fixed points is an EXPTIME-hard problem. Hence we use an approximate, conservative technique for equivalence detection which is safe and can be efficiently applied. First, we check if two formulas are equivalent based on the algorithm in [3]. The algorithm states that syntactically identical formula expressions are semantically equivalent. If the equivalence between formula expressions is not readily understood from their structure, we apply the technique developed in [6]. This technique relies on converting the formula into a labeled transition system, called *formula graphs*, where each state is annotated by a formula expressions and transitions are labeled by various syntactic constructs of $C\mu$-calculus, e.g., diamond modal action. The equivalence between two formula expressions are determined by checking whether the corresponding formula graphs refine each other. Such graph-based equivalence detection algorithm is more powerful than that relying on textual representation of syntax [3] as the former can effectively extract dependencies between formula variables (see [6]).

Convergence acceleration. To ensure convergence and termination, we develop a widening algorithm that over-approximates a relaxing sequence of φ_i'' and under-approximates the contracting sequence of φ_i'. The core of the technique is to examine two consecutive formula expressions φ_i and φ_j in a sequence and determine their differences. For example, if the formulas are members of a relaxing sequence ($\varphi_i \Rightarrow \varphi_j$), the difference is identified as a disjunct in φ_j. Widening amounts to removing this disjunct and generate a new formula φ_a such that $\varphi_j \Rightarrow \varphi_a$. Similarly, for contracting sequence, we remove the divergence-causing conjuncts. Note that, this type of widening is only applicable to safety and reachability properties where all the boolean connectives in the formula are either $\wedge$ or $\vee$, respectively.

Note that widening leads to an approximation of the limit of the sequence. As such, given a parameterized system P^n and formula φ, if limit φ_ω of a relaxing sequence is realized via widening and $0 \models \varphi_\omega$, we cannot infer that $\exists n.P^n \models \varphi$. However, $0 \not\models \varphi_\omega \Rightarrow \forall n.P^n \not\models \varphi$. Similarly, for contracting sequence, if φ_ω is the limit reached after widening, then $0 \models \varphi_\omega \Rightarrow \forall n.P^n \models \varphi$, while $0 \not\models \varphi_\omega \not\Rightarrow \exists n.P^n \not\models \varphi$.

5 Optimizations

In general, the transformation rules may generate a number of redundant formulas, e.g., two sub-formulas that are equivalent. Redundancies result in formulas that are large and virtually un-manageable. In order to apply the partial model checker to any practical application, we need to develop techniques to remove such redundancies.

In this section, we propose several optimization techniques to reduce the number of formulas generated by transformation. In [6], the redundancy removal technique was solely focused on removing equivalent sub-formulas and used heavy-weight bisimulation checking algorithm on graphical representation of formulas. Such a technique was used off-line, after the formulas have been generated in the first place. In contrast, here we present a number of light-weight techniques that are tightly-coupled with the transformation rules and help to significantly reduce the size of the resulting formulas.

Symmetry Reduction. When the partial model checker generates new formula variables, it names them based on the corresponding process expressions (see Rule 6 in Figure 3). The number of formulas generated can be reduced considerably by exploiting a form of symmetry reduction. For instance, let X be a formula variable, and P and Q be arbitrary process expressions. Note that $\Pi(P|Q)(X) = \Pi(P)(\Pi(Q)(X))$ is a new formula variable of the form $X_{Q,P}$. On the other hand, $\Pi(Q|P)(X) = \Pi(Q)(\Pi(P)(X))$ is $X_{P,Q}$. Hence $X_{P,Q}$ and $X_{Q,P}$ are semantically identical. We avoid creating the two formula variables in the first place, by reducing the suffix process expression to a symmetrically equivalent canonical form. This is done by first reducing the expression to a sequence of parallel-free process expressions (exploiting the associativity of parallel composition), and sorting the sequence by imposing a global total order on the elements (exploiting the commutativity of parallel composition). This optimization is light-weight and may dramatically reduce the number of formulas generated even for applications where symmetry is not obvious (see Section 6).

Optimizing the Choice Rule. The choice rule in Figure 3 may generate redundant formulas. Consider the process definition $p(x,y) \stackrel{\text{def}}{=} x(v).p(x,y) + y(w).p(x,y)$ and the formula $\varphi =_\nu \langle \tau \rangle tt$. $\Pi(p(x,y))(\varphi)$ generates the following formulas.

$$X_1(x,y) =_\nu \langle \tau \rangle tt \vee X_2(x,y) \vee X_3(x,y)$$
$$X_2(x,y) =_\nu \langle \tau \rangle tt \vee \langle \overline{x}\{v\} \rangle X_1(x,y) \qquad X_3(x,y) =_\nu \langle \tau \rangle tt \vee \langle \overline{y}\{w\} \rangle X_1(x,y)$$

From the above, we can infer that $X_1(x,y) = \langle \tau \rangle tt \vee \langle \tau \rangle tt \vee \langle \overline{x}\{v\} \rangle X_1(x,y) \vee \langle \tau \rangle tt \vee \langle \overline{y}\{w\} \rangle X_1(x,y)$. We can, however, avoid generating the two redundant sub-formulas $\langle \tau \rangle tt$ using the following revised "+" rule.

$$\Pi(P_1 + P_2)(\langle \alpha \rangle \varphi) = \langle \alpha \rangle \Pi(P_1 + P_2)(\varphi) \vee \Pi'(P_1)(\langle \alpha \rangle \varphi) \vee \Pi'(P_2)(\langle \alpha \rangle \varphi)$$

Π' differs from Π in Rule 13 where modal obligation $\langle \alpha \rangle$ is not imposed on the environment.

Simplification Techniques. Apart from symmetry-based simplification, we also remove redundant sub-formulas and use the simplifying equations originally proposed in [3]. The most frequently used simplification techniques are constant propagation (e.g. $X = \langle \alpha \rangle X_1, X_1 = tt \Rightarrow X = \langle \alpha \rangle tt$), and unguardedness removal(e.g. $X = \langle \alpha \rangle X_1, X_1 = $

$X_2 \Rightarrow X = \langle \alpha \rangle X_2$). These simplification techniques help to quickly detect if two formulas are equivalent.

Environment-Based Reduction. Consider Rule 13 in Figure 3. Process $a.P$ either leaves the environment to perform an α action (1st disjunct) or an $\bar{a}$ action if $\alpha = \tau$ (3rd disjunct), or $a.P$ itself performs an α action (2nd disjunct). However, if the environment cannot perform an α or an $\bar{a}$ action, then the 1st and the 3rd disjuncts need not be generated. For instance, consider the example given in Figure 1. Given a formula φ, we first use $p(x)$ to transform φ under the environment $q(x) \mid \ldots \mid q(x)$. From the specification, process $q(x)$ cannot synchronize with itself, thus the model checker does not need to leave the environment to perform a τ action. However, this optimization requires the knowledge of the environment, thereby rendering the model checker of Figure 3 no longer compositional. Moreover, the assertion $(P|Q) \models \varphi \Leftrightarrow Q \models \Pi(P)(\varphi)$ now holds only for those Q that are consistent with the knowledge of the environment used to perform this optimization.

When using P to transform a formula under the environment Q, we check: 1) What are the actions of P with which Q cannot synchronize? 2) Can Q perform a τ transition? These can be easily determined for value-passing calculus by parsing the specification, but are more difficult for the π-calculus due to link passing. Thus we compute the set of actions conservatively: if we do not know whether one process can synchronize with another, then we conservatively assume that such synchronization exists between the two processes. The environment information is propagated in the model checker. The details are given in [34]. This optimization may reduce the size of each formula and sometimes reduces the number of formulas generated (see Section 6).

Eliminating Constraints Based on the Types of Channels. This optimization is applied to whenever the formulas generated are guarded by equality and disequality constraints. Under certain conditions, we can determine whether a constraint generated is unsatisfiable. For instance, assume that we keep track of the set of all names that have been extruded from their initial scope. Then if x has never been extruded and y is a bound name of an input action, then $x = y$ is never true. We use a simple type system to determine whether a channel could have been extruded.

6   Preliminary Experimental Results

In this section, we show the effectiveness of our technique to verify parameterized versions of several small but non-trivial examples. The examples include those with a fixed process interconnection, namely, *Token ring*, a ring of n token-passing processes, and *Spin lock*, a simple locking protocol where n processes compete to acquire a single common resource. We also include examples with dynamically changing interconnection between processes, namely *Printer*, where n clients use a single print server to mediate access to a printer, and *Server* [9], where n file readers serve web page read requests. We also evaluate the performance of our model checker on the *Handover procedure* [29] (which maintains the connectedness of a mobile station in a cellular network when the station crosses cell boundaries) to verify a single instance of the system.

The experimental results are shown in Fig. 5. All reported performance data were obtained on a 1.4GHz Pentium M machine with 512MB of memory running Red Hat

Benchmark	Property	Summary		# Formulas					Time (sec.)				
		# Iter	Widen (Y/N)	Orig	Sym	Env	All	Conv	Orig	Sym	Env	All	Conv
Token ring	deadlock freedom	3	Y	86	45	–	45	40	1.93	0.56	–	0.56	0.37
Spin lock	mutual exclusion	3	N	398	192	364	181	181	34.96	7.8	23.37	5.11	5.29
	deadlock freedom	3	Y	160	80	160	80	64	6.89	1.49	4.62	0.99	1.35
Printer	deadlock freedom	3	Y	55	29	–	29	22	1.03	0.29	–	0.29	0.20
Server	order preservation	4	Y	1440	1270	241	239	172	361.58	280	10.17	10.07	5.24

Fig. 5. Experimental Results

Linux 9.0. The figure is divided broadly into three parts. The verification results for the different systems and properties are summarized in the first part (columns under "Summary"). In that part, the number of iterations for the sequence to converge, and whether widening was needed appear in columns "# Iter", and "Widen" respectively. For all the cases listed in the figure, we can conclude that the property holds for all instances of the parameterized system, even when widening was used to enforce convergence.

The second and third parts of the table, namely, columns under "# Formulas" and "Time", present the performance results (number of formulas processed and the CPU time taken, resp.) for the examples. The columns "Conv" list the total number of formulas and time to compute the formula sequence, including the time taken to perform convergence check and widening (when needed). The other columns list the same statistics to compute the formula sequence (length of the sequence is same as the number of iterations) but without checking for convergence or applying widening. The columns "Orig", "Sym", "Env" and "All" list the statistics when no optimizations, symmetry reduction, environment-based reduction and all optimizations described in Section 5 (resp.) are applied. In the table "–" indicates that the optimization is inapplicable. The performance results show the effectiveness of the optimizations: the overheads of performing the optimizations are easily offset by the reductions enabled by the optimizations. Widening sometimes reduces formula sizes sufficiently (see Token Ring, Printer, Server), consequently saving enough time to offset that needed to perform the operation. In all benchmarks, the memory requirement of the model checker without optimizations is always higher than that with optimizations (all < 12MB), and hence the corresponding results are not shown.

Finally, we applied the compositional model checker to verify a single instance of the Handover protocol (1 mobile and 2 base stations). Even with all optimizations enabled, it takes 12s to verify the deadlock freedom property for this instance. In contrast, the non-compositional model checker MMC can verify this instance in less than a second. This indicates that the compositional checker is unsuitable for use, as it stands, for routine verification of non-parameterized systems. When we attempted to verify another instance of the protocol (with 2 mobile stations), the compositional checker generated more formulas than can be handled by our prototype implementation.

7 Conclusion

In this paper, we presented an automatic technique for verifying parameterized systems that consist of a number of instances of finite-control π-calculus processes. This technique uses a sufficiently expressive logic, Cμ-calculus, to represent properties, and is based on a compositional model checker for the π-calculus.

Since the technique is based on a compositional model checker, each process instance is verified in an "open" (unknown) environment. Hence in this approach, we consider a lot more potential system behaviors than any instance of the parameterized system can exhibit. This leads to generation of large number of formulas at each step. Optimization aim at reducing this potential blow-up. Among these, the environment-based reduction attempts to construct an environment for each process that is significantly more restricted than the open environment. This is based on the capabilities of the other processes in the parameterized system (e.g. channels they can communicate on). Even a relatively simple version of this optimization presented in this paper, which is based on a very coarse notion of capabilities of processes, results in significant reduction in verification time (e.g. Server example in Fig. 5). We are currently investigating heavier-weight but more effective optimizations that would make it possible to use our technique on realistic parameterized systems such as the Handover protocol.

References

1. R. Alur and T. Henzinger. Reactive modules. In *LICS*, 1996.
2. R. Alur, P. Madhusudan, and W. Nam. Symbolic compositional verification by learning assumptions. In *CAV*, pages 548–562, 2005.
3. H.R. Andersen. Partial model checking (extended abstract). In *LICS*, 1995.
4. H.R. Andersen, C. Stirling, and G. Winskel. A compositional proof system for the modal mu-calculus. In *LICS*, 1994.
5. T. Arons, A. Pnueli, S. Ruah, J. Xu, and L. Zuck. Parameterized verification with automatically computed inductive assertions. In *Computer Aided Verification*, 2001.
6. S. Basu and C. R. Ramakrishnan. Compositional analysis for verification of parameterized systems. In *Proceedings of TACAS*, pages 315–330, 2003.
7. S. Berezin and D. Gurov. A compositional proof system for the modal mu-calculus and CCS. Technical Report CMU-CS-97-105, CMU, 1997.
8. J. Bradfield and C. Stirling. *Modal logics and mu-calculi: an introduction (In the Handbook of Process Algebra)*, pages 293–330. Elsevier, 2001.
9. S. Chaki, S.K.Rajamani, and J. Rehof. Types as models: model checking message-passing programs. In *Proceedings of POPL*, pages 45 – 57, 2002.
10. E. M. Clarke, O. Grumberg, and S. Jha. Verifying parameterized networks. *ACM Transactions on Programming Languages and Systems*, 1997.
11. M. Dam. Proof systems for pi-calculus logics. *Logic for Concurrency and Synchronisation*, 2001.
12. G. Delzanno. Automatic verification of parameterized cache coherence protocols. In *Computer Aided Verification*, 2000.
13. E.A. Emerson and K.S. Namjoshi. Reasoning about rings. In *POPL*, 1995.
14. E.A. Emerson and K.S. Namjoshi. Automated verification of parameterized synchronous systems. In *Computer Aided Verification*. Lecture Notes in Computer Science, 1996.
15. E.A. Emerson and K.S. Namjoshi. On model checking for non-deterministic infinite state systems. In *LICS*, 1998.
16. J. Esparza, A. Finkel, and R. Mayr. On the verification of broadcast protocols. In *LICS*, 1999.
17. R. Cleaveland G. Bhat. Efficient model checking via the equational μ-calculus. In *LICS*, pages 304–312, 1996.
18. O. Grumberg and D.E. Long. Model checking and modular verification. *ACM Transactions on Programming Languages and Systems*, 1994.

19. T. Henzinger, S. Qadeer, and S.K. Rajamani. You assume, we guarantee. In *CAV*, 1998.
20. G. J. Holzmann. The model checker SPIN. *IEEE Transactions on Software Engineering*, 23(5):279–295, May 1997.
21. A. Igarashi and N. Kobayashi. A generic type system for the pi-calculus. *Theoretical Computer Science*, 311(1–3):121–163, 2004.
22. C.N. Ip and D.L. Dill. Verifying systems with replicated components in murphi. *Formal Methods in System Design*, 1999.
23. Y. Kesten and A. Pnueli. Control and data abstraction:the cornerstones of pratical formal verification. *International Journal on Software tools for Technology*, 2000.
24. D. Kozen. Results on the propositional μ-calculus. *Theoretical Computer Science*, 1983.
25. H. Lin. Symbolic bisimulation and proof systems for the π-calculus. Technical report, School of Cognitive and Computer Science, U. of Sussex, UK, 1994.
26. K.L. McMillan. Compositional rule for hardware design refinement. In *CAV*, 1997.
27. R. Milner. *Communication and Concurrency*. Prentice Hall, 1989.
28. R. Milner, J. Parrow, and D. Walker. A calculus of mobile processes, Parts I and II. *Information and Computation*, 100(1):1–77, 1992.
29. F. Orava and J. Parrow. An algebraic verification of a mobile network. *Journal of Formal Aspects of Computing*, 4:497–543, 1992.
30. A. Pnueli, S. Ruah, and L. Zuck. Automatic deductive verification with invisible invariants. In *Tools and Algorithms for the Construction and Analysis of Systems*, 2001.
31. A. Pnueli and E. Shahar. Liveness and acceleration in parameterized verification. In *Computer Aided Verification*, 2000.
32. H. Song and K. J. Compton. Verifying pi-calculus processes by Promela translation. Technical Report CSE-TR-472-03, Univ. of Michigan, 2003.
33. B. Victor. The Mobility Workbench user's guide. Technical report, Department of Computer Systems, Uppsala University, Sweden, 1995.
34. P. Yang, S. Basu, and C. R. Ramakrishnan. Parameterized verification of π-calculus systems, 2006. Available at http://www.lmc.cs.sunysb.edu/~pyang/ptech.pdf.
35. P. Yang, C. R. Ramakrishnan, and S. A. Smolka. A logical encoding of the π-calculus: Model checking mobile processes using tabled resolution. In *Proceedings of VMCAI*, 2003. Extended version in *Software Tools for Technology Transfer*, 6(1):38-66,2004.
36. P. Yang, C. R. Ramakrishnan, and S. A. Smolka. A provably correct compiler for efficient model checking of mobile processes. In *Proceedings of PADL*, 2005.
37. L. Zuck and A. Pnueli. Model checking and abstraction to the aid of parameterized systems (a survey). *Computer Languages, Systems & Structures*, 30(3–4):139–169, 2004.

Easy Parameterized Verification of Biphase Mark and 8N1 Protocols

Geoffrey M. Brown[1] and Lee Pike[2],[*]

[1] Indiana University, Bloomington
geobrown@cs.indiana.edu
[2] Galois Connections
leepike@galois.com

Abstract. The Biphase Mark Protocol (BMP) and 8N1 Protocol are physical layer protocols for data transmission. We present a generic model in which timing and error values are parameterized by linear constraints, and then we use this model to verify these protocols. The verifications are carried out using SRI's SAL model checker that combines a *satisfiability modulo theories* decision procedure with a bounded model checker for highly-automated induction proofs of safety properties over infinite-state systems. Previously, parameterized formal verification of real-time systems required mechanical theorem-proving or specialized real-time model checkers; we describe a compelling case-study demonstrating a simpler and more general approach. The verification reveals a significant error in the parameter ranges for 8N1 given in a published application note [1].

1 Introduction

The Biphase Mark Protocol (BMP) and 8N1 Protocol are common physical layer protocols used in data transmission – BMP in CDs, Ethernet, and Tokenring and 8N1 in UARTs. Decoders for protocols such as these present challenging formal verification problems because their correctness depends upon reasoning about interacting real-time events. BMP was first verified using the Boyer-Moore Theorem Prover (Nqthm) [2]. Subsequently, it was verified using a Duration Calculus model in the PVS theorem prover [3], with the HyTech model checker [4, 5] and also using a combination of the Uppaal model checker and PVS [6]. In this paper, we show how a parameterized specification of BMP can be verified easily with the SAL tool set using its built-in bounded model checker in conjunction with a satisfiability modulo theories (SMT) decision procedure to complete induction proofs over infinite-state systems [7].[1]

Compared to interactive mechanical theorem proving – the usual method for parameterized verification – this approach is substantially simpler. For example,

---

[*] The majority of this work was completed while this author was a member of the Formal Methods Group at the NASA Langley Research Center in Hampton, Virginia.

[1] The SAL specifications and a proof script are available at http://www.cs.indiana.edu/~lepike/pub_pages/bmp.html.

H. Hermanns and J. Palsberg (Eds.): TACAS 2006, LNCS 3920, pp. 58–72, 2006.
© Springer-Verlag Berlin Heidelberg 2006

the proof of Vaandrager and de Groot using PVS requires 37 invariants whereas ours requires only five. Because invariants can be combined, a more meaningful (and striking) metric may be the number of user-directed proof steps required: their initial verification effort required more than 4000 steps whereas each of our five invariants is proved automatically by SAL. As another comparison, the verification reported by Hung has such complexity that PVS requires approximately five hours just to *check* the validity of the manually-created proof script. In our approach, the proofs are *generated* by the bounded model checker and decision procedure in just a few seconds. We emphasize the simplicity of the invariants necessary in our verification, the "push-button" technique used to prove them, and the robustness of the proofs under modifications to the underlying model. In fact, we demonstrate that with a few trivial changes to the model, the proof for BMP naturally leads to a similar proof for 8N1. Finally, in verifying the 8N1 decoder, we found a significant error in a published application note that incorrectly defines the relationship between various real-time parameters which, if followed, would lead to unreliable operation [1].

While the verification approach described in this paper can be orders-of-magnitude easier than mechanical theorem-proving, it is less general. In the models presented, we fix two small integer constants, and the constraints on the model are parameterized with respect to these. The fixed constants are sufficiently small, and the verification is sufficiently fast, so that these values can be enumerated, and the constraints can be checked for each value. Alternatively, an anonymous referee pointed out an alternative formulation of the constraints that allows for a fully parameterized verification of BMP (the limitation of the SAL's ICS decision procedure described in Section 5 prevents a fully parameterized verification of 8N1). We present a fully parameterized model similar to the one suggested by the referee in the SAL specifications provided on-line, and we briefly describe the approach in Section 7. We also make a more detailed comparison to other verifications, including those carried out using specialized real-time model checkers, in Section 7.

To motivate the design of this sort of protocol, consider Figure 1 where the top stream is the signal to be transmitted, while the middle stream is a digital clock that defines the boundaries between the individual bits. In a digital circuit, the clock signal is transmitted separately from the data; however, this is not feasible

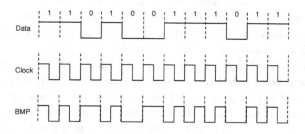

Fig. 1. Data and Synchronization Clock

in most communication systems (e.g., serial lines, Ethernet, SONET, Infrared) in which a single signal is transmitted. A general solution to this problem is to merge the clock and data information using a coding scheme such as BMP, illustrated as the lower stream. In BMP, every bit is guaranteed to begin with a transition marking a clock event. The value of the bit is determined by the presence (to encode a 1) or absence (to encode a 0) of a transition in the middle of the bit period. Thus, 0's are encoded as the two symbols 00 or 11, while 1's are encoded as 01 or 10. 8N1 is a simpler encoding scheme in which a transition is guaranteed to occur only at the beginning of each *frame*, a sequence of bits that includes a start bit, stop bit, and eight data bits. Data bits are encoded by the identity function – a 1 is a 1 and a 0 is a 0. Consequently, the clock can only be recovered once in each frame in which the eight data bits are transmitted.

Thus, the central design issue for a *data decoder* is reliably extracting a clock signal from the combined signal. Once the locations of the clock events are known, extracting the data is relatively simple. Although the clock events have a known relationship to signal transitions, detecting these transitions precisely is usually impossible because of distortion in the signal around the transitions, clock jitter, and other effects. The transmitter and receiver of the data do not share a common time base, and hence the estimation of clock events is affected by differences in the reference clocks used. Constant delay is largely irrelevant; however, transition time and variable delay (e.g., jitter) are not. Furthermore, differences in receiver and transmitter clock phase and frequency are significant. Any correctness proof of a BMP (or 8N1) decoder must be valid over a range of parameters defining limits on jitter, transition time, frequency, and clock phase.

The remainder of this paper is organized as follows. In Section 2, the SAL tool set and the k-induction proof technique are described. In Section 3, we present the general SAL models of the transmitter, receiver, and data transmission used in the verifications. The specifics of the BMP model are provided in Section 4, and the small changes necessary for the 8N1 model are in Section 5. The verification of the two protocols is described in Section 6, and concluding remarks follow in Section 7.

2   Introduction to SAL

The protocols are specified and verified in the Symbolic Analysis Laboratory (SAL), developed by SRI, International [7]. SAL is a verification environment that includes symbolic and bounded model checkers, an interactive simulator, integrated decision procedures, and other tools.

SAL has a high-level modeling language for specifying transition systems. A transition system is specified by a *module*. A module consists of a set of state variables and guarded transitions. Of the enabled transitions, one is nondeterministically executed at a time. Modules can be composed both synchronously (||) and asynchronously ([]), and composed modules communicate via shared variables. In a synchronous composition, a transition from each module is simultaneously applied; a synchronous composition is deadlocked if either module has no enabled transition. In an asynchronous composition, an enabled transition from one of the modules is nondeterministically chosen to be applied.

The language is typed, and predicate sub-typing is possible. Types can be both interpreted and uninterpreted, and base types include the reals, naturals, and booleans; array types, inductive data-types, and tuple types can be defined. Both interpreted and uninterpreted constants and functions can be specified. This is significant to the power of these models: the parameterized values are uninterpreted constants from some parameterized type.

Bounded model checkers are usually used to find counterexamples, but they can also be used to prove invariants by induction over the state space [8]. SAL supports k-induction, a generalization of the induction principle, that can prove some invariants that may not be strictly inductive. By incorporating a satisfiability modulo theories decision procedure, SAL can do k-induction proofs over infinite-state transition systems. We use SRI's ICS decision procedure [9], the default SAT-solver and decision procedure in SAL, but others can be plugged in.

Let $(S, I, \rightarrow)$ be a transition system where S is a set of states, $I \subseteq S$ is a set of initial states, and $\rightarrow$ is a binary transition relation. If k is a natural number, then a k-trajectory is a sequence of states $s_0 \rightarrow s_1 \rightarrow \ldots \rightarrow s_k$ (a 0-trajectory is a single state). Let k be a natural number, and let P be property. The k-induction principle is then defined as follows:

- Base Case: Show that for each k-trajectory $s_0 \rightarrow s_1 \rightarrow \ldots \rightarrow s_k$ such that $s_0 \in I$, $P(s_j)$ holds, for $0 \leq j < k$.
- Induction Step: Show that for all k-trajectories $s_0 \rightarrow s_1 \rightarrow \ldots \rightarrow s_k$, if $P(s_j)$ holds for $0 \leq j < k$, then $P(s_k)$ holds.

The principle is equivalent to the usual transition-system induction principle when $k = 1$. In SAL, the user specifies the depth at which to attempt an induction proof, but the attempt itself is automated. The main mode of user-guidance in the proof process is in iteratively building up inductive invariants. While arbitrary LTL safety formulas can be verified in SAL using k-induction, only state predicates may be used as lemmas in a k-induction proof. Lemmas strengthen the invariant. We have more to say about the proof methodology for k-induction in Section 6.

3   Modeling

In this section, we discuss the general model of physical layer protocols, postponing the details of the BMP and 8N1 protocols to Sections 4 and 5, respectively. We model the protocols using three processes asynchronously composed – a transmitter (tx), a receiver (rx), and a global clock unit (clock). The general arrangement of the three major modules along with the details of the transmitter (tx) module are illustrated in Figure 2. The modules tx and rx model the transmitters and receivers of the protocols; the clock is a modeling artifact that records the passage of the global real time.

```
system : MODULE = clock [] rx [] tx;
```

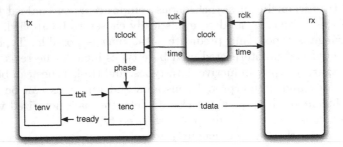

Fig. 2. System Block Diagram

The clock unit provides a single real output variable – `time` – and two inputs, `rclk` and `tclk`, which are the timeout variables of the receiver and transmitter, respectively. The basic idea, described as *timeout automata* by Dutertre and Sorea, is that the progress of time is enforced cooperatively (but nondeterministically) [10, 11]. The receiver and transmitter have *timeouts* that mark the real time at which they will respectively make transitions (timeouts are always in the future and may be updated nondeterministically). Each module is allowed to execute only if its timeout equals the value of `time`. When no module can execute, `clock` updates `time` to be equal to the next timeout. The SAL module below describes the transitions of the global clock.

```
TIME : TYPE = REAL;

clock: MODULE =
  BEGIN
    INPUT  rclk, tclk : TIME
    OUTPUT time : TIME
  INITIALIZATION time = 0
  TRANSITION
    [    time < rclk AND rclk <= tclk --> time' = rclk
     [] time < tclk AND tclk <= rclk --> time' = tclk ]
  END;
```

The transmitter consists of a local clock module (`tclock`) that manages the transmitter's timeout variable, an encoder (`tenc`) module that implements the basic protocol, and an environment module (`tenv`) that generates the data to be transmitted. These modules are synchronously composed.

```
tx : MODULE = tclock || tenc || tenv;
```

The environment and clock modules, defined in Figure 3, are protocol independent and used in both the BMP and 8N1 models. The `tenv` module determines when new input data should be generated and is regulated by `tenc` (which is protocol dependent and described in the following two sections). Whenever `tready` is true, a random datum is selected from {0, 1}; otherwise the old datum is preserved (the syntax "var' IN Set" defines the value of variable `var` after the transition to be a random value from the set Set).

The `tclock` module regulates the `tenc` module. To model periods when the value of a signal is either in transition or uncertain, we divide each period of the transmitter into a settling phase TSETTLE, in which the wire might have a value other than `Zero` or `One`, and a stable phase TSTABLE, in which the wire may only be `Zero` or `One`. In our models, TSETTLE and TSTABLE are uninterpreted constants; however they are parameterized, which allows us to verify the models for any combination of settling time and receiver clock error (described subsequently). The transmitter settling time can be used to capture the effects of jitter and dispersion in data transmission as well as jitter in the transmitter's clock. In the case of the settling period, the model can be viewed as less deterministic than an actual implementation which might reach stable transmission values sooner. This means we verify the model under more pessimistic conditions than an actual implementation would face.

```
tenv : MODULE =
  BEGIN
    INPUT  tready  : BOOLEAN
    OUTPUT tbit    : [0..1]
    INITIALIZATION tbit = 1;
    TRANSITION
      [    tready --> tbit' IN {0,1};
        [] ELSE    --> tbit' = tbit; ]
  END;

PHASE: TYPE = {Stable, Settle};

tclock : MODULE =
  BEGIN
    INPUT  time   : TIME
    OUTPUT tclk   : TIME
    OUTPUT phase  : PHASE
  INITIALIZATION
    phase = Stable;
    tclk  IN {x : TIME | 0 <= x AND x <= TSTABLE};
  TRANSITION
    [    time = tclk AND phase = Stable --> tclk' = time + TSETTLE;
                                            phase' = Settle;
      [] time = tclk AND phase = Settle --> tclk' = time + TSTABLE;
                                            phase' = Stable; ]
  END;
```

Fig. 3. Transmitter Environment and Clock

The decoders are protocol dependent, and are described in the following two sections. Each decoder is composed of a receiver clock, `rclock`, which enforces the timing discipline, and a decoder state machine, `rdec`.

```
rx : MODULE = rclock || rdec;
```

The receiver clock, operating at a multiple of the (nominal) transmitter clock frequency, is used to digitally sample the received signal. These samples are used to detect both transitions and level values which are in turn used to decode the received data. As described in Section 1, the received signal is not purely digital in nature – there are substantial periods when the received signal is neither 1 nor 0 (i.e., it falls outside of specified voltage bands). Sampling the received signal in or near these transition bands can result in non-deterministic behavior. To model these transition bands, we let a wire have four possible values:

```
WIRE: TYPE = {Zero, One, ToZero, ToOne};
```

Only three values are required, but in practice it is convenient to use the two transition values (`ToZero`, `ToOne`) to store trajectory information. At the receiver we use non-deterministic transition rules of the form `var' IN sample(tdata)` where `sample(wire)` defines the set of possible values obtained when sampling a wire that may be in transition.

```
sample(w : WIRE) : [WIRE -> BOOLEAN] =
  IF (w = ToZero OR w = ToOne) THEN {Zero, One} ELSE {w} ENDIF;
```

The result is always binary but is chosen randomly from the set {`Zero`, `One`} whenever the wire has a transition value (`ToZero`, `ToOne`). Thus, the extra data transition values in the model do not "leak" to the receiver.

We do not model constant transmission delay – the settling phase need only capture the variable delay. While our proofs relate the state of the transmitter and receiver at an instant in time, the results hold for a delayed version of the transmitter state in the presence of a constant transmission delay.

As mentioned above, the transmitter clock period is constant (TSTABLE + TSETTLE). The receiver's clock is based upon this nominal period; however, in order to capture the effects of frequency mismatch and receiver clock jitter, the receiver's timeout period has a random error component that can affect every cycle. We model the transmitter clock as an integer number of unit length ticks (e.g., 16). The receiver clock error is defined on a per-tick basis. For a given nominal timeout of length T ticks, the actual receiver timeout value falls in the range

$$time + T * (1 - ERROR) \leq rclk \leq time + T * (1 + ERROR) \,,$$

which we implement in SAL with the following timeout function:

```
timeout (min : TIME, max : TIME) : [TIME -> BOOLEAN] =
  {x : TIME | min <= x AND x <= max};
```

As we shall show when we discuss the protocols, the receiver uses different nominal timeout periods depending upon its state. The value of ERROR is parameterized by protocol-specific linear inequalities that depend upon TSETTLE, which is constrained by the nominal clock periods – together they define the region of reliable operation.

4   Biphase Mark Protocol

Recall from Section 1 that the BMP protocol encodes every bit as two symbols – 00 or 11 for bit 0 and 01 or 10 for bit 1 – guaranteeing a transition at the beginning of every encoded bit (called a *cell*). Our encoder module, illustrated below, is a straightforward translation where the first two guarded commands implement the basic protocol and are enabled only at end of the "stable" period discussed in Section 3; the third command is enabled only at the end of the "Settle" period and returns the output wire tdata to one of the two stable values (One, Zero). The tready signal, which controls the environment module tenv (Section 3), is defined as a function from the current state and phase that is true only when the encoder transitions from state 1 to state 0.

Note that our implementation of the transmitter clock (Section 3) assumes the two halves of a cell are of identical length.[2] To modify the model in order to support asymmetric cells requires a small change to the tclock module to make the timeout period state-dependent.

```
tenc : MODULE =
  BEGIN
    INPUT   phase      : PHASE
    OUTPUT  tdata      : WIRE
    OUTPUT  tstate     : [0..1]
    OUTPUT  tready     : BOOLEAN
    INPUT   tbit       : [0..1]
    LOCAL   ttoggle    : WIRE
  INITIALIZATION
    tdata  = One;
    tstate = 1;
  DEFINITION
    tready  = phase = Stable AND tstate = 1;
    ttoggle = IF (tdata = Zero) THEN ToOne ELSE ToZero ENDIF;
  TRANSITION
    [    phase = Stable AND tstate = 1 --> tdata' = ttoggle;
                                          tstate' = 0;
      [] phase = Stable AND tstate = 0 --> tdata' = IF (tbit = 1)
                                           THEN ttoggle ELSE tdata ENDIF;
                                           tstate' = 1;
      [] phase = Settle -->
         tdata' = IF tdata = ToOne THEN One ELSIF tdata = ToZero
                                       THEN Zero ELSE tdata ENDIF; ]
  END;
```

Recall from Section 3 that to model wires in transition, we use a two-phase clock model for the transmitter. At the beginning of a clock cycle, the transmitter either leaves its output tdata at its current value (Zero or One) or initiates a transition to the other stable value by setting tdata to the appropriate intermediate value (ToOne or ToZero). After an appropriate settling time, the wire is restored to a stable value.

The Biphase receiver is composed of two modules – a receiver clock rclock which enforces the timing discipline and a decoder state machine rdec. The receiver clock enables state transitions when time = rclk and it determines the next receiver timeout based upon the decoder's next state (either scanning for an edge or sampling data). Notice that the timeouts are selected randomly from ranges that are bound by the receiver clock error. The values of the various constants are discussed shortly.

---

[2] Although Moore [2] suggests that there are advantages to an asymmetric cell, this is not generally done in practice because it alters the DC balance and transmitted bandwidth of the signal.

```
rclock : MODULE  =
  BEGIN
    INPUT time   : TIME
    INPUT rstate : [1..2]
    OUTPUT rclk  : TIME
  INITIALIZATION
    rclk IN { x : TIME | 0 <= x AND x < RSCANMAX };
  TRANSITION
    [ time = rclk -->
        rclk' IN IF (rstate' = 2)
                 THEN timeout(time + RSCANMIN, time + RSCANMAX)
                 ELSE timeout(time + RSAMPMIN, time + RSAMPMAX) ENDIF; ]
  END;

rdec   : MODULE =
  BEGIN
    INPUT  tdata  : WIRE
    OUTPUT rdata  : WIRE
    OUTPUT rstate : [1..2]
    OUTPUT rbit   : [0..1]
  INITIALIZATION
    rstate = 2;
    rdata = One;
    rbit  = 1;
  TRANSITION
    [    rstate = 1  -->
         rdata' IN sample(tdata);
         rbit' = IF (rdata = rdata') THEN 0 ELSE 1 ENDIF;
         rstate' = 2;
     [] rstate = 2  -->
         rdata' IN sample(tdata);
         rstate' = IF (rdata = rdata') THEN 2 ELSE 1 ENDIF; ]
  END;
```

The decoder has two states – in state 2, the decoder scans for an edge while in state 1 it determines the value of the transmitted bit.

We define the nominal transmitter clock period TPERIOD, the length of a half-cell, as an constant integer number of units. The nominal number of ticks from the beginning of the cell until the middle of the next half-cell is the constant TSAMPLE. In practice, verification of the model is sufficiently fast that it's feasible to run the verification for any choice of TPERIOD and TSAMPLE.

```
TIME     : TYPE = REAL;
TPERIOD : TIME = 16;
TSAMPLE : INTEGER = 23
```

The receiver runs at two rates – when it is "scanning" for an edge, its clock rate is nominally 1 time unit. After detecting an edge, the receiver waits until the middle of the next half cell. The actual receiver clock (timeout) depends upon the per tick frequency error giving us the four constants used in generating the receiver timeout, as shown in Figure 4.

```
RSAMPMAX : TIME = TSAMPLE * (1 + ERROR);
RSAMPMIN : TIME = TSAMPLE * (1 - ERROR);
RSCANMAX : TIME = 1 + ERROR;
RSCANMIN : TIME = 1 - ERROR;
```

Fig. 4. Receiver Rate Bounds

The limits on ERROR are related by a pair of linear inequalities to TSETTLE. Even if ERROR = 0, there is a practical limit on TSETTLE – reading of the second half-cell value must occur after the settling time but before the end of the cell. This results in the following type constraints for the uninterpreted constants TSETTLE and TSTABLE. Notice their values are both dependent on the value of TPERIOD.

```
TSETTLE : {x : TIME | (0 <= x) AND (x + TPERIOD < TSAMPLE) AND
                      (x + TSAMPLE + 1 < 2 * TPERIOD)};
TSTABLE : TIME = TPERIOD - TSETTLE;
```

Finally, we derive the frequency error bounds. Again, we examine where the reading of the second half-cell value occurs. It must occur after the mid-cell transition, but before the end of the cell. The earliest the reading may occur is RSAMPMIN after the beginning of the cell and the latest the reading may occur is TSETTLE + RSCANMAX + RSAMPMAX. This observation leads to a bound on ERROR.

```
ERROR : {x : TIME | 0 <= x AND TPERIOD + TSETTLE < TSAMPLE * (1-x) AND
                    TSAMPLE * (1+x) + (1+x) + TSETTLE < 2 * TPERIOD};
```

Note that the type for ERROR is parameterized by linear inequalities since TSAMPLE is an interpreted constant.

5 8N1 Protocol

In contrast with BMP, where the receiver clock is re-synchronized on every cell, 8N1, illustrated in Figure 5, is a frame-based protocol where re-synchronization occurs once per frame. Each frame consists of a start bit (0), eight data bits, and one or more stop bits (1), making 10 bits in total.

The 8N1 encoder module is very similar to the Biphase encoder. It contains additional transitions for the special cases of delivering the start and stop bits. The transmitter has ten states. In state 9, the encoder nondeterministically idles, or it sends a start bit by transitioning tdata to Zero and transitioning to state 0. In states 1 through 8, the encoder sends data bits that are generated by the tenv module described in Section 3. However, the interaction between the two modules differs slightly. tenv is directed to generate a new value for tbit when

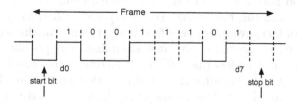

Fig. 5. 8N1 Code

phase = Stable and tstate < 8 – the states during which data bits are sent. In state 8, the encoder generates a stop bit by transitioning tdata to One.

The 8N1 decoder model is also a simple adaption of the Biphase decoder model. The 8N1 decoder has ten states. In state 10, the decoder samples for the start bit; in state 9, it samples for the stop bit, and in the other states it samples for data bits. As with the BMP decoder, detection of the start of the frame causes the 8N1 decoder to wait until the middle of the first data bit to take its next sample, skipping over the start bit (which has already been detected).

The timing parameters are similar to those in the Biphase model. Again, a nominal transmitter clock period TPERIOD is defined. The 8N1 receiver runs at three rates. While scanning for an edge, its nominal bit rate is 1 time unit. After detecting a start bit, the receiver waits until the middle of the first data cell to sample the data. The constraints on sampling and scanning are the same as in Figure 4. To read the remaining data, the receiver waits for TPERIOD nominal ticks to sample the middle of the next cell. RPERIODMAX and RPERIODMIN bound the error of the receiver's clock.

```
RPERIODMAX : TIME = TPERIOD * (1 + ERROR);
RPERIODMIN : TIME = TPERIOD * (1 - ERROR);
```

As with BMP, we can derive bounds on both TSETTLE and ERROR (we discuss TSETTLE shortly). The basic intuition behind parameterizing ERROR is that the accumulated error at the point of reading the stop bit must fall in the stable part of the received signal. There are two bounds – the end of the stop bit and the beginning of the stable period of the stop bit. Together, these define bounds on the clock error value. Notice the similarity with the constraint for BMP.

```
ERROR : {x : TIME | 0 <= x AND 9 * TPERIOD + TSETTLE <
    8 * TPERIOD * (1-x) + TSAMPLE * (1-x) AND
    8 * TPERIOD * (1+x) + TSAMPLE * (1+x) + (1+x) + TSETTLE <
    10 * TPERIOD};
```

ICS is unable to handle the ERROR constant parameterized by an uninterpreted TSETTLE in this protocol. Thus, we parameterize ERROR by the worst-case settling time calculated by hand. For example, if we bound the uninterpreted constant TSETTLE such that 0 <= TSETTLE < TPERIOD/4, then we calculate from the above formula that 0 <= ERROR < 3/151.

As we mention in Section 1, we discovered significant errors in the analysis in an application note for UARTs [1]. The authors suggest that if TSTABLE is TPERIOD/2 (they call this the "nasty" scenario), then a frequency error of ±2% is permissible. In fact, even with zero frequency mismatch, the stable period is too short – if we assume "infinitely" fast sampling, it is possible to show that the settling time must be less than 50% of TPERIOD – otherwise it is impossible to sample the first data bit after the settling period but before the end of the bit period. With our choice of time constants, the longest settling time must be less than 7 (43.75%). In reading the article, it becomes clear that the authors neglected the temporal error introduced by sampling the start bit. They describe a "normal" scenario with TSETTLE = TPERIOD/4 and assert that a frequency error of ±3.3% is permissible. As our derivation above illustrates, the frequency error in this case is limited to ±3/151 ≈ ±1.9%.

6   Verification

Our main goal is to prove that the Biphase and 8N1 decoders reliably extract the data from the combined signal they receive. The statement of the main correctness theorem for BMP is expressible in the LTL temporal logic, where the G operator denotes that its argument holds in all states on a trajectory through the transition system, and the X operator denotes that its argument holds in the next state.

```
BMP_Thm : THEOREM
   system |- G(rstate = 1 AND time = rclk =>
                 (time /= tclk) AND (tstate = 1) AND X(rbit = tbit));
```

Informally, suppose that rstate = 1, and the time has come for the receiver to make a transition (time = rclk). At this time, the wire's value should correspond to the second half of a transmitted cell, and the transmitter should *not* be changing the value of the wire at this time. Furthermore, in the next state – just after the receiver has sampled the wire – the receiver should record the same data bit as the receiver had encoded in that cell. Thus, rbit = tbit should hold.

The main theorem for the 8N1 decoder is essentially the same. The only substantial difference is that we prove that the decoder must reliably extract the data over an entire frame (i.e., for states rstate < 9).

For both BMP and 8N1, supporting lemmas are necessary to prove the main theorem. When a k-induction proof attempt fails, two options are available to the user: the proof can be attempted at a greater depth, or supporting lemmas can be added to restrict the state-space. A k-induction proof attempt is automated, but if the attempt is not successful for a sufficiently small k (i.e., the attempt takes too long or too much memory), additional invariants are necessary to reduce the necessary proof depth. The user must formulate the supporting invariants manually, but their construction is facilitated by the counterexamples returned by SAL for failed proof attempts. If the property is indeed invariant, the counterexample is a trajectory that fails the induction step but lies outside the set of reachable states, and the state-space can be appropriately constrained by an auxiliary lemma based on the counterexample. The following lemmas are built by examining the counterexamples returned from proof attempts for the main theorem and the successive intermediary lemmas.

For both models, we begin by proving three simple preliminary invariants that describe the behavior of the transmitter in both models, irrespective of the receivers. The first invariant, 10, states that either the wire is in its settling phase, or it is high or low. Invariants 11 and 12 constrain the transmitter's timeout tclk during the stable and settle phases: it will never be updated more than TSTABLE and TSETTLE, respectively. Each lemma is inductive, so it is proved at a depth of one.

```
10 : LEMMA system |- G(phase = Settle OR tdata = One OR tdata = Zero);
11 : LEMMA system |- G(phase = Stable => (tclk <= (time + TSTABLE)));
12 : LEMMA system |- G(phase = Settle => (tclk <= (time + TSETTLE)));
```

One additional lemma is proved for the 8N1 transmitter stating that the stable value of the stop bit is One. This lemma is proved at a depth of 13, using invariants 10 - 12 as lemmas.

The essential part of the proof is an invariant describing the relationship between the transmitter and receiver. We must relate them both temporally and with respect to their discrete state (e.g., tstate with rstate and tdata with rdata). The number of and the complexity of the supporting lemmas necessary to prove the main results is significantly reduced by proving a *disjunctive invariant* [12]. A disjunctive invariant has the form $\bigvee_{i \in I} P_i$ where each P_i is a state predicate (predicates P_i and P_j need not be disjoint for $i \neq j$). Disjunctive invariants are easier to generate iteratively than conjunctive invariants. If a disjunctive invariant fails to cover the reachable states, additional disjuncts can be incrementally added to it (in a conjunctive invariant, additional conjunctions must hold in all the reachable states). Although this is a general proof technique, it is particularly easy to build a disjunctive invariant in SAL. The counterexamples SAL returns can be used to iteratively weaken the disjunction until it is invariant.

There are seven disjuncts in the both the BMP and the 8N1 disjunctive invariants. To get an idea about how the invariants are constructed, consider the typical state predicate from the BMP model below. In general, each disjunct states the phase, relates tstate and rstate, and then describes the relative difference between tclk and rclk:

```
... OR ((phase = Settle) AND (rstate = tstate + 1) AND
        (rclk - tclk - TPERIOD > 0) AND
        (tclk + TPERIOD + TSTABLE - rclk > 0)) OR ...
```

Using lemmas 10, 11, 12 described above, the BMP disjunctive invariant is proved at depth five. Using these lemmas and lemma 13, the 8N1 disjunctive invariant is proved at depth three. All that remains is to prove the main theorems, BMP_Thm and the corresponding theorem for the 8N1 decoder. Using the respective disjunctive invariants as lemmas, the former is proved at depth two, and the latter is proved at depth six.

7   Discussion

We have described a general model of physical layer data transmission, and we have used this model to verify the correctness of BMP and 8N1 under parameterized timing constraints. We also present an error in a published application note discovered during the verification. The verification is highly-automated using k-induction implemented with a SMT decision procedure and a bounded model checker in SAL.

As mentioned in Section 1, a referee suggested an alternative approach that fully parameterizes the BMP verification. The central idea is to leave TPERIOD and TSAMPLE as uninterpreted constants and then constrain the times when the receiver scans and samples directly in terms of TPERIOD, TSETTLE, and TSTABLE:

```
RSCANMIN : {x : TIME | 0 < x};
RSCANMAX : {x : TIME | RSCANMIN <= x AND x < TSTABLE};
RSAMPMIN : {x : TIME | TPERIOD + TSETTLE < x};
RSAMPMAX : {x : TIME | RSAMPMIN <= x AND x < 2 * TSTABLE - RSCANMAX};
```

Thus, no error term is necessary, and the verification is fully parameterized. The BMP specification otherwise remains the same, and its proof of correctness succeeds using the same lemmas, proved at the same depth. The constraints on the error can be easily recovered by hand from the fully parameterized verification by replacing the constants RSCANMIN, RSAMPMIN, and RSCANMAX in the type definitions above by their definitions from Figure 4. The referees also point out that because the error bounds are not explicit in this fully parameterized model in SAL, it is less general than the verification by Vaandrager and de Groot using mechanical theorem-proving [6]. Although the parameterized verification in SAL with error bounds recovered by hand is neither fully automated nor machine-checked, it is a more economical approach than mechanical theorem-proving.

As compared to real-time model checking, our SAL verification appears to be more parameterized than the verifications reported by Ivanov and Griffioen in Hytech [4] and at least as parameterized as the one suggested (but not described) by Henzinger, Preussig, and Wong-Toi, also using Hytech, in which the verification is fully automatic [5]. The tool TReX has similar capabilities to HyTech [13]. Note, however, that SAL is not specifically a real-time model checker.

The verification technology employed in SAL is recent, and only a few non-trivial verifications using it exist [11, 14]. This work, along with recent work by one of the authors, is the first known application of these techniques to the verification of physical-layer protocols [15].

Acknowledgments. We thank Leonardo de Moura, John Rushby, and our three anonymous TACAS referees for their careful comments and suggestions.

References

1. Maxim Integrated Products, Inc. *Determining Clock Accuracy Requirements for UART Communications*, June 2003. Available at http://www.maxim-ic.com/appnotes.cfm/appnote_number/2141.
2. J Strother Moore. A formal model of asynchronous communication and its use in mechanically verifying a biphase mark protocol. *Formal Aspects of Computing*, 6(1):60–91, 1994.

3. D. V. Hung. Modelling and verification of biphase mark protocols using PVS. In *Proceedings of the International Conference on Applications of Concurrency to System Design (CSD'98)*, pages 88–98. IEEE Computer Society Press, 1998.
4. S. Ivanov and W. O. D. Griffioen. Verification of a biphase mark protocol. Technical Report CSI-R9915, University of Nijmegen Computing Science Institute, 1999.
5. T. Henzinger, J. Preussig, and H. Wong-Toi. Some lessons from the Hytech experience. In *Proceedings of the 40th Annual Conference on Decision and Control*, pages 2887–2892, 2001.
6. F. W. Vaandrager and A. L. de Groot. Analysis of a Biphase Mark Protocol with Uppaal and PVS. Technical Report NIII-R0455, Nijmegen Institute for Computing and Information Science, 2004.
7. Leonardo de Moura, Sam Owre, Harald Rueß, John Rushby, N. Shankar, Maria Sorea, and Ashish Tiwari. SAL 2. In *Computer-Aided Verification, CAV'04*, volume 3114 of *LNCS*, pages 496–500, Boston, MA, July 2004. Springer-Verlag.
8. Leonardo de Moura, Harald Rueß, and Maria Sorea. Bounded model checking and induction: From refutation to verification. In *Computer-Aided Verification, CAV'03*, volume 2725 of *LNCS*, 2003.
9. Leonardo de Moura, Sam Owre, Harald Ruess, John Rushby, and N. Shankar. The ICS decision procedures for embedded deduction. In *2nd International Joint Conference on Automated Reasoning (IJCAR)*, volume 3097 of *LNCS*, pages 218–222, Cork, Ireland, July 2004. Springer-Verlag.
10. Bruno Dutertre and Maria Sorea. Timed systems in SAL. Technical Report SRI-SDL-04-03, SRI International, 2004.
11. Bruno Dutertre and Maria Sorea. Modeling and verification of a fault-tolerant real-time startup protocol using calendar automata. In *FORMATS/FTRTFT*, pages 199–214, 2004.
12. John Rushby. Verification diagrams revisited: Disjunctive invariants for easy verification. In *Computer-Aided Verification, CAV'00*, volume 1855 of *LNCS*, pages 508–520, Chicago, IL, July 2000. Springer-Verlag.
13. Aurore Annichini, Ahmed Bouajjani, and Mihaela Sighireanu. TReX: A tool for reachability analysis of complex systems. In *Computer-Aided Verification, CAV'01*, pages 368–372, London, UK, 2001. Springer-Verlag.
14. Lee Pike and Steven D. Johnson. The formal verification of a reintegration protocol. In *EMSOFT '05: Proceedings of the 5th ACM international conference on Embedded software*, pages 286–289, New York, NY, USA, 2005. ACM Press.
15. Geoffrey M. Brown. Verification of a data synchronization circuit for all time. Unpublished, 2005.

Evaluating the Effectiveness of Slicing for Model Reduction of Concurrent Object-Oriented Programs

Matthew B. Dwyer[1], John Hatcliff[2], Matthew Hoosier[2], Venkatesh Ranganath[2], Robby[2], and Todd Wallentine[2]

[1] University of Nebraska, Lincoln, NE 68588, USA
dwyer@cse.unl.edu
[2] Kansas State University, Manhattan, KS 66506, USA
{hatcliff, matt, rvprasad, robby, tcw}@cis.ksu.edu

Abstract. Model checking techniques have proven effective for checking a number of non-trivial concurrent object-oriented software systems. However, due to the high computational and memory costs, a variety of model reduction techniques are needed to overcome current limitations on applicability and scalability. Conventional wisdom holds that static program slicing can be an effective model reduction technique, yet anecdotal evidence is mixed, and there has been no work that has systematically studied the costs/benefits of slicing for model reduction in the context of model checking source code for realistic systems.

In this paper, we present an overview of the sophisticated Indus program slicer that is capable of handling full Java and is readily applicable to interesting off-the-shelf concurrent Java programs. Using the Indus program slicer as part of the next generation of the Bandera model checking framework, we experimentally demonstrate significant benefits from using slicing as a fully automatic model reduction technique. Our experimental results consider a number of Java systems with varying structural properties, the effects of combining slicing with other well-known model reduction techniques such as partial order reductions, and the effects of slicing for different classes of properties. Our conclusions are that slicing concurrent object-oriented source code provides significant reductions that are orthogonal to a number of other reduction techniques, and that slicing should always be applied due to its automation and low computational costs.

1 Introduction

1.1 Motivation

Model checking techniques have proven effective for debugging a number of non-trivial software systems. Due to the high computational and memory costs, a variety of model reduction techniques such as data abstraction [11], predicate abstraction [2], systematic application of data and resource bounds, heuristic search strategies [16], and partial order reduction techniques driven by synchronization and heap-structure properties [36, 12] are needed to overcome current limitations on applicability and scalability. In model reduction, the resulting transition system should be small enough to make automatic checking tractable, yet it should be large enough to capture all information relevant to the property being checked. One of the primary difficulties is determining which parts of the program are relevant to the property being checked.

H. Hermanns and J. Palsberg (Eds.): TACAS 2006, LNCS 3920, pp. 73–89, 2006.

Conventional wisdom holds that static program slicing can be an effective model reduction technique for software model checking. Given a program and a *slicing criterion* – a set of program points (e.g., statements) that a user is interested in, a program slicer automatically calculates the portions of the program that are relevant for carrying out the computation at the statements given in the criterion. All features of the program (e.g., statements, fields, classes, methods, threads) that are irrelevant for the computation at the criterion statements are "sliced away." Thus, by including the features of the program mentioned in a property/specification to be model checked as a slicing criterion, slicing will remove from the program features that are irrelevant for (i.e., do not influence) the property to be checked.

However, existing experience with slicing for model reduction is sometime inconclusive. For example, Holzmann's experience shows that slicing in Spin usually does not yield much reduction for realistic Promela design models [20]. While there have been extensive experimental studies to evaluate the effectiveness of model reduction techniques such as partial order reductions [15, 36, 12, 14] and abstraction [2] for software model checking, there have been no such studies to evaluate the effectiveness of slicing as a model reduction technique. In fact, there seem to be several factors that prevent researchers and practitioners from drawing strong conclusions about the effectiveness of slicing as a model reduction technique.

First, due to the lack of robustness of many model checking tools and the relative immaturity of the field in general, researchers often tried to evaluate the effectiveness of slicing using only small "text book" examples such as Dining Philosophers or Bakery Algorithm in which the system under consideration has already been boiled down to its bare essentials and possesses no property-irrelevant information to be sliced away. In contrast, larger realistic systems often have many aspects that are irrelevant to specific properties being checked.

Second, few software model checking frameworks include or make use of existing program slicing frameworks (quite sophisticated static analysis frameworks themselves – especially in the context of concurrent object-oriented programming languages). The Bandera model checking framework was the first to include slicing capabilities with Spin following shortly thereafter with a Promela slicing capability. Although one could imagine applying existing C program slicers in the context of model checking C programs, we know of no other software model checking frameworks with integrated slicing capabilities.

Lack of available slicing infrastructure in general has further hindered progress in evaluating the effectiveness of slicing for model reduction. Simply put, building a slicing framework capable of scaling to realistic applications and handling challenging language features such as one would find, e.g., in full Java, is a very challenging task.

1.2   This Paper

In this paper, we present an overview of our Java program slicer available as part of Indus, a program analysis tool kit, and we use this slicer to carry out wide-ranging experimental studies that demonstrate program slicing to be a valuable model reduction technique for model-checking concurrent object-oriented software. Both the slicer and our extensible model checking framework Bogor [33] are components of the next generation of the Bandera Java model checking framework that translates Java programs into models in the Bandera Intermediate Representation (BIR). Bogor model checks BIR models, using state of the art techniques for heap symmetry, collapse compression for object-oriented data structures, and partial order reductions driven by synchronization and escape analysis.

We believe this work presents a number of results that will be of interest to both researchers and practitioners working in the area of software model checking.

- It represents the first study to systematically demonstrate the effectiveness of program slicing as a model reduction technique for an interesting range of Java programs. Specifically, we consider ten different programs including an example from the Java Grande benchmarks as well as programs based on Siena – a generic scalable publish/subscribe Internet event-notification framework.
- It considers the relative benefits of state-of-the-art Java slicing techniques with state-of-the-art implementations of other model reduction techniques such as partial order reductions, and demonstrates that reductions provided by slicing are largely orthogonal to the effect of these other techniques.
- It considers the effects of slicing for model reduction when considering different classes of properties including deadlock checking and assertions.
- It shows that slicing can be applied as a low-cost (the costs are a very small percentage of the overall cost of model checking) and completely automated model reduction technique that almost always yields both space and time reductions (often, significant reductions) while almost never causing an increase in end-to-end run time.
- The Indus tool kit provides a sophisticated program slicer capable of handling full Java and scaling to interesting off-the-shelf concurrent Java programs of more than 10,000 application bytecodes (49,314 application + library bytecodes). Indus is freely available, and has been downloaded over 1100 times since its public release in June 2004. Thus, the techniques described in this paper can be *immediately* applied to other Java model checking frameworks such as JPF [5] and jMoped [37]. In fact, Indus is already being used by researchers at Fujitsu for reduction when model checking with JPF.

The rest of the paper is organized as follows. Section 2 overviews the architecture of the Bandera Java model checking tool set. Section 3 gives a brief summary of slicing and the Indus analysis framework. Section 4 explains how slicing can be used for model reduction, and presents the hypotheses and research questions that we seek to answer with our experimental studies. Section 5 provides an overview of the different examples that we consider along with metrics capturing various static characteristics of their implementation (no. of bytecodes, no. of classes, no. of fields, etc.). Section 6 presents the results of our experiments and provides assessment with respect to the previously given research hypotheses. Section 7 surveys related work and Section 8 concludes.

The Indus web site [29] provides the Indus distribution as well as an extended version of this paper that gives an expanded discussion of experimental results.

2 Bandera Overview

Bandera is a tool framework for model checking concurrent Java programs. The tool framework is organized as a *modular pipeline* – each tool in the pipeline communicates with its predecessor and successor purely through its inputs and outputs. To create a run of Bandera for a specific program and property, the user creates a *session file* that indicates the components of the pipeline that should be applied as well as particular settings or options for each component.

In the pipeline that we use for the experiments in this paper, the **Soot** tool [39] first reads Java class files to be model checked and translates them to Jimple [39] – Soot's three-address code intermediate representation for Java. The **Indus** tool takes the resulting Jimple program along with information about the property to be checked and produces a sliced Jimple program. The **Jimple-To-BIR (J2B)** tool takes the sliced Jimple program and translates it to BIR, which is then model checked by **Bogor**.

We are interested in determining the extent to which slicing can improve performance *beyond* the best reduction strategies currently available in Bogor.

These reduction strategies include heap symmetry/canonicalization which represents all execution states of a Java program that differ only in the physical addresses of objects or in the unreclaimed garbage using a single representative state, thread symmetry, and collapse compression which reduces the space required to store a state by sharing common parts of distinct states [34].

In this paper, we will be most interested in Bogor's partial order reduction framework that minimizes the set of paths that need to be explored in the state-space during model checking. Classical partial order reductions (POR) (e.g., [15]) leverage the *independence* of transitions to induce equivalence classes of paths such that it is sufficient to explore a single path from each class. For multi-threaded Java programs, we leverage the structure of the Java heap and Java synchronization idioms to infer more precise information about transition independence [12]. For example, transitions that access *thread-local* objects (i.e., objects that are reachable from a single thread) are independent because no transition in another thread can possibly access such an object (until the object becomes shared). Transitions that operate on a *properly locked* object (e.g, where the set of locks held by each thread when accessing the object always contains at least one common lock) are also independent as are operations on *read-only* objects. An additional feature of Bogor's POR implementation is that it biases the search to coalesce transitions in a method into a consecutive run of transitions. By doing this, the model checker is able to defer state-storage until the end of the run of independent transitions effectively implementing on-the-fly detection of *atomic blocks* of transitions. The combination of partial order reduction techniques in Bogor yields orders of magnitude reduction in the space and time required for model checking nearly all of the Java programs we have encountered.

3 Program Slicing and the Indus Java Slicing Framework

3.1 A Brief Overview of Slicing Concurrent Java Programs

There are many variants of slicing (forward/backward, static/dynamic) [38]. We consider *static backward* slicing – the variant usually applied for model reduction [6, 18, 26].

Static backward slicing uses *static* program analysis to look *backwards* along data and control flows to discover the set S_C of all program statements that influence the given slicing criterion C – a set of select program statements. S_C is guaranteed to contain all the statements upon which computations at statements in C depend; S_C will usually contain additional program statement beyond those that actually influence C due to the conservative nature of static analysis.

Slicing for concurrent Java programs is based on several notions of program statement dependence, and it is well beyond the scope of this paper to present detailed definitions for each of these. Our previous work presents formalizations and correctness proofs for the definitions of data and control dependence [18, 31] and dependences for concurrent Java [17] that we use in this paper. Control and data dependences are well-understood, so we focus below on the less familiar, but crucial, notions of dependence needed to treat concurrency. Briefly, a node n is data-dependent on node m if, for a variable v referenced at n, a definition of (*i.e.*, an assignment to) v at m reaches n; a node n is *control-dependent* on a conditional statement m if one of the branches of m must always lead to n but the other branch of m can bypass n and reach the program's (i.e., method's) end node.

For the definitions below, if a statement at control-flow graph (CFG) node n is in the slice set S_C and n depends on a statement at node m, then node m is also in S_C. Intuitively, the slicer begins with the statements in the slicing criteria C and computes a transitive closure using data and control dependence along with the dependences below (modulo some optimizations enabled by further static analysis) to obtain S_C.

Divergence: To preserve behaviors with *infinite delay* (e.g., as required for checking liveness properties or certain classes of deadlocks), our earlier work [18, 31] notes that it is important to consider additional notions of control dependence that preserve diverging executions (e.g., as caused by infinite loops). One method for capturing dependences caused by diverging loops is to use the notion of *strong post-domination* and *weak control dependence* introduced by Podgurski and Clarke [28]. Node n *strongly post-dominates* node m if n post-dominates m and there is an integer $k \geq 1$ such that every path from node m of length $\geq k$ passes through n [28]. The difference between strong post-domination and the simple definition of post-domination above is that even though node n occurs on every path from m to e (and thus n post-dominates m), it may be the case that n does not strongly post-dominate m due to a loop in the CFG between m and n that admits an infinite path beginning at m and not containing n. Hence, strong post-domination is sensitive to the possibility of non-termination along paths from m to n. Node n_j is *weakly control dependent* on n_i if n_i has at least two successors, n_k and n_l, n_j strongly postdominates n_k, n_j does not strongly postdominate n_l. We will typically refer to control dependence and weak control dependence as *termination insensitive* and *termination sensitive* control dependence, respectively. The experiments in this paper will use the notion of weak control dependence – which guarantees that if n is in the slice and there exists a (possibly infinite) loop in the CFG that could prevent control from reaching n, then the control structure associated with the loop is also included in the slice.

Interference dependence: To capture data dependence across threads, node n from thread t_n is *interference dependent* on node m from thread t_m with $t_n \neq t_m$ if there exists a variable $v \in def(m) \cap ref(n)$ and there exists a schedule in which m's execution is followed by n's execution with no intervening definition of m [25]. A precise *static* calculation of schedules that may give rise interference dependence is prohibitively expensive for large systems (exact precision is equivalent to the model checking problem itself). Cheap but conservative/imprecise strategies [17, 26] simply assume that an interference exists whenever $v \in def(m) \cap ref(n)$ even though there may never be a schedule that gives rise a flow of data between m and n. Other approaches use exponential symbolic execution algorithms to try to detect realizable execution paths leading to such flows [25, 27]. Indus strikes a balance between these by pruning infeasible interference edges using escape/alias analysis and various "happens before" relations [32].

Ready dependence: Just as diverging loops may give rise to infinite delays within a single thread, indefinite delays can also be generated due to interactions between threads via synchronization primitives such as locking (synchronized statements) and wait/notify. When the completion of a statement n of thread t_n (e.g., an lock acquire or a wait) depends of the completion of node m of thread t_m (e.g., a lock release or a notify), n is said to be *ready dependent* on m [17]. In addition, ready dependences can also arise within a single thread t_m: if node p is reachable in t_m's control flow graph from m where m is either a lock acquire or wait statement, then p is ready dependent on m since m's failure to complete could cause p to never be executed.

Effects of references/aliasing: The calculation of above data dependences, interference dependences, and ready dependences both in sequential and concurrent setting, becomes much more challenging (and the results much less precise) when aliasing is introduced. In the presence of aliasing, two variables can refer to the same data/object, and so, it is possible that an update via a.f will affect the value of b.f when a and b are aliases. Our previous work [32], describes the various forms of alias and escape analyses that are used in Indus to address this issue.

3.2 Indus

The goal of the Indus project is to provide a Java library of program analyses and transformations for Java to enable sophisticated program analyses such as program slicing and program specialization via partial evaluation. In its current state, the project provides a large collection of program analyses, a Java program slicing framework, and a sophisticated user interface for the slicer [23] built as an Eclipse [13] plug-in.

Static analysis support provided by Indus includes a general flow analysis framework in which an *object-sensitive object-flow analysis* [30] is implemented that provides points-to information for objects, a *call graph analysis* of varying levels of precision, a *thread graph analysis* that calculates the method-to-thread containment relation in a given program, an *alias-aware interprocedural use-def analysis* that provides use-def information for reference type variables across procedural boundaries, and a *side-effect analysis*. Indus also provides two basic concurrency specific analyses: an *escape analysis* [32] that detects if an object allocation is thread local and a *monitor analysis* that calculates containment relation between various statements and locks in the program. Building on these analyses, a rich set of dependence analyses calculate data and control dependences in *intra-procedural, inter-procedural, intra-thread, inter-thread, non-termination sensitive,* and/or *non-termination insensitive* settings. These analyses subsume all dependences mentioned in Section 3.1. Further, the precision of interference and ready dependence analyses is improved by leveraging escape analysis to prune dependence based on non-thread local access to objects [32] and safe-lock analysis to prune divergence based dependence due to synchronization constructs [17].

4   Slicing for Model Reduction

4.1   Issues

Property-directed slicing: In earlier work [18], we presented the foundations of slicing as a model reduction technique with emphasis on the notion of "property-directed slicing" – program features mentioned in the property to be checked formed the slicing criteria, hence, leading to the automatic removal of program features that can be statically shown to be irrelevant to the property. In this paper, we evaluate the effectiveness of slicing with respect to two classes of properties: deadlock checking and assertions.

For deadlock checking, the slicing criteria consists of all synchronized and wait/notify statements. The sophisticated analyses of Indus allow us to optimize this in several ways, e.g., if Indus escape analysis indicates that objects being used in a synchronized statement are non-escaping, such statements can be omitted from the criteria since there is no contention for these locks. For assertion checking, the slicing criteria simply consists of the assertion statements in the program.

Call-graph reachability vs. slicing: Researchers familiar with static analysis might initially conceive of obtaining functionality related to slicing by simply constructing the call graph of the program to be checked and then eliminating code for methods that are not reachable in the call graph. This is especially relevant in model checking frameworks like Bandera that *translate* a program representation to a lower-level language (e.g., BIR) for model checking. Removing the code for unreachable methods via call-graph construction/analysis reduces overhead in the translation phase (code for unreachable methods does not have to be translated). Precise call graph construction in a concurrent OO language is non-trivial; it must be intertwined with points-to/alias analysis to resolve virtual method invocations, it must take control flow due to exceptions into account, and it must account for the invocation of class initializers done implicitly by the virtual machine and not by explicit invocation sites in the program.

The major drawback of mere call-graph reachability is that it does not eliminate parts of the system that are reachable in the system but do not affect the property being verified. For example, while checking for deadlocks, every reachable call to System.out.println() in the system will be included when these calls (almost always) do not affect the deadlocking behavior of the system. Inclusion of such calls increases model checking cost due to simulation of unnecessary transitions and storage of data entities required by such transitions in the state vector. On the other hand, slicing can detect and exclude such unnecessary calls and provide increased reduction in terms of model checking cost in comparison with call-graph reachability.

Bandera implements pruning of unreachable methods and data using the static analyses of Indus. Since such analyses are well-known in the static analysis community, we consider an approach that includes them as the *baseline* for our experiments: we seek to demonstrate the benefits of slicing *beyond* the already substantial reductions derived from such analyses.

4.2 Research Questions

We have focused our empirical study on four specific questions related to the use of slicing as a reduction technique.

(RQ 1) How does the net effect of applying program slicing to reduce the cost of model checking multi-threaded Java programs vary with program size and complexity?

(RQ 2) What is the incremental benefit of program slicing compared to call-graph based reachability optimizations in reducing the cost of model checking multi-threaded Java programs?

(RQ 3) What is the incremental benefit of program slicing compared to state-of-the-art partial order and thread symmetry reductions in reducing the cost of model checking multi-threaded Java programs?

(RQ 4) Does program slicing yield greater reductions for model checking assertion-based specifications of non-trivial multi-threaded Java programs in comparison to checking for deadlock?

The lack of significant experimental has left the research community with intuitions and opinions, but no definitive evidence on the effectiveness of slicing for model reduction. While some initial case studies point to the effectiveness of slicing [6, 8, 26] some experts have developed what can only be described as negative intuitions about the effectiveness of slicing as a model reduction technique. In the latter case, the best justified of these intuitions have been arrived at via formative studies of slicers implemented in verification frameworks and applied to collections of transition system descriptions as opposed to program source code. For example, Holzmann indicates that he has found SPIN's slicing capabilities useful for finding small redundancies in Promela models, but not that effective for reduction in realistic Promela properties/systems [20]. Holzmann notes that experience with program slicing on Java source code might be different, and in fact, we hypothesize that one reason why slicing has not been widely recognized as a reduction technique is that it has not been applied to realistic source code. With **(RQ 1)** we seek to provide evidence to indicate whether software model checking reductions can be achieved in analyzing realistic Java code bases. To answer this question, we have selected both relatively small, and well-studied, examples from the software model checking literature and larger examples that have not previously been analyzed via model checking.

Section 4.1 explains how sophisticated, but well-understood static analyses, could remove *unreachable/non-accessed* program components. However, these analyses do not eliminate code fragments that are reachable but yet *irrelevant* with respect to the property (e.g. writes to standard output via System.out.println()). Slicing is more costly and much more difficult to implement, yet it is more precise and it is able to eliminate reachable but irrelevant features. Answering **(RQ 2)** will provide evidence on both the relative cost of these two analyses and their relative benefit. Given the exponential complexity of model checking, if static call graph and slicing provide clear benefits in terms of reduction then it is likely that those benefits would outweigh any increase in static analysis cost. Such an answer would indicate that existing Java model checking should always employ call-graph analysis or program slicing as a pre-phase.

Research on reduction techniques for model checking has produced significant results over the past decades. Partial order reductions [36, 12] and heap symmetry/canonicalization reductions [21, 34] are completely automated reductions that have been applied to reduce the state space of concurrent OO software models. We believe that the model checking research community is in broad agreement that these techniques should *always* be used when model checking non-trivial programs. Note that while counter-example guided predicate abstraction [2] has been applied with good success in sequential settings where programs do not include a lot of heap data manipulation, it has yet to be applied in the concurrent OO setting in a completely automatic way. Moreover, tool-based data abstraction techniques for Java [11] still require some user intervention. Thus, in **(RQ 3)**, we seek evidence on the incremental improvement in reduction that can be achieved by slicing (a completely automated technique) relative to existing completed automated reduction techniques concurrent OO programs. We believe that slicing should only be considered worthwhile for incorporating into tools if it can provide reductions over-and-above what can be achieved by existing automated state-space reductions.

As noted in Section 4.1, slicing for model reduction is *property driven*. Answering **(RQ 4)** will provide evidence on the degree to which model reduction via program slicing is sensitive to the class of property under analysis. We have selected two classes of properties: deadlocks and assertions. A deadlocks can be considered a relatively *global* property since it is potentially related to every blocking statement in the program. It has been observed, e.g., [1, 7], that in many cases *data* manipulation can be relatively cleanly separated from *control* structures involved in synchronization. Thus, one might anticipate that significant data portions of the program could be removed when slicing for deadlock. Unfortunately, distinctions between data and synchronization are often blurred in the context of object-oriented programming where synchronization is achieved by locking data structures. Thus, slicing multi-threaded Java programs for deadlock preservation may not yield as significant a reduction as one might expect. Assertions, in contrast, are often considered *local* properties since they reference a single control point and an expression over variables in a program scope. In practice, the locality of an assertion can vary widely depending on complexity of the asserted expression. Similar expressions form the definition of *observable propositions* [9] that are used in defining temporal logic properties of programs. Thus, we expect that reduction results for assertional specifications will be indicative of the results for model checking temporal logic formulae. In answering this question, we seek to determine whether slicing on localized properties can yield additional reduction in model checking. To emphasize the *locality* of assertions we defined a collection of simple parameter and object field assertions that are enforced on method entry and that reflect comments in the source code; we did not apply slicing to assertions attempting to capture data structure properties of programs.

5 Description of Code Bases

We evaluate the effectiveness of slicing as a model reduction technique relative to the research questions stated in Section 4.2 over a collection of multi-threaded Java programs. In this section, we describe these Java code bases and characterize them in terms of static measures of their control, data and synchronization complexity. Table 1 presents the counts for several measures of each example: bytecodes, classes, methods, fields, new expressions, calls to Thread.start(), catch blocks, synchronized statements and methods, wait statements, and notify/notifyall statements. For each example, the first table row gives these measures both for the total of the application and library code that comprise the program and, independently, for just the application code; the values are given separated by a /. We provide the application measures for reference, but the tools process both the application and referenced library code. The second row gives the measures for the call-graph reachability based pruning from Section 4.1 and deadlock-preserving slicing (separated by '/') when applied to the complete code base (application+libraries). For example, 34479 bytecodes in the complete RAX system are reduced to 768 bytecodes by call-graph reachability and to 101 bytecodes by slicing. It is important to understand that these are static measures that the code base complexity presented to the program slicer, rather than the state space complexity presented to the model checker. For example, the static number of Thread.start() calls and new expressions typically underestimate the number of running threads and object instances in a system since these calls often appear in loops.

The set of programs includes five *standard* examples, that are commonly used in experiments in the concurrency literature, but which are best thought of as implementations of algorithm sketches rather than realistic Java code bases. *BBuffer* implements a thread-safe queue using an array and wait/notify synchronization and includes very simple producer and consumer threads. *Pipeline* implements a dynamically assembled sequence of threads that are used to parallelize a simple staged computation on integer data. *SBarbers* is a classic synchronization problem that is presented in many operating systems textbooks (e.g., [1]). *RW* includes an abstract class that implements a concurrent-read and exclusive-write policy for controlling access to program regions of implemented as methods that override abstract methods; a simple set of reader and writer threads complete this example. *RAX* is the distillation of a bug in the NASA remote experiment platform that was presented in [5].

Two *small* programs implement simple discrete-event simulators for a *DiskScheduler* and a non-trivial *AlarmClock*. In general, these examples are significantly more heap-data intensive than the standard examples.

Of the three *larger* applications we considered, one is from the literature *RepWorker* [3], one from the JavaGrande benchmark [22], *RayTracer*, and one is an Internet-scale publish-subscribe infra-structure, named *Siena*, that has been the subject of several studies of software testing techniques [10]. The *RepWorker* implements a highly-configurable client-server data-distribution framework with a sample Jacobi relaxation example running atop it as an application. The JavaGrande benchmark implements a non-trivial scientific calculations whose synchronization is achieved through the use of barriers.

Table 1. Static measures of examples

Name	Bytecode	Class	Method	Field	New	Thrd	Except	Synch	Wait	Nfy
AlarmClock	34728/319	349/6	3245/25	1295/19	1461/13	4/3	473/18	252/15	3/2	3/2
Reach/Slice	1020/345	49/25	98/41	57/18	45/18	3/3	23/17	18/15	2/2	2/2
BBuffer	34577/168	351/8	3238/18	1294/8	1455/7	4/3	462/7	241/4	3/2	3/2
Reach/Slice	873/194	50/23	91/30	151/15	38/10	3/3	12/7	8/5	2/2	2/2
DiskSched	35181/793	348/5	3238/18	1297/21	1510/63	2/1	458/3	239/2	3/2	2/1
Reach/Slice	1314/643	48/25	92/36	52/15	79/52	1/1	12/7	8/5	2/2	1/1
Pipeline	34475/66	347/4	3229/9	1280/4	1452/4	3/2	456/1	239/2	2/1	2/1
Reach/Slice	764/97	46/19	80/20	42/6	35/7	2/2	6/1	6/3	1/1	1/1
SBarber	34564/155	347/4	3229/9	1287/11	1455/7	3/2	474/19	245/8	4/3	4/3
Reach/Slice	853/184	46/19	80/20	48/12	38/10	2/2	24/19	12/9	3/3	3/3
RAX	34479/70	347/4	3229/9	1283/7	1452/4	3/2	456/1	239/2	2/1	2/1
Reach/Slice	768/101	46/19	80/20	45/9	35/7	2/2	6/1	6/3	1/1	1/1
RW	34699/290	348/5	3246/26	1287/11	1455/7	5/4	473/18	247/10	3/2	3/2
Reach/Slice	945/268	47/20	95/34	49/13	39/11	4/4	23/18	14/11	2/2	2/2
RepWorker	34885/574	356/14	3265/47	1317/42	1471/23	2/1	460/5	255/18	6/5	7/6
Reach/Slice	1792/1460	69/57	158/131	82/47	81/74	1/1	22/19	6/6	5/5	6/6
RayTracer	35544/1783	361/19	3327/109	1351/76	1538/91	2/1	486/31	142/15	1/1	1/1
Reach/Slice	2757/2520	72/65	195/179	126/95	119/114	1/1	29/26	12/12	1/1	1/1
Siena	49314/9229	489/74	4700/620	1688/296	2119/389	5/4	644/186	384/139	10/7	14/8
Reach/Slice	14213/13491	198/194	844/909	424/306	574/565	3/3	164/164	105/110	4/4	8/7

As the data indicate, slicing can yield reductions ranging up to two orders of magnitude in the size of the code base to be analyzed by the model checker. While the call-graph reachability reduction can also yield significant reductions, program slicing always achieves better reductions. As we will see in the next section, the elimination of additional statements and fields can give rise to substantial reductions in model check times and more than compensate for the relatively modest slicer run-time which for even the largest examples was at most several seconds.

6 Experimental Results

In this section, we report on the performance of model checking selected properties of the examples described in Section 5 using different state-space reduction options. We present statistics from different subsets of these model checking runs and discuss how those results help to answer the research questions from Section 4.2.

Table 2 presents a sampling of the model check runs we performed. For the systems we studied, we model checked a total of 31 different variations of those systems; variations were either applying fixes to known bugs or activating additional specifications encoded as assertions in the code base. To conserve space, we only list runs for variations on a given program that are substantially different in performance. We differentiate runs that found errors from those that did not by using an *e* subscript on example names; note that several of our examples have buggy versions. For each system variation we

Table 2. Effect of slicing on model checking

Name	Conf.	States	Trans.	Memory	Time
AlarmClock$_e$	dR	11204	28931	2.45	25.2
	dRP	106	870	0.12	11.1
	dS	4867	11593	0.12	13.1
	dSP	83	693	0.12	10.3
AlarmClock	dR	1469917	5117602	4.49	57:56.4
	dRP	2305	49801	2.55	50.6
	dS	724666	2501705	3.69	13:1.6
	dSP	1204	25298	2.19	20.1
	aS	724666	2501705	3.22	12:56.4
	aSP	1204	25298	2.13	20.4
BBuffer	dR	36405	90882	3.9	1:1.2
	dRP	138	3980	0.12	14.4
	dS	7484	18578	0.11	13.9
	dSP	28	630	0.12	10.7
	aS	7484	18578	0.12	13.9
	aSP	28	630	0.12	10.2
DiskSched$_e$	dR	7687219	2044564	5.71	9:48:1.8
	dRP	7690	858963	4.16	30:59.7
	dS	5487745	14302033	5.88	1:16:34.5
	dSP	7688	816991	1.81	5:17.6
	aS	5487745	14302033	5.88	1:16:26.7
	aSP	7688	816991	3.65	5:11.8
Pipeline	dR	9892140	43821449	5.52	5:41:5.7
	dRP	7379	76307	4.21	45.6
	dS	9881030	43771450	5.43	5:28:4.4
	dSP	7379	76303	4.21	40.6

Name	Conf.	States	Trans.	Memory	Time
SBarber$_e$	dR	197	197	0.12	13.4
	dRP	31	197	0.12	11.6
	dS	193	193	0.12	10.7
	dSP	31	193	0.12	12.1
RAX$_e$	dR	268	279	0.80	28.4
	dRP	33	252	0.80	27.2
	dS	266	277	0.57	26.8
	dSP	33	250	0.84	26.2
RW	dR	25197913	26780595	5.86	13:21:24.6
	dRP	603	44621	4.13	1:11.2
	dS	113727	415098	4.15	1:29.8
	dSP	134	2103	0.12	11.3
RepWorker	dR	2818232	8102858	4.77	2:9:59.9
	dRP	3091	96798	1.65	2:43.2
	dS	2736984	7867615	4.74	1:25:34.9
	dSP	2676	90735	3.52	2:1.1
RayTrace	dR	2404257*	4754057*	6.26*	20:0:0*
	dRP	11610	2923881	5.35	9:8:45.4
	dS	2803535*	5552993*	6.34*	20:0:0*
	dSP	10932	2776238	5.18	6:53:13.9
Siena$_e$	dR	11465	11475	2.8	9:37.4
	dRP	116	11475	3.86	12:1.2
	dS	11310	11319	3.93	6:30.4
	dSP	114	11319	4.13	7:51.5

ran the model checker in at least four configurations. In each of these configurations, the model checker was configured to terminate when the first error was encountered in the state space search. The tables list statistics for different configurations of the model checking tools where d indicates deadlock check, a indicates assertion check, R indicates call-graph reduction, S indicates slicing, and P indicates the use of POR. For each configuration, we give the total number of stored states, the number of transitions searched, the maximum memory consumption of the toolset in giga-bytes, and the total run-time for the toolset in hours:minutes:seconds format. The model checks were run as the only application on an Opteron 250 processor with 12 Gigabytes of RAM running Linux using the SDK 1.5. The small number of runs that exceeded 20 hours were terminated and they are noted in the table with *. Consequently, the reduction results presented below should be viewed as lower bounds.

6.1 Analysis of Data and Research Questions

Our analysis of the experimental data confirms that slicing is a cost-effective state space reduction technique, however the data do illustrate some of the limitations of program slicing and suggest opportunities for additional approaches to refining slicing to achieve greater reductions.

To assess the cost-effectiveness of slicing we calculate *reduction factors* that capture the ratio of the total run-time of our toolset for specific pairs of configurations. The mean of a reduction factor is calculated over a specified subset of the 31 model check runs and positive outliers are removed; a positive outlier is a reduction factor that exceeds the mean by more than two standard deviations. We consider different pairs of configurations of the model checker to address the different research questions. In the discussions below, we focus on run-time reduction factors as opposed to factors related to memory consumption or state-space size, since this measure best captures the total time to apply slicing reductions which happen before the actual model checks run. We have observed, however, that space reductions seem to follow the same trend as time reductions.

(**RQ 1**) is concerned with the variation in effectiveness of slicing as a reduction with program size and complexity. For this question, we consider the reduction factor dR/dS which is a measure of the effectiveness of slicing. To assess this question, we group the examples into the set of *larger* examples and the rest. The mean of dR/dS over set of larger examples is 1.4 and for the smaller examples it is 2.7.

This data seems to suggest that slicing scales poorly as a state-space reduction. It is well-understood, however, that static code measures, such as lines of code, are poor indicators of state-space size and our real intention is to understand the reduction of slicing as the size of the state-space scales. Furthermore, we believe that the real benefit of slicing, and of many state-space reductions, is only apparent when the search is *stateful*. To assess this, we compared the number of matched states to the number of stored states during model checking. We term a model check run *sparse* if the ratio of matched to stored states is less than 0.1. Most, but not all, of our error runs were classified as sparse, for example, there were runs of SBarber, RAX and Siena that required no or only minimal backtracking to find the error. The non-sparse searches included all of the model checks that verified the property being checked and several error revealing checks where the error was found late in the search. Recalculating the mean of dR/dS for this grouping of runs yields reduction factors of 1.9 for sparse and 4.0 for non-sparse searches. Even without this secondary analysis, it is clear that program slicing is an effective reduction technique since the reduction factors account for the cost of slicing.

(**RQ 2**) is concerned with the relative effectiveness of call-graph reachability and slicing model reductions. The mean of dR/dS across all runs in our study was 2.5 indicating a non-trivial net benefit to slicing.

(**RQ 3**) is concerned with the relative effectiveness of partial-order reduction and slicing. The mean of dRP/dSP over the total set of runs in our study was 2.1; the means for sparse and non-sparse subsets of runs were 1.2 and 2.9, respectively. Clearly slicing yields non-trivial additional reduction over POR. POR appears to be a more *powerful* than slicing based on the fact that the mean of dR/dRP over the total set of runs in our study was 48.3; the means for sparse and non-sparse subsets of runs were 1.2 and 105.5, respectively. Not surprisingly, POR and slicing appear to both provide benefit only when a substantial portion of the state space is searched.

(**RQ 4**) is concerned with the relative reduction power of slicing when the property being analyzed is deadlock or a simple assertion. The data indicate that there is no statistically significant difference. For the set of examples on which both deadlock and assertional specifications were checked the mean of dRP/dSP was 2.8 and the mean of aRP/aSP was 2.7. This was surprising to us since we expected that a more localized specification would require less of the program to be included in the slice. In the programs we studied, however, there always existed a chain of dependences from the assertion expression to a program point that is part of the programs *synchronization skeleton*. Once one such point is drawn into the slice so to is the rest of the skeleton. This is an unfortunate consequence of high-degree of synchronization coupling in the set of multi-threaded Java programs we studied.

7   Related Work

Since its development, the concept of slicing has been applied to a wide variety of problems including: program understanding, debugging, differencing, integration, and testing; we refer the reader to Tip's survey article for a broad view of slicing [38]. Here, we focus on other work related to slicing for model reduction and verification and slicing Java programs.

Millett and Teitelbaum [26] study static slicing of Promela (the model description language for the model-checker SPIN [19]) and its application to model checking, simulation, and protocol understanding. Their work formed the basis of the Promela slicing framework that is now included in the SPIN distribution. Both [26] and the SPIN Promela slicer support slicing with criteria formed from assertions and never claims (and thus LTL formulae), but do not include support for slicing to preserve deadlock. Slicing systems in a modeling language like Promela is considerably simpler than slicing Java programs due to the absence of challenging features like heap-allocated data, exceptions, methods and dynamic dispatch, threads associated with object references, etc. However, care must be taken to deal correctly with Promela features such as channels, richer intra-thread non-deterministic choice constructs, and more sophisticated notions of blocking due to Promela's rich guarded command language (as we noted earlier, Java programs can only block due to lock acquisitions and wait statements.

The IF Validation Framework [4] also provides a slicing capability for the IF modeling language which is similar to Promela in its level of abstraction. In a case-study of using IF to verify properties of the MASCARA protocol for a wireless asynchronous transfer protocol, Graf and Jia [24] report reductions from 1-2 orders of magnitude for four different properties of the protocol while acknowledging that it is difficult to make general conclusions about the effectiveness of slicing since amount of reduction depends significantly on the particular property and system considered.

Clarke *et al.*[6] present a tool for slicing VHDL programs with dependence graphs. Using the VHDL description of the controller logic for a RISC processor and two accompanying CTL properties (a safety and a liveness property), they show that slicing reduces the reachable state space from roughly 10^{38} states to 10^{22} states. They also observe a *reverse scalability* effect for slicing – smaller VHDL programs tend to have fewer irrelevant components, and thus the benefits of slicing to improve (percentage-wise) as programs grow in size. Sen *et al.*[35] use a substantively different technique called *computation slicing* for model reduction in verification of "systems on a chip" hardware designs.

8   Conclusion

Most researchers have developed strong opinions about the potential effectiveness of program slicing as a reduction technique for software model checking. Many of those opinions are in the negative. We believe that the study presented in this paper provides convincing evidence that slicing is efficient to apply, taking no more than 40 seconds on even the largest code base we considered, and yields non-trivial reductions in model check time, averaging a factor of 4 improvement for non-trivial model checks. Given the long-running nature of model checks, this magnitude of reduction can significantly increase productivity. Furthermore, these reductions are orthogonal to existing state-space reductions and can thus be considered an extension to the state of the art.

As with any experimental study, one can question the external validity of these conclusions, and we plan to increase the number of examples in our study and vary the sources from which we draw those examples to provide more evidential force to our findings. In spite of such questions, given that we never encountered a model check run where slicing caused a non-trivial increase in run-time in our study, we believe that concluding that slicing is a cost-effective model checking reduction is justified.

References

1. G. R. Andrews. *Concurrent Programming: Principles and Practice*. Addison-Wesley, 1991.
2. T. Ball, R. Majumdar, T. Millstein, and S. Rajamani. Automatic predicate abstraction of C programs. In *Proceedings of the ACM SIGPLAN '01 Conference on Programming Language Design and Implementation (PLDI-01)*, pages 203–213, June 2001.
3. Bandera. +http://bandera.projects.cis.ksu.edu+. SAnToS Laboratory.
4. M. Bozga, J.-C. Fernandez, L. Ghirvu, S. Graf, J.-P. Krimm, and L. Mounier. IF: A validation environment for timed asynchronous systems. In *12th International Conference on Computer Aided Verification (CAV 2000)*, LNCS 1855, pp. 543–547, July 2000.
5. G. Brat, K. Havelund, S. Park, and W. Visser. Java PathFinder – A second generation of a Java model-checker. In *Proceedings of the Workshop on Advances in Verification*, July 2000.
6. E. Clarke, M. Fujita, S. Rajan, T.Reps, S. Shankar, and T. Teitelbaum. Program slicing of hardware description languages. In *Proceedings of CHARME'99*, September 1999.
7. E. M. Clarke and E. A. Emerson. Design and synthesis of synchronization skeletons using branching-time temporal logic. In *Logic of Programs, Workshop*, pages 52–71, London, UK, 1982. Springer.
8. J. C. Corbett, M. B. Dwyer, J. Hatcliff, S. Laubach, C. S. Păsăreanu, Robby, and H. Zheng. Bandera: Extracting finite-state models from Java source code. In *Proceedings of the 22nd International Conference on Software Engineering*, June 2000.
9. J. C. Corbett, M. B. Dwyer, J. Hatcliff, and Robby. Expressing checkable properties of dynamic systems: The Bandera Specification Language. *International Journal on Software Tools for Technology Transfer*, 2002.
10. H. Do, S. Elbaum, and G. Rothermel. Infrastructure support for controlled experimentation with software testing and regression testing techniques. In *2004 International Symposium on Empirical Software Engineering (ISESE 2004)*, pages 60–70. IEEE Computer Society, 2004.
11. M. B. Dwyer, J. Hatcliff, R. Joehanes, S. Laubach, C. S. Păsăreanu, Robby, W. Visser, and H. Zheng. Tool-supported program abstraction for finite-state verification. In *Proceedings of the 23rd International Conference on Software Engineering*, May 2001.
12. M. B. Dwyer, J. Hatcliff, V. R. Prasad, and Robby. Exploiting object escape and locking information in partial order reductions for concurrent object-oriented programs. *Formal Methods in System Designs*, 25(2–3):199–240, September–November 2004.
13. Eclipse Consortium. Eclipse website. http://www.eclipse.org.

14. C. Flanagan and P. Godefroid. Dynamic partial-order reduction for model checking software. In J. Palsberg and M. Abadi, editors, *Proceedings of the 32nd ACM SIGPLAN-SIGACT Symposium on Principles of Programming Languages, POPL*, pages 110–121, Long Beach, California, USA, January 2005. ACM.
15. P. Godefroid. *Partial Order Methods for the Verification of Concurrent Systems*, volume 1032 of *Lecture Notes in Computer Science*. Springer, 1996.
16. A. Groce and W. Visser. Model checking Java programs using structural heuristics. In *Proceedings of the International Symposium on Software Testing and Analysis*, pages 12–21. ACM Press, 2002.
17. J. Hatcliff, J. C. Corbett, M. B. Dwyer, S. Sokolowski, and H. Zheng. A formal study of slicing for multi-threaded programs with JVM concurrency primitives. In *Proceedings of the 6th International Static Analysis Symposium (SAS'99)*, volume 1694 of *Lecture Notes in Computer Science*, Sept. 1999.
18. J. Hatcliff, M. B. Dwyer, and H. Zheng. Slicing software for model construction. *Journal of Higher-order and Symbolic Computation*, 13(4):315–353, 2000.
19. G. J. Holzmann. The model checker SPIN. *IEEE Transactions on Software Engineering*, 23(5):279–294, May 1997.
20. G. J. Holzmann. Personal communication, Oct. 2005.
21. R. Iosif. Symmetry reduction criteria for software model checking. In *Proceedings of Ninth International SPIN Workshop*, volume 2318 of *Lecture Notes in Computer Science*, pages 22–41. Springer, Apr. 2002.
22. Java Grande Benchmarking Project. Java Grande forum benchmark suite – thread version 1.0. http://www.epcc.ed.ac.uk/computing/research_activities/java_grande/.
23. G. Jayaraman, V. P. Ranganath, and J. Hatcliff. Kaveri: Delivering Indus Java program slicer to Eclipse. In *Proceedings of the Fundamental Approaches to Software Engineering, FASE 2005*. Springer, April 2005.
24. G. Jia and S. Graf. Verification experiments on the MASCARA protocol. In M. B. Dwyer, editor, *Model Checking Software: 8th International SPIN Workshop*, volume 2057 of *LNCS*, pages 123–142, Toronto, Canada, May 2001. Springer.
25. J. Krinke. Static slicing of threaded programs. In *Proceedings ACM SIGPLAN/SIGFSOFT Workshop on Program Analysis for Software Tools and Engineering (PASTE'98)*, pages 35–42, Montreal, Canada, June 1998. ACM SIGPLAN Notices 33(7).
26. L. I. Millett and T. Teitelbaum. Slicing Promela and its applications to model checking, simulation, and protocol understanding. In *Proceedings of the 4th International SPIN Workshop*, LNCS, 1998.
27. M. G. Nanda and S. Ramesh. Slicing concurrent programs. In *Proceedings of International Symposium on Software Testing and Analysis (ISSTA'00)*, pages 180–190, 2000.
28. A. Podgurski and L. Clarke. A formal model of program dependences and its implications for software testing, debugging, and maintenance. *IEEE Transactions on Software Engineering*, 16(8):965–979, 1990.
29. V. P. Ranganath. Indus. +http://indus.projects.cis.ksu.edu+.
30. V. P. Ranganath. Object-flow analysis for optimizing finite-state models of Java software. Master's thesis, Kansas State University, 2002.
31. V. P. Ranganath, T. Amtoft, A. Banerjee, M. B. Dwyer, and J. Hatcliff. A new foundation for control-dependence and slicing for modern program structures. In *Programming Languages and Systems, Proceedings of 14th European Symposium on Programming, ESOP 2005*. Springer, April 2005.
32. V. P. Ranganath and J. Hatcliff. Pruning interference and ready dependences for slicing concurrent Java programs. In E. Duesterwald, editor, *Proceedings of Compiler Construction (CC'04)*, *Lecture Notes in Computer Science* 2985, pages 39–56. March 2004.

33. Robby, M. B. Dwyer, and J. Hatcliff. Bogor: An extensible and highly-modular model checking framework. In *Proceedings of the 9th European Software Engineering Conference / 11th ACM SIGSOFT Symposium on the Foundations of Software Engineering*, 2003.

34. Robby, M. B. Dwyer, J. Hatcliff, and R. Iosif. Space-reduction strategies for model checking dynamic systems. In *Proceedings of the 2003 Workshop on Software Model Checking*, July 2003.

35. A. Sen, J. Bhadra, V. K. Garg, and J. A. Abraham. Formal verification of a system-on-chip using computation slicing. In *International Test Conference ITC*, pages 810–819, October 2004.

36. S. Stoller. Model-checking multi-threaded distributed Java programs. In *International Journal on Software Tools for Technology Transfer*. Springer, 2002.

37. D. Suwimonteerabuth, S. Schwoon, and J. Esparza. jMoped: A Java bytecode checker based on Moped. In *Proceedings of the 11th Conference on Tools and Algorithms for the Construction and Analysis of Systems (TACAS 2007)*, number 3440 in Lecture Notes in Computer Science, pages 541–545, 2005.

38. F. Tip. A survey of program slicing techniques. *Journal of programming languages*, 3:121–189, 1995.

39. R. Vallée-Rai, L. Hendren, V. Sundaresan, P. Lam, E. Gagnon, and P. Co. Soot – A Java optimization framework. In *Proceedings of CASCON'99*, Nov. 1999.

New Metrics for Static Variable Ordering
in Decision Diagrams*

Radu I. Siminiceanu[1] and Gianfranco Ciardo[2]

[1] National Institute of Aerospace, Hampton, Virgina 23666
[2] University of California, Riverside, CA 92521

Abstract. We investigate a new class of metrics to find good variable orders for decision diagrams in symbolic state-space generation. Most of the previous work on static ordering is centered around the concept of minimum variable span, which can also be found in the literature under several other names. We use a similar concept, but applied to event span, and generalize it to a family of metrics parameterized by a moment, where the metric of moment 0 is the combined event span. Finding a good variable order is then reduced to optimizing one of these metrics, and we design extensive experiments to evaluate them. First, we investigate how the actual optimal order performs in state-space generation, when it can be computed by evaluating all possible permutations. Then, we study the performance of these metrics on selected models and compare their impact on two different state-space generation algorithms: classic breadth-first and our own saturation strategy. We conclude that the new metric of moment 1 is the best choice. In particular, the saturation algorithm seems to benefit the most from using it, as it achieves the better performance in nearly 80% of the cases.

1 Introduction

In automated system verification, the performance of symbolic model checking algorithms based on binary decision diagrams (BDD) [4] is strongly influenced by the variable ordering of the model. While the boundaries of what is now amenable to BDD technology have been constantly pushed, many industrial-size applications are still out of reach. A critical factor is that finding the optimal BDD variable order is an NP-complete problem. Not knowing what the optimum BDD performance could be, leaves the issue of what is actually achievable by this method still uncertain.

Various heuristics have been proposed to tackle the variable order issue. One direction is to attempt to find a good variable order statically [1, 2, 3, 20, 23], i.e., *prior* to generating the state space, hoping to keep the peak size of the BDD as small as possible. The other direction is to dynamically alter the variable ordering *during* state-space generation [24], usually when the size of the BDD becomes too large, to reduce the current BDD size.

---

* Work supported in part by the National Aeronautics and Space Administration under grant NCC1-02043 and by the National Science Foundation under grants CNS-0501747 and CNS-0501748.

H. Hermanns and J. Palsberg (Eds.): TACAS 2006, LNCS 3920, pp. 90–104, 2006.

Most of the previous efforts on static ordering is centered around the concept of *minimum variable span*, variants of which have been described as normalized average lifetime [22], smallest communication graph [1], and diagonal dependency matrix [15]. At its core is the idea that clustering variables that are interrelated (in the transition relation expression, combinatorial circuit design, dependency matrix, etc.) yields better results. This was hinted as early as in [6] and also supports the idea of event locality [9], which ultimately produced the saturation strategy [10], an efficient state-space generation algorithm.

However, simply minimizing the span as a metric does not always guarantee good results in practice. Indeed, variable orders with the same span may produce drastically different results. In the process of developing the saturation strategy, we observed that the dynamics of the BDD growth can be significantly different than for the classic breadth-first iterations. In general, the complexity of symbolic state-space generation depends not only on the overall number of BDD nodes, but also on the location of the region of BDD levels affected by each event. In most cases, some regions tend to grow much larger than the rest. Precisely pinpointing where those levels are concentrated cannot be done in advance, as this is largely model-dependent, but experience indicates that the BDDs grow larger mostly in the middle or middle-bottom area. Therefore, BDD node operations tend to be more costly if performed at the top levels, as the recursive calls propagate downstream. In this paper, we propose a metric focused on the *event span* (over variables), rather than the *variable span*, and propose a generalized version of this metric that takes into account the location of the span with respect to the range of state variables.

The remainder of the paper is structured as follows. Section 2 contains a brief digest of previous work on variable ordering. Section 3 recalls the background on symbolic state-space generation and introduces the new metrics. Section 4 discusses the experimental results to evaluate the significance of these metrics in the context of the saturation and breadth-first iteration strategies. Section 5 concludes and discusses future work.

2 Related Work

The importance of clustering interdependent variables was first pointed out by Burch, Clarke, and Long [6]. Fujita et al. [15] provided an early overview and evaluation of BDD variable orderings. On a closely related subject, a first static heuristic for image computation with a partitioned transition relation was proposed by Geist and Beer [13], based on the idea of ordering the conjuncts depending on the number of affected variables. IWLS95, another successful but quite elaborate heuristic, was proposed in [25] and is still widely used in various BDD packages. Aziz et al. [1] also suggested clustering variables that depend on each other based on an underlying communication graph.

Moon et al. [22] discusses the normalized average lifetime metric in the context of efficiently applying the transition relation of a system using BDDs, either disjunctively or conjunctively. They report significant improvements over previous heuristics in performing image computation within a unified framework that combines conjunctive and splitting methods. In the same context, Chauhan et al. [7] studied different algorithms for optimizing the lifetime metric and concluded that the simulated annealing algorithm achieves the best results. They also proved that the problem of minimizing the normalized average lifetime metric is NP-complete.

Closer to our approach, [3] attempts to alter the minimum event span method. Variables are assigned different weights, according to how many events in the model affect them, then they are statically arranged in decreasing weight order. MINCE [2] is a similar heuristic in the context of both BDD and SAT-based verification, which exploits information from the conjunctive normal form.

Solving the BDD minimization problem by means of genetic algorithms is seen in [14, 23]. One drawback in this type of work is that the evaluation function of the chromosomes is the actual size of the resulting BDD for that order, hence the optimization process is extremely time consuming. In Section 4.5, we propose a much faster approach, where the fitness function is the value of the weighted event span metric, which can be computed statically from the model information for each order.

Other techniques for variable ordering that do not directly employ optimizing a metric are found in [20], which proposes a sampling heuristic, [18], which introduces the scatter search, and [17], which studies a learning based method.

3 Variable Ordering in Symbolic State-Space Generation

We focus on the important problem of symbolically generating the state-space $\mathcal{S}$ of a discrete-state model. We assume a high-level description of the model where each state $\mathbf{i}$ is a K-tuple of integer variables, $\mathbf{i} = (i_K, ..., i_1)$. Each of these variables i_k is in some range $\mathcal{S}_k = \{0, 1, ..., n_k - 1\}$, so that the *potential state space* of the model is $\widehat{\mathcal{S}} = \mathcal{S}_K \times \cdots \times \mathcal{S}_1$. The model has an initial state, or, in full generality, an initial set of states $\mathcal{S}^{init} \subseteq \widehat{\mathcal{S}}$. A *next-state function* of the form $\mathcal{N} : \widehat{\mathcal{S}} \rightarrow 2^{\widehat{\mathcal{S}}}$ specifies the set of states reachable from each state, we can also think of it as a *transition relation* of the form $\mathcal{R} \subseteq \widehat{\mathcal{S}} \times \widehat{\mathcal{S}}$, where $\mathbf{j} \in \mathcal{N}(\mathbf{i}) \Leftrightarrow (\mathbf{i}, \mathbf{j}) \in \mathcal{R}$. We are interested in computing and storing the state space $\mathcal{S}$, which can be defined as the smallest set containing $\mathcal{S}^{init}$ and satisfying the fixed-point equation $\mathcal{X} = \mathcal{X} \cup \mathcal{N}(\mathcal{X})$.

Symbolic methods to compute $\mathcal{S}$ use *decision diagrams*. We consider *quasi-reduced ordered multi-valued decision diagrams (MDDs)* [19], formally defined as a directed acyclic edge-labeled multi-graph where:

- Each node p belongs to a *level* $k \in \{K, ..., 1, 0\}$, denoted $p.lvl$.
- There is a single *root* node r at level K
- Level 0 can only contain the two *terminal* nodes *Zero* and *One*.
- A node p at level $k > 0$ has n_k outgoing edges, labeled from 0 to $n_k - 1$. The edge labeled by i_k points to a node q at level $k - 1$; we write $p[i_k] = q$.
- Given nodes p and q at level $k > 0$, if $p[i_k] = q[i_k]$ for all $i_k \in \mathcal{S}_k$, then $p = q$, i.e., there are no *duplicates*.

The set of states encoded by an MDD is $\mathcal{B}(r)$, defined recursively as

$$\mathcal{B}(p) = \begin{cases} \bigcup_{i_k \in \mathcal{S}_k} \{i_k\} \times \mathcal{B}(p[i_k]) & \text{if } p.lvl = k > 1 \\ \{i_1 : p[i_1] = One\} & \text{if } p.lvl = 1 \end{cases}.$$

A basic *breadth-first-search* (BFS) algorithm to generate $\mathcal{S}$ implements exactly the fixed-point definition of $\mathcal{S}$, by initializing $\mathcal{S}$ to $\mathcal{S}^{init}$, then repeatedly updating it to include the states reachable from it in one (more) application of $\mathcal{N}$, until no more new states are found, i.e., until $\mathcal{N}(\mathcal{S}) \subseteq \mathcal{S}$. A $2K$-level MDD, fixed for the duration of the iterations, is used to store the next-state function $\mathcal{N}$, while a K-level MDD, which grows and shrinks during the iterations, is used to store $\mathcal{S}$. The *peak size* of this second MDD is critical, as it can exceed the available memory.

To reduce the peak memory requirements of symbolic state-space generation, especially for *globally-asynchronous locally-synchronous systems (GALS)*, we proposed an alternative algorithm called *saturation* [10]. At its core is the recognition that, in GALS, most events exhibit strong *locality*, i.e., they affect only a small subset of the state variables, while the other state variables are subject to *identity transformations*, i.e., they do not change.

Saturation requires a next-state function *disjunctively-partitioned* according to a set $\mathcal{E}$ of (asynchronous) *events* in the high-level model, $\mathcal{N} = \bigcup_{e \in \mathcal{E}} \mathcal{N}_e$. As initially defined, saturation also requires that each $\mathcal{N}_e$ be *conjunctively-partitioned* into K *local* functions, $\mathcal{N}_e = \mathcal{N}_{K,e} \times \cdots \times \mathcal{N}_{1,e}$, each one describing the interaction between event e and a state variable k, $\mathcal{N}_{k,e} : \mathcal{S}_k \to 2^{\mathcal{S}_k}$. Such a decomposition always exists. However, for Petri nets, for example, the $\mathcal{N}_{k,e}$ functions always exist regardless of how many places are grouped into a single state variable while, in other formalisms, this conjunctive decomposition might exist only if we merge state variables or split events, potentially leading to exponential growth of the node sizes or of the number of events. A more recent version of saturation allows the conjuncts to be functions of multiple state variables [12], but we limit our discussion to the original version for simplicity (the findings of this paper are equally applicable to this general version of saturation).

We say that level k does not *depend* on event e, and vice-versa, if $\mathcal{N}_{k,e} = \mathcal{I}_k$, the identity function, i.e., $\mathcal{N}_{k,e}(i_k) = \{i_k\}$ for every local state $i_k \in \mathcal{S}_k$. Then, we define $Top(e) = \max\{k : \mathcal{N}_{k,e} \neq \mathcal{I}_k\}$ and $Bot(e) = \min\{k : \mathcal{N}_{k,e} \neq \mathcal{I}_k\}$ to be the highest and lowest levels that depend on event e. Letting $\mathcal{N}_k = \bigcup_{e : Top(e)=k} \mathcal{N}_e$ and $\mathcal{N}_{\leq k} = \bigcup_{e : Top(e) \leq k} \mathcal{N}_e$, saturation applies $\mathcal{N}_1$ to each node p at level 1 in the MDD encoding of $\mathcal{S}^{init}$, by modifying it *in place*, until it has reached a fixed-point, i.e., $\mathcal{B}(p) = \mathcal{B}(p) \cup \mathcal{N}_{\leq 1}(\mathcal{B}(p))$; then it moves to each node q at level 2 and applies $\mathcal{N}_2$ to it, and $\mathcal{N}_1$ to any node at level 1 created by this application, so that $\mathcal{B}(q) = \mathcal{B}(q) \cup \mathcal{N}_{\leq 2}(\mathcal{B}(q))$; then it moves to the nodes at level 3, and so on. Once the root r is saturated in this manner, it encodes the desired state space $\mathcal{S}$. Saturation has been shown to have memory and time requirements several orders of magnitude smaller than those of BFS in many models of GALS.

3.1   BDD vs. MDD Variables and Their Order

It is well-known that the variable order can greatly affect the size of a BDD, thus the efficiency of the symbolic iterations. Moreover, finding the optimal order that minimizes the size of a BDD (or of multiple BDDs stored in a BDD forest to share nodes) is an NP-complete problem [5]. The same applies to MDDs, of course, but, in addition, the MDD variables themselves offer a greater degree of freedom, thus more opportunities to introduce improvements, but also inefficiencies. For example, we can choose to partition the P places of a Petri net into $K \leq P$ groups, each one corresponding to a state variable. We do not address the issue of defining these groups of MDD variables, but simply observe that it can be seen as an improvement to be applied *after* having decided the order of the finest possible partition (in the case of Petri nets, this means assigning a different place to each level of the MDD, i.e., $K = P$). Thus, since we focus on the problem of finding a good order for the finest set of MDD state variables, the results that follow are applicable to BDDs as well.

3.2   Event Span Metrics

A variable ordering is a permutation π of the K state variables $(i_K, \ldots, i_1)$, so that variable i_k is assigned to level $\pi(k)$ of the MDD. In the following, we write $Top_\pi(e)$ and $Bot_\pi(e)$ to mean the value of $Top(e)$ and $Bot(e)$ when we use the permutation π. We can also envision a boolean matrix describing the dependence between levels and events, $\mathbf{A} \in \{0,1\}^{|\{K,\ldots,1\}| \times |\mathcal{E}|}$ where $\mathbf{A}(k,e) = 1$ iff $\mathcal{N}_{k,e} \neq \mathcal{I}_k$ and, for a given permutation π, let $\mathbf{A}_\pi$ be matrix obtained by permuting the rows of $\mathbf{A}$ according to π, i.e., row k of $\mathbf{A}$ equals row $\pi(k)$ of $\mathbf{A}_\pi$.

For a given variable ordering π, we define the Normalized Event Span (*NES*) metric as

$$NES(\pi) = \sum_{e \in \mathcal{E}} \frac{Top_\pi(e) - Bot_\pi(e) + 1}{K \cdot |\mathcal{E}|}$$

The *NES* metric computes the average span of all events (the span is then normalized by K) and its value is always between 0 and 1. A low *NES* indicates that the event spans are small, i.e., that most events affect only state variables close to each other in the order π.

We generalize this concept by introducing the Weighted Event Span metric of moment i, $WES^{(i)}$ for variable ordering π as:

$$WES^{(i)}(\pi) = \sum_{e \in \mathcal{E}} \left(\frac{Top_\pi(e)}{K/2} \right)^i \cdot \frac{Top_\pi(e) - Bot_\pi(e) + 1}{K \cdot |\mathcal{E}|}$$

We observe that $WES^{(0)}$ is exactly equivalent to *NES*. The $WES^{(1)}$ metric, instead, adds to it a component that reflects the *location* of the affected region, by assigning higher weights to locations closer to the top. This takes into account that operations applied to nodes in the lower portion of the MDD tend to have lower cost than those applied to higher nodes. Therefore the span of an event is scaled by $\alpha_\pi(e) = \frac{Top_\pi(e)}{K/2}$, the relative position of the topmost level compared to the average level, $K/2$. The weight of an event is thus between $(2/K)^i$ and 2^i, but the average over all events, if their tops were uniformly distributed over the MDD, should have an expected value of 1 for $WES^{(1)}$, like for NES. For larger moments i, the emphasis on the location grows, as the weight multiplies in powers of 2, while strong clustering is relatively less important.

The Normalized Average Lifetime (NAL) metric introduced in [22] is very similar to our NES, but it is employed in a different context: that of finding a good ordering of the conjuncts in the transition relation expression when performing symbolic image computations. In essence, the target in [22] is still to minimize the average span of rows, but computed on the transpose of our dependence matrix. Therefore, the object of optimizing NAL can be ultimately viewed as clustering *events* (the rows in our matrix), as opposed to variables (the columns).

3.3 NP-Completeness of Our Metric

Intuitively, our $WES^{(i)}$ metric arises from two components, the size of the span for each event, and the (i^{th} power of the) position of the span for each event.

Given our matrix $\mathbf{A} \in \{0,1\}^{|\{K,...,1\}| \times |\mathcal{E}|}$ and considering all the matrices $\mathbf{A}_\pi$ obtained by permuting its rows according to π, the question ($SUM\text{-}OF\text{-}SPANS$, i.e., NES)

$$\text{"Is there an } \mathbf{A}_\pi \text{ s.t. } \sum_{e \in \mathcal{E}} \frac{Top_\pi(e) - Bot_\pi(e) + 1}{K \cdot |\mathcal{E}|} \leq T\text{"},$$

was proven in [7] to be NP-complete by reducing the *directed optimal linear arrangement* problem (GT43 in [16]) to it.

Focusing on the position of the spans alone, the question ($SUM\text{-}OF\text{-}TOPS$)

$$\text{"Is there an } \mathbf{A}_\pi \text{ s.t. } \sum_{e \in \mathcal{E}} Top_\pi(e) \leq T\text{"}$$

can also be shown to be NP-complete [26] by reducing the *interval graph completion* problem (GT35 in [16]) to it.

The corresponding question for our more general metric $WES^{(i)}$,

$$\text{"Is there an } \mathbf{A}_\pi \text{ s.t. } \sum_{e \in \mathcal{E}} \left(\frac{Top_\pi(e)}{K/2} \right)^i \cdot \frac{Top_\pi(e) - Bot_\pi(e) + 1}{K \cdot |\mathcal{E}|} \leq T\text{"}$$

is clearly solvable in non-deterministic polynomial time, by simply evaluating the metric for each non-deterministically chosen permutation π, but, while we strongly suspect that it is NP-complete, just like $SUM\text{-}OF\text{-}SPANS$ and $SUM\text{-}OF\text{-}TOPS$, we have not yet been able to prove its NP-hardness so far. The major obstacle in achieving the completeness result is posed by the non-linearity of the target function for higher moments.

4 Results

Extensive tests were performed to shed light on the properties of the *WES* metrics. We attempted as many exhaustive experiments as we could afford, given that the number of runs required to determine the optimal ordering can be huge.

4.1 Methodology

We designed three set of experiments, which we ran on a 2.4GHz Linux workstation with 1GB of memory. Our goal is to look for a connection between optimizing one of the metrics, i.e., finding the variable ordering that results in the smallest value for the metric, and optimizing the MDD performance, i.e., having the smallest peak number of MDD nodes during state-space generation. Since the runtime and memory consumption are strongly related for MDD-based algorithms, we can restrict ourselves to peak memory as a measure of the overall performance. In all the experiments, we limited ourselves to comparing the metrics for the first three moments: $WES^{(0)}$, $WES^{(1)}$, and $WES^{(2)}$.

Finding the optimum peak MDD size among all possible K-variable orders requires $K!$ runs. This becomes infeasible for relatively small values of K. In our first set of experiments, then, we tried this exhaustive search on a set of five random models with $K = 6$ variables (for a total of $5 \times 6! = 3600$ runs). The question we wanted to answer was whether variable orders that minimize the MDD size coincide with orders that minimize any of the WES metrics, and how often. This test was completed only for the saturation strategy, due to the enormous amount of time required to finish the same tests on BFS.

The second set of experiments considered the inverse question: which metric we should choose to minimize in order to achieve the best MDD performance. We randomly generated 900 models of different size for which the minimum value of the metric (not the state-space) for all $K!$ variable orders can be computed in a reasonable amount of time. We stopped at a maximum of $K = 10$ variables, since after evaluating the $10! = 3,628,800$ possible permutations, the optimum one is run by BFS, for each model and each $WES^{(i)}$, in roughly ten minutes on average. For all 900 models, the total runtime for BFS was 29 days. In contrast, the same experiments took only 16 hours when running saturation, which is more than 40 times faster.

The next value of $K = 11$ would have taken an estimated two hours per run for BFS, for a grand total of close to one year. Even so, computing the value of the *WES* functions statically for 10! orders and then generating the state space for (one of) the order(s) that minimizes each metric takes much less time than executing 6! different MDD-based state-space generation runs. While it was not the purpose of this study, it would be of interest to generate *all* distinct models of a given size K. The total number of such models is $2^{K(K-1)}$, since, in our setting, this is the number of all sub-digraphs of the complete digraph of K nodes, as described in more detail in Section 4.2 (without considering any symmetries, equivalences, or other possible reductions). At the same time, the 900 models used in this experiment are still relevant, precisely because they are randomly generated: they represent an unbiased statistical sample and offer a reasonably even coverage of all possible models.

The first two sets of experiments can only be performed on small models. The last set is instead taken from larger, more practical models. The methodology in this case is different, as generating all models or all orders is out of the question. We generated various orders, ranging from nearly optimal to nearly random, by running a basic genetic algorithm for permutations [21]. The algorithm is stopped after a varying number of generations, and the fittest chromosome (order) at the end is fed into the state-space generator. The resulting MDD size is then used to compare how the variations in the metric value relate to the MDD performance.

4.2 The Random Model Generator

A small program written in C++ generates models as bounded Petri nets to be fed to the SMART [8] tool. The user specifies the number of Petri net places (state variables) and transitions (model events), and the maximum number of tokens allowed in each place (range of each state variable). Each transition is adjacent to one input and one output arc. Hence, this technique of "filling out" the Petri net with transitions is very similar to randomly filling a directed graph with arcs between its nodes. The program rejects disconnected models, but allows sinks, traps, and deadlocks.

4.3 Experiments Where the MDD Optimum Is Known

Table 1 presents a synopsis of the results from the first set of experiments. We generate all possible 720 permutations of six variables and report the number of permutations ("per") that led to the smallest peak MDD size. The next three pairs of columns report the minimum value of each WES metric on these orders, and also how many of those reached the MDD optimum. For comparison, we also list, in the last three pairs of columns, the overall optimum of each metric and in how many instances this was reached.

Figure 1 illustrates the five random models used in this experiment, as directed graphs (instead of Petri nets). An arrow represents a transition that removes a token from (i.e., decreases the value of) the source place (variable) and adds it to (i.e., increments) the target place (variable). The initial value of p_0 is written inside the place p_0.

Table 1. Experiment 1: MDD optimum vs. WES optimums

		smallest MDD					overall metric optimum					
	per	metric value on smallest MDDs					$WES^{(0)}$		$WES^{(1)}$		$WES^{(2)}$	
		$WES^{(0)}$	per	$WES^{(1)}$	per	$WES^{(2)}$	per	min	per	min	per	min	per
model 1	10	0.444	1	0.648	1	0.977	1	0.426	2	0.623	1	0.949	1
model 2	10	0.407	1	0.574	1	0.819	1	0.407	2	0.574	1	0.819	1
model 3	2	0.438	1	0.674	1	1.111	1	0.396	4	0.542	1	0.806	1
model 4	4	0.467	4	0.689	2	1.081	2	0.467	16	0.689	4	1.081	2
model 5	4	0.467	2	0.661	1	1.046	1	0.450	4	0.661	1	1.046	1

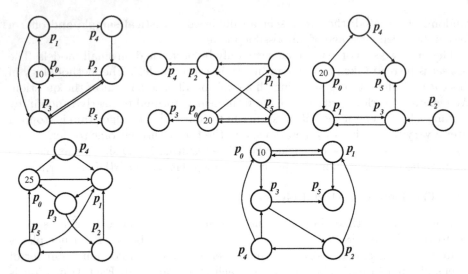

Fig. 1. The five random models used in the first set of experiments

Note that the minimums for the metrics differ substantially, depending on the moment. This is because our assumption about the expected value of the scalars $\alpha_\pi(e)$ was imprecise. The average on the top level of all events is actually higher than $K/2$ as the width of the affected region pushes this value up. Similarly, the average bottom level would sit lower than $K/2$. To achieve a better common ground when comparing the metrics, we should consider the middle level as a scalar:

$$\alpha_\pi(e) = \frac{(Top_\pi(e) + Bot_\pi(e))/2}{K/2}$$

However, that would be a completely different metric, which will not capture the effect we were targeting: the top level is most important, because that is where the recursive calls in MDD operations start. Therefore, we will forgo the property of having common expected values for the metrics in our present study.

The results show that in two of the five models (1 and 3), none of the metrics' optimums led to a MDD optimum. In two other models (2 and 4), all metrics reach the MDD optimum. However, for the $WES^{(0)}$ metric, there are multiple orderings that have minimum value and only a fraction of them are also among those that coincide with the smallest MDD (1/2 and 4/16). For the other two metrics this proportion is better (1/1 and 2/4). For the last model, $WES^{(0)}$ does not reach the MDD optimum, while the others do, and they do so for a single value. Moreover, we observe that overall (and this trend continues in the next batch of experiments) $WES^{(0)}$ has multiple minimums, making it difficult to choose the particular order among them that might lead to the MDD optimum. With the other metrics, the number of minimums is much smaller, thus the selection has a greater chance to succeed in matching the MDD's best. Most encouraging are cases such as models 2 and 5, where $WES^{(1)}$ has a *unique* minimum which *coincides* with the MDD optimum.

4.4 Experiments Where the *WES* Optimums Are Known

This set of experiments used three parameters for generating the random nets:

- number of variables P: from 8 to 10;
- number of transitions T: from 11 to 25;
- number of tokens in the initial marking (i.e., the range of variables): from 5 to 100, in increments of 5.

for a total of 900 cases.

In many instances, the best order was the same for two, or even all three metrics. A synopsis of the results is presented in Figure 2, as the percentage of runs where each metric performed best among the three (there are many ties, thus the sum of the three plots is over 100%). While for BFS the choice of metric does not appear to have a large impact, this is not the case for saturation. The table in the left of Figure 3 (left) presents a digest of the results for saturation, where it can be seen that $WES^{(1)}$ clearly performs the best.

At first glance, $WES^{(1)}$ is the best choice among the three metrics. It also appears that models that are not "dense" with transitions favor higher moment metrics ($WES^{(1)}$ and $WES^{(2)}$). Since $WES^{(1)}$ seems to be consistently slightly better than $WES^{(2)}$, it is then interesting to examine when it also "beats" $WES^{(0)}$. Figure 3 (right) shows the percentage of runs where $WES^{(1)}$ is at least as good as $WES^{(0)}$, as a function of T, for the choices $P = 8$ and $P = 10$. The overall percentage is 79%.

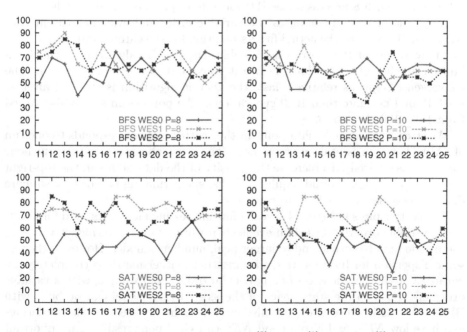

Fig. 2. Experiment 2: % of runs where $WES^{(0)}$, $WES^{(1)}$, or $WES^{(2)}$ is best, as a function of T (x-axis) and P, for BFS (top) and saturation (bottom)

	$WES^{(0)}$	$WES^{(1)}$	$WES^{(2)}$
$P = 8, T = 15$	35%	80%	65%
$P = 8, T = 20$	50%	75%	65%
$P = 8, T = 25$	50%	70%	60%
$P = 8$, total	51%	73%	70%
$P = 10, T = 15$	50%	85%	50%
$P = 10, T = 20$	45%	85%	65%
$P = 10, T = 25$	50%	55%	60%
$P = 10$, total	48%	66%	55%

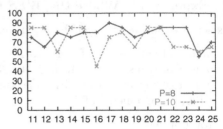

% of runs where each metric is best   % of runs where $WES^{(1)}$ beats $WES^{(0)}$
(for saturation)   as a function of the number of events

Fig. 3. Experiment 2 results: focus on saturation

4.5   Experiments Where Optimums Are Not Known

The collection of experimental results presented here is trying to answer the question: "Is $WES^{(1)}$ more appropriate than $WES^{(0)}$, i.e., NES, to evaluate good variable orderings in large models?". We compare the effect of NES and $WES^{(1)}$ in generating the state space with the two algorithms, saturation and BFS, and measure the runtime and peak number of nodes in the MDD (final number of nodes, as well as peak and final memory consumption are also collected, but not shown in the graphs for conciseness). The experiments are set up in SMART for three models: dining philosophers of size 10, slotted ring with 6 slots, and round robin mutex with 8 processes (see [11] for a description of these models).

A genetic algorithm computes the variable order and evaluates the metrics NES and $WES^{(1)}$ (as the actual fitness function for the chromosomes). To cover as many values of the metrics as possible, the genetic algorithm is run for a limited number of generations, before it converges to a good solution. As the convergence happens relatively fast, the genetic algorithm is stopped after at least 10 and no more than 1000 generations. The population size is also varied from 10 to 100 chromosomes.

We stress that a single data point in the scatter plots corresponds to one run of SMART, which can take up to an hour (the script aborts a run if the one hour timeout has expired). To increase the density of the data points in the top-right corners of the graphs would require months, spent running bad orders, so more data in those sections is hard to come by.

The scatter plots in Figure 4 reveal a few interesting facts. First and foremost, static variable ordering based on event span works: as a trend, higher values of the metric tend to correspond to larger peak number of nodes. However, there is some dispersion for both metrics, showing that neither metric is completely accurate in predicting the effect of a particular order. For example, with a variable order of NES 0.35 the state space of the slotted ring model can be built with BFS as fast as in 80 seconds, but also as slow as in 550 seconds. Bad orderings can have low NES, and also a good NES can yield poor results. An important question is then: are the $WES^{(1)}$ plots less scattered? The answer is yes, even if not impressively so. Nonetheless, a conclusion is that, using the $WES^{(1)}$ metric

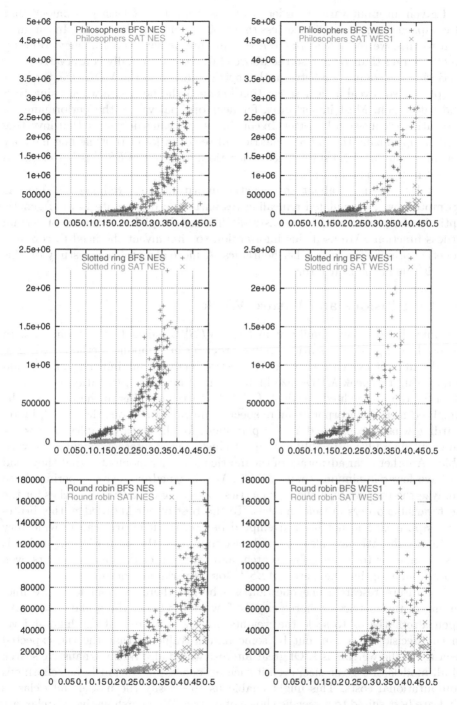

Fig. 4. Peak no. of nodes as a function of the $NES/WES^{(1)}$ metric: BFS vs. saturation

and given an input variable order of fitness 0.35, it is at least guaranteed that state-space generation will take less than 350 seconds for this model. In conjunction to this, we recall that the $WES^{(1)}$ minimums have the tendency to be up to 80% larger than NES's, so the above statement is actually conservative.

Beside the connection between the metric values and the MDD size, the scatter plots also reveal a clear separation between the peak size when using BFS and saturation. Most importantly, for near optimal values the performance of saturation is consistently better. In conclusion, we can safely state that investing time in optimizing the $WES^{(1)}$ metric will result in lower runtime and memory consumption for MDD state-space generation, and that $WES^{(1)}$ is better suited for saturation than for BFS.

Finally, a remark about the genetic algorithm employed here is due. As prompted by [7], simulated annealing (essentially a degenerate form of genetic optimization) was found to be faster at finding the global optimum of certain fitness functions. We used this information to circumvent the need to compare genetic optimization with other heuristics. A more comprehensive study on this issue is due in the near future.

5   Conclusions and Future Work

We introduced a new family of metrics $WES^{(i)}$, indexed by a moment i, to be used as a guide for static variable ordering in symbolic methods. We provided sufficient evidence that the connection between minimizing $WES^{(1)}$ and minimizing the peak MDDs size in symbolic state-space generation is stronger than for the unweighted metric $WES^{(0)}$. We attribute this to the fact that the weighted metrics incorporate more specific information about the model, by rewarding what is considered a good placement for the state variables affected by an event, in addition to only a compact clustering of interdependent state variables. Another clear advantage of the metrics of higher moment is that they tend to have fewer minimums than $WES^{(0)}$. We designed extensive experiments to analyze the properties of the new metrics, including exhaustive searches for the best variable orders in small models. To the best of our knowledge, this brute-force approach had not been attempted before, yet it clearly can provide very useful insight. We have also attested once more that the saturation algorithm is vastly superior to breadth-first search, and, quite interestingly, it benefits even more from adopting the metric $WES^{(1)}$ for its variable ordering.

For future research, one question is whether there is room for more fine-tuning of the metrics or more "creative" ways to choose the scalars $\alpha_\pi(e)$. An open alternative is to scale the weights not by the index of the highest level in the decision diagram, but by some middle value so that the the expected average of the weights is 1. Of great interest would also be an exhaustive search of all models of a given size, even if such an endeavour obviously has enormous computational costs. This might enable us to classify the models into classes that are best suited to a specific choice of metric. Where exhaustive searches are not possible, data of statistical nature should be collected from more extensive experiments. The behavior of the metrics near the optimums for the metrics, and how this behavior relates to the minimization of the peak MDD size should be considered. From the algorithmic standpoint, heuristics to minimize the metrics, other than genetic optimization, and approximation methods should be studied and compared.

References

1. A. Aziz, S. Tasiran, and R.K. Brayton. BDD Variable Ordering for Interacting Finite State Machines. In *31st ACM/IEEE Design Automation Conference (DAC)*, San Diego, CA, June 1994. San Diego Convention Center. ch. 18.3.
2. F. A. Aloul, I. L. Markov, and K. A. Sakallah. MINCE: A static global variable-ordering heuristic for SAT search and BDD manipulation. *J. UCS*, 10(12):1562–1596, 2004.
3. D. Borrione and J. Vidal. Improving static ordering of BDDs for reachability analysis, Apr. 29 2002.
4. R. E. Bryant. Graph-based algorithms for boolean function manipulation. *IEEE Trans. Comput.*, 35(8):677–691, Aug. 1986.
5. R. E. Bryant. Symbolic boolean manipulation with ordered binary-decision diagrams. *ACM Comp. Surv.*, 24(3):293–318, 1992.
6. J. R. Burch, E. M. Clarke, and D. E. Long. Symbolic model checking with partitioned transistion relations. In *VLSI*, pages 49–58, 1991.
7. P. Chauhan, E. Clarke, S. Jha, J. Kukula, H. Veith, and D. Wang. Using combinatorial optimization methods for quantification scheduling. *Lecture Notes in Computer Science*, 2144:293–302, 2001.
8. G. Ciardo, R. L. Jones, A. S. Miner, and R. Siminiceaunu. Logical and stochastic modeling with SMART. In *Proc. Modelling Techniques and Tools for Computer Performance Evaluation*, LNCS 2794, pages 78–97, Urbana, IL, USA, Sept. 2003. Springer-Verlag.
9. G. Ciardo, G. Lüttgen, and R. Siminiceanu. Efficient symbolic state-space construction for asynchronous systems. In *Proc. 21th Int. Conf. on Applications and Theory of Petri Nets*, LNCS 1825, pages 103–122, Aarhus, Denmark, June 2000. Springer-Verlag.
10. G. Ciardo, G. Lüttgen, and R. Siminiceanu. Saturation: An efficient iteration strategy for symbolic state space generation. In T. Margaria and W. Yi, editors, *Proc. TACAS*, LNCS 2031, pages 328–342, Genova, Italy, Apr. 2001. Springer-Verlag.
11. G. Ciardo, R. Marmorstein, and R. Siminiceanu. Saturation unbound. In *Proc. Tools and Algorithms for the Construction and Analysis of Systems (TACAS)*, LNCS 2619, pages 379–393, Warsaw, Poland, Apr. 2003. Springer-Verlag.
12. G. Ciardo and J. Yu. Saturation-based symbolic reachability analysis using conjunctive and disjunctive partitioning. In *Proc. CHARME*, Saarbrücken, Germany, Oct. 2005. Springer-Verlag. To appear.
13. D. Geist and I. Beer. Efficient model checking by automated ordering of transition relation. In David L. Dill, editor, *Proceedings of the sixth International Conference on Computer-Aided Verification CAV*, volume 818, pages 299–310, Standford, California, USA, 1994. Springer-Verlag.
14. R. Drechsler, B. Becker, and N. Gockel. A genetic algorithm for variable ordering of OBDDs. In *Int'l Workshop on Logic Synthesis*. ACM/IEEE, May 1995.

15. M. Fujita, H. Fujisawa, and Y. Matsunaga. Variable ordering algorithms for ordered binary decision diagrams and their evaluation. *IEEE Transactions on Computer-Aided Design of Integrated Circuits and Systems*, 12(1):6–12, Jan. 1993.

16. M. R. Garey and D. S. Johnson. *Computers and Intractability: A Guide to the Theory of NP-Completeness.* Freeman Press, 1979.

17. O. Grumberg, S. Livne, and S. Markovitch. Learning to order BDD variables in verification. *Journal of Artificial Intelligence Research*, 18:83–116, 2003.

18. W. N. N. Hung and X. Song. BDD variable ordering by scatter search. In *ICCD*, pages 368–373, 2001.

19. T. Kam, T. Villa, R. Brayton, and A. Sangiovanni-Vincentelli. Multi-valued decision diagrams: theory and applications. *Multiple-Valued Logic*, 4(1–2):9–62, 1998.

20. Y. Lu, J. Jain, E. M. Clarke, and M. Fujita. Efficient variable ordering using a BDD based sampling. In *Design Automation Conference*, pages 687–692, 2000.

21. Z. Michalewicz. *Genetic Algorithms + Data Structures = Evolution Programs.* Springer-Verlag, New York, NY, USA, 1996.

22. I.-H. Moon, J. H. Kukula, K. Ravi, and F. Somenzi. To split or to conjoin: the question in image computation. In *Proceedings of the 37th Conference on Design Automation (DAC-00)*, pages 23–28, NY, June 5–9 2000. ACM/IEEE.

23. A. M. Moreira, D. Déharbe, and U. S. Costa. Advances in BDD reduction using parallel genetic algorithms, May 2001.

24. R. Rudell. Dynamic Variable Ordering for Ordered Binary Decision Diagrams. In *IEEE /ACM International Conference on CAD*, pages 42–47, Santa Clara, California, Nov. 1993. ACM/IEEE, IEEE Computer Society Press.

25. R. Ranjan, A. Aziz, R. Brayton, B. Plessier, and C. Pixley. Efficient BDD algorithms for FSM synthesis and verification, May 1995.

26. Y. Wu and J. Robert. Personal communication, Oct. 2005.

Widening ROBDDs with Prime Implicants

Neil Kettle[1], Andy King[1], and Tadeusz Strzemecki[2]

[1] University of Kent, Canterbury, CT2 7NF, UK
[2] Fordham University, New York, NY 10023, USA

Abstract. Despite the ubiquity of ROBDDs in program analysis, and extensive literature on ROBDD minimisation, there is a dearth of work on approximating ROBDDs. The need for approximation arises because many ROBDD operations result in an ROBDD whose size is quadratic in the size of the inputs. Furthermore, if ROBDDs are used in abstract interpretation, the running time of the analysis is related not only to the complexity of the individual ROBDD operations but also the number of operations applied. The number of operations is, in turn, constrained by the number of times a Boolean function can be weakened before stability is achieved. This paper proposes a widening that can be used to both constrain the size of an ROBDD and also ensure that the number of times that it is weakened is bounded by some given constant. The widening can be used to either systematically approximate from above (i.e. derive a weaker function) or below (i.e. infer a stronger function).

Keywords: ROBDD, widening, approximation, abstract interpretation.

1 Introduction

Reduced-Ordered Binary Decision Diagrams (ROBDDs) have numerous applications in model checking [4], program analysis [25] and abstract interpretation [1]. The popularity of ROBDDs stems from their memory-efficient encoding of Boolean functions and a canonical representation that supports the memoisation of ROBDD operations. The worst-case complexity of many ROBDD operations is quadratic in the size of the inputs [2], but the inherent intractability of Boolean function manipulation inevitably manifests itself; even though ROBDDs are constructed so as to factor out all replicated sub-ROBDDs, Boolean functions exist whose size is exponential in the number of variables no matter what variable ordering is employed [3]. Intractably large ROBDDs can [6] and do [11] arise in program analysis. In particular, when an analysis associates each program variable with n attributes and m program variables appear in scope, then an ROBDD over $m\lceil \lg(n) \rceil$ propositional variables are required to encode the dependencies between the attributes of the program variables. Even with the use of sophisticated tree-automata techniques to improve the encoding [12], problematically large ROBDDs still arise even when $m \approx 100$ [11].

ROBDDs are not only problematic in terms of space but also in terms of time. This is not only due to the complexity of individual ROBDD operations, but because the number of ROBDD operations is itself potentially exponential. In

H. Hermanns and J. Palsberg (Eds.): TACAS 2006, LNCS 3920, pp. 105–119, 2006.
© Springer-Verlag Berlin Heidelberg 2006

the context of abstract interpretation, this has particular relevance as analysis is typically formulated as a fixpoint. Suppose, for example, that the result of an analysis is conceived as the least fixpoint of a series of equations:

$$f_1 = F_1(f_1, \ldots, f_n)$$
$$\vdots \quad \vdots \qquad \vdots$$
$$f_n = F_n(f_1, \ldots, f_n)$$

where each f_i is a propositional function over m variables $x_1, \ldots, x_m$ and each F_i is an operation on $f_1, \ldots, f_n$ obtained by, say, composing monotonic operations such as disjunction $f_i \vee f_j$, conjunction $f_i \wedge f_j$ and existential quantification $\exists_{x_i}(f_j)$. The least fixpoint can be computed by setting $f_i = false$ and then reapplying the n equations until stability is achieved. In the worst-case, each application of n equations might weaken exactly one f_i by adding a single model. Since each f_i can possess 2^m models, a chain of $n2^m$ iterates are required in the worst-case which violates the general requirement for a polynomial analysis. (The reader is referred to [6] for examples that manifest this behaviour).

In program analysis, it is generally better to return an approximate answer in an acceptable time than an exact answer in an exorbitant time. To this end, widening operators have been proposed [9] that accelerate convergence on computational domains that possess either infinite or very long chains. This use of widening trades precision for time. However, widening can also be used to trade precision for space, for example, replace one ROBDD with another that has more models yet has a more compact representation [11, 15, 18, 21]. Despite extensive literature on reducing the size of an ROBDD by selecting a propitious variable ordering (the reader is referred to citations of the classic paper [19] on variable reordering and minimisation), the problem of widening ROBDDs has received relatively scant attention. This paper plugs this gap by proposing a new widening for ROBDDs based upon the enumeration of prime implicants [8] that has a number of attractive properties:

- The widening can ensure that each f_i is not weakened more than a prescribed number of times. Previous attempts at bounding the iterations have confined the analysis to a fixed sub-domain of Boolean formulae [13]. The widening can support richer classes of dependencies without sacrificing scalability.
- The widening can compute dense approximations of an ROBDD. Moreover, by constructing the new ROBDD in terms of the progressively longer implicants, the widening can be tuned to achieve the desired degree of precision.
- The widening is not dependent on the variable ordering. State-of-the-art in ROBDD approximation is represented by heuristic algorithms [21, 18] that prune branches from an ROBDD by checking whether each branch is subsumed by its sibling. These algorithms are syntactic in that they are informed only by the structure of the ROBDD. In this paper, widening is formulated in terms of the prime implicants of the underlying Boolean function. The advantage of this semantic approach is that the widening is not sensitive to the variable ordering, hence improving the predictability of the analysis.

- The widening can be realised in a surprisingly straightforward manner by introducing a cardinality constraint into the algorithm of Coudert and Madre [8] that removes all prime implicants of excessive length. Experimental work suggests that although this widening produces accurate approximations, the running time of our implementation is not significantly worse than state-of-the-art methods [21, 18].

The paper is structured as follows: Section 2 presents the necessary preliminaries. Section 3 specifies a widening for ROBDDs and Sect. 4 details algorithms for realising it. Section 5 presents the experimental results. Finally, Sect. 6 surveys the related work and Sect. 7 concludes.

2   Preliminaries

2.1   Boolean Functions

A Boolean function is a mapping $f : Bool^n \to Bool$ where $Bool = \{0, 1\}$ that is conventionally written as a propositional formula defined over a totally ordered set of propositional variables $X = \{x_1, \ldots, x_n\}$. For instance, $x_1 \vee x_2$ represents the dyadic function $\{\langle 0, 0 \rangle \mapsto 0, \langle 0, 1 \rangle \mapsto 1, \langle 1, 0 \rangle \mapsto 1, \langle 1, 1 \rangle \mapsto 1\}$. The set of propositional formulae over X is denoted $Bool_X$ and henceforth functions and formulae will be used interchangeably. We define the set of models of a Boolean function f as the mapping $model_X(f) : Bool_X \to \wp(Bool^n)$ such that $model_X(f) = \{\langle b_1, \ldots, b_n \rangle \mid f(b_1, \ldots, b_n) = 1\}$ where $\wp$ denotes the power-set operator. For example, if $X = \{x_1, x_2, x_3\}$ then $model_X(x_1 \wedge (x_2 \to x_3)) = \{\langle 1, 0, 0 \rangle, \langle 1, 0, 1 \rangle, \langle 1, 1, 1 \rangle\}$. One Boolean function f_1 entails another f_2, denoted $f_1 \models f_2$ iff $model_X(f_1) \subseteq model_X(f_2)$. The structure $\langle Bool_X, \models, \vee, \wedge, 0, 1 \rangle$ is a finite lattice where 0 and 1 abbreviate the Boolean functions $\lambda b.0$ and $\lambda b.1$ respectively and $b \in Bool^n$. A chain of Boolean functions C is a set $C \subseteq Bool_X$ such that either $f \models f'$ or $f' \models f$ for all $f, f' \in C$. An anti-chain of Boolean functions A is a set $A \subseteq Bool_X$ such that $f \not\models f$ or $f = f'$ for all $f, f' \in A$. The Shannon co-factor of a Boolean function f w.r.t. a variable x_i and a Boolean constant b is defined by $f|_{x_i \leftarrow b} = f(x_1, \ldots, x_{i-1}, b, x_{i+1}, \ldots, x_n)$. Finally, we denote existential quantification w.r.t. a variable x_i by $\exists_{x_i}(f)$ which can be computed using Schröder elimination, that is, by $\exists_{x_i}(f) = f|_{x_i \leftarrow 0} \vee f|_{x_i \leftarrow 1}$.

A cube p is a Boolean function of the form $(\wedge_{y \in Y} y) \wedge (\wedge_{z \in Z} \neg z)$ such that $Y \cup Z \subseteq X$ and $Y \cap Z = \emptyset$ where Y, Z are sets of variables; moreover, the length of p is denoted $\|p\|$ and defined by $\|p\| = \|Y\| + \|Z\|$. An implicant p of a Boolean function f is a cube p such that $p \models f$. The Boolean function 1 is the cube obtained by putting $Y = Z = \emptyset$. A prime implicant p of a Boolean function f is an implicant p of f such that there exists no other implicant p' of f where $p \models p'$ and $p' \neq p$. Let $primes(f)$ denote the set of prime implicants of the Boolean function f. To illustrate, consider $f = (\neg x_1 \vee \neg x_2) \wedge (\neg x_1 \vee \neg x_3) \wedge (\neg x_3 \vee x_4)$ and $p = (\neg x_1 \wedge \neg x_3)$. Observe that $p \models f$ and therefore p is a implicant of f. Further, suppose $p \models p'$ and $p \neq p'$. Then $p' = \neg x_1$ or $p' = \neg x_3$ and, in either case, $p' \not\models f$. Hence p is a prime implicant of f. In fact, $primes(f) = \{\neg x_1 \wedge \neg x_3, \neg x_2 \wedge \neg x_3, \neg x_1 \wedge x_4\}$. Finally, observe $primes(1) = \{1\}$ and $primes(0) = \emptyset$.

2.2 Binary Decision Diagrams

A Binary Decision Diagram (BDD) [2] is a rooted directed acyclic graph where each internal node is labelled with a variable x_i. Each internal node has one successor node connected via an edge labelled 0, and another successor connected via an edge labelled 1. An external (leaf) node is represented by one of two nodes labelled with the Boolean constants 0 or 1. The Boolean function represented by a BDD can be evaluated for a given variable assignment by traversing the graph from the root, taking the 1 edge at a node when the variable is assigned to 1 and the 0 edge when the variable is assigned to 0. The external node reached in this traversal indicates the value of the Boolean function for the assignment. Observe that each sub-BDD of a BDD also itself represents a Boolean function.

An ROBDD is a BDD that obeys the following restrictions to obtain a canonical representation and thereby permit constant-time equivalence checks. Firstly, the label of a node x_i is always less than the label x_j of any internal node immediately reachable via its successors, that is, $i < j$. Secondly, there can exist no sub-ROBDD that is rooted at a node labelled with x_i that represents the function f such that $f|_{x_i \leftarrow 0} = f|_{x_i \leftarrow 1}$. Thirdly, there are no two nodes labelled with the same variable that have identical successor nodes.

3 Specification of the Widening

To decouple the widening from implementation concerns, we first specify how to widen Boolean functions for both space and time using prime implicants.

3.1 Widening for Space

The ROBDD approximation algorithms of Shiple [21] and Ravi et al [18] seek to improve the density of an ROBDD which is defined as the ratio of minterms in the represented function to the number of nodes in the representing ROBDD. Both algorithms identify the non-dense sub-ROBDDs within a ROBDD and substitute them with other sub-ROBDDs which are denser and yet possess more models. Ultimately this culminates in a dense upper-approximation. Although this approach is well-intended, density comparisons and ROBDD restructuring is limited to those sub-ROBDDs that actually arise in the ROBDD whose presence, in turn, depends on the variable ordering. Our thesis is that prime implicants are natural variable order-independent candidates for reasoning about density. To illustrate this, consider the set of implicants $S = \{p \mid p \models f\}$ of a function f. Any $S' \subseteq S$ is a sound under-approximation of f in the sense that $\vee S' \models f$ yet different S', even of the same size, can yield better approximations. For instance, consider an implicant $p \in S$ and a prime implicant p' strictly contained within it, that is, $p \models p'$ and $p \neq p'$. Then $\|p'\| < \|p\|$. Hence p' contributes $2^{n-\|p'\|}$ minterms to f whereas p contributes only $2^{n-\|p\|}$. Thus p' is a better candidate for inclusion in S' than p. Moreover, since p' is shorter than p, it is likely to contribute a shorter path in an ROBDD that represents $\vee S'$. The following family of widening operators draw together these ideas to compute a sound over-approximation by combining negation with systematic under-approximation.

Definition 1. The family of operators $\nabla_k : Bool_X \to Bool_X$ where $k \in \mathbb{N} \cup \{0\}$ are defined by $\nabla_k(f) = \bigwedge\{\neg p \mid p \in primes(\neg f) \wedge \|p\| \leq k\}$.

The proposition asserts that ∇_k is anti-monotonic in its parameter k and hence ∇_k is uniformly more precise than ∇_{k-1}. Furthermore, in the limit, $\nabla_k(f)$ converges onto f from above. The widening is also monotonic in its argument f.

Proposition 1. Suppose $\|X\| = n$. Then

- If $f \in Bool_X$ then $f = \nabla_n(f) \models \nabla_{n-1}(f) \models \ldots \models \nabla_0(f) = 1$
- If $f, f' \in Bool_X$, $f \models f'$ and $0 \leq k \leq n$ then $\nabla_k(f) \models \nabla_k(f')$.

Proof.

- Since $f = \bigvee primes(f)$ (Blake canonical form [10]), $f = \nabla_n(f)$. Let $0 \leq k < n$. Note $\{\neg p \mid p \in primes(\neg f) \wedge \|p\| \leq k\} \subseteq \{\neg p \mid p \in primes(\neg f) \wedge \|p\| \leq k+1\}$, hence $\nabla_{k+1}(f) \models \nabla_k(f)$. Finally observe $\nabla_0(f) = \bigwedge \emptyset = 1$ as required.
- Let $0 \leq k \leq n$, $p' \in primes(\neg f')$ and $\|p'\| \leq k$. Then $p' \models \neg f' \models \neg f$. There exists $p \in primes(\neg f)$ such that $p' \models p$. Thus $\|p\| \leq \|p'\| \leq k$. Since $p' \models p$, $\neg p \models \neg p'$, hence $\nabla_k(f) = \bigwedge\{\neg p \mid p \in primes(\neg f) \wedge \|p\| \leq k\} \models \neg p'$. Therefore $\nabla_k(f) \models \nabla_k(f')$ as required. $\square$

3.2 Widening for Time

To explain the role of implications in widening for time, consider a chain of functions $\{f_1, f_2, \ldots\} \subseteq Bool_X$ where $f_{i+1} = F(f_i)$ and $F : Bool_X \to Bool_X$ is a monotonic operator. The problem is to extract an invariant from that chain, that is, find a function g such that $f_i \models g$ for all f_i. Such an invariant can be found, whilst applying F only a bounded number of times, by constructing a set of m Boolean functions $S_1 = \{g_1, \ldots, g_m\}$ such that $f_1 \models g_i$ for all g_i. This set is then iteratively pruned until stability is reached. This is realised by constructing $S_{i+1} = \{g \in S_i \mid F(\wedge S_i) \models g\}$. By construction $f_1 \models \wedge S_1$ and, because F is monotonic, it follows by induction that $f_i \models \wedge S_i$. If S_l denotes the limit, that is $S_l = S_{l+1}$, then $f_i \models \wedge S_l$ for all f_i, hence $\wedge S_l$ is an invariant. The key point about this construction is that F is applied at most m iterations rather than possibly $2^{\|X\|}$ times. This gives a performance guarantee and a parameter m that can be increased (if necessary) to improve precision. This merely leaves the problem of constructing S_1.

An uninformed approach to computing S_1 is to extract m arbitrary implicants of $\neg f_1$, that is, $p \models \neg f_1$. Then each $\neg p$ is a clause of f_1. However, consider a prime implicant p' of $\neg f_1$ such that $p \models p'$. Then $\neg p' \models \neg p$, therefore substituting a prime implicant p' for p we obtain a more accurate initial $\wedge S_1$, without increasing its size. This motivates constructing S_1 from prime implicants. Furthermore, consider two prime implicants p and p' such that $\|p'\| < \|p\|$. Then p' is a more propitious candidate for inclusion in S_1 since the clause $\neg p'$ possesses fewer minterms than $\neg p$ which motivates a greedy approach to constructing S_1 in terms of prime implicants of minimal length.

One may wonder whether a bound k on the length of prime implicants, induces a bound on the number m of primes, and hence a bound on the number of iterates. A straightforward relationship between k and m follows from the observation that there are $^nC_1 2^1, {}^nC_2 2^2, \ldots, {}^nC_k 2^k$ different cubes of length $1, 2, \ldots, k$ respectively where $^iC_j = \frac{i!}{(i-j)!j!}$. Hence a bound on m is $\min(\{2^n, \sum_{i=1}^k {}^nC_k 2^k\})$ where $n = \|X\|$. However, by adapting an argument relating to anti-chains of implicants [5, proof of Theorem 2.2], the following tighter bound can be obtained:

Proposition 2. $\|\{p \in primes(f) \mid \|p\| \le k\}\| \le \max(\{^nC_1 2^1, \ldots, {}^nC_k 2^k\})$.

Proof. Let $f \in Bool_X$, $X = \{x_1, \ldots, x_n\}$, C denote the set of cubes over X and $P = \{p \in primes(f) \mid \|p\| \le k\}$. P is anti-chain of $Bool_X$ and also C. It has been shown [14] that in a poset such as $\langle C, \models \rangle$, there exists a maximal anti-chain which is invariant under any isomorphism of C. Let A be such an anti-chain. Now let $c, c' \in A$ such that $\|c\| = \|c'\|$ and consider a mapping $F : Y \to Y$ where $Y = \{x_1, \neg x_1, \ldots, x_n, \neg x_n\}$ such that $F(x_i) = \neg F(\neg x_i)$. Suppose that $F(c) = c'$ where F is extended from Y to C in the natural way. Since F is an automorphism, it follows that $c' \in A$, hence $\{c'' \in C \mid |c| = |c''|\} \subseteq A$. Since A is an anti-chain, then if $p \in C$ and $\|p\| < \|c\|$ then there exists $c'' \in A$ such that $p \models c''$ and $p \ne c''$. Hence $p \notin A$. Similarly, if $\|p\| > \|c\|$ then $p \notin A$. Therefore $\|A\| = {}^nC_{\|c\|} 2^{\|c\|}$ and, since $\|P\| \le \|A\|$, the result follows. □

Whenever $3k \le 2(n+1)$ the above bound on m collapses to $^nC_k 2^k$. This follows since $^nC_1 2^1 \le \ldots \le {}^nC_{k-1} 2^{k-1} \le {}^nC_k 2^k$ iff $\frac{1}{(n-k+1)} \le \frac{2}{k}$ iff $3k \le 2(n+1)$. Because this bound is so conservative, a more pragmatic tactic is needed for generating the shortest m prime implicants. One such tactic is to compute all prime implicants of length 1 for f_1, then all primes whose length does not exceed 2, then all primes whose length does not exceed 3 *etc*, until m prime implicants are discovered. The following section presents new algorithm that is designed for solving this specific form of the prime implicant enumeration problem.

4   Implementation of the Widening

The complexity of finding the shortest prime implicant given a DNF formula over n variables is in $GC(\log^2 n, coNP)$-complete [24], hence at least as hard as $coNP$, and therefore one would expect the widening to be completely intractable. However, Coudert and Madre [8] give an elegant algorithm for computing all the prime implicants of a Boolean function presented as an ROBDD. The primes are, in turn, represented in an ROBDD and hence the complexity of prime enumeration is not necessarily reliant on the number of implicants but the size of the ROBDD. Alas, a detailed analysis of the complexity of this algorithm has not been forthcoming and it is unknown whether the algorithm is polynomial in the size of the input ROBDD [7]. Furthermore, it remains unclear how the results of Umans [24] relate to the complexity of this algorithm.

This section proposes a refinement to the algorithm of Coudert and Madre [8] that enumerates all primes implicants whose length does not exceed k. This refined algorithm can be applied iteratively to find a shortest prime implicant and thus is unlikely to be polynomial. The essence of the Coudert and Madre [8] scheme is a transformation that maps an ROBDD representing f over the variables X to another representing a function f' over the variables $o_1, s_1, \ldots, o_n, s_n$ where $n = \|X\|$. The idea is that any implicant p' of f' can be reinterpreted as a prime implicant of f in the sense that p is a prime implicant of f whenever:

$$p = (\wedge\{x_i \mid p' \models o_i \wedge p' \models s_i\}) \wedge (\wedge\{\neg x_i \mid p' \models o_i \wedge p' \models \neg s_i\})$$

The intuition is that o_i indicates whether the variable x_i occurs within a prime and s_i encodes the polarity of that occurrence. Coudert and Madre [8] present an ROBDD transformation that recursively builds f' from f. Our new insight is that it is possible to build f' from f whilst enforcing the cardinality constraint $\sum_{i=1}^{n} o_i \leq k$. The following algorithm builds toward the refined algorithm by generating an ROBDD which expresses the cardinality constraint. The constraint is realised as a cascade of n full-adders that together output the sum that is expressed in $\lceil \lg(n) \rceil$ bits. These bits are then constrained so as to not exceed k.

Algorithm 1. CONSTRAIN(k)

---

for $i \leftarrow 1$ **to** $\lceil \lg n \rceil$ **do**
  $sum[i] \leftarrow 0$
for $i \leftarrow 1$ **to** n **do**
  $c \leftarrow o_i$
  for $j \leftarrow 1$ **to** $\lceil \lg n \rceil$ **do**
    $c' \leftarrow c \wedge sum[j]$
    $sum[j] \leftarrow sum[j] \oplus c$
    $c \leftarrow c'$
$f \leftarrow 0$
for $i \leftarrow 1$ **to** n **do**
  $f \leftarrow (\neg sum[i] \wedge k[i]) \vee ((sum[i] \leftrightarrow k[i]) \wedge f)$
return f

In the above algorithm, the bound k is represented as an array of $\lceil \lg n \rceil$ bits $k[i]$ such that $k = k[1] + 2k[2] + \ldots + 2^{\lceil \lg n \rceil} k[\lceil \lg n \rceil]$. The first loop initialises the elements of the temporary array $sum[i]$ to $false$. The second loop iteratively calculates $o_1 + \ldots + o_n$ and stores the result in the temporary array sum. The ith iteration of the loop initialises the carry c to be o_i and then proceeds to add the carry into the sum that has accumulated thus far. The formula $sum[j] \oplus c$ merely denotes the exclusive-or of the jth bit of sum with the carry c. The third loop constrains the array sum to not exceed the k vector. Algorithm 2 details how this constraint can be integrated in the algorithm of Coudert and Madre [8]. Because of reasons of space, those readers who wish to follow the structure of the algorithm and the underlying meta-product construct are referred to [8].

Algorithm 2 repeatedly imposes the cardinality constraint which trims the size of all intermediate ROBDDs. The astute reader will notice that each call to PRIMESLEQ operates on a sub-ROBDD that is only defined over $\{x_j, \ldots, x_n\}$.

Algorithm 2. PRIMESLEQ(f, k)

$x_i \leftarrow \text{var}(f)$
$g \leftarrow$ PRIMESLEQ($f|_{x_i \leftarrow 0} \wedge f|_{x_i \leftarrow 1}, k$)
$g' \leftarrow$ PRIMESLEQ($f|_{x_i \leftarrow 1}, k$) $\wedge \neg g$
$g'' \leftarrow$ PRIMESLEQ($f|_{x_i \leftarrow 0}, k$) $\wedge \neg g$
return $((\neg o_i \wedge g) \vee (o_i \wedge s_i \wedge g') \vee (o_i \wedge \neg s_i \wedge g'')) \wedge$ CONSTRAIN(k)

However, CONSTRAIN(k) imposes a constraint over $\{x_1, \ldots, x_n\}$. This is no error since $\sum_{i=1}^{n} o_i \leq k$ entails $\sum_{i=j}^{n} o_i \leq k$ and therefore it is not necessary to manufacture a different cardinality constraint for each level in the ROBDD.

When widening for time, it is necessary to extract m primes from the transformed ROBDD. This can be accomplished by a partial, depth-first traversal that sweeps the ROBDD until m primes have been retrieved. When widening for space, an ROBDD over-approximation is required. The following algorithm details how this can be constructed by applying existential quantification:

Algorithm 3. PRIMES2BDD(f)

---
for $i \leftarrow 0$ **to** n **do**
  $f' \leftarrow \exists_{s_i}(\exists_{o_i}(f \wedge (o_i \rightarrow (x_i \leftrightarrow s_i))))$
  $f \leftarrow f'$
return f

---

5   Experimental Results

To assess the precision and tractability of the widening, it was implemented within the CUDD [22] Decision Diagram package. This package supports the algorithms of Shiple [21] and Ravi *et al.* [18] which, following the CUDD naming scheme, will henceforth be referred to as bddOverApprox and remapOverApprox respectively. Table 1 presents details of the Boolean functions, drawn from the MCNC and ISCAS benchmark circuits, used to assess the widening. For ease of reference, all Boolean functions are labelled with a numeric identifier. The second and third columns give the circuit name and specific output number taken from the circuits; outputs were selected so as to evaluate the widening on ROBDDs with varying size. The fourth, fifth, sixth and seventh columns respectively give the number of variables, number of ROBDD nodes, the number of minterms of the Boolean function represented by the ROBDD and the density of the ROBDD. All experiments were performed on an UltraSPARC IIIi 900MHz based system, equipped with 16GB RAM, running the Solaris 9 Operating System, and using getrusage to calibrate CPU usage in seconds.

5.1   Our Method

The topmost graph of Fig. 1 presents the time required to apply Algorithm 2 and then Algorithm 3 to the benchmarks for various k. (Note that this time is dom-

Table 1. Benchmark formulae

ID	Circuit	#	$\|\mathbf{X}\|$	size	minterms	density
1.	pair	177	51	26253	1.86×10^{14}	7.08×10^{9}
2.		182	53	33190	8.12×10^{14}	2.45×10^{10}
3.	mm9b	420	31	94328	1.61×10^{9}	1.71×10^{4}
4.		421	31	96875	1.62×10^{9}	1.67×10^{4}
5.	s9234	288	76	655192	3.59×10^{22}	5.48×10^{16}
6.		488	75	1304371	1.95×10^{22}	1.49×10^{16}
7.	rot	149	53	1315	5.18×10^{15}	3.94×10^{12}
8.		172	55	1700	1.08×10^{16}	6.35×10^{12}

inated by the cost of applying Algorithm 2 and therefore the times reported in the table closely tally with the times required to apply Algorithm 2 and then walk the ROBDD to extract a bounded number of primes). Interestingly, Coudert and Madre [8] suggest that "[their] procedures have costs that are independent of the sizes of [the prime] sets", "since there is no relation between the size of a set and the size of the [ROBDD] that denotes it". However, this does not square with our results which suggest that the size of the ROBDDs depends, at least to some extent, on the number of primes that it represents. This is witnessed by the sharp increase in runtime that occurs for some circuits as k increases. However, the crucial point is not that the runtime spikes, but the degree of precision achieved before the escalation in complexity. To this end, the middle graph plots the ratio of minterms of the original Boolean function against that of the approximation for increasing values of k. Observe that the quality of the approximation rapidly converges onto 1 as k increases. This suggests the tactic of incrementally increasing k until either the precision is acceptable or a timeout is reached. Applying this tactic achieves precision rates of $70, 80$, and 90% yielding runtimes of less than $5, 20$ and 60 seconds respectively. On the other hand, repeatedly incrementing k until the accumulated runtime exceeds 30 seconds, achieves minterm precision rates for benchmarks 1–8 of $99, 99, 99, 99, 99, 92, 96, 95\%$ respectively. This realises an anytime approach to prime generation and ROBDD approximation in which the quality of the result is limited only be the quantity of resource available. Incrementing k until at least 1024 prime implicants are found (which if anything is rather high for the purposes of analysis), requires the following values of k: 5, 5, 7, 7, 5, 6, 7, 7.

It should be noted that these figures are, if anything, rather pessimistic for many types of program analysis. For example, in the context of groundness analysis that is widely used in logic programming, it has been observed that the vast majority of clauses that arise during analysis are very small in length [13]. This implies that widening with small k is unlikely to have any discernable impact on the overall precision.

The value of an approximation algorithm has traditionally been reported in terms of density [21, 18] which gives an indication as to the compactness of the approximating ROBDD. The lower graph thus reports how the density varies

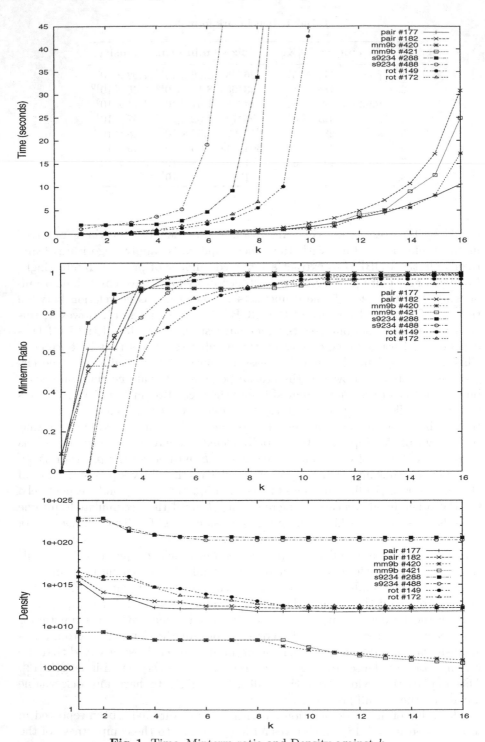

Fig. 1. Time, Minterm ratio and Density against k

with k. By comparing the densities reported in Table 1 against those presented in the graph, it can be seen that the widening can significantly improve on the density of the original ROBDD.

5.2 Comparison Against Existing Methods

Table 2 summaries the results obtained by exercising the `bddOverApprox` and `remapOverApprox` algorithms on the circuits in our benchmark suit. The table is partitioned horizontally, into three groups of rows according to whether the `bddOverApprox` algorithm, `remapOverApprox` algorithm, or the widening algorithm proposed in this paper was applied. The second and third columns give the size of the approximating ROBDD and the number of minterms in its underlying Boolean function. The fourth and fifth columns detail the ratio of these values with respect to the size and number of minterms in the original ROBDD (as given in Table 1). The `bddOverApprox` and `remapOverApprox` algorithms are parameterised by a quality parameter $q \in [0, 1]$, that specifies the minimal acceptable density improvement. That is, these algorithms ensure that the new

Table 2. Comparison of approximation

ID		Approximation		Ratios		Time	Notes
	size	minterms	size	minterms		
[18] 1.	8382	3.40×10^{14}	0.32	1.83	4.61	q: 0.94
2.	9711	1.47×10^{15}	0.29	1.81	6.32	q: 0.84
3.	933	1.88×10^{9}	0.01	1.16	10.85	q: 0.75
4.	722	1.88×10^{9}	0.01	1.16	11.96	q: 0.84
5.	15	5.68×10^{22}	0.01	1.58	1086.12	q: 0.88
6.	11	2.89×10^{22}	0.01	1.49	2321.68	q: 0.92
7.	91	7.30×10^{15}	0.07	1.41	1.13	q: 0.96
8.	838	2.96×10^{16}	0.49	2.75	1.50	q: 0.98
[21] 1.	8385	1.72×10^{15}	0.32	10.85	4.86	q: 0.92
2.	9714	8.06×10^{15}	0.29	9.93	6.35	q: 0.81
3.	933	1.88×10^{9}	0.01	1.16	12.39	q: 0.75
4.	722	1.88×10^{9}	0.01	1.16	13.10	q: 0.84
5.	15	5.68×10^{22}	0.01	1.58	1057.62	q: 0.87
6.	11	2.89×10^{22}	0.01	1.49	2562.30	q: 0.92
7.	168	8.10×10^{15}	0.13	1.56	1.25	q: 0.92
8.	837	1.73×10^{16}	0.49	1.60	1.67	q: 0.94
§3 1.	11027	2.06×10^{14}	0.42	1.11	0.58	k: 5
2.	7301	8.32×10^{14}	0.22	1.03	0.85	k: 6
3.	44334	1.68×10^{9}	0.47	1.02	6.38	k: 12
4.	39718	1.69×10^{9}	0.41	1.05	8.19	k: 11
5.	75	3.64×10^{22}	0.01	1.01	20.36	k: 7
6.	103	1.96×10^{22}	0.01	1.01	47.53	k: 6
7.	289	6.29×10^{15}	0.22	1.21	0.88	k: 7
8.	527	1.09×10^{16}	0.31	1.01	1.66	k: 7

density d' satisfies $q \geq d/d'$ where d is the density of the original ROBDD. As Shiple himself says [21], "The bddUnderApprox method is highly sensitive to the [quality] parameter". Added to this, there is no clear way to choose q so as to obtain a desired reduction in ROBDD size.

For purposes of comparison, we chose to reduce the size of an ROBDD by at least 50%, but ideally not significantly more than 50% (it was the desire to solve this particular analysis problem that motivated this study). Both bddOverApprox and remapOverApprox were called repeatedly under the bisection algorithm to search for a quality value that yielded an acceptable reduction in size. The algorithm terminated when the difference between the high and lower quality bounds was less than 0.01. The notes column gives the particular quality values that achieved the best ROBDD approximation and the time column presents the total time required to call bisection which, of course, was dominated by the time to approximate the ROBDDs. Despite the systematic use of bisection, the reduction in ROBDD size was often significantly more than 50%. This was due to the ROBDD collapsing at certain quality thresholds.

The lower rows of the Table 2 summarise the results of incrementing k until a space reduction of at least 50% was obtained. The notes column gives the required values of k and the cumulative execution time. Observe that the minterm ratios thus obtained compare favourably with those derived using bddOverApprox and remapOverApprox whilst the overall execution time is also reduced. Note that other variable orderings may give different results for the bddOverApprox and remapOverApprox. (As a sanity check, the widening was tested to verify that it delivered the same approximations under different variable orderings.)

6   Related Work

Quite apart from the heuristic algorithms of Shiple [21] and Ravi et al. [18] that both reside in $O(\|G\|^2)$ where $\|G\|$ is the number of nodes in the ROBDD, other less well-known widenings have been proposed in the literature. Mauborgne [15] shows how to perform strictness analysis with an ROBDD variant referred to as a typed decision graph (TDG). Mauborgne advocates widening TDGs for space, using an operator $\nabla(l, f)$ that takes, as input, a TDG that encodes a Boolean function f and returns, as output, a TDG g with at most l nodes such that $f \models g$. The first widening he proposes is in $O(\|G\|^4)$ where $\|G\|$ is the number of nodes in the TDG. To improve efficiency, Mauborgne suggests a second widening that resembles those of Shiple and Ravi et al. This algorithm computes the TDGs $f_1, \ldots, f_n$ obtained by replacing each node i with 1. The f_i are filtered to remove those TDGs whose size exceed $\|G\|/2$. Of the remaining f_i, an f_{max} is selected which "gives best results" and the widening is reapplied to f_{max} if its TDG contains more than l nodes. More recently, Schachte and Søndergaard [20] have presented elegant ROBDD algorithms for approximating functions to various sub-domains of Boolean formulae. Although complexity theoretic issues still remain, these algorithms are potentially useful as widenings.

Algorithm 4. EquivVars(f)

$x_i \leftarrow \mathbf{var}(f)$
if $f|_{x_i \leftarrow 0} = true$ **then**
    return $\langle i, 0, 1 \rangle :: \epsilon$
if $f|_{x_i \leftarrow 1} = true$ **then**
    return $\langle i, 1, 0 \rangle :: \epsilon$
if $f|_{x_i \leftarrow 0} = false$ **then**
    return $\langle i, 1, 0 \rangle ::$EquivVars$(f|_{x_i \leftarrow 1})$
if $f|_{x_i \leftarrow 1} = false$ **then**
    return $\langle i, 0, 1 \rangle ::$EquivVars$(f|_{x_i \leftarrow 0})$
$v_1 \leftarrow \langle i, 0, 1 \rangle ::$EquivVars$(f|_{x_i \leftarrow 0})$
$v_2 \leftarrow \langle i, 1, 0 \rangle ::$EquivVars$(f|_{x_i \leftarrow 1})$
return $\mathtt{anti\_unify}(v_1, v_2)$

The widening presented in this paper relies upon the generation of prime implicants. This problem was first addressed by Quine [17] and, since then, there has been much interest in developing efficient prime implicant enumeration algorithms (interested readers should consult [23] for a detailed history of the problem and known algorithms). Interestingly, the ROBDD literature already suggests an approach to widening ROBDDs that is based on prime implicants (albeit of a restricted form). Bagnara and Schachte [1] propose an $O(n^2 \|G\|)$ ROBDD algorithm for finding all pairs $x, y \in X$ such that $\neg(x \leftrightarrow y) \models f$ where

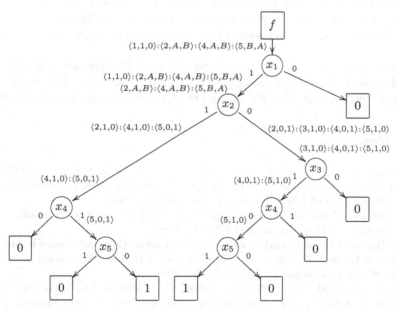

Fig. 2. Algorithm 4 when applied to $f = (x_1 \wedge (x_2 \vee x_3)) \wedge (x_2 \leftrightarrow x_4) \wedge (x_2 \leftrightarrow \neg x_5)$

$n = \|X\|$. The formula $\neg(x \leftrightarrow y) = (x \wedge \neg y) \vee (\neg x \wedge y)$ is actually a quadratic prime implicant and this hints at an ROBDD widening. The algorithm sketched in Algorithm 4 applies Plotkin's anti-unification algorithm [16] to detect all quadratic prime implicants of the form $\neg(x \leftrightarrow y)$ and $(x \leftrightarrow y)$ whilst reducing the complexity from $O(n^2\|G\|)$ [1] to $O(n \lg n\|G\|)$ where n is the number of variables in the ROBDD. A run of the algorithm is illustrated for an ROBDD representing $f = (x_1 \wedge (x_2 \vee x_3)) \wedge (x_2 \leftrightarrow x_4) \wedge (x_2 \leftrightarrow \neg x_5)$. The intuition behind the algorithm is that lists such as $\langle 2, 1, 0 \rangle : \langle 4, 1, 0 \rangle : \langle 5, 0, 1 \rangle$ and $\langle 2, 0, 1 \rangle : \langle 3, 1, 0 \rangle : \langle 4, 0, 1 \rangle :$ $\langle 5, 1, 0 \rangle$ represent $x_2 \wedge x_4 \wedge \neg x_5$ and $\neg x_2 \wedge x_3 \wedge \neg x_4 \wedge x_5$. Anti-unification can then be applied to these lists to obtain $\langle 2, A, B \rangle : \langle 4, A, B \rangle : \langle 5, B, A \rangle$ which encodes $(x_2 \leftrightarrow x_4) \wedge (x_4 \leftrightarrow \neg x_5)$ where A and B are special symbols that represent simple dependencies between variables. The algorithm finally returns a list that represents $x_1 \wedge (x_2 \leftrightarrow x_4) \wedge (x_4 \leftrightarrow \neg x_5)$ which, indeed, is a safe upper approximation of f. By adapting an argument given in [13], it can be shown that this algorithm returns an upper-approximation in a sub-class of Boolean formulae that admits chains of maximal length $2n$. Although not as general as the approach proposed in this paper, this algorithm offers a compromise between efficiency and generality that might suit some analyses [13].

7   Conclusions

The paper has proposed a new widening for ROBDDs and an algorithm for realising it. The widening can be used to either bound the number of times that an ROBDD is updated in an iterative analysis or approximate an ROBDD with another that has a more space-efficient representation. Empirical evidence suggests that the widening is potentially useful and surprisingly tractable.

Acknowledgements. We thank Jacob Howe, Laurent Mauborgne, Axel Simon, Peter Schachte and Harald Søndergaard for useful discussions. This work was funded by EPSRC Grant EP/C015517 and the British Council Grant PN 05.021.

References

[1] R. Bagnara and P. Schachte. Factorizing Equivalent Variable Pairs in ROBDD-Based Implementations of *Pos*. In *Algebraic Methodology and Software Technology*, volume 1548 of *LNCS*, pages 471–485. Springer, 1999.

[2] R. E. Bryant. Graph-based Algorithms for Boolean Function Manipulation. *IEEE Transactions on Computers*, 35(8):677–691, 1986.

[3] R. E. Bryant. On the Complexity of VLSI Implementations and Graph Representations of Boolean Functions with Application to Integer Multiplication. *IEEE Transactions on Computers*, 40(2):205–213, 1991.

[4] J. R. Burch, E. M. Clarke, K. L. McMillan, D. L. Dill, and L. J. Hwang. Symbolic Model Checking: 10^{20} States and Beyond. *Information and Compututation*, 98(2):142–170, 1992.

[5] A. K. Chandra and G. Markowsky. On The Number of Prime Implicants. *Discrete Mathematics*, 24(1):7–11, 1978.

[6] M. Codish. Worst-Case Groundness Analysis using Positive Boolean Functions. *Journal of Logic Programming*, 41(1):125–128, 1999.

[7] O. Coudert. Two Open Questions On ROBDDs and Prime Implicants. http://www.informatik.uni-trier.de/Design_and_Test/abstract30.html.

[8] O. Coudert and J. C. Madre. Implicit and Incremental Computation of Primes and Essential Primes of Boolean Functions. In *Proceedings of the Design Automation Conference*, pages 36–39. IEEE, 1992.

[9] P. Cousot and R. Cousot. Abstract Interpretation: a Unified Lattice Model for Static Analysis of Programs by Construction or Approximation of Fixpoints. In *Symposium on Principles of Programming Languages*, pages 238–252, 1977.

[10] Y. Crama and P. L. Hammer. *Boolean Functions*. To appear.

[11] C. Fecht. *Abstrakte Interpretation logischer Programme: Theorie, Implementierung, Generierung*. PhD thesis, Universität des Saarlandes, 1997.

[12] J. P. Gallagher, K. S. Henriksen, and G. Banda. Techniques for Scaling Up Analyses Based on Pre-interpretations. In *International Conference on Logic Programming*, volume 3668 of *LNCS*, pages 280–296. Springer, 2005.

[13] A. Heaton, M. Abo-Zaed, M. Codish, and A. King. A Simple Polynomial Groundness Analysis for Logic Programs. *Journal of Logic Programming*, 45:143–156, 2000.

[14] D. J. Kleitman, M. Edelberg, and D. Lubell. Maximal Sized Antichains in Partial Orders. *Discrete Mathematics*, 1(1):47–53, 1971.

[15] L. Mauborgne. Abstract Interpretation Using Typed Decision Graphs. *Science of Computer Programming*, 31(1):91–112, 1998.

[16] G. Plotkin. A Note on Inductive Generalisation. In *Machine Intelligence*, volume 5, pages 153–163. Edinburgh University Press, 1970.

[17] W. V. Quine. The Problem of Simplifying Truth Functions. *American Mathematical Monthly*, (52):521–531, 1952.

[18] K. Ravi, K. L. McMillan, T. R. Shiple, and F. Somenzi. Approximation and Decomposition of Binary Decision Diagrams. In *Proceedings of the Design Automation Conference*, pages 445–450. IEEE, 1998.

[19] R. Rudell. Dynamic Variable Ordering for Ordered Binary Decision Diagrams. In *International Conference on Computer-Aided Design*, pages 42–47. IEEE, 1993.

[20] P. Schachte and H. Søndergaard. Closure Operators for ROBDDs. In *Proceedings of the Seventh International Conference on Verification, Model Checking and Abstract Interpretation*, volume 3855 of *LNCS*, pages 1–16. Springer, 2006.

[21] T. R. Shiple. *Formal Analysis of Synchronous Circuits*. PhD thesis, University of California at Berkeley, Electronics Research Laboratory, 1996.

[22] F. Somenzi. CUDD Package, Release 2.4.1. http://vlsi.colorado.edu/~fabio/.

[23] T. Strzemecki. Polynomial-time Algorithms for Generation of Prime Implicants. *ACM Journal of Complexity*, 8(1):37–63, 1992.

[24] C. Umans. On the Complexity and Inapproximability of Shortest Implicant Problems. In *International Colloqium on Automata, Languages and Programming*, volume 1644 of *LNCS*, pages 687–696. Springer, 1999.

[25] J. Whaley and M. S. Lam. Cloning-Based Context-Sensitive Pointer Alias Analysis Using Binary Decision Diagrams. In *Programming Language Design and Implementation*, pages 131–144. ACM Press, 2004.

Efficient Guided Symbolic Reachability Using Reachability Expressions

Dina Thomas[1], Supratik Chakraborty[1], and Paritosh Pandya[2]

[1] Indian Institute of Technology, Bombay, India
dina@cfdvs.iitb.ac.in, supratik@cse.iitb.ac.in
[2] Tata Institute of Fundamental Research, India
pandya@tifr.res.in

Abstract. Asynchronous systems consist of a set of transitions which are non-deterministically chosen and executed. We present a theory of guiding symbolic reachability in such systems by scheduling clusters of transitions. A theory of reachability expressions which specify the schedules is presented. This theory allows proving equivalence of different schedules which may have radically different performance in BDD-based search. We present experimental evidence to show that optimized reachability expressions give rise to significant performance advantages. The profiling is carried out in the NuSMV framework using examples from discrete timed automata and circuits with delays. A variant tool called NuSMV-DP has been developed for interpreting reachability expressions to carry out the experiments.

1 Introduction

Asynchronous systems consist of a set of processes which execute independently of each other and synchronize occasionally. A standard model of their execution consists of non-deterministically interleaving the actions of individual processes. Activities of such processes can be modeled by a *global transition system* consisting of a set of guarded transitions $(G \mapsto A)$. The system starts non-deterministically in one of a set of designated initial states. In any state, one of the enabled transitions is non-deterministically chosen and executed atomically. This causes a state change. This process is then repeated until no new state is reached. Safety verification of such systems typically reduces to exploring whether some undesirable state is reachable by some execution.

Symbolic model checking [7] has emerged as an important technique for program verification and for finding deep logical bugs in reactive systems. Programs are modeled as finite state transition systems. BDD-based [3] symbolic search techniques, e.g. those used in NuSMV [6], can explore very large but finite state spaces efficiently. However, there is wide variability in the computational efficiency of BDD-based searches. It is well-known that the performance of these techniques strongly depends on the size of the BDD representation of transition relations and of intermediate sets of states.

H. Hermanns and J. Palsberg (Eds.): TACAS 2006, LNCS 3920, pp. 120–134, 2006.

Earlier work in this area has addressed this issue by identifying good variable orders for BDDs representing transition relations [1], by partitioning the transition relation conjunctively or disjunctively [8], and by determining good quantification schedules for conjunctive partitioning [4, 5]. Yet another technique is to use guided search where hints [2] are used to direct initial parts of the search.

In this paper, we propose using clusters of individual guarded transitions within the global transition system in ways that generalize conjunctive and disjunctive partitioning. We introduce a notation called *reachability expressions* and investigate its algebraic properties. Each reachability expression denotes a way of computing the set of final states from a set of initial states. Thus, each reachability expression is a predicate transformer. Reachability expressions are rich enough to specify diverse search strategies such as symbolic breadth-first, round-robin etc. They also include familiar operations like sequential composition, union and Kleene closure. Importantly, they allow us to encode more efficient ways of computing the set of reachable states than symbolic breadth-first search.

We have implemented an interpreter for reachability expressions in a tool called NuSMV-DP that works as a wrapper on top of the reachability engine of NuSMV [6]. Using the semantics of reachability expressions, we show that several distinct reachability expressions are equivalent, i.e. they compute the same predicate transformation. However, as our experiments show, the computational effort involved in applying these equivalent predicate transformers to a given predicate using our BDD-based NuSMV-DP tool can vary significantly. We discuss some equivalence transformations which improve the efficiency of evaluating reachability expressions on finite state systems. A Kleene algebra of reachability expressions has also been investigated by Pandya and Raut [9].

We apply our theory to some examples drawn from discrete timed automata. Such automata can be represented as finite state global transition systems, as discussed in [11]. We experimentally evaluate the performance of BDD-based symbolic reachability analysis on these examples using multiple equivalent reachability expressions. A previous technical report [11] gives details of experiments carried out using NuSMV-DP with diverse problems such as the Fischer protocol, the job-shop scheduling problem and some asynchronous circuits with delays. These experiments show a significant improvement in the efficiency of computing reachable states using our technique. For example, we have been able to model check the Fischer protocol with 100 processes, whereas classical techniques such as symbolic search using polyhedra or difference bound matrices can handle instances of this protocol with only up to 20 processes. On other examples, the relative gains are significant but more modest.

The remainder of this paper is organized as follows. In Section 2, we present the basic theory of reachability expressions. Section 3 gives experimental results obtained by applying this theory to improve the efficiency of reachability analysis. The experiments are carried out using the NuSMV-DP tool. Finally, we conclude the paper in Section 4.

2   A Theory of Reachability Expressions

We consider a state transition system as a 4-tuple (V, Q, Q_0, Υ), where V is a finite set of *state variables*, Q is the set of states, $Q_0 \subseteq Q$ is the set of initial states, and Υ is a finite set of *guarded actions*. Each variable $v_i \in V$ has an associated domain $\mathcal{D}_i$. A state $q \in Q$ is an assignment of a value from $\mathcal{D}_i$ to each variable v_i in V. The set of all such assignments constitutes the set of states Q. A *guarded action* is a pair $(G \mapsto A)$, where the guard G denotes a Boolean combination of predicates on the variables in V or a constant in $\{\mathsf{True}, \mathsf{False}\}$. The action A is either a multiple assignment statement denoting simultaneous assignments to a finite set of variables in V, or the special action skip. We leave the concrete syntax of guarded actions unspecified. Note that each state variable $v_i \in V$ may be assigned a value from $\mathcal{D}_i$ at most once in A. The execution semantics of guarded actions is as usual: If A consists of the special action skip, the values of all state variables remain unchanged. If the system is in state s_1, and if the corresponding assignment of values to variables in V satisfies the guard G, we say that the guarded action $(G \mapsto A)$ is *enabled* in state s_1. The new state reached after executing the action A from state s_1 is obtained by simultaneously assigning to all variables that have been assigned in A, their corresponding values. All state variables that have not been assigned in A retain their values from state s_1 in state s_2.

Let $B = (V, Q, Q_0, \Upsilon)$ be a state transition system. We define a *cluster* to be a non-empty set of guarded actions of B. We also define a special singleton set δ consisting of the guarded action $(\mathsf{True} \mapsto \mathsf{skip})$. Thus, the action in δ can be executed from every state, and its execution takes every state to itself. The empty set of guarded actions is denoted by Θ. An *extended cluster* of the state transition system B is either a subset of Υ or δ or Θ. Every extended cluster C defines a relation, R_C, on the set Q of states. We say that $(s_1, s_2) \in R_C$ iff there exists a guarded action $(G \mapsto A) \in C$ such that G evaluates to True in s_1, and action A takes the system from s_1 to s_2. Given an extended cluster T and a set of states $S (\subseteq Q)$, the *image* of S under T is $Im_T(S) = \{s \mid \exists s' \in S, \ R_T(s', s)\}$. It is easy to see that $Im_T : 2^Q \rightarrow 2^Q$ is a monotone function.

2.1   Syntax and Semantics

Let $\mathcal{T} = \{\tau_1, \dots \tau_k\}$ be a set of extended clusters of B. Syntactically, a *reachability expression* over $\mathcal{T}$ is a terminal string obtained from the following grammar:

$$E \ \rightarrow \ E + E \ \mid E \, ; \, E \ \mid E \circ E \ \mid (E) \ \mid {*}E \ \mid \mathbf{T_1} \mid \dots \mid \mathbf{T_k}$$

In the above syntax, we have used $\mathbf{T_1}, \dots, \mathbf{T_k}$ to denote reachability expressions corresponding to the extended clusters $\tau_1, \dots, \tau_k$ in B. We will use this notation throughout this paper.

The notion of evaluating reachability expressions can be formalized by defining their semantics. The semantics of a reachability expression is defined with respect to an underlying state transition system, and is naturally described as a mapping from sets of states to sets of states. Let $B = (V, Q, q_o, \Upsilon)$ be a state transition system, and T be a set of extended clusters of B. Let σ be a reachability expression over T and let $S \subseteq Q$. The semantics of σ with respect to B, denoted by $[\![\sigma]\!]_B$, is a mapping from 2^Q to 2^Q defined inductively as follows. We shall henceforth omit the subscript B when it is clear from the context.

- $[\![T_i]\!](S) = Im_{\tau_i}(S)$, for all $\tau_i \in T$
- $[\![\sigma_1 + \sigma_2]\!](S) = [\![\sigma_1]\!](S) \cup [\![\sigma_2]\!](S)$
- $[\![\sigma_1 \circ \sigma_2]\!](S) = [\![\sigma_2]\!]([\![\sigma_1]\!](S))$
- $[\![\sigma_1 ; \sigma_2]\!](S) = [\![(\sigma_1 + \delta) \circ (\sigma_2 + \delta)]\!](S)$
- $[\![(\sigma)]\!](S) = [\![\sigma]\!](S)$
- $[\![*\sigma]\!](S) = \bigcup_{i=0}^{\infty} [\![(\sigma)^i]\!](S)$

Although ";" is seen to be a derived operator, we retain it for notational convenience.

2.2 Properties of Reachability Expressions

Let σ_1 and σ_2 be reachability expressions over a set T of symbolic extended clusters. We say that σ_1 is *covered by* σ_2 iff $[\![\sigma_1]\!]_B(S) \subseteq [\![\sigma_2]\!]_B(S)$ for every state transition system B, for every subset S of states of B, and for every instantiation of symbolic clusters in T with extended clusters of B. We denote this by $\sigma_1 \sqsubseteq \sigma_2$. We say that $\sigma_1 = \sigma_2$, iff $\sigma_1 \sqsubseteq \sigma_2$ and $\sigma_2 \sqsubseteq \sigma_1$. For example, it can be shown from the semantics of reachability expressions that $(\sigma_1 ; \sigma_2) = \delta + \sigma_1 + \sigma_2 + (\sigma_1 \circ \sigma_2)$.

Given a set T of extended clusters, let $\Pi(T)$ denote the set of all reachability expressions over T. It can be shown that $(\Pi(T), +)$ forms an idempotent, commutative monoid with Θ as the identity element. Similarly, $(\Pi(T), \circ)$ forms a monoid with δ as the identity element, and $(\Pi(T), +, \circ)$ forms an idempotent semiring. In particular, "$\circ$" distributes over "$+$" from both left and right. Detailed proofs of these properties are given in the extended version of this paper [10].

Lemma 1. *Let $\sigma_1, \sigma_2, \sigma_3, \sigma_4$ be reachability expressions.*

(a) If $\sigma_1 \sqsubseteq \sigma_2$ and $\sigma_3 \sqsubseteq \sigma_4$, then $(\sigma_1 \; op \; \sigma_3) \sqsubseteq (\sigma_2 \; op \; \sigma_4)$, where $op \in \{+, \circ, ; \}$.
(b) $(\sigma_1 ; \sigma_2)^i \sqsubseteq (\sigma_1 ; \sigma_2)^{i+1}$ for all $i \geq 0$.
(c) If $\sigma_1 \sqsubseteq \sigma_2$, then $(\sigma_1)^i \sqsubseteq (\sigma_2)^i$ for all $i \geq 0$, and $(*\sigma_1) \sqsubseteq (*\sigma_2)$.
(d) $(*\sigma_1)^i = (*\sigma_1)$ for all $i \geq 1$, and $*(*\sigma_1) = (*\sigma_1)$.

Proof sketch. Part (a) follows from the semantics of reachability expressions. Parts (b) through (d) are proved by induction on i. Detailed proofs are given in the extended version of this paper [10].

Lemma 2. *For all reachability expressions σ_1 and σ_2, $*(\sigma_1 ; \sigma_2) = *(\sigma_1 ; (*\sigma_2)) = *((*\sigma_1) ; \sigma_2) = *((*\sigma_1) ; (*\sigma_2))$.*

Proof sketch. By the semantics of "$*$", we have $\sigma_2 \sqsubseteq (*\sigma_2)$. Therefore, by Lemma 1(a), $(\sigma_1 ; \sigma_2) \sqsubseteq (\sigma_1 ; (*\sigma_2))$, and by Lemma 1(c), $*(\sigma_1 ; \sigma_2) \sqsubseteq *(\sigma_1 ; (*\sigma_2))$.

To show that $*(\sigma_1 ; (*\sigma_2)) \sqsubseteq *(\sigma_1 ; \sigma_2)$, we first prove that $(\sigma_1 ; (*\sigma_2)) \sqsubseteq *(\sigma_1 ; \sigma_2)$. Details of this proof are available in the extended version of our paper [10].

Applying Lemmas 1(c) and (d), we then get $*(\sigma_1 ; (*\sigma_2)) \sqsubseteq *(\sigma_1 ; \sigma_2)$. Since we also have $*(\sigma_1 ; \sigma_2) \sqsubseteq *(\sigma_1 ; (*\sigma_2))$, it follows that $*(\sigma_1 ; \sigma_2) = *(\sigma_1 ; (*\sigma_2))$. The proof of $*(\sigma_1 ; \sigma_2) = *((*\sigma_1) ; \sigma_2)$ is similar with the roles of σ_1 and σ_2 interchanged.

If we substitute $*\sigma_1$ for σ_1 in the result proved above, we get $*((*\sigma_1) ; \sigma_2) = *((*\sigma_1) ; (*\sigma_2))$. However, $*((*\sigma_1) ; \sigma_2) = *(\sigma_1 ; \sigma_2)$, as argued above. Therefore, $*(\sigma_1 ; \sigma_2) = *((*\sigma_1) ; (*\sigma_2))$.

Theorem 1. *Let $\{\sigma_1, \ldots, \sigma_k\}$, $k \geq 1$, be a finite set of reachability expressions. Then* $*(\sigma_1 + \cdots + \sigma_k) = *(\sigma_1 ; \cdots ; \sigma_k)$.

Proof sketch. We prove the theorem by induction on k.
Basis $(k = 1)$: The result holds trivially.
Hypothesis: Assume the result holds for all k in 1 through m.
Induction step: Consider a set of $m + 1$ reachability expressions, and let $\sigma_Y = (\sigma_2 + \cdots + \sigma_{m+1})$. We first prove that $*(\sigma_1 + \sigma_Y) = *(\sigma_1 ; \sigma_Y)$. Details of this proof are given in the extended version of this paper [10].

By Lemma 2, we know that $*(\sigma_1 ; \sigma_Y) = *(\sigma_1 ; (*\sigma_Y))$. By the induction hypothesis, $(*\sigma_Y) = (*\sigma_Z)$, where $\sigma_Z = (\sigma_2 ; \ldots ; \sigma_{m+1})$. Therefore, $*(\sigma_1 + \sigma_Y) = *(\sigma_1 ; (*\sigma_Z))$. Applying Lemma 2 again, we get $*(\sigma_1 + \sigma_Y) = *(\sigma_1 ; \sigma_Z)$. The proof is completed by noting that "$+$" and "$;$" are associative.

Theorem 2. *Let $\{\sigma_1, \ldots, \sigma_k\}$, $k \geq 2$, be a finite set of reachability expressions. Let $\sigma_Y = (\sigma_1 + \cdots + \sigma_k)$ and $\sigma_Z = (\sigma_1 ; \cdots ; \sigma_k)$.*

(a) For all $n \geq 0$, $(\overset{n}{\underset{j=0}{+}} (\sigma_Y)^j) \sqsubseteq (\sigma_Z)^n$.

(b) Furthermore, if $(\sigma_p)^2 \sqsubseteq \sigma_p$ for all p, then $(\overset{n}{\underset{j=0}{+}} (\sigma_Y)^j) \sqsubseteq (\sigma_Z)^{n-(\lfloor n/k \rfloor -1)}$.

Proof sketch.

(a) Since $\sigma_Y \sqsubseteq \sigma_Z$, by Lemma 1(c), $(\sigma_Y)^j \sqsubseteq (\sigma_Z)^j$ for all $j \geq 0$. Therefore, $(\overset{n}{\underset{j=0}{+}} (\sigma_Y)^j) \sqsubseteq (\overset{n}{\underset{j=0}{+}} (\sigma_Z)^j)$. Applying Lemma 1(b), it can now be shown that $(\overset{n}{\underset{j=0}{+}} (\sigma_Z)^j) = \sigma_Z^n$. Hence, $(\overset{n}{\underset{j=0}{+}} (\sigma_Y)^j) \sqsubseteq \sigma_Z^n$.

(b) Let $n = k.i + r$, where $i \geq 0$ and $0 \leq r < k$. Using induction on k, it can be shown that $(\overset{k.i}{\underset{j=0}{+}} (\sigma_Y)^j) \sqsubseteq (\sigma_Z)^{(k-1).i+1}$ for $k \geq 2$. The detailed proof is presented in the extended version of this paper [10].

Since $(\overset{k.i+r}{\underset{j=0}{+}} (\sigma_Y)^j) = (\overset{k.i}{\underset{j=0}{+}} (\sigma_Y)^j) \circ (\overset{r}{\underset{j=0}{+}} (\sigma_Y)^j)$ and $(\overset{r}{\underset{j=0}{+}} (\sigma_Y)^j) \sqsubseteq \sigma_Z^r$ (by Theorem 2(a)), we can apply Lemma 1(a) to show that $(\overset{k.i+r}{\underset{j=0}{+}} (\sigma_Y)^j) \sqsubseteq \sigma_Z^{(k-1).i+1} \circ \sigma_Z^r = \sigma_Z^{(k.i+r-(i-1))}$. The theorem is proved by noting that $k.i + r = n$ and $i = \lfloor n/k \rfloor$.

Let $B = (V, Q, Q_0, \Upsilon)$ be a finite state transition system, and let $\{\tau_1, \ldots \tau_k\}$ be a set of extended clusters, satisfying $\bigcup_{i=1}^{k} \tau_i = \Upsilon$. From the definition of the semantics of reachability expressions, the set of reachable states of B, denoted $reach(B)$, is given by $[\![*(\mathbf{T_1} + \cdots + \mathbf{T_k})]\!] (Q_0)$. By Theorem 1, this is also given by $[\![*(\mathbf{T_1} ; \ldots ; \mathbf{T_k})]\!] (Q_0)$. Furthermore, Theorem 2(a) guarantees that the number of image computation iterations using $*(\mathbf{T_1} ; \ldots ; \mathbf{T_k})$ never exceeds that required with $*(\mathbf{T_1} + \cdots + \mathbf{T_k})$. Therefore, if computing $[\![(\sigma_Y)^{i+1}]\!] (S)$ and computing $[\![(\sigma_Z)^{i+1}]\!] (S)$ (using the terminology of Theorem 2) are of comparable complexity, it is advantageous to use $*(\mathbf{T_1} ; \ldots ; \mathbf{T_k})$. This advantage is also demonstrated by our experiments, as reported in Section 3. If $(\sigma_p)^2 \sqsubseteq \sigma_p$ for all p, Theorem 2(b) improves the upper bound of Theorem 2(a) even further. Note that we can have $(\sigma_p)^2 \sqsubseteq \sigma_p$ under several circumstances, e.g. if σ_p is of the form $*\sigma_q$.

Theorem 3. *Let $B = (V, Q, Q_0, \Upsilon)$ be a finite state transition system with extended clusters $\{\tau_1, \ldots \tau_k\}$, such that $\bigcup_{i=1}^{k} \tau_i = \Upsilon$ and $\mathbf{T_k} \not\sqsubseteq *(\mathbf{T_1} + \cdots + \mathbf{T_{k-1}})$. Let σ_X denote $(\mathbf{T_1} + \cdots + \mathbf{T_{k-1}})$, and $\widehat{\sigma}$ denote $(*\sigma_X) \circ *(\mathbf{T_k} ; (*\sigma_X))$.*

(a) $[\![\widehat{\sigma}]\!] (Q_0) = reach(B)$.

(b) Let σ be any reachability expression over $\{\tau_1, \ldots \tau_k\}$ such that $[\![\sigma]\!] (Q_0) = reach(B)$. Let $N_k(\sigma, Q_0)$ denote the number of times image under $\mathbf{T_k}$ is computed until the complete set of states reachable from Q_0 is obtained during evaluation of $[\![\sigma]\!] (Q_0)$. Then $N_k(\widehat{\sigma}, Q_0) \leq N_k(\sigma, Q_0) + 1$.

Proof sketch.

(a) From Lemma 2 and Theorem 1, $*(\mathbf{T_k} ; (*\sigma_X)) = *(\mathbf{T_k} ; \sigma_X) = *(\mathbf{T_k} + \sigma_X)$. Since $\delta \sqsubseteq *\sigma_X$, by composing both sides with $*(\mathbf{T_k} + \sigma_X)$ (or, equivalently with $*(\mathbf{T_k} ; (*\sigma_X))$) and by applying Lemma 1(a), we get $*(\mathbf{T_k} + \sigma_X) \sqsubseteq (*\sigma_X) \circ *(\mathbf{T_k} ; (*\sigma_X))$. Therefore, $*(\mathbf{T_k} + \sigma_X) \sqsubseteq \widehat{\sigma}$. However, $\widehat{\sigma} \sqsubseteq *(\mathbf{T_k} + \sigma_X)$. Hence, $\widehat{\sigma} = *(\mathbf{T_k} + \sigma_X)$. Since $[\![*(\mathbf{T_k} + \sigma_X)]\!] (Q_0)) = reach(B)$, it follows that that $[\![\widehat{\sigma}]\!] (Q_0) = reach(B)$.

(b) Let σ be an arbitrary reachability expression over $\{\tau_1, \ldots, \tau_k\}$ such that $[\![\sigma]\!] (Q_0) = reach(B)$. The theorem is proved by showing that the computation of the set of reachable states with σ can be mimicked by $\widehat{\sigma}$ with no more than $N_k(\sigma, Q_0) + 1$ iterations of evaluation of $(\mathbf{T_k} ; (*\sigma_X))$. Details of the proof are given in the extended version of this paper [10].

Given a finite-state system, Theorem 3 gives us a reachability expression that guarantees that the number of image computations under τ_k is at worst 1 more than the minimum number needed to compute the reachable state space using any reachability expression. This is particularly useful when we have clusters with disparate image computation costs. For example, when performing reachability analysis of a network of timed automata, the discrete (or non-time-elapse) transitions of individual automata might be represented by τ_1 through τ_{k-1}, while a combined time-elapse transition for all automata might be represented by τ_k. Since clocks of all automata change synchronously, computing the image under τ_k requires synchronizing all the processes and updating the clocks of *all* automata, unlike computing the image under τ_1 through τ_{k-1}. Consequently, image computation under τ_k is expected to be more expensive (in terms of memory usage and CPU time) in general compared to image computation under τ_1 through τ_{k-1}. In such cases, it may be advantageous to minimize the number of expensive image computations by application of Theorem 3(b).

Often the set of extended clusters in a state transition system are related in such a way that starting from an initial set of states S_0, if we compute the image under a cluster σ_j, no *new* states are reached unless the image under another cluster σ_i has already been computed. As an illustration, consider a combinational circuit in which the behaviour of each gate is modeled as a finite state transition system. Suppose the circuit contains a single-input gate g_1 that is fed by another gate g_2. Suppose further that the circuit starts from a stable internal state (i.e., the output of no gate is scheduled to change). The inputs of the circuit are then changed after some delay, leading to a new state. If we compute the image of this new state under a cluster modeling the behaviour of g_1, the set of reachable states cannot change unless the image under clusters corresponding to g_2 has already been computed. The following theorem shows that such dependencies can be exploited to simplify reachability expressions.

Theorem 4. *Let* $\{\sigma_1, \ldots \sigma_k\}$ *be a set of extended clusters and S be a set of states satisfying the following conditions:*

C1: $(\sigma_i \circ ((*\sigma_{i+1}) \circ \cdots (*\sigma_k)) \circ \sigma_i) \sqsubseteq (\sigma_i \circ ((*\sigma_i) \circ \cdots (*\sigma_k)))$ *for all* $1 \leq i < k$.
C2: There exists m, $1 \leq m \leq k$ such that
    C21: $(\sigma_i \circ \sigma_j) \sqsubseteq (\sigma_i + \sigma_j)$ *for* $1 \leq i, j \leq m$ *and* $i \neq j$.
    C22: $[\![*\sigma_i]\!] (S) = S$, *for all* $i > m$.

Then $[\![*(\sigma_1; \cdots; \sigma_k)]\!] (S) = [\![(*\sigma_1); \cdots; (*\sigma_k)]\!] (S)$.

Proof sketch. We first note that $[\![*(\sigma_1; \cdots \sigma_k)]\!] (S) = [\![*((*\sigma_1); \cdots; (*\sigma_k))]\!] (S)$ by Lemma 2. The theorem is then proved by using induction on r to show that $[\![((*\sigma_1); \cdots; (*\sigma_k))^r]\!] (S) \sqsubseteq [\![(*\sigma_1); \cdots; (*\sigma_k)]\!] (S)$ for all $r \geq 0$. Details of the proof are given in the extended version of this paper [10].

Condition C1 in Theorem 4 formalizes an ordering of dependencies between the σ_i's. Effectively, C1 states that the effect of computing the image under expressions $\{\sigma_{i+1}, \ldots \sigma_k\}$ does not affect the computation of image under σ_i for all $1 \leq i < k$. Condition C21 asserts that the first few expressions in the above ordering do not depend on any other expressions. Hence, computing the image under the composition of two such expressions gives the same result as computing the image under the expressions individually and then taking their union. Condition C22 states an additional ordering requirement: unless the image of S under one of $\{\sigma_1, \ldots \sigma_m\}$ is computed, the reachability expressions $\{\sigma_{m+1}, \ldots \sigma_k\}$ do not result in any new states being reached. If all three conditions are satisfied, Theorem 4 permits a simplification in the computation of reachable states. In particular, it allows us to obtain the entire set of reachable states by computing the reachable states under each σ_i only once.

3   Experimental Results and Their Analysis

In the previous section, we presented theorems on reachability expressions which embody heuristic strategies for improving the efficiency of symbolic search. These include strategies such as replacing symbolic breadth-first search by round-robin search, and minimizing the number of applications of costly transitions. In order to evaluate the effectiveness of these heuristics, we have implemented an inter-preter for reachability expressions in a tool called NuSMV-DP. Our tool acts as a wrapper on top of the reachability analysis engine of NuSMV [6]. It takes as inputs: (a) a description of a finite state transition system as a collection of named clusters, (b) a reachability expression, and (c) an initial set of states. Our tool explores the reachable state space according to the reachability expression and reports performance statistics on termination of the search.

Brief overview of example suite: We have used two classes of examples for our experiments – Fischer protocol and gate-level circuits with delays. Our choice of examples is motivated by their popularity in the domain of timed system analysis, and also by the ease of scaling their sizes.

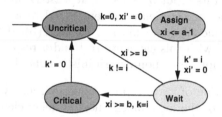

Fig. 1. Fischer's mutual exclusion protocol

Fischer protocol: This is a distributed timed protocol used to ensure mutual exclusion when a number of processes access a shared resource. Each process P_i is modeled as a timed automaton, as shown in Figure 1, where x_i is the clock of P_i and k is a shared variable for communication between processes. In Figure 1, a and b are integer constants that bound the time spent by each process in the "Assign" and "Wait" states. For an n-process Fischer protocol, a network of timed automata is obtained by asynchronous parallel composition of n automata. Details of the model can be found in our technical report [11].

A natural clustering for an n-process Fischer protocol is to have one cluster per process, containing all *discrete* or non-time-elapse guarded actions of the process. Additionally, we must have one cluster containing the guarded action representing the synchronous advancement of time for all processes.

Circuits with inertial and bi-bounded delays: Our second set of examples consists of gate-level circuits. Each gate is modeled as consisting of three parts:

– A *boolean logic block* that gives the boolean value of the output as a function of the boolean values of the inputs.

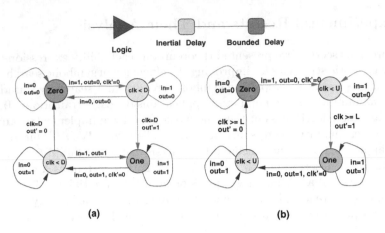

Fig. 2. (a) Inertial delay model (b) Bi-bounded pure delay model

- The output of the logic block is fed to an *inertial delay element* modeled as in Figure 2(a). If the inertial delay is D, the output of this element changes only if a change in its input persists for at least D units of time.
- The output of the inertial delay element is fed to a *bi-bounded pure delay element* which is modeled as shown in Figure 2(b). If the lower and upper bounds associated with this element are l and u respectively, it delays each transition on its input by a non-deterministic delay between l and u units.

Given an interconnection of gates representing a circuit, we compose the state transition behaviours of the logic block, inertial delay element and bi-bounded delay element of each gate to form a network of timed automata. To simplify the model, we assume that D, l and u are identical for all gates. To ensure that every pure delay element causes its output to change once between two consecutive changes at its input, we also assume that $u < D$. When the output of a gate feeds the input of another gate, we ensure during composition that the corresponding output and input transitions occur simultaneously. Time is assumed to flow synchronously for all gates.

A natural clustering for an n-gate circuit modeled as above is to have a cluster for the discrete (non-time-elapse) transitions of each logic function, inertial and bi-bounded delay element, and an additional cluster for the synchronous advancement of time for all clocks. When the output of a gate feeds the input of another gate, we must combine the corresponding guarded actions at the output and input. For our experiments, the circuit inputs are modeled as signals that non-deterministically change their boolean values after a predefined delay Δ_{in}. The exact circuits used in our experiments as well as details about our model can be found in [11]. For both classes of examples, we assume that time is discrete, and model the timed behaviour using bounded-counter automata.

Performance comparisons: For the examples described above, let $\{\tau_1, \ldots, \tau_k\}$ be the set of extended clusters representing non-time-elapse transitions, and let

τ_t be the cluster representing synchronous advancement of time. Let Γ be the monolithic transition relation obtained by combining all transitions into a single cluster. Then, the reachability expression $S_0 = *\Gamma$ mimics symbolic breadth-first search using this monolithic transition relation, as in the original NuSMV tool. Γ can also be disjunctively partitioned into its component clusters and the image computed using the reachability expression $S_1 = *(\mathbf{T_1} + \cdots + \mathbf{T_k} + \mathbf{T_t})$. While this reduces the effort for each image computation, the number of image computations increases significantly. To control this, we apply Theorem 2, and consider the reachability expression $S_2 = *(\mathbf{T_1} ; \cdots ; \mathbf{T_k} ; \mathbf{T_t})$ instead.

We have experimentally profiled the performance of reachability analysis using the expressions S_0, S_1 and S_2. All our experiments were run on a 3 GHz Intel Pentium 686 processor with 1 GB of main memory, and running Fedora Core Linux 3.4.3-6.fc3.

For the Fischer protocol examples, we computed the set of backward reachable states starting from a set of states in which mutual exclusion is violated. For simplicity, the parameters a and b were set to 1 and 2 respectively, for all processes. The results are shown as bar graphs in Figures 3 and 4. The total number of image computation iterations needed to compute the reachable states using S_0, S_1 and S_2 respectively are shown as triples within parentheses along the abscissa in Figure 3. The missing data corresponds to experiments that did not terminate in 30 minutes. For the circuit examples, we computed the set of forward reachable states starting from a given set of initial states. The results are shown as bar graphs in Figures 5 and 6. In these figures, bar graphs corresponding to experiments on the same circuit but with different values of the parameters l, u, D and Δ_{in} have been grouped together. The total number of image computation iterations needed to compute the reachable states using S_1 and S_2 respectively are shown as comma-separated pairs along the abscissa in Figure 5. For each circuit with r different combinations of l, u, D and Δ_{in} (r ranges from 2 to 4 in our experiments), there are r sets of bar graphs and r lines of comma-separated pairs above the circuit's name. The ith pair from the top and the ith set of bar graphs from the left represent data obtained with the same set of parameters for a given circuit. The number of iterations using S_0 and S_1 were identical for all our circuit experiments. Details of the parameter values used for each circuit are available in a detailed version of this paper [10].

In Figures 3 and 5, "Time (s)" denotes the time in seconds to compute the reachable state space. In Figures 4 and 6, "max BDD" denotes the maximum number of BDD nodes required to store the (partially computed) state space at any time during the state space search.

It can be seen that unguided disjunctive partitioning of the transition relation, as in S_1, results in worse performance than reachability search using a monolithic transition relation. In the absence of guidance, disjunctive partitioning is, therefore, not an effective strategy. Theorem 2 guarantees that S_2 requires no more iterations of image computation than S_1. This is clearly seen in the iteration counts in Figures 3 and 5. A reduction in CPU time is expected from the combined effect of fewer iterations and operations on smaller BDDs. In the

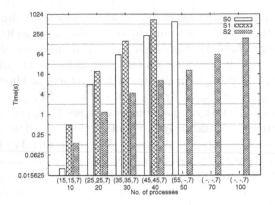

Fig. 3. Analysis of Fischer processes: Time and iteration counts for S_0, S_1, S_2

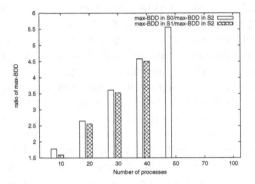

Fig. 4. Analysis of Fischer processes: Ratios of "max BDD"

Fischer protocol examples, S_2 has the best performance. The only exception is the example with 10 processes. Here, the BDDs are small even when using S_0, and no significant gains are obtained by decomposing the transition relation. Instead, iterating through the clusters incurs time overhead when using S_2. For circuits, the ratios in Figure 6 are always greater than 1. Thus, S_2 results in the minimum "max BDD" value. However, as seen in Figure 5, circuits 6, 7 and 8 show better performance using S_0 with respect to time. These circuits were found to have very low "max BDD" values compared to the largest transition cluster size. This is in contrast to circuits 2, 3 and 4 where this ratio was much higher. Therefore, unlike in circuits 2, 3 and 4, BDD sizes of partially computed state sets do not significantly influence the performance of reachability analysis in circuits 6, 7 and 8. Since the largest transition cluster size is large compared to "max BDD", reducing the total number of image computation iterations gives better performance. Thus S_0 performs better than S_2 for circuits 6, 7 and 8.

The BDD representation of the cluster "τ_t" is usually larger than that of other τ_i's since the transitions in τ_t involve clock variables of *all* processes. These large BDDs, in turn, lead to higher costs for computing the image under τ_t vis-a-vis the cost of computing the image under a τ_i. We have seen above that Theorem 3

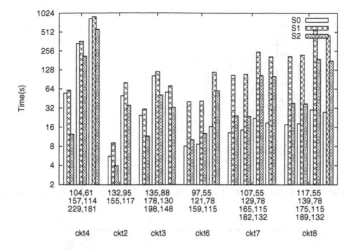

Fig. 5. Analysis of circuits: Time and iteration counts for S_1, S_2. Iteration counts for S_0 are identical to those for S_1.

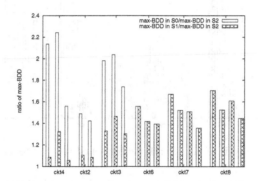

Fig. 6. Analysis of circuits: Ratios of "max BDD"

gives us a way to reduce the number of costly image computations, potentially leading to performance improvements. To validate this experimentally, we measured and recorded the performance of computing the reachable state set using a reachability expression obtained from Theorem 3. In the Fischer protocol examples, the size of the BDD representation of τ_t is comparable to that of the other τ_i clusters. Hence, the effect of minimizing applications of τ_t does not produce a significant performance difference for the Fischer examples, and we report results for only the circuits. Let $\sigma_x = (\mathbf{T_1} ; \cdots ; \mathbf{T_k})$ and let $S_3 = (*\sigma_x) \circ *(\mathbf{T_t} ; (*\sigma_x))$. As seen in Theorem 3, S_3 minimizes the number of image computations under τ_t (up to 1 additional computation). We now compare its performance with an equivalent schedule S_4, which is defined as: $S_4 = *(\mathbf{T_1} ; \cdots ; \mathbf{T_k} ; *\mathbf{T_t})$.

Figure 7 shows the ratios of "max BDD" using S_4 to that using S_3 for the circuit examples. For each circuit, we used different sets of delay parameters, as in the earlier experiments. Within the set of experiments for each circuit, the

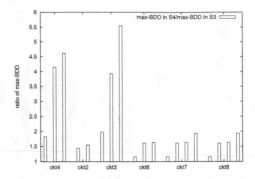

Fig. 7. Analysis of circuits: Ratios of "max BDD" using S_4 to that using S_3

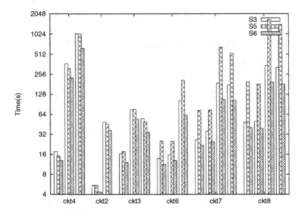

Fig. 8. Analysis of circuits: Time for schedules S_3, S_5 and S_6

number of image computations under τ_t until all reachable states are computed, increases from left to right for both S_4 and S_3. As the number of computations increases, the effect of minimizing applications of τ_t becomes more pronounced, as can be seen from the rising ratio of "max BDD" using S_4 to that using S_3.

Theorem 4 relates to the effect of applying a sequence of clusters consistently with the topological dependencies between them. To evaluate the effectiveness of this Theorem, we performed an additional set of experiments with the circuit examples. In these examples, one can obtain a topological ordering of the gates and circuit elements from the inputs to the outputs. When computing this order, a sub-circuit with a loop must be considered as a single circuit element without exposing the loop. Since the output of each gate/circuit element is fed to a gate or element with a higher topological index, there is an ordering of dependencies between the non-time-elapse clusters τ_i. By choosing the initial state S to be such that all gates are stable (i.e. no gate is scheduled to change its output), we ensure that condition C22 required in Theorem 4 is satisfied.

Let the input-to-output topological ordering of the non-time-elapse clusters be $\tau_1 < \cdots < \tau_k$. Let $\sigma_x = (\mathbf{T_1} ; \cdots ; \mathbf{T_k})$ as before, and let $\sigma_y = (\mathbf{T_k} ; \cdots ; \mathbf{T_1})$

compute images of the clusters in reverse topological order. Moreover, let $\sigma_z = (*\mathbf{T_1} \,; \cdots \,; *\mathbf{T_k})$. Then, by Theorem 1, we have $*\sigma_x = *\sigma_y$ and by Theorem 4, we have $*\sigma_x = \sigma_z$. Earlier, we have considered the reachability expression $S_3 = (*\sigma_x) \circ *(\mathbf{T_t} \,; (*\sigma_x))$ that minimizes (up to 1 additional computation) the number of image computations under time transition cluster τ_t. We now consider the reachability expressions $S_5 = (*\sigma_y) \circ *(\mathbf{T_t} \,; (*\sigma_y))$ and $S_6 = \sigma_z \circ *(\mathbf{T_t} \,; \sigma_z)$. Using the above mentioned identities, it is easy to see that that $S_3 = S_5 = S_6$, i.e. all three reachability expressions compute the same set of reachable states.

Using S_3, S_5, and S_6 in the circuit examples, "max BDD" was found to be nearly identical. However, the CPU times were different because of additional fix-point checks in S_5 and S_3 compared to those in S_6. In Figure 8, the circuits are arranged from left to right in order of increasing topological depth. The increased number of fix-point checks due to an increase in the number of ordered clusters results in the increased time difference between schedules S_5 and S_3 from circuit 4 to 8 as seen in Figure 8. For circuits with short topological depth, the performance of S_5 and S_3 are similar. However, as the topological depth increases, computing images in topologically sorted order leads to significant improvements compared to computing in reverse topological order. Furthermore, S_6 improves over S_3, albeit marginally, in most cases. This is because all clusters τ_i other than the time transition cluster τ_t are self-disabling; hence computing the image under $\mathbf{T_i}$ and $*\mathbf{T_i}$ require similar computational effort.

4   Discussion and Conclusion

Reachability expressions give the user the ability to specify the heuristics of symbolic state space search. Semantically equivalent reachability expressions can have radically different costs of computation. In this paper, we presented a theory to reason about the equivalence and relative performance of alternative reachability expressions, and validated our predictions with experiments.

Our experimental investigations indicate that when the absolute size of the BDD representation of a monolithic transition relation is small, it is advantageous to perform classical symbolic breadth-first search using the monolithic relation directly. Similarly, when the maximum BDD size encountered in representing (partially) computed state sets is small compared to the BDD size of the monolithic transition relation or the BDD size of the largest transition cluster, it helps to minimize the number of image computation iterations by using classical symbolic breadth-first search. However, if the maximum BDD size for representing (partially) computed state sets is large and there is a dominant cluster represented as a large BDD, it is advantageous to adopt a round-robin scheduling of clusters in a way that minimizes the image computations under the dominant cluster. Further, in round-robin scheduling, ordering the clusters in topological order is effective in examples such as deep circuits, which have considerable forward propagation of events.

The experiments and conclusions reported in this paper are promising, although preliminary. Much more data on a wider set of examples is needed before a comprehensive evaluation of the effectiveness of reachability expressions in improving the performance of state space search can be done. However, we believe that reachability expressions will serve as a useful addition to the existing repository of tools and techniques for making symbolic reachability analyzers more efficient.

Acknowledgments. We thank Varun Kanade for help with the experiments.

References

1. D. Beyer, C. Lewerentz, and A. Noack. Rabbit: A tool for BDD-based verification of real-time systems. In *Proceedings of CAV*, LNCS 2725, pages 122–125, 2003.
2. R. Bloem, K. Ravi, and F. Somenzi. Symbolic guided search for CTL model checking. In *Proceeding of ACM/IEEE DAC*, pages 29–34, 2000.
3. R. E. Bryant. Graph-based algorithms for boolean function manipulation. *IEEE Transactions on Computers*, 35(8):677–691, 1986.
4. P. Chauhan, E. M. Clarke, S. Jha, J. Kukula, T. Shiple, H. Veith, and D. Wang. Non-linear quantification scheduling in image computation. In *Proceedings of ACM/IEEE ICCAD*, pages 293–298, 2001.
5. P. Chauhan, E. M. Clarke, S. Jha, J. Kukula, H. Veith, and D. Wang. Using combinatorial optimization methods for quantification scheduling. In *Proceedings of CHARME*, LNCS 2144, pages 293–309, 2001.
6. A. Cimatti, E. Clarke, E. Giunchiglia, F. Giunchiglia, M. Pistore, M. Roveri, R. Sebastiani, and A. Tacchella. NuSMV version 2: An opensource tool for symbolic model checkin. In *Proceedings of CAV*, LNCS 2404, pages 359–364, 2002.
7. J. R. Burch, E. M. Clarke, K. L. McMillan, D. L. Dill, and L. J. Hwang. Symbolic Model Checking: 10^{20} States and Beyond. In *Proceedings of LICS*, pages 1–33, 1990.
8. A. Narayan, A. J. Isles, J. Jain, R. K. Brayton, and A. L. Sangiovanni-Vincentelli. Reachability analysis using partitioned-robdds. In *Proceedings of ACM/IEEE ICCAD*, pages 388–393, 1997.
9. P. K. Pandya and M. Raut. A kleene algebra of reachability expressions and its use in efficient symbolic guided search. Technical Report (in preparation), STCS, Tata Institute of Fundamental Research, 2005.
10. D. Thomas, S. Chakraborty, and P. K. Pandya. Efficient guided symbolic reachability using reachability expressions. Technical Report TR-06-1 (http://www.cfdvs.iitb.ac.in/reports/techrep06.php3), CFDVS, IIT Bombay, January 2006.
11. D. Thomas, P. K. Pandya, and S. Chakraborty. Scheduling clusters in model checking of real time systems. Technical Report TR-04-16 (http://www.cfdvs.iitb.ac.in/reports/techrep04.php3), CFDVS, IIT Bombay, September 2004.

SDSAT: Tight Integration of *Small Domain Encoding* and *Lazy* Approaches in a Separation Logic Solver

Malay K Ganai[1], Muralidhar Talupur[2], and Aarti Gupta[1]

[1] NEC LABS America, Princeton, NJ, USA
[2] Carnegie Mellon University, Pittsburgh, PA, USA

Abstract. Existing Separation Logic (*a.k.a Difference Logic, DL*) solvers can be broadly classified as *eager* or *lazy,* each with its own merits and de-merits. We propose a novel Separation Logic Solver *SDSAT* that combines the strengths of both these approaches and provides a robust performance over a wide set of benchmarks. The solver *SDSAT* works in two phases: *allocation* and *solve*. In the *allocation phase*, it allocates non-uniform *adequate* ranges for variables appearing in separation predicates. This phase is similar to previous small domain encoding approaches, but uses a novel algorithm *Nu-SMOD* with 1-2 orders of magnitude improvement in performance and smaller ranges for variables. Furthermore, the Separation Logic formula is not transformed into an equi-satisfiable Boolean formula in one step, but rather done lazily in the following phase. In the *solve phase*, *SDSAT* uses a lazy refinement approach to search for a satisfying model *within the allocated ranges*. Thus, any partially DL-theory consistent model can be discarded if it can not be satisfied within the allocated ranges. Note the crucial difference: *in eager approaches, such a partially consistent model is not allowed in the first place, while in lazy approaches such a model is never discarded.* Moreover, we dynamically refine the allocated ranges and search for a feasible solution within the updated ranges. This combined approach benefits from both the smaller search space (as in eager approaches) and also from the theory-specific graph-based algorithms (characteristic of lazy approaches). Experimental results show that our method is robust and always better than or comparable to state-of-the art solvers.

1 Introduction

Separation Logic, (*a.k.a Difference Logic*, DL) extends propositional logic with predicates of the form $x+c \triangleright y$ where $\triangleright \in \{>, \geq\}$, c is a constant, and x, y are variables of some ordered infinite type *integer* or *real*. All other equalities and inequalities can be expressed in this logic. Uninterpreted functions can be handled by reducing to Boolean equalities [1]. Separation predicates play a pivotal role in verification of timed systems [2] and hardware models with ordered data structures like queues and stacks, and modeling job scheduling problem [3]. Deciding a Separation Logic problem is *NP-Complete*. Decision procedures based on graph algorithms use a weighted directed graph to represent Separation predicates; with nodes representing variables

H. Hermanns and J. Palsberg (Eds.): TACAS 2006, LNCS 3920, pp. 135–150, 2006.

appearing in the predicates and edges representing the predicates. A predicate of the form $x+c \geq y$ is represented as directed edge from node x to node y with weight c. A conjunction of separation predicates is consistent if and only if the corresponding graph does not have a cycle with negative accumulated weight. The task for decision procedures is reduced to finding solutions without negative cycles. Note, some decision procedures can decide the more general problem of linear arithmetic where the predicates are of the form $\Sigma_i a_i x_i \geq c$ where a_i, c are constants and x_i are variables. Most of them *ICS* [4], *HDPLL* [5], *PVS* [6], and *ASAP* [7] are based on a variable elimination technique like Fourier-Motzkin [8]. Here, we restrict ourselves to a discussion of decision procedures dedicated for Separation Logic.

Satisfiability of a Separation formula can be checked by translating the formula into an equi-satisfiable Boolean formula and checking for a satisfying model using a Boolean satisfiability solver (SAT). In the past, several dedicated decision procedures have taken this approach to leverage off recent advances in SAT engines [9]. These procedures can be classified as either *eager* or *lazy*, based on whether the Boolean model is refined (i.e., transformed) eagerly or lazily, respectively. In eager approaches [10-14] , the Separation formula is reduced to an equi-satisfiable Boolean formula in one step and SAT is used to check the satisfiability. Reduction to Propositional Logic is done either by deriving adequate ranges for formula variables (*a.k.a small domain encoding*) [12] or by deriving all possible transitivity constraints (*a.k.a per-constraint encoding*) [11]. A hybrid method [13] combines the strengths of the two encoding schemes and was shown to give robust performance over the two. In lazy approaches [15-19], SAT is used to obtain a possibly feasible model corresponding to a conjunction of separation predicates and feasibility of the conjunct is checked separately using graph-based algorithms. If the conjunct is infeasible, the Boolean formula is refined and thus, an equi-satisfiable Boolean formula is built lazily by adding the transitivity constraints on a need-to basis.

Both the eager and lazy approaches have relative strengths and weaknesses. Though the small model encoding approaches [12, 20] reduce the range space allocated to a finite domain, Boolean encoding of the formula often leads to large propositional logic formula, eclipsing the advantage gained from the reduced search space. Researchers [14] have also experimented with the pseudo-Boolean Solver *PBS* [21] to obtain a polynomial size formula, but without any significant performance gain. In a *per-constraint encoding*, the formula is abstracted by replacing each predicate with a Boolean variable, and then pre-emptively adding all transitivity constraints over the predicates. Often the transitivity constraints are redundant and adding them eagerly can lead to an exponentially large formula. The Boolean SAT solvers are often unable to decide "smartly" in the presence of such overwhelmingly large number of constraints. As a result the advantage gained from reduced search often takes a backseat due to lack of proper search guidance. Lazy approaches overcome this problem by adding the constraints as required. Moreover, they use advanced graph algorithms based on Bellman-Ford shortest path algorithm [22] to detect infeasible combination of predicates in polynomial time in the size of the graph. These approaches exploit incremental propagation and efficient backtracking schemes to obtain improved performance. Moreover, several techniques have been proposed [17, 18] to add pre-emptively some subset of infeasible combination of predicates. This approach has been shown to reduce the number of backtracks significantly in some cases. Note, the feasibility check is based on detection of a negative cycle (negative accumulation of edge weights) in the graph. Potentially, there could be an exponential number of such cycles and eliminating them lazily can be quite costly. Due to this reason, lazy approaches do not perform as well as eager approaches on benchmarks like *diamonds* which have an exponential number of cycles ($\sim 2^n$ cycles where n is the number of variables). Thus, we are naturally motivated to combine the strength of the two approaches as tightly as possible.

We propose a robust Separation Logic Solver *SDSAT* (short for $\underline{S}$mall $\underline{D}$omain $\underline{SAT}$isfiability solver) that combines the strengths of both eager (small domain encoding) and lazy approaches and gives a robust performance over a wide set of benchmarks. Without overwhelming the SAT solver with a large number of constraint clauses and thereby adversely affecting its performance, we take advantage of both the (finite) reduced search space and the need-to basis transitivity constraints which are able to guide the SAT solver more efficiently.

Outline: We give a short background on Separation Logic and the state-of-the-art solvers in Section 2. We describe our solver *SDSAT* in detail, highlighting the technicalities and novelties in Section 3. This is followed by experiments and conclusions in Sections 4 and 5, respectively.

2 Background: Separation Logic

Separation predicates are of the form $x+c \vartriangleright y$ where $\vartriangleright \in \{>, \geq\}$, c is a constant and x, y are variables of some ordered infinite type *integer* or *real*, D. Separation Logic is a decidable theory combining Propositional Logic with these predicates. If all variables are integers then a strict inequality $x + c > y$ can be translated into a weak inequality $x + (c-1) \geq y$ without changing the decidability of the problem. Similar transformations exist for mixed types, by decreasing c by small enough amounts determined by remaining constants in the predicates [16]. Note, an inequality of the form $x \vartriangleright c$, can be also be translated into a weak inequality of two variables, by introducing a reference node z. Henceforth, we will consider separation predicates of the form $x+c \geq y$.

2.1 State-of-the-Art Lazy Approach: Negative-Cycle Detection

We discuss briefly the essential components in the state-of-the-art Separation Logic solvers based on lazy approaches as shown in Figure 1.

Problem Formulation: In this class of decision procedures, a Separation formula φ is abstracted into Boolean formula φ_B by mapping predicates $x+c \geq y$ and $y+ (-1-c) \geq x$ to a Boolean variable and its negation respectively (or vice versa, depending on some ordering of x and y.) An assignment (or interpretation) is a function mapping each variable to value in D and each Boolean variable to $\{T, F\}$. An assignment α is extended to map a Separation formula ψ to $\{T, F\}$ by defining the following mapping over the Separation predicates, i.e., $\alpha (x+c \geq y) = T$ iff $\alpha (x)+c \geq \alpha (y)$. A Boolean SAT solver is used to obtain a consistent assignment for Boolean variables in φ_B. If such an assignment does not exist, it declares the problem *unsatisfiable*. On the other hand, for any satisfying assignment to φ_B, an additional consistency check is required for the underlying separation predicates. Note, incremental solvers [17, 19, 23] perform this check on a partial assignment to detect conflict early. The problem is declared SAT only when the satisfying assignment is consistent under the check.

Constraint Feasibility: Any partial assignment (also referred to as a partial Boolean model) to variables in φ_B represents a conjunction of separation predicates. The Boolean model is represented as a weighted directed graph (*a.k.a* constraint graph) [24], where an edge $x \rightarrow y$ with weight c (denoted as (x,y,c)) corresponds to the predicate e $\equiv (x+c \geq y)$ where $\alpha(e)=T$. The constraint graph is said to be consistent if and only if it does not have an accumulated negative weighted cycle (or simply, negative cycle.) Intuitively, a negative cycle violates the transitivity property of the separation predicates. The building of the constraint graph and detection of negative cycles, as shown in Figure 1, are done incrementally to amortize the cost of constraint propagation. It has been shown [25] that addition of a predicate and update of a feasible assignment α can be done in $O(m+n \log n)$ where m is the number of predicates and n is the number of variables. After the constraint graph is detected consistent i.e. feasible (shown by the feasible arc in Figure 1), more assignments are made to the unassigned variables in φ_B leading to a more constraint graph. Problem is declared *satisfiable* by Boolean SAT, if there are no more assignments to make.

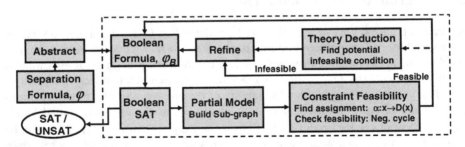

Fig. 1. Overview of state-of-the-art Separation Logic Solver based on lazy approach

Refinement: Whenever a negative cycle is encountered during constraint feasibility (*a.k.a.* constraint propagation), a transitivity constraint not yet implied by φ_B is learnt and added to φ_B as a conflicting clause. For example, if the subgraph corresponding to a conjunction of predicates, i.e., $e_1 \wedge e_2 \wedge e_3 \wedge \neg e_4$ has a negative cycle, then a clause $(\neg e_1 \vee \neg e_2 \vee \neg e_3 \vee e_4)$ is added to φ_B to avoid re-discovering it. As shown in [16], instead of stopping at the first negative cycle, one can detect all negative cycles and then choose a clause with minimum size representing a stronger constraint. Note, due to large overhead, addition of all detected negative cycle clauses, though possible, is not done usually. Moreover, like in Boolean SAT solvers, incremental solvers [17, 19, 23] restore the assignments to the variables to a state just before the inconsistency was detected, instead of starting from scratch.

Pre-emptive Learning (Theory Deduction): Some solvers [17, 18] have capabilities to add transitivity constraints preemptively to φ_B so as to avoid finding them later.

However, as the overhead of adding all transitivity constraints can be prohibitive as observed in *per-constraint* eager approach, solvers often use heuristics to add them selectively and optionally (shown as dotted arrow in Figure 1).

2.2 Eager Approach: Finite Instantiation

Range allocation (*a.k.a. small domain encoding*) approaches find the adequate set of values (*a.k.a.* ranges) for each variable in the finite model. We briefly describe the range allocation problem for Separation Logic which has been discussed at greater depth in [20, 26]. Let $Vars(\varphi)$ denote the set of variables used in a Separation formula φ over the set of integers Z. We assume φ is in Non-Negated Form (NNF), i.e., every predicate occurring negatively in the formula is converted into its dual positive predicate a priori (e.g., $\neg(x+c< y) \Rightarrow x+c \geq y$) A domain (or range) $R(\varphi)$ of a formula φ is a function from $Vars(\varphi)$ to 2^Z. Let $Vars(\varphi) = \{v_1,...,v_n\}$ and $|R(v_i)|$ denote the number of elements in the set $R(v_i)$, domain of v_i. The size of domain $R(\varphi)$, denoted by $|R(\varphi)|$ is given by $|R(\varphi)| = |R(v_1)| \cdot |R(v_2)| \cdots |R(v_n)|$. Let $SAT_R(\varphi)$ denote that φ is *satisfiable* in a domain R. The goal is to find a small domain R such that

$$SAT_R(\varphi) \Leftrightarrow SAT_Z(\varphi) \tag{1}$$

We say that a domain R is *adequate* for φ if it satisfies formula (1). As finding the smallest domain for a given formula is at least as hard as checking the satisfiability of φ, the goal (1) is relaxed to finding the adequate domain for the set of all separation formulas with the *same set of predicates* as φ, denoted by $\Phi(\varphi)$ as adequacy for $\Phi(\varphi)$ implies adequacy for φ. As discussed in the previous section, separation predicates can be represented by a constraint directed graph $G(V,E)$. Thus, the set of all the subgraphs of G represents the set $\Phi(\varphi)$. Given G, the range allocation problem is setup to finding a domain R such that every consistent sub graph of G can be satisfied from the values in R.

It has been shown [12] that for a Separation formula with n variables, a range $[1..n+maxC]$ is adequate for each variable, with $maxC$ being equal to the sum of absolute constants in the formula. This leads to a state space of $(n+maxC)^n$ where all variables are given uniform ranges regardless of the formula structure. This small model encoding approach in *UCLID* [12], would require $\lceil log_2|R(x)| \rceil$ Boolean variables to encode the range $R(x)$, allocated for variable x. There has been further work [20] to reduce the overall ranges and hence, the size of the Boolean formula. In [20], a method *SMOD* was proposed to allocate non-uniform ranges to variables, exploiting the problem structure. The method builds cut-point SCC graph recursively in top-down manner and allocates ranges to the nodes in a bottom-up style, propagating the range values. The approach is based on enumeration of all cycles and therefore, the worst-case complexity of such an approach is exponential. In this paper, we propose an efficient and robust technique *Nu-SMOD* that computes non-uniform ranges in polynomial-time; polynomial in the number of predicate variables and size of the constants. Moreover, the ranges are comparable to or better than the non-uniform ranges obtained using *SMOD*, and consistently better than the uniform ranges obtained using *UCLID* [12]. In experimental evaluation, *Nu-SMOD* completes allocation for all the benchmarks unlike *SMOD*, with 1-2 orders of magnitude performance improvement over *SMOD*. Unlike *SMOD*, we do not compute cutpoint-graph or enumerate cycles in our new procedure *Nu-SMOD*; rather we propagate only distinct values along a path from a cut-point. As the ranges will be used subsequently by the lazy search-engine, we emphasize improvement in performance instead of ranges. Thus, our objective differs slightly from *SMOD* procedure.

3   SDSAT: Integrating Small Domain and Lazy Approaches

We propose a Separation Logic Solver *SDSAT* as shown in Figure 2, that combines the strengths of both eager (small domain encoding) and lazy approaches and gives a robust performance over a wide set of benchmarks. This combined approach benefits both from the reduced search space (as in eager approaches) and also from the need-to basis refinement of the Boolean formula with the transitivity constraints (as in lazy approaches). The solver *SDSAT* proceeds in two phases: *allocation* and *solve*.

In the *allocation* phase (shown as *Phase I* in Figure 2), it computes *non-uniform adequate ranges* using an efficient technique *Nu-SMOD* that runs in polynomial time; polynomial in the number of predicate variables and size of the constants. This phase is similar to previous small domain encoding approaches; however, the Separation Logic formula is not transformed into an equi-satisfiable Boolean formula in one step, but rather done lazily in the following phase.

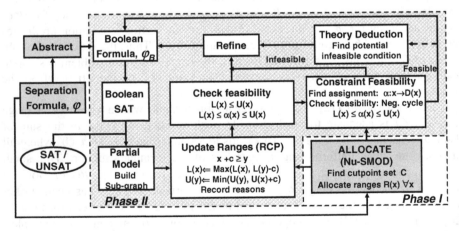

Fig. 2. Overview of our Separation Logic solver *SDSAT*

In the *solve phase* (shown as *Phase II* in Figure 2), *SDSAT* searches for a satisfying model *within the allocated ranges* using a lazy refinement approach. Thus, any partially DL-theory consistent model is discarded if it can not be satisfied within the allocated ranges (The check is done in the blocks "Check feasibility" and "Constraint feasibility" in Figure 2). Note the key difference: *in eager approaches, such a partially consistent model is not allowed in the first place, while in lazy approaches such a model is never discarded.* By focusing on adequate ranges and not just consistency of the separation predicates we are able to learn more constraints leading to larger reductions in search space. Furthermore, we dynamically refine the ranges allocated to variables in the *allocation phase* using range constraint propagation (described in Section 3.2.2) and search for a feasible solution within the updated ranges (shown in the block "Updated Ranges (RCP)" in Figure 2). Another novelty is in the use of cutpoints to determine whether an added edge (to a consistent model) leads to an infeasible condition, based on the observation that any cycle will have at least one cutpoint (Given a directed graph G (V, E), a *cutpoint* set $C \subseteq V$ is a set of nodes whose removal breaks all the cycles in G). If an added edge $x \rightarrow y$ (corresponding to the predicate $x + c \geq y$) is not reachable from some cutpoint and x is not a cutpoint, then a previously consistent subgraph modified with this new edge is guaranteed *not to* have a negative cycle. Moreover like in most lazy approaches, *SDSAT* has incremental propagation and cycle detection, and preemptive learning of infeasible condition (theory deduction shown as dotted arrow in Figure 2).

3.1 Allocation Phase: Non-uniform Range Allocation

We discuss the algorithm *Nu-SMOD* to allocate non-uniform ranges to the variables in the predicates. The algorithm assumes that the constraint directed graph $G(V,E)$ is a Strongly Connected Component (SCC). Extension to non-SCCs is straightforward: compute the ranges for SCCs individually and then offset the ranges appropriately to account for the edges between the SCCs starting from some root SCC. As far as validity of the Separation Logic problem is concerned, it is easy to see that these edges can be removed from the problem as they will never contribute to a cycle.

Algorithm *Nu-SMOD*: We first derive a cutpoint set C using polynomial approximation [27], as finding a minimal cutpoint set is an NP-Hard problem. Using the set C, we invoke the procedure (line 1 of the procedure *NU-SMOD*, Figure 3) *Nu-SMOD-1* which is described as follows (lines 11-19, Figure 3): Range of each node x, denoted by $R(x)$, is divided into several sets; each identified with unique id or simply *level*. Let the level k set of the node x be denoted by $L^k(x)$. Note, $R(x) = \cup_k L^k(x)$. Initially, all the level sets are empty. The nodes in Level 1 set, denoted by I, are allocated 0 value, i.e., $L^1(x) = \{0\}$, $\forall x \in I$. To compute Level $(k+1)$ values, i.e., $L^{k+1}(y)$ for node y (line 17), we use the Level k values of the nodes x that have a direct edge, i.e., fanout (x,y,c) (corresponding to the predicate $x + c \geq y$) to y and offset with edge weight c. Note, we include only the cutpoints C in the set I. Once the ranges for the cutpoints C are obtained using *Nu-SMOD-1*, another pass is made (in lines 2-5) to obtain *reverse_dfs* values $Q[y]$ for each non-cutpoint y. Starting from each cutpoint (line 4-5) with value M (equal to maximum range value allocated among the cutpoints), we do a *reverse_dfs* (lines 7-10) to update Q values (line 9) of all the non-cutpoints by reverse propagating a tight value (higher than the previous Q value, line 8) without traversing through any other cutpoints (line 7). Note that the reverse dfs path from a cutpoint to non-cutpoint is a simple path as there is no cycle. All the inequalities from non-cutpoint to cutpoint are satisfied using *reverse_dfs* Q values.

```
/Range Allocation for an          13. foreach k, 1≤k<|V| do
//SCC G(V,E)                      14.  foreach node x∈V do
                                  15.   foreach(x,y,c)∈fanouts(x)do
Input: G(V,E), Cutpoint set C     16.    foreach value v ∈ Lᵏ(x) do
Output: R(x) for ∀x∈V             17.     Lᵏ⁺¹(y)=Lᵏ⁺¹(y)∪{v+c}
Procedure: Nu-SMOD                18.
1.Nu-SMOD-1 {INPUT: G(V,E), I=C   19. ∀x∈V  R(x)=∪₁≤k≤|V| Lᵏ(x)
             OUTPUT: R(x)∀x∈V }
2.∀y∈V-C Q[y]=-∞                  //Assignment for subgraph D of G
3.M=max(∪∀x∈cR(x))               Input: D(Vᵈ,Eᵈ)
4.foreach x∈C do                  Output: {(x,vₓ)|x∈Vᵈ, vₓ∈R(x)}
5.   reverse_dfs(x,M);            Procedure: ASSIGN
6.end                             20. S = {set of root nodes}
                                  21. ∀y ∈ Vᵈ-S vᵧ = +∞;
reverse_dfs(x,v)                  22. foreach x ∈ S do
7.foreach (y,x,w) s.t. y∉C do     23.    vₓ = 0; enqueue(x)
8.  if (Q[y]+w ≥ v) continue;     24.    bfm(x);
9.  Q[y] = v - w;                 25. end
10. reverse_dfs(y,Q[y])           26. ∀y∈Vᵈ-S if (vᵧ == +∞) vᵧ=Q[y]


                                  bfm(x)
Input: G(V,E), I⊆V                27. while (x = dequeue())!=null)
Output: R(x) for ∀x∈V             28.  foreach(x,y,c)∈fanouts(x)do
Procedure: Nu-SMOD-1              29.   if (vₓ+c >= vᵧ) continue;
                                  30.   vᵧ = vₓ+c;
11. L¹(x)={0}∀x∈I, L¹(x)={}∀x∈V\I 31.   enqueue(y);
12. Lᵏ(x)={} ∀x∈V, 1<k≤|V|        32.  end
                                  33. end
```

Fig. 3. Pseudo-code for the algorithm *Nu-SMOD* and *ASSIGN* procedures

Theorem 1: Ranges allocated by *Nu-SMOD* are adequate.

Proof Sketch: We now show that the ranges allocated by *Nu-SMOD* are *adequate*, i.e., any satisfiable sub-graph $D(V^d,E^d)$ of $G(V,E)$ ($V^d \subseteq V$, $E^d \subseteq E$) has a satisfying assignment from the allocated set of ranges. We further assume D is connected. If not, then each component is a satisfiable sub-graph of G and ranges can be assigned to variables in each component independently of the other.

We construct the adequacy proof by devising an assignment procedure *ASSIGN* as shown in Figure 3 (lines 20-33) which will generate a satisfying solution from the allocated set of ranges. We first construct a set S of *root* nodes (those nodes in $V^d \cap C$ that can not be reached from any other node in $V^d \cap C$) in D (line 20). If S is empty either $V^d \cap C$ is empty or all nodes are in some cycle. In the former case, we skip to line 26, else we pick any node in $V^d \cap C$ and continue. We initially assign all the nodes not in S with $+\infty$ (a large positive value, line 21). We denote the value assigned to a node x as v_x. Starting from each node in S (with initial value 0 as in line 23), we call *bfm* (similar to Bellman-Ford-Moore Shortest Path algorithm [22]) procedure to assign *tight* values on the nodes that can be reached. The edge (x,y,c) is said to be stable if the current value of x and y is said to satisfy the constraint $(x+c \geq y)$. Note that the value of the node can change only if the current value is lower than the previously assigned value (line 30). Such an operation is also called an *edge relaxation* [22]. Only under such a scenario, the node is en-queued (line 31). Those nodes whose value are still $+\infty$, are given *reverse_dfs* Q values (line 26). To show that the given assignment procedure *ASSIGN* generates a satisfying solution from the ranges allocated, we need to prove the following lemmas (Contact author for proof details).

Lemma 1: The procedure *ASSIGN* terminates.

Lemma 2: All inequalities corresponding to edges of D are satisfied.

Lemma 3: Each assigned value v_x belongs to $R(x)$.

The above theorem guarantees the existence of the solution for a satisfying subgraph D with all the *root nodes* in $V^d \cap C$ having special value 0 and the other nodes in $V^d \backslash C$ having either *tight* values or *reverse_dfs* values Q, depending on whether they are reachable from root nodes or not, respectively. Note that the cutpoints do not need Q values as they are the root nodes. As we will see shortly, the *solve phase* is based primarily on this observation.

3.2 Solve Phase

Similar to standard lazy solvers, we first build an abstract Boolean formula φ_B from the given Separation formula φ and search for a partial consistent Boolean model. As the partial model is being incrementally built up, we search for a satisfying model using *cutpoint-relaxation algorithm* (described in Section 3.2.1) within the dynamically updated ranges achieved by *range constraint propagation* (described in Section 3.2.2). We build these algorithms by augmenting the procedure *ASSIGN* (described above) with

- inconsistency detection due to negative cycles,
- range violations check, and
- pre-emptive learning.

In the following, we restrict our discussion to novelties in detecting the inconsistencies. (For details on pre-emptive learning please refer [17, 18]).

3.2.1 Incremental Cycle Detection Using Cutpoint Relaxation

In the past [23, 28], the detection of negative cycles and finding satisfying assignments are done incrementally in a weighted digraph that is built incrementally. Each of these algorithms uses a variant (mostly in the ordering of the relaxed edges) of Bellman-Ford-Moore (BFM) Shortest Path algorithm and extends it with an ability to detect negative cycle. Our approach is also based on BFM with the following difference: *For a satisfiable sub-graph D, we consider only those solutions which lie within the ranges allocated by the Nu-SMOD procedure.* Note, a satisfying assignment set $\{\alpha(x)\}$ represents a class of satisfying assignments $\{\alpha(x)+k\}$ for some constant k.

As shown in the procedure *ASSIGN*, the existence of the solution for a satisfying subgraph D is guaranteed with all the *root nodes* in $V^d \cap C$ having special value 0 and the other nodes in $V^d \backslash C$ having either *tight* values or *reverse_dfs* values Q, depending on whether they are reachable from root nodes or not, respectively. Thus, in our approach, we restrict the set of satisfying assignments such that $\alpha(x)=0$ for the *root nodes* $x \in V^d \cap C$. We discuss the implication of such restriction in our incremental cycle detection algorithm *cutpoint relaxation*. As will be clear shortly, the theoretical complexity of the algorithm is not different from BFM and its variants. In our *cutpoint relaxation* algorithm (unlike *ASSIGN* procedure) we do not change $\alpha(x)$ from $+\infty$ to $Q[x]$ if a node x is not reachable from a root node (due to incremental addition of edges, such a node may be reachable later). Now, we discuss how the incremental addition and deletion of edges affect the negative cycle detection.

Edge Addition: Suppose, we add an edge (x,y,c) to D and obtain a subgraph D'. If $\alpha(x) \neq +\infty$, x is reachable from some root node in D and we do the usual BFM. If $\alpha(x) = +\infty$, we consider two cases depending on $x \in C$ or $x \notin C$.

Case $x \in C$: Clearly, x is root node in D' as it is not reachable from any other root node in D. We choose $\alpha(x)=0$ and do usual BFM with negative cycle detection after relaxing (x,y,c).

Case $x \notin C$: Note, x is not reachable from any node in $V^d \cap C$. As any cycle will have at least one cutpoint and since x is not a cutpoint in G, there cannot be any cycle in subgraph D' (of G) with the edge (x,y,c). Based on this observation, we skip edge relaxation and cycle detection for this case.

Edge Deletion: When an edge (x,y,c) is deleted, we need to restore the previous $\alpha(y)$ value only if it is different from $+\infty$. Since, deletion of edges takes place at the time of backtracking, we restore only those $\alpha(y)$ that got affected after the backtrack level. We use a standard stack-based approach for efficient backtracking.

Thus, our algorithm *cutpoint relaxation* has two main novelties: First, the approach allows us to identify cases where we guarantee no negative cycles in a subgraph *without* edge relaxation. Second, we reduce the search space by restricting our solution space in a spirit similar to finite instantiation. Though maintaining such a restriction on assignment values on root nodes has an overhead, yet we did not find it to be a significant bottleneck. Besides using cutpoints and restricted solutions to reduce the search space, we can further reduce the search space by dynamically updating the ranges of the variables as discussed in the following section.

3.2.2 Range Constraint Propagation (RCP)

Ranges computed by the *allocation phase* guarantee the adequacy for a satisfiable subgraph D; however, the ranges are often more than those required to obtain a satisfying solution for D. We allow range constraint propagation (RCP) to dynamically refine the ranges of the variables for the given subgraph D, while maintaining the range adequacy (Theorem 2). This approach is similar to the more general approach for interval arithmetic [29, 30]. We achieve RCP as follows: Let the minimum and maximum values in the range of a variable x be denoted by $L(x)$ and $U(x)$, respectively. Initially, these limits are obtained during the *allocation phase*. RCP on an edge $x+c \geq y$, denoted by RCP($x + c \geq y$), updates the limits $L(x)$ and $U(y)$ as follows:

$$L(x) \Leftarrow \text{MAX}\{L(x), L(y)\text{-}c\}$$
$$U(y) \Leftarrow \text{MIN}\{U(y), U(x)\text{+}c\}$$

We apply this process recursively, i.e., whenever the L (or U) value of a node changes, we update the L (or U) values of all the nodes with a direct edge to (or from) the node. The process stops when either a range violation is detected, i.e. $L(x) > U(x)$ or all the limits have stabilized. As constraint propagation reduces the range sizes monotonically, the process is guaranteed to terminate. A conflict can also be detected due to range violation of the invariant $L(x) \le \alpha(x) \le U(x)$ where $\alpha(x)$ is a satisfying assignment for x reachable from some *root node*. Note, these range violations can occur in a subgraph *even without a negative cycle*. (These checks are carried out in the block "Check feasibility" in Figure 2. We illustrate this with an example later.) *Thus, the reduced range space leads to faster detection of conflicts and hence, reduced search.* We can also obtain the set of conflicting edges by storing the edges as reasons for the change in minimum and maximum limits. The following theorem addresses the range adequacy after RCP (please contact authors for proof details).

Theorem 2: Reduced ranges obtained by RCP are adequate for subgraph D.

Example: We illustrate RCP and its roles in reducing the search space on a diamond example shown in Figure 4. Let the Separation formula F be $e_1 \wedge e_4 \wedge e_5 \wedge e_8 \wedge e_9 \wedge (e_2 \vee e_3) \wedge (e_6 \vee e_7)$ where e_i represents a separation predicate. Let $n_0...n_5$ represent the integer variables. The separation predicates are shown as edges e_i in Figure 4(a) (with weights in brackets). For example: $e_1 \equiv (n_0 \ge n_1)$ and $e_9 \equiv (n_5-1 \ge n_0)$. The previous approaches based on *only* negative cycle detection have to find all four negative cycles before F is declared unsatisfiable. Using our approach of combined negative cycle detection with RCP, we decide unsatisfiability with detection of two negative cycles and one range violation as described below.

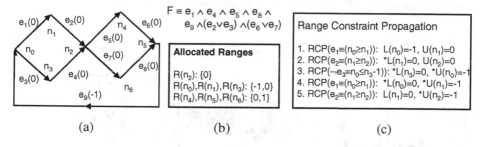

(a)   (b)   (c)

Fig. 4. (a) Example (b) Allocated Ranges (c) RCP w/ negative cycle detection

As shown in Figure 4(b), L and U of each variable are initially set to corresponding minimum and maximum range R values as obtained by *Nu-SMOD* (for example: $L(n_0)=-1$, $U(n_0)=0$). Note, that these ranges are adequate for this graph. Consider the subgraph $e_1 \wedge e_2 \wedge \neg e_3$. When we apply RCP as shown in the Figure 4(c), we detect a range violation as follows (note, $*L$ and $*U$ denote changes from the previous step): As $U(n_0)$ changes in step 3, we change $U(n_1)$ to -1 in step 4 as the edge e_1 is incident on n_1 and $U(n_2)$ to -1 in step 5 as the edge e_2 is incident on n_2. Now, as $L(n_2)=0 > U(n_2)=-1$, we detect a range violation and learn a clause $(\neg e_1 \vee \neg e_2 \vee e_3)$ by doing conflict analysis. The learnt clause $(\neg e_1 \vee \neg e_2 \vee e_3)$, together with the formula clause $(e_2 \vee e_3)$ implies a clause $(\neg e_1 \vee e_3)$; which in turn with formula clause (e_1) implies (e_3). When we detect two negative cycles with edge pairs (e_3, e_7) and (e_3, e_6), we learn that

e_3 *implies* $(\neg e_6 \wedge \neg e_7)$. As $(e_6 \vee e_7)$ is a formula clause, we could declare the formula F unsatisfiable without the need to detect further negative cycles.

4 Experimental Results

We have integrated our incremental cycle detection using cutpoint relaxation and RCP with the zChaff Boolean SAT solver [31]. We have also implemented pre-emptive learning but have not done controlled experiments to ascertain its usefulness. We conducted experiments on a set of six public benchmark suites generated from verification and scheduling problems: *diamonds, DTP, DLSAT, mathsat, sal* and *uclid*. We ran our experiments on a workstation with 3.0 GHz Intel Pentium 4 processor and 2 GB of RAM running Red Hat Linux 7.2. First, we compare the range allocation algorithms; second, we evaluate the effectiveness of RCP in *SDSAT* and third, we compare it with the state-of-the-art solvers.

Comparison of Range Allocations Algorithms: We compared our approach *Nu-SMOD* with previous approaches *SMOD* [20] and *UCLID* [12] on these benchmarks and present results in Figure 5. We used a time limit of 2 minutes for each run. Note, the *UCLID* procedure allocates each of n nodes in an SCC a continuous range from 1 to $n + maxC$ where $maxC$ is the sum of all constant absolute values. We compare the number of Boolean variables required to encode the ranges assigned by the different approaches as the *ratio between the approach and Nu-SMOD*. Note, for range set $R(y)$, we require $\lceil log_2(|R(y)|) \rceil$ Boolean variables to encode the set $R(y)$.

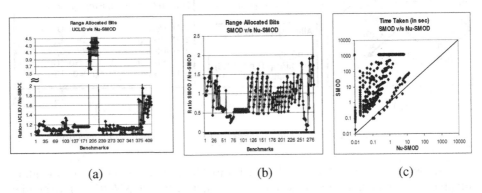

(a)   (b)   (c)

Fig. 5. Ratio of range bits allocated between (a) UCLID v/s Nu-SMOD, (b) SMOD v/s Nu-SMOD. (c) Scatter plot of time taken (in sec) between SMOD v/s Nu-SMOD.

UCLID v/s Nu-SMOD: As shown in Figure 5(a), compared to *UCLID*, *Nu-SMOD* allocates on average about 40% less range bits (about 4X less on *diamond set*). Note that such linear reductions amount to exponential reduction in range space.

SMOD v/s Nu-SMOD: Of 432 benchmarks, *SMOD* could complete only 262 in the given time limit of 2 minutes. If we increase the time limit to 20 minutes, it solves 23 more cases. Not surprisingly, time-out occurs mostly for dense graph as also observed by the authors [20]. Baring a few benchmarks, the ranges allocated by *Nu-SMOD* are comparable to *SMOD* as seen in Figure 5(b). Moreover, *SMOD* is 1-2 orders of magnitude slower on the completed benchmarks as compared to *Nu-SMOD* as shown in the scatter plot (in logarithmic scale) in Figure 5(c).

Allocation and Role of RCP in SDSAT: In the second set of experiments, we present the results of *allocation phase* and compare the effectiveness of refinement in *SDSAT* with and without RCP as shown in Table 1. In our experience, the number of refinements did not distinct the role of RCP. We observed performance improvement using RCP with more refinements as well as with fewer refinements. Thus, instead of using the number of refinements, we introduce two metrics to measure its effectiveness: *refinement overhead* and *refinement penalty*. We define *refinement overhead* as the time taken in the corresponding graph algorithm per refinement, and *refinement penalty* as the time taken by Boolean SAT per refinement. The former metric measures the cost in detecting the inconsistency, whereas the latter measures the cost of Boolean search after refinement, evaluating its effectiveness. Ideally, we would like to have a low number for both the metrics. In the Table 1, Column 1 shows the benchmarks suites with the number in brackets indicating the number of problems considered. Columns 2-3 show the results of *allocation phase*: especially, Column 2 shows the average size of range bits per variable computed in the *allocation phase*. Column 3 shows the average time taken for *allocation phase*. Columns 4-5 show the result of incremental negative cycle detection without RCP. Column 4 shows the average refinement overhead (in milliseconds) and Column 5 gives the average refinement penalty (in milliseconds). Similarly, Columns 6-8 show the result of incremental negative cycle detection with RCP. Column 6 shows the average refinement overhead (in milliseconds), Column 7 shows the average refinement penalty (in milliseconds), and Column 8 shows the average percentage of refinements due to RCP.

Note first that the time overhead in the *allocation phase* is not very significant. The bits allocated for the ranges averages around 10 bits per variable. Though the solution space is reduced, the bit blasted translation of the formula could be quite large if we were to apply small domain encoding [12]. Note that in the presence of RCP the refinement overhead is not affected significantly. Moreover, a lower refinement penalty with RCP indicates improvement in quality of refinements and Boolean search. We also observe that, except for diamonds, on average 50% refinements are due to range violations discovered during RCP.

Comparison with other Separation Logic Solvers: In the third set of experiments, we compare our approach *SDSAT* (the *solve phase*) with other latest available state-of-the-art tools, including *UCLID[13], MathSAT[17], ICS[4], TSAT++[16],* and *DPLL(T)[18]*. As *allocation phase* has a constant time overhead, we use the solver phase run-time for comparison to understand the results better. We used a common platform and 1 hour time limit for each of the benchmarks. We present the cumulative results in Table 2. Due to unavailability of appropriate translators, we could not compare on *uclid* benchmarks for this experiment. Pairs of the form *(n t)* represent that the particular approach timed out in n number of cases for that benchmark suite. Overall, we observe that *SDSAT* and *DPLL(T)* have superior performance compared to other lazy and eager approaches by several orders of magnitude. Comparing *SDSAT* with *DPLL(T)*, we see an improvement in some suites, in particular, *diamonds* and *math-sat*. Especially for *diamonds*, *SDSAT* is able to detect unsatisfiability in less than 1 sec for 32 out of 36 problems. Though there are many negative cycles in these *diamonds* problems, RCP is able to take advantage of the significantly reduced ranges as shown in Column 2 in Table 1. On the whole, *SDSAT* times out in 7 cases as compared to 10 cases for *DPLL(T)*. Thus, overall our approach is relatively more robust than the pure lazy approaches which can also benefit using our ideas.

Table 1. SDSAT: Allocation and role of RCP

Bench	Allocation		-ve cycle w/o RCP		-ve cycle with RCP		
	Avg. Range bits per var	Avg.Time taken (s)	Ref ovhd (ms)	Ref pnlty (ms)	Ref ovhd (ms)	Ref Pnlty (ms)	Range violation (%)
DTP (59)	13	0.46	0.2	0.3	0.2	0.18	48
diamonds(36)	0.99	0.14	0.1	0.12	0.006	0.02	100
mathsat (147)	9.97	0.94	32	713	32	371	48
DLSAT (31)	11.9	3	0.2	1.6	0.3	0.9	45
sal (99)	10.9	3.34	1	36	1	19	49

Table 2. Performance comparison (in sec) of state-of-the-art Separation Logic Solvers

Bench	TSAT++	UCLID	MathSAT	ICS	DPLL(T)	SDSAT
DTP (59)	642	122590 (34 t)	120	188592 (48 t)	10	202
diamonds(36)	6571	32489 (9 t)	24302 (1 t)	51783 (11 t)	679	41
mathsat (147)	62863 (15 t)	73751 (20 t)	41673 (9 t)	51789 (13 t)	37696 (8 t)	31279 (6 t)
DLSAT (31)	276	97334 (27 t)	429	12671 (2 t)	13	46
sal (99)	135909 (34 t)	156399 (43 t)	57401 (15 t)	107313 (28 t)	18721 (2 t)	22178 (1 t)

5   Conclusions

We proposed a novel Separation Logic Solver *SDSAT* that takes advantage of the small domain property of Separation logic to perform a lazy search of the state space. The solver tightly integrates the strengths of both lazy and eager approaches and gives a robust performance over a wide range of benchmarks. It first allocates non-uniform adequate ranges efficiently and then uses the graph-based algorithms to search *lazily* for a satisfying model within the allocated ranges. It combines a state-of-the-art negative cycle detection algorithm with range constraint propagation to prune out infeasible search space very efficiently. Moreover, it also benefits from incremental propagation and cycle detection using cutpoint relaxation algorithm. Experimental evidence presented here bears out the efficacy of our technique.

References

[1] W. Ackermann, "Solvable Cases of the Decision Problem," in *Studies in Logic and the Foundations of Mathematics*, 1954.

[2] P. Niebert, M. Mahfoudh, E. Asarin, M. Bozga, O. Maler, and N. Jain, "Verification of Timed Automata via Satisfiability Checking," in *Proc. of Formal Techniques in Real-Time and Fault Tolerant Systems*, 2002.

[3] J. Adams, E. Balas, and D. Zawack, "The shifting bottleneck procedure for job shop scheduling," in *Management Science*, 1988.

[4] J.-C. Filliatre, S. Owre, H. Rueβ, and N. Shankar, "ICS: Integrated Canonizer and Solver," in *Proceedings of CAV*, 2001.

[5] G. Parthasarathy, M. K. Iyer, K.-T. Cheng, and C. Wang, "An Efficient Finite-Domain Constraint Solver for RTL Circuits," in *Proceedings of DAC*, 2004.

[6] S. Owre, J. M. Rushby, and N. Shankar, "PVS: A Prototype Verification System," in *Proceedings of CADE*, 1992.

[7] D. Kroening, J. Ouaknine, S. A. Seshia, and O. Strichman, "Abstraction-Based Satisfiability Solving of Presburger Arithmetic," in *Proceedings of CAV*, 2004.

[8] A. J. C. Bik and H. A. G. Wijshoff, "Implementation of Fourier-Motzkin Elimination.," in *Technical Report 94-42, Dept. of Computer Science, Leiden University*, 1994.

[9] L. Zhang and S. Malik, "The Quest for Efficient Boolean Satisfiability Solvers," in *Proceeding of CAV*, 2002.

[10] A. Pnueli, Y. Rodeh, O. Strichman, and M. Siegel, "The Small Model Property: How small can it be?," in *Information and computation*, vol. 178(1), Oct 2002, pp. 279-293.

[11] O. Strichman, S. A. Seshia, and R. E. Bryant, "Deciding Separation Formulas with SAT," in *CAV*, July 2002.

[12] R. E. Bryant, S. K. Lahiri, and S. A. Seshia, "Modeling and Verifying Systems using a Logic of Counter Arithmetic with Lambda Expressions and Uninterpreted Functions," in *Computer-Aided Verification*, 2002.

[13] S. A. Seshia, S. K. Lahiri, and R. E. Bryant, "A Hybrid SAT-based Decision Procedure for Separation Logic with Uninterpreted Functions," in *Proceedings of DAC*, 2003.

[14] R. E. Bryant, S. K. Lahiri, and S. A. Seshia, "Deciding CLU logic formulas via Boolean and peudo-Boolean encodings," in *Workshop on Constraints in Formal Verification*, 2002.

[15] C. Barrett, D. L. Dill, and J. Levitt, "Validity Checking for Combination of Theories with Equality," in *Proceedings of FMCAD*, 1996.

[16] A. Armando, C. Castellini, E. Giunchiglia, M. Idini, and M. Maratea, "TSAT++: An Open Platform for Satisfiability Modulo Theories," in *Proceedings of Pragmatics of Decision Procedures in Automated Resonings (PDPAR'04)*, 2004.

[17] M. Bozzano, R. Bruttomesso, A. Cimatti, T. Junttila, P. V. Rossum, S. Schulz, and R. Sebastiani, "An Incremental and Layered Procedure for the Satisfiability of Integer Arithmetic Logic," in *Proceedings of TACAS*, 2005.

[18] R. Nieuwenhuis and A. Oliveras, "DPLL(T) with Exhaustive Theory Propogation and its Application to Difference Logic," in *CAV*, 2005.

[19] C. Wang, F. Ivancic, M. Ganai, and A. Gupta, "Deciding Separation Logic Formulae with SAT by Incremental Negative Cycle Elimination," in *Proceeding of Logic for Programming, Artificial Intelligence and Reasoning*, 2005.

[20] M. Talupur, N. Sinha, and O. Strichman, "Range Allocation for Separation Logic," in *CAV*, 2004.

[21] F. Aloul, A. Ramani, I. Markov, and K. Sakallah, "PBS: A backtrack search pseudo-Boolean solver," in *Symposium on the Theory and Applications of Satisfiability Testing (SAT)*, 2002.

[22] T. H. Cormen, C. E. Leiserson, and R. L. Rivest, *Introduction to Algorithms*. Cambridge, MA: MIT Press, 1990.

[23] S. Cotton, "Satisfiability Checking with Difference Constraints," in *IMPRS Computer Science, Saarbruceken*, 2005.

[24] V. Pratt, "Two Easy Theories Whose Combination is Hard," in *Technical report, MIT*, 1977.

[25] G. Ramalingam, J. Song, L. Joscovicz, and R. Miller, "Solving difference constraints incrementally," in *Alogrithmica*, 1999.

[26] O. Strichman, "http://iew3.techninon.ac.il/~ofers."

[27] D. S. Hochbaum, *Approximation Algorithms for NP-hard Problems*: PWS Publishing Company, 1997.

[28] B. V. Cherkassky and E. Goldberg, "Negative-cycle Detection Algorithms," in *European Symposium on Algorithms*, 1996.

[29] R. E. Moore, *Interval Analysis*. NJ: Prentice-Hall, 1966.

[30] T. Hickey, Q. Ju, and H. V. Emden, "Interval Arithmetic: from principles to implementation," in *Journal of the ACM*, 2001.

[31] M. Moskewicz, C. Madigan, Y. Zhao, L. Zhang, and S. Malik, "Chaff: Engineering an Efficient SAT Solver," in *Proceedings of Design Automation Conference*, 2001.

SAT-Based Software Certification

Sagar Chaki

Carnegie Mellon Software Engineering Institute
chaki@sei.cmu.edu

Abstract. We formalize a notion of witnesses for satisfaction of linear temporal logic specifications by infinite state programs. We show how such witnesses may be constructed via predicate abstraction, and validated by generating verification conditions and proving them. We propose the use of SAT-based theorem provers and resolution proofs in proving these verification conditions. In addition to yielding extremely compact proofs, a SAT-based approach overcomes several limitations of conventional theorem provers when applied to the verification of programs written in real-life programming languages. We also formalize a notion of witnesses of simulation conformance between infinite state programs and finite state machine specifications. We present algorithms to construct simulation witnesses of minimal size by solving pseudo-Boolean constraints. We present experimental results on several non-trivial benchmarks which suggest that a SAT-based approach can yield extremely compact proofs, in some cases by a factor of over 10^5, when compared to existing non-SAT-based theorem provers.

1 Introduction

There is an evident and urgent need for objective measures of confidence in the *behavior* of software obtained from untrusted sources. In general, the lack of trust in a piece of code stems from two sources: (i) the code producer, and (ii) the mechanism of delivery of the code to the consumer. Unfortunately, the vast majority of current software assurance techniques target the above sources of mistrust in isolation, but fail to account for them both.

For instance, cryptographic techniques are typically unable to say anything substantial about the run-time behavior of the program. Techniques such as sandboxing and analytic redundancy require mechanisms for run-time monitoring and appropriate responses to failure. Additionally, such approaches are inherently dynamic and unable to provide adequate levels of static correctness guarantees. Extrinsic software quality standards typically have a heavy focus on process and are usually quite subjective. Moreover, software qualities are weakly related to desired behavior, if at all.

This article presents a technique that uses *proofs* to certify software. More specifically, we certify a rich set of safety and *liveness* policies on C source code. Our approach consists of two broad stages. We first use model checking [13, 11] in conjunction with CounterExample Guided Abstraction Refinement (CEGAR) [12] and predicate abstraction [17] to verify that a C program

H. Hermanns and J. Palsberg (Eds.): TACAS 2006, LNCS 3920, pp. 151–166, 2006.

C satisfies a policy S. The policy S may be expressed either as a linear temporal logic (LTL) formula or a finite state machine.

Subsequently, we use information generated by the verification procedure to extract a witness Ω. We show how the witness may be used to generate a verification condition VC. We also prove that C respects the policy S iff VC is valid. The witness Ω is constructed and shipped by the code producer along with C and the proof P of VC. The code consumer uses Ω to reconstruct VC and verify that P truly corresponds to VC. Therefore, in our setting, the witness Ω and the proof P may together be viewed as the certificate that C respects S.

While the above strategy is theoretically sound, it must overcome two key pragmatic obstacles. First, since certificates have to be transmitted and verified, they must be small and efficiently checkable. Unfortunately, proofs generated by conventional theorem-provers, such as CVC and VAMPYRE, are often prohibitively large. Second, conventional theorem provers are usually unfaithful to the semantics of C. For example, they often do not support features of integer operations such as overflow and underflow. This means that certificates generated by such theorem provers are, in general, not trustworthy. For example, the following VC is declared valid by most conventional theorem provers, including CVC and VAMPYRE: $\forall x \cdot (x + 1) > x$. However, the above statement is actually invalid according to the semantics of the C language due to the possibility of overflow.

In this article, we propose the use of Boolean satisfiability (SAT) to solve both these problems. More specifically, we translate VC to a propositional formula Φ such that VC is valid iff Φ is unsatisfiable. Therefore, a resolution refutation (proof of the unsatisfiability) of Φ serves as a proof of the validity of VC. We use the state-of-the-art SAT solver ZCHAFF [25], which also generates resolution refutations, to prove that Φ is unsatisfiable. The translation from VC to Φ is faithful to the semantics of C and therefore handles issues such as overflow.

We have implemented our proposed technique in the COMFORT [10] reasoning framework and experimented with several non-trivial benchmarks. Our results indicate that the use of SAT leads to extremely compact (in some cases over 10^5 times smaller) proofs in comparison to conventional theorem-provers. Further details of our experiments can be found in Section 7.

We believe that this paper contributes to not just the area of software certification, but to the much broader spectrum of scientific disciplines where compact proofs are desirable. Algorithms to compress proof representations are currently a topic of active research. This article demonstrates that the use of SAT technology is a very promising idea in this context. In the rest of this paper, we omit proofs of lemmas and theorems for the sake of brevity. Detailed proofs can be found in an extended version of this paper [6].

2   Related Work

Necula and Lee [28, 30, 31] proposed PCC as a means for checkably certifying that untrusted *binaries* respect certain fundamental safety (such as memory safety) criteria. Foundational PCC [2, 18] attempts to reduce the trusted computing base of PCC to solely the foundations of mathematical logic. Bernard and Lee [5] propose a new temporal logic to express PCC policies for machine code.Non-SAT-based techniques for minimizing PCC proof sizes [29, 32] and formalizing machine code semantics [24] have also been proposed. Our work uses proofs to certify software but is applicable to safety as well as liveness specifications, and at the *source code* level.

Certifying model checkers [26, 22] emit an independently checkable certificate of correctness when a temporal logic formula is found to be satisfiable by a *finite state* model. Namjoshi [27] has proposed a two-step technique for obtaining proofs of μ-calculus specifications on *infinite-state* systems. In the first step, a proof is obtained via certifying model checking. In the second step, the proof is *lifted* via an abstraction. This approach is more general than ours as far as LTL model checking is concerned, but does not handle simulation. It also does not propose the use of SAT or provide experimental validation.

Magill et al. [23] have proposed a two-step procedure for certifying simulation conformance between an infinite-state system and a finite state machine specification. In the first step they certify that a finite-state abstraction simulates the infinite-state system. In the second step they prove simulation between the finite-state abstraction and the specification. Their approach does not cover LTL specifications, and in particular, is unable to handle liveness policies. Also, it does not propose the use of SAT.

Predicate abstraction [17] in combination with CEGAR [12] has been applied successfully by several software model checkers such as SLAM [4], BLAST [20] and MAGIC [7]. Out of these SLAM and MAGIC do not generate any proof certificates when claiming the validity of program specifications. BLAST includes a method [19] for lifting linear time safety proofs through the abstraction computed by their algorithm into a checkable proof of correctness for the original program. It does not handle liveness specifications and uses the non-SAT-based theorem prover VAMPYRE for proof generation. The use of SAT for software model checking has also been explored in the context of both sequential ANSI-C programs [14] and asynchronous concurrent Boolean programs [15]. Proving program termination via ranking functions is also a rich, and developing, research area [16, 3].

3 Preliminaries

In this section we present preliminary definitions and results. Let *Act* be a denumerable set of actions. We begin with the notion of labeled transition systems.

Definition 1 (LTS). *A Labeled Transition System (LTS) is a quadruple* $(S, Init, \Sigma, T)$ *where: (i)* S *is a finite set of states, (ii)* $Init \subseteq S$ *is a set of initial states, (iii)* $\Sigma \subseteq Act$ *is a finite alphabet, and (iv)* $T \subseteq S \times \Sigma \times S$ *is a transition relation.*

Given an LTS $M = (S, Init, \Sigma, T)$ we write $s \xrightarrow{\alpha} s'$ to mean $(s, \alpha, s') \in T$. Also for any $s \in S$ and any $\alpha \in \Sigma$ we denote by $Succ(s, \alpha)$ the set of successors of s under α. In other words: $Succ(s, \alpha) = \{s' \mid s \xrightarrow{\alpha} s'\}$.

Linear Temporal Logic. We now define our notion of linear temporal logic (LTL). Unlike standard practice, the flavor of LTL we use is based on actions instead of propositions. This distinction is, however, inessential as far as this article is concerned. The syntax of LTL is defined by the following BNF-style grammar (where $\alpha \in Act$): $\phi := \alpha \mid \neg\phi_1 \mid \phi_1 \wedge \phi_2 \mid \mathbf{X}\phi_1 \mid \phi_1 \mathbf{U}\phi_2$.

The semantics of LTL is fairly standard and we do not describe it here. In fact, we do not deal with LTL specifications directly but rather via an equivalent automata-theoretic formalism called Büchi automata.

Definition 2 (Büchi Automaton). *A Büchi automaton (or simply an automaton) is 5-tuple $(S, Init, \Sigma, T, F)$ where: (i) S is a finite set of states, (ii) $Init \subseteq S$ is a set of initial states, (iii) $\Sigma \subseteq Act$ is a finite alphabet, (iv) $T \subseteq S \times \Sigma \times S$ is a transition relation, and (v) $F \subseteq S$ is a set of final (or accepting) states.*

As in the case of LTSs, given a Büchi Automaton $B = (S, Init, \Sigma, T, F)$, we write $s \xrightarrow{\alpha} s'$ to mean $(s, \alpha, s') \in T$. Also for any $s \in S$ and any $\alpha \in \Sigma$, we denote by $Succ(s, \alpha)$ the set $\{s' \mid s \xrightarrow{\alpha} s'\}$.

Language. A *trace* $t \in Act^\omega$ is an infinite sequence of actions. The language accepted by an automaton is a set of traces defined as follows. Let $B = (S, Init, \Sigma, T, F)$ be any automaton and $t = \langle \alpha_0, \alpha_1, \ldots \rangle$ be any trace. A *run* r of B on t is an infinite sequence of states $\langle s_0, s_1, \ldots \rangle$ such that: (i) $s_0 \in Init$ and (ii) $\forall i \geq 0 \cdot s_i \xrightarrow{\alpha_i} s_{i+1}$. For any run r we write $Inf(r)$ to denote the set of states appearing infinitely often in r. Then a trace t is accepted by B iff there exists a run r of B on t such that $Inf(r) \cap F \neq \emptyset$. The language of B, denoted by $\mathcal{L}(B)$ is the set of traces accepted by B. We define the product between an LTS and an automaton in the standard manner as follows:

Definition 3 (Product Automaton). *Let $M = (S_1, Init_1, \Sigma_1, T_1)$ be an LTS and $B = (S_2, Init_2, \Sigma_2, T_2, F_2)$ be an automaton such that $\Sigma_1 = \Sigma_2$. Then the product of M and B is denoted by $M \otimes B$ and defined as the automaton $(S, Init, \Sigma, T, F)$ where: (i) $S = S_1 \times S_2$, (ii) $Init = Init_1 \times Init_2$, (iii) $\Sigma = \Sigma_1$, (iv) $F = S_1 \times F_2$ and (v) T is defined as follows: $(s_1, s_2) \xrightarrow{\alpha} (s_1', s_2') \iff s_1 \xrightarrow{\alpha} s_1' \wedge s_2 \xrightarrow{\alpha} s_2'$.*

Program. We have applied our ideas to actual C programs. However, for clarity and simplicity of presentation, we use a programming language based on guarded commands. Let *Var* be a denumerable set of integer variables. The set of expressions *Expr* is defined over *Var* using the following operators : $+, -, \times, \div, =, <, \neg, \wedge$ and the C bit-wise operators.

Program Syntax. An assignment is a pair (v, e) where $v \in Var$ denotes the left-hand-side (LHS) and $e \in Expr$ denotes the right-hand-side (RHS). The set of assignments is denoted by *Asgn*. A guarded command is a triple (*Grd*, *Evt*, *Cmd*) where *Grd* $\in$ *Expr* is a guard, *Evt* $\in$ *Act* is an event and *Cmd* $\in$ *Asgn* is an assignment. The set of guarded commands is denoted by *GrdCmd*. Given a guarded command $gc = (g, e, c)$ we write *Grd(gc)*, *Evt(gc)* and *Cmd(gc)* to denote g, e and c respectively. Finally, a program is a pair (I, C) where $I \in$ *Expr* expresses constraints on the initial states of the program and $C \subseteq$ *GrdCmd* is a finite set of guarded commands.

Store. A *store* is a function $\sigma : Var \rightarrow \mathbb{Z}$ from variables to integers. The set of all stores is denoted by *Sto*. Any store σ naturally induces a function from expressions to integers: $\sigma(e)$ is the integer obtained by evaluating e under σ.

Our language has a C-like semantics as far as variables and operators are concerned. Integers are treated as 32-bit vectors. Also, the arithmetic, relational, Boolean and bit-wise operators are interpreted in a C-like manner. In particular, there is overflow and underflow, zero is treated as FALSE, while all other integers are treated as TRUE.

Definition 4 (Store Update). *Given a store* σ *and an assignment* $a = (v, e)$ *we write* $a[\sigma]$ *to denote the store resulting after executing* a *from* σ. *In other words,* $a[\sigma]$ *is the same as* σ *for all variables other than* v, *while* $a[\sigma](v) = \sigma(e)$.

Definition 5 (Satisfaction). *Given a store* σ *and an expression* e *we say that* σ *satisfies* e *iff* $\sigma(e) \neq 0$. *We denote the satisfaction of* e *by* σ *as* $\sigma \models e$ *and write* $\sigma \not\models e$ *to mean* $\neg(\sigma \models e)$.

In the rest of this article we use the terms formula and expression synonymously since, as we have seen, any expression e can also be viewed as a logical formula. The models of e are simply the stores satisfying e.

Program Semantics. We now define the semantics of a program *Prog* in terms of a labeled transition system. Intuitively, the states of the LTS are stores, its initial states are determined by the initial condition of *Prog*, and its transitions are determined by the guarded commands in *Prog*. Formally, let *Prog* $= (I, C)$ be a program. Then the semantics of *Prog*, denoted by $[\![Prog]\!]$, is an LTS $(S, Init, \Sigma, T)$ such that: (i) $S = Sto$, (ii) $Init = \{\sigma \mid \sigma \models I\}$, (iii) $\Sigma = \{Evt(gc) \mid gc \in C\}$, and (iv) $\sigma \xrightarrow{\alpha} \sigma'$ iff: $\exists gc \in C . \sigma \models Grd(gc) \wedge \alpha = Evt(gc) \wedge \sigma' = Cmd(gc)[\sigma]$. Given a specification as a *negated* automaton *Spec*, we say that *Prog* satisfies *Spec*, and denote this by *Prog* $\models$ *Spec*, iff $\mathcal{L}([\![Prog]\!] \otimes Spec) = \emptyset$.

4   Temporal Logic Witness

In this section we present our proof framework for programs. We consider a program *Prog* $= (I, C)$. We begin with the notion of strongest postconditions. For any expression e, variable v and expression t, we denote the expression obtained by simultaneously replacing all occurrences of v in e by t as $e[v/t]$.

Definition 6 (Strongest Postcondition). *Let* $Prog = (I, C)$ *be a program, e be an expression and α be an action. Then the strongest postcondition of e w.r.t. α is denoted by* $\mathcal{SP}[e]\{\alpha\}$ *and defined as follows:* $\mathcal{SP}[e]\{\alpha\} = \exists v' \,.\, \bigvee_{(g,\alpha,(v,t))\in C}(g \wedge e)[v/v'] \wedge (v = t[v/v'])$.

The concept of strongest postconditions is quite standard. In particular, the following fact about strongest postconditions is fairly well-known. Recall that a state of *Prog* is a store. Consider any expression e and any action α. Let σ and σ' be stores such that $\sigma \models e$ and $\sigma \xrightarrow{\alpha} \sigma'$. Then $\sigma' \models \mathcal{SP}[e]\{\alpha\}$. This idea is captured by the following well-known fact.

Fact 1. *Let Prog be a program and* $[\![Prog]\!] = (S, Init, \Sigma, T)$ *be its semantics. Let e be any expression. Then the following holds:* $\forall \sigma \in S \,.\, \forall \sigma' \in S \,.\, \forall \alpha \in \Sigma \,.\, ((\sigma \models e) \wedge (\sigma \xrightarrow{\alpha} \sigma')) \Rightarrow (\sigma' \models \mathcal{SP}[e]\{\alpha\})$.

Lemma 1. *Let e_1, e_2 be any expressions and α be any action. Then the following holds:* $(\mathcal{SP}[e_1]\{\alpha\} \vee \mathcal{SP}[e_2]\{\alpha\}) \iff \mathcal{SP}[e_1 \vee e_2]\{\alpha\}$.

We are now ready to present the formal notion of a proof of $Prog \models Spec$. Recall that our goal is to prove $\mathcal{L}([\![Prog]\!] \otimes Spec) = \emptyset$. Such a proof essentially encodes a *stratified ranking function* between $[\![Prog]\!]$ and $Spec$. Let us write $M_\otimes$ to mean $[\![Prog]\!] \otimes Spec$. Let $M_\otimes = (S_\otimes, Init_\otimes, \Sigma, T_\otimes, F_\otimes)$ and R be a finite set of integral ranks. Suppose that there exists a ranking function $\rho : S_\otimes \to R$ such that the following holds:

- **(RANK1)** $Init_\otimes \subseteq Domain(\rho)$, i.e., all initial states of $M_\otimes$ have a rank.
- **(RANK2)** $\forall s \xrightarrow{\alpha} s' \,.\, s \notin F_\otimes \Rightarrow \rho(s) \geq \rho(s')$.
- **(RANK3)** $\forall s \xrightarrow{\alpha} s' \,.\, s \in F_\otimes \Rightarrow \rho(s) > \rho(s')$.

Then there is no infinite path of $M_\otimes$ that visits an accepting state infinitely often, i.e., $\mathcal{L}(M_\otimes) = \emptyset$. We use a witness to encode a ranking function. We also use appropriate side-conditions to ensure that the ranking function satisfies the three conditions mentioned above. We now state this formally:

Theorem 1. *Let $Prog = (I, C)$ be a program and $Spec = (S, Init, \Sigma, T, F)$ be a specification automaton. Let R be a finite set of integral ranks. Suppose that there exists a function* $\Omega : S \times R \to Expr$ *that satisfies the following four conditions:*

(C1) $\forall s \in S \,.\, \forall r \in R \,.\, \forall r' \in R \,.\, r \neq r' \Rightarrow \neg(\Omega(s,r) \wedge \Omega(s,r'))$
(C2) $\forall s \in Init \,.\, I \Rightarrow \bigvee_{r \in R} \Omega(s,r)$
(C3) $\forall s \in S \setminus F \,.\, \forall \alpha \,.\, \forall r \in R \,.\, \forall s' \in Succ(s,\alpha) \,.\, \mathcal{SP}[\Omega(s,r)]\{\alpha\} \Rightarrow \bigvee_{r' \leq r} \Omega(s',r')$
(C4) $\forall s \in F \,.\, \forall \alpha \,.\, \forall r \in R \,.\, \forall s' \in Succ(s,\alpha) \,.\, \mathcal{SP}[\Omega(s,r)]\{\alpha\} \Rightarrow \bigvee_{r' < r} \Omega(s',r')$
Then $[\![Prog]\!] \models Spec$ *and we say that Ω is a witness to* $[\![Prog]\!] \models Spec$.

Suppose we are given $Prog$, $Spec = (S, Init, \Sigma, T)$ and a candidate witness Ω over a set of ranks R. Since S, Σ and R are all finite, it is straightforward to generate a formula equivalent to the conditions **C1 – C4** enumerated in Theorem 1. We call such a formula our *verification condition* and denote it by $VC(Prog, Spec, \Omega)$.

In essence, on account of Theorem 1, a valid proof of $VC(Prog, Spec, \Omega)$ is also a valid proof of $Prog \models Spec$.

Theorem 1 is useful in checking the validity of a proposed witness Ω. However, it yields no technique to construct such a Ω. In this section we present a procedure called predicate abstraction. In the next section we show how to construct a valid witness using predicate abstraction. More specifically, if our procedure actually results in a witness Ω, then Ω is guaranteed to be valid. In other words, the verification condition $VC(Prog, Spec, \Omega)$ is guaranteed to be a valid formula. We begin with some preliminary definitions:

Definition 7 (Predicate). *A predicate is simply an expression. Let $\mathcal{P}$ be a finite set of predicates. A valuation of $\mathcal{P}$ is a function from $\mathcal{P}$ to $\{\text{TRUE}, \text{FALSE}\}$. The set of all valuations of $\mathcal{P}$ is denoted by $\mathcal{V}(\mathcal{P})$. Given a valuation $V \in \mathcal{V}(\mathcal{P})$ of $\mathcal{P}$, the concretization of $\mathcal{P}$ w.r.t. V is denoted by $\gamma^{\mathcal{P}}(V)$ and is the expression defined as follows: $\gamma^{\mathcal{P}}(V) = \bigwedge_{p \in \mathcal{P}} p^{V(p)}$, where for any predicate p, we have $p^{\text{TRUE}} = p$ and $p^{\text{FALSE}} = \neg p$.*

In this article we only consider finite sets of predicates. We write $\gamma(V)$ to mean $\gamma^{\mathcal{P}}(V)$ when $\mathcal{P}$ is clear from context. The notion of concretization presented above means that any valuation V can also be thought of as the expression $\gamma(V)$. This leads naturally to the notion of consistency between valuations and expressions and between two valuations.

Definition 8 (Consistency). *Let V be a valuation of a set of predicates $\mathcal{P}$ and e be an expression. We say that V is consistent with e, and denote this by $V \Vdash e$, iff the expression $\gamma(V) \Rightarrow \neg e$ is invalid. In other words: $V \Vdash e \iff \exists \sigma \in Sto$. $\sigma \models \gamma(V) \wedge \sigma \models e$. Equivalently, $\neg(V \Vdash e)$ iff the expression $\gamma(V) \Rightarrow \neg e$ is valid.*

Consistency essentially means that a valuation and an expression are not mutually exclusive. We now define weakest preconditions, a concept closely related to strongest postconditions. Recall that for any expression e, variable v and expression t, we denote the expression obtained by simultaneously replacing all occurrences of v in e by t as $e[v/t]$.

Definition 9 (Weakest Precondition). *Let $Prog = (I, C)$ be a program, e be an expression and α be an action. Then the weakest precondition of e w.r.t. α is denoted by $\mathcal{WP}[e]\{\alpha\}$ and defined as: $\mathcal{WP}[e]\{\alpha\} = \bigvee_{(g,\alpha,(v,t)) \in C} g \wedge e[v/t]$.*

The relationship between strongest postconditions and weakest preconditions is expressed formally by the following lemma.

Lemma 2. *Let e, e' be expressions and α be an action. Then the following holds: $(e \Rightarrow \neg \mathcal{WP}[e']\{\alpha\}) \Rightarrow (\mathcal{SP}[e]\{\alpha\} \Rightarrow \neg e')$.*

Predicate Abstraction. Let $Prog = (I, C)$ be a program and $\mathcal{P}$ be a set of predicates. Let $[\![Prog]\!] = (S, Init, \Sigma, T)$ be the semantics of $Prog$. Then the predicate abstraction of $Prog$ w.r.t. $\mathcal{P}$ is denoted by $\{\!\{Prog\}\!\}^{\mathcal{P}}$ and is defined as an LTS $(\widehat{S}, \widehat{Init}, \widehat{\Sigma}, \widehat{T})$ where: (i) $\widehat{S} = \mathcal{V}(\mathcal{P})$: the states are the valuations of $\mathcal{P}$,

(ii) $\widehat{Init} = \{V \in \mathcal{V}(\mathcal{P}) \mid V \Vdash I\}$, (iii) $\widehat{\Sigma} = \Sigma$, and (iv) $\widehat{T}$ is defined as follows: $V \xrightarrow{\alpha} V' \iff V \Vdash \mathcal{WP}[\gamma(V')]\{\alpha\}$.

Predicate abstraction enables us to create finite LTS abstractions of our infinite state programs. More importantly, it can be automated. Given $Prog$ and $\mathcal{P}$ it is easy to construct $\{\!\{Prog\}\!\}^{\mathcal{P}}$ from the definition given above. In order to check for consistency we use an automated theorem-prover. More specifically, suppose we want to check if $V \Vdash e$. Then, in accordance with Definition 8, we check for the validity of $\gamma(V) \Rightarrow \neg e$ using a (sound) theorem prover. We assume $\neg(V \Vdash e)$ iff the theorem says that $\gamma(V) \Rightarrow \neg e$ is valid.

Generating LTL Witnesses. We now present an algorithm **WitGen** for constructing a valid witness to $[\![Prog]\!] \models Spec$. The input to **WitGen** is: (i) a set of predicates $\mathcal{P}$ such that $\{\!\{Prog\}\!\}^{\mathcal{P}} \models Spec$, and (ii) a ranking function ρ from the states of $\{\!\{Prog\}\!\}^{\mathcal{P}} \otimes Spec$ to a finite set of ranks R that obeys conditions **RANK1 – RANK3** given in Section 4. We defer the question as to how such a set of predicates $\mathcal{P}$ and ranking function ρ may be constructed till later. The output of **WitGen** is a valid witness Ω. The following theorem conveys the key ideas behind our algorithm.

Theorem 2 (Valid Witness). *Let* $Prog = (I, C)$ *be a program,* $Spec = (S, Init, \Sigma, T, F)$ *be a finite specification automaton and* $\mathcal{P}$ *be a set of predicates such that* $\{\!\{Prog\}\!\}^{\mathcal{P}} \models Spec$. *Let* $\{\!\{Prog\}\!\}^{\mathcal{P}} = (\mathcal{V}(\mathcal{P}), \widehat{Init}, \widehat{\Sigma}, \widehat{T})$. *Let* R *be a finite set of integral ranks and* $\rho : \mathcal{V}(\mathcal{P}) \times S \to R$ *be a ranking function that obeys conditions* **RANK1 – RANK3** *given in Section 4. Now consider the witness* $\Omega : S \times R \to Expr$ *defined as follows:* $\Omega(s, r) = \bigvee_{V : \rho(V, s) = r} \gamma(V)$. *Then* Ω *is a valid witness to* $[\![Prog]\!] \models Spec$.

Getting Predicates and Ranking Functions. Theorem 2 immediately leads to an algorithm **WitGen** to construct a valid witness Ω to $Prog \models Spec$. However, **WitGen** requires as input an appropriate set of predicates $\mathcal{P}$ such that $\{\!\{Prog\}\!\}^{\mathcal{P}} \models Spec$, as well as a ranking function ρ satisfying the conditions mentioned in Theorem 2. A suitable $\mathcal{P}$ may be constructed by combining predicate abstraction with CEGAR. Full details of such a procedure can be found elsewhere [9]. Due to the fundamental undecidability of the problem, such an approach is not always guaranteed to terminate. However, CEGAR-based techniques have been reported to be quite successful [4, 20, 7] in software verification in recent times.

Generating the Ranking Function. Once an appropriate set of predicates $\mathcal{P}$ has been found by the above procedure, we have to construct a ranking function ρ. More precisely, suppose that $\{\!\{Prog\}\!\}^{\mathcal{P}} = (\mathcal{V}(\mathcal{P}), \widehat{Init}, \widehat{\Sigma}, \widehat{T})$ and $Spec = (S, Init, \Sigma, T, F)$. Then we have to construct: (i) a finite set of integral ranks R, and (ii) a ranking function $\rho : \mathcal{V}(\mathcal{P}) \times S \to R$ that obeys conditions **RANK1 – RANK3** given in Section 4. We now give an algorithm to achieve these two goals.

Let us denote $\{\!\{Prog\}\!\}^{\mathcal{P}} \otimes Spec$ by $M_{\otimes}$ and let $M_{\otimes} = (S_{\otimes}, Init_{\otimes}, \Sigma, T_{\otimes}, F_{\otimes})$. Without loss of generality we assume that both $S_{\otimes}$ and $F_{\otimes}$ only contain the states of $M_\otimes$ that are reachable from $Init_\otimes$ via the transition relation. Our ranking function is defined on only $S_\otimes$, and undefined for unreachable states of $M_\otimes$.

First, we note that $M_\otimes$ can be viewed as a directed graph $G_\otimes = (N, E)$ such that: $(N = S_\otimes) \bigwedge (E = \{(s, s') \mid \exists \alpha \in \Sigma \cdot s \xrightarrow{\alpha} s'\})$. Given any two nodes s and s' we say that $s \rightsquigarrow s'$ iff there is a path from s to s' in G. In other words, $s \rightsquigarrow s'$ iff there exists a finite *non-empty* sequence of states $s_1, s_2, \ldots, s_k$ such that: $(s = s_1) \bigwedge (s' = s_k) \bigwedge (\forall i \in \{1, \ldots, k-1\} \cdot (s_i, s_{i+1}) \in E)$. A strongly connected component (SCC) of $G_\otimes$ is a set of nodes $X \subseteq N$ such that: $\forall s \in X \cdot \forall s' \in X \cdot s \rightsquigarrow s'$. A node of $G_\otimes$ that does not belong to any SCC is called a *finitary* node. It is evident that a node n is finitary iff for every run x of $M_\otimes$ we have $n \notin Inf(x)$. We also know that $\{\!\{Prog\}\!\}^{\mathcal{P}} \models Spec$ and hence $\mathcal{L}(M_\otimes) = \emptyset$. This means that every accepting state $s \in F_\otimes$ must be finitary.

It is also well known that every directed graph G induces a directed acyclic graph G^{SCC}. The nodes of G^{SCC} are the maximal strongly connected components and the finitary nodes of G while its edges are induced by those of G. Let $G_\otimes^{SCC}$ be the directed acyclic graph induced by $G_\otimes$. Let $\mathcal{O} = \langle n_1, n_2, \ldots, n_k \rangle$ be a topological ordering of the nodes of $G_\otimes^{SCC}$ such that if $n_i \rightsquigarrow n_j$, then n_j appears before n_i in $\mathcal{O}$. We now fix our set of ranks R to be $\{1, 2, \ldots, k\}$ where $k = |\mathcal{O}|$. We first define a ranking function ρ^{SCC} for the nodes of $G_\otimes^{SCC}$ as follows: $\rho^{SCC}(n) = i$ iff $n = n_i$ according to the ordering $\mathcal{O}$. We then use ρ^{SCC} to define a ranking function ρ for $G_\otimes$ as follows:

- If n is a finitary node then it is also a node of $G_\otimes^{SCC}$. Then $\rho(n) = \rho^{SCC}(n)$.
- Otherwise n belongs to an unique maximal SCC n^{SCC} which is a node of $G_\otimes^{SCC}$. In this case $\rho(n) = \rho^{SCC}(n^{SCC})$.

We now show that ρ satisfies conditions **RANK1** – **RANK3** given in Section 4. Condition **RANK1** holds because $Init_\otimes \subseteq S_\otimes = Domain(\rho)$. For condition **RANK2**, consider any transition $s \xrightarrow{\alpha} s'$ of $M_\otimes$ such that $s \notin F_\otimes$. Now since $s \rightsquigarrow s'$ we have $\rho(s) \geq \rho(s')$ which is precisely **RANK2**. For condition **RANK3**, consider any transition $s \xrightarrow{\alpha} s'$ of $M_\otimes$ such that $s \in F_\otimes$. Recall that in this case s must be a finitary node. Hence $\rho(s) \neq \rho(s')$. Since $s \rightsquigarrow s'$ we have $\rho(s) > \rho(s')$ which is precisely **RANK3**.

The use of ranking functions for proofs of liveness properties is well studied and ours is but another instance of this methodology. The use, and limitations, of CEGAR for generating appropriate predicates is orthogonal to the witness construction procedure. In practice, any oracle capable of providing a suitable set of predicates can be substituted for CEGAR. For instance, some of the predicates can be manually supplied and the remaining predicates may be constructed automatically.

5 SAT-Based Certificates

Suppose we are given a program *Prog*, a specification *Spec* and a candidate witness Ω. We wish to check the validity of Ω. To this end we construct the verification condition $VC = VC(Prog, Spec, \Omega)$ and prove that VC is valid. One way to achieve this goal is to pass VC as a query to an existing proof-generating automated theorem-prover such as CVC or VAMPYRE. However, there are at least two shortcomings of this approach:

First, most theorem provers treat integers, as well as operations on integers, in a manner that is incompatible with the semantics of our programming language. For example, our language defines integers to be 32-bit vectors and operations such as addition and multiplication are defined in accordance with two's-complement arithmetic. In contrast, for most theorem provers, integers have an infinite domain and operations on them are the ones we learn in primary school. An important consequence of this discrepancy is that certificates generated by conventional theorem provers may be untrustworthy for our purposes. For example, the following verification condition is declared valid by most conventional theorem provers, including CVC and VAMPYRE: $\forall x . (x + 1) > x$. However, the above statement is actually invalid according to our language semantics due to the possibility of overflow.

In addition, the proofs generated by such theorem provers are usually quite large (cf. Figure 2). We propose the use of a SAT-based proof-generating decision procedure to overcome both these hurdles. Recall that the verification conditions we are required to prove are essentially expressions. Given a verification condition VC, we check its validity as follows:

1. We translate VC to a SAT formula Φ in conjunctive normal form such that VC is valid iff Φ is unsatisfiable. In essence Φ represents the negation of VC.
2. We check for the satisfiability of Φ using a SAT solver. If Φ is found to be satisfiable then VC is invalid. Otherwise, Φ is unsatisfiable and therefore VC is valid. In such a case our SAT solver also emits a resolution[1] proof P that refutes Φ. We use P as the proof of validity of VC.

In our implementation, we use the CPROVER [21] tool to perform Step 1 above. Step 2 is performed by the state-of-the-art SAT solver ZCHAFF [25] which is capable of generating resolution-based refutation proofs [34]. The ZCHAFF distribution also comes with a proof checker which we use to verify the correctness of the proofs emitted by ZCHAFF as a sanity-check. We discuss our experimental results in detail in Section 7. We note here that in almost all cases, SAT-based proofs are over 100 times (in one case over 10^5 times) more compact than those generated by CVC and VAMPYRE. Of course, our proofs are additionally faithful to the semantics of our programming language.

It is important to understand how our approach addresses the two shortcomings of conventional theorem provers presented at the beginning of this section. The first problem regarding language semantics is handled by the translation from VC to Φ in Step 1 above. Of course, the translator itself now becomes part of our trusted computing base. However, we believe that such a decision is amply justified by the resulting benefits.

The second difficulty with large proof sizes is mitigated by the fact that a Φ generated from real-life programs and specifications often has an extremely

---

[1] Resolution is a sound and complete inference rule for refuting propositional formulas.

compact resolution refutation. Intuitively, if a program is correct, it is usually correct because of some simple reason. In practice, this results in Φ having a much smaller unsatisfiable core C. In essence, C is a subset of the clauses in Φ that is itself unsatisfiable. Since Φ is in CNF form, it is possible to refute Φ by simply refuting C. State-of-the-art SAT solvers, such as ZCHAFF, leverage this idea by first computing a small unsatisfiable core of the target formula and then generating a refutation for only the core. Section 7 contains more details about the kind of compression we are typically able to obtain by using the unsatisfiable core.

Finally, we note that the use of SAT guarantees trustworthiness of the generated certificate even if we use a non-SAT-based theorem prover, such as SIMPLIFY [33], for predicate abstraction. This enables us to use fast, but potentially unfaithful, theorem provers during the verification stage and still remain faithful to C semantics as far as certification is concerned.

6   Simulation

While LTL allows us to reason about both safety and liveness properties, it is nevertheless restricted to a purely linear notion of time. Simulation enables us to reason about branching time properties of programs since it preserves all ACTL* specifications.

Definition 10 (Simulation). Let $M_1 = (S_1, Init_1, \Sigma, T_1)$ and $M_2 = (S_2, Init_2, \Sigma, T_2)$ be two LTSs. Note that M_1 and M_2 have the same alphabet. A relation $\mathcal{R} \subseteq S_1 \times S_2$ is said to be a simulation relation if it satisfies the following condition: **(SIM)** $\forall s_1 \in S_1 . \forall s_1' \in S_1 . \forall s_2 \in S_2 . \forall \alpha \in \Sigma . (s_1, s_2) \in \mathcal{R} \wedge s_1 \xrightarrow{\alpha} s_1' \Rightarrow \exists s_2' \in S_2 . s_2 \xrightarrow{\alpha} s_2' \wedge (s_1', s_2') \in \mathcal{R}$. We say that M_1 is simulated by M_2, and denote this by $M_1 \preccurlyeq M_2$, iff there exists a simulation relation $\mathcal{R} \subseteq S_1 \times S_2$ such that $\forall s_1 \in Init_1 . \exists s_2 \in Init_2 . (s_1, s_2) \in \mathcal{R}$.

Simulation Witness. We are now ready to present the formal notion of a proof of $Prog \preccurlyeq Spec$. Such a proof essentially encodes a simulation relation between $Prog$ and $Spec$. The idea is to use a mapping Ω from states of $Spec$ to expressions such that for any state s of $Spec$, $\Omega(s)$ is satisfied by those states of $Prog$ that are simulated by $Spec$. We now state this formally:

Theorem 3. Let $Prog = (I, C)$ be a program and $Spec = (S, Init, \Sigma, T)$ be a finite LTS. Suppose that there exists a function $\Omega : S \rightarrow Expr$ that satisfies the following two conditions: **(D1)** $I \Rightarrow \bigvee_{s \in Init} \Omega(s)$ and **(D2)** $\forall s \in S . \forall \alpha \in \Sigma . \mathcal{SP}[\Omega(s)]\{\alpha\} \Rightarrow \bigvee_{s' \in Succ(s, \alpha)} \Omega(s')$. Then $[\![Prog]\!] \preccurlyeq Spec$ and we say that Ω is a witness to $[\![Prog]\!] \preccurlyeq Spec$.

Suppose we are given $Prog$, $Spec = (S, Init, \Sigma, T)$ and a candidate witness Ω. Since both S and Σ are finite, it is straightforward to generate a formula equivalent to the conditions $\mathbf{D1} - \mathbf{D2}$ enumerated in Theorem 3. We call such a formula our *verification condition* and denote it by $VC(Prog, Spec, \Omega)$. In essence, on account of Theorem 3, a valid proof of $VC(Prog, Spec, \Omega)$ is also a valid proof of $Prog \preccurlyeq Spec$.

Generating Simulation Witnesses. We now present an algorithm **WitGenSimul** for constructing a valid witness to $[\![Prog]\!] \preccurlyeq Spec$. The input to **WitGenSimul** is a set of predicates $\mathcal{P}$ such that $\{\!\{Prog\}\!\}^{\mathcal{P}} \preccurlyeq Spec$, and a simulation relation $\mathcal{R}$ between the states of $\{\!\{Prog\}\!\}^{\mathcal{P}}$ and the states of $Spec$. We defer the question as to how such a set of predicates $\mathcal{P}$ and simulation relation $\mathcal{R}$ may be constructed till later. The output of **WitGenSimul** is a valid witness Ω. The following theorem conveys the key ideas behind our algorithm.

Theorem 4 (Valid Witness). *Let* $Prog = (I, C)$ *be a program,* $Spec = (S, Init, \Sigma, T)$ *be a finite LTS and* $\mathcal{P}$ *be a set of predicates such that* $\{\!\{Prog\}\!\}^{\mathcal{P}} \preccurlyeq Spec$. *Let* $\{\!\{Prog\}\!\}^{\mathcal{P}} = (\mathcal{V}(\mathcal{P}), \widehat{Init}, \widehat{\Sigma}, \widehat{T})$ *and* $\mathcal{R} \subseteq \mathcal{V}(\mathcal{P}) \times S$ *be a simulation relation such that:* (**A1**) $\forall V \in \widehat{Init} \,.\, \exists s \in Init \,.\, (V, s) \in \mathcal{R}$. *Let us also define a function* $\theta : S \to 2^{\mathcal{V}(\mathcal{P})}$ *as follows:* (**A2**) $\forall s \in S \,.\, \theta(s) = \{V \mid (V, s) \in \mathcal{R}\}$. *Now consider the witness* $\Omega : S \to Expr$ *defined as follows:* (**A3**) $\forall s \in S \,.\, \Omega(s) = \bigvee_{V \in \theta(s)} \gamma(V)$. *Then* Ω *is a valid witness to* $[\![Prog]\!] \preccurlyeq Spec$.

Getting Simulation Predicates. Theorem 4 immediately leads to an algorithm **WitGenSimul** to construct a valid witness Ω to $Prog \preccurlyeq Spec$. However, **WitGenSimul** requires as input an appropriate set of predicates $\mathcal{P}$ such that $\{\!\{Prog\}\!\}^{\mathcal{P}} \preccurlyeq Spec$. As in the case of LTL model checking, such a $\mathcal{P}$ may be constructed by combining predicate abstraction with CEGAR. Full details of such a procedure can be found elsewhere [8]. As in the case of LTL, due to the fundamental undecidability of the problem, such an approach is not always guaranteed to terminate, but has been found to be quite effective in practice.

Witness Minimization. It is clear from Theorem 4 that the size of witnesses and proofs generated by **WitGenSimul** is directly related to the size of the simulation relation $\mathcal{R}$ between $\{\!\{Prog\}\!\}^{\mathcal{P}}$ and $Spec$. In this section we describe an algorithm to construct a *minimal* simulation relation between two finite LTSs if such a relation exists. Clearly, such an algorithm can be used to construct an $\mathcal{R}$ of minimal size which would in turn lead to a witness Ω of small size.

Our algorithm relies on a well-known technique [7] to check for simulation between finite LTSs using satisfiability for weakly negated HORNSAT formulas. More specifically suppose we are given two finite LTSs $M_1 = (S_1, Init_1, \Sigma, T_1)$ and $M_2 = (S_2, Init_2, \Sigma, T_2)$. Then one can construct a propositional CNF formula Ψ such that the set of variables appearing in Ψ is $S_1 \times S_2$. Intuitively, a variable (s_1, s_2) stands for the proposition that state s_1 can be simulated by state s_2.

The clauses of Ψ encode constraints imposed by a simulation relation and are constructed as follows. For each $s_1 \in S_1$, each $s_2 \in S_2$, each $\alpha \in \Sigma$, and each $s_1' \in Succ(s_1, \alpha)$ we add the following clause to Ψ: $(s_1, s_2) \Rightarrow \bigvee_{s_2' \in Succ(s_2, \alpha)} (s_1', s_2')$. Intuitively the above clause expresses the requirement that for s_2 to simulate s_1, at least one α-successor of s_2 must simulate s_1'. Also, for each $s_1 \in Init_1$ we add the following clause to Ψ: $\bigvee_{s_2 \in Init_2} (s_1, s_2)$. These clauses assert that every initial state of M_1 must be simulated by some initial state of M_2. Now, Ψ has the following simple property. Let X be any satisfying assignment of Ψ and for any variable $v = (s_1, s_2)$ let us write $X(s_1, s_2)$ to mean the Boolean value assigned to v by X. Then the relation $\mathcal{R} = \{(s_1, s_2) \mid X(s_1, s_2) = \text{TRUE}\}$ is a simulation relation between M_1 and M_2.

Therefore, we can construct a minimal simulation between M_1 and M_2 by constructing Ψ and then looking for a satisfying assignment X such that the number of variables assigned TRUE by X is as small as possible. This can be achieved by using a solver for pseudo-Boolean formulas [1]. A pseudo-Boolean formula is essentially a propositional formula coupled with an arithmetic constraint over the propositional variables (where TRUE is treated as one and FALSE as zero). More specifically, recall that the set of variables of Ψ is $S_1 \times S_2$. We thus solve for Ψ along with the constraint that the following sum be minimized: $\Upsilon = \sum_{s \in S_1 \times S_2} s$. We then construct a minimal simulation relation using any satisfying assignment to Ψ that also minimizes Υ.

Hardness of Finding Minimal Simulation Relations. One may complain that solving pseudo-Boolean formula satisfiability (an NP-complete problem) to verify simulation (for which polynomial time algorithms exist) is overkill. However, the use of a pseudo-Boolean solver is justified by the fact that finding a *minimal* simulation between two finite LTSs is actually an NP-hard problem.

We now prove this claim by reducing *sub-graph isomorphism*, a well-known NP-complete problem, to the problem of finding a minimal simulation relation between two LTSs. In the rest of this section, whenever we mention a simulation relation between two LTSs M_1 and M_2 we also tacitly assume that every initial state of M_1 is simulated by some initial state of M_2.

Definition 11 (Graph). *An undirected graph is a pair (V, E) where V is a set of vertices and $E \subseteq V \times V$ is a symmetric irreflexive relation denoting edges.*

Definition 12 (Subgraph Isomorphism). *Given two graphs $G_1 = (V_1, E_1)$ and $G_2 = (V_2, E_2)$ such that $|V_1| < |V_2|$, we say that G_1 is sub-graph isomorphic to G_2 iff there exists an injection $\mu : V_1 \to V_2$ that obeys the following condition: $\forall v \in V_1 \cdot \forall v' \in V_1 \cdot (v, v') \in E_1 \iff (\mu(v), \mu(v')) \in E_2$.*

Note that we do not allow self-loops in graphs. It is well-known that given two arbitrary graphs G_1 and G_2, the problem of deciding whether G_1 is sub-graph isomorphic to G_2 is NP-complete. We now show that this problem has a logspace reduction to the problem of finding a minimal simulation relation between two LTSs. In essence, from G_1 and G_2, we construct two LTSs M_1 and M_2 such that G_1 is sub-graph isomorphic to G_2 iff a minimal simulation relation between M_1 and M_2 has the same size as G_1.

Recall that $G_1 = (V_1, E_1)$. We construct $M_1 = (S_1, Init_1, \Sigma, T_1)$ as follows: (i) the states of M_1 are exactly the vertices of V_1, i.e., $S_1 = V_1$, (ii) all states of M_1 are initial, i.e., $Init_1 = S_1$, (iii) M_1 has two actions a and b, i.e., $\Sigma = \{a, b\}$, and (iv) the transitions T_1 of M_1 are set up as follows: (i) for each $(v, v') \in E_1$ we add $v \xrightarrow{a} v'$ and $v' \xrightarrow{a} v$ to T_1, and (ii) for each $(v, v') \notin E_1$ we add $v \xrightarrow{b} v'$ and $v' \xrightarrow{b} v$ to T_1. The LTS M_2 is constructed from graph G_2 in an analogous manner. As an example, Figure 1 shows two graphs G_1 and G_2 as well

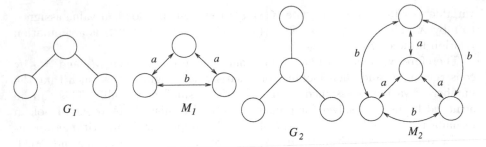

Fig. 1. Example graphs and LTSs constructed from them. A bi-directional arrow between two states represents a pair of transitions – one from each state to the other.

as the LTSs M_1 and M_2 constructed from them. Note that M_1 and M_2 can be constructed using logarithmic additional space. Now our NP-hardness reduction is completed by the following theorem.

Theorem 5. *Let n be the number of states of M_1, i.e., $n = |S_1|$. Then G_1 is sub-graph isomorphic to G_2 iff a minimal simulation relation between M_1 and M_2 has n elements.*

7   Experimental Results

We implemented our techniques in COMFORT [10] and experimented with a set of Linux and Windows NT device drivers, OpenSSL, and the Micro-C operating system. All our experiments were carried out on a dual Intel Xeon 2.4 GHz machine with 4 GB RAM and running Redhat 9. Our results are summarized in Figure 2. The Linux device drivers were obtained from kernel 2.6.11.10. We checked that the drivers obey the following conventions with spin_lock and spin_unlock: (i) locks must be acquired and released alternately beginning with an acquire (*safe*), and (ii) every acquire must be eventually followed by a release (*live*). The Windows drivers are instrumented so that an ERROR location is reached if any illegal behavior is executed. We certified that ERROR is unreachable for all the drivers we experimented with. For OpenSSL (version 0.9.6c) we certified that the initial handshake between a server and a client obeys the protocol specified in the SSL 3.0 specification. For Micro-C (version 2.72) we certified that the calls to OS_ENTER_CRITICAL and OS_EXIT_CRITICAL obey the two locking conventions mentioned above.

In almost all cases, SAT-based proofs are over 100 times more compact than those generated by CVC and VAMPYRE. In one instance – *tlan.c (live)* – the improvement is by a factor of more than 10^5. We also find that an important reason for such improvement is that the UNSAT-cores are much smaller (by over two to three orders of magnitude) than the actual SAT formulas. Upon closer inspection, we discovered that this is due to the simplicity of the verification conditions (VCs). For instance, the device drivers satisfy the locking conventions because of local coding conventions (every procedure with a lock has a matching

Name	LOC	CVC	Vampyre	SAT	Cert	Core	Improve
ide.c (safe)	7428	80720	×	100	703	>2000	807
ide.c (live)	7428	82653	×	100	1319	>2000	827
tlan.c (safe)	6523	11145980	×	517	4663	>200	21559
tlan.c (live)	6523	90155057	×	572	74281	>200	157614
aha152x.c (safe)	10069	247435	×	210	2102	>1500	1178
aha152x.c (live)	10069	247718	×	210	3968	>1500	1180
synclink.c (safe)	17104	9822	×	53	185	>500	185
synclink.c (live)	17104	9862	×	53	327	>500	186
hooks.c (safe)	30923	597642	×	369	2004	>1500	1629
hooks.c (live)	30923	601175	×	368	3102	>1500	1624
cdaudio.c (safe)	17798	248915	156787*	209	2006	>1000	750
diskperf.c (safe)	4824	117172	×	106	955	>2500	1105
floppy.c (safe)	17386	451085	60129*	318	2595	>3000	189
kbfiltr.c (safe)	12131	56682	7619*	51	528	>2500	149
parclass.c (safe)	26623	460973	×	262	2156	>4500	1759
parport.c (safe)	61781	2278120	102967*	529	3568	>5000	195
SSL-srvr (simul)	2483	1287290	19916	261	1055	>150	76
SSL-clnt (simul)	2484	189401	27189	155	740	>200	175
Micro-C (safe)	6272	416930	118162	262	2694	>5500	451
Micro-C (live)	6272	435450	×	263	7571	>5500	1656

Fig. 2. Comparison between CVC, VAMPYRE and SAT-based proof generation. A ×
indicates that results are not available. Best figures are highlighted. *LOC* = lines of
code. *CVC*, *Vampyre* and *SAT* = proof size in bytes (after compressing with the `gzip`
utility) with CVC, VAMPYRE and SAT. CVC statistics obtained via COMFORT, BLAST
statistics obtained from version 2.0 or existing publication [19] (indicated by *). *Cert*
= gzipped certificate (i.e., witness + proof of the verification condition) size with SAT.
Core = factor by which the unsatisfiable core is smaller than the original SAT formula.
Improve = factor by which SAT-based proofs are smaller than nearest other proofs.

unlock). In practice, this results in very simple VCs. Proofs generated by CVC
and VAMPYRE suffer from redundancies and inefficient encodings and therefore
turn out to be large even for such simple formulas. In contrast, SAT formulas
generated from these simple VCs are characterized by small unsatisfiable cores.

  We note that the total size of the certificate is usually dominated by the size of
the witness. Finally, we find that certificates for liveness policies tend to be larger
than those for the corresponding safety policies. This is due to the additional
information required to encode the ranking function, which is considerably more
complex for liveness specifications.

Acknowledgment. We are grateful to Stephen Magill, Aleksandar Nanevski,
Peter Lee and Edmund Clarke for insight on PCC and model checking. We also
thank Rupak Majumdar and Ranjit Jhala for providing us with the Windows
driver benchmarks, and Anubhav Gupta for advice on ZCHAFF.

References

1. F. Aloul, A. Ramani, I. Markov, and K. Sakallah. PBS: A backtrack search pseudo
   Boolean solver. In *Proc. of SAT*, 2002.
2. A. Appel. Foundational proof-carrying code. In *Proc. of LICS*, 2001.

3. I. Balaban, A. Pnueli, and L. Zuck. Shape analysis by predicate abstraction. In *Proc. of VMCAI*, 2005.
4. T. Ball and S. Rajamani. Automatically validating temporal safety properties of interfaces. In *Proc. of SPIN*, 2001.
5. A. Bernard and P. Lee. Temporal logic for proof-carrying code. In *CADE*, 2002.
6. S. Chaki. SAT-based Software Certification. Technical report CMU/SEI-2006-TN-004, Carnegie Mellon Software Engineering Institute, Pittsburgh, USA, 2006.
7. S. Chaki, E. Clarke, A. Groce, S. Jha, and H. Veith. Modular verification of software components in C. *IEEE TSE*, 30(6):388–402, 2004.
8. S. Chaki, E. Clarke, S. Jha, and H. Veith. An iterative framework for simulation conformance. *Journal of Logic and Computation*, 15(4), 2005.
9. S. Chaki, E. Clarke, J. Ouaknine, N. Sharygina, and N. Sinha. State/event-based software model checking. In *Proc. of IFM*, 2004.
10. S. Chaki, J. Ivers, N. Sharygina, and K. Wallnau. The ComFoRT reasoning framework. In *Proc. of CAV*, 2005.
11. E. Clarke and E. A. Emerson. Synthesis of synchronization skeletons for branching time temporal logic. In *Proceedings of WLP*, 1981.
12. E. Clarke, O. Grumberg, S. Jha, Y. Lu, and H. Veith. Counterexample-guided abstraction refinement for symbolic model checking. *J. ACM*, 50(5), 2003.
13. E. Clarke, O. Grumberg, and D. Peled. *Model Checking*. MIT Press, 2000.
14. E. Clarke, D. Kroening, and F. Lerda. A tool for checking ANSI-C programs. In *Proc. of TACAS*, 2004.
15. B. Cook, D. Kroening, and N. Sharygina. Symbolic model checking for asynchronous boolean programs. In *Proc. of SPIN*, 2005.
16. B. Cook, A. Podelski, and A. Rybalchenko. Abstraction refinement for termination. In *Proc. of SAS*, 2005.
17. S. Graf and H. Saïdi. Construction of abstract state graphs with PVS. In *CAV'97*.
18. N. Hamid, Z. Shao, V. Trifonov, S. Monnier, and Z. Ni. A syntactic approach to foundational proof-carrying code. In *Proc. of LICS*, 2002.
19. T. Henzinger, R. Jhala, R. Majumdar, G. Necula, G. Sutre, and W. Weimer. Temporal-safety proofs for systems code. In *Proc. of CAV*, 2002.
20. T. Henzinger, R. Jhala, R. Majumdar, and G. Sutre. Lazy abstraction. *POPL'02*.
21. D. Kroening. Application specific higher order logic theorem proving. *VERIFY'02*.
22. O. Kupferman and M. Vardi. From complementation to certification. *TACAS'04*.
23. S. Magill, A. Nanevski, E. Clarke, and P. Lee. Simulation-based safety proofs by MAGIC. In preparation.
24. N. Michael and A. Appel. Machine instruction syntax and semantics in higher order logic. In *Proc. of CADE*, 2000.
25. M. Moskewicz, C. Madigan, Y. Zhao, L. Zhang, and S. Malik. Chaff: Engineering an efficient SAT solver. In *Proc. of DAC*, 2001.
26. K. Namjoshi. Certifying model checkers. In *Proc. of CAV'01*.
27. K. Namjoshi. Lifting temporal proofs through abstractions. In *VMCAI'03*.
28. G. Necula. Proof-carrying code. In *POPL'97*.
29. G. Necula and P Lee. Efficient representation and validation of proofs. In *LICS'98*.
30. G. Necula and P. Lee. Safe kernel extensions without run-time checking. *OSDI'96*.
31. G. Necula and P. Lee. Safe, untrusted agents using proof-carrying code. In *Proc. of Mobile Agents and Security*, 1998.
32. G. Necula and S. P. Rahul. Oracle-based checking of untrusted software. *POPL'01*.
33. G. Nelson. *Techniques for Program Verification*. PhD thesis, 1980.
34. L. Zhang and S. Malik. Validating sat solvers using an independent resolution-based checker: Practical implementations and other applications. In *DATE'03*.

Expressiveness + Automation + Soundness: Towards Combining SMT Solvers and Interactive Proof Assistants

Pascal Fontaine, Jean-Yves Marion, Stephan Merz,
Leonor Prensa Nieto, and Alwen Tiu

LORIA – INRIA Lorraine – Université de Nancy

Abstract. Formal system development needs expressive specification languages, but also calls for highly automated tools. These two goals are not easy to reconcile, especially if one also aims at high assurances for correctness. In this paper, we describe a combination of Isabelle/HOL with a proof-producing SMT (Satisfiability Modulo Theories) solver that contains a SAT engine and a decision procedure for quantifier-free first-order logic with equality. As a result, a user benefits from the expressiveness of Isabelle/HOL when modeling a system, but obtains much better automation for those fragments of the proofs that fall within the scope of the (automatic) SMT solver. Soundness is not compromised because all proofs are submitted to the trusted kernel of Isabelle for certification. This architecture is straightforward to extend for other interactive proof assistants and proof-producing reasoners.

1 Introduction

Deductive tools for system verification can be classified according to the axes of *expressiveness*, *degree of automation* and *guarantees of soundness*. An ideal tool would score high everywhere: expressive input languages such as higher-order logic or set theory allow a user to write natural and concise models, automatic verification takes care of a large fraction of the proof obligations, and the assurance of soundness gives confidence in the result. In practice, these goals are in conflict. For example, interactive proof assistants encode rich logics, which are at the basis of highly expressive (and user-extensible) modeling languages. Their verification environment is usually built around a small trusted code base, ensuring that theorems can only be produced from explicitly stated axioms and proof rules. At the other end of the spectrum one finds automatic verification tools, including model checkers and decision procedures. These tools come with fixed input languages in which to express the models, and they implement fully automatic verification algorithms tailored for these languages. Using sophisticated optimizations, they aim to scale up to large problems; however, it is all too easy to inadvertently introduce bugs that compromise soundness.

It is clearly desirable to combine interactive and automatic verification tools in order to benefit from their respective strengths. Proof assistants often provide a back door for using automated tools in the form of trusted *oracles*: it suffices to translate the formulas to prove into the input language of the automatic reasoner and to invoke it. If the proof succeeds, the proof assistant will accept the formula as a theorem. However,

H. Hermanns and J. Palsberg (Eds.): TACAS 2006, LNCS 3920, pp. 167–181, 2006.

this mechanism makes the oracle a part of the trusted code base, and therefore weakens the guarantees of soundness. Even if one may be inclined to trust the external reasoner, the translation function can be non-trivial, for example when translating from higher-order to first-order logic; moreover, the translation will often undergo much less testing than the external reasoner itself.

One way to avoid this problem is to make the external reasoner produce proof traces that can be checked independently. Usually, checking a proof is a much simpler problem than finding it in the first place, so the checker can be accepted as part of the trusted code base. Even more, proof checking can be implemented relatively easily within an interactive proof assistant so that the size of the trusted kernel does not augment beyond what users of the proof assistant accept anyway. The combined tool offers the full expressiveness of the proof assistant, but provides the automation of the external reasoner over its domain, without compromising soundness guarantees.

An alternative would be to verify the algorithm of the automatic prover within a proof assistant and to extract an implementation whose soundness is guaranteed, without the need of checking individual proofs. (Note that code extraction or interpretation becomes part of the trusted code base.) It is not clear yet that this approach can produce implementations whose efficiency can compete with reasoners implemented as, say, highly optimized C programs. Mahboubi [14] describes ongoing work with the aim of implementing cylindrical algebraic decomposition in Coq.

In this paper we describe an implementation of proof certification for a decision procedure for the quantifier-free first-order language of uninterpreted function and predicate symbols implemented in haRVey [7] within Isabelle/HOL [23], the encoding of higher-order logic in Isabelle. The SMT (Satisfiability Modulo Theories) solver haRVey combines a SAT solver with decision procedures. In a nutshell, the SAT solver maintains a Boolean abstraction of the input formula. Whenever a propositional model for this abstraction is found, it is submitted to the decision procedure(s). If the model is found to be incompatible with a theory, a *conflict clause* is produced in order to exclude a class of models. This process continues until either a model is found, in which case the input formula is satisfiable, or until the SAT solver determines the Boolean abstraction to be unsatisfiable. Because the SAT solver plays a central role in haRVey, we first introduce in Sect. 3 proof reconstruction in Isabelle for SAT solvers. In Sect. 4 we describe how haRVey has been extended to produce proof traces and how we implement proof reconstruction for these traces (Sect. 5). The overall approach generalizes to other theories implemented in SMT solvers, including fragments of arithmetic and set-theoretical constructions.

Related Work. We are not aware of any existing combination of SMT solvers and proof assistants, but the use of proof certification for tool combination is widely accepted. For example, an interface between Coq and the rewriting system ELAN [21] lets ELAN compute proof objects (as λ-terms) that are submitted to Coq, and a similar approach has been implemented for Coq and the first-order theorem provers Bliksem [4] and Zenon. Because explicit proof objects can be huge, Necula and Lee [18] propose techniques to compress them. In contrast, we do not compute full proof objects but just "hints" that guide Isabelle during proof reconstruction. Meng et al. describe a combination of Isabelle and resolution-based first-order theorem provers [16], and a similar approach underlies the combination of Gandalf and HOL within the Prosper project [13]. The work on the TRAMP system reported by Meier [15] is used in the Omega system [25], and it appears to be closely related to ours because the target logic is similar; also, our "proof hints" can be understood as a form of proof planning.

2 Motivation for Tool Integration

Our motivation for combining interactive proof assistants and SMT solvers comes from case studies that we performed for the verification of distributed algorithms, including a framework for clock synchronization protocols [3, 26]. These case studies were carried out in Isabelle/HOL, and this formalism allowed us to write easily understandable system specifications. When it came to verification, we would typically instantiate the higher-order abstractions in a few initial proof steps, leaving us with first-order verification conditions. Many of these subgoals would fall within the domain of automatic decision procedures. A typical example is provided by the following lemma that appears within the context of clock synchronization:

> **lemma** *bounded-drift*:
>   **assumes** $s \leq t$ **and** *correct p t* **and** *correct q t*
>   **and** *rbound1 C* **and** *rbound2 C* **and** *rbound1 D* **and** *rbound2 D*
>   **shows** $|C\,p\,t - D\,q\,t| \leq |C\,p\,s - D\,q\,s| + 2 \times \rho \times (t - s)$

The lemma establishes a bound on the drift between two ρ-bounded clocks C and D for processors p and q that are supposed non-faulty (*correct*) at time t. It relies on the following definition of ρ-boundedness:

$$rbound1\ C \stackrel{\Delta}{=} \forall p, s, t.\ correct\ p\ t \wedge s \leq t \longrightarrow C\,p\,t - C\,p\,s \leq (1 + \rho) \times (t - s)$$
$$rbound2\ C \stackrel{\Delta}{=} \forall p, s, t.\ correct\ p\ t \wedge s \leq t \longrightarrow (1 - \rho) \times (t - s) \leq C\,p\,t - C\,p\,s$$

The Isabelle proof of this lemma in [26] requires a series of intermediate lemmas, which were rather tedious to prove. In particular, Isabelle's built-in tactic for linear arithmetic is unable to prove the lemma, even after manual instantiation of the quantifiers. This is mainly due to the appearance of the subterm $\rho \times (t - s)$, which falls outside the scope of linear arithmetic. In contrast, it is not hard to see that the lemma is correct, and CVC-Lite [2] was able to prove it automatically. CVC-Lite is an SMT solver whose core consists of a combination of decision procedures for fragments of first-order logic; other tools in this category include MathSAT [5], ICS [10] and Yices.

As a first step towards tool combination, we tried an oracle-style integration and implemented ML functions that translate a fragment of Isabelle/HOL to the input languages of SMT solvers. The recent emergence of the common SMT-LIB input format [24] turned out to be very helpful, because the same translations worked for many different tools. By using SMT solvers as oracles, we could concentrate on the high-level structure of the verification and leave tedious details such as the above lemma to the external tools.

However, we were also quickly reminded of the dangers with oracle-style integration: a simple typo in the translation functions was enough to corrupt soundness. The translation from a higher-order setting to a (multi-sorted) first-order language is non-trivial. In short, it was all too easy to introduce bugs in the translation, which suggested to us that we should investigate techniques of proof certification.

3   Proof Reconstruction for Propositional Logic

SAT solvers decide the satisfiability problem for propositional logic, and they are an essential component of SMT solvers. Given a propositional formula, a SAT solver either computes a satisfying valuation or reports that the formula is unsatisfiable. Modern SAT solvers implement the DPLL algorithm [6] due to Davis, Putnam, Logemann, and Loveland, enhanced by optimizations such as conflict analysis and non-chronological backtracking, good branching heuristics, and efficient data structures [29]. These solvers expect the input to be presented as a set (i.e., conjunction) of clauses, which are disjunctions of literals. In preparation for using a SAT solver, we must convert arbitrary propositional formulas into conjunctions of clauses, preserving satisfiability.

A naive conversion to conjunctive normal form (CNF) simply distributes disjunctions over conjunctions. However, this could result in a conjunction whose size is exponential in the size of the original formula. For example, the formula

$$(a_1 \wedge b_1) \vee \ldots \vee (a_n \wedge b_n)$$

gives rise to 2^n conjuncts. For our purposes, we do not need to produce an equivalent CNF formula, but only have to preserve (un)satisfiability, and it is well known that a conversion of linear complexity is possible in this case. The classical technique, due to Tseitin [1, 27], is to introduce new Boolean variables to represent complex subformulas. In the above example, we would introduce additional variables $x_1, \ldots, x_n$ and obtain the clauses

$$x_1 \vee \ldots \vee x_n, \ \neg x_i \vee a_i, \ \neg x_i \vee b_i, \ x_i \vee \neg a_i \vee \neg b_i \quad (i = 1, \ldots, n).$$

The first clause represents the original formula, whereas the remaining clauses arise from "definitional" equivalences $x_i = a_i \wedge b_i$. This idea can be implemented in Isabelle by a tactic that repeatedly applies the theorem

$$(A \wedge B) \vee C = (\exists x.(x = A \wedge B) \wedge (x \vee C))$$

in order to obtain a quantified Boolean formula $\exists \mathbf{x}.c_1 \wedge \ldots \wedge c_m$ that is equivalent to the original formula. The clauses $c_1, \ldots, c_m$ are then passed on to the SAT solver.

SAT solvers try to compute a satisfying assignment of truth values to atoms by repeatedly applying two basic operations [17]: Boolean constraint propagation determines the values of Boolean variables that appear in *unit clauses*, i.e. clauses that contain a single unassigned literal. Second, truth values are guessed for variables whose value has not yet been determined. In case these guesses are found to be incompatible with the input clauses, the search backtracks, remembering the unsuccessful guesses as a *learned clause* that is added to the original set of clauses in order to help direct the search.

In a theorem-proving context, we show a formula to be valid by establishing the unsatisfiability of its negation, and we are therefore mostly interested in verdicts of unsatisfiability. As explained in [30], SAT solvers such as MiniSAT [9] or zChaff [29] can produce justifications of unsatisfiability verdicts as lists of binary resolution steps. Each step operates on two clauses $c_1 \equiv a_1 \vee \ldots \vee a_k$ and $c_2 \equiv b_1 \vee \ldots \vee b_l$ that contain a complementary literal (say, $b_1 \equiv \overline{a_1}$) to produce the clause $a_2 \vee \ldots \vee a_k \vee b_2 \vee \ldots \vee b_l$; hence, a step can be represented as a triple of integers identifying the two participating clauses and the propositional variable to resolve on. The proof ends with establishing the empty clause, which is trivially unsatisfiable.

The proof trace produced by the SAT solver is passed to Isabelle, where it is used to guide a proof of the unsatisfiability of the formula $\exists \mathbf{x}.c_1 \wedge \ldots \wedge c_m$ obtained by the CNF transformation. The unsatisfiability of this latter formula is easily reduced to the proof of the sequent $[\![c_1; \ldots; c_m]\!] \Longrightarrow False$, i.e. to deriving a contradiction from the hypotheses $c_1, \ldots, c_m$. At this point, the representation of the clauses c_i in Isabelle becomes important. A naive representation of clauses as disjunctions of literals in Isabelle/HOL requires associativity and commutativity of disjunction to be applied prior to each resolution step so that the complementary literal appears, say, as the first disjunct. This complication can be circumvented when clauses are encoded as sequents, observing that the clause $a_1 \vee \ldots \vee a_k$ can be represented as the sequent $[\![\overline{a_1}; \ldots; \overline{a_k}]\!] \Longrightarrow False$ where $\overline{a_i}$ denotes the complement of the literal a_i. With this representation, binary resolution essentially becomes an application of the cut rule. More precisely, given two clauses $c_1 \equiv [\![a_1; \ldots; a_k]\!] \Longrightarrow False$ and $c_2 \equiv [\![b_1; \ldots; b_l]\!] \Longrightarrow False$ in sequent representation such that, say, $b_j \equiv \overline{a_i}$, we deduce from c_1 the equivalent sequent

$$c_1' \equiv [\![a_1; \ldots; a_{i-1}; a_{i+1}; \ldots; a_k]\!] \Longrightarrow \overline{a_i}$$

and then join the two sequents using a primitive operation provided by Isabelle to obtain the sequent representation of the resolvent, i.e.

$$[\![a_1; \ldots; a_{i-1}; a_{i+1}; \ldots; a_k; b_1; \ldots; b_{j-1}; b_{j+1}; \ldots; b_l]\!] \Longrightarrow False.$$

We have tested our method with proofs generated by MiniSAT and by zChaff, and it is now available as the sat and satx tactics (the latter based on the definitional CNF conversion described above) in the Isabelle 2005 standard distribution. Table 1 shows experimental results for several examples taken from the TPTP benchmark, based on the solver zChaff. We can successfully check proofs for problems of a few hundred clauses and that require about 10000 binary resolutions. As for the execution time (given in seconds, measured on a Pentium-IV with 1.6 GHz and 512 MB main memory under

Table 1. Running time for SAT proof reconstruction

Problem	# clauses	SAT time	Total time
MSC007-1.008	204	0.208	11.546
PUZ015-2.006	184	0.005	2.435
PUZ016-2.005	117	0.003	1.158
PUZ030-2	63	0.002	0.485
PUZ033-1	13	0.003	0.078
SYN090-1.008	65	0.002	0.492
SYN093-1.002	26	0.005	0.133
SYN094-1.005	82	0.005	0.742

Linux), "SAT time" refers to the running time of the SAT solver alone whereas "Total time" includes the time taken by Isabelle to reconstruct the proof. One can see that proof checking by Isabelle takes at least two orders of magnitude longer than it takes zChaff to determine unsatisfiability and to produce the proof. This mainly comes from the underlying representation of formulas and theorems in Isabelle, which accommodates arbitrary higher-order syntax, and is not optimized for propositional logic. On the other hand, the default automated tactics offered by Isabelle cannot solve any but the smallest problems of Tab. 1.

Weber [28] has independently suggested a way to perform proof reconstruction in Isabelle from proof traces obtained from SAT solvers. His approach is based on rewriting entire sets of clauses, whereas our sequent representation allows us to operate on comparatively small objects, and our implementation is about an order of magnitude faster for most of the examples of Tab. 1.

4 Proof Traces from SMT Solvers

The integration of SAT solving with Isabelle is essential for supporting SMT solvers that handle more expressive, though still quantifier-free, languages. Roughly, SMT solvers are SAT solvers working together with theory reasoners, as illustrated in Fig. 1. The information exchanged at the interface are conflict clauses of the theory reasoner, introduced in Sections 4.1 and 4.2. These clauses also contain the essence of a formal proof: the conjunction of the clauses implies the unsatisfiability of the goal formula by purely propositional reasoning. The conflict clauses themselves are proved by laws of equational logic (reflexivity, symmetry, transitivity, and congruence), and in Sect. 4.3 we address the generation of these proofs from the data structures of the underlying decision procedure.

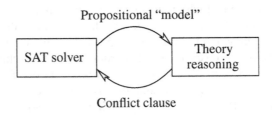

Fig. 1. Cooperation between a SAT solver and a theory reasoner

4.1 SAT Solvers Beyond Boolean Logic

Assume that we wish to decide the satisfiability of the formula

$$x = y \wedge \left(f(x) \neq f(y) \vee (\neg p(x) \wedge p(z)) \right). \qquad (1)$$

We first construct a Boolean abstraction by consistently replacing first-order atoms by Boolean variables. For our example, we obtain the propositional formula

$$p_1 \wedge \left(\neg p_2 \vee (\neg p_3 \wedge p_4) \right) \qquad (2)$$

where the Boolean variables p_1, p_2, p_3 and p_4 correspond to the first-order atoms $x = y$, $f(x) = f(y)$, $p(x)$ and $p(z)$. This Boolean abstraction has two (sets of) models that respectively satisfy the literals $\{p_1, \neg p_2\}$ and $\{p_1, \neg p_3, p_4\}$. The first abstract model (i.e. the one that makes p_1 true and p_2 false) does not correspond to a model for the original formula (1), because it is not possible to have a model that would make $x = y$ true and $f(x) = f(y)$ false. The second abstract model corresponds to a concrete one, since $\{x = y, \neg p(x), p(z)\}$ is satisfiable. In general, a formula is satisfiable if and only if there exists a model for the Boolean abstraction of the formula that corresponds to a satisfiable set of literals. Formula (1) is indeed satisfiable.

Notice that this process of first building a Boolean abstraction to extract an abstract model, and then checking the corresponding sets of first-order literals, allows the theory reasoner to operate on sets of literals only. The Boolean structure of formulas is managed efficiently by the SAT solver.

Now if in Formula (1) we replace $p(z)$ by $p(y)$, we obtain the unsatisfiable formula

$$x = y \wedge \left(f(x) \neq f(y) \vee (\neg p(x) \wedge p(y)) \right).$$

Its Boolean abstraction is still (2) but p_4 now represents $p(y)$. The models for the abstraction do not correspond to models for the original formula, since the sets of literals $\{x = y, f(x) \neq f(y)\}$ and $\{x = y, \neg p(x), p(y)\}$ are both unsatisfiable. To reduce the satisfiability problem to a purely propositional one, it is sufficient to add conjunctively to (2) *conflict clauses* that express the unsatisfiability of the abstract models in the first-order theory. In our example, we obtain the conflict clauses $\neg p_1 \vee p_2$ and $\neg p_1 \vee p_3 \vee \neg p_4$, corresponding to the valid formulas $x \neq y \vee f(x) = f(y)$ and $x \neq y \vee p(x) \vee \neg p(y)$.

To summarize, the cooperation between the SAT solver and the decision procedure for sets of literals is depicted in Fig. 1. The SAT solver produces models for the Boolean abstraction (that are not necessarily models for the original formula). If the sets of first-order literals that correspond to those models are unsatisfiable, they are rejected by the theory reasoning module, and the Boolean abstraction is *refined* by a conflict clause. For a satisfiable input, an abstract model corresponding to a satisfiable set of first-order literals will eventually be found. For an unsatisfiable input, the successive refinements with conflict clauses will eventually produce an unsatisfiable propositional formula.

4.2 Improving Efficiency

In practice, the Boolean abstraction of a given formula will have many models. It is therefore important to find conflict clauses that eliminate not just one, but many abstract models.

The first ingredient to remove several abstract models simultaneously is to extract *partial models* from the propositional abstraction rather than full models. A partial model assigns a truth value to a subset of the propositional variables used in the abstraction, such that every interpretation that extends this partial model is a (full) model. A partial model assigning n variables for a formula using m variables represents 2^{m-n} full models. Adding a conflict clause to reject a partial model allows us to reject a large number of full models. In [11] we introduced a simple technique to efficiently compute a minimal partial model from a full model for a set of clauses.

Second, the set of literals L corresponding to an abstract (partial) model can still be huge. On the contrary, the very reason for which this set is unsatisfiable is often quite small: it can be expressed as a small subset of L that is unsatisfiable with respect to the theory, the remaining literals being irrelevant. Generating conflict clauses that correspond to small unsatisfiable subsets will, in practice, contribute to an efficient cooperation of the SAT solver with the theory reasoner. The theory reasoner should therefore be able, given an unsatisfiable set of literals, to detect those literals that were really useful to conclude that the set is unsatisfiable. The congruence closure algorithm described in Sect. 4.3 has been designed for this purpose.

Because proof reconstruction essentially relies on the conflict clauses produced by the theory reasoner, it also benefits from this effort to compute small conflict clauses.

4.3 Congruence Closure

A congruence closure algorithm decides the satisfiability of a set of ground first-order logic literals in the theory of uninterpreted predicates and functions. It does so by constructing equivalence classes of terms. Two terms belong to the same class if and only if the equalities from the input force the terms to be equal: disequalities play no role in building equivalence classes. A set of literals may be unsatisfiable for two reasons. First, if it contains a pair of complementary literals built from the same predicate such that the corresponding arguments are in the same congruence class as in $\{a = b, p(a,b), \neg p(b,a)\}$. Second, if there is a disequality between two terms in a single congruence class: for instance the set $\{a = b, f(a) \neq f(b)\}$ is unsatisfiable.

Many implementations of congruence closure exist, notably the Nelson-Oppen algorithm [20], and the algorithm due to Downey, Sethi and Tarjan (DST for short) [8]. The simple Nelson-Oppen algorithm has a complexity of $O(n^2)$ where n is the total number of nodes in the tree or DAG representations of the set of literals. The DST algorithm is more complicated but is of complexity $O(n \log n)$, as long as enter and query operations on a hash table are assumed to be constant in time. haRVey implements a variant of DST: its complexity is $O(n \log n)$, and terms are represented as DAGs for maximal sharing of subterms. This algorithm is described in detail in [11].

Very abstractly, the congruence closure algorithms work on a partition of a set of terms. This set must be closed under the subterm relation. Initially each term is alone in its own class. The partition of terms is successively updated to take into account a set of equalities. When an equality $t = t'$ is given to the algorithm, the classes for terms t and t' are merged. Any class merge may produce the merge of further classes because of the congruence rule

$$\frac{t_1 = t_1' \quad \cdots \quad t_n = t_n'}{f(t_1, \ldots t_n) = f(t_1', \ldots t_n')} \tag{3}$$

For instance, assume x and y belong to two classes that are merged. Then, if $f(x)$ and $f(y)$ belong to two different classes, those two classes should also be merged. Implementations of congruence closure algorithms rely on efficient data structures to represent classes of terms, and on indexing techniques to quickly find the classes that have to be merged because of the congruence rule.

As an example, consider the set of terms

$$\{a, b, f(a), g(a), g(b), g(g(a)), f(g(b)), g(f(a))\}.$$

This set is closed under the subterm relation. Assume that we wish to compute the equivalence classes of this set of terms for the equalities $a = f(a)$, $f(a) = f(g(b))$, $f(g(b)) = g(f(a))$ and $g(b) = g(g(a))$. Initially every term is in its own class. Processing the equality $a = f(a)$ merges the classes for a and $f(a)$. Because of congruence, the classes for $g(a)$ and $g(f(a))$ will also be merged. Taking into account the equality $f(a) = f(g(b))$ merges the classes for the two terms, without inducing any further merging operations. At this point, the partition of terms is

$$\{\{a, f(a), f(g(b))\}, \{b\}, \{g(a), g(f(a))\}, \{g(b)\}, \{g(g(a))\}\}.$$

Now, processing the equality $f(g(b)) = g(f(a))$ merges the classes for those two terms, that is, the classes for a and $g(a)$. This entails, by congruence, that $g(a)$ and $g(g(a))$ are equal. Processing the last equality $g(b) = g(g(a))$ results in all terms except for b forming a single class.

Notice that only the congruence axiom is applied explicitly: the data structure (i.e. a partition of terms) makes implicit the equivalence properties of equality, i.e. the laws of reflexivity, symmetry, and transitivity. Two classes are merged because two terms are found to be equal, either because a literal in the input equates them, or by propagation according to the congruence rule. If we want to store that information for later use, we can store the pair of terms that are responsible for a merge, together with its reason. This information is enough to reconstruct, for any two terms of a class, a small set of equations that entail their equality.

Back to the previous example, we can draw a graph that summarizes the successive merges. The nodes of the graph are just the terms handled by the algorithm. Each time two classes are merged because of an equation in the input (for instance $a = f(a)$), we draw a plain edge between the left- and right-hand side terms of the equation, and label the edge by the equation. If two classes are merged because of an application of the congruence rule (for instance $g(a)$ and $g(f(a))$), we draw a dashed edge. The full merge-history graph for the congruence closure algorithm applied to our example appears in Fig. 2.

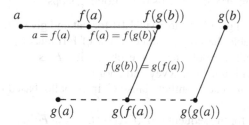

Fig. 2. Merge-history graph

It is easy to verify that merge-history graphs enjoy the following properties:

- the equality of two terms is entailed by a set of equations (i.e. the two terms are in the same class), if and only if there is a path between the corresponding nodes in the merge-history graph;
- there is a unique path between any two terms in the same class;

- the equality between two terms in the same class follows by reflexivity, symmetry, and transitivity of equality from the conjunction of the edge labels along the path between the two terms;
- two terms connected by a dashed edge have the same topmost symbol, and the corresponding subterms are in the same classes. The equality between those two terms follows, by congruence only, from equalities between direct subterms.

As a consequence, it is easy to use a merge-history graph to decompose[1] the justification of the equality of two terms into elementary steps that involve either only congruence or only reflexivity, symmetry, and transitivity of equality.

Assume that the algorithm concludes the unsatisfiability of a set containing the equalities $a = f(a)$, $f(a) = f(g(b))$, $f(g(b)) = g(f(a))$ and $g(b) = g(g(a))$ and the disequality $a \neq g(b)$, possibly among many other literals. It does so by building the classes of terms according to the equalities in the input, and then discovering a conflict with the disequality $a \neq g(b)$. At this point, the algorithm uses the merge-history graph to produce a minimal unsatisfiable subset of the input literals and outputs a justification of the unsatisfiability of this set that will be used for proof reconstruction.

The idea of using representations similar to merge-history graphs to extract small conflict sets has appeared before [19, 12, 22], but we are not aware of a previous use of these graphs to justify *a posteriori* the equality of terms by elementary proof steps.

5   Proof Reconstruction for Congruence Closure

In this section we describe our implementation of the interface between Isabelle and haRVey, with the focus on proof reconstruction for the congruence closure reasoning part of haRVey, as it is described in Section 4. This interface is implemented as a proof method called rv in Isabelle, i.e., as an ML program.

The idea behind the interface is not to use haRVey to give a complete proof for a given goal, rather, it is used to provide a list of intermediate lemmas, namely the conflict clauses described in Section 4, to guide proof search in Isabelle. More precisely, given a goal formula F, the interface performs the following steps:

1. Convert the negated goal ($\neg F$) to SMT-LIB format and give it to haRVey.
2. If $\neg F$ is unsatisfiable, haRVey produces a list of formulas $C_1, \ldots, C_n$ (the conflict clauses) along with a proof trace for each C_i. If $\neg F$ is satisfiable, the interface displays the model found by haRVey and aborts.
3. Construct a proof for each conflict clause C_i in Isabelle, based on the justification output by haRVey.
4. Construct a proof for the sequent $[\![\neg F; C_1; \cdots; C_n]\!] \Longrightarrow False$.
5. Apply modus ponens to the formulas obtained in (3) and (4) to get $\neg F \Longrightarrow False$, and hence prove F.

Step (5) is implemented straightforwardly in Isabelle using resolution. Step (4) applies the SAT interface described in Section 3. We now describe the proof reconstruction for each conflict clause C_i.

---

[1] Decomposition terminates due to the inductive construction of merge-history graphs from the two elementary merge operations.

The haRVey prover produces a compact proof trace for each conflict clause, summarizing the kind of reasoning needed to prove the clause. These proof traces consist of lists of sequents labeled with hints how they can be proved, as follows:

```
TRANS: <sequent>
CONGR: <sequent>
PRED : <sequent>
INEQ : <sequent>
```

and end with the line

```
CONFL: <formula>
```

The formula following the keyword CONFL is the conflict clause. We shall look at the overall structure of the proof trace, before explaining in details the meaning of the other keywords. Implicit in the proof format is the (backward) resolution proof for deriving the conflict clause. More precisely, suppose that the list of sequents preceding the conflict clause are

$$l_1 : [\![C_{11}; \cdots ; C_{1k_1}]\!] \Longrightarrow B_1$$
$$\vdots \qquad\qquad \vdots$$
$$l_n : [\![C_{n1}; \cdots ; C_{nk_n}]\!] \Longrightarrow B_n$$

where each label l_i is either TRANS, CONGR, PRED or INEQ. The first sequent is always a statement of a contradiction, i.e., B_1 is *False*. The assumptions C_{ij} in the sequent i satisfy the following requirement: each of them either appears in negated form in the conflict clause, or it is the conclusion of a later sequent, i.e. it is B_k, for some $k > i$. The conflict clause is therefore proved by contradiction, as the result of resolving its negation with all the intermediate sequents above until *False* is derived. The corresponding inference in Isabelle looks something like:

$$\frac{[\![\neg C; C_{n1}; \cdots ; C_{nk_n}]\!] \Longrightarrow B_n \quad \cdots \quad [\![\neg C; C_{11}; \cdots ; C_{1k_1}]\!] \Longrightarrow False}{C}$$

where C is the conflict clause. This is a valid inference because each C_{ij} is either justified by $\neg C$, or it is B_k for some $k > i$. In the implementation, this inference scheme is realized by a series of resolution steps between sequent i, for several (possibly all) $i > 1$, with the first sequent.

We shall now turn to the proofs of the intermediate sequents. The keywords preceding the sequents indicate the kind of reasoning needed to prove the sequent. The keyword PRED indicates that the sequent can be proved using one substitution and followed by proof-by-contradiction. That is, the sequent in this case is of the form:

$$[\![s = t; P\, s; \neg(P\, t)]\!] \Longrightarrow False.$$

The keyword INEQ indicates that the sequent contains a contradictory pair of equalities:

$$[\![s = t; s \neq t]\!] \Longrightarrow False.$$

Proof reconstruction for both cases are easily done in Isabelle using substitution and proof by contradiction.

The keyword TRANS means that the sequent is provable by using the reflexivity, symmetry, and transitivity of equality alone. We have implemented a special tactic in Isabelle to do this type of equality reasoning. We could have used the built-in simplifier tactics (based on rewriting) but these may not terminate in case of equalities that result in looping rewrite rules.

The label CONGR indicates that the sequent is provable by using the congruence rule (3). As in the case with TRANS, we could use Isabelle's built-in rewriting engine, but faster proofs are obtained using a custom-built tactic. Because terms are represented in curried notation in Isabelle/HOL, we only need to rely on a single axiom scheme, independently of the arity of the function symbol:

$$[\![f = g; \; x = y]\!] \Longrightarrow f \, x = g \, y.$$

Proof construction proceeds recursively from the last argument of a function application: to prove $f \, x_1 \cdots x_n = g \, y_1 \cdots y_n$, first show $x_n = y_n$ and then recursively construct a proof for $f \, x_1 \cdots x_{n-1} = g \, y_1 \cdots y_{n-1}$.

Example. Given the formula (cf. Fig. 2)

$$a = f \, a \wedge f \, a = f \, (g \, b) \wedge f \, (g \, b) = g \, (f \, a) \wedge g \, b = g \, (g \, a) \Longrightarrow a = g \, b,$$

haRVey produces one conflict clause, which is just the formula itself, but in CNF. It also produces a proof trace for the conflict clause, which appears in Fig. 3. For better readability, we have presented in boldface letters the (dis)equations that come from the conflict clause (the last line of the proof trace). The remaining (dis)equations appear as conclusions of sequents below in the proof trace. It is straightforward to construct a refutation proof from the above sequents.

> INEQ: $[\![a = g \, b; \; \mathbf{a \neq g \, b}]\!] \Longrightarrow \textit{False}$
> TRANS: $[\![\mathbf{a = f \, a}; \; \mathbf{f \, a = f \, (g \, b)}; \; \mathbf{f \, (g \, b) = g \, (f \, a)};$
> $\quad\quad\quad g \, (f \, a) = g \, (g \, a); \; \mathbf{g \, b = g \, (g \, a)}]\!] \Longrightarrow a = g \, b$
> CONGR: $f \, a = g \, a \Longrightarrow g \, (f \, a) = g \, (g \, a)$
> TRANS: $[\![g \, (f \, a) = g \, a; \; \mathbf{f \, (g \, b) = g \, (f \, a)}; \; \mathbf{f \, a = f \, (g \, b)}]\!] \Longrightarrow f \, a = g \, a$
> CONGR: $\mathbf{a = f \, a} \Longrightarrow g \, (f \, a) = g \, a$
> CONFL: $a = g \, b \vee a \neq f \, a \vee f \, a \neq f \, (g \, b) \vee f \, (g \, b) \neq g \, (f \, a) \vee g \, b \neq g \, (g \, a)$

Fig. 3. Proof trace for a conflict clause

Benchmark. We have tested our interface to haRVey with proof reconstruction with a number of example formulas. The running times needed to solve these problems using the rv tactic are given in Tab. 2. The benchmarks were run on a machine with a 1.5 GHz Intel Pentium-IV processor and 1024 MB memory under Linux. For each formula, we indicate the number of nodes in the dag representation of the formula, the number of distinct atoms that occur in the formula, and the number of conflict clauses produced by haRVey. We also indicate the times taken by haRVey to refute the formula and output the proof trace, and by Isabelle to parse the proof trace and check the proof.

For all these examples, the running time it took for haRVey to find a refutation is negligible (less than a second). For formulas of small size, the number of conflict clauses

Table 2. Running time for proof reconstruction for congruence closure

Formula	Size		# confl.	Times (s)	
	nodes	atoms	clauses	haRVey	Isabelle
SEQ004-size5	18795	6967	143	0.41	115.68
SEQ011-size2	7355	3471	73	0.02	9.69
SEQ015-size2	331	47	20	0.02	3.10
SEQ020-size2	7963	3775	74	0.02	7.16
SEQ032-size2	255	43	20	0.01	2.66
SEQ042-size2	947	293	49	0.09	11.17
SEQ050-size2	779	213	105	0.11	32.42

produced is up to 20 clauses. In those cases, proof reconstruction succeeds within one to five seconds. For larger test cases, we make use of some of the benchmark problems used in the SMT 2005 competition. Note that "small problems" in the competition are actually quite large formulas, in comparison to the kind of lemmas shown in Sect. 2. We see that the times taken for proof reconstruction in Isabelle are again more than two orders of magnitude larger than the running times of haRVey, and that they depend mostly on the number of conflict clauses produced (remember also that each conflict clause is justified by a number of low-level reasoning steps).

None of these examples succumbs to Isabelle's existing automatic proof methods. Isabelle 2005 contains a preliminary implementation, without proof reconstruction, of the combination of resolution-based theorem provers and Isabelle described by Meng et al. [16], and we have not succeeded in using this implementation to prove the examples of Tab. 2: for the larger examples, the first-order prover did not complete within 5 minutes. For the smaller examples, Isabelle was unable to parse the result of the prover, which also took orders of magnitude longer than haRVey. This experiment seems to indicate to us that the combination with an SMT solver can be useful for certain problems.

6 Conclusion

We have proposed a technique for combining interactive proof assistants and proof-producing SMT solvers. Because proofs are certified by the trusted kernel of the interactive prover, theorems established in this way come with the same soundness guarantees as those theorems established interactively. The combination with an efficient external reasoner allows us to significantly raise the degree of automation while retaining the expressiveness of the input language for specification. Our current implementation combines Isabelle/HOL with the fragment of haRVey that handles quantifier-free first-order logic with uninterpreted function and predicate symbols. However, the overall approach extends to other interactive provers and to other decidable fragments of first-order logic. In particular, we plan to address linear arithmetic along the same lines by making haRVey output compact proof traces that can be replayed within Isabelle/HOL.

On the implementation level, we observe that the time Isabelle takes to replay a proof trace significantly exceeds the time taken by haRVey to find the proof, although basically no proof search is required. We believe that a significant part of this run-time penalty comes from the overhead incurred by the support for higher-order abstract syntax, but more investigation will be necessary into this matter. It also remains to be seen whether efficiency of proof reconstruction is a big issue for those verification conditions that we expect to see in practical applications (where we are mostly interested in stronger theories). Also, proof reconstruction can be done off-line, whereas an oracle-style combination should be sufficient for interactive proof.

On a conceptual level, we propose to study and identify uniform formats for proof traces for SMT solvers, akin to the SMT-LIB input format, to enable comparisons between different solvers and to standardize the interface towards interactive proof assistants (and, in fact, independent proof checkers).

Acknowledgements. We are grateful to Kamal Kant Gupta, who contributed to the syntactic translation from Isabelle to the SMT format, and to Tjark Weber for his help with integrating and maintaining our code for SAT proofs within the Isabelle distribution.

References

1. M. Baaz, U. Egly, and A. Leitsch. Normal form transformations. In J. A. Robinson and A. Voronkov, editors, *Handbook of Automated Reasoning*, volume I, chapter 5, pages 273–333. Elsevier Science B.V., 2001.
2. C. Barrett and S. Berezin. CVC Lite: A new implementation of the cooperating validity checker. In *CAV*, volume 3114 of *LNCS*, pages 515–518. Springer, Apr. 2004.
3. D. Barsotti, L. Prensa-Nieto, and A. Tiu. Verification of clock synchronization algorithms: Experiments on a combination of deductive tools. In *Proc. of the Fifth Workshop on Automated Verification of Critical Systems (AVOCS)*, ENTCS, 2005. to appear.
4. M. Bezem, D. Hendriks, and H. de Nivelle. Automated proof construction in type theory using resolution. *J. Autom. Reasoning*, 29(3-4):253–275, 2002.
5. M. Bozzano, R. Bruttomesso, A. Cimatti, T. Junttila, P. van Rossum, S. Schulz, and R. Sebastiani. The MathSAT 3 System. In *CADE*, volume 3632 of *LNCS*, pages 315–321, Tallinn, Estonia, 2005. Springer.
6. M. Davis, G. Logemann, and D. Loveland. A machine program for theorem-proving. *Comm. of the ACM*, 5(7):394–397, 1962.
7. D. Déharbe and S. Ranise. Light-weight theorem proving for debugging and verifying units of code. In *Software Engineering and Formal Methods (SEFM)*, pages 220–228. IEEE Comp. Soc., Sept. 2003.
8. P. J. Downey, R. Sethi, and R. E. Tarjan. Variations on the common subexpressions problem. *Journal of the ACM*, 27(4):758–771, 1980.
9. N. Eén and N. Sörensson. An extensible SAT-solver. In E. Giunchiglia and A. Tacchella, editors, *SAT*, volume 2919 of *LNCS*, pages 502–518. Springer, 2003.
10. J.-C. Filliâtre, S. Owre, H. Rueß, and N. Shankar. ICS: integrated canonizer and solver. In G. Berry, H. Comon, and A. Finkel, editors, *CAV*, volume 2102 of *LNCS*, pages 246–249. Springer, 2001.
11. P. Fontaine. *Techniques for verification of concurrent systems with invariants*. PhD thesis, Institut Montefiore, Université de Liège, Belgium, Sept. 2004.
12. P. Fontaine and E. P. Gribomont. Using BDDs with combinations of theories. In M. Baaz and A. Voronkov, editors, *LPAR*, volume 2514 of *LNCS*, pages 190–201. Springer, 2002.
13. J. Hurd. Integrating Gandalf and HOL. In *Theorem Proving in Higher-Order Logics (TPHOLs'99)*, volume 1690 of *LNCS*, pages 311–322, Nice, France, 1999. Springer.

14. A. Mahboubi. Programming and certifying the CAD algorithm inside the coq system. In T. Coquand, H. Lombardi, and M.-F. Roy, editors, *Mathematics, Algorithms, Proofs*, volume 05021 of *Dagstuhl Seminar Proceedings*, Schloss Dagstuhl, Germany, 2005.

15. A. Meier. TRAMP: Transformation of machine-found proofs into ND-proofs at the assertion level. In D. McAllester, editor, *CADE*, volume 1831 of *LNCS*, pages 460–464, Pittsburgh, PA, 2000. Springer.

16. J. Meng, C. Quigley, and L. C. Paulson. Automation for interactive proof: First prototype. *Information and Computation*, to appear.

17. D. G. Mitchell. A SAT solver primer. *EATCS Bulletin*, 85:112–133, 2005.

18. G. Necula and P. Lee. Efficient representation and validation of logical proofs. In *Logics in Computer Science (LICS'98)*, pages 93–104. IEEE Press, 1998.

19. G. C. Necula. *Compiling with Proofs*. PhD thesis, Carnegie Mellon University, Oct. 1998. Available as Technical Report CMU-CS-98-154.

20. G. Nelson and D. C. Oppen. Fast decision procedures based on congruence closure. *Journal of the ACM*, 27(2):356–364, 1980.

21. Q. H. Nguyen, C. Kirchner, and H. Kirchner. External rewriting for skeptical proof assistants. *J. Autom. Reason.*, 29(3-4):309–336, 2002.

22. R. Nieuwenhuis and A. Oliveras. Union-find and congruence closure algorithms that produce proofs. In C. Tinelli and S. Ranise, editors, *PDPAR*, 2004.

23. T. Nipkow, L. Paulson, and M. Wenzel. *Isabelle/HOL. A Proof Assistant for Higher-Order Logic*. Number 2283 in LNCS. Springer, 2002.

24. S. Ranise and C. Tinelli. The SMT-LIB standard : Version 1.1, Mar. 2005.

25. J. H. Siekmann and many others. Proof development with OMEGA. In *CADE*, pages 144–149, 2002.

26. A. Tiu. Formalization of a generalized protocol for clock synchronization in Isabelle/HOL. Archive of Formal Proofs: http://afp.sourceforge.net, 2005.

27. G. S. Tseitin. On the complexity of derivation in propositional calculus. In A. O. Slisenko, editor, *Studies in Constructive Mathematics and Mathematical Logic*, volume II, pages 115–125. 1970.

28. T. Weber. Using a SAT solver as a fast decision procedure for propositional logic in an LCF-style theorem prover. In J. Hurd, E. Smith, and A. Darbari, editors, *Theorem Proving in Higher Order Logics (TPHOLs 2005), Emerging Trends*, pages 180–189. Oxford Univ. Comp. Lab., Prog. Res. Group, 2005. Report PRG-RR-05-02.

29. L. Zhang and S. Malik. The quest for efficient Boolean satisfiability solvers. In A. Voronkov, editor, *CADE*, volume 2392 of *LNCS*, pages 295–313. Springer, 2002.

30. L. Zhang and S. Malik. Validating SAT solvers using an independent resolution-based checker. In *Design, Automation and Test in Europe (DATE 2003)*, pages 10880–85, Munich, Germany, 2003. IEEE Comp. Soc.

Exploration of the Capabilities of Constraint Programming for Software Verification

Hélène Collavizza and Michel Rueher

Université de Nice–Sophia-Antipolis – I3S/CNRS,
930, route des Colles - B.P. 145, 06903 Sophia-Antipolis, France
{helen, rueher}@essi.fr

Abstract. Verification and validation are two of the most critical issues in the software engineering process. Numerous techniques ranging from formal proofs to testing methods have been used during the last years to verify the conformity of a program with its specification. Recently, constraint programming techniques have been used to generate test data. In this paper we investigate the capabilities of constraint programming techniques to verify the conformity of a program with its specification. We introduce here a new approach based on a transformation of both the program and its specification in a constraint system. To establish the conformity we demonstrate that the union of the constraint system derived from the program and the negation of the constraint system derived from its specification is inconsistent (for the considered domains of values). This verification process consists of three steps. First, we generate a Boolean constraint system which captures the information provided by the control flow graph. Then, we use a SAT solver to solve the Boolean constraint system. Finally, for each Boolean solution we build a new constraint system over finite domains and solve it. The latter system captures the operational part of the program and the specification. Boolean constraints play an essential role since they drastically reduce the search space before the search and enumeration processes start. Moreover, in the case where the program is not conforming with its specification, Boolean constraints provide a powerful tool for finding wrong behaviours in different execution paths of the program. First experimental results on standard benchmarks are very promising.

1   Introduction

Verification and validation are two of the most critical issues in the software engineering process. These expensive and difficult tasks may account for up to 50% of the cost of software development [12]. Numerous techniques ranging from formal proofs to testing methods have been used during the last years to verify the conformity of a program with its specification. The goal of the SLAM project is to build "tools that can do actual proofs about the software and how it works in order to guarantee the reliability"[1].

---

[1] See http://research.microsoft.com/slam

H. Hermanns and J. Palsberg (Eds.): TACAS 2006, LNCS 3920, pp. 182–196, 2006.

Constraint programming techniques have been used to generate test data (e.g., [9, 10, 22, 23]) and to develop efficient model checking tools (e.g. [17, 6]). SAT based model checking platforms have been able to scale and perform well due to many advances in SAT solvers [20]. Recently Bouquet et al [3] developed a symbolic animator for specifications written in Java Modeling Language (JML) [15]. Their JML animator– based on constraint programming techniques– allows to simulate the execution of a JML specification and to verify on the fly class invariant properties.

In this paper we investigate the capabilities of constraint programming techniques to verify the conformity of a program with its specification. We introduce a new approach based on a transformation of both a program and its specification in a constraint system. To establish the conformity we demonstrate that the union of the constraints derived from the program and the negation of the constraints derived from its specification is inconsistent. Roughly speaking, pruning techniques -that reduce the domain of the variables- are combined with search and enumeration heuristics to demonstrate that this constraint system has no solutions.

The verification process consists of three steps:

1. Generating of a Boolean constraint system which captures the information provided by the control flow graph of the program and the specification;
2. Using a SAT solver to find the solutions of the Boolean constraint system. For each Boolean solution a new constraint system over finite domains – denoted CSP in the following– is built; the latter captures the operational part of the program and the specification.
3. Solving the CSP with a finite domain solver.

Boolean constraints play an essential role since they drastically reduce the search space before the search and enumeration processes start on the generated CSP. Moreover, in the case where the program is not conforming with its specification, Boolean constraints provide a powerful tool for finding wrong behaviors in different execution paths of the program. An essential observation is that in this approach we do not transform all assignments and numerical instructions into Boolean constraints[2]. The point is that it is much more convenient to transform these instructions in finite domain constraints and to solve them with a CSP solver. So the collaboration between the SAT solver and the CSP solver is the cornerstone of our approach. Indeed, since we first identify the feasible paths, the finite domain solver will work with both smaller constraint systems and reduced domains.

The prototype system we have developed takes as input a JAVA program and its specification written in JML [15]. Currently, we only consider JAVA unit code without function calls, without return inside loops, and without inheritance. Moreover, we assume that all numerical operations only concern integers.

---

[2] Contrary to the most popular Model Checking approaches based on SAT Solvers [4, 5].

The rest of this paper is organised as follows. Section 2 gives an overview of our approach whereas Section 3 recalls some basics on constraint programming techniques. Section 4 details the verification process we propose and introduces the translation process we use to generate the constraint systems. Section 5 describes the experimental results and discusses some critical issues.

Before going into the details, let us illustrate the capabilities of our approach on a well-known benchmark.

2   Motivating Example

We illustrate our approach on the well-known `tritype` program for classification of triangles [7]. We first describe the program, then we show very informally how the transformation process works, and finally we describe different experimentations.

2.1   The Problem

The `tritype` program is a basic benchmark in test case generation since it contains numerous non feasible paths. `tritype` takes three positive integers as inputs (the triangle sides) and returns 1 if the inputs correspond to any triangle, 2 if the inputs correspond to an isoscele triangle, 3 if the inputs correspond to an equilateral one, 4 if the inputs do not correspond to any triangle. Figure 1 gives the `tritype` program in JAVA with its specification in JML. Note that \result in JML corresponds to the value returned by the program.

2.2   The Verification Process

We first translate this program and the negation of its specification into a set of constraints, using the process detailed in Section 4.2.

Then, in order to delay the enumeration on integers, we introduce boolean variables for each decision on input variables, e.g., we introduce variable eq_{ij} for condition $i = j$, variable eq_{ik} for condition $i = k$, and so on. So the resolution process is decomposed into two parts:

1. Finding a set of paths that correspond to potential non-conformities;
2. Solving the CSP which corresponds to the identified set of paths.

For instance, if the boolean solver finds the solution $\{eq_{ij} = true, eq_{jk} = true, eq_{ik} = false\}$ we generate the CSP $\{i = j, j = k, i \neq k\}$; the domain of i, j, k being $\{0,...,65635\}$. If the CSP has a solution we have found a test case which corresponds to a non-conformity. If none of the generated CSP has a solution the verification is done.

The constraints generated for lines 4 to 7 in Fig. 1 are displayed in Fig. 2. $cond \rightarrow c$ denotes a guarded constraint: roughly speaking, constraint c has to be satisfied when condition $cond$ holds (see section 3.3 for the exact semantic). $r0$ and $r1$ are the two first renamings of variable r. nul_i (resp. nul_j, nul_k) is the boolean variable that captures the decision $i = 0$ (resp. $j = 0$, $k = 0$). eq_{ij} is the boolean

```
/*@ public normal_behavior
  @ requires (i>=0)&&(j>=0)&&(k>=0);
  @ ensures
  @ ((i+j<=k)||(j+k<=i)||(i+k<=j)) ==> \result == 4 &&
  @ !((i+j<=k)||(j+k<=i)||(i+k<=j))&&((i==j)&&(j==k)) ==> \result == 3 &&
  @ !((i+j<=k)||(j+k<=i)||(i+k<=j))&&!((i==j)&&(j==k))
  @        &&((i==j)||(j==k)||(i==k)) ==> \result == 2 &&
  @ !((i+j<=k)||(j+k<=i)||(i+k<=j))&&!((i==j)&&(j==k))
  @        &&!((i==j)||(j==k)||(i==k)) ==> \result == 1;
@*/
```

```
1  public static int tritype(int i, int j, int k){
2    int trityp ;
3    // not a triangle
4    if ((i==0)||(j==0)||(k==0)) trityp = 4 ; //ERR: trityp = 3
5    else {
6      trityp = 0 ;
7      if (i==j) trityp = trityp + 1 ;
8      if (i==k) trityp = trityp + 2 ;
9      if (j==k) trityp = trityp + 3 ;
10     if (trityp==0){
11       // triangular inequality not verified
12       if ((i+j <= k)||(j+k <= i)||(i+k <= j)) trityp = 4 ;
13       else trityp = 1 ; // any triangle
14     }
15     else {
16       if (trityp > 3) trityp = 3 ; // equilateral
17       else
18         //i=j and triangular inequality verified
19         if ((trityp==1)&&(i+j>k)) trityp = 2 ;
20         else
21           //i=k and triangular inequality verified
22           if ((trityp==2)&&(i+k>j)) trityp = 2 ; //ERR: (trityp == 1)
23           else
24             //j=k and triangular inequality verified
25             if ((trityp==3)&&(j+k>i)) trityp = 2 ;
26             else trityp = 4 ; // not a triangle
27         }
28     }
29   return trityp;
30 }
```

Fig. 1. tritype program in java with a specification in JML

variable for decision $i == j$. The constraint $((nul_i = 1) \vee (nul_j = 1) \vee (nul_k = 1)) \rightarrow r0 = 4$ corresponds to the if part of instruction on line 4 in Fig. 1, the following constraint corresponds to the else part. The last two constraints correspond to the if instruction on line 7 in Fig. 1. The full constraint system for the tritype program can be found in http://www.essi.fr/ rueher/appendix-tacas06.pdf.

// SSA variables for multiple definitions of result in the program
r0 : {0,...,65635}, r1 : {0,...,65635},
// boolean variables
nul_i : {0,1}, nul_j : {0,1}, nul_k : {0,1}, eq_{ij} : {0,1}
//constraints of line 4 to 7 of the program

$$((nul_i{=}1) \vee (nul_j{=}1) \vee (nul_k{=}1)) \qquad\qquad \rightarrow \text{r0=4}$$
$$\neg\,((nul_i{=}1) \vee (nul_j{=}1) \vee (nul_k{=}1)) \qquad\qquad \rightarrow \text{r0=0}$$
$$\neg\,((nul_i{=}1) \vee (nul_j{=}1) \vee (nul_k{=}1)) \wedge (eq_{ij}{=}1) \qquad \rightarrow \text{r1=r0} + 1$$
$$\neg\,((nul_i{=}1) \vee (nul_j{=}1) \vee (nul_k{=}1)) \wedge \neg\,(eq_{ij}{=}1) \quad \rightarrow \text{r1=r0}$$

Fig. 2. Constraints generated for lines 4 to 7 of the `tritype` program

2.3   Experimentations

We have introduced two errors into the `tritype` program:

1. A wrong return value when one of the inputs is zero (line 4 of the java program);
2. A wrong test on the trityp variable (line 22 of the java program).

These two errors occur in two different execution paths of the program. Figure 3 displays the four first non-conformities we have found: we successively display the path (i.e the value of decision variables), then three solutions of the corresponding integer system, and finally the value returned by the specification and the program.

The two first non-conformities are due to the wrong test on variable *trityp*, line 22 of the program. The first one is generated when "i=k", and so "trityp=2". Since the test on line 22 is "trityp==1" instead of "trityp==2", the execution goes through the else part on line 25, so the value of result equals 4 instead of 2.

The second non-conformity corresponds to the case where "i=j". So "trityp=1" and due to the wrong test on line 22 result equals 2 instead of 4 since the triangular inequality is verified.

The other errors we have found are those where at least one of the input is zero. Since we have introduced the error "trytyp = 3" instead of "trytyp = 4" on line 4 of Fig. 1, the program returns 3 instead of 4 whenever an input is equal to zero. The overall process finds 15 non-conformities in less than 5 seconds CPU time.[3]

We did also run the verification process with a correct program. It required 2.36 seconds CPU time to perform the complete verification. Note that we explored only 92 solutions of the Boolean constraint system although there are 9 variables, and thus 2^9 combinations. This clearly shows that the constraint system is strong enough to prune the search space, and to avoid a costly enumeration of all paths.

---

[3] All experimentations have been performed with ILOG Solver (see http://www.ilog.com/products/solver) and run on a Intel(R) Pentium(R) 4 CPU 2.00GHz computer with 256 Mb memory.

Error 1
Path : !(i=j), i=k, !(j=k), !(i+j≤ k), !(j+k ≤ i), !(i+k ≤ j), !(i=0), !(j=0), !(k=0)
Input values : i:2, j:1, k:2 – i:2, j:3, k:2 – i:3, j:1, k:3
Specification : 2, program : 4
Error 2
Path :i=j, !(i=k), !(j=k), i+j ≤ k , !(j+k ≤ i), !(i+k ≤ j), !(i=0), !(j=0), !(k=0)
Input values : i:1, j:1, k:2 – i:1, j:1, k:3 – i:1, j:1, k:4
Specification : 4, program : 2,
Error 3
Path : !(i=j), !(i=k), !(j=k), !(i+j ≤ k) , !(j+k ≤ i), i+k ≤ j, !(i=0), !(j=0), k=0
Input values : i:1, j:2, k:0 – i:1, j:3, k:0 – i:1, j:4, k:0
Specification : 4, program : 3
Error 4
Path : !(i=j), !(i=k), !(j=k), !(i+j ≤ k), j+k ≤ i, !(i+k ≤ j), !(i=0), !(j=0), k=0
Input values: i:2, j:1, k:0 – i:3, j:1, k:0 – i:3, j:2, k:0
Specification : 4, program : 3

Fig. 3. Four first non-conformities for the `tritype` program with two errors

3 Constraint Programming

This section recalls some basic concept of constraint programming which are useful to understand this paper. More details can be found in [21, 18, 13].

3.1 Definition of a CSP

Constraint programming is a paradigm that is tailored to hard search problems. The main application areas are planning, scheduling, timetabling, routing, placement, investment, configuration, design and insurance. Constraint programming incorporates techniques from mathematics, artificial intelligence and operational research; it offers significant advantages in these areas since it supports fast program development, economic program maintenance, and efficient runtime performance.

Constraint programming solvers are based on a *branch and prune* algorithm that combines local consistencies and efficient search heuristics.

More precisely, a *Constraint Satisfaction Problem* (CSP) is defined as:

- a set of *variables* $X = \{x_1, ..., x_n\}$,
- a finite set D_i of possible values for each variable x_i, called *domain*,
- a set of *constraints* $C = \{c_1, ..., c_n\}$ restricting the values that the variables can simultaneously take; X_j denotes the set of variables that occur in constraint c_j.

Note that the domains are a convenient way to express some specific constraints.

A *solution of a CSP* is an assignment of a value from its domain to every variable, in such a way that all constraints are satisfied.

3.2   Solving a CSP

To solve a CSP pruning techniques -that reduce the domain of the variables- are combined with search and enumeration heuristics. We only detail here local consistencies techniques.

Local consistencies are a key issue in finite domains where arc–consistency [19, 16] is very popular. A constraint c_j is arc-consistent if for any variable x_i in X_j, each value in D_i has a support in the domains of all other variables of X_j. In other words, a constraint c is arc–consistent for variable x, if values exist in the domains of all other variables such that constraint c holds when x is assigned to any value of its domain. The essential observation is that local consistency filtering algorithms try to reduce the size of the domain of some variable by considering only one constraint.

The following example shows in a very informal way how arc–consistency works. Consider the constraint system $C_1 = \{c_1 : x_1 + x_2 > 2, c_2 : x_1^2 + x_2^2 \leq 4, D_1 = \{0, 1, 2\}, D_2 = \{0, 1, 2\}\}$.

Constraint c_1 cannot be satisfied when either x_1 or x_2 are equal to 0. So arc–consistency will remove value 0 from domain D_1 and domain D_2. Now, constraint c_2 can no longer be satisfied when x_1 or x_2 are equal to 2, and thus value 2 will be removed from both domains. However, since the domain of one of the variables of constraint c_1 has been modified, we have to reconsider this constraint. Now, c_1 can no more be satisfied, the value 1 is removed from its domain which become empty; thus arc-consistency has detected the inconsistency of the whole constraint system.

Constraint system C_2 (see below) shows a case where the constraint system is arc-consistent but no solution satisfying all constraints exists.

$$C_2 = \{c_1 : x_1 \neq x_2, c_2 : x_2 \neq x_3, c_1 : x_3 \neq x_2\}, D_1 = D_2 = D_3 = \{0, 1\}.$$

3.3   Guarded Constraints

In this paper we also use guarded constraints. Guarded constraints are conditional constraints whose evaluation depends upon other constraints. $C_0 \rightarrow C_1$ denotes a guarded constraint where C_0 and C_1 are conjunctions of basic constraints. Relation $C_0 \rightarrow C_1$ states that constraints C_1 have to be added to the current constraint store when the solver can prove that constraints C_0 hold. More precisely, let C_0 be a boolean expression and C_1 a set of constraints, the guarded constraint $C_0 \rightarrow C_1$ behaves as follows:

- When the solver can prove that C_0 is true, then constraints C_1 are added to the store of constraints;
- When the solver can prove that C_0 is false, then the guarded constraint is just discarded;
- When the solver can neither prove that C_0 is true, nor prove that C_0 is false, that is when not enough variables of C_0 are instantiated, then the guarded constraint is suspended.

The solver tries to prove that the guard C_0 of a suspended constraint holds whenever the domain of some variable occurring in C_0 has been reduced. Of course, some guarded constraints may never become active.

One major difficulty with guarded constraints is that nothing can be done before the solver can demonstrate that the condition is either *true* or *false*. Let us consider a very simple piece of code:

```
//@ ensures \result ≥ 0
public int absolute(int i, int j) {
    if (i<j) return j-i;
        else return i - j;
}
```

This code is translated into the following set of constraints:

$$\{i < j \rightarrow r = j - i, \neg(i < j) \rightarrow r = i - j, r < 0, D_i = D_j = D_r = \{0, ..., 65635\}\}$$

A standard CSP solver cannot achieve any pruning on this system since nothing is known about i and j. So a very costly enumeration process is started: the inconsistency is only detected when the domain of i and j are reduced to one value. The advantages of combining SAT solver and CSP are obvious here. After having introduced a boolean variable for modeling $i < j$, the SAT solver enumerates the two paths, that is to say the two CSP $\{r = j - i, i < j, r < 0\}$ and $\{r = i - j, i \geq j, r < 0\}$. When the constraints of the CSP are transformed in binary constraints, arc-consistency immediately detects the inconsistency.

4   Verification Process

In this section we describe the overall verification process and explain how we transform the program and its specification into a set of constraints.

4.1   Verification Steps

The different operations which are performed during the verification process are detailed in Fig. 4.

Note that in step 3, we introduce boolean variables only to model decisions about input variables. This is sufficient to delay the enumeration process induced by guarded constraints (see Section 3.3). On the other hand, assignments are modeled using integer variables. Thus, we lose less information than with a translation of any statement into a boolean variable.

4.2   Translating the Program into a Set of Constraints

We first transform the program into its SSA form: for each new definition of a program variable, we introduce a fresh variable. In order to manage control instructions, we use ϕ–functions for **if then else** statements and we unfold loops. We use guarded constraints to model conditional execution flow (see part 3.3).

1. Put the program into a simplified Single State Assignment (SSA) form [14] and translate the SSA program into a set of constraints.
2. Add the constraints corresponding to the negation of the property to be proved.
3. Introduce a boolean variable for each decision on an input variable; Let *BoolSystem* be the constraint system obtained after steps 1, 2, and 3.
4. Start a solving process on *BoolSystem* and for **each** solution of *BoolSystem*:
   a. Build a CSP *IntSystem* that corresponds to the boolean values found in the current solution of *BoolSystem*
   b. Start a solving on IntSystem and for **each** solution of IntSystem print the current values of boolean variables (path trace) and find some errors of *IntSystem* (wrong input values).
5. If *BoolSystem* has no solution or if for each boolean solution *IntSystem* has no solution, print "the program is conform with is specification".

Fig. 4. Verification process

Basic Statements. Each assignment $var \leftarrow value$ is translated as a constraint $var = value$. Each boolean condition is translated as the corresponding constraint. We denote $SSA(s)$ the constraint corresponding to the basic statement s where each new definition of a variable has been replaced by the current renaming of this variable.

The If then Statement. For the sake of clarity, we only focus on the assignment of a single variable. Trivially, the same process could be applied individually for each variable appearing in a block with many variable assignments. Let us consider the statement S : if (cond) {var=val1;var=val2; ...; var=valq;}. Assume that var has already been defined p times before this statement. S is translated into the following set of guarded constraints:

$$SSA(cond) \quad \rightarrow \quad var_{p+1} = SSA(val_1)$$
$$SSA(cond) \quad \rightarrow \quad var_{p+2} = SSA(val_2)$$
...
$$SSA(cond) \quad \rightarrow \quad var_{p+q} = SSA(valq)$$
// else part
$$SSA(\neg cond) \quad \rightarrow \quad var_{p+1} = var_p$$
$$SSA(\neg cond) \quad \rightarrow \quad var_{p+2} = var_p$$
...
$$SSA(\neg cond) \quad \rightarrow \quad var_{p+q} = var_p$$

The else part is useful to ensure that the q fresh variables will not remain uninstantiated in the corresponding CSP.

The If then else Statement. Let us consider the statement S : if (cond) {var=val11;var=val12; ...;var=val1q;} else {var=val21;var=val22;... var=val2r;}. Assume that var has already been defined p times before this statement and assume that $q < r$. Since var has not the same number of definitions in the `if` part and the `else` part, we need to introduce a guarded constraint to take the place of the ϕ function. So, S is translated into the following set of guarded constraints:

```
// if part
```
$$\text{SSA(cond)} \quad \rightarrow \quad var_{p+1} = \text{SSA}(val_{11})$$
$$\text{SSA(cond)} \quad \rightarrow \quad var_{p+2} = \text{SSA}(val_{12})$$
...
$$\text{SSA(cond)} \quad \rightarrow \quad var_{p+q} = \text{SSA}(val_{1q})$$
```
// else part
```
$$\text{SSA}(\neg\text{cond}) \quad \rightarrow \quad var_{p+1} = \text{SSA}(val_{21})$$
$$\text{SSA}(\neg\text{cond}) \quad \rightarrow \quad var_{p+2} = \text{SSA}(val_{22})$$
...
$$\text{SSA}(\neg\text{cond}) \quad \rightarrow \quad var_{p+r} = \text{SSA}(val_{2q})$$
```
// φ function
```
$$\text{SSA(cond)} \quad \rightarrow \quad var_{p+q+1} = var_{p+q}$$
$$\text{SSA(cond)} \quad \rightarrow \quad var_{p+q+2} = var_{p+q}$$
...
$$\text{SSA(cond)} \quad \rightarrow \quad var_{p+r} = var_{p+q}$$

Remark: If $q > r$ the same principle is applied and the guarded constraints of the ϕ function are guarded by $SSA(\neg\ cond)$. If q=r then no ϕ function is required.

Figure 5 gives the translation of an overlapped `if then else`.

```
1  if (i < j) x = 0;          (i<j) → x1=0
       else {                 (¬(i<j)∧(i<30))→ (x1=x0+1∧x2=x1+y0)
2          if (i < 30) {      (¬(i<j)∧ ¬(i<30)∧(j>43))→ x1=2
               x = x+1;       (¬(i<j)∧ ¬(i<30)∧ ¬(j>43))→ x1=3
               x = x+y;       // φ-function for #2 if
           }                  (¬(i<j)∧¬(i<30)) → x2=x1
           else {             // φ-function for #1 if
3              if (j > 43) x=2;   (i<j) → x2=x1
               else x=3;
           }
       }
```

Fig. 5. Example of if then else translation

The `Loop` Statement. We first transform any loop into the equivalent while loop. Then we unfold the while loop using an overestimate of the number of loop steps. This overestimate may be the worst case complexity of the loop or could be given by the user. To describe all possible paths inside the loop, we guard the constraints of the loop with the entrance condition. Our process is close to the one described in [4] except that we use guarded constraints instead of boolean operators to combine condition and assignment. More precisely, let us consider the following while loop L : while (cond) var = value;. We assume that this loop is executed at most max time and that var was defined p times before this statement. Then the loop statement L is translated into the following set of guarded constraints:

$$
\begin{aligned}
cond_1 &\rightarrow var_{p+1} = val_{p+1} \\
\neg\, cond_1 &\rightarrow var_{p+1} = var_p \\
cond_1 \wedge cond_2 &\rightarrow var_{p+2} = val_{p+2} \\
\neg\, (cond_1 \wedge cond_2) &\rightarrow var_{p+2} = var_{p+1} \\
\ldots\ldots & \\
cond_1 \wedge cond_2 \wedge \ldots \wedge cond_{max} &\rightarrow var_{p+max} = val_{p+max} \\
\neg\, (cond_1 \wedge cond_2 \wedge \ldots \wedge cond_{max}) &\rightarrow var_{p+max} = var_{p+max-1}
\end{aligned}
$$

where val_i denotes the ith SSA form of value.

With this system of guarded constraints, if the loop condition has never been true, then $var_{p+max} = var_p$, if it has been true only once then $var_{p+max} = var_{p+1} = val_{p+1}$, if it has been true max times then $var_{p+max} = val_{max}$.

Remarks

- The number of unfoldings may not be sufficient to detect all non-conformities especially when an error in the program entails more iterations than specified by the theoretical bound.

- When the bound of a *for* loop is well-known and when the index variable is not modified inside the loop block, it is more efficient to generate n constraint systems, one for each value of the decision variable. This is due to the fact that the guarded constraints are expensive to manage, even when the conditions are instantiated very early.

5   Experimental Results and Discussion

In this section we analyse the experimentations we have performed on three non-trivial academic examples.

5.1   The tritype Program

The first example we consider is the tritype program. As we mentioned in the introduction, we can find some errors in the program as well as prove the correctness of the program. Introducing boolean variables only for decisions on input variables gave very good results in this case. Indeed, tritype is a typical example of pure decisional program, so the proof mainly consists in showing that the same decision in program and specification gives the same code condition return value.

5.2   The merge Example

This merge program referenced in [11] computes five outputs from five inputs[4]. A partial order is given on the inputs and the property to be proved is that the

---

[4] The merge program and its JML specification can be found in http://www.essi.fr/~rueher/appendix-tacas06.pdf

outputs are sorted in decreasing order. In this program, a contrario to tritype program, the link between the specification and the program goes through the operational part. So we need to introduce boolean variables not only to model decisions but also to model the assignments. We have introduced the same error as in [11]. We found four error paths including the one shown in [11]. For each error path we search five different integer values for the inputs. The overall process took 159.71 seconds CPU time whereas the proof of the correctness required 310.67 seconds CPU time (no CPU time is given in [11]).

5.3 The bsearch Program

The bsearch program[5] takes as input an array of integers t sorted by increasing order, an integer value val to search in the array, and returns the index of the value if it is found or -1 otherwise. The worst case complexity of this program is $O(log_2(n))$ where n is the size of the array.

To perform the verification, we introduce boolean variables for condition tests on input variables (i.e $t[i] = val$, $t[i] < val$, $t[i] < t[i+1]$). Since the worst case complexity of bsearch is $O(log_2(n))$ we unfold the program loop $\lceil (log_2(n)) \rceil$ times. We successively introduce two errors. The first one is to return the value $middle + 1$ when the $t[middle] = val$. This error was detected by the CSP solver. The errors found by the solver correspond to all the possible paths through the loop when it stops with $t[middle] = val$. The second error consists in assigning the right bound with $middle$ instead of $middle + 1$ when $t[middle] < val$. With this second error the program will not terminate in some cases, for example when searching a value which is bigger than all the values in the array. This error was also detected.

The correctness proof was also performed. The required time exponentially increases according to the length of the array. The solver runs out of memory for arrays of size > 8 and values in $[0, 2^{16}]$.

6   Discussion and Related Work

The new framework we have introduced in this paper has of course some limitations, e.g., there is no way to prove temporal properties, it works well with JAVA program but it would be difficult to handle C programs with pointers. Even for JAVA programs there are some restrictions: inheritance and functions calls are currently not handled[6].

A critical issue concerns the detection of inconsistencies in the CSP generated for each Boolean constraint system. Indeed, the constraints in some CSP may be too weak to achieve any pruning of the solution space, even when this CSP has no solution. In this case, a very costly search process is required to demonstrate

---

[5] The bsearch program and its JML specification can be found in http://www.essi.fr/~rueher/appendix-tacas06.pdf

[6] As long as we only consider finite structures, it should be possible to incorporate these features into our framework without major difficulties.

that the CSP is inconsistent. To overcome - at least partly - this problem some dedicated solvers could be used. For instance, when the finite domain constraints are linear, linear programming solvers could be used to reduce the domains. Formal simplifications of the constraint system could also be useful in some cases.

Of course, this problem is highly dependent from the modelling of the program and its specification. In other words, the kind of constraints that are generated will have strong influence on the performances of the solver [7].

Ganziger et al [8] have introduced a general DPLL(X) engine, where parameter X can be instantiated with a specialized solver $Solver_T$. That's to say DPLL(X) is a general engine for propositional solving. The authors illustrate their approach on their solver for EUF(logic with equality with uninterpreted functions). The goal of the approach introduced in this paper is not to integrate a CSP solver in a general DPLL engine. In our framework the essential role of the SAT solver is to boost the CSP solver by reducing the search space.

Armando et al [1] have recently proposed to use SMT solvers instead of SAT solvers for bounded model checking of software. We have compared our solver with their SMT-CBMC solver, which use CVC Lite for the theory of bit vectors. We have performed experimentations on the two sorting benchmarks contained in their last paper [1]. SMT-CBMC requires more than 600 seconds to analyse a bubble sort program with an array of size 26 whereas our solver analyses the same program with an array of size 100 in less than one second. Similarly, SMT-CBMC requires more about 200 seconds to analyse a selection sort program with an array of size 29 whereas our solver analyses the same program with an array of size 100 in less than 3 seconds.

We have also started an evaluation of our framework on standard SMT benchmarks (http://www.csl.sri.com/users/demoura/smt-comp/2005/). First results are promising; for instance we did prove the unsatisfiability of DTP_k2_n35_c210-s7.smt and DTP_k2_n35_c245_s10.smt in less than one second.

7   Conclusion

In this paper we have performed a first exploration of the capabilities of constraint techniques for verifying the conformity of a program with its specification.

First experimentations show that these techniques can be very efficient on some non trivial problems. Further work concerns the inclusion of dedicated solvers or simplifiers in our framework as well as a deeper study of the modelling issue.

Acknowledgements. Many thanks to Laurent ARDITI and Claude MICHEL for numerous and enriching discussions on this work.

---

[7] This is a well known problem in constraint programming: the performances of a solver may be very different on two constraint systems that are logically equivalent.

References

1. Armando, A., Mantovani, J., and Platania, L.: Bounded Model Checking of C Programs using a SMT solver instead of a SAT solver Technical Report, AI-Lab, DIST, University of Genova, December 19, 2005, 16 pages.
2. Ball T., Rajamani S. K., : Boolean Programs : A Model and Process For Software Analysis. Technical Report MSR TR 200-14, 2000
3. Bouquet, F., Dadeau, F., Legeard, B. and Utting, M: JML-Testing-Tools: a Symbolic Animator for JML Specifications using CLP. Procs of the 11th Int. Conf. on Tools and Algorithms for the Construction and Analysis of Systems, Tool session (TACAS'05). Springer-Verlag. LNCS 3440, pp. 551–556, 2005.
4. Clarke E., Kroenig D., Lerda F. : A Tool for Checking ANSI-C programs. TACAS 2004, LNCS 2988, pp. 168-176, 2004
5. Clarke E., Kroenig D., Sharygina N., Yorav K. : Predicate abstraction of ANSI-C Programs using SAT. Formal Methods in System Design, Vol 25, pp. 105-127, Kluwer Academic Press, 2004
6. Edmund M. Clarke, Daniel Kroening, Natasha Sharygina, Karen Yorav: SATABS: SAT-Based Predicate Abstraction for ANSI-C. Procs of the 11th Int. Conf. on Tools and Algorithms for the Construction and Analysis of Systems, Tool session (TACAS'05). Springer-Verlag. LNCS 3440, pp. 570–574, 2005.
7. Demillo R. A., Offut A.J. : Experimental Results from an Automatic Test Case Generator. ACM Transactions on Software Engineering Methodology. vol. 2, number 2, 1993, pp. 109-175
8. Ganzinger,H., Hagen,G., Nieuwenhuis, R.,Oliveras, A., and C. Tinelli: DPLL(T): Fast Decision Procedures. Proc. of CAV 2004. Springer-Verlag. LNCS 3114, pp. 175-188, 2004.
9. Gotlieb A., Botella B. and Rueher M : Automatic Test Data Generation using Constraint Solving Techniques. Proc. ISSTA 98, ACM SIGSOFT, vol. 2, pp. 53-62, 1998.
10. Gotlieb A., Botella B. and Rueher M : A CLP Framework for Computing Structural Test Data Proc of Computational Logic (CL2000), pp. 399-413, 2000.
11. Keller C. W., Saha D., Basu S., Smolka S.A. : FocusCheck : A tool for Model Checking and Debugging Sequantial C Programs. TACAS 2005, LNCS 3440, pp. 563-569, 2005
12. Kon O. and Castanet R. : Test generation for interworking systems. Computer Communications,vol. 23, pp. 642–652, 2000.
13. Krzystof R. Apt : Principles of Constraint Programming Cambridge University Press, 2003.
14. Ron Cytron, Jeanne Ferrante, Barry K. Rosen, Mark N. Wegman, and F. Kenneth Zadeck. Efficently Computing Static Single Assignment Form and the Control Dependence Graph. *Transactions on Programming Languages and Systems*, 13(4):451–490, October 1991.
15. Leavens Gary T. and Cheon Yoonsik : Design by Contract with JML. www.jmlspecs.org, August 2005.
16. A. Mackworth : Consistency in networks of relations. *Journal of Artificial Intelligence*, pages 8(1):99–118, 1977.
17. Malay K. Ganai, Aarti Gupta, Pranav Ashar: DiVer: SAT-Based Model Checking Platform for Verifying Large Scale Systems. Procs of the 11th Int. Conf. on Tools and Algorithms for the Construction and Analysis of Systems, Tool session (TACAS'05). Springer-Verlag. LNCS 3440, pp. 575–580, 2005.

18. Michela Milano (editor): Constraint and integer programming Kluwer Academic Publisher, 2004.
19. U. Montanari : Networks of constraints : Fundamental properties and applications to image processing. *Information science*, 7:95–132, 1974.
20. M. Moskewicz, C. Madigan, Y. Zhao, L. Zhang, and S. Malik,M: Chaff: Engineering an Efficient SAT Solver. Proc of DAC, pp. 530–535, 2001
21. Rina Dechter: Constraint Processing. Morgan Kaufmann publisher, 2003
22. Sy N.T. and Deville Y.: Automatic test data generation for programs with integer and float variables. Proc of. 16th IEEE International Conference on Automated Software Engineering(ASE01), 2001.
23. Sy N.T. and Deville Y.: Consistency Techniques for interprocedural Test Data Generation. Proc. of the Joint 9th European Software Engineering Conference and 11th ACM SIGSOFT Symposium on the Foundation of Software Engineering (ESEC/FSE03), Helsinki, Finland, 2003.

Counterexample-Guided Abstraction Refinement for the Analysis of Graph Transformation Systems*

Barbara König and Vitali Kozioura

Institut für Formale Methoden der Informatik, Universität Stuttgart, Germany
{koenigba, koziouvi}@fmi.uni-stuttgart.de

Abstract. Graph transformation systems are a general specification language for systems with dynamically changing topologies, such as mobile and distributed systems. We propose a counterexample-guided abstraction refinement technique which is based on the over-approximation of graph transformation systems (GTS) by Petri nets. We show that a spurious counterexample is caused by merging nodes during the approximation. We present a technique for identifying these merged nodes and splitting them using abstraction refinement, which removes the spurious run. The technique has been implemented in the AUGUR tool and experimental results are discussed.

1 Introduction

In the last years verification techniques based on counterexample-guided abstraction refinement [8] have been very successful. The idea behind this approach is to start with a coarse initial over-approximation and to refine this abstraction by eliminating spurious counterexamples. The technique has been used successfully in several tools such as SLAM [6], BLAST [10] or MAGIC [7].

Abstraction is also important for graph structures that can arise in several applications, for instance as evolving pointer structures on the heap, as object graphs or as networks with mobile processes. So far, little work has been done in this area concerning abstraction refinement. We are only aware of [12] where models of a 3-valued logics representing pointer structures are refined in the framework of shape analysis [16] by generating new instrumentation relations.

Here we are working in a different framework where we are using graph transformation systems (GTS)—instead of 3-valued logics—in order to represent and transform graph structures. Graph transformation systems are an expressive and useful specification formalism, allowing to describe dynamic properties of concurrent and distributed systems [15]. They can be used to model systems such as pointer structures, object-oriented languages and mobile processes.

In this paper the technique of counterexample-guided abstraction refinement is applied to the verification of graph transformation systems. Our approach is based on a (partial order) technique that approximates GTSs by Petri nets via

---

* Research supported by DFG project SANDS and SFB 627 (NEXUS).

H. Hermanns and J. Palsberg (Eds.): TACAS 2006, LNCS 3920, pp. 197–211, 2006.

an unfolding construction [3]. More specifically, in this approach a finite over-approximation called Petri graph is constructed, which consists of a graph and a Petri net having the edges of the graph as places. The important property of the approximation obtained in this way is that each graph reachable from the start graph in the GTS can be mapped, by merging some of its nodes, to a reachable marking of the over-approximating Petri net. On the other hand there may be some markings reachable in the obtained Petri graph, which have no counterpart in the original GTS. The sequence of events in the approximation leading to such a graph is called a spurious run.

In our case spurious runs are caused by the merging of graph nodes in the construction of the over-approximation. This is similar to the concept of summary nodes in shape analysis [16]. This paper describes how to construct a more exact over-approximation by separating merged nodes for which these spurious runs disappear. This procedure can be performed repeatedly for any number of spurious runs.

We believe that the technique of identifying the reason for the spurious run is independent of the abstraction mechanism used in this paper and could also be used in other frameworks dealing with approximations of graph structures.

The techniques presented here are implemented as an extension of the tool AUGUR[1]. The experimental part of the paper compares this approach with an already existing abstraction refinement technique which reduces the number of spurious examples by constructing an over-approximation which is exact up to some pre-defined depth [5]. It is shown experimentally that counterexample-guided abstraction refinement is faster and produces smaller Petri graphs.

A long version of this paper is available as a technical report [11].

2   Basic Notions

In this section we describe the notions of hypergraph, GTS, Petri net and Petri graph and also show in an informal way how to construct over-approximating Petri graphs.

Definition 1 (hypergraphs and hypergraph morphisms). *Let Λ be a set of labels where each label $l \in \Lambda$ has an arity $ar(l) \in \mathbb{N}$. A labelled hypergraph G is a tuple (V_G, E_G, c_G, l_G), where V_G is a finite set of nodes, E_G is a finite set of edges, $c_G : E_G \to V_G^*$ is a connection function and $l_G : E_G \to L$ is the labeling function satisfying $ar(l_G(e)) = |c_G(e)|$ for every $e \in E_G$. The nodes are not labelled.*

Let G and G' be two labelled hypergraphs. A hypergraph morphism (or simply morphism) $\varphi : G_1 \to G_2$ consists of a pair of total functions $\varphi_V : V_{G_1} \to V_{G_2}$ and $\varphi_E : E_{G_1} \to E_{G_2}$ such that for every $e \in E_{G_1}$ it holds that $l_{G_1}(e) = l_{G_2}(\varphi_E(e))$ and $\varphi_V(c_{G_1}(e)) = c_{G_2}(\varphi_E(e))$. A morphism is called edge-bijective (edge-injective) whenever it is bijective (injective) on edges. It is an isomorphism whenever it is bijective on nodes and edges.

Hypergraphs can be rewritten using rules of the following kind.

---

[1] Available from `http://www.fmi.uni-stuttgart.de/szs/tools/augur/`

Definition 2 (rewriting rule). *A rewriting rule r is a triple (L, R, α), where L and R are hypergraphs, called left-hand side and right-hand side respectively and $\alpha : V_L \to V_R$ is an injective mapping, indicating how nodes are preserved.*

We demand that there are no isolated nodes in the left-hand side L and no isolated nodes in $V_R - \alpha(V_L)$. Additionally E_L must not be empty.

The first condition says that we abstract from isolated nodes, whereas the second is a standard requirement for unfolding-based techniques, where every rule must be consuming. Note furthermore that we do not consider rules that preserve edges of the left-hand side.

For convenience we will in the following often assume that α is an inclusion denoted by *id*, which can be enforced by renaming the nodes of the left or right-hand side appropriately, and that the node and edge sets of L and R are disjoint otherwise. That is, we demand that $V_L \subseteq V_R$ and $E_L \cap E_R = \emptyset$ which implies that the union $L \cup R$ is well-defined.

Given a hypergraph, a rewriting rule and a match of the left-hand side, we can apply this rule and replace the left-hand side by the right-hand side in the following way. Additionally we define a partial morphism ν from the original graph to the rewritten graph, keeping track of preserved nodes and edges.

Definition 3 (rewriting step). *Let $r = (L, R, id)$ be a rewriting rule. A match of r in a hypergraph G is any morphism $\varphi : L \to G$ injective on edges. We can apply r to G according to the match φ and obtain a new graph H, written $G \Rightarrow_r H$, which is defined as follows: $V_H = V_G \uplus (V_R - V_L)$, $E_H = (E_G - \varphi(E_L)) \uplus E_R$ and, defining $\overline{\varphi} : V_R \to V_H$ by $\overline{\varphi}(v) = \varphi(v)$ if $v \in V_L$ and $\overline{\varphi}(v) = v$ otherwise, the connection and labelling functions are given by $c_H(e) = c_G(e)$, $l_H(e) = l_G(e)$ if $e \in E_G - \varphi(E_L)$ and $c_H(e) = \overline{\varphi}(c_R(e))$, $l_H(e) = l_R(e)$ if $e \in E_R$.*

We also define an injective partial morphism $\nu : G \to H$ where $\nu_V : V_G \to V_H$ and $\nu_E : (E_G - \varphi(E_L)) \to E_H$ with $\nu(x) = x$ for every node or edge x.

A *graph transformation system (*GTS*) $\mathcal{G} = (\mathcal{R}, G_0)$ is a finite set of rules together with a start hypergraph (also called initial graph).

Example: We illustrate the definitions of this chapter with an example describing a firewall system similar to the one introduced in [4]. This system contains an (arbitrarily large) set of processes running behind a firewall (safe processes) and one process in a public area (unsafe process). Any number of safe processes (SP) and connected locations (L) can be generated during runtime. The property to verify is that the unsafe process from the public area does not penetrate the firewall. If this situation is detected, rule "Error" will be applied and an edge labelled *Error* is created.

Fig. 1 and Table 1 depict the initial graph and the rules of the firewall system. A double-headed arrow in a rule means that the rule can be applied in both directions. Numbers close to the nodes indicate the mapping α. The private and public areas are connected by the firewall (F), and initially there is one unsafe processes (UP) in the public area. Only safe processes will be generated and the firewall can be crossed in one direction only. Our aim is to show that no reachable graph contains the 0-ary edge *Error*.

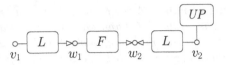

Fig. 1. Initial graph of the firewall system

Table 1. Rules of the firewall system

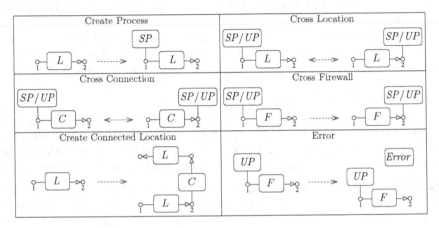

In order to approximate GTSs we will employ Petri nets, which, as multi-set rewriting systems, can be seen as a special case of graph rewriting. Petri nets are an easier model than GTS and hence more amenable to analysis. Several algorithms and tools are available for their verification. Furthermore, by approximating with Petri nets we will be able to preserve nice properties of the GTS model, such as locality (state changes are only described locally) and concurrency (no unnecessary interleaving of events) in the approximation.

We will now introduce a notation for Petri nets.[2]

Definition 4 (Petri net). *Let Δ be a finite set of labels. A Δ-labelled Petri net is a tuple $N = (S, T, {}^{\bullet}(), ()^{\bullet}, p)$, where S is the set of places, T is a set of transitions, ${}^{\bullet}(), ()^{\bullet} : T \to S^{\oplus}$ assign to each transition its pre-set and post-set and $p : T \to \Delta$ assigns a label to each transition. A marked Petri net is a pair (N, m_N), where N is a Petri net and $m_N \in S^{\oplus}$ is the initial marking.*

3   Approximated Unfolding

In this section we will give a short overview of a technique that approximates a graph transformation system by a structure that is both a Petri net and a hypergraph [3, 4, 5].

---

[2] By $A^{\oplus}$ we denote a multiset over A and for a function $f : A \to B$ we denote by $f^{\oplus} : A^{\oplus} \to B^{\oplus}$ its extension to multisets. Furthermore for $m \in A^{\oplus}$ and $a \in A$ we denote by $m(a)$ the multiplicity of a in m.

First we define the notion of Petri graph which will be used to represent an over-approximation for a given GTS. Note that the edges of the graph are at the same time the places of the net and that the transitions are labelled with rules of the GTS.

Definition 5 (Petri graph). *Let $\mathcal{G} = (\mathcal{R}, G_0)$ be a GTS. A Petri graph (over $\mathcal{R}$) is a tuple $P = (G, N, \mu)$, where G is a hypergraph, $N = (E_G, T_N, {}^\bullet(), ()^\bullet, p_N)$ is an $\mathcal{R}$-labelled Petri net where the places are the edges of G and μ associates to each transition $t \in T_N$, with $p_N(t) = (L, R, id)$, a hypergraph morphism $\mu(t) : L \cup R \to G$ such that ${}^\bullet t = \mu(t)^\oplus(E_L)$ and $t^\bullet = \mu(t)^\oplus(E_R)$.*
A Petri graph for the GTS $\mathcal{G}$ is a pair (P, ι), where $P = (G, N, \mu)$ is a Petri graph over $\mathcal{R}$ and $\iota : G_0 \to G$ is a graph morphism. A marking is reachable (coverable) in Petri graph if it is reachable (coverable) in the underlying Petri net with the multiset $\iota^\oplus(E_{G_0})$ as the initial marking.

We view Petri graphs as symbolic representations of transition systems with graphs as states. Specifically each marking m of a Petri graph (G, N, m_0) can be seen as representation of a graph, denoted by $graph(m)$, according to the following definition: We take the marked subgraph of G and duplicate each edge as indicated by the marking.

Alternatively one can define $graph(m)$ as the unique graph H, up to isomorphism, such that H has no isolated nodes and there exists a morphism $\psi : H \to G$, injective on nodes, with $\psi^\oplus(E_H) = m$. Furthermore, whenever there exists a morphism $\varphi : G' \to G$ such that $\varphi^\oplus(E_{G'}) \leq m$, then there exists an edge-injective morphism $e_{m,\varphi} : G' \to graph(m)$ such that $\psi \circ e_{m,\varphi} = \varphi$.

In order to obtain a Petri graph approximating a GTS, we first need—as building blocks—Petri graphs that describe the effect of a single rule.

Definition 6 (Petri graph for a rewriting rule). *Let $r = (L, R, id)$ be a rewriting rule. By $P(t, r) = (G, N, \mu)$ we denote a Petri graph with $G = L \cup R$ and N is a net with places $S_N = E_L \cup E_R$ and one transition t such that $p_N(t) = r$, ${}^\bullet t = E_L$ and $t^\bullet = E_R$. Furthermore the morphism $\mu(t) : L \cup R \to G$ is the identity.*

Given a GTS $\mathcal{G} = (\mathcal{R}, G_0)$ one can construct an over-approximating Petri graph $\mathcal{C}_\mathcal{G}$ (also called the *covering* of $\mathcal{G}$), using the following algorithm (see [3]). It starts with a Petri graph P_0 that consists only of the start graph and computes $\mathcal{C}_\mathcal{G}$ iteratively. It is based on an unfolding technique which is combined with over-approximating folding steps which guarantee a finite approximation.

Algorithm 7 (approximated unfolding). We set $P_0 = (G_0, N_0, m_0)$, where N_0 contains no transitions, $m_0 = E_{G_0}$ and let $\iota_0 : G_0 \to G_0$ be the identity. As long as one of the following steps is applicable, transform P_i into P_{i+1} according to the possibilities given below (where folding steps take precedence over unfolding steps).

Unfolding: Find a rule $r = (L, R, id) \in \mathcal{R}$ and a match $\varphi : L \to G_i$. Then choose a new transition t and extend P_i by attaching $P(t, r)$, i.e., take the disjoint union of both Petri graphs and factor through the equivalence $\equiv$ generated by $e \equiv \varphi(e)$ for every $e \in E_L$.

Folding: Find a rule $r = (L, R, id) \in \mathcal{R}$ and two matches $\varphi, \varphi' : L \to G_i$ such that $\varphi^{\oplus}(E_L)$ and $\varphi'^{\oplus}(E_L)$ are coverable in N_i and the second match is causally dependent on the transition unfolding the first match. Then merge the two matches by setting $\varphi(e) \equiv \varphi'(e)$ for each $e \in E_L$ and factoring through the resulting equivalence relation $\equiv$.

If neither possibility applies the Petri graph P_i obtained in the last step is returned. The result is denoted by $\mathcal{C_G}$. In [3] it has been shown that the algorithm always terminates with a result unique up to isomorphism.

In our running example, the constructed over-approximation consists of the hypergraph in Fig. 2 and the Petri net in Fig. 3. (Ignore the highlighted transitions for the moment.) Note that the set of edges of the graph corresponds exactly to the set of places of the net (the correspondence is indicated by giving indices to the labels).

Before we can show in what way Petri graphs can be considered as abstractions of GTSs and before we discuss how they can be analyzed, we first need the definition of an abstract run of a GTS and a notion of correspondence of two abstract runs. Then we can define how Petri graphs can be seen as abstractions of GTSs.

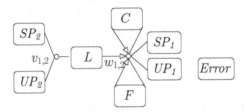

Fig. 2. Hypergraph component of the approximating Petri graph (firewall example)

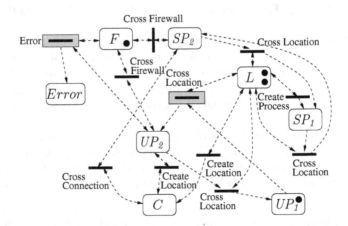

Fig. 3. Petri net component of the approximating Petri graph (firewall example)

Definition 8 (Abstract run). *An* abstract run *of a* GTS $(\mathcal{R}, G_0)$ *is a sequence of hypergraphs* $\mathcal{J} = (J_0 \Rrightarrow_{r_1} J_1 \Rrightarrow_{r_2} \ldots \Rrightarrow_{r_n} J_n)$, *where* r_i *is a rule name, together with morphisms* $\varphi_i : L_{i+1} \to J_i$ *for each* $i = 1, \ldots, n-1$, *where* L_i *is the left-hand side of rule* $r_i \in \mathcal{R}$.

Note that we do not demand that J_i *can be derived from* J_{i-1} *by applying rule* r_i *at match* φ_i. *In this case* $\mathcal{J}$ *will be called a* real run *and we will also use the symbol* $\Rightarrow$ *instead of* $\Rrightarrow$.

Let $\mathcal{J}' = (J_0' \Rrightarrow_{r_1} J_1' \Rrightarrow_{r_2} \ldots \Rrightarrow_{r_n} J_n')$ *be another abstract run with morphisms* $\varphi_i' : L_{i+1} \to J_i'$ *for each* $i = 1, \ldots, n-1$. *We say that* $\mathcal{J}'$ *weakly corresponds to* $\mathcal{J}$ *(in symbols* $\mathcal{J}' \ll \mathcal{J}$*) if for each* $i = 1, \ldots, n-1$ *there exist edge-bijective morphism* $\xi_i : J_i' \to J_i$ *for* $i = 0, \ldots, n$. *If furthermore the following diagram commutes we say that* $\mathcal{J}'$ corresponds to $\mathcal{J}$ *and write* $\mathcal{J}' \lll \mathcal{J}$.

$$L_{i+1} \xrightarrow{\varphi_i'} J_i' \xrightarrow{\xi_i} J_i$$
$$\underbrace{\qquad\qquad\qquad}_{\varphi_i}$$

Petri graphs can, as mentioned above, be seen as symbolic representations of graph transition systems and also as representations of sets of abstract runs.

Definition 9 (Abstract runs of a Petri graph). *Let* (P, ι) *with* $P = (G, N, \mu)$ *be a Petri graph for a* GTS $(\mathcal{R}, G_0)$. *Furthermore let* $m_0[t_1\rangle \ldots [t_n\rangle m_n$ *be a firing sequence of the net* N *and let* $r_i = p_N(t_i)$ *be the rules corresponding to the transitions. We define morphisms* $\varphi_i = e_{m_i, \mu(t_{i+1})|_{L_{i+1}}} : L_{i+1} \to graph(m_i)$, *where* L_{i+1} *is the left-hand side of rule* r_{i+1}. *The sequence* $graph(m_0) \Rrightarrow_{r_1} graph(m_1) \Rrightarrow_{r_2} \ldots \Rrightarrow_{r_n} graph(m_n)$ *together with the morphisms* φ_i *is an abstract run. We denote by* $Run_A(P, \iota)$ *the set of all abstract runs of the Petri graph* (P, ι).

Each real run $\mathcal{J}_r = (G_0 \Rightarrow_{r_1} G_1 \Rightarrow_{r_2} \ldots \Rightarrow_{r_n} G_n)$ of the GTS $(\mathcal{R}, G_0)$ can be considered as an abstract run where the $\varphi_i : L_{i+1} \to G_i$ represent the matches of the left-hand sides of the rules r_i.

Proposition 1. *Let* $\mathcal{C}_\mathcal{G}$ *be an over-approximation for a* GTS $\mathcal{G}$ *computed by Algorithm 7. Then, for every real run* $\mathcal{J}_r$ *of the graph transformation system there exists an abstract run* $\mathcal{J} \in Run_A(\mathcal{C}_\mathcal{G})$ *such that* $\mathcal{J}_r$ *corresponds to* $\mathcal{J}$, *i.e.,* $\mathcal{J}_r \lll \mathcal{J}$.

An abstract run $\mathcal{J}$ for which there does not exist a real run corresponding to $\mathcal{J}$ is called *spurious*. If, at the same time, it violates the property we attempt to verify, it is called a *counterexample* or *error trace*.

We can now verify the GTS by analyzing the Petri graph underlying the Petri net. For instance, in order to show that no reachable graph contains a subgraph G_s we add a new rule to the GTS with G_s as left-hand side and an edge with a new label *Error* in the right-hand side (see rule "Error" in Table 1). If we can show that either no place labelled *Error* exists in the net or every such place is not coverable (this can be done using coverability graphs or backward reachability algorithms [1]), then we can deduce that this property holds.

However, if the approximation is too coarse, we might not be able to verify the property. We have shown in [5] how to construct a sequence of subsequently better unfolding—which however grow in size fairly rapidly—by forbidding folding steps up to depth k. Therefore we will now show how to successfully apply the technique of counterexample-guided abstraction refinement in our framework.

4   Abstraction Refinement

In order to eliminate spurious runs, we will show that they are always caused by the fact that certain nodes were merged. We will identify these nodes and show how to avoid their being merged in the next iteration, thereby avoiding this particular spurious run and all other abstract runs corresponding to it in a sense made precise later. Merging of nodes is harmful since it might produce new left-hand sides, thereby leading to additional rewriting steps.

4.1   Spurious Runs

For a given abstract run $\mathcal{J} = (graph(m_0) \Rightarrow_{r_1} graph(m_1) \Rightarrow_{r_2} \cdots \Rightarrow_{r_n} graph(m_n))$ of the Petri graph with morphisms $\varphi_i : L_{i+1} \to graph(m_i)$ we define $\mathcal{H}$ to be the set of real runs corresponding to the prefixes of $\mathcal{J}$. Furthermore let $\mathcal{H}_i$ be the set of hypergraphs reachable after i steps in a real run $\mathcal{J}_r \in \mathcal{H}$. It holds that $\mathcal{H}_0 = \{G_0\}$.

An abstract run $\mathcal{J}$ is spurious if $\mathcal{H}_n = \emptyset$. If the run is spurious, there exists a k such that $\mathcal{H}_k \neq \emptyset$, but $\mathcal{H}_{k+1} = \emptyset$ (and therefore also $\mathcal{H}_l = \emptyset$ for $l > k$). It will be shown in the following how to construct a new refined over-approximation $\mathcal{C}'_{\mathcal{G}}$, which does not contain $\mathcal{J}$ and some other spurious runs corresponding to $\mathcal{J}$.

Example: We illustrate the idea of a spurious abstract run with the run corresponding to the firing of the highlighted transitions "Cross Location" and "Error" in Fig. 3. In fact, there is not real run in the original GTS that corresponds to it.

4.2   Relations on Nodes for Refining Abstract Runs

According to Algorithm 7 and Definition 8 it holds that $\mathcal{H}_k \neq \emptyset$ and $\mathcal{H}_{k+1} = \emptyset$ if and only if for each $G \in \mathcal{H}_k$ there exists *no* edge-injective morphism $\eta : L_{k+1} \to G$ such that the following diagram commutes, where ξ_k is an edge-bijective morphism derived from the correspondence property (see Definition 8). In other words: there is no way to find a match of the left-hand side in G that agrees with the abstract run.

$$L_{k+1} \overset{\eta}{\dashrightarrow} G \overset{\xi_k}{\longrightarrow} graph(m_k)$$
$$\underset{\varphi_k}{\underbrace{\phantom{L_{k+1} \dashrightarrow G}}}$$

For if there were such a match morphism η, we could rewrite G to G' with rule r_{k+1} corresponding to the transition transforming m_k to m_{k+1}. Because of the construction of the Petri graph, where the right-hand side of r_{i+1} has been attached during an unfolding step, we would then be able to find an edge-bijective morphism $\xi_{k+1}: G' \to graph(m_{k+1})$ thus continuing the correspondence.

Such a situation is only possible if ξ_k is non-injective on some nodes of G, i.e., these nodes were merged during construction of the over-approximation $\mathcal{C}_{\mathcal{G}}$, which is the reason for the spurious run.

Example: In our running example (see Fig. 1 and 2) the nodes v_1 and v_2 as well as w_1 and w_2 of the initial hypergraph have been merged by the over-approximation, becoming $v_{1,2}$ and $w_{1,2}$. This led to the spurious abstract run described above.

We will now show how to determine the node merges which caused the spurious run. Consider, for a fixed graph G and a morphism ξ_k, the set Θ of possible equivalence relations $\sim$ on nodes for a graph $G \in \mathcal{H}_k$ such that, after merging the nodes in each equivalence class, we can find an appropriate match of the left-hand side L_{k+1} in the graph $G/\sim$. More formally, we demand the existence of an edge-injective morphism $\eta' : L_{k+1} \to G/\sim$ such that the following diagram commutes, where $\xi_k' : G/\sim \to graph(m_k)$ is obtained by quotienting ξ_k according to $\sim$.

$$ L_{k+1} \xrightarrow{\;\eta'\;} G/\sim \xrightarrow{\;\xi_k'\;} graph(m_k) $$
$$ \underset{\varphi_k}{\longrightarrow} $$

In order to characterize the smallest equivalence in Θ consider a node v of the left-hand side and determine a set Q_v of nodes in G which have to be fused into one node which is the image of v under η'. Let $v \in V_{L_{k+1}}$ and let e be an edge of L_{k+1} with[3] $c_i(e) = v$ for some i. For every edge e' in G with $\xi_k(e') = \varphi_k(e)$ we require that $c_i(e') \in Q_v$.

Consider the relation $\mathcal{Q}$, where for each $v \in V_{L_{k+1}}$ all nodes in Q_v are related and the relation $\widehat{\mathcal{Q}}$ which is the smallest equivalence containing $\mathcal{Q}$.

Proposition 2. *The equivalence $\widehat{\mathcal{Q}}$ constructed above is the smallest equivalence contained in Θ.*

Example: We consider again the abstract error trace $\mathcal{J}$ which can be obtained by firing transitions "Cross Location" and "Error". However, this error trace has no real runs that correspond to it, which can be seen by computing the set $\mathcal{H}$ of runs corresponding to prefixes of $\mathcal{J}$. Here, the set $\mathcal{H}_0$ consists of the initial hypergraph and the set $\mathcal{H}_1$ contains one graph G_1. The next rule "Error" cannot be applied to G_1 in such a way that the corresponding diagram commutes and therefore the set $\mathcal{H}_2$ is empty.

Fig. 4 shows the left-hand side of rule "Error", $G_1 \in \mathcal{H}_1$ and $graph(m_1)$, the graph corresponding to the marking reached after one step. One notices that no appropriate morphism η can be found unless the nodes w_1 and w_2 in G_1 are merged. Therefore we have $Q_{w_1'} = \{w_1, w_2\}$, $Q_{w_2'} = \{w_2\}$ and the smallest

---

[3] Note that by $c_i(e)$ we denote the i-the node in the sequence $c(e)$.

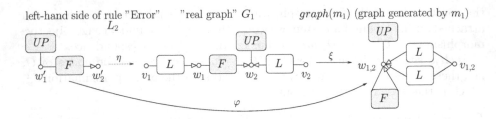

Fig. 4. Hypergraphs $G_1 \in \mathcal{H}_1$, L_2 and $graph(m_1)$ from the firewall example

equivalence relation $\widehat{\mathcal{Q}}$ relates the nodes w_1 and w_2 and no other nodes. Note for instance that w_2 must be contained in $Q_{w_1'}$ since both are attached to the unary edge labelled UP.

4.3   Elimination of Spurious Runs

The general idea for destroying spurious runs is to avoid the merging of nodes from the same equivalence class of $\widehat{\mathcal{Q}}$. For this reason we assign colours to the nodes of the graphs contained in $\mathcal{H}$ and disallow the merging of nodes corresponding to nodes with the same colour. For reasons that will become clear below a node may have several colours, i.e., a node v is associated to a set $cols(v)$ of colours.

For each $G \in \mathcal{H}_k$ we and each morphism $\xi_k : G \to graph(m_k)$ we consider the corresponding relation $\mathcal{Q}_{G,\xi_k}$. Then we assign colours to nodes in such a way that there exists at least one pair v_1, v_2 of nodes such that $v_1 \mathcal{Q}_{G,\xi_k} v_2$ and $cols(v_1) \cap cols(v_2) \neq \emptyset$. There are several ways to do this and all of them will help to eliminate the counterexample. In our implementation we choose a color for each set of nodes Q_v and assign it to all nodes contained in Q_v.

In order to catch "bad" mergings as early as possible, these colours have to be distributed to the remaining graphs contained in $\mathcal{H}$. Let us recall here that according to Definition 3 for each real run $\mathcal{J}_r = (G_0 \Rightarrow_{r_1} G_1 \ldots \Rightarrow_{r_k} G_k)$ from $\mathcal{H}$ we have injective partial morphisms $\nu_i : G_i \to G_{i+1}$ for $i = 0, \ldots, k-1$. Using these partial morphisms we assign the colours of G_k to the remaining graphs G_i contained in $\mathcal{H}$. We start from G_k and proceed as follows: if a node $v \in G_{i+1}$ has a colour then we also assign this colour to the node $\nu^{-1}(v)$ if such a node exists. In this way a node may obtain several colours, due to the branching structure of the runs contained in $\mathcal{H}$. We denote by $cols(v)$ the set of colours of the node $v \in V_{G_j}$ where $G_j \in \mathcal{H}_j$.

We are now ready to give the algorithm for computing the refined over-approximation.

Algorithm 10 (Refined approximated unfolding).

Input: A GTS $\mathcal{G}$, a set $\mathcal{H}$ of runs corresponding to prefixes of the counterexample and a function $cols$ assigning sets of colours to the nodes of the graphs in $\mathcal{H}$.

Output: The refined over-approximation $\mathcal{C}_\mathcal{G}'$.

We start constructing the new over-approximation $\mathcal{C}'_\mathcal{G}$ with the initial graph G_0. Unfolding steps will be performed as described in Algorithm 7.

For a folding step we disallow the merging of nodes corresponding to nodes in $\mathcal{H}$ having the same colour. More specifically, consider the over-approximation $\mathcal{C}'_\mathcal{G}$, which is currently being constructed. Now for each run $\mathcal{J}_r = G_0 \Rightarrow_{r_1} \ldots \Rightarrow_{r_\ell} G_\ell$ in $\mathcal{H}$ where $\ell < k$ check the following:

We consider all abstract runs $\mathcal{J} = graph(m_0) \Rightarrow_{r_1} \ldots \Rightarrow_{r_\ell} graph(m_\ell)$ of the current Petri graph $\mathcal{C}'_\mathcal{G}$ for which $\mathcal{J}_r \ll \mathcal{J}$ and all edge-bijective morphisms $\xi \colon G_i \to graph(m_i)$ for $i = 0, \ldots, \ell$. Whenever there are two nodes v_1, v_2 in G_i with $cols(v_1) \cap cols(v_2) \neq \emptyset$ and $\xi(v_1) = \xi(v_2)$, we have erroneously merged two nodes in the approximation which should not have been merged. Consequently this folding step is undone.

Previously rejected folding steps are recorded and are not any more considered by the algorithm.

In this way we will eliminate not only the spurious run but several more runs which are characterized below (see Proposition 5).

Example: Fig. 5 depicts the hypergraph obtained for the firewall example after the abstraction refinement procedure. As one can see, the "critical nodes" of the hypergraph, namely the nodes w_1 and w_2, are now separated.

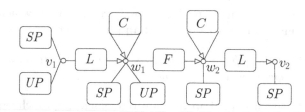

Fig. 5. Hypergraph obtained after abstraction refinement

4.4   Correctness

In the following we will show that Algorithm 10 terminates and that the refined over-approximation is correct and more exact then the previous one.

Let $\mathcal{C}_\mathcal{G}$ be an over-approximation with a spurious run $\mathcal{J}$ and let $\mathcal{C}'_\mathcal{G}$ be the corresponding refined over-approximation. In [3] it is shown that the algorithm constructing the over-approximating Petri graph terminates. We modified the algorithm by forbidding some of the folding steps and hence we have to reprove termination for the new version of the algorithm.

Proposition 3. *The algorithm computing the refined over-approximation $\mathcal{C}'_\mathcal{G}$ for a given GTS $\mathcal{G}$ and a (spurious) abstract run $\mathcal{J}$ of $\mathcal{C}_\mathcal{G}$ terminates.*

Furthermore the new over-approximation is still a valid over-approximation as before.

Proposition 4. *Let C'_G be the refined over-approximation of the* GTS. *Then, for every real run J_r of the graph transformation system there exists an abstract run $J \in Run_A(C'_G)$ such that J_r corresponds to J, i.e., $J_r \ll J$.*

In the following two propositions we will show that we have eliminated the given spurious counterexample and have not added any new ones. First we should answer the following question: what kind of runs have we eliminated by abstraction refinement? It is easy to see that in the refined over-approximation we have lost the initial spurious counter-example J. In fact we have not only eliminated J, but some more runs as described below.

Definition 11 (Correspondence with respect to runs). *Let (P, ι) and (P', ι') be two Petri graphs for a* GTS (R, G_0). *Furthermore let $J \in Run_A(P, \iota)$ and $J' \in Run_A(P', \iota')$ be two abstract runs of these Petri graphs and let H be the set of real runs considered earlier. We say that J' corresponds to J with respect to H if J' corresponds to J and a run $J'' \in H$ of maximal length weakly corresponds to a prefix of J'.*

Using this definition we can now state and prove the following propositions.

Proposition 5. *The refined over-approximation C'_G, constructed above does not contain any run J' corresponding to the spurious run J of C_G with respect to H.*

We can also show that no new spurious runs have appeared, which means that the new approximation is strictly better than the old one.

Proposition 6. *If the refined over-approximation C'_G contains a spurious run J', then it corresponds to some spurious run J in C_G.*

We remark that the considered abstraction refinement approach can also be implemented in the case of any number of spurious counterexamples by iteratively refining the abstraction. Naturally, due to undecidability and the fact that GTSs are in general Turing-complete, there is no guarantee that it will ever terminate.

5   Implementation and Experimental Results

In this section we consider examples of GTSs and compare the experimental results obtained by refining the approximation by forbidding folding steps up to a certain depth (see [5]) and counterexample-guided abstraction refinement as presented in this paper. It is shown that for practical purposes the new technique is usually more efficient.

The algorithm was implemented in C++ under Linux and the computer parameters are 2*Xeon 2.4 GHz, 2 GB RAM.

For case studies we have chosen two distributed systems: the running example of this paper (firewall example) and a system of public and private servers (for a description of the second example see [11]). If we compare the results in

Table 2. Verification results (abstraction refinement by forbidding folding steps up to a certain depth k, i.e., by computing k-coverings)

example	k (depth)	nodes	edges	transitions	time (sec)	verified
Public/private servers I	0	1	9	13	0.05	no
Public/private servers I	1	2	19	34	**0.72**	yes
Public/private servers II	0	1	10	14	0.05	no
Public/private servers II	1	1	11	16	0.07	no
Public/private servers II	2	3	31	63	**7.16**	yes
Firewall I	0	2	8	13	0.05	no
Firewall I	1	6	25	50	2.4	no
Firewall I	2	10	51	148	138.18	no
Firewall II	0	2	8	13	0.14	no
Firewall II	1	8	39	82	13.7	no
Firewall II	2	14	79	242	858.4	no

Table 3. Verification results (counterexample-guided abstraction refinement)

example	nodes	edges	transitions	time (sec)	verified
Public/private servers I	2	16	25	**0.67**	yes
Public/private servers II	2	17	26	**0.68**	yes
Firewall I	4	11	17	**0.16**	yes
Firewall II	4	12	18	**0.33**	yes

Tables 2 and 3 it can be seen that in the case of counterexample-guided abstraction refinement we have an advantage both in runtime for computing the approximation and in the size of the over-approximations, which are consequently easier to analyze. The difference is especially pronounced for versions II, which use larger start graphs.

The efficiency of the abstraction refinement approach can be explained by the fact that we forbid to merge only those parts of the unfolding which are responsible for the spurious counterexample. This means that the over-approximation remains rather compact compared to the depth-based (or k-covering) approach, where we are not allowed to merge all items having depth smaller than k. Note that for the firewall example it was not possible to verify the properties using the depth-based approached.

6   Conclusion

In this paper we have shown how counterexample-guided abstraction refinement can be applied to the analysis of dynamically evolving graphical structures in a fully automatic way. In this case we are not concerned with the abstraction of data values, but rather with graphs that are abstracted by merging nodes and edges, using the concept of graph morphisms. Hence, abstraction refinement can in this case be described by exploiting commutativity or rather non-commutativity of morphisms as described in Section 4. Also, since we are dealing with the approximation of graph structures rather than data values, no theorem prover is needed in order to determine the initial abstraction, instead we use techniques for approximated unfolding developed in [3].

Apart from smaller case studies we have used our approximated unfolding technique to verify a mutual exclusion protocol [9] and to verify insertion of elements into red-black trees [2]. We are currently working on an encoding of simple pointer programs into graph rewriting which will enable us to directly verify operations on pointer structures.

Research concerned with the verification of dynamically evolving graph structures which can be used to model distribution and mobility is fairly recent. There are contributions coming from the area of dataflow analysis such as shape analysis [16] as well as work directed more specifically towards the analysis of graph transformation systems [14, 13, 17, 9]. We believe that introducing counterexample-based abstraction refinement is an important step in order to make such verification techniques usable in practice. We also think that some of the techniques presented here can be employed in fairly general settings.

Compared to shape analysis [16, 12] which is also concerned with over-approximation techniques for graphical structures and which represents these structures as models of a 3-valued logic, we follow a different approach where graphs are represented directly and graph morphisms are used as a convenient abstraction mechanism. Furthermore we approximate with Petri nets, which enable us to talk about multiplicities of edges and can be conveniently analyzed using a variety of existing Petri net tool.

Acknowledgments. We would like to thank Tobias Heindel, Paolo Baldan and Andrea Corradini for many interesting discussions on the topics of this paper.

References

1. P.A. Abdulla, B. Jonsson, M. Kindahl, and D. Peled. A general approach to partial order reductions in symbolic verification. In *Proc. of CAV '98*, pages 379–390. Springer, 1998. LNCS 1427.
2. P. Baldan, A. Corradini, J. Esparza, T. Heindel, B. König, and V. Kozioura. Verifying red-black trees. In *Proc. of COSMICAH '05*, 2005. Proceedings available as report RR-05-04 (Queen Mary, University of London).
3. P. Baldan, A. Corradini, and B. König. A static analysis technique for graph transformation systems. In *Proc. of CONCUR '01*, pages 381–395. Springer, 2001. LNCS 2154.
4. P. Baldan, A. Corradini, and B. König. Static analysis of distributed systems with mobility specified by graph grammars - a case study. In *Proc. of IDPT '02*. Society for Design and Process Science, 2002.
5. P. Baldan and B. König. Approximating the behaviour of graph transformation systems. In *Proc. of ICGT '02*, pages 14–29. Springer, 2002. LNCS 2505.

6. T. Ball and S.K. Rajamani. Automatically validating temporal safety properties of interfaces. In *Proc. of SPIN '01*, pages 103–122. Springer, 2001. LNCS 2057.
7. S. Chaki, E. Clarke, A. Groce, S. Jha, and H. Veith. Modular verification of software components in C. In *Proc. of ICSE '03*, pages 385–395. IEEE Computer Society, 2003.
8. E. Clarke, S. Grumberg, S. Jha, Y. Lu, and H. Veith. Counterexample-guided abstraction refinement. In *Proc. of CAV '00*, pages 154–169. Springer, 2000. LNCS 1855.
9. F.L. Dotti, L. Foss, L. Ribeiro, and O. Marchi Santos. Verification of distributed object-based systems. In *Proc. of FMOODS '03*, pages 261–275. Springer, 2003. LNCS 2884.
10. T.A. Henzinger, R. Jhala, R. Majumdar, and G. Sutre. Lazy abstraction. In *Proc. of POPL '02*, pages 58–70. ACM, 2002.
11. Barbara König and Vitali Kozioura. Counterexample-guided abstraction refinement for the analysis of graph transformation systems. Technical Report 01/2006, Universität Stuttgart, 2006.
12. A. Loginov, T. Reps, and M. Sagiv. Abstraction refinement via inductive learning. In *Proc. of CAV '05*, pages 519–533. Springer, 2005. LNCS 3576.
13. A. Rensink. Canonical graph shapes. In *Proc. of ESOP '04*, pages 401–415. Springer, 2004. LNCS 2986.
14. A. Rensink. State space abstraction using shape graphs. In *Proc. of AVIS '04*, ENTCS, 2004. to appear.
15. G. Rozenberg, editor. *Handbook of Graph Grammars and Computing by Graph Transformation, Vol. 1: Foundations*. World Scientific, 1997.
16. M. Sagiv, T. Reps, and R. Wilhelm. Parametric shape analysis via 3-valued logic. *TOPLAS*, 24(3):217–298, 2002.
17. D. Varró. Towards symbolic analysis of visual modeling languages. In *Proc. of GT-VMT '02*, volume 72 of *ENTCS*. Elsevier, 2002.

Why Waste a Perfectly Good Abstraction?

Arie Gurfinkel and Marsha Chechik

Department of Computer Science, University of Toronto,
Toronto, ON M5S 3G4, Canada
{arie, chechik}@cs.toronto.edu

Abstract. Software model-checking based on the CEGAR framework can be made more precise by separating non-determinism from the lack of information due to abstraction. The two can be modeled individually using four-valued Belnap logic. In addition, this logic allows reasoning about negations effectively and thus enables checking of full CTL. In this paper, we present YASM – a new symbolic software model-checker. Preliminary experience with YASM shows that our implementation can effectively construct and analyze Belnap models without a substantial overhead when compared to its classical counterparts.

1 Introduction

Symbolic software model-checking, pioneered by the Microsoft's SLAM [1] project, is a technique that works directly on code and checks the program by combining automated *predicate abstraction* [13] with *counterexample-guided abstraction refinement* (CEGAR) [6]. The approach is divided into three phases: abstraction, model-checking, and refinement. During the abstraction phase, a theorem-prover is typically used to construct, using a list of predicates, a finite model that approximates the program being verified. The model is analyzed by the model-checker, and counterexamples generated by it are used to find additional predicates, if necessary. The process continues until either the property is successfully proved or disproved, or resources are exhausted.

For example, suppose our goal is to verify whether the line labelled P1 can be reached in the (deterministic) C program shown in Figure 1(a). This can be expressed in CTL as $AG(pc \neq \text{P1})$. Figure 1(c)-(e) gives a series of predicate programs which are automatically constructed while checking this property. The abstraction in Figure 1(c) is just the control-flow graph of the program, where the symbol '*' indicates that the condition was abstracted away, and its value is not known. '*' is thus interpreted as "either true or false", and treated as a non-deterministic choice during model-checking. Verifying $AG(pc \neq \text{P1})$ on this abstraction yields false. It is possible to resolve non-determinism so as to reach the line labeled P1, i.e., by exiting the while and entering the if statement. We then check the feasibility of this execution in the concrete program, with the goal of replacing the undesired non-determinism. Specifically, a predicate $x = 2$ is needed to determine whether the control flow enters the if statement. The new abstraction is shown in Figure 1(d): $x = 2$ becomes true during initialization, is not affected by the body of the loop, and is checked in the condition of the if statement. Now, the analysis yields that the property is violated if the loop terminates, and the condition $y \leq 2$ of the loop is added to the list of predicates, yielding an abstraction in Figure 1(e). The statement y = y − 1 is abstracted as follows: if $y \leq 2$ is true, then

H. Hermanns and J. Palsberg (Eds.): TACAS 2006, LNCS 3920, pp. 212–226, 2006.

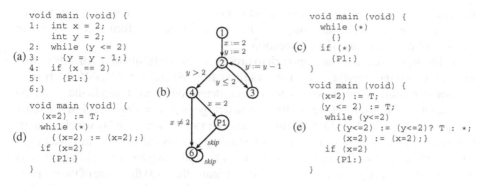

```
        void main (void) {
     1:   int x = 2;
          int y = 2;
     2:   while (y <= 2)
(a)  3:     {y = y - 1;}
     4:   if (x == 2)
     5:     {P1:}
     6:}

        void main (void) {
          (x=2)  := T;
          while (*)
(d)       { (x=2) := (x=2);}
          if (x=2)
            {P1:}
        }
```

```
        void main (void) {
          while (*)
          {}
(c)       if (*)
            {P1:}
        }

        void main (void) {
          (x=2)  := T;
          (y <= 2) := T;
          while (y<=2)
(e)       { (y<=2) := (y<=2)? T : *;
            (x=2)  := (x=2);}
          if (x=2)
            {P1:}
        }
```

Fig. 1. A simple C program (a), its control-flow graph (b) and its predicate abstractions: (c): no predicates; (d): after adding $x = 2$; (e): after adding $y \leq 2$

```
        int x;           if (*)        int x = 0;                      if (NONDET)
        x = 0;           {}            if (fopen (...) != NULL)        { if (*)
        if (x > 0)       else          { if (x > 0)                      {}
(a)       {x++}    (b)   {}      (c)       {x++;}               (d)       else
        else             P1:           else                              {}
          {x--}                           {x--}                          P1:
        P1:                            P1:                             }
                                       }
```

Fig. 2. (a): a C program where line P1 is not reachable; (b): abstraction of (a) without predicates; (c): a non-deterministic C program; (d) abstraction of (c)

decrementing y leaves it as true; otherwise, its value is unknown. The predicate $x = 2$ is not affected. The predicate program in Figure 1(e) is sufficient to determine that the loop does not terminate, and thus the property $AG(pc \neq P1)$ holds.

Now consider an example in Figure 2(a). Here, the property $\varphi = AG(pc \neq P1)$ fails in the concrete program. However, existing techniques (i.e., SLAM or BLAST) will not be able to determine this from the abstract program in Figure 2(b). To find a possible counterexample to φ, e.g., an execution which passes through the else part of the if statement, these techniques need to add another predicate, $x > 0$, and repeat the refinement and the model-checking phases. On the other hand, a human can easily determine that φ fails just by looking at the abstract program in Figure 2(b): line P1 is reachable along *every* path, regardless of which of these are feasible. Thus, the abstraction in Figure 2(b) is conclusive for φ, and we will use it in our analysis. Specifically, given an abstraction and a property $AG(pc \neq x)$ for some line x, we first attempt to prove it directly, just like other approaches. If the proof fails, we then attempt to prove its negation, i.e., that $pc = x$ is *always* reachable, without considering which abstract executions are possible. If this proof fails as well, we gather additional predicates and proceed to the refinement phase.

So far, we have assumed that programs are deterministic. This assumption is unrealistic even for sequential programs, e.g., because of user input or other external factors, such as presence or absence of files that the program attempts to use. For example, consider the program in Figure 2(d) which abstracts the one in Figure 2(c). Here, the computation not leading to P1 occurs when the file cannot be opened; since this behaviour is controlled by the environment, there exists a concrete execution leading to P1. Thus, we can conclude $AG(pc \neq \text{P1})$ fails, without any further refinements or analysis of the feasibility of this execution.

In this paper, we present an approach to proving truth and falsity of reachability properties. It is based on treating unknowns resulting from abstraction, '$*$', differently from unknowns resulting from the environment, non-determinism, as shown in the above example. Our approach is similar to the one taken by Reps and Sagiv [26] in the sense that it uses a logic with additional truth values (we use Belnap logic [4] which is an extension of Kleene logic [22] used in [26]) enabling us to perform both checks during a single analysis phase. The analysis yields one of the following answers: (1) the property holds; (2) the property fails (as in the model in Figure 2(d)); (3) the value of the property depends on the resolution of '$*$', and thus the abstraction needs to be further refined.

We also present an implementation of this approach via a symbolic software model-checker YASM[1]. Although similar approaches have been studied theoretically, e.g. see [8, 12], we believe this to be the first efficient implementation with performance that is comparable to SLAM and BLAST. The implementation makes use of a number of ideas from existing CEGAR approaches, which we have generalized for our purposes. In particular, our implementation is applicable to programs with non-deterministic control-flow, and is not restricted to reachability analysis.

The rest of this paper is organized as follows. After giving the necessary background in Section 2, we describe, in Section 3, the process of creating and interpreting abstractions of programs we want to check. We discuss three abstract semantics: over-approximation, under-approximation and exact approximation, used in YASM. In Section 4, we describe model-checking of the models constructed via the exact approximation and the use of counterexamples for conclusiveness, generated by the model-checker, for computing refined abstractions. Exact approximations enable the use of effective techniques for improving the speed and the precision of the analysis. We discuss a few of them in Section 5. We describe the tool and give its performance data in Section 6, and conclude in Section 7 with a comparison of our approach with related work, a summary of the paper, and a discussion of future research directions.

2   Background

In this section, we review multi-valued logics, define multi-valued Kripke, and a multi-valued version of the modal μ-calculus.

Logics. Boolean logic **2** is a set $\{t, f\}$ together with the truth ordering relation $\sqsubseteq$, s.t. $f \sqsubseteq t$. Conjunction $\wedge$ and disjunction $\vee$ represent meet and join with respect to the truth ordering. Additionally, a negation operator is defined as $\neg t \triangleq f$ and $\neg f \triangleq t$. Kleene logic [22] **3** extends **2** with an additional element $\bot$, representing "unknown" information. In this paper, $\bot$ is used to represent '$*$', discussed in Section 1. The truth ordering of the logic is extended as $f \sqsubseteq \bot$ and $\bot \sqsubseteq t$, and negation as $\neg\bot = \bot$. We define an additional ordering $\preceq$, that relates values based on the amount of *information*; thus $\bot \preceq t$ and $\bot \preceq f$, so that $\bot$ represents the least amount of information. Belnap logic [4]

---

[1] YASM stands for a **Y**et **A**nother **S**oftware **M**odel-checker.

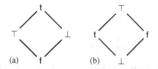

Fig. 3. Belnap logic: (a) truth order; (b) information order

4 extends **3** with an additional element $\top$. The truth ordering is extended so that $f \sqsubseteq \top$ and $\top \sqsubseteq t$, and negation as $\neg\top = \top$, i.e., $\top$ is equivalent to $\bot$ with respect to this ordering. Finally, the information ordering is extended by making $\top$ be the largest element, i.e., $f \preceq \top$ and $t \preceq \top$. This makes **4** into the smallest structure containing **2** that is a complete distributive lattice under both truth and information orderings. The truth and information orderings of **4** are shown in Figure 3.

Temporal Logic. Temporal logic properties are specified in propositional μ-calculus $L_\mu(AP)$ [23]. Properties are often expressed in CTL, which is a subset of L_μ [7].

Definition 1. *Let* Var *be a set of variable names, and* AP *be a set of atomic propositions. The logic* $L_\mu(AP)$ *is the set of formulas defined as:*

$$\varphi ::= Z \mid p \mid \neg\varphi \mid \varphi \wedge \varphi \mid \Diamond\varphi \mid \mu Z \cdot \varphi(Z)$$

where $p \in AP$, $Z \in$ Var, *and* $\varphi(Z)$ *is syntactically monotone in* Z.

We use the following syntactic abbreviations:

$$\varphi \vee \psi = \neg(\neg\varphi \wedge \neg\psi) \qquad \Box\varphi = \neg\Diamond\neg\varphi \qquad \nu Z \cdot \varphi(Z) = \neg\mu Z \cdot \neg\varphi(\neg Z)$$

The semantics of L_μ is defined with respect to an $\mathcal{L}$-valued Kripke structures.

Definition 2. *An* $\mathcal{L}$-*valued Kripke structure over a set of atomic propositions* AP *is a tuple* $K = \langle S, \mathcal{L}, R, I \rangle$, *where* S *is a set of states,* $\mathcal{L} \in \{2, 3, 4\}$ *is a logic,* $R : S \times S \to \mathcal{L}$ *is a transition relation, and* $I : AP \to [S \to \mathcal{L}]$ *is an interpretation of atomic propositions that assigns to each atomic proposition a mapping from states to values in* $\mathcal{L}$.

We often refer to $\mathcal{L}$-valued Kripke structures simply as Kripke structures when $\mathcal{L}$ is irrelevant or clear from the context. For a transition relation $R : S \times S \to \mathcal{L}$, we define the *preimage* of $Q : S \to \mathcal{L}$ w.r.t. R, $pre[R] : [S \to \mathcal{L}] \to [S \to \mathcal{L}]$, as

$$pre[R](Q) \triangleq \lambda s \in S \cdot \bigvee_{t \in S} R(s, t) \wedge Q(t)$$

$pre[R](Q)$ is a set of states that have an R-successor in Q. A dual of *pre* is *wp*:

$$wp[R](Q) \triangleq \neg pre[R](\neg Q)$$

$wp[R](Q)$ is a set of states whose R-successors are all in Q.

The semantics of L_μ formula φ in a Kripke structure K, written $||\varphi||_\sigma^K$, is defined inductively on the structure of the formula, where $\sigma : $ Var $\to \mathcal{L}^S$ is an object assignment for free variables:

$$||p||_\sigma^K \triangleq I(p) \qquad\qquad ||z||_\sigma^K \triangleq \sigma(z)$$
$$||\varphi \wedge \psi||_\sigma^K \triangleq ||\varphi||_\sigma^K \wedge ||\psi||_\sigma^K \qquad ||\neg\varphi||_\sigma^K \triangleq \neg||\varphi||_\sigma^K$$
$$||\mu x \cdot \varphi||_\sigma^K \triangleq \mathrm{lfp}^\sqsubseteq \left(\lambda S \cdot ||\varphi||_{\sigma[x \mapsto S]}^K \right) \qquad ||\Diamond\varphi||_\sigma^K \triangleq pre[R](||\varphi||_\sigma^K)$$

where $\mathrm{lfp}^\sqsubseteq f$ is the $\sqsubseteq$-least fixpoint of f. For a closed L_μ formula φ, $||\varphi||_\sigma^K = ||\varphi||_{\sigma'}^K$, for any σ and σ', written as $||\varphi||^K$. For a Kripke structure K and a state s, we write $K, s \models \varphi$ to mean $||\varphi||^K(s) = \text{true}$. Note that when K is 4-valued, $K, s \not\models \varphi$ does not mean that $K, s \models \neg\varphi$, i.e., proving that φ is false is not the same as failing to prove that φ is true. Finally, we define $\Box L_\mu$ and $\Diamond L_\mu$ to be subsets of L_μ, where the modal operations are just $\Box$ and $\Diamond$, respectively, and negation is allowed only at the level of atomic propositions.

3 Program Abstraction

In this section, we show how programs are approximated by Boolean programs and present three approximation semantics.

3.1 Programs

Operations. Let V denote the set of program variables. A program is built out of operations Ops of which there are two kinds: (1) an assignment $l := e$, where l is a variable from V and e is an expression over program variables, and (2) an operation $assume(e)$, where e is a boolean expression. Assume operations are used to model conditional branches. We also use an operation $skip$ as a syntactic abbreviation for $assume(\mathsf{t})$.

Programs as Control Flow Graphs. A *Control Flow Graph* CFG is a structure $G = \langle Loc, \delta \rangle$, where Loc is a finite set of locations, and $\delta : Loc \times Loc \to \mathbf{2}$ is a transition relation. A program is modeled by a labeled CFG $\langle G, \tau \rangle$, where τ labels each edge of the CFG G with an operation from Ops. A CFG corresponding to the program in Figure 1(a) is shown in Figure 1(b).

Programs as Kripke Structures. A *state* is a type-correct valuation of all program variables. We use S to denote the set of all states, and $s(x)$ to denote the value of the variable x in s. Each operation op corresponds to a transition relation $\mathsf{S}(op)$ defined as:

$$\mathsf{S}(op)(s,t) \Leftrightarrow t = \begin{cases} s & \text{if } op \text{ is } assume(e) \text{ and } s \models e \\ s[l \mapsto s.e] & \text{if } op \text{ is } l := e \end{cases}$$

Finally, a program $Prg = \langle G, \tau \rangle$ corresponds to a Kripke structure $K_{Prg} \triangleq \langle Loc \times S, \mathbf{2}, R_{Prg}, I_{Prg} \rangle$, where R and I are defined as:

$$R_{Prg}(\langle l, s \rangle, \langle k, t \rangle) \triangleq \delta(l, k) \wedge (\mathsf{S}(\tau(l, k)))(s, t)$$
$$I_{Prg}(pc = j)(\langle l, s \rangle) \triangleq (l = j)$$
$$I_{Prg}(e)(\langle l, s \rangle) \triangleq s \models e$$

and e is a boolean expression.

The semantics of L_μ is extended to programs in the obvious way: a program Prg satisfies φ iff the corresponding Kripke structure K_{Prg} satisfies φ.

3.2   Boolean Programs

Boolean Operations. Let $P = \{p_1, \ldots, p_n\}$ be a set of quantifier-free first-order boolean predicates over program variables V. A Boolean (or Predicate) program [2] is a program constructed out of Boolean operations $BOps$. As before, the operations are divided into two kinds: (1) a parallel assignment $p_1 := e_1, \ldots, p_n := e_n$, and (2) an operation $assume(e)$. We refer to elements of a parallel assignment as *updates*, e.g., $p_1 := e_1, p_2 := e_2$ consists of two updates, for predicates p_1 and p_2, respectively. The expressions on the right-hand-side of the assignment and in the argument of the assume operation are *partial boolean expressions* with the following grammar:

$$pb\_expr ::= * \mid choice(bool\_expr, bool\_expr) \mid \neg pb\_expr \mid bool\_expr$$

Intuitively, $*$ stands for an unknown expression, and $choice(a, b)$ – for an expression that evaluates to true when a is true, to false when b is true, and whose value is unknown otherwise. In Boolean programs, we use *skip* as a syntactic abbreviation for a parallel assignment $p_1 := choice(p_1, \neg p_1), \ldots, p_n := choice(p_n, \neg p_n)$, and $\neg choice(a, b)$ for $choice(b, a)$. As before, a Boolean program is a CFG whose edges are labeled with operations from $BOps$.

Syntactic Abstraction. We now show how a Boolean program $BPrg$ is used to approximate a program Prg by describing the behavior of Prg using a finite set of predicates. We present the approximation in a bottom-up fashion, starting with approximation of expressions, and ending with approximation of programs.

A partial boolean expression pe approximates a boolean expression e (denoted as $pe \preceq e$), if (a) pe is a boolean expression logically equivalent to e, (b) pe is the $*$ expression, (c) pe is of the form $choice(a, b)$ and a logically implies e, and b logically implies $\neg e$. For example, $y > 0$ is approximated by $choice(y > 1, \mathsf{f})$. Note that from the perspective of the approximation, $*$ is equivalent to $choice(\mathsf{f}, \mathsf{f})$.

The approximation is extended to the assume operations in the obvious way: $assume(pe) \preceq assume(e)$ iff $pe \preceq e$, e.g., $assume(y > 0)$ is approximated by $assume(choice(y > 1, \mathsf{f}))$. A single update $p := choice(a, b)$ approximates an assignment $l := e$ if $choice(a, b)$ approximates the weakest pre-condition of the predicate p with respect to the assignment. In other words, a approximates the condition under which p becomes true after the assignment, and b approximates the condition under which p becomes false. For example, a program assignment $y := y - 1$ is approximated by $(y \leq 2) := choice(y \leq 2, \mathsf{f})$. Finally, a parallel assignment A approximates an assignment $l := e$ if all update operations of A approximate $l := e$. For example, $y := y - 1$ is approximated by $(y \leq 2) := choice(y \leq 2, \mathsf{f}), (x = 2) := choice((x = 2), \neg(x = 2))$.

We say that a Boolean program $BPrg = \langle G, \tau_B \rangle$ approximates a program $Prg = \langle G, \tau \rangle$ if each operation of $BPrg$ approximates the corresponding operation of Prg. Since we have not yet given an operational semantics to Boolean programs, we call this approximation a *syntactic predicate abstraction*. There are standard techniques to compute such abstractions [1, 13].

3.3   Three Semantics of Boolean Programs

In order to evaluate temporal properties on Boolean programs, we must equip them with Kripke semantics. The only difficulty is to find a proper way to model the partial expressions, i.e., $*$ and $choice(a, b)$. In this section, we describe three choices for this approximation: (a) an *over-approximating* semantics where "unknown" is modeled as a non-deterministic choice between true and false – this is the semantics used by most existing model-checkers such as SLAM [2] and BLAST [20]; (b) an *under-approximating* semantics where "unknown" is modeled by a partial assignment; and (c) the *exact* semantics that uses Belnap logic to combine over- and under-approximation – this is the semantics used by our model-checker YASM. The three semantics are illustrated on a parallel assignment $A : (y \leq 2) := choice(y \leq 2, \mathsf{f}), (x = 2) := choice((x = 2), \neg(x = 2))$ that approximates $y := y - 1$ using predicates $y \leq 2$ and $x = 2$.

Over-Approximation. In this case, a state is a boolean valuation of predicates, i.e., it is an element of 2^P. Each operation bop in BOp is associated with a transition relation $\mathsf{O}(bop) \subseteq 2^P \times 2^P$, such that abstract states a and b are not connected if we can conclude from the boolean operation that there is no transition between the corresponding states of the concrete program. That is, if the current state a does not satisfy the precondition for p to become false, a has a successor, b, in which p is true.

Formally, the semantics of an update operation is

$$\mathsf{O}(p := choice(q, r))(a, b(p)) \Leftrightarrow (b(p) = \mathsf{t} \text{ and } a \not\models r) \text{ or } (b(p) = \mathsf{f} \text{ and } a \not\models q)$$

and semantics of a parallel assignment is the conjunction of all of its updates:

$$\mathsf{O}(\{p_i := choice(q_i, r_i)\}_{i=1}^n)(a, b) \Leftrightarrow \bigwedge_{i=1}^n (\mathsf{O}(p_i := choice(q_i, r_i))(a, b(p_i)))$$

For our running example, a part of a transition relation $\mathsf{O}(A)$ is shown in Figure 4(a). Note that a state a_1 corresponding to concrete states where $(y \not\leq 2)$ and $x = 2$ has two outgoing transitions, to states a_0 and a_1, indicating that it is possible for $y \leq 2$ to non-deterministically become true or false in the next state. That is, the fact that the value of $y \leq 2$ is unknown in the next state is modeled by non-determinism.

Finally, the semantics of the assume operator is:

$$\mathsf{O}(assume(e))(a, b) \Leftrightarrow a \not\models \neg e \text{ and } \mathsf{O}(skip)(a, b)$$

Under-Approximation. In this case, a state is a partial valuation of predicates, i.e, an element of 3^P, or a "tri-vector" [1]. Each operation $bop \in BOp$ is associated with a transition relation $\mathsf{U}(bop) \subseteq 3^P \times 3^P$, such that each predicate p is true in the next state, b, only if the current state, a, satisfies a precondition for p to become true.

Formally, the semantics of an update operation is

$$\mathsf{U}(p := choice(q, r))(a, b(p)) \Leftrightarrow (b(p) = \mathsf{t} \text{ and } a \models q) \text{ or } (b(p) = \mathsf{f} \text{ and } a \models r) \text{ or } (b(p) = \bot)$$

and semantics of a parallel assignment is the conjunction of all of its updates:

$$\mathsf{U}(\{p_i := choice(q_i, r_i)\}_{i=1}^n)(a, b) \Leftrightarrow \bigwedge_{i=1}^n (\mathsf{U}(p_i := choice(q_i, r_i))(a, b(p_i)))$$

For our running example, a part of a transition relation $\mathsf{U}(A)$ is shown in Figure 4(b). Here, state a_1 has a single outgoing transition to state a_3 indicating that in the next state the value of $y \leq 2$ is unknown, and $x = 2$ remains true.

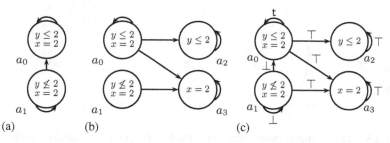

Fig. 4. Fragment of a transition relation: (a) over-approximation, (b) under-approximation, and (c) exact approximation

Finally, the semantics of the assume operator is:

$$U(assume(e))(a, b) \Leftrightarrow a \models e \text{ and } U(skip)(a, b)$$

Exact Approximation. This approximation combines the over- and under-approximating semantics in a single 4-valued model. Thus, the states are partial valuations of predicates, i.e., elements of 3^P. Each operation bop in BOp is associated with a 4-valued transition relation $E(bop) : 3^P \times 3^P \to 4$. Intuitively, a transition is t if it appears both in the over- and the under-approximations, $\bot$ if it appears only in the over-approximation, and $\top$ if it appears only in the under-approximation. For our running example, a part of a transition relation $E(A)$ is shown in Figure 4(c).

To define the semantics formally, we first introduce a function $eval()$:

$$eval(\varphi, a) \triangleq \begin{cases} t & \text{if } a \models \varphi \\ f & \text{if } a \models \neg\varphi \\ \bot & \text{if } a \not\models \varphi \text{ and } a \not\models \neg\varphi \end{cases}$$

Then, the semantics of an update is

$$E(p := choice(q, r))(a, b(p)) = \begin{cases} eval(choice(q, r), a) & \text{if } b(p) = t \\ eval(\neg choice(q, r), a) & \text{if } b(p) = f \\ \top & \text{if } b(p) = \bot \end{cases}$$

and the semantics of a parallel assignment is the conjunction of all of its updates:

$$E(\{p_i := choice(q_i, r_i)\}_{i=1}^n)(a, b) \Leftrightarrow \bigwedge_{i=1}^n (E(p_i := choice(q_i, r_i))(a, b(p_i)))$$

Finally, the semantics of the assume operation is:

$$E(assume(e))(a, b) \triangleq eval(e, a) \wedge E(skip)(a, b)$$

The semantics of operations is extended to Boolean programs in an obvious way. Thus, each semantics associates a Boolean program with a Kripke structure. For example, the Kripke structure corresponding to the boolean program in Figure 2(d) is shown in Figure 5(a). The following theorem shows that over- and under-approximating semantics preserve universal and existential fragments of L_μ, respectively, whereas the exact semantics preserves full L_μ.

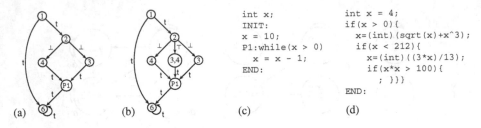

```
int x;              int x = 4;
INIT:               if(x > 0){
x = 10;                 x=(int)(sqrt(x)+x^3);
P1:while(x > 0)         if(x < 212){
    x = x - 1;             x=(int)((3*x)/13);
END:                       if(x*x > 100){
                               ; }}}
                    END:
```

(a)   (b)   (c)   (d)

Fig. 5. (a) a Kripke structure corresponding to the Boolean program in Figure 2(d); (b) improving precision of `if`; (c) and (d) two example programs

Theorem 1. *Let Prg and $BPrg$ be a program and its Boolean abstraction, respectively. Then, for an abstract state, a, and a corresponding concrete state, s, the following holds:*

$$1.\ \forall \varphi \in \Box L_\mu \cdot O(BPrg), a \models \varphi \quad \Rightarrow \quad Prg, s \models \varphi$$
$$2.\ \forall \varphi \in \Diamond L_\mu \cdot U(BPrg), a \models \varphi \quad \Rightarrow \quad Prg, s \models \varphi$$
$$3.\ \forall \varphi \in L_\mu \quad \cdot E(BPrg), a \models \varphi \quad \Rightarrow \quad Prg, s \not\models \varphi$$

The over-approximating semantics has been used in standard software model-checking tools to prove truth of AG properties. Our approach uses the exact semantics, which enables us to prove truth and falsity of such properties. We discuss it in the next section.

4   Abstract Model-Checking

To model-check a temporal logic formula φ in a state s and location l of a Boolean program $BPrg$, we use the techniques of Section 3 to construct a 4-valued Kripke structure K_{BPrg} and then compute the value of $||\varphi||^{K_{BPrg}}(\langle l, s \rangle)$. The latter step involves multi-valued model-checking, e.g., using the algorithm implemented in XChek [5]. In Section 4.1, we describe how to perform model-checking with Belnap logic using standard BDD packages. In Section 4.2, we show how to find additional predicates to refine the abstraction if the result of model-checking a formula φ is inconclusive.

4.1   Model-Checking

A symbolic multi-valued model-checking algorithm depends on an efficient representation and manipulation of Belnap functions, i.e., functions from some set S into **4**. These functions are represented in YASM as BDDs using the ideas below. First, any set S can be encoded by r boolean variables $v_1, \ldots, v_r$, for a sufficiently large r. Thus, we only need to find a representation for Belnap functions whose domain is 2^r. Second, any Belnap function $f : 2^r \to 4$ can be represented by a pair of boolean functions $\langle f_\top, f_\bot \rangle$ over 2^r [16], where $f_\top$ is $\lambda x \cdot f(x) \sqsupseteq \top$ and $f_\bot$ is $\lambda x \cdot f(x) \sqsupseteq \bot$. With this decomposition, $f(x)$ is equivalent to $(f_\top(x) \wedge \top) \vee (f_\bot(x) \wedge \bot)$. The following equivalences enable the direct computation of conjunction and disjunction of Belnap functions: (a) $f \wedge g = \langle f_\top \wedge g_\top, f_\bot \wedge g_\bot \rangle$; (b) $f \vee g = \langle f_\top \vee g_\top, f_\bot \vee g_\bot \rangle$; (c) $\neg f = \neg \langle f_\top, f_\bot \rangle = \langle \neg f_\bot, \neg f_\top \rangle$. Thus, we can represent each Belnap function by a pair of BDDs, one for each boolean function in the decomposition. Third, a pair of boolean functions $\langle f, g \rangle$ over variables $v_1, \ldots, v_r$ is represented by a single boolean function h with a new boolean variable z, using the encoding $h = z \wedge f \vee \neg z \wedge g$. So, Belnap functions can be represented and manipulated as standard BDDs at the expense of one additional variable. Furthermore, as many other symbolic model-checkers, we use the control-flow graph to partition the transition relation and its pre-image computation.

4.2 Abstraction Refinement

Whenever model-checking φ is inconclusive, our model-checker produces a behaviour of the system explaining why this is the case [15, 14]. So, we can use any of the existing techniques, e.g., [21], to determine whether this trace is feasible and use it to obtain additional predicates to refine the abstraction. However, in the multi-valued framework, checking feasibility of the trace is not necessary: we know exactly which part is inconclusive, and concentrate the refinement on it.

For example, consider the program in Figure 2(c), its abstraction in Figure 2(d), and the corresponding Kripke structure in Figure 5(a). Since the abstraction is built without any predicates, the Kripke structure is essentially equivalent to the CFG of the program. In this abstraction, $||EF(pc = \mathtt{P1})||(1)$ is inconclusive, i.e., $\bot$, which is exemplified by a path 1, 2, 4, P1 with an $\bot$-transition between states 2 and 4. In this example, the $\bot$-transition is the result of executing a boolean operation $assume(*)$ that syntactically abstracts $assume(x > 0)$ in the concrete program. Thus, the value of the predicate $x > 0$ is required to make the proof conclusive, which is done by refining the abstraction with this predicate, and repeating model-checking on the refined program.

In general, a path exemplifying why the result of model-checking is inconclusive always contains at least one $\bot$-transition. Suppose such a transition is between states $\langle k, a \rangle$ and $\langle l, b \rangle$, where k and l are program locations, and a and b are boolean valuations of predicates. By construction, this transition corresponds to a boolean operation bop such that $\mathsf{E}(bop)(a, b) = \bot$. If bop is a parallel assignment, then by the definition of the exact semantics there exists a predicate p and an update of the form $p := choice(q, r)$ in bop such that $a \not\models q$ and $a \not\models r$. The idea is to refine the update, by strengthening the expressions q and r by the precondition for p to become true after execution of the concrete operation op corresponding to bop. This is done by refining the Boolean program with the predicate corresponding to the weakest precondition of p with respect to op, i.e., $wp[op](p)$.

For example, suppose we have model-checked a Boolean program with two predicates $y \leq 2$ and $x = 2$, and the cause of inconclusiveness is a $\bot$-transition between states $a = \{(y \leq 2) \mapsto \mathsf{f}, (x = 2) \mapsto \mathsf{t}\}$ and $b = \{(y \leq 2) \mapsto \mathsf{t}, (x = 2) \mapsto \mathsf{t}\}$ Further, assume that the corresponding boolean operation is $(y \leq 2) := choice(y \leq 2, \mathsf{f}), (x = 2) := choice(x = 2, x \neq 2)$, which is the result of abstracting the concrete operation $y := y - 1$. The transition is unknown since the prestate a does not guarantee that $y \leq 2$ is true or false in the next state, i.e., $a \not\models y \leq 2$ and $a \not\models \mathsf{f}$. We can then refine the Boolean program by adding the predicate $wp[y := y - 1](y \leq 2) = (y \leq 3)$.

The above approach to abstraction-refinement is not limited to reachability properties. Our multi-valued model-checker can provide explanations to inconclusiveness of arbitrary CTL properties in the form of *proofs* [15], which we mine for additional predicates.

5   Exploiting Exact Approximations

The use of precise (Belnap) abstractions, described in Section 3, opens way to creating a number of techniques for improving the speed and the precision of the analysis. In this section, we discuss two of them.

Reusing Results of Previous Abstractions. One of the obvious limitations of the CE-GAR framework is the fact that intermediate results are not shared between successive abstraction-refinement iterations. For example, consider applying the framework to check whether the property $EF(pc = \text{END})$ holds in location INIT in the program in Figure 5(c).

In the first iteration, we conclude that reachability of END depends on the value of $x > 0$, which is added to the list of predicates. During the model-checking phase of the second iteration, it is proved that END is reachable from P1 if $x \leq 0$, i.e., $||EF(pc = \text{END})||(\langle \text{P1}, \{(\text{x} > 0) \mapsto \mathsf{f}\}\rangle)$ holds in the corresponding Kripke structure. Additionally, during the refinement phase, a new predicate $x > 1$ is added. The third iteration once again reproves that END is reachable from P1 provided that $x \leq 0$ or $x \leq 1$, adding a predicate $x > 2$. The process continues, repeating the work done at the previous iterations, until all predicates of the form $x > i$, where $0 \leq i \leq 10$, are added, and termination of the loop is established.

To reuse results of previous computations, we must first identify which results are preserved between iterations. For a program Prg, let K_P be a Kripke structure abstracting Prg using predicates $P = \{p_1, \ldots, p_n\}$, constructed during an iteration i, and let $K_{P'}$ be a Kripke structure constructed during the $i + 1$ iteration using predicates $P' = P \cup \{p_{n+1}\}$. From the construction of the abstractions, $||\varphi||^{K_P}(\langle l, u \rangle) \preceq ||\varphi||^{K_{P'}}(\langle l, v \rangle)$ for a formula φ and those states $\langle l, v \rangle$ of K_P and $\langle l, u \rangle$ of $K_{P'}$, where $v(p_i) = u(p_i)$ for all $i \leq n$ (i.e., v and u agree on the values of the first n predicates). In particular, if the concretization of v is not empty, then, if φ is either t or f in $\langle l, u \rangle$, it is correspondingly t or f in $\langle l, v \rangle$. This allows us to use $||\varphi||^{K_P}$, the result of model-checking φ on K_P, to help compute $||\varphi||^{K_{P'}}$ Formally, we define D_P as follows:

$$D_P(\langle l, \langle u_1, \ldots, u_{n+1} \rangle \rangle) = \begin{cases} \mathsf{t} & \text{if } ||\varphi||^{K_P}(\langle l, \langle u_1, \ldots, u_n \rangle \rangle) = \mathsf{t} \\ \mathsf{f} & \text{otherwise} \end{cases}$$

The function D_P is an under-approximation of $||\varphi||^{K_{P'}}$: for any state s of $K_{P'}$ with a non-empty concretization, $D_P(s) \sqsubseteq ||\varphi||^{K_{P'}}(s)$. If φ is computed using a least fixpoint, e.g., $\varphi = EF\psi$, D_P can be used as the starting point in computing φ on $K_{P'}$. For formulas that are computed using a greatest fixpoint, an over-approximation with respect to the truth ordering can be constructed and used in a similar manner. For a formula $\varphi = EF\psi$, the above optimization computes, at iteration $i + 1$, reachability of states proved to satisfy $EF\psi$ at iteration i. In our example, this results in $EF(pc = \text{END})$ during the first and the second iteration, $EF(pc = \text{END} \vee (pc = \text{P1} \wedge x \leq 0))$ during the third, $EF(pc = \text{END} \vee (pc = \text{P1} \wedge x \leq 1))$ during the fourth, etc. In the standard approach, we would have been checking $EF(pc = \text{END})$ from scratch after each refinement.

Handling Conditional Statements. In this paper, every abstract state corresponds to a unique control flow location, which simplifies construction of the abstract model but limits its precision. Recall that the goal of checking our program in Figure 2(d) and its corresponding Kripke structure in Figure 5(a) was to establish whether the location $pc = \text{P1}$ is reachable. Intuitively, model-checking begins by labeling node P1 by t, i.e., P1 is reachable from itself, and then propagates this labeling along the edges of the Kripke structure. Thus, in the second iteration, nodes $pc = 4$ and $pc = 3$ are labeled by t, i.e., $pc = \text{P1}$ is definitely reachable from these nodes. In the third iteration, we run into a problem. We would like to conclude that $pc = \text{P1}$ is reachable from the node $pc = 2$ – it is reachable from both branches of the if-statement. However, according to our algorithm, the value at $pc = 2$ is obtained by (a) propagating the labeling of $pc = 3$ through the $(2, 3)$-edge, (b) propagating the labeling of $pc = 4$ through the $(2, 4)$-edge, and (c) taking a disjunction of (a) and (b). Thus, after the third iteration, the node $pc = 2$ is labeled with $(\perp \wedge \text{t}) \vee (\perp \wedge \text{t}) = \perp$, allowing us to conclude only that $pc = \text{P1}$ is $\perp$-reachable from $pc = 2$.

The cause of this problem is that in our abstract domain, we cannot express that one of the branches of the if-statements is taken, although we do not know which. One solution is to increase the abstract domain to include a state corresponding to several control flow locations. Figure 5(b) shows a possible abstraction with an additional abstract state $pc = (3, 4)$, corresponding to the set of program states in which the control location is either 3 or 4. It has a t-transition to $pc = \text{P1}$ since all states corresponding to it have a transition there, and has a $\top$-transition from $pc = 2$, indicating that the execution of the if-statement *definitely* results in the control passing to either location 3 or 4. In this case, after the second iteration of the model-checking algorithm, nodes P1, 3, 4, and $(3, 4)$ are labeled with t, and the third iteration results in the desired result: $(\perp \wedge \text{t}) \vee (\top \wedge \text{t}) \vee (\perp \wedge \text{t}) = \text{t}$.

Additional abstract states solve our problem; however, they can significantly increase the size of the abstract model and complicate the abstraction process. In YASM, we take a different approach, similar in spirit to "hyper-transitions" (e.g., [24, 27, 9]). Instead of increasing the abstract domain, we use the fact that for any concrete (2-valued) left-total transition relation R, $wp[R](Q) \subseteq pre[R](Q)$ – if all successors of a state s are in Q, then at least one successor is in Q. Thus, the pre-image computation of an abstract transition relation R_a can be augmented from $pre[R_a](Q)$ to $pre[R_a](Q) \vee (wp[R_a](Q) \succeq \text{t})$, i.e., a state is assigned t if either it has a definite successor in Q, or all of its non-f successors are definitely in Q. In our example, this changes the third iteration of model-checking of the Kripke structure in Figure 5(a) as follows: in addition to computing *pre* along the edges $(2, 3)$ and $(2, 4)$, *wp* along each edge is computed to be $\neg\perp \vee \text{t} = \text{t}$, and the node $pc = 2$ is marked with t as desired. Thus, we can obtain a conclusive abstraction without the need to add the predicate $x > 0$.

Our approach also enables us to give definite results for certain programs with non-linear predicates. Consider the program in Figure 5(d). If the goal of a successful model-checking run is to *examplify* the path to END (as is the case in standard software model-checking approaches), the presence of complex mathematical operations will make the theorem-proving quite difficult, if not impossible. Our approach enables us to avoid these problems: we simply conclude that the path to END exists, whether it goes through the nested if statement or not. For such cases, we effectively perform context-sensitive slicing, removing parts of the abstraction which are not necessary to achieve a conclusive answer.

6   Experiments

The techniques described in this paper have been implemented in a software model-checker YASM. YASM is written in JAVA and uses theorem prover CVC Lite [3] to approximate program statements, and CUDD [28] library as a decision diagram engine.

Table 1 summarizes the performance of YASM on several programs based on the examples distributed with BLAST [20]. The experiments were performed on a Pentium 4 2.4 GHz machine running Linux 2.4.20. For each experiment, we list the number of iterations required by the abstraction-refinement phase, the final number of predicates, the overall model-checking time, and the final analysis result. For example, running YASM on a 4065-line qpmouse program took three iterations and yielded two predicates, in 2.5 seconds, whereas BLAST solved this problem in 1 second, also using two predicates. For every example, we checked whether an error condition is unreachable, which holds everywhere except qpmouse_err.

Table 1. Experimental results

Name	LOC	YASM			Result	BLAST	
		Iterations	# of Pred	Time (sec)		Time (sec)	# of Pred
tlan	6885	4	3	15.4	t	52	9
qpmouse	4065	3	2	2.5	t	1	2
qpmouse_err	4065	12	20	5.7	f	−	−
s3_srvr	2261	3	30	2.9	t	16.6	15
s3_srvr.3	2240	3	38	25.1	t	152	20

For these experiments, YASM was configured to prefer adding new predicates instead of computing a more precise abstraction. Our results clearly show that the running time of YASM is comparable to that of BLAST. We ran the latter as a baseline, to determine a reasonable performance for a software model-checker: a more direct comparison is not possible because the techniques used in the two model-checkers are significantly different. We do not report the results of running BLAST on qpmouse_err because the answer it gives when error is reachable is unsound: the paths reported by the tool are often infeasible.

7   Conclusion and Related Work

In this paper, we have presented YASM − a BDD-based software model-checker that combines automatic predicate abstraction-refinement with reasoning over Belnap logic. Our experience indicates that the CEGAR framework can be successfully extended to do proofs of reachability and proofs of unreachability, using the same abstraction. This approach allows us to shorten the abstraction-refinement cycle, is applicable to programs with non-deterministic control-flow, and provides support for model-checking of arbitrary CTL formulas.

There has been a lot of progress in applying automatic predicate abstraction of Graf and Saïdi [13] to software model-checking. The approach closest to ours is the one taken by SLAM [1] – YASM simply reinterprets SLAM's boolean programs using 4-valued semantics. Like our work, [25] makes a distinction between "non-deterministic" and "unknown" transitions and shows that performance of an explicit-state software model-checker is improved by guiding it towards the former. In our terminology, this would mean guiding the search to prefer non-$\bot$ transition, which happens automatically in our (symbolic) approach.

4-valued Kripke structures and their application to abstraction are equivalent to Mixed Transition Systems [8, 18]. They can also be seen as an extension of Modal Transition Systems [11] that are defined using Kleene logic.

We are not the first to use multi-valued logic to model abstraction in model-checking. Specifically, Kleene logic has been previously applied to reason about abstractions [26], and suggested as a basis for abstract model-checking [11]. Belnap logic has also been used to model abstraction in the context of (G)STEs [19] in a manner similar to ours.

Models based on Kleene logic have been used in [10] to separate handling of "unknown" and "non-determinism". Unlike our work or that of [8], it does not account for the relationship between abstract states, i.e., the case where $\gamma(a) \subseteq \gamma(b)$ for some abstract states a and b. It uses a (rather expensive [10, 17]) *generalized model-checking* approach and does not address the issue of generating counterexamples which are essential for an application of the CEGAR framework.

We are currently working on an implementation of YASM that combines exact approximations with function summaries for handling recursive functions. This is subject of a forthcoming paper.

Acknowledgments

We are grateful to Xin Ma, Kelvin Ku and Shiva Nejati for their help implementing, evaluating and improving YASM, and to Ou Wei for thoroughly reading an earlier draft of this paper and for many interesting discussions. We would like to acknowledge the financial support provided by NSERC. The first author has also been partially supported by an IBM Ph.D. Fellowship.

References

1. T. Ball, A. Podelski, and S. Rajamani. "Boolean and Cartesian Abstraction for Model Checking C Programs". *STTT*, 5(1):49–58, 2003.
2. T. Ball and S. Rajamani. "The SLAM Toolkit". In *Proceedings of CAV'01*, volume 2102 of *LNCS*, pages 260–264, 2001.
3. C. Barrett and S. Berezin. "CVC Lite: A New Implementation of the Cooperating Validity Checker". In *Proceedings of CAV'04*, volume 3114 of *LNCS*, pages 515–518, 2004.
4. N.D. Belnap. "A Useful Four-Valued Logic". In Dunn and Epstein, editors, *Modern Uses of Multiple-Valued Logic*, pages 30–56. Reidel, 1977.

5. M. Chechik, B. Devereux, and A. Gurfinkel. "XChek: A Multi-Valued Model-Checker". In *Proceedings of CAV'02*, volume 2404 of *LNCS*, pages 505–509, 2002.

6. E. Clarke, O. Grumberg, S. Jha, Y. Lu, and H. Veith. "Counterexample-Guided Abstraction Refinement for Symbolic Model Checking". *Journal of the ACM*, 50(5):752–794, 2003.

7. E. Clarke, O. Grumberg, and D. Peled. *Model Checking*. MIT Press, 1999.

8. D. Dams, R. Gerth, and O. Grumberg. "Abstract Interpretation of Reactive Systems". *ACM TOPLAS*, 2(19):253–291, 1997.

9. L. de Alfaro, P. Godefroid, and R. Jagadeesan. "Three-Valued Abstractions of Games: Uncertainty, but with Precision". In *Proceedings of LICS'04*, pages 170–179, 2004.

10. P. Godefroid. "Reasoning about Abstract Open Systems with Generalized Module Checking". In *Proceedings of EMSOFT'2003*, volume 2855 of *LNCS*, pages 223–240, 2003.

11. P. Godefroid, M. Huth, and R. Jagadeesan. "Abstraction-based Model Checking using Modal Transition Systems". In *Proceedings of CONCUR'01*, volume 2154 of *LNCS*, pages 426–440, 2001.

12. P. Godefroid and R. Jagadeesan. "Automatic Abstraction Using Generalized Model-Checking". In *Proceedings of CAV'02*, volume 2404 of *LNCS*, pages 137–150, 2002.

13. S. Graf and H. Saïdi. "Construction of Abstract State Graphs with PVS". In *Proceedings of CAV'97*, volume 1254 of *LNCS*, pages 72–83, 1997.

14. O. Grumberg, M. Lange, M. Leucker, and S. Shoham. "Don't Know in the μ-Calculus". In *Proceedings of CAV'05*, volume 3385 of *LNCS*, pages 233–249, 2005.

15. A. Gurfinkel and M. Chechik. "Generating Counterexamples for Multi-Valued Model-Checking". In *Proceedings of FME'03*, volume 2805 of *LNCS*, 2003.

16. A. Gurfinkel and M. Chechik. "Multi-Valued Model-Checking via Classical Model-Checking". In *Proceedings of CONCUR'03*, volume 2761 of *LNCS*, pages 263–277, 2003.

17. A. Gurfinkel and M. Chechik. "How Thorough is Thorough Enough". In *Proceedings of CHARME'05*, volume 3725 of *LNCS*, pages 65–80, 2005.

18. A. Gurfinkel, O. Wei, and M. Chechik. "Systematic Construction of Abstractions for Model-Checking". In *Proceedings of VMCAI'06*, volume 3855 of *LNCS*, pages 381–397, 2006.

19. S. Hazelhurst and C. H. Seger. "Model Checking Lattices: Using and Reasoning about Information Orders for Abstraction". *Logic Journal of the IGPL*, 7(3):375–411, May 1999.

20. T. Henzinger, R. Jhala, R. Majumdar, and G. Sutre. "Lazy Abstraction". In *Proceedings of POPL'02*, pages 58–70, 2002.

21. T. A. Henzinger, R. Jhala, R. Majumdar, and K. L. McMillan. "Abstractions from Proofs". In *Proceedings of POPL'04*, pages 232–244, 2004.

22. S. C. Kleene. *Introduction to Metamathematics*. New York: Van Nostrand, 1952.

23. D Kozen. "Results on the Propositional μ-calculus". *Theoretical Computer Science*, 27: 334–354, 1983.

24. K.G. Larsen and L. Xinxin. "Equation Solving Using Modal Transition Systems". In *Proceedings of LICS'90*, 1990.

25. C. Pasareanu, M. Dwyer, and W. Visser. "Finding Feasible Counter-examples when Model Checking Abstracted Java Programs". In *Proceedings of TACAS'03*, volume 2031 of *LNCS*, pages 284–298, 2003.

26. T.W. Reps, M. Sagiv, and R. Wilhelm. "Static Program Analysis via 3-Valued Logic". In *Proceedings of CAV'04*, volume 3114 of *LNCS*, pages 15–30, 2004.

27. S. Shoham and O. Grumberg. "Monotonic Abstraction-Refinement for CTL". In *Proceedings of TACAS'04*, volume 2988 of *LNCS*, 2004.

28. F. Somenzi. "CUDD: CU Decision Diagram Package Release", 2001.

Efficient Abstraction Refinement in Interpolation-Based Unbounded Model Checking*

Bing Li and Fabio Somenzi

University of Colorado at Boulder
{Bing.Li, Fabio}@Colorado.EDU

Abstract. It has been pointed out by McMillan that modern satisfiability (SAT) solvers have the ability to perform on-the-fly model abstraction when examining it for the existence of paths satisfying certain conditions. The issue has therefore been raised of whether explicit abstraction refinement schemes still have a role to play in SAT-based model checking. Recent work by Gupta and Strichman has addressed this issue for bounded model checking (BMC), while in this paper we consider unbounded model checking based on interpolation. We show that for passing properties abstraction refinement leads to proofs that often require examination of shorter paths. On the other hand, there is significant overhead involved in computing efficient abstractions. We describe the techniques we have developed to minimize such overhead to the point that even for failing properties the abstraction refinement scheme remains competitive.

1 Introduction

Model checking algorithms that employ propositional satisfiability (SAT) as basic decision procedure have enjoyed considerable success in the last few years. Bounded Model Checking (BMC, [2]) can often find counterexamples to properties of models that are too complex for other techniques. In BMC the problem of finding a trace violating a linear-time property is formulated as the satisfiability of a formula derived from the transition relation of the model, the initial state condition, and the property to be disproved. The practical success of this approach is due in part to the great efficiency achieved by today's SAT solvers, and in part to the fact that storing a representation of the set of reachable states of the model is not required.

Although theoretically complete for finite-state systems, the basic BMC algorithm is not useful to prove properties (rather than refuting them). Auxiliary techniques have been developed to provide termination conditions for true properties. The method of [17] checks for simple paths of certain lengths that either start from initial states or end in *bad* states. From the non-existence of such paths it is possible to deduce the non-reachability of the bad states, and hence to prove an invariant. A criterion for all linear-time properties also relying on simple paths was proposed in [1]; it is based on representing the property as a Büchi automaton.

A different approach to proving termination is taken in [15], which relies on the notion of Craig's interpolant of an unsatisfiability proof. A properly chosen interpolant of the proof that no counterexample of length L to an invariant exists can be interpreted as

---

* This work was supported in part by SRC contract 2004-TJ-920.

H. Hermanns and J. Palsberg (Eds.): TACAS 2006, LNCS 3920, pp. 227–241, 2006.

a set of states with two properties: It includes all states reachable in one transition from the initial states; and it contains no state that can reach a state violating the invariant in $L - 1$ transitions or less. This observation suggests an iterative procedure which, if it converges without discovering any (possibly spurious) counterexample, guarantees the unreachability of the bad states. The advantage of interpolation-based termination check is that the paths to be encoded in the SAT instances are never longer than those examined by the simple-path method and sometimes much shorter. Both approaches turn bounded model checking algorithms into unbounded ones. There also exist SAT-based algorithms that are not extensions of BMC (e.g., [14]) but so far they have proved competitive only for a limited class of problems.

Abstraction refinement [10] is another technique that has greatly improved the capacity of model checkers. To prove a (universal) linear-time property, one starts with a coarse abstraction that simulates the given model. If no counterexample is found in the abstract model, the property is known to hold in the original, concrete system as well. If a counterexample is found, which is not also a counterexample of the concrete model, the abstraction is too coarse and is refined. Refinement may aim at removing the error trace that was discovered [5], or all error traces of a certain length [16, 4, 20, 12].

Whether SAT-based model checking and abstraction refinement can be profitably combined is an interesting question. It has been argued convincingly by McMillan that modern SAT solvers effectively perform an on-the-fly abstraction of the model. They can prove unsatisfiability of a formula without ever assigning values to many of its variables. The heuristics used to choose decision variables indeed tend to identify a good subset of the variables and mostly work on them. With abstraction already taking place inside the SAT solver, it is not clear that abstraction outside the solver would provide additional benefit. On the other hand, there may be significant overhead in checking spurious counterexamples and computing the corresponding refinements.

Gupta and Strichman [8] have addressed this issue for BMC, that is, for failing properties. They observed that SAT solvers may spend time on needless Boolean constraint propagation and local conflicts if working directly on a large concrete model.

In this paper we look at the combination of abstraction refinement and interpolation-based model checking. We show that termination test carried out on the abstract model increases the ability to prove properties for large models by reducing the length of the paths to be examined. This improvement depends on the model checker ability to keep the abstract model small. Therefore, our algorithm invests considerable time in identifying small refinements. This, however, adds a significant overhead in the case of failing properties, for which the ability to prove termination sooner is immaterial. Therefore, we present several techniques that we have devised to speed up the computation of refinements without compromising their quality. The resulting algorithm outperforms the corresponding one without abstraction refinement for passing properties, while remaining competitive for the failing ones.

The rest of the paper is organized as follows. Section 2 reviews background material. Sections 3 and 4 present the abstraction refinement algorithm with termination check based on interpolation. Experimental results are discussed in Sect. 5 and conclusions are drawn in Sect. 6.

2 Preliminaries

2.1 Open Systems and Safety Properties

Let $V = \{v_1, \ldots, v_n\}$ and $W = \{w_1, \ldots, w_m\}$ be sets of Boolean variables. We designate by V' the set $\{v'_1, \ldots, v'_n\}$ consisting of the primed version of the elements of V, and by V^i the set $\{v^i_1, \ldots, v^i_n\}$. Likewise, $W^i = \{w^i_1, \ldots, w^i_m\}$. An *open system* is a 4-tuple $\langle V, W, I, T \rangle$, where V is the set of (current) state variables, W is the set of combinational variables, $I(V)$ is the initial state predicate, and $T(V, W, V')$ is the transition relation. The variables in V' are the next state variables. We assume that $T(V, W, V')$ is given by a *circuit graph*, that is, by a labeled graph $\mathcal{C} = (V \cup W, E)$ such that $m \geq n$, node $v_i \in V$ is labeled by $w_i \in W$, node $w_i \in W$ is labeled by a Boolean formula $T_i = w_i \leftrightarrow \delta_i(V, W)$, $(w_i, v_i) \in E$ for $i \in \{1, \ldots, n\}$, and, for $x \in V \cup W$, $w_i \in W$, $(x, w_i) \in E$ iff x appears in δ_i. The transition relation is then defined by:

$$T(V, W, V') = \bigwedge_{1 \leq i \leq n} (v'_i \leftrightarrow w_i) \wedge \bigwedge_{1 \leq i \leq m} T_i(W, V) \ . \tag{1}$$

In this paper, we use a form of circuit graph known as And-Inverter Graph [9] from the only types of gates allowed in it. AIGs can be manipulated efficiently.

An open system Ω defines a labeled transition structure in the usual way, with states Q_Ω corresponding to the valuations of the variables in V, and transition labels corresponding to the valuations of the variables in W. Conversely, a set of states $S \subseteq Q_\Omega$ corresponds to a predicate $S(V)$ or $S(V')$. Predicate $S(V)$ $(S(V'))$ is the characteristic function of S expressed in terms of the current (next) state variables. State $q \in Q_\Omega$ is an initial state if it satisfies $I(V)$. State set $S \subseteq Q_\Omega$ is *reachable* from state set S' in k steps if there is a path of length k in the labeled transition structure defined by Ω that connects some state in S' to some state in S; equivalently if

$$S'(V^0) \wedge \bigwedge_{1 \leq i \leq k} T(V^{i-1}, W^i, V^i) \wedge S(V^k) \tag{2}$$

is satisfiable. State set S is reachable from S' if there exists $k \in \mathbb{N}$ such that S is reachable in k steps from S'. A state set is reachable (in k steps) if it is reachable (in k steps) from I. A sequence of states $\rho \in Q^*_\Omega$ $(\in Q^\omega_\Omega)$ is a *run* of Ω if the first state is initial, and every other state is reachable from its predecessor in one step.

An *invariant* is a property that states that a certain predicate holds of all reachable states of Ω. Let P be the set of states that satisfy that predicate. We identify the property with the set of states that satisfy it. Hence, property P is satisfied by Ω if there is no $k \in \mathbb{N}$ such that

$$I(V^0) \wedge \bigwedge_{1 \leq i \leq k} T(V^{i-1}, W^i, V^i) \wedge \neg P(V^k) \tag{3}$$

is satisfiable. This approach extends to all safety properties. (See, for instance, [12].)

The search for a k such that (3) is satisfiable can obviously be restricted to the range $\{0, \ldots, |Q_\Omega| - 1\}$. Hence, in theory, the process is guaranteed to terminate. In practice, the number of states is too large to be of any practical use, and tighter upper bounds for k are sought [17, 15].

2.2 Abstraction Refinement

Open system $\widehat{\Omega} = \langle \widehat{V}, \widehat{W}, \widehat{I}, \widehat{T} \rangle$ is an *abstraction* of Ω if

- $\widehat{V} \subseteq V$;
- $\widehat{W} = \widehat{W}_1 \cup (V \setminus \widehat{V})$;
- $\widehat{W}_1 \subseteq W$ such that $v_i \in \widehat{V}$ implies $w_i \in \widehat{W}_1$;
- $\widehat{I}(\widehat{V}) = \exists (V \setminus \widehat{V}) . I(V)$;
- $\widehat{T}(\widehat{V}, \widehat{W}, \widehat{V}') = \exists (W \setminus \widehat{W}) . \exists (V' \setminus \widehat{V}') . T(V, W, V')$.

(Note that w_i is the combinational variable associated to v_i'). This definition entails that every run of Ω has a matching run in $\widehat{\Omega}$. Property $\widehat{P}$ is the abstraction of property P with respect to $\widehat{\Omega}$ if $\widehat{P}(\widehat{V}) = \forall (V \setminus \widehat{V}) . P(V)$. If $\widehat{\Omega}$ satisfies (or models) $\widehat{P}$, then Ω satisfies P. That is, $\widehat{\Omega} \models \widehat{P} \rightarrow \Omega \models P$. This preservation result is the basis for the following abstraction refinement approach to the verification of P. One starts with a coarse abstraction $\widehat{\Omega}_0$ of the *concrete* open system Ω and checks whether $\widehat{\Omega}_0 \models \widehat{P}_0$. If that is the case, then $\Omega \models P$; otherwise, there exists a least $k' \in \mathbb{N}$ such that

$$\widehat{I}(\widehat{V}^0) \wedge \bigwedge_{1 \le i \le k'} T(\widehat{V}^{i-1}, \widehat{W}^i, \widehat{V}^i) \wedge \neg \widehat{P}(\widehat{V}^{k'}) \tag{4}$$

is satisfiable. The satisfying assignments to (4) are the shortest-length *abstract counterexamples* (ACEs). If $\widehat{\Omega}_0 \not\models \widehat{P}_0$ one or more ACEs are checked for *concretization*. That is, one checks whether (3) has solutions that agree with the ACE(s) being checked. Because of the additional constraints provided by the ACEs, a concretization test is often less expensive that the satisfiability check of (3). However, its failure only indicates that the abstract error traces are spurious. Therefore, if the concretization test fails, one chooses a refined abstraction $\widehat{\Omega}_1$ and repeats the process, until one of these cases occurs.

1. $\widehat{\Omega}_i \models \widehat{P}_i$ for some i, in which case $\Omega \models P$ is inferred.
2. The concretization test passes for some i, in which case it is concluded that $\Omega \not\models P$ and the satisfying assignment to (3) found is returned as counterexample to P.
3. The refinement eventually produces $\widehat{\Omega}_i = \Omega$. In this final case, the satisfiability check of (4) answers the model checking question conclusively.

The cone of influence (COI), or direct support, of a property is the union of the COIs (direct supports) of all the variables mentioned in the predicate P that defines the property. COI reduction refers to the abstraction in which $\widehat{V}$ is the COI of the property. It is commonly applied before any model checking is attempted, because it satisfies

$$\widehat{\Omega} \models \widehat{P} \leftrightarrow \Omega \models P. \tag{5}$$

2.3 Satisfiability Solvers, Proofs of Unsatisfiability, and Interpolants

The Davis-Putnam-Logemann-Loveland (DPLL) procedure is the basic algorithm for most modern SAT solvers, which add conflict-driven learning and non-chronological backtracking [18] to the basic branching and backtracking approach.

Conflict-driven learning is an important feature of many modern SAT solvers, which is normally based on conflict clause recording. Whenever SAT solvers detect a conflicting assignment to a formula f (one that causes f to evaluate to false), they conjoin a *conflict clause* to f. The clause is generated by analyzing the so-called *implication graph*, which shows which decisions and clauses are responsible for the conflict. The new clause prevents the solver from attempting the same assignment again. It may also exclude from future consideration other parts of the search space that can be inferred to contain no satisfying assignments.

The clauses that make up the edges of an implication graph can be used to explain the conflict clause deduced from it. Keeping track of the explanations of conflict clauses results in the ability to identify an *unsatisfiable core (or unsatisfiability proof)* [7, 21] of the given formula when it is indeed unsatisfiable. This can be done by recursively replacing conflict clauses with those that produced them, the resolvent of which is exactly the conflict clause. The process starts from the final empty clause (final unsolvable conflict) and terminates when only clauses of the original formula are left.

When the check for existence of counterexamples of a certain length fails, the unsatisfiable core produced by the SAT solver can be used to guide the refinement of the abstract model. AROSAT [11] is a specialized SAT solver that tries to find an unsatisfiability proof that relies on a small number of state variables of the model, so as to speed up the computation of a minimal refinement.

From the proof of unsatisfiability it is also possible to extract interpolants, that is, formulae that summarize part of the proof, while depending only on a specified set of variables [15]. Interpolants can be computed in time linear in the size of the resolution tree associated with the unsatisfiability proof.

3 Algorithm

Our algorithm is called IPAR because it combines interpolation and abstraction refinement. The pseudocode of our main procedure is shown in Fig. 1. The input to the algorithm is an open system $\Omega = \langle V, W, I, T \rangle$ whose transition relation T is specified by a circuit graph $\mathcal{C} = (V \cup W, E)$, and a predicate $P(V)$ describing a set of accepting states. The return value is TRUE if the property passes, FALSE otherwise.

Initially, an abstract model $\widehat{\Omega}$ is computed by collecting in $\widehat{V}$ only the state variables that appear in $P(V)$; hence, $\widehat{P} = P$ throughout. Then the procedure of GETREFINEMENTFROMREFPREDICT is applied to get probable future refinement and add it to $\widehat{\Omega}$. After the initial abstract model is created, the algorithm progressively increases L from its initial value 0 until either a counterexample of length L is found in the concrete system Ω, or it is concluded that no counterexample exists in the current abstract model $\widehat{\Omega}$. For each abstract model, the procedure CHECKINTERPOLATION is invoked to detect the existence of counterexamples as well as prove absence of counterexamples by detecting convergence of the interpolants, which is similar to what is described in [15], with the differences that 1) the constraint due to the property is added only to the last timeframe, 2) each time the length is increased, its new value is the sum of the previous length and the number of iterations in the previous termination check minus one [13].

CHECKINTERPOLATION returns two parameters. The first is CEXFOUND; if it is FALSE, there is no counterexample of any length in the abstract model, and the prop-

```
boolean IPAR(Ω, P, C) {
1      L = 0;
2      Ω̂ = CREATEINITIALABSTRACTION(Ω,P);
3      refinement = GETREFINEMENTFROMREFPREDICT(Ω,Ω̂);
4      Ω̂ = ADDREFTOABSMODEL(Ω̂, refinement);
5      while (Ω̂ ≠ Ω) {
6          (CEXFOUND,L) = CHECKINTERPOLATION(Ω̂,P,L)
7          if (¬ CEXFOUND)
8              return TRUE;
9          Ω̃ = ADDLAYER(Ω̂, Ω, C);
10         while (EXISTCEX(Ω̃,P,L)) {
11             if (Ω̃ == Ω)
12                 return FALSE;
13             else
14                 Ω̃ = ADDLAYER(Ω̃, Ω, C);
15         }
16         Ω̂ = GENERATENEWABSTRACTION(Ω̂,Ω̃,P,L);
17         L = L + 1;
18     }
19     (CEXFOUND,L) = CHECKINTERPOLATION(Ω̂,P,L);
20     return ¬ CEXFOUND;
21 }
```

Fig. 1. The IPAR algorithm

erty is true of the concrete model. Otherwise, an abstract counterexample has been found, and we should try to find a corresponding real counterexample. The other parameter is L; if CEXFOUND is TRUE, there is no counterexample of length $< L$, but at least one counterexample of length L in the abstract model. If CHECKINTERPOLATION fails to prove termination, we try to find a sufficient model—one that has no counterexample up to length L—by incrementally adding, with ADDLAYER, latches to the current abstract model one layer at the time, until we either find a sufficient model or a real counterexample. Function EXISTCEX decides whether a counterexample exists by calling the SAT solver. Lines 9–15 in Fig. 1 implement a procedure called *incremental concretization*; more details can be found in [12]. Line 16 shows that if a sufficient model is found, a refinement is computed and added to the abstract model; the detailed pseudocode is shown in Fig. 2. Once a new abstract model is generated, we increase the length L by one and iterate. The abstract model may eventually equal the concrete model; in this case we just apply the interpolation algorithm to the concrete model, as shown in Lines 19–20.

The pseudocode of GENERATENEWABSTRACTION is shown in Fig. 2. It takes four input parameters—concrete model Ω, abstract model $\widehat{\Omega}$, property P, current checking length L—and returns a new abstract model. In this procedure, first a compact unsatisfiability proof is generated in procedure GENERATEUNSATPROOFFROMIAROSAT by utilizing IAROSAT (see Sect. 3.1); then *bridge abstraction* is applied to extract a sufficient refinement candidate set which, if added to $\widehat{\Omega}$, would kill all abstract counterexamples of length up to L. All *latch variables* (variables corresponding to some

model GENERATENEWABSTRACTION($\Omega, \widehat{\Omega}, P, L$) {
   Ψ = GENERATEUNSATPROOFFROMIAROSAT(Ω, P, L);
   ζ = GENERATESUFFISETBYBRIDGEABS($\Omega, \widehat{\Omega}, \Psi$);
   RCArray = COMPUTERELATIVECORRELATIONARRAY($\zeta, \Omega, \widehat{\Omega}$);
   refinement = UNSATPROOFGUIDEDRM($\widehat{\Omega}$, RCArray);
   $\widehat{\Omega}$ = ADDREFTOABSMODEL($\widehat{\Omega}$, refinement);
   refinement = GETREFINEMENTFROMREFPREDICT($\Omega, \widehat{\Omega}$);
   $\widehat{\Omega}$ = ADDREFTOABSMODEL($\widehat{\Omega}$, refinement);
   return $\widehat{\Omega}$
}

Fig. 2. The refinement algorithm

latch in the AIG) in the unsatisfiability proof would guarantee a sufficient set; however, too many latch variables in the proof may lead to too many refinement candidates and a time-consuming refinement minimization procedure. Oftentimes, some latch variables can be eliminated without affecting unsatisfiability. If we define the *latch-bridge-pair* for a latch to be the pair of the present and the next state variables of a latch for the same time frame, we can claim that a latch can be eliminated without damaging the unsatisfiability of the formula if none of its *latch-bridge-pairs* appears in the proof [11]. So if we pick all latches that have at least one *latch-bridge-pair* in the unsatisfiability proof, we can build a sufficient set. Since each such latch works like a bridge for propagating the implications, we call this kind of abstraction extraction *bridge abstraction*.

After refinement candidates are generated, to keep the abstract model compact after refining, we use the structural guidance provided by *relative correlation* [12] to order the candidates for the unsatisfiability proof-guided refinement procedure, UN-SATPROOFGUIDEDRM, the result of which is a minimal refinement set (see Sect. 3.2). This refinement will be added to the current abstract model to obtain a new abstraction. Then a refinement prediction procedure, GETREFINEMENTFROMREFPREDICT, described in Sect. 3.3, is applied to it to generate another refinement. The final new abstract model, which will be returned to the main procedure, will be obtained by adding the second refinement to the abstract model.

In the abstraction refinement approach, if abstract models become close to concrete models, due to the inner abstraction refinement mechanism of SAT solver, we may not gain much by using abstraction refinement even after various techniques like IAROSAT, URM and RP—descibed in the sequel—have been used. So, at each length, we calculate what percentage the abstract model is in the concrete model. If it is larger than a threshold, we switch to flat model checking. We call this simple, yet effective technique *abstraction switching*.

3.1 Improved AROSAT

Given a circuit C, let V be a set of variables of C, and $\{V_1, V_2, \ldots, V_n\}$ a partition of V. Then $V_1, V_2, \ldots, V_n$ are called *layers* of C. AROSAT [12] is a SAT algorithm designed especially for the abstraction and refinement approach, to generate unsatisfiability proofs that use latch variables corresponding to fewer different latches. In

AROSAT, layered constraints are enforced on the choice of decision variables and on implication propagation to make sure only necessary latch variables are involved in the SAT search. AROSAT normally obtains much better unsatisfiability proof than an ordinary SAT solver, however, the speed of AROSAT is much slower, 5 times slower according to [11]. Here we propose an improved version of the old AROSAT which is called IAROSAT. Compared to AROSAT, IAROSAT has the following features:

In AROSAT, only latch variables are divided into different layers and given higher priority to be selected as decision variables than other variables. This causes the decision variables to be just latch variables in most cases. In [6] the observation was made that the choice of branching variables should be very dynamic. Accordingly, in IAROSAT, instead of concentrating only on latch variables for decision variable selection, we divide the whole variable space into different layers, and all variables in the same layer have the same priority. We first form clusters of latches according to the latch order with respect to their *relative correlation* values. We then start from latches in higher priority clusters, cluster by cluster, to do *cone-of-influence* search. We generate the layers by collecting all variables which are in the direct *cone-of-influence*, DCOI for short, of latches in a certain cluster but not in the DCOI of any latch in any higher priority clusters, as the corresponding layer.

In AROSAT, latch variables are divided into different layers and implications can be propagated beyond the border of a certain layer if and only if all variables in higher priority layer have all been assigned. Hence, we have the following lemma:

Lemma 1. *In AROSAT, if a variable in Layer i has been assigned a value, the sub-SAT instance formed by collecting the clauses containing only variables belonging to the $i - 1$ highest priority layers is satisfiable.*

From Lemma 1, we see that once a variable has been assigned, keeping layers at higher priority separate is meaningless because unless some variables outside these layers are involved, there is no way that we can get an unsatisfiability proof. So, in IAROSAT, if any layer is involved in the SAT searching process, we just merge this layer with all the layers with higher priority. In IAROSAT, to gain more speed, score decay is allowed, but only within each layer to guarantee the different priorities of layers. From our experiments, the speed of IAROSAT is only 2.8 times slower than a conventional SAT solver while AROSAT is 5 times slower.

3.2   Unsatisfiability Proof-Guided Refinement Minimization (URM)

In PureSAT [12], refinement minimization is an important technique to guarantee the final refinement is minimal so that the cumulative abstract models do not grow too quickly. However, even after we apply IAROSAT, the refinement candidates generated directly from unsatisfiability proofs may still be numerous, which results in a time-consuming refinement minimization procedure.

Here we propose an unsatisfiability proof-guided refinement minimization procedure which works as follows: After the refinement candidates are generated, they are given to the refinement minimization engine to be tested one by one. During each test, an unsatisfiability proof is generated. Since we are trying to find a small set of latches, which, when added to the old abstraction, can form a new abstraction without any current counterexamples, any untested latches that do not appear in the current unsatisfiability proof can be eliminated from the candidate list. In this way, one test may eliminate multiple candidates.

3.3   Refinement Prediction (RP)

The refinement minimization engine is only responsible for finding a sufficient set to kill all counterexamples up to the current length without any concern about future refinements. Such an approach guarantees a minimal refinement. However, some latches which are also eliminated would prevent spurious abstract counterexamples and decrease the number of refinement iterations.

Here we propose a refinement prediction approach that utilizes current available information. The criteria we use for judging whether a latch is a good candidate for future refinements are the following:

1. Including this latch into the current abstract model will not add too much burden to the model checking engine.
2. This latch is closely related to the current abstraction.

For the first criterion, since we only add all the gates in the DCOI of a latch into our abstract model once we include this latch into the current abstraction, we tend to add those latches such that most gates of their direct cones are already in the current abstraction. For the second criterion, we have two assumptions: 1) If most gates in the DCOI of a latch are in the current abstraction, then this latch is closely related to current abstract model. 2) If we take the current abstraction as core and do a DFS and we only consider latches, then a latch with a smaller DFS level is more closely related to the current abstract model than a latch with a larger DFS level. Considering all these criteria and assumptions, we regard a latch as a future refinement and add it to current abstraction if most gates in its DCOI are already in the current abstraction and it has a very small DFS level.

4   Implementation

4.1   AIG-Based Implementation

Our implementation is based on AIG, which is a Boolean circuit containing only AND gates and inverters. To reuse the AIG nodes previously built as much as possible, when we unfold the AIG, we directly build it for the whole concrete model. Then, for each abstraction, we mark all the nodes which are in the current abstract model, and only these nodes marked are involved in the SAT solving process.

If the SAT instance turns out to be unsatisfiable and an interpolant needs to be generated, a resolution graph is then created, the leaves of which are CNF clauses translated from AIG nodes, and the root of which is the empty clause. The interpolant is then computed based on this resolution graph.

4.2   Elimination of Pseudo-global Variables

In the interpolation-based model checking algorithm [15], the model checking problem is first translated into a SAT instance in the form of CNF clauses, and then all clauses are

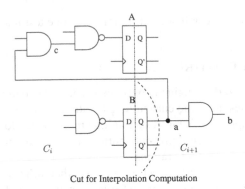

Cut for Interpolation Computation

Fig. 3. Elimination of pseudo-global variables

divided into disjoint subset $\{C_1, C_2\}$, which corresponds to placing a cut in the original circuit. A variable is a *global variable* if it appears in both subsets; otherwise, it is a *local variable*. Only global variables can appear in interpolants. If an interpolant is to be an overapproximation of the reachable states, the global variables are normally latch variables. However, if interpolants are computed on abstract models, we may introduce *pseudo-global variables*, PGV for short.

Figure 3 illustrates this problem. In the figure, A and B are two latches. In the concrete model, a is a global variable since it appears in both clauses of $(\neg c \lor a)$ and $(\neg c \lor b)$, which belong to C_1 and C_2, respectively. However, if we assume A is in the abstract model while B is not, then a is treated as a pseudo-input, that is, all the logic feeding latch B is eliminated. After this abstraction, a remains a global variable because it still appears in C_1 and C_2, which means that a may appear in the computed interpolant, while an expression in terms of only visible latch variables is desired here.

There may be various ways to deal with this problem. In this paper, we use a method called *variable-splitting*, which works as follows: Before the SAT instance is sent to the SAT solver, a preprocessing step finds all the possible PGVs, and splits each of them into two variables; one is connected to the nodes of C_i, the other is connected to the nodes of C_{i+1}. After the preprocessing step, only visible latch variables are global variables. A postprocessing step for recovering those PGVs is also utilized after the interpolant is generated.

5   Experimental Results

To evaluate the efficiency of our algorithm, we compared different algorithms on 21 test cases using models from both industry and the VIS verification benchmarks [3, 19]. Thirteen of the properties fail; the other 8 pass. In the following tables, failing examples are shown on top, and both kinds of examples are sorted by increasing number of latches in the concrete model. A line is used to separate the two kinds of examples. All the experiments were run under Linux on an IBM IntelliStation with a 1.7 GHz Intel Pentium 4 CPU and 2 GB of RAM.

Table 1 shows the comparison among five algorithms: 1) the algorithm of [12], named PureSAT, 2) the PureSAT+AROSAT algorithm [11], named AROSAT, 3) our

Table 1. Experimental results

model	size	Fail/Pass	PureSAT		AROSAT		AigIP		IP		IPAR	
			time	len.	time	len.	time	len.	time	len.	time	len.
D14-p1	96	F	486	14	824	14	158	14	36	14	31	14
28-batch	108	F	443	14	3723	14	155	14	51	14	36	14
03-batch	119	F	300	32	736	32	157	32	72	32	97	32
bj-2	122	F	88	17	201	17	54	17	65	17	40	17
18-batch	133	F	2148	23	TO	(21)	1391	23	571	23	426	23
06-batch	140	F	1936	31	TO	(29)	1935	31	257	31	218	31
04-batch	252	F	72	24	96	24	36	24	25	24	22	24
D5-p1	319	F	51	31	32	31	15	31	27	31	14	31
D18-p1	506	F	MO	(22)	1185	23	154	23	64	23	63	23
D20-p1	562	F	MO	(9)	3154	14	848	14	20	14	82	14
24-batch-3	701	F	MO	(21)	TO	(12)	6447	24	2425	24	1956	24
24-batch-1	766	F	MO	(20)	TO	(12)	5435	24	1133	24	2179	24
24-batch-2	766	F	MO	(21)	TO	(12)	6874	24	1760	24	2786	24
bj-3	122	P	TO	(48)	TO	(49)	TO	(16-14)	7352	13-14	507	6-10
bj-4	122	P	TO	(37)	TO	(52)	242	7-8	TO	(25-2)	578	7-12
02-batch-2	140	P	TO	(109)	TO	(86)	6.7	7-19	1.2	4-12	6.8	7-19
02-batch-1	141	P	MO	(111)	TO	(84)	133	24-24	993	66-18	134	24-24
25-batch	218	P	7	9	20	9	3.8	6-4	1.2	4-4	3.1	5-3
motoro	222	P	2100	14	1219	14	39	4-3	70	3-6	45	4-3
IU-p1	4494	P	MO	(69)	TO	(19)	664	24-17	TO	(35-6)	2136	72-8
IU-p2	4494	P	780	11	868	11	192	8-8	73	3-6	92	2-5

basic algorithm which combines together interpolation, abstraction by localization reduction, and refinement based on unsatisfiability proof and bridge abstraction, named AigIP, 4) the flat interpolation algorithm of [15], named IP, and 5) our final algorithm, which is built on top of AigIP by adding various techniques described in Sect. 3, called IPAR. A comparison to PureSAT and AROSAT shows that our baseline algorithm, AigIP, is competitive, and that our implementation of interpolation is efficient.

In Table 1, the first column gives the names of models, the second column shows the size of each model in terms of latches in the COI of the property. The third column tells whether the property of the model is passing or failing. In this and the following tables, MO means memory out, and TO means time out where the time limit is set to 12000 s. Columns 4–13 indicate the results for the five algorithms. For each algorithm, the left column is the total time, and the right one is the termination length: for a failing property, it is the length of the shortest counterexample; for a passing property, it is the length at which the property is proved. For a passing property, in PureSAT and AROSAT, the termination length is the longest simple path +1 [17], while for AigIP, IP, and IPAR, the first number is the length on termination, the second number is the number of iterations at the length on termination. For example, for IU-p1, IPAR terminated at the 8th iteration of length 72. Since we increase the current checking length by $L = L+$ iterations -1, it is fair to think of termination length as the sum of length on termination and the number of iterations for this length. In this and the following tables, a number in parentheses indicates the length at which the run was aborted due to insufficient resources. From Table 1, if we compare PureSAT, AROSAT vs. IPAR, we see that we got a substantial improvement over our starting point, which is due to two factors: one is interpolation is more efficient than simple path checking in terms of termination length and computational cost, the other is that various techniques we developed, which are described in Sect. 3, prove to be very efficient in the abstraction refinement procedure. If we compare IP and IPAR, we can see that for true properties, IPAR wins most of the time, especially in large examples. For some passing examples, like IU-p2, even though IPAR loses because of the overhead, it still wins if we consider the termination length. For false properties, IPAR is a bit better, but generally, comparable to IP. Hence, we can conclude that abstraction helps to shorten termination length.

Comparison of AigIP and IP shows that the former is significantly faster for passing properties, but correspondingly slower for failing properties. Table 2 shows that the problem is due to excessive time spent in refinement. The improvements brought by the various techniques described in Sect. 3 (except for *abstraction switching*) are also shown in Table 2, which compares the algorithms AigIP and IPAR3. Algorithm IPAR is not used here because the information on refinement in algorithm IPAR may not be accurate enough due to *abstraction switching*. Columns 4–6 and 7–9 represent data from algorithms AigIP and IPAR3, respectively. In each algorithm, we collect the data for refinement time, total time, and the percentage of total time spent for refinement. From this table, we can see that the techniques in Sect. 3 drastically decrease refinement

Table 2. Impact of refinement computation on CPU time

Model	Size	F/P	AigIP			IPAR3		
			Ref.	Total	Perc.	Ref.	Total	Perc.
D14-p1	96	14	128	158	81	29	54	54
28-batch	108	14	121	155	78	27	60	45
03-batch	119	32	106	157	68	42	142	30
bj-2	122	17	6	54	11	4	53	8
18-batch	133	23	920	1391	66	558	1432	39
06-batch	140	31	1643	1935	85	376	547	69
04-batch	252	24	20	36	56	8	21	38
D5-p1	319	31	4	15	27	3	13	23
D18-p1	506	23	120	154	78	93	128	73
D20-p1	562	14	760	848	90	736	814	90
24-batch-3	701	24	4930	6447	76	1380	2964	47
24-batch-1	766	24	4741	5435	87	1375	2198	63
24-batch-2	766	24	4455	6874	65	2038	2901	70
bj-3	122	P	58	>12000	<0.5	49	504	10
bj-4	122	P	109	242	45	47	180	26
02-batch-2	140	P	0.17	6.7	3	0.1	6.8	1
02-batch-1	141	P	0.16	133	0.1	0.16	48	0.3
25-batch	218	P	1.15	3.8	30	0.5	3	17
motoro	222	P	12	39	31	17	44	38
IU-p1	4494	P	101	664	15	452	2127	21
IU-p2	4494	P	11	192	6	0	92	0

Table 3. Impact of different speedup techniques

model	size	F/P	AigIP	IPAR1	IPAR2	IPAR3	IPAR
D14-p1	96	14	158	133	118	54	31
28-batch	108	14	155	96	99	60	36
03-batch	119	32	157	168	144	142	97
bj-2	122	17	54	40	38	53	40
18-batch	133	23	1391	1272	1057	1432	426
06-batch	140	31	1935	658	535	547	218
04-batch	252	24	36	18	19	21	22
D5-p1	319	31	15	13	13	13	14
D18-p1	506	23	154	126	127	128	63
D20-p1	562	14	848	803	582	814	82
24-batch-3	701	24	6447	5793	5312	2964	1956
24-batch-1	766	24	5435	2046	1921	2198	2179
24-batch-2	766	24	6874	4123	3954	2901	2786
bj-3	122	P	TO	502	498	504	507
bj-4	122	P	242	575	545	180	578
02-batch-2	140	P	6.7	3.4	3.4	6.8	6.8
02-batch-1	141	P	133	132	132	48	134
25-batch	218	P	3.8	2.5	2.6	3.1	3.1
motoro	222	P	39	46	42	44	45
IU-p1	4494	P	664	2232	2212	2127	2136
IU-p2	4494	P	192	128	128	92	92

time for failing properties. Even for examples like 24-batch-2, in which the percentage of refinement time increases, we still get a much smaller absolute refinement time. However, for passing properties, we don't see much improvement, and even occasional deterioration. The reasons are two: First, most time for passing properties is spent on convergence checking instead of refinement, while techniques we described in Sect. 3 are mainly designed to tackle the problem of time-consuming refinement. Second, the termination lengths for passing properties are not very stable.

A detailed examination of different techniques we described in Sect. 3 is shown in Table 3, which compares five variants of the IPAR algorithm. The basic one is AigIP in Table 1, the other four algorithms are formed by adding techniques one at the time: 1) IAROSAT gives IPAR1, 2) Unsatisfiability proof based refinement minimization gives IPAR2, 3) Refinement prediction results in IPAR3, and 4) Abstraction switching, which finally gives IPAR. Columns 4–8 show the results for these algorithms, respectively. For failing properties, a clear trend of improvements can be seen over these five algorithms from this table. For passing properties, we don't gain much because of the same reasons as we pointed out in the discussion for Table 2.

6 Conclusions

We have presented an abstraction refinement algorithm for model checking that uses interpolants to prove termination. Experimental results show that, in most cases, abstraction helps prove termination for passing properties. The challenge of combining the two techniques lies in the overhead associated with the computation of refinement, which incurs a significant overhead for failing properties. We have therefore developed a set of techniques designed to speed up refinement to the point that the new algorithm is competitive for failing properties, while retaining its advantage for passing properties. Our results support the conclusion that, in spite of the abstraction implicitly performed by a modern SAT solver, there is benefit in applying an explicit abstraction refinement scheme.

References

[1] M. Awedh and F. Somenzi. Proving more properties with bounded model checking. In R. Alur and D. Peled, editors, *Sixteenth Conference on Computer Aided Verification (CAV'04)*, pages 96–108. Springer-Verlag, Berlin, July 2004. LNCS 3114.

[2] A. Biere, A. Cimatti, E. Clarke, and Y. Zhu. Symbolic model checking without BDDs. In *Fifth International Conference on Tools and Algorithms for Construction and Analysis of Systems (TACAS'99)*, pages 193–207, Amsterdam, The Netherlands, Mar. 1999. LNCS 1579.

[3] R. K. Brayton et al. VIS: A system for verification and synthesis. In T. Henzinger and R. Alur, editors, *Eighth Conference on Computer Aided Verification (CAV'96)*, pages 428–432. Springer-Verlag, Rutgers University, 1996. LNCS 1102.

[4] P. Chauhan, E. Clarke, J. Kukula, S. Sapra, H. Veith, and D. Wang. Automated abstraction refinement for model checking large state spaces using SAT based conflict analysis. In M. D. Aagaard and J. W. O'Leary, editors, *Formal Methods in Computer Aided Design*, pages 33–51. Springer-Verlag, Nov. 2002. LNCS 2517.

[5] E. Clarke, A. Gupta, J. Kukula, and O. Strichman. SAT based abstraction-refinement using ILP and machine learning. In E. Brinksma and K. G. Larsen, editors, *Fourteenth Conference on Computer Aided Verification (CAV 2002)*, pages 265–279. Springer-Verlag, July 2002. LNCS 2404.

[6] E. Goldberg and Y. Novikov. BerkMin: A fast and robust SAT-solver. In *Proceedings of the Conference on Design, Automation and Test in Europe*, pages 142–149, Paris, France, Mar. 2002.

[7] E. Goldberg and Y. Novikov. Verification of proofs of unsatisfiability for CNF formulas. In *Design, Automation and Test in Europe (DATE'03)*, pages 886–891, Munich, Germany, Mar. 2003.

[8] A. Gupta and O. Strichman. Abstraction refinement for bounded model checking. In *Seventeenth Conference on Computer Aided Verification (CAV'05)*, pages 112–124. Springer-Verlag, Berlin, July 2005. LNCS 3576.

[9] A. Kuehlmann and F. Krohm. Equivalence checking using cuts and heaps. In *Proceedings of the Design Automation Conference*, pages 263–268, Anaheim, CA, June 1997.

[10] R. P. Kurshan. *Computer-Aided Verification of Coordinating Processes*. Princeton University Press, Princeton, NJ, 1994.

[11] B. Li and F. Somenzi. Efficient computation of small abstraction refinements. In *Proceedings of the International Conference on Computer-Aided Design*, pages 518–525, San Jose, CA, Nov. 2004.

[12] B. Li, C. Wang, and F. Somenzi. Abstraction refinement in symbolic model checking using satisfiability as the only decision procedure. *Software Tools for Technology Transfer*, 7(2):143–155, Apr. 2005.

[13] J. P. Marques-Silva. Improvements to the implementation of interpolant-based model checking. In *Correct Hardware Design and Verification Methods (CHARME'05)*, pages 367–370, Saarbrucken, Germany, Oct. 2005. Springer-Verlag. LNCS 3725.

[14] K. L. McMillan. Applying SAT methods in unbounded symbolic model checking. In E. Brinksma and K. G. Larsen, editors, *Fourteenth Conference on Computer Aided Verification (CAV'02)*, pages 250–264. Springer-Verlag, Berlin, July 2002. LNCS 2404.

[15] K. L. McMillan. Interpolation and SAT-based model checking. In W. A. Hunt, Jr. and F. Somenzi, editors, *Fifteenth Conference on Computer Aided Verification (CAV'03)*, pages 1–13. Springer-Verlag, Berlin, July 2003. LNCS 2725.

[16] K. L. McMillan and N. Amla. Automatic abstraction without counterexamples. In *International Conference on Tools and Algorithms for Construction and Analysis of Systems (TACAS'03)*, pages 2–17, Warsaw, Poland, Apr. 2003. LNCS 2619.

[17] M. Sheeran, S. Singh, and G. Stålmarck. Checking safety properties using induction and a SAT-solver. In W. A. Hunt, Jr. and S. D. Johnson, editors, *Formal Methods in Computer Aided Design*, pages 108–125. Springer-Verlag, Nov. 2000. LNCS 1954.

[18] J. P. M. Silva and K. A. Sakallah. Grasp—a new search algorithm for satisfiability. In *Proceedings of the International Conference on Computer-Aided Design*, pages 220–227, San Jose, CA, Nov. 1996.

[19] URL: http://vlsi.colorado.edu/~vis.

[20] C. Wang, B. Li, H. Jin, G. D. Hachtel, and F. Somenzi. Improving Ariadne's bundle by following multiple threads in abstraction refinement. In *Proceedings of the International Conference on Computer-Aided Design*, pages 408–415, Nov. 2003.

[21] L. Zhang and S. Malik. Validating SAT solvers using an independent resolution-based checker: Practical implementations and other applications. In *Design, Automation and Test in Europe (DATE'03)*, pages 880–885, Munich, Germany, Mar. 2003.

Approximating Predicate Images for Bit-Vector Logic*

Daniel Kroening[1] and Natasha Sharygina[2]

[1] Computer Systems Institute, ETH Zürich
[2] University of Lugano, Switzerland

Abstract. Predicate abstraction refinement is a successful technique for verifying large ANSI-C programs. However, computing the image of the predicates with respect to the transition relation is computationally expensive. Recent results have shown that predicate images can be computed by transforming a *proof* of a formula over integers into a Boolean formula that is satisfiable if and only if the original formula is satisfiable. However, the existing algorithms compute the closure of the proof rules that are used to axiomatize the logic, and thus, rely on the fact that the set of axioms is small. They are therefore limited to logics of low complexity, such as difference logic.

We describe a proof-based algorithm that computes an over-approximation of the predicate image but in turn allows a rich set of axioms. The algorithm can be used to compute images of predicates using a combination of bit-vector logic, the theory of arrays, and pointer arithmetic. The proof-based approach can also be used to refine the image. We quantify the performance of the algorithm in comparison with a Das/Dill-like greedy incremental refinement of the image and a proof-based incremental refinement.

1 Introduction

In the hardware industry, formal verification is well established. Introduced in 1981, *Model Checking* [1, 2] is one of the most commonly used formal verification techniques in a commercial setting. However, it suffers from the state-space explosion problem. In case of BDD-based symbolic model checking this problem manifests itself in the form of unmanageably large BDDs [3].

A principal method for addressing the state-space explosion problem is *abstraction*. Abstraction techniques reduce the state space by mapping the set of states of the actual, concrete system to an abstract, and smaller, set of states in a way that preserves the relevant behaviors of the system.

Predicate abstraction [4, 5] is one of the most popular and widely applied methods for systematic abstraction of programs. It abstracts data by only keeping track of certain predicates on the data. Each predicate is represented by a Boolean variable in the abstract program, while the original data variables are eliminated. Verification of a software system with predicate abstraction consists of constructing and evaluating a finite-state system that is an abstraction of the original system with respect to a set of predicates.

---

* Ideas of this paper first appeared as a position paper at "Verified Software: Theories, Tools, Experiments", an international conference of Working Group 2.3 (Programming Methodology) of the International Federation for Information Processing.

H. Hermanns and J. Palsberg (Eds.): TACAS 2006, LNCS 3920, pp. 242–256, 2006.

The abstraction refinement process using predicate abstraction has been promoted by the success of the SLAM [6, 7, 8, 9, 10, 11, 12] project at Microsoft Research. One starts with a coarse abstraction of the program. If the property holds on the abstract model, we can conclude that the property holds on the original model as well. If the abstract model contains an error trace, the algorithm attempts to simulate this error trace on the original model. If this succeeds, the error trace is reported to the user.

If it is found that the error-trace reported by the model checker is not realistic, the error trace is used to refine the abstract program, and the process proceeds until no spurious error traces can be found or the simulation succeeds. The actual steps of the loop follow the *abstract-verify-refine* paradigm [13] and depend on the abstraction and refinement techniques used [14].

A main task of the refinement loop is to compute an abstract model $\hat{M}$ from the concrete model M given a set of n predicates $\Pi = \{\pi_1, \ldots, \pi_n\}$. An abstract state $\hat{x}$ is a valuation of the n predicates. Most algorithms that aim at verifying safety properties compute an *existential abstraction* [15], i.e., any concrete transition in M has a corresponding abstract transition in the transition relation $\hat{R}$ of $\hat{M}$. Formally, the abstract transition relation $\hat{R}$ is the image of the current state vector $\hat{x}$ and next state vector $\hat{x}'$ under the concrete transition relation R of M.

Computationally, this corresponds to an existential quantification of the concrete state vectors x and x'. This computation, if done in a precise manner, is very expensive and typically exponential in the number of predicates n. All existing tools, with the exception of MAGIC, therefore compute over-approximations $\hat{R}' \supseteq \hat{R}$. Computing such an over-approximation can be substantially faster than computing the exact image. This is a safe and sound technique if the goal is to show safety properties, as any safety property that holds on $\hat{M}$ also holds on M.

However, the over-approximation in $\hat{M}$ may result in additional spurious counterexamples, which are costly to eliminate. There therefore exists a trade-off between the cost of computing the initial abstraction and the cost related to successive refinements. A wide range of options exists between the two extremes of a) computing the precise image and b) using $\hat{R}'(\hat{x}, \hat{x}') = \text{true}$ as initial abstraction.

Most existing approaches that compute or refine predicate images are based on decision procedures for the respective logic. In contrast to that, the authors of [16] generate a generic *proof* that the transition $\hat{x}, \hat{x}'$ does not exist. They then extract a Boolean formula from the proof steps. This formula is satisfiable if and only if the transition from $\hat{x}$ to $\hat{x}'$ exists in the concrete model. This Boolean formula is then used as the abstract transition relation. For equality and difference logic, the approach is shown to be polynomial instead of exponential. Results on a more expressive logic, e.g., full linear arithmetic, are not reported.

Most program analysis tools use theories for arithmetic over unbounded integers or even the reals to reason about the program variables. As motivated in [17], these theories are a poor fit for program analysis, especially when applied to low-level software. Programs in languages such as Java, C or C++ require reasoning for bounded-width bit-vector arithmetic that takes overflow into account, and allows bit-wise operators.

We proposed the use of propositional SAT-solvers as a reasoning engine for the verification of low-level software in [18]. The astonishing progress SAT solvers made in the past few years is the enabling technology for this approach. As in Bounded Model Checking (BMC), the arithmetic operators in the formula are replaced by corresponding circuits. The resulting net-list is converted into CNF and passed to a propositional SAT solver. This allows supporting all operators as defined in the ANSI-C standard.

We report experimental results that quantify the impact of replacing ZAPATO, a decision procedure for integers, with Cogent, a decision procedure built using a SAT solver [17]: The increased precision of Cogent improves the performance of SLAM, while the support for bit-level operators resulted in the discovery of a previously unknown bug in a Windows device driver.

The disadvantage of such a bit-level representation of arithmetic operators is that the variables are split into individual bits and the word-level information is lost. For example, encoding an addition in propositional logic results in one XOR per bit, which are chained together through the carry bit. It is known that such XOR chains can result in very hard SAT instances. As a result, there are many programs (and circuits) that cannot be verified by means of a bit-level SAT solver. This is a justification for using a solver for linear arithmetic for program verification, as the reasoning is done at the word-level, and not at the bit-level.

Contribution. This paper makes two contributions.

1. We present a word-level algorithm for approximating predicate images in bit-vector logic. The algorithm is based on the approach in [16]. In contrast to [16], we compute an over-approximation instead of the precise image. This allows us to support a rich logic, as the size of the formula that is generated no longer explodes as the number of proof rules grows. The implementation reported in [16] is limited to difference predicates. In contrast to that we implement combined theories for bit-vector-, array-, and pointer-logic, including non-linear arithmetic. In contrast to [16], we also support transition relations with a non-trivial propositional structure.
2. The Boolean formulas obtained from proof trees contain fresh Boolean variables. These variables have to be quantified in order to obtain a formula over the predicates. The implementation reported in [16] is enumerating the cubes of a BDD for this task, whereas we are integrating this step into the model checker used for the abstract model.

We present experimental results on software model checking benchmarks that show that the new algorithm outperforms a predicate abstraction refinement loop that uses proof-based refinement of transitions.

Related Work. Abstract interpretation [19] is a very general framework to reason about transition systems. ASTRÉE implements static program analysis [20] using abstract interpretation and widening. It automatically refines abstractions of programs in order to prove the specification. However, if the proof fails, no simulation step is attempted, and thus, the algorithm may generate false alarms.

MAGIC [21] implements predicate abstraction and computes the exact image. The individual transitions $\hat{x}, \hat{x}'$ are enumerated and checked individually using Simplify [22]. Lahiri et al. [23] use SAT-based existential quantification taken from [18] to compute the exact image. The quantification is performed over reductions from linear arithmetic over integers to propositional logic computed using UCLID.

In the SLAM framework, the abstract model is computed by the C2BP component [7]. It enumerates Boolean combinations of a bounded number of current state predicates in order to infer constraints on the next state. C2BP has been replaced by FASTABS, which computes faster, but also more coarse abstractions. In order to address the spurious traces introduced this way, SLAM uses a component called CONSTRAIN [9]. CONSTRAIN uses the decision procedure ZAPATO [24] in order to decide if a given abstract transition is spurious or not. ZAPATO implements a fragment of linear arithmetic over integers.

A completely demand-driven way of constructing $\hat{M}$ was proposed by Das and Dill [25]: starting with no restrictions on abstract transitions, the spurious abstract transitions are removed following the counterexamples produced by the model checker. A similar approach is implemented in BLAST [26]: initially, BLAST computes an abstraction based on the Cartesian product, which is refined subsequently. This refinement is done using Craig interpolants in the current version of BLAST [27].

The first efficient proof-based reduction from integer and real valued linear arithmetic to propositional logic was introduced by Strichman [28]. The proof is generated using Fourier-Motzkin variable elimination for the reals and the Omega test for the integers. These algorithms come with various heuristics to guide the proof, a fact which promises more compact proofs.

Decision procedures for bit-vector arithmetic have been found in tools such as SVC and ICS for years. ICS uses BDDs in order to represent the arithmetic operators, whereas SVC is based on a computation of a canonizer and a solver [29]. SVC has been superseded by CVC, and then CVC-Lite [30], which uses a propositional SAT-solver to decide satisfiability of a circuit-based translation of the bit-vector formula.

The related work on bit-vector decision procedures is mostly in the hardware verification domain. Wedler et al. normalize bit-vector formulas in order to simplify the generated SAT instance in [31]. Word-level reasoning using a decision procedure such as the Omega test or the like is typically not employed. One exception is Brinkmann and Drechsler [32], who use an encoding of linear bit-vector arithmetic into ILP in order to decide properties of circuit data-paths given at the RT-level. The Omega test is used as a decision procedure for the ILP instance. However, [32] only aims at the data-paths, and thus, does not allow a Boolean part within the original formula. This is mended by [33] using a lazy encoding with a modified DPLL search.

Outline. In Section 2, we provide background information about lazy and eager encodings of decision problems. We describe how to use proof encodings as over-approximations of abstractions in Section 3. Experimental results are reported in Section 4.

2 Background

2.1 Bit-Vector Arithmetic

The subset of bit-vector arithmetic we consider is defined by the language L_B according to the following grammar:

$$formula : formula \lor formula \mid formula \land formula \mid \neg formula \mid atom$$

$$atom : term \; rel \; term \mid Boolean\text{-}Identifier$$

$$rel := \; \mid \neq \mid \leq \mid \geq \mid < \mid >$$

$$term : term \; op \; term \mid identifier \mid \sim term \mid constant \mid atom \, ? \, term : term$$

$$op : \oplus \mid \ominus \mid \otimes \mid \oslash \mid << \mid >> \mid \& \mid \mid \mid \,\hat{}$$

With each expression, we associate a type. The type is the width of the expression in bits and whether it is signed (two's complement encoding) or unsigned (binary encoding). Assigning semantics to this language is straight-forward, e.g., as done in [32].

We do not consider bit-extraction and concatenation operators, as they are not offered by ANSI-C. However, adding these operators as part of the bit-wise operators is a simple extension. We use the ANSI-C symbols to denote the bit-wise operators, e.g., & denotes bit-wise AND, while ^ denotes bit-wise XOR. The trinary operator $c?a:b$ is a case-split: the operator evaluates to a if c holds, and to b otherwise.

We use $\oplus$ to distinguish addition on bit-vectors with modular arithmetic from addition on unbounded integers. Note that the relational operators $>, <, \leq, \geq$, the multiplicative operators $\otimes, \oslash$ and the right-shift operator depend on whether an unsigned, binary encoding or a two's complement encoding is used. We assume that the type of the expression is clear from the context.

Following the notation in [32], we add an index to the operator and operands in order to denote the bit-width. As an example, $a_{[32]} \otimes_{[32]} b_{[32]}$ denotes the 32-bit multiplication of a and b. Both the result and the operands are 32 bits wide, the remaining 32 bits of the result are discarded.

Example 1. As a motivating example, the following formula obviously holds on the integers:

$$(x - y > 0) \iff (x > y) \tag{1}$$

However, if x and y are interpreted as bit-vectors, this equivalence no longer holds, due to possible overflow on the subtraction operation.

Definition 1. *Let ϕ^B denote a formula. The set of all atoms in ϕ^B that are not Boolean identifiers is denoted by $\mathcal{A}(\phi^B)$. The i-th distinct atom in ϕ^B is denoted by $\mathcal{A}_i(\phi^B)$. The* Propositional Skeleton ϕ_{sk} *of a bit-vector formula ϕ^B is obtained by replacing all atoms $a \in \mathcal{A}(\phi^B)$ by fresh Boolean identifiers $e_1, \ldots, e_\nu$, where $\nu = |\mathcal{A}(\phi^B)|$.*

As an example, the propositional skeleton of $\phi^B = (x = y) \land ((a \oplus b = c) \lor (x \neq y))$ is $e_1 \land (e_2 \lor \neg e_1)$, and $\mathcal{A}(\phi^B) = \{x = y, a \oplus b = c\}$.

We denote the vector of the variables $E = \{e_1, \ldots, e_\nu\}$ by $\bar{e}$. Furthermore, let $\psi(a, p)$ denote the atom a with polarity p:

$$\psi(a, p) := \begin{cases} a & : p \\ \neg a & : \text{otherwise} \end{cases}. \tag{2}$$

2.2 Encoding Decision Problems into Propositional Logic

Lazy vs. Eager Encodings. There are two basic ways to compute an encoding of a decision problem ϕ into propositional logic. In both cases, the propositional part ϕ_{sk}

of the formula is converted into CNF first. Linear-time algorithms for computing CNF for ϕ_{sk} are well-known [34]. The algorithms differ in how the non-propositional part is handled.

The vector of variables $\bar{e} : \mathcal{A}(\phi) \longrightarrow \{\text{true}, \text{false}\}$ as defined above denotes a truth assignment to the atoms in ϕ. Let $\Psi_{\mathcal{A}(\phi)}(\bar{e})$ denote the conjunction of the atoms $\mathcal{A}(\phi)_i$, where the atom number i is in the polarity given by e_i:

$$\Psi_{\mathcal{A}(\phi)}(\bar{e}) := \bigwedge_{i=1}^{\nu} \psi(\mathcal{A}_i(\phi), e_i) \tag{3}$$

An *Eager Encoding* considers all possible truth assignments $\bar{e}$ before invoking the SAT solver, and computes a Boolean constraint $\phi_E(\bar{e})$ such that

$$\phi_E(\bar{e}) \iff \Psi_{\mathcal{A}(\phi)}(\bar{e}) \tag{4}$$

The number of cases considered while building ϕ_E can often be dramatically reduced by exploiting the polarity information of the atoms, i.e., whether $\mathcal{A}_i(\phi)$ appears in negated form or without negation in the negation normal form (NNF) of ϕ. After computing ϕ_E, ϕ_E is conjoined with ϕ_{sk}, and passed to a SAT solver. A prominent example of a decision procedure implemented using an eager encoding is UCLID [35].

A *Lazy Encoding* means that a series of encodings ϕ_L^1, ϕ_L^2 and so on with $\phi \implies \phi_L^i$ is built. Most tools implementing a lazy encoding start off with $\phi_L^1 = \phi_{sk}$. In each iteration, ϕ_L^i is passed to the SAT solver. If the SAT solver determines ϕ_L^i to be unsatisfiable, so is ϕ. If the SAT solver determines ϕ_L^i to be satisfiable, it also provides a satisfying assignment, and thus, an assignment $\bar{e}^i$ to $\mathcal{A}(\phi)$.

The algorithm proceeds by checking if $\Psi_{A\phi}(\bar{e}^i)$ is satisfiable. If so, ϕ is satisfiable, and the algorithm terminates. If not so, a subset of the atoms $\mathcal{A}' \subseteq \mathcal{A}(\phi)$ is determined that is already unsatisfiable under $\bar{e}^i$. The algorithm builds a *blocking clause* b, which prohibits this truth assignment to $\mathcal{A}'$. The next encoding ϕ_L^{i+1} is $\phi_L^i \wedge b$. Since the formula becomes only stronger, the algorithm can be tightly integrated into one SAT-solver run, which preserves the learning done in prior iterations.

Among many others, CVC-Lite [30] implements a lazy encoding of integer linear arithmetic. The decision problem for the conjunction $\Psi_{A\phi}(\bar{e}^i)$ is solved using the Omega test.

2.3 Encodings from Proofs

A proof is a sequence of transformations of facts. The transformations follow specific rules, i.e., proof rules, which are usually derived from an axiomatization of the logic at hand. A proof of a formula ϕ in a particular logic can be used to obtain another formula ϕ_P in propositional logic that is valid if and only if the original formula is valid, i.e., $\phi \iff \phi_P$. Let $\mathscr{F}$ denote the set of facts used in the proof.

Given a proof of ϕ, a propositional encoding of ϕ can be obtained as follows:

1. Assign a fresh propositional variable v_f to each fact $f \in \mathscr{F}$ that occurs anywhere in the proof.

2. For each proof step i, generate a constraint c_i that captures the dependencies between the facts. As an example, the derivation

$$\frac{A, B}{C}$$

with variables v_A, v_B, v_C for the facts A, B, and C generates the constraint $(v_A \wedge v_B) \longrightarrow v_C$.

3. The formula ϕ_P is obtained by conjoining the constraints:

$$\phi_P := \bigwedge_i c_i$$

However, the generation of such a proof is often difficult to begin with. In particular, it often suffers from a blowup due to case-splitting caused by the Boolean structure present in ϕ. This is addressed by a technique introduced by Strichman in [28]. His paper describes an eager encoding of linear arithmetic on both real numbers and integers into propositional logic using the Fourier-Motzkin transformation for the reals and the Omega-Test [36] for the integers. The idea of [28] is applicable to any proof-generating decision-procedure:

- All atoms $\mathcal{A}(\phi)$ are passed to the prover *completely disregarding the Boolean structure* of ϕ.
- For facts f that are also atoms assign $v_f := e_f$.
- The prover must be modified to obtain *all* possible proofs, i.e., must not terminate even if the empty clause is resolved.

Since the formula that is passed to the prover does not contain any propositional structure, obtaining a proof is considerably simplified. The formula ϕ_P obtained from the proof as described above is then conjoined with the propositional skeleton ϕ_{sk}. The conjunction of both is equi-satisfiable with ϕ. As $\phi_P \wedge \phi_{sk}$ is purely propositional, it can be solved by an efficient propositional SAT-solver.

3   Computing Predicate Images

3.1   Existential Abstraction

Let S denote the set of concrete states, and $R(x, x')$ denote the concrete transition relation. As an example, consider the basic block

```
i++;
j=i;
```

We use $x.v$ to denote the value of the variable v in state x. The transition relation corresponding to this basic block is then $x'.i = x.i + 1 \wedge x'.j = x'.i$.

Let $\Pi = \{\pi_1, \ldots, \pi_n\}$ denote the set of predicates. The abstraction function $\alpha(x)$ maps a concrete state $x \in S$ to an abstract state $\hat{x} \in \{\mathsf{true}, \mathsf{false}\}^n$:

$$\alpha(x) := (\pi_1(x), \ldots, \pi_n(x))$$

Definition 2 (Abstract Transition Relation). *The abstract model can make a transition from an abstract state $\hat{x}$ to $\hat{x}'$ iff there is a transition from x to x' in the concrete model and x is abstracted to $\hat{x}$ and x' is abstracted to $\hat{x}'$. We denote abstract transition relation by $\hat{R}$:*

$$\hat{R} := \{(\hat{x}, \hat{x}') \mid \exists x, x' \in S : R(x, x') \wedge \alpha(x) = \hat{x} \wedge \alpha(x') = \hat{x}'\}$$

$\hat{R}$ is also called the image of the predicates Π over R. In [23], $\hat{R}$ is computed following the definition above by means of SAT or BDD-based quantification. Due to the quantification over the concrete states this corresponds to an all-SAT instance. Solving such instances is usually exponential in n.

3.2 Predicate Images from Proofs

As an alternative, $\hat{R}$ can be computed using a generic *proof of validity* of the following formula:
$$R(x, x') \wedge \alpha(x) = \hat{x} \wedge \alpha(x') = \hat{x}'$$

Within this formula, only R contains propositional operators, as the predicates in α are assumed to be atomic. The computation of ϕ_{sk} therefore only has to take the propositional structure of R into account. In case of software, the propositional structure of R is typically trivial, as the abstraction is performed for each basic block separately. Thus, the facts (atoms) given to the prover are:

1. All the predicates evaluated over state x, i.e., $\pi_i(x)$,
2. all the predicates evaluated over state x', i.e., $\pi_i(x')$,
3. the atoms in the transition relation $R(x, x')$.

We then obtain ϕ_P as described in section 2.3. Both ϕ_P and ϕ_{sk} contain fresh propositional variables for the atoms $\mathcal{A}(R)$ in R, for the predicates Π over x and x', and for the facts $f \in \mathscr{F}$ found during the derivation. Let V_R denote the set of propositional variables corresponding to atoms in R that are not predicates, and let V_F denote the set of propositional variables corresponding to facts $f \in \mathscr{F}$ that are not predicates.

The propositional variables that do not correspond to predicates are quantified existentially to obtain the predicate image. Let $\overline{v}_R$ denote the vector of variables in V_R, let $\overline{v}_F$ denote the vector of variables in V_F, and let $\mu_R = |V_R|$ and $\mu_F = |V_F|$ denote the number of such variables.

$$\hat{R} := \{(\hat{x}, \hat{x}') \mid \exists \overline{v}_R \in \{0, 1\}^{\mu_R}, \overline{v}_F \in \{0, 1\}^{\mu_F} : \\ \phi_{sk}(\hat{x}, \hat{x}', v_R) \wedge \phi_P(\hat{x}, \hat{x}', v_F)\} \tag{5}$$

Thus, we replace the existential quantification of concrete program variables $x, x' \in S^2$ by an existential quantification of $\mu_R + \mu_F$ Boolean variables. The authors of [23,37] report experiments in which this quantification is actually performed by means of either BDDs or the SAT-engine of [18].

The authors of [16] use BDDs to obtain all cubes over the variables in V_F, and then enumerate these cubes. This operation is again worst-case exponential. The next two sections describe how to overcome the limitations of the proof-based predicate image computation.

3.3 Quantification as Part of the Abstract Model

Instead of performing the quantification in equation 5 upfront, we propose to perform this step inside the model checker for the abstract model. When performing the fixed-point iteration, a symbolic model checker computes an image of the given transition relation, and usually contains algorithms that are well optimized for this task. Furthermore, the image only has to be computed with respect to the set of reachable states, whereas performing the quantification upfront has to consider all possible state pairs $(\hat{x}, \hat{x}')$.

It is important to point out that most model checkers for abstract models do not require modifications for this purpose. As an example, consider the following abstract transition relation over state variables x, y, and their next-state versions x' and y':

$$\exists v_1 \in \{0,1\}.(x' \iff v_1) \wedge (v_1 \iff x \vee y) \wedge (y' \iff v_1) \tag{6}$$

This abstract transition relation can be translated into a closed form by enumerating the values of v_1, as done in [16]:

$$\begin{array}{c}(\neg x' \wedge \neg (x \vee y) \wedge \neg y') \vee \\ (x' \wedge (x \vee y) \wedge y')\end{array} \tag{7}$$

However, if we add v_1 as a state variable to the abstract model, we can use the following equivalent SMV code without having to resort to existential quantification[1]:

```
TRANS  next(x)=next(v1)  &
       next(v1)=(x|y)  &
       next(y)=next(v1)
```

Integration in Boppo. The addition of state variables comes at an expense. Since these variables never have direct constraints that relate their current state to their next-state value, it is not actually necessary to store any representation of their values. BOPPO [38] is a symbolic model checker for Boolean programs, i.e., abstract models of C programs. It uses symbolic simulation for checking reachability. We have modified BOPPO to allow the definition of variables that can be used in constrain clauses, but are not part of the state vector and are therefore disregarded during the fixed-point detection. Our experiments indicate that the additional variables do not noticeably increase the run-time of BOPPO.

3.4 Predicate Images in Bit-Vector Logic

As motivated above, reasoning for integers is a bad fit for system-level software. We would therefore like a proof-based method for a bit-vector logic. The main challenge is that any axiomatization for a reasonably rich bit-vector logic permits too many ways of proving the same fact, as the procedure as described above relies on enumerating *all* proofs.

---

[1] We use next(v1) instead of v1 in order to avoid a transition relation that is not total.

Even if great care is taken to obtain a small set of axioms, the number of proofs is still too large. Furthermore, the proofs include derivations that are based on reasoning about single bits of the vectors involved, resulting in a flattening of the formula, which resembles the circuit-based models used for encodings of bit-vector logic into propositional logic.

We therefore sacrifice precision in order to be able to reason about bit-vectors, and compute an over-approximation of $\hat{R}$. This is a commonly applied technique, e.g., used by SLAM and BLAST. If this over-approximation results in a spurious transition, it can be refined by any of the existing refinement methods, e.g., based on UNSAT cores as in [39] or based on interpolants as in [27].

The over-approximation of $\hat{R}$ is obtained as follows: Instead of aiming at a minimalistic set of axioms, we aim at the richest possible set of axioms. This permits proofs (or refutations) of facts with very few proof steps. It also allows to support a very rich logic, which is bit-vector logic including bit-wise shifts, extraction, concatenation, non-linear arithmetic, the theory of arrays, and pointer logic permitting pointer arithmetic in our case.

Definition 3. *The* derivation depth $d(f)$ *of a fact* $f \in \mathcal{F}$ *is defined recursively as follows:*

- *Axioms and the facts given as input have depth zero.*
- *Any new fact* f *derived from a set of existing facts* $f_1, \ldots, f_k$ *has depth* $d(f) = \max\{d(f_1), \ldots, d(f_k)\} + 1$.

In order to avoid that $d(f)$ depends on the order the facts are derived, we generate the facts in a BFS manner, i.e., new facts are derived preferably from existing facts with a low number of derivation steps.

Definition 4. *Given a maximum depth* δ, *a depth-bounded* derivation tree *is a set of derivations of facts* f_i *such that* $d(f_i) \leq \delta$.

Note that a depth-bounded derivation tree not necessarily constitutes a proof or refutation of any of the facts that are given as input, as the shortest proof or refutation could require more than δ steps.

Claim. Let ϕ_P^δ denote the formula corresponding to a derivation tree with maximum depth δ. The formula corresponding to the full unbounded proof tree ϕ_P implies ϕ_P^δ.

Let $\hat{R}^\delta$ denote the transition relation obtained by using ϕ_P^δ instead of ϕ_P. $\hat{R}^\delta$ is an over-approximation of $\hat{R}$, i.e., $\hat{R}(\hat{x}, \hat{x}') \longrightarrow \hat{R}^\delta(\hat{x}, \hat{x}')$, and thus, $\hat{R}^\delta$ is a conservative abstraction for reachability properties.

Example. Assume we have, among others, the following derivation rules:

$$\frac{}{(a|b)\&b == b} \quad (8) \qquad\qquad \frac{b\&c == 0}{(a|b)\&c == a\&c} \quad (9)$$

The predicates we consider are $\pi_1 \Longleftrightarrow (x\&1 = 0)$ and $\pi_2 \Longleftrightarrow (x\&2 = 0)$, and the statement to be executed is:

```
x|=2;
```

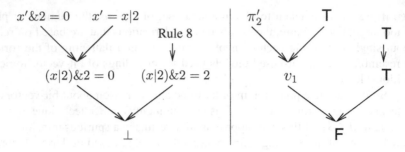

Fig. 1. Derivation of constraints for π'_2

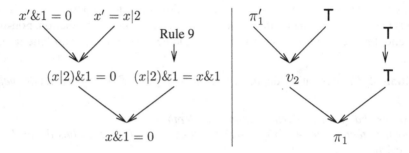

Fig. 2. Derivation of constraints for π'_1

The facts passed to the prover are $x\&1 = 0$, $x\&2 = 0$, $x'\&1 = 0$, $x'\&2 = 0$, and $x' = x|2$. Figure 1 shows a derivation on the left hand side and on the right hand side the same derivation tree in which the atoms are replaced by their propositional variables. The derivation results in the constraint $(\pi'_2 \longrightarrow v_1) \wedge (v_1 \longrightarrow \mathsf{F})$, which is equivalent to $\neg\pi'_2$. Figure 2 shows a derivation that ends in an existing atom π_1 rather than F. The constraint generated is equivalent to $\pi'_1 \longrightarrow \pi_1$.

We collected a set of over 100 (highly redundant) proof rules for bit-vector arithmetic, pointer arithmetic, and the theory of arrays; we typically limit the depth of the proofs to 3 derivation steps.

4   Experimental Results

We implemented the proof-based predicate image approximation as described above in SATABS [40]. SATABS uses an abstraction refinement loop to prove reachability properties of ANSI-C programs. We make our implementation available to other researchers[2] for experimentation. We have three different configurations:

1. The first configuration ("Greedy Ref.") follows the suggestions by Das/Dill [25]: a syntactic heuristic is used to compute the initial image. The image is subsequently refined using a greedy heuristic.

---

[2] http://www.inf.ethz.ch/personal/daniekro/satabs/

Table 1. Summary of results: the column "Max. n" shows the largest number of predicates in any program location. The columns under "Greedy Ref." show the number of iterations, the time spent during refinement, and the total run-time of SATABS using the Greedy heuristic described in [25]. The columns under "Proof Ref." show the results using a proof-based refinement. The columns under "Proof Image+Ref." show the results using the technique proposed in this paper in order to obtain the initial predicate image and to refine the image. A star denotes that the one hour timeout was exceeded.

Benchmark	Result	Max. n	Greedy Ref.			Proof Ref.			Proof Image+Ref.			
			It.	Ref.	Total	It.	Ref.	Total	It.	Abstr.	Ref.	Total
B1	T	25	85	$\star$	$\star$	180	$\star$	$\star$	2	1.3s	0.2s	2.0s
B2	F	11	51	4.8s	5.9s	46	3.5s	5.2s	8	0.1s	0.8s	1.2s
B3	T	7	14	8.4s	9.5s	15	4.8s	5.3s	6	0.1s	1.9s	2.2s
B4	F	21	102	65.2s	70.2s	78	15.1s	20.9s	20	2.1s	13.6s	18.3s
MD2	T	10	62	58.8s	67.9s	50	19.1s	24.7s	14	0.3s	9.2s	11.1s
B5'	F	81	242	$\star$	$\star$	241	$\star$	$\star$	80	123.1s	843.7s	1112.7s
AP1	F	149	31	$\star$	$\star$	154	$\star$	$\star$	201	210.8s	1532.2s	2102.8s

2. The second configuration ("Proof Ref.") replaces the greedy heuristic proposed in [25] by a proof-based refinement strategy that uses the proof of unsatisfiability to refine the transitions.
3. The third configuration ("Proof Image+Ref.") combines the proof-based refinement with the word-level proof-based initial abstraction as proposed in this paper.

To the best of our knowledge, a comparison of these image approximation heuristics on software given in C has not yet been made; Das/Dill [25] use examples from protocol verification.

For all configurations, we use the modified version of BOPPO [38] as Model Checker for the abstract model. All configurations use the following simulation phase: the path generated by model checker is transformed into SSA (static single assignment) form. The resulting bit-vector formula is translated using a circuit representation and passed to a propositional SAT-solver. We are using Booleforce[3] for our experiments. We also experimented with ZChaff 2003, but Booleforce outperformed ZChaff on all benchmarks.

The refinement phase depends on whether the spurious trace is due to predicate image over-approximation or due to a lack of sufficiently strong predicates. This is determined by the simulation phase. If a transition is found to be spurious due to image over-approximation, the incremental approach described in [25] uses a greedy heuristic to generalize the transition and refine the abstract transition relation. In contrast to that, configuration 2) and 3) use the proof of unsatisfiability to generalize the transition.

If the spurious counterexample is due to insufficient predicates, we use weakest preconditions to compute new predicates. The set of new predicates is limited to those transitions found in the UNSAT core of the SAT instance used for simulation.

The experiments have been performed on an Intel Xenon Processor with a clock frequency of 2.8 GHz running Linux. The results are summarized in table 1. The bench-

---

[3] A recent SAT-solver based on MiniSAT written by A. Biere.

marks are C programs that require a moderate to large number of predicates per program location (the table shows the largest number of predicates required in any program location). All benchmarks make use of bit-vector and pointer arithmetic, and arrays. The benchmark AP1 is an array-bounds property of the Apache httpd server, which makes heavy use of pointers and pointer arithmetic.

The experiments show that a small additional expense for computing an initial predicate image can reduce the number of iterations required and the time spent for refinement dramatically. The larger the number of predicates, the bigger the benefit of using an initial abstraction usually is. Due to the depth bound of the proofs, the abstraction phase never uses an excessive amount of time.

5 Conclusion

This paper shows two things:

1. When extracting predicate images for abstract models, it is not necessary to perform the existential quantification upfront. It can be performed within the model checker instead. Potentially expensive methods, such as BDD-based enumeration as in [16], can be avoided that way.
2. A rich logic, including bit-vector logic, can be supported if we sacrifice some precision and abort proofs after a small number of steps. The experiments show that we in many cases still right away obtain an abstract model that is strong enough to terminate without many refinement iterations, and thus, often as good as a model computed using the precise image.

Future Work. The algorithm presented here uses the propositional encoding ϕ_{sk} to handle a complex Boolean structure of the transition relation. The transition relation of software programs, when partitioned using a program counter construction, usually only contains very few facts (one per statement of any basic block). As future work, we plan to experiment with the algorithm using larger transition relations, e.g., those of circuits given in Verilog.

We also plan to investigate even richer logics, e.g., non-standard logics such as separation logic [41] in order to reason about dynamic data structures.

Acknowledgment

The authors would like to thank Ofer Strichman for valuable comments, and Armin Biere for his proof-generating SAT solver Booleforce.

References

1. Clarke, E., Grumberg, O., Peled, D.: Model Checking. MIT Press (1999)
2. Clarke, E.M., Emerson, E.A.: Synthesis of synchronization skeletons for branching time temporal logic. In: Logic of Programs: Workshop. Volume 131 of LNCS. Springer (1981) 52–71

3. Burch, J.R., Clarke, E.M., McMillan, K.L., Dill, D.L., Hwang, L.J.: Symbolic model checking: 10^{20} states and beyond. Information and Computation **98** (1992) 142–170
4. Graf, S., Saïdi, H.: Construction of abstract state graphs with PVS. In: Computer Aided Verification (CAV). Volume 1254 of LNCS. Springer (1997) 72–83
5. Colón, M., Uribe, T.: Generating finite-state abstractions of reactive systems using decision procedures. In: Computer Aided Verification (CAV). Volume 1427 of LNCS. Springer (1998) 293–304
6. Ball, T., Rajamani, S.: Boolean programs: A model and process for software analysis. Technical Report 2000-14, Microsoft Research (2000)
7. Ball, T., Majumdar, R., Millstein, T., Rajamani, S.K.: Automatic predicate abstraction of C programs. In: Programming Language Design and Implementation (PLDI), ACM (2001) 203–213
8. Ball, T., Rajamani, S.K.: Generating abstract explanations of spurious counterexamples in C programs. Technical Report MSR-TR-2002-09, Microsoft Research (2002)
9. Ball, T., Cook, B., Das, S., Rajamani, S.K.: Refining approximations in software predicate abstraction. In: Tools and Algorithms for the Construction and Analysis of Systems (TACAS). Volume 2988 of LNCS. Springer (2004)
10. Ball, T., Rajamani, S.K.: Bebop: A symbolic model checker for Boolean programs. In: SPIN. Volume 1885 of LNCS. Springer (2000) 113–130
11. Ball, T., Rajamani, S.K.: Automatically validating temporal safety properties of interfaces. In: SPIN. Volume 1885 of LNCS. Springer (2000) 113–130
12. Ball, T., Rajamani, S.K.: Bebop: A path-sensitive interprocedural dataflow engine. In: Proceedings of the 2001 ACM SIGPLAN-SIGSOFT workshop on Program analysis for software tools and engineering, ACM (2001) 97–103
13. Kurshan, R.: Computer-Aided Verification of Coordinating Processes. Princeton University Press, Princeton (1995)
14. Clarke, E., Grumberg, O., Jha, S., Lu, Y., Veith, H.: Counterexample-guided abstraction refinement. In: Computer Aided Verification (CAV). Volume 1855 of LNCS. Springer (2000) 154–169
15. Clarke, E., Grumberg, O., Long, D.: Model checking and abstraction. In: Principles of Programming Languages (POPL), ACM (1992) 343–354
16. Lahiri, S.K., Ball, T., Cook, B.: Predicate abstraction via symbolic decision procedures. In: Computer Aided Verification (CAV). Volume 3576 of LNCS., Springer (2005) 24–38
17. Cook, B., Kroening, D., Sharygina, N.: Cogent: Accurate theorem proving for program verification. In: Computer Aided Verification (CAV). Volume 3576 of LNCS., Springer (2005)
18. Clarke, E., Kroening, D., Sharygina, N., Yorav, K.: Predicate abstraction of ANSI–C programs using SAT. Formal Methods in System Design **25** (2004) 105–127
19. Cousot, P.: Abstract interpretation. Symposium on Models of Programming Languages and Computation, ACM Computing Surveys **28** (1996) 324–328
20. Cousot, P., Cousot, R., Feret, J., Mauborgne, L., Miné, A., Monniaux, D., Rival, X.: The ASTREÉ analyzer. In: European Symposium on Programming (ESOP). Volume 3444 of LNCS. Springer (2005) 21–30
21. Chaki, S., Clarke, E., Groce, A., Strichman, O.: Predicate abstraction with minimum predicates. In: Correct Hardware Design and Verification Methods (CHARME). Volume 2860 of LNCS. Springer (2003) 19 – 34
22. Detlefs, D., Nelson, G., Saxe, J.B.: Simplify: A theorem prover for program checking. Technical Report HPL-2003-148, HP Labs (2003)
23. Lahiri, S.K., Bryant, R.E., Cook, B.: A symbolic approach to predicate abstraction. In: Computer-Aided Verification (CAV). Volume 2725 of LNCS. Springer (2003) 141–153

24. Ball, T., Cook, B., Lahiri, S.K., Zhang, L.: Zapato: Automatic theorem proving for predicate abstraction refinement. In: Computer Aided Verification (CAV). Volume 3114 of LNCS., Springer (2004)
25. Das, S., Dill, D.: Successive approximation of abstract transition relations. In: Logic in Computer Science (LICS). (2001) 51–60
26. Henzinger, T.A., Jhala, R., Majumdar, R., Sutre, G.: Lazy abstraction. In: Principles of programming languages (POPL). (2002) 58–70
27. Henzinger, T., Jhala, R., Majumdar, R., McMillan, K.: Abstractions from proofs. In: Principles of Programming Languages (POPL), ACM (2004) 232–244
28. Strichman, O.: On solving presburger and linear arithmetic with SAT. In: Formal Methods in Computer-Aided Design (FMCAD). Volume 2517 of LNCS. Springer (2002) 160–170
29. Barret, C.W., Dill, D.L., Levitt, J.R.: A decision procedure for bit-vector arithmetic. In: Design Automation Conference (DAC), ACM (1998)
30. Barrett, C., Berezin, S.: CVC Lite: A new implementation of the cooperating validity checker. In: Computer-Aided Verification. Volume 3114 of LNCS. Springer (2004)
31. Wedler, M., Stoffel, D., Kunz, W.: Normalization at the arithmetic bit level. In: Design Automation Conference (DAC), ACM (2005) 457–462
32. Brinkmann, R., Drechsler, R.: RTL-datapath verification using integer linear programming. In: VLSI Design, IEEE (2002) 741–746
33. Parthasarathy, G., Iyer, M.K., Cheng, K.T., Wang, L.C.: An efficient finite-domain constraint solver for circuits. In: Design Automation Conference (DAC), ACM (2004) 212–217
34. Plaisted, D.A., Greenbaum, S.: A structure-preserving clause form translation. Symbolic Computation 2 (1986) 293–304
35. Bryant, R.E., Lahiri, S.K., Seshia, S.A.: Modeling and verifying systems using a logic of counter arithmetic with lambda expressions and uninterpreted functions. In: Computer-Aided Verification. Volume 2404 of LNCS. Springer (2002)
36. Pugh, W.: The Omega test: a fast and practical integer programming algorithm for dependence analysis. Communications of the ACM (1992) 102–114
37. Lahiri, S.K., Bryant, R.E.: Constructing quantified invariants via predicate abstraction. In: Verification, Model Checking and Abstract Interpretation (VMCAI). Volume 2937 of LNCS. Springer (2004) 267–281
38. Cook, B., Kroening, D., Sharygina, N.: Symbolic model checking for asynchronous Boolean programs. In: SPIN. Volume 3639 of LNCS. Springer (2005) 75–90
39. Jain, H., Kroening, D., Sharygina, N., Clarke, E.: Word level predicate abstraction and refinement for verifying RTL Verilog. In: Design Automation Conference (DAC), ACM (2005) 445–450
40. Clarke, E., Kroening, D., Sharygina, N., Yorav, K.: SATABS: SAT-based predicate abstraction for ANSI-C. In: Tools and Algorithms for the Construction and Analysis of Systems (TACAS). Volume 3440 of LNCS. Springer (2005) 570–574
41. Reynolds, J.: Separation logic: A logic for shared mutable data structures. In: Logic in Computer Science (LICS), IEEE (2002) 55–74

Finitary Winning in ω-Regular Games[*]

Krishnendu Chatterjee[1] and Thomas A. Henzinger[1,2]

[1] University of California, Berkeley, USA
[2] EPFL, Switzerland
{c_krish, tah}@eecs.berkeley.edu

Abstract. Games on graphs with ω-regular objectives provide a model for the control and synthesis of reactive systems. Every ω-regular objective can be decomposed into a safety part and a liveness part. The liveness part ensures that something good happens "eventually." Two main strengths of the classical, infinite-limit formulation of liveness are robustness (independence from the granularity of transitions) and simplicity (abstraction of complicated time bounds). However, the classical liveness formulation suffers from the drawback that the time until something good happens may be unbounded. A stronger formulation of liveness, so-called *finitary* liveness, overcomes this drawback, while still retaining robustness and simplicity. Finitary liveness requires that there exists an unknown, fixed bound b such that something good happens within b transitions. While for one-shot liveness (reachability) objectives, classical and finitary liveness coincide, for repeated liveness (Büchi) objectives, the finitary formulation is strictly stronger. In this work we study games with finitary parity and Streett (fairness) objectives. We prove the determinacy of these games, present algorithms for solving these games, and characterize the memory requirements of winning strategies. Our algorithms can be used, for example, for synthesizing controllers that do not let the response time of a system increase without bound.

1 Introduction

Games played on graphs are suitable models for multi-component systems: vertices represent states; edges represent transitions; players represent components; and objectives represent specifications. The specification of a component is typically given as an ω-regular condition [9], and the resulting ω-regular games have been used for solving control and verification problems (see, e.g., [3, 11, 12]).

Every ω-regular specification (indeed, every specification) can be decomposed into a safety part and a liveness part [1]. The safety part ensures that the component will not do anything "bad" (such as violate an invariant) within any finite number of transitions. The liveness part ensures that the component will do something "good" (such as proceed, or respond, or terminate) within some finite number of transitions. Liveness can be violated only in the limit, by infinite sequences of transitions, as no bound is stipulated on when the "good" thing

---

[*] This research was supported in part by the AFOSR MURI grant F49620-00-1-0327 and the NSF ITR grant CCR-0225610.

H. Hermanns and J. Palsberg (Eds.): TACAS 2006, LNCS 3920, pp. 257–271, 2006.

must happen. This infinitary, classical formulation of liveness has both strengths and weaknesses. A main strength is robustness, in particular, independence from the chosen granularity of transitions. Another main strength is simplicity, allowing liveness to serve as an abstraction for complicated safety conditions. For example, a component may always respond in a number of transitions that depends, in some complicated manner, on the exact size of the stimulus. Yet for correctness, we may be interested only that the component will respond "eventually." However, these strengths also point to a weakness of the classical definition of liveness: it can be satisfied by components that in practice are quite unsatisfactory because no bound can be put on their response time. It is for this reason that alternative, stronger formulations of liveness have been proposed. One of these is *finitary* liveness [2, 4]: finitary liveness does not insist on response within a known bound b (i.e., every stimulus is followed by a response within b transitions), but on response within some unknown bound (i.e., there exists b such that every stimulus is followed by a response within b transitions). Note that in the finitary case, the bound b may be arbitrarily large, but the response time must not grow forever from one stimulus to the next. In this way, finitary liveness still maintains the robustness (independence of step granularity) and simplicity (abstraction of complicated safety) of traditional liveness, while removing unsatisfactory implementations.

In this paper, we study graph games with finitary winning conditions. The motivation is the same as for finitary liveness. Consider, for example, the synthesis of an elevator controller as a strategy in a game where one player represents the environment (i.e., the pushing of call buttons on various floors, and the pushing of target buttons inside the elevators), and the other player represents the elevator control (i.e., the commands to move an elevator up or down, and the opening and closing of elevator doors). Clearly, one objective of the controller is that whenever a call button is pushed on a floor, then an elevator will eventually arrive, and whenever a target button is pushed inside an elevator, then the elevator will eventually get to the corresponding floor. Note that this objective is formulated in an infinitary way (the key term is "eventually"). This is because, for robustness and simplicity, we do not wish to specify for each state the exact number of transitions until the objective must be met. However, a truly unbounded implementation of elevator control (where the response time grows from request to request, without bound) would be utterly unsatisfactory. A finitary interpretation of the objective prohibits such undesirable control strategies: there must exist a bound b such that the controller meets every call request, and every target request, within b transitions.

We formalize finitary winning for the normal form of ω-regular objectives called *parity* conditions [13]. A parity objective assigns a non-negative integer priority to every vertex, and the objective of player 1 is to make sure that the lowest priority that repeats infinitely often is even. This is an infinitary objective, as player 1 can win by ensuring that every odd priority that repeats infinitely often is followed by a smaller even priority "eventually" (arbitrarily many transitions later). The *finitary* parity objective, by contrast, insists that

Fig. 1. A simple game graph

player 1 ensures that there exists a bound b such that every odd priority that repeats infinitely often is followed by a smaller even priority within b transitions. The finitary parity objective is stronger than the classical parity objective, as is illustrated by the following example.

Example 1. Consider the game shown in Figure 1. The square-shaped states are player 1 states, where player 1 chooses the successor state, and the diamond-shaped states are player 2 states (we will follow this convention throughout this paper). The priorities of states are shown next to each state in the figure. If player 1 follows a memoryless strategy σ that chooses the successor s_2 at state s_0, this ensures that against all strategies π for player 2, the minimum priority of the states that are visited infinitely often is even (either state s_3 is visited infinitely often, or both states s_0 and s_1 are visited finitely often). However, consider the strategy π_w for player 2: the strategy π_w is played in rounds, and in round $k \geq 0$, whenever player 1 chooses the successor s_2 at state s_0, player 2 stays in state s_2 for k transitions, and then goes to state s_3 and proceeds to round $k+1$. The strategy π_w ensures that for all strategies σ for player 1, either the minimum priority visited infinitely often is 1 (i.e., both states s_0 and s_1 are visited infinitely often and state s_3 is visited finitely often); or states of priority 1 are visited infinitely often, and the distances between visits to states of priority 1 and subsequent visits to states of priority 0 increase without bound (i.e., the limit of the distances is ∞). Hence it follows that in this game, although player 1 can win for the parity objective, she cannot win for the finitary parity objective. ∎

We prove that games with finitary parity objectives are determined: for every state either there is a player 1 strategy (a winning strategy for player 1) that ensures that the finitary parity objective is satisfied against all player 2 strategies, or there is a player 2 strategy (a winning strategy for player 2) that ensures that the finitary parity objective is violated against all player 1 strategies. Similar to games with infinitary parity objectives, we establish the existence of winning strategies that are *memoryless* (independent of the history of the play) for player 1. However, winning strategies for player 2 in general require infinite memory; this is in contrast to infinitary parity objectives, where memoryless winning strategies exist also for player 2 [5]. We present an algorithm to compute the winning sets in time $O(n^{2d-3} \cdot d \cdot m)$ for game graphs with n states and m edges, and for finitary parity objectives with d priorities. Games with infinitary parity objectives can be solved in time $O(n^{\lfloor \frac{d}{2} \rfloor} \cdot m)$ [8]. Since in the case of finitary parity objectives, winning strategies for player 2 require infinite memory in general, the analysis and the algorithm for games with finitary parity objectives is more involved. We also show that polynomial-size witnesses exist for the winning strategies of both players; in particular, even though the winning strategies for player 2 may require infinite memory, there exist polynomial witnesses for these strategies. This allows us to conclude that, similar to games with infinitary parity objectives, the winning sets for games with finitary parity objectives can be decided in NP ∩ coNP.

In addition to finitary parity, we study finitary Streett objectives. Streett objectives require that if some stimuli are repeated infinitely often, then the corresponding responses occur infinitely often. The finitary interpretation requires, in addition, that there exists a bound b on all required response times (i.e., on the number of transitions between stimulus and corresponding response). We show that games with finitary Streett objectives can be solved by a reduction to finitary parity objectives (on a different game graph). The reduction establishes that games with finitary Streett objectives are determined. It also gives an algorithm that computes the winning sets in time $(n \cdot d!)^{O(d)} \cdot O(m)$ for game graphs with n states, m edges, and finitary Streett objectives with d pairs. Hence, the winning sets can be decided in EXPTIME. The decision problem for winning sets for games with infinitary Streett objectives is coNP-complete [5], and the winning sets can be computed in time $O(n^d \cdot d! \cdot m)$ [7]. For classical as well as finitary Streett games, finite-memory winning strategies exist for player 1. However, while in the classical case memoryless winning strategies exist for player 2 [5], in the finitary case the winning strategies for player 2 may require infinite memory.

We focus on finitary parity and Streett objectives. The finitary parity objectives are a canonical form to express finitary versions of ω-regular objectives; they subsume finitary reachability, finitary Büchi, and finitary co-Büchi objectives as special cases. The Streett objectives capture liveness conditions that are of particular interest in system design, as they correspond to strong fairness (compassion) constraints [9]. The finitary Streett objectives, therefore, give the finitary formulation of strong fairness.

2   Games with ω-Regular Objectives

Game graphs. A *game graph* $G = ((S, E), (S_1, S_2))$ consists of a directed graph (S, E) with a finite state space S and a set E of edges, and a partition (S_1, S_2) of the state space S into two sets. The states in S_1 are player 1 states, and the states in S_2 are player 2 states. For a state $s \in S$, we write $E(s) = \{t \in S \mid (s, t) \in E\}$ for the set of successor states of s. We assume that every state has at least one out-going edge, i.e., $E(s)$ is non-empty for all states $s \in S$.

Plays. A game is played by two players: player 1 and player 2, who form an infinite path in the game graph by moving a token along edges. They start by placing the token on an initial state, and then they take moves indefinitely in the following way. If the token is on a state in S_1, then player 1 moves the token along one of the edges going out of the state. If the token is on a state in S_2, then player 2 does likewise. The result is an infinite path in the game graph; we refer to such infinite paths as plays. Formally, a *play* is an infinite sequence $\langle s_0, s_1, s_2, \ldots \rangle$ of states such that $(s_k, s_{k+1}) \in E$ for all $k \geq 0$. We write Ω for the set of all plays.

Strategies. A strategy for a player is a recipe that specifies how to extend plays. Formally, a *strategy* σ for player 1 is a function $\sigma: S^* \cdot S_1 \to S$ that, given a finite sequence of states (representing the history of the play so far) which ends in a player 1 state, chooses the next state. The strategy must choose only available successors, i.e., for all $w \in S^*$ and $s \in S_1$, if $\sigma(w \cdot s) = t$, then $t \in E(s)$. The strategies for player 2 are defined analogously. We write Σ and Π for the sets of all strategies for player 1 and player 2, respectively. Strategies in general require memory to remember the history of plays. An equivalent definition of strategies is as follows. Let M be a set called *memory*. A strategy with memory can be described as a pair of functions: (a) a *memory-update* function $\sigma_u: S \times M \to M$ that, given the memory and the current state, updates the memory; and (b) a *next-state* function $\sigma_n: S \times M \to S$ that, given the memory and the current state, specifies the successor state. The strategy is *finite-memory* if the memory M is finite. The strategy is *memoryless* if the memory M is a singleton set. The memoryless strategies do not depend on the history of a play, but only on the current state. Each memoryless strategy for player 1 can be specified as a function $\sigma: S_1 \to S$ such that $\sigma(s) \in E(s)$ for all $s \in S_1$, and analogously for memoryless player 2 strategies. Given a starting state $s \in S$, a strategy $\sigma \in \Sigma$ for player 1, and a strategy $\pi \in \Pi$ for player 2, there is a unique play, denoted $\omega(s, \sigma, \pi) = \langle s_0, s_1, s_2, \ldots \rangle$, which is defined as follows: $s_0 = s$ and for all $k \geq 0$, if $s_k \in S_1$, then $\sigma(s_0, s_1, \ldots, s_k) = s_{k+1}$, and if $s_k \in S_2$, then $\pi(s_0, s_1, \ldots, s_k) = s_{k+1}$.

Classical winning conditions. We first define the class of ω-regular objectives and the classical notion of winning.

Objectives. Objectives for the players in non-terminating games are specified by providing the sets $\Phi, \Psi \subseteq \Omega$ of *winning plays* for player 1 and player 2, respectively. We consider zero-sum games, where the objectives of both players are complementary, i.e., $\Psi = \Omega \setminus \Phi$. The class of *$\omega$-regular objectives* [13] are of special interest since they form a robust class of objectives for verification and synthesis. The ω-regular objectives, and subclasses thereof, can be specified in the following forms. For a play $\omega = \langle s_0, s_1, s_2, \ldots \rangle \in \Omega$, we define $\mathrm{Inf}(\omega) = \{s \in S \mid s_k = s$ for infinitely many $k \geq 0\}$ to be the set of states that occur infinitely often in ω.

1. *Reachability and safety objectives.* Given a set $F \subseteq S$ of states, the reachability objective $\mathrm{Reach}(F)$ requires that some state in F be visited, and dually, the safety objective $\mathrm{Safe}(F)$ requires that only states in F be visited. Formally, the sets of winning plays are $\mathrm{Reach}(F) = \{\langle s_0, s_1, s_2, \ldots \rangle \in \Omega \mid \exists k \geq 0. s_k \in F\}$ and $\mathrm{Safe}(F) = \{\langle s_0, s_1, s_2, \ldots \rangle \in \Omega \mid \forall k \geq 0. s_k \in F\}$.
2. *Büchi and co-Büchi objectives.* Given a set $F \subseteq S$ of states, the Büchi objective $\mathrm{Buchi}(F)$ requires that some state in F be visited infinitely often, and dually, the co-Büchi objective $\mathrm{coBuchi}(F)$ requires that only states in F be visited infinitely often. Thus, the sets of winning plays are $\mathrm{Buchi}(F) = \{\omega \in \Omega \mid \mathrm{Inf}(\omega) \cap F \neq \emptyset\}$ and $\mathrm{coBuchi}(F) = \{\omega \in \Omega \mid \mathrm{Inf}(\omega) \subseteq F\}$.
3. *Rabin and Streett objectives.* Given a set $P = \{(E_1, F_1), \ldots, (E_d, F_d)\}$ of pairs of sets of states (i.e, for all $1 \leq j \leq d$, both $E_j \subseteq S$ and $F_j \subseteq S$), the

Rabin objective Rabin(P) requires that for some pair $1 \leq j \leq d$, all states in E_j be visited finitely often, and some state in F_j be visited infinitely often. Hence, the winning plays are Rabin(P) = $\{\omega \in \Omega \mid \exists 1 \leq j \leq d. \ (\mathrm{Inf}(\omega) \cap E_j = \emptyset$ and $\mathrm{Inf}(\omega) \cap F_j \neq \emptyset)\}$. Dually, given $P = \{(E_1, F_1), \ldots, (E_d, F_d)\}$, the Streett objective Streett(P) requires that for all pairs $1 \leq j \leq d$, if some state in F_j is visited infinitely often, then some state in E_j be visited infinitely often, i.e., Streett(P) = $\{\omega \in \Omega \mid \forall 1 \leq j \leq d. \ (\mathrm{Inf}(\omega) \cap E_j \neq \emptyset$ or $\mathrm{Inf}(\omega) \cap F_j = \emptyset)\}$.

4. *Parity objectives.* Given a function $p \colon S \to \{0, 1, 2, \ldots, d-1\}$ that maps every state to an integer *priority*, the parity objective Parity(p) requires that of the states that are visited infinitely often, the least priority be even. Formally, the set of winning plays is Parity(p) = $\{\omega \in \Omega \mid \min\{p(\mathrm{Inf}(\omega))\}$ is even$\}$. The dual, co-parity objective has the set coParity(p) = $\{\omega \in \Omega \mid \min\{p(\mathrm{Inf}(\omega))\}$ is odd$\}$ of winning plays.

Every parity objective is both a Rabin objective and a Streett objective. Hence, the parity objectives are closed under complementation. The Büchi and co-Büchi objectives are special cases of parity objectives with two priorities, namely, $p \colon S \to \{0, 1\}$ for Büchi objectives with $F = p^{-1}(0)$, and $p \colon S \to \{1, 2\}$ for co-Büchi objectives with $F = p^{-1}(2)$. The reachability and safety objectives can be turned into Büchi and co-Büchi objectives, respectively, on slightly modified game graphs.

Winning. Given an objective $\Phi \subseteq \Omega$ for player 1, a strategy $\sigma \in \Sigma$ is a *winning strategy* for player 1 from a set $U \subseteq S$ of states if for all player 2 strategies $\pi \in \Pi$ and all states $s \in U$, the play $\omega(s, \sigma, \pi)$ is winning, i.e., $\omega(s, \sigma, \pi) \in \Phi$. The winning strategies for player 2 are defined analogously. A state $s \in S$ is winning for player 1 with respect to the objective Φ if player 1 has a winning strategy from $\{s\}$. Formally, the set of *winning states* for player 1 with respect to the objective Φ is $W_1(\Phi) = \{s \in S \mid \exists \sigma \in \Sigma. \ \forall \pi \in \Pi. \ \omega(s, \sigma, \pi) \in \Phi\}$. Analogously, the set of winning states for player 2 with respect to an objective $\Psi \subseteq \Omega$ is $W_2(\Psi) = \{s \in S \mid \exists \pi \in \Pi. \ \forall \sigma \in \Sigma. \ \omega(s, \sigma, \pi) \in \Psi\}$. We say that there exists a (memoryless; finite-memory) winning strategy for player 1 with respect to the objective Φ if there exists such a strategy from the set $W_1(\Phi)$; and similarly for player 2.

Theorem 1 (Classical determinacy and strategy complexity).

1. [6] *For all game graphs, all Rabin objectives Φ for player 1, and the complementary Streett objective $\Psi = \Omega \backslash \Phi$ for player 2, we have $W_1(\Phi) = S \backslash W_2(\Psi)$.*

2. [5] *For all game graphs and all Rabin objectives for player 1, there exists a memoryless winning strategy for player 1.*

3. [6] *For all game graphs and all Streett objectives for player 2, there exists a finite-memory winning strategy for player 2. However, in general no memoryless winning strategy exists.*

3   Finitary Winning Conditions

We now define a stronger notion of winning, namely, *finitary winning*, in games with parity and Streett objectives.

Finitary winning for parity objectives. For parity objectives, the finitary winning notion requires that for each visit to an odd priority that is visited infinitely often, the distance to a stronger (i.e., lower) even priority be bounded. To define the winning plays formally, we need the concept of a distance sequence.

Distance sequences for parity objectives. Given a play $\omega = \langle s_0, s_1, s_2, \ldots \rangle$ and a priority function $p \colon S \to \{0, 1, \ldots, d-1\}$, we define a sequence of distances $dist_k(\omega, p)$, for all $k \geq 0$, as follows: $dist_k(\omega, p) = 0$ if $p(s_k)$ is even, and $dist_k(\omega, p) = \inf\{k' \geq k \mid p(s_{k'})$ is even and $p(s_{k'}) < p(s_k)\}$ if $p(s_k)$ is odd. Intuitively, the distance for a position k in a play with an odd priority at position k, denotes the shortest distance to a stronger even priority in the play. We assume the standard convention that the infimum of the empty set is ∞.

Finitary parity objectives. The finitary parity objective finParity(p) for a priority function p requires that the sequence of distances for the positions with odd priorities that occur infinitely often be bounded. This is equivalent to requiring that the sequence of all distances be bounded in the limit, and captures the notion that the "good" (even) priorities that appear infinitely often do not appear infinitely rarely. Formally, the sets of winning plays for the finitary parity objective and its complement are finParity(p) = $\{\omega \in \Omega \mid \limsup_{k \to \infty} dist_k(\omega, p) < \infty\}$ and infParity(p) = $\{\omega \in \Omega \mid \limsup_{k \to \infty} dist_k(\omega, p) = \infty\}$, respectively. Observe that if a play ω is winning for a co-parity objective, then the lim sup of the distance sequence for ω is ∞, that is, coParity(p) $\subseteq$ infParity(p). However, if a play ω is winning for a (classical) parity objective, then the lim sup of the distance sequence for ω can be ∞ (as shown in Example 1), that is, finParity(p) $\subsetneq$ Parity(p). Given a game graph G and a priority function p, solving the finitary parity game requires computing the two winning sets W_1(finParity(p)) and W_2(infParity(p)).

Remark 1. Recall that Büchi and co-Büchi objectives correspond to parity objectives with two priorities. A finitary Büchi objective is in general a strict subset of the corresponding classical Büchi objective; a finitary co-Büchi objective coincides with the corresponding classical co-Büchi objective. However, it can be shown that for parity objectives with two priorities, the classical winning sets and the finitary winning sets are the same; that is, for all game graphs G and all priority functions p with two priorities, we have W_1(finParity(p)) = W_1(Parity(p)) and W_2(infParity(p)) = W_2(coParity(p)). Note that in Example 1, we have $s_0 \in W_1$(Parity(p)) and $s_0 \notin W_1$(finParity(p)). This shows that for priority functions with three or more priorities, the winning set for a finitary parity objective can be a strict subset of the winning set for the corresponding classical parity objective, that is, W_1(finParity(p)) $\subsetneq W_1$(Parity(p)). ∎

Finitary winning for Streett objectives. The notion of distance sequence for parity objectives has a natural extension to Streett objectives.

Distance sequences for Streett objectives. Given a play $\omega = \langle s_0, s_1, s_2, \ldots \rangle$ and a set $P = \{(E_1, F_1), \ldots, (E_d, F_d)\}$ of Streett pairs of state sets, the d sequences of distances $dist_k^j(\omega, P)$, for all $k \geq 0$ and $1 \leq j \leq d$, are defined as follows: $dist_k^j(\omega, P) = 0$ if $s_k \notin F_j$, and $dist_k^j(\omega, P) = \inf\{k' \geq k \mid s_{k'} \in E_j\}$ if $s_k \in F_j$. Let $dist_k(\omega, P) = \max\{dist_k^j(\omega, P) \mid 1 \leq j \leq d\}$ for all $k \geq 0$.

Finitary Streett objectives. The finitary Streett objective finStreett(P) for a set P of Streett pairs requires that the distance sequence be bounded in the limit, i.e., the winning plays are finStreett$(P) = \{\omega \in \Omega \mid \limsup_{k \to \infty} dist_k(\omega, P) < \infty\}$.

Example 2. Consider the game graph of Figure 2. Player 2 generates requests of type Req_1 and Req_2; these are shown as labeled edges in the figure. Player 1 services a request of type Req_i by choosing an edge labeled $Serv_i$, for $i = 1, 2$. Whenever a request is received, further requests of the same type are disabled until the request is serviced; then the requests of this type are enabled again. The state s_0 represents the case when there are no unserviced requests; the states s_1 and s_2 represent the cases when there are unserviced requests of type Req_1 and Req_2, respectively; and the states s_7 and s_8 represent the cases when there are unserviced requests of both types, having arrived in either order. On arrival of a request of type Req_i, a state in F_i is visited, and when a request of type Req_i is serviced, a state in E_i is visited, for $i = 1, 2$. Hence $F_1 = \{s_1, s_8\}$, $F_2 = \{s_2, s_7\}$, $E_1 = \{s_5, s_{12}\}$, and $E_2 = \{s_6, s_{11}\}$. The Streett objective Streett(P) with $P = \{(E_1, F_1), (E_2, F_2)\}$ requires that if a request of type Req_i is received infinitely often, then it be serviced infinitely often, for both $i = 1, 2$. The player 1 strategy $s_9 \to s_{11}$ and $s_{10} \to s_{12}$ is a *stack* strategy, which always services first the request type received last. The player 1 strategy $s_9 \to s_{12}$ and $s_{10} \to s_{11}$ is a *queue* strategy, which always services first the request type received first. Both the stack strategy and the queue strategy ensure that the classical Streett objective Streett(P) is satisfied. However, for the stack strategy, the number of transitions between the arrival of a request of type Req_i and its service can be unbounded. Hence the stack strategy is not a winning strategy for player 1 with respect to the finitary Streett objective finStreett(P). The queue strategy, by contrast, ensures not only that every request that is received infinitely often is serviced, but it also ensures that the number of transitions between the arrival

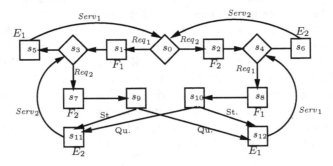

Fig. 2. A request-service game graph

of a request and its service is at most 6. Thus the queue strategy is winning for player 1 with respect to finStreett(P).   ∎

4 Finitary Determinacy and Algorithmic Analysis

We present an algorithm to solve games with finitary parity objectives. The correctness argument for the algorithm also proves determinacy for finitary parity games.[1] We then show that games with finitary Streett objectives can be solved via a reduction to finitary parity games.

Solving games with finitary parity objectives. We start with some preliminary notation and facts that will be required for the analysis of the algorithm.

Closed sets. A set $U \subseteq S$ of states is a *closed set* for player 2 if the following two conditions hold: (a) for all states $u \in (U \cap S_2)$, we have $E(u) \subseteq U$, i.e., all successors of player 2 states in U are again in U; and (b) for all $u \in (U \cap S_1)$, we have $E(u) \cap U \neq \emptyset$, i.e., every player 1 state in U has a successor in U. The closed sets for player 1 are defined analogously. Every closed set U for player ℓ, for $\ell \in \{1,2\}$, induces a sub-game graph, denoted $G \restriction U$. For winning sets W_1 and W_2, we write W_1^G and W_2^G to explicitly specify the game graph G.

Proposition 1. *Consider a game graph G, and a closed set U for player 2. For every objective Φ for player 1, we have $W_1^{G \restriction U}(\Phi) \subseteq W_1^G(\Phi)$.*

Attractors. Given a game graph G, a set $U \subseteq S$ of states, and a player $\ell \in \{1,2\}$, the set $Attr_\ell(U,G)$ contains the states from which player ℓ has a strategy to reach a state in U against all strategies of the other player; that is, $Attr_\ell(U,G) = W_\ell^G(\text{Reach}(U))$. The set $Attr_1(U,G)$ can be computed inductively as follows: let $R_0 = U$; let $R_{i+1} = R_i \cup \{s \in S_1 \mid E(s) \cap R_i \neq \emptyset\} \cup \{s \in S_2 \mid E(s) \subseteq R_i\}$ for all $i \geq 0$; then $Attr_1(U,G) = \bigcup_{i \geq 0} R_i$. The inductive computation of $Attr_2(U,G)$ is analogous. For all states $s \in Attr_1(U,G)$, define $rank(s) = i$ if $s \in R_i \setminus R_{i-1}$, that is, $rank(s)$ denotes the least $i \geq 0$ such that s is included in R_i. Define a memoryless strategy $\sigma \in \Sigma$ for player 1 as follows: for each state $s \in (Attr_1(U,G) \cap S_1)$ with $rank(s) = i$, choose a successor $\sigma(s) \in (R_{i-1} \cap E(s))$ (such a successor exists by the inductive definition). It follows that for all states $s \in Attr_1(U,G)$ and all strategies $\pi \in \Pi$ for player 2, the play $\omega(s,\sigma,\pi)$ reaches U in at most $|Attr_1(U,G)|$ transitions.

Proposition 2. *For all game graphs G, all players $\ell \in \{1,2\}$, and all sets $U \subseteq S$ of states, the set $S \setminus Attr_\ell(U,G)$ is a closed set for player ℓ.*

Notation. Given a priority function $p: S \to \{0,1,\ldots,d-1\}$, and a priority $j \in \{0,1,\ldots,d-1\}$, we write $p^{-1}(j) \subseteq S$ for the set of states with priority j. For $\bowtie \in \{<,\leq,>,\geq\}$, let $p^{-1}(\bowtie j) = \bigcup_{j' \bowtie j} p^{-1}(j')$. Moreover, let

---

[1] The determinacy of games with finitary parity objectives can also be proved by reduction to Borel objectives, using the determinacy of Borel games [10]; however, our proof is direct.

$even(p) = \bigcup_{2j<d} p^{-1}(2j)$ be the set of states with even priorities. We define the set $\text{ReachSafe}(p) = \bigcup_{2j+1<d}(\text{Reach}(p^{-1}(2j+1)) \cap \text{Safe}(p^{-1}(\geq 2j+1)))$ of plays, i.e., the objective $\text{ReachSafe}(p)$ requires that a state of some odd priority $2j + 1$ be reached, and that the play stay within the set of states with priorities at least $2j + 1$. The complementary objective is $\Omega \setminus \text{ReachSafe}(p) = \bigcap_{2j+1<d}((\Omega \setminus \text{Reach}(p^{-1}(2j+1))) \cup \text{Reach}(p^{-1}(\leq 2j) \cap even(p)))$.

Informal description of Algorithm 1. The algorithm takes as input a game graph G and a priority function $p\colon S \to \{0, 1, \ldots, d-1\}$ with d priorities. The algorithm iteratively computes the winning sets $W_1(\text{finParity}(p))$ and $W_2(\text{infParity}(p))$ for player 1 and player 2, respectively. We describe one iteration of the algorithm (i.e., one execution of the loop body at Step 2). Let G^i be the game graph at iteration i, and let (S^i, E^i) be the underlying directed graph. In Step 2.1, the set $A = Attr_1(p^{-1}(0), G^i)$ is computed as the set of states from which player 1 can reach a state of priority 0. In the sub-game $G^i \upharpoonright B$, where $B = S^i \setminus A$, the set C denotes the set of player 2 states that have an edge into A. In Step 2.3, the set $D = Attr_2(C, G^i \upharpoonright B)$ is computed and the sub-game $G^i \upharpoonright H$ is solved recursively, where $H = B \setminus D$. If a non-empty player 1 winning set U_1 is discovered in the sub-game $G^i \upharpoonright H$, then U_1 and $Attr_1(U_1, G^i)$ are identified as subsets of $W_1(\text{finParity}(p))$, removed from G^i, and the algorithm proceeds to iteration $i + 1$ (Step 2.5). Otherwise, the game graph $G^i \upharpoonright B$ is solved with the objective $\text{ReachSafe}(p)$ for player 2 (and the complementary objective for player 1). If the winning set for player 2 is empty, then all of S^i is identified as a subset of $W_1(\text{finParity}(p))$, and the algorithm stops (Step 2.7). Otherwise, let X_2 be the winning set for player 2 in the sub-game $G^i \upharpoonright B$ with respect to the objective $\text{ReachSafe}(p)$, and let $L = Attr_2(X_2, G^i)$. The sub-game $G^i \upharpoonright Q$ is solved recursively, where $Q = S^i \setminus L$. If a non-empty player 1 winning set Z_1 is discovered in $G^i \upharpoonright Q$, then Z_1 and $Attr_1(Z_1, G^i)$ are identified as subsets of $W_1(\text{finParity}(p))$, removed from G^i, and the algorithm proceeds to iteration $i+1$ (Step 2.8.3). Otherwise, all of S^i is identified as a subset of $W_2(\text{infParity}(p))$, and the algorithm stops (Step 2.8.4).

Claim 1: Correctness of Step 2.5. We first argue that the set H defined in Step 2.3 is a closed set for player 2. Observe that for all states $s \in (S_2 \cap B)$, if $E(s)$ is not a subset of B, then $s \in C$. Hence for all states in $s \in B \setminus C$, we have $E(s) \subseteq B$. It follows from Proposition 2 that $H = B \setminus Attr_2(C, G^i \upharpoonright B)$ is a player 2 closed set in the game graph G^i. It follows from Proposition 1 that the set $U_1 = W_1^{G^i \upharpoonright H}(\text{finParity}(p))$ in the sub-game $G^i \upharpoonright H$ is winning for player 1. Hence U_1 and $Attr_1(U_1, G^i)$ are correctly identified as subsets of the player 1 winning set $W_1(\text{finParity}(p))$. ∎

Claim 2: Correctness of Step 2.7. Observe that if Step 2.7 is executed, then $X_2 = \emptyset$, and hence player 1 wins with respect to the objective $\Phi = \bigcap_{2j+1\leq d}((\Omega \setminus \text{Reach}(p^{-1}(2j+1))) \cup \text{Reach}(p^{-1}(\leq 2j) \cap even(p)))$ from every state $s \in B$ in the sub-game $G^i \upharpoonright B$. Recall that $B = S^i \setminus A$, and $A = Attr_1(p^{-1}(0), G^i)$. It follows that player 1 wins with respect to the objective Φ from all states $s \in S^i$

Algorithm 1. FinitaryParity

Input: a game graph G and a priority function p.
Output: the sets $W_1 = W_1(\text{finParity}(p))$ and $W_2 = W_2(\text{infParity}(p))$.

1. $W_1 = \emptyset$; $W_2 = \emptyset$; $G^0 = G$; $i = 0$;
2. **repeat**
   2.1. $A = Attr_1(p^{-1}(0), G^i)$; $B = S^i \setminus A$;
   2.2. $C = \{s \in (B \cap S_2) \mid E^i(s) \cap A \neq \emptyset\}$;
   2.3. $D = Attr_2(C, G^i \upharpoonright B)$; $H = B \setminus D$;
   2.4. $(U_1, U_2) = \text{FinitaryParity}(G^i \upharpoonright H, p)$;
   2.5. **if** $U_1 \neq \emptyset$ **then**
       2.5.1. $W_1 = W_1 \cup Attr_1(U_1, G^i)$; $S^{i+1} = S^i \setminus Attr_1(U_1, G^i)$;
       2.5.2. **goto** Step 2.9;
   2.6. $(X_1, X_2) = \text{GameSolve}(G^i \upharpoonright B, \Omega \setminus \text{ReachSafe}(p))$;
   2.7. **if** $X_2 = \emptyset$ **then**
       2.7.1. $W_1 = W_1 \cup S^i$;
       2.7.2. **return** (W_1, W_2);
   2.8. **else**
       2.8.1. $L = Attr_2(X_2, G^i)$; $Q = S^i \setminus L$;
       2.8.2. $(Z_1, Z_2) = \text{FinitaryParity}(G^i \upharpoonright Q, p)$;
       2.8.3. **if** $Z_1 \neq \emptyset$ **then**
           2.8.3.1. $W_1 = W_1 \cup Attr_1(Z_1, G^i)$; $S^{i+1} = S^i \setminus Attr_1(Z_1, G^i)$;
           2.8.3.2. **goto** Step 2.9;
       2.8.4. **else**
           2.8.4.1. $W_2 = W_2 \cup S^i$;
           2.8.4.2. **return** (W_1, W_2);
   2.9. $G^{i+1} = G^i \upharpoonright S^{i+1}$; $i := i + 1$;
   until $S^i = \emptyset$;
3. **return** (W_1, W_2).

---

in the game graph G^i. Hence $p^{-1}(2j + 1) \subseteq Attr_1(p^{-1}(\leq 2j) \cap even(p), G^i)$ for all $2j + 1 < d$. We inductively define the following sets: let $A_0 = A = Attr_1(p^{-1}(0), G^i)$; and let $A_{2j} = Attr_1(p^{-1}(2j), G^i \upharpoonright (S^i \setminus A_{2j-2}))$ for $2 \leq 2j < d$. Observe that $p^{-1}(2j + 1) \subseteq \bigcup_{j' \leq j} A_{2j'}$. A memoryless strategy σ for player 1 can be constructed as follows: in A_0, reach $p^{-1}(0)$ within $|A_0|$ transitions; and in the sub-game $G^i \upharpoonright (S^i \setminus A_{2j-2})$, reach $p^{-1}(2j)$ within $|A_{2j}|$ transitions from all states in A_{2j}. If player 1 follows the strategy σ, then for all player 2 strategies π, if the play visits a state in $p^{-1}(2j + 1)$, then it visits $p^{-1}(\leq 2j) \cap even(p)$ within $|S^i|$ transitions. Thus, for all states s and all player 2 strategies π, we have $dist_k(\omega(s, \sigma, \pi), p) \leq |S^i|$ for all $k \geq 0$, and therefore $\limsup_{k \to \infty} dist_k(\omega(s, \sigma, \pi), p) < \infty$. ∎

Claim 3: Correctness of Step 2.8.3. Observe that $L = Attr_2(X_2, G^i)$, and hence $Q = S^i \setminus L$ is a closed set for player 2 (by Proposition 2). It follows from arguments similar to the correctness of Step 2.5 that Z_1 and $Attr_1(Z_1, G^i)$ are correctly identified as subsets of $W_1(\text{finParity}(p))$. ∎

Claim 4: Correctness of Step 2.8.4. Observe that if Step 2.8.4 is executed, then the following two conditions hold: (i) player 2 has a winning strategy π_H from H with respect to the objective infParity(p) in the sub-game $G^i \upharpoonright H$ (because the test of Step 2.5 fails); and (ii) player 2 has a winning strategy π_Q from Q with respect to the objective infParity(p) in the sub-game $G^i \upharpoonright Q$ (because the test of Step 2.8.3 fails). We construct a winning strategy π for player 2 from S^i which is played in rounds. In every round, there are five stages, and we describe each stage of the strategy π for round r as follows:

Stage 1. [play in Q] As long as the play stays in Q, play the strategy π_Q (the player 2 winning strategy from Q in the sub-game $G^i \upharpoonright Q$ with respect to the objective infParity(p)). If the play enters $L = S^i \setminus Q$, proceed to Stage 2.

Stage 2. [play in L] Play a strategy π_L to reach X_2 within $|L|$ transitions, and proceed to Stage 3 when the play reaches X_2.

Stage 3. [play in X_2] Play a winning strategy π_{X_2} with respect to the objective ReachSafe(p) in the sub-game $G^i \upharpoonright B$. After the play reaches a state in $p^{-1}(2j+1) \cap B$, and stays in $p^{-1}(\geq 2j+1) \cap B$ for r transitions, proceed to Stage 4.

Stage 4. [play in H] As long as the play stays in H, play the strategy π_H (the player 2 winning strategy from H in the sub-game $G^i \upharpoonright H$ with respect to the objective infParity(p)). If the play enters $D = B \setminus H$, proceed to Stage 5.

Stage 5. [play in D] Play a strategy to reach C within $|D|$ transitions, then leave B via an edge from C to A, and proceed to Stage 1 of round $r+1$.

Given the player 2 strategy π, consider a player 1 strategy σ and a state $s \in S^i$. Observe that if the play $\omega(s, \sigma, \pi)$ reaches Stage 2 of a round r, then Stages 3 and 4 of round r are also reached. Similarly, if stage 5 of round r is reached, then Stages 1 or 2 of round $r+1$ are also reached. If the play $\omega(s, \sigma, \pi)$ remains forever in Stage 1 or Stage 4 for some round r, then by properties of π_H and π_Q (conditions (i) and (ii) from above), it follows that $\omega(s, \sigma, \pi) \in$ infParity(p). Otherwise, the play proceeds through infinitely many rounds. Stage 3 of the strategy π ensures that in round r, there is a position $k \geq 0$ such that $dist_k(\omega(s, \sigma, \pi), p) \geq r$. Hence it follows that $\limsup_{k \to \infty} dist_k(\omega(s, \sigma, \pi), p) = \infty$, and thus again $\omega(s, \sigma, \pi) \in$ infParity(p). ∎

The claims 1–4 establish the correctness of Algorithm 1, and also establish the determinacy of games with finitary parity objectives.

Theorem 2 (Finitary determinacy). *For all game graphs and all priority functions p, we have $W_1(\text{finParity}(p)) = S \setminus W_2(\text{infParity}(p))$.*

Running time of Algorithm 1. Recall from Remark 1 that for priority functions p with two priorities, the winning sets for the classical parity objective Parity(p) and for the finitary parity objective finParity(p) coincide. Hence, for two priorities the winning set $W_1(\text{finParity}(p))$ can be computed in $O(n \cdot m)$ time, where n is the number of states and m is the number of edges (by algorithms for solving Büchi and co-Büchi games). For priority functions with d priorities, let $T(n, m, d)$ be the running time of Algorithm 1 to compute $W_1(\text{finParity}(p))$ and

$W_2(\text{infParity}(p))$. The running time of one iteration of the algorithm (i.e., one execution of the loop body at Step 2) can be bounded by $n \cdot (T(n, m, d-1) + O(d \cdot m))$. Since in each iteration at least one state is removed from the game graph, we obtain the recurrence $T(n, m, d) = n^2 \cdot (T(n, m, d-1) + O(d \cdot m))$ for $d > 2$. This yields the time bound in the following theorem.

Theorem 3 (Algorithm 1). *Given a game graph with n states and m edges, and a priority function p with d priorities, Algorithm 1 computes the winning sets $W_1(\text{finParity}(p))$ and $W_2(\text{infParity}(p))$ in $O(n^{2d-3} \cdot d \cdot m)$ time.*

Winning strategies for finitary parity objectives. We first show that winning strategies for player 2 with respect to the objective infParity(p) in general require infinite memory. To see this, recall Example 1: the player 2 winning strategy π_w constructed in the example requires infinite memory, and against any finite-memory strategy π_f for player 2, the player 1 strategy σ that chooses the successor s_2 at state s_0, ensures that in the play $\omega(s_0, \sigma, \pi_f)$ the distances between states of priority 1 and priority 0 are always bounded. In contrast to winning strategies for player 2, which may require infinite memory, we now argue that memoryless winning strategies exist for player 1. This follows from the analysis of Steps 2.5, 2.7, and 2.8.3 of Algorithm 1. In the correctness argument for Step 2.7, a memoryless winning strategy is constructed. The existence of memoryless winning strategies for Steps 2.5 and 2.8.3 follow from inductive arguments (induction on the number of priorities for Step 2.5, and induction on the size of the state space for Step 2.8.3).

Witness sizes for winning strategies. Since memoryless winning strategies exist for player 1, there exist polynomial-size witnesses (in fact, linear-size witnesses) for player 1 winning strategies. We now argue that although player 2 winning strategies may require infinite memory, there exist polynomial-size witnesses for these strategies as well. Consider the correctness argument for Step 2.8.4 of Algorithm 1. The sets used in the analysis can serve as witness for the player 2 winning strategy. The witness consists of the following components: (a) the sets $A = Attr_1(p^{-1}(0), G^i)$ and $B = S^i \setminus A$; (b) the sets C and $D = Attr_2(C, G^i \upharpoonright B)$ and $H = B \setminus D$; (c) the set $X_2 = W_2^{G^i \upharpoonright B}(\text{ReachSafe}(p))$, and a player 2 winning strategy in X_2 with respect to the objective ReachSafe(p); (d) the set $L = Attr_2(X_2, G^i)$, and a player 2 winning strategy in L to reach X_2; and (e) player 2 winning strategies in the sub-games $G^i \upharpoonright H$ and $G^i \upharpoonright Q$. Given such a witness, the existence of a player 2 winning strategy follows from the construction presented in the correctness argument for Step 2.8.4. It is easy to argue that linear-size witnesses exist for parts (a)–(d). The witness for part (e) is recursive. A key observation to obtain a polynomial-size witness is the following: in Stage 1 of the strategy construction, in the set $Q \cap H$ player 2 can follow the winning strategy in H of the sub-game $G^i \upharpoonright H$. Hence the witness in Q can follow the witness of H in the set $Q \cap H$, and we need to exhibit a different witness in Q only for the subset that is disjoint from H. Let $Size(t)$ denote the size of the witness for a set of size t. Hence the witness consists of the witness in H of $Size(|H|)$, the witness in Q of size $Size(|Q \setminus H|)$, and witnesses of linear size. Thus we have the recurrence $Size(n) \leq \max\{Size(h)+Size(n-h)+O(n) \mid 1 \leq h \leq n\}$, where h denotes the size of the set H, that is, $h = |H|$. This recurrence is satisfied by $Size(n) = O(n^2)$.

Theorem 4 (Finitary strategy complexity). *For all game graphs and all priority functions p, there exists a memoryless winning strategy for player 1 with respect to the objective* finParity(p). *However, in general no finite-memory winning strategy exists for player 2 with respect to the complementary objective* infParity(p). *For game graphs with n states, there are witnesses of size $O(n)$ and $O(n^2)$ for the winning strategies for player 1 and player 2, respectively.*

Computational complexity. The existence of memoryless winning strategies for player 1 implies that whether a given state lies in $W_1(\text{finParity}(p))$ can be decided in NP. Moreover, because of the existence of polynomial-size witnesses for player 2 winning strategies, also whether a given state lies in $W_2(\text{infParity}(p))$ can be decided in NP.

Corollary 1. *For all game graphs, all priority functions p, and all states s, whether $s \in W_1(\text{finParity}(p))$ can be decided in* NP $\cap$ coNP.

It remains an open problem if there is a polynomial-time algorithm to compute $W_1(\text{finParity}(p))$. The existence of memoryless winning strategies for finitary parity objectives also gives the following refined characterization of the winning set, which shows that distances can be bounded by the size of the state space.

Corollary 2. *For all game graphs with n states, and all priority functions p, we have $W_1(\text{finParity}(p)) = \{s \in S \mid \exists\sigma \in \Sigma. \forall\pi \in \Pi.$ $\limsup_{k\to\infty} dist_k(\omega(s,\sigma,\pi),p) \leq n\}$.*

Solving games with finitary Streett objectives. The *index appearance record* (IAR) construction [13] translates games with player 1 Streett objectives into games with parity objectives, preserving the abilities of both players to win. Given a game graph G with n states and m edges, and a set $P = \{(E_1, F_1), \ldots, (E_d, F_d)\}$ of d Streett pairs, the IAR construction yields a game graph G' with $n \cdot d! \cdot d^2$ states and $m \cdot d! \cdot d^2$ edges, and a priority function p with $O(d)$ priorities. We only sketch the construction here. An IAR is a triple (τ, e, f), where τ is a permutation of $(1, 2, \ldots, d)$, and $e, f \in \{1, 2, \ldots, d\}$. The permuation τ remembers the order of the latest appearances of the sets E_j, for $1 \leq j \leq d$, and the indices e and f remember the previous positions in τ of the most recent sets E_j and F_j, respectively. The new game graph G' is obtained as the synchronous product of the original game graph G and the IAR; see [13]. For a state $\langle s, (\tau, e, f)\rangle$ of G' (where s is a state of G), the priority function p is defined such that $p(\langle s, (\tau, e, f)\rangle) = 2e$ if $f \leq e$, and otherwise $p(\langle s, (\tau, e, f)\rangle) = 2f - 1$. The IAR reduction from Streett to parity games ensures that for every play in G, the limsup of the Streett distance sequence is bounded by $d! \cdot d^2$ times the limsup of the parity distance sequence for the corresponding play in G'.

Theorem 5 (Finitary Streett games). *Given a game graph G with n states, m edges, and a set P of d Streett pairs, let G' be the game graph with $n \cdot d! \cdot d^2$*

states and $m \cdot d! \cdot d^2$ edges, and let p be the corresponding priority function with $O(d)$ priorities, obtained by the IAR construction. For a play ω' in G', let ω be the corresponding play in G. If $\limsup_{k \to \infty} dist_k(\omega', p) = \alpha < \infty$, then $\limsup_{k \to \infty} dist_k(\omega, P) \leq \alpha \cdot d! \cdot d^2$, and if $\limsup_{k \to \infty} dist_k(\omega', p) = \infty$, then $\limsup_{k \to \infty} dist_k(\omega, P) = \infty$.

Hence solving games with finitary Streett objectives can be reduced to solving games with finitary parity objectives. Using Theorem 2, Theorem 3, and Theorem 4 we obtain the following corollary.

Corollary 3. *For all game graphs with n states and m edges, and all sets P of d Streett pairs, the following assertions hold.*

1. $W_1(\text{finStreett}(P)) = S \setminus W_2(\Omega \setminus \text{finStreett}(P))$.
2. $W_1(\text{finStreett}(P))$ *can be computed in* $O((n \cdot d! \cdot d^2)^{2d-3} \cdot m \cdot d! \cdot d^3)$ *time.*
3. *There exists a finite-memory winning strategy for player 1 with respect to the objective* $\text{finStreett}(P)$. *However, in general no finite-memory strategy exists for player 2 with respect to the complementary objective* $\Omega \setminus \text{finStreett}(P)$.

It follows that whether a state lies in $W_1(\text{finStreett}(P))$ can be decided in EXPTIME. The exact complexity of the problem remains open.

References

1. B. Alpern and F.B. Schneider. Defining liveness. *Information Processing Letters*, 21:181–185, 1985.
2. R. Alur and T.A. Henzinger. Finitary fairness. In *Proc. Logic in Computer Science*, pages 52–61. IEEE Computer Society, 1994.
3. R. Alur, T.A. Henzinger, and O. Kupferman. Alternating-time temporal logic. *J. ACM*, 49:672–713, 2002.
4. N. Dershowitz, D.N. Jayasimha, and S. Park. Bounded fairness. In *Verification: Theory and Practice*, pages 304–317. LNCS 2772, Springer, 2003.
5. E.A. Emerson and C. Jutla. The complexity of tree automata and logics of programs. In *Proc. Foundations of Computer Science*, pages 328–337. IEEE Computer Society, 1988.
6. Y. Gurevich and L. Harrington. Trees, automata, and games. In *Proc. Symp. Theory of Computing*, pages 60–65. ACM, 1982.
7. F. Horn. Streett games on finite graphs. *Workshop on Games in Design and Verification*, 2005.
8. M. Jurdzinski. Small progress measures for solving parity games. In *Symp. Theoretical Aspects of Computer Science*, pages 290–301. LNCS 1770, Springer, 2000.
9. Z. Manna and A. Pnueli. *The Temporal Logic of Reactive and Concurrent Systems: Specification*. Springer, 1992.
10. D.A. Martin. Borel determinacy. *Annals of Mathematics*, 102:363–371, 1975.
11. A. Pnueli and R. Rosner. On the synthesis of a reactive module. In *Proc. Principles of Programming Languages*, pages 179–190. ACM, 1989.
12. P.J. Ramadge and W.M. Wonham. Supervisory control of a class of discrete-event processes. *SIAM J. Control and Optimization*, 25:206–230, 1987.
13. W. Thomas. Languages, automata, and logic. In *Handbook of Formal Languages*, volume 3, pages 389–455. Springer, 1997.

Efficient Model Checking for LTL with Partial Order Snapshots

Peter Niebert[1] and Doron Peled[2]

[1] Laboratoire d'Informatique Fondamentale de Marseille,
CMI, 39, rue Joliot Curie, 13453 Marseille Cedex 13, France
[2] Department of Computer Science, University of Warwick,
Coventry CV4 7AL, United Kingdom

Abstract. Certain behavioral properties of distributed systems are difficult to express in interleaving semantics, whereas they are naturally expressed in terms of partial orders of events or, equivalently, Mazurkiewicz traces. Examples of such properties are serializability of a database or *snapshots*. Recently, a modest extension for LTL by an operator that expresses snapshots has been proposed. It combines the ease of linear (interleaving) specification with this useful partial order concept. The new construct allows one to assert that a global snapshot (also called a *slice* or a *cut*) was passed, perhaps not in the observed (interleaved) execution sequence, but possibly in a (trace) equivalent one. A model checking algorithm was suggested for a subset of this logic, with PSPACE complexity in the size of the system and the checked formula. For the whole logic, a solution that is in EXSPACE in the size of the system (PSPACE in the number of its global states) was given.

In this paper, we provide a model checking algorithm in PSPACE in the size of a system of communicating sequential processes when restricting snapshots to boolean combinations of local properties of each process. Concerning size of the formula, it is PSPACE for the case of snapshot properties expressed in DNF, and EXPSPACE where a translation to DNF is necessary.

1 Introduction

Automatic verification of concurrent systems is highly challenging. The exponential growth of the state space with the number of processes makes the problem intractable, as well as all the more important. Except for the intractability issue, one needs also to consider expressiveness, i.e., the ability to formulate the desired properties of the verified system. These two issues are not independent, as increasing the expressiveness may also increase complexity. The goal is therefore to find a formalism that can express common and useful specifications in a compact way, while still having a relatively efficient decision procedure.

Traditionally, concurrent systems are modeled using interleaving semantics, where occurrence of actions from different processes appear in either order in different execution sequences. Intuitively, sequences that differ only in the relative order of such occurrences can be considered as two representations for the same behavior. However, the interleaving model does not make any use of this

H. Hermanns and J. Palsberg (Eds.): TACAS 2006, LNCS 3920, pp. 272–286, 2006.
© Springer-Verlag Berlin Heidelberg 2006

observation. The interleaving model is rather simple, and as such enjoys the benefit of using powerful mathematical tools for verification, e.g., based on finite automata [11]. The partial order model has been extensively studied within concurrency theory. It offers a more intuitive view than the interleaving semantics, as concurrent occurrences appear unordered, rather than one after another. However, formalisms that are based on that model and include global states have turned out to have highly intractable computational complexity. For example, EXSPACE-complete for the *until-free* version of ISTL [8, 1], and non-elementary for LTrL [1, 10].

This situation promoted a debate about the practicality of using the partial order model in automatic verification. Independent of this debate, practice shows that to a large extent, using the interleaving model for concurrency is sufficient in most cases. On the other hand, there are some cases where it is highly beneficial to exploit the connection between the interleaving and partial order models. In particular, one can consider all the linearizations (completions into total orders) of a partial order as equivalent; indistinguishable from each other for an observer that can simultaneously compare local states at multiple processes. Although not very common, such a distinction is made in some concurrent algorithms. One example of this is the calculation of global *snapshots* [2], i.e., a distributed global state of the system. Such a snapshot may not appear on an interleaving sequence in which it is accumulated, but rather on an equivalent one. Another example is database serializability, where transactions are designed to appear one after another in at least one representative out of every equivalence class of sequences.

The challenge here is therefore to design a specification formalism that allows using the traditional interleaving view, yet allow expressing some useful partial order aspects. Moreover, we would like to keep the complexity as low as possible. As learned from the high complexity of temporal logics with global states, we aim at a modest extension. We follow [4], where the logic LTL was expanded with the *snapshot operator* $[p]$, with p a propositional formula. The new operator asserts that a global snapshot satisfying p appears in the past on some interleaving sequence equivalent to the current one. This logic was titled in [4] *SLTL*, for Snapshot Linear Temporal Logic.

A model checking algorithm for SLTL was given in [4]. The complexity of this logic was rather high. Given a verified system B with set of actions Σ and an SLTL property φ, the space complexity was polynomial in $2^{|B|+|\Sigma|} + |\varphi|$, where $|B|$ is the size of the system calculated by adding the size of the local processes. For comparison, model checking for LTL can be done in space complexity polynomial in $\mathcal{O}(|B| + |\varphi|)$.

In this paper we provide a more efficient algorithm tailored for synchronous communication systems in the style of CSP [5]. This means that each action is either local to one process or synchronously involving groups (pairs) of processes (changing their local states simultaneously). Moreover, we restrict specifying snapshots by using Boolean combinations of propositional assertions expressing properties of local states. For example, we do not allow a proposition q that asserts that the sum of a variable x of process p_1 and y of process p_2 is even.

Instead, we may need to have a proposition q_1 representing that x is *even* and q_2 representing that y is even, and can replace q by $q_1 \leftrightarrow q_2$.

Under these definitions, we give a new model checking algorithm for SLTL with space complexity polynomial in $(|B| + 2^{|\varphi|})$. The substantial improvement over previous work is that the current algorithm is PSPACE in terms of the system description, which is typically the big part of the input. Moreover, the exponential complexity in the formula results from the requirement of the construction that occurrences of the snapshot operator $[p]$ are applied to propositional formulas in disjunctive normal form. In transforming arbitrary boolean properties to DNF, an exponential blowup may occur. When restricting occurrences of the snapshot operator to formulae in DNF, the space complexity is polynomial in $(|B| + |\varphi|)$.

Our construction introduces *freeze automata*, which are capable of determining the first state in the computation where we subsumed some global snapshot from an equivalent execution.

We believe that our model checking algorithm, whose complexity is not far worse than that for LTL, makes model checking using partial order with snapshot practical, as opposed to the high complexity of using previous such temporal logics.

The paper is structured as follows. In Section 2, we formalize communication sequential processes as a model of concurrent systems. In Section 3, we recall Snapshot LTL, slightly adapted to the model proposed in Section 2. In Section 4, we present the new model checking algorithm, prove its correctness and analyze its complexity.

2   Preliminaries

Communicating Sequential Processes

We first give a simple model of communicating sequential processes [5]. A system of communicating sequential processes is a structure B with the following components:

1. *Proc* is a finite set of processes,
2. Σ_x an alphabet of actions for every $x \in Proc$.
3. P_x a set of local properties for every $x \in Proc$, such that $P_x \cap P_y = \emptyset$ for $x \neq y$.
4. S_x a set of local-states of the process x for every $x \in Proc$, $s_x^0 \in S_x$ the initial state.
5. $\lambda_x : S_x \longrightarrow 2^{P_x}$ an evaluation function of local properties for every $x \in Proc$.
6. $\delta_x : S_x \times \Sigma_x \longrightarrow S_x$ the deterministic transition function. The functions δ_x are *partial* in the sense that $\delta_x(s_x, a)$ does not have to be defined. If it is defined, we say that a is *enabled* at s_x, otherwise, a is *disabled*.

Note that we do not require the local alphabets to be disjoint. Common actions are used to synchronize local processes, giving rise to a global transition system.

The *transition system* for B is a structure $T_B = \langle S, \Sigma, \delta, s_0, P, \lambda \rangle$, where

1. $S = \prod_{x \in Proc} S_x$,
2. $\Sigma = \bigcup_{x \in Proc} \Sigma_x$ the global alphabet of actions,

3. $\delta : S \times \Sigma \longrightarrow S$ the global transition relation with $\delta(\Pi_{x \in Proc}(s_x), a) = \Pi_{x \in Proc}(t_x)$ iff for all x with $a \notin \Sigma_x$ it holds that $s_x = t_x$ (non participants do not change state), $t_x = \delta_x(s_x, a)$ and a is enabled from s_x for each process x such that $a \in \Sigma_x$.
4. $s_0 = \Pi_{x \in Proc}(s_x^0)$,
5. $P = \bigcup_{x \in Proc} P_x$.
6. $\lambda : S \longrightarrow 2^P$ such that for $p \in P_y$ it holds that $p \in \lambda(\Pi_{x \in Proc}(s_x))$ iff $p \in \lambda_y(s_y)$.

For convenience, we inductively extend the transition function δ to words: $\delta(s, \varepsilon) = s$ and $\delta(s, ua) = \delta(\delta(s, u), a)$. Denote $proc(a) = \{x | a \in \Sigma_x\}$, and extend it to $proc(v) = \bigcup_i \{proc(a_i) | v = a_1 a_2 \ldots a_n\}$.

For simplicity, we assume that δ is total, i.e., for every state $s \in S$ there exists some $a \in \Sigma$ and $s' \in S$ such that $\delta(s, a) = s'$. An *execution* of B is an infinite sequence $v \in \Sigma^\omega$ such that $v = a_0 a_1 a_2 \ldots$ and there exists an infinite sequence of states from S, $g_0 g_1 g_2 \ldots$ where,

1. $g_0 = s_0$, i.e., the sequence starts with the initial state of B.
2. $s_{i+1} = \delta(s_i, a_i)$, for $i \geq 0$.

Trace Equivalence

Based on B, we define an independence relation on Σ, the irreflexive and symmetric relation $I \subseteq \Sigma \times \Sigma$, such that $a \, I \, b$ iff $proc(a) \cap proc(b) = \emptyset$. For two words $u, v \in \Sigma^*$, write $u \stackrel{1}{\equiv} v$ if there exist words w_1, w_2 and letters a, b such that $(a, b) \in I$, $u = w_1 ab w_2$ and $v = w_1 ba w_2$, i.e., if u is obtained from v by exchanging the order of two adjacent independent letters. Let $\equiv$ be the reflexive and transitive closure of the relation $\stackrel{1}{\equiv}$. We say that u and v are *trace equivalent* [6] over (Σ, I) if $u \equiv v$. That is, u is trace equivalent to v if u can be obtained from v by repeatedly commuting adjacent independent letters.

By simple induction, if u and v are trace equivalent, then $\delta(s, u) = \delta(s, v)$ and this holds in particular at $s = s_0$, the initial state. Let $a \in \Sigma$ and $p \in P_x$ for some x. Then we say that a is *visible* w.r.t. p if $a \in \Sigma_x$, *invisible* otherwise. If a is invisible w.r.t. p, then in particular $p \in \lambda(s)$ iff $p \in \lambda(\delta(s, a))$ for any state s.

A *global execution sequence* (or *interleaving sequence*) $\xi = g_0 a_0 g_1 a_1 g_2 \ldots$ of B is an infinite (alternating) sequence in $(S \times \Sigma)^\omega$ such that $g_0 = s_0$, and for each $i \geq 0$ we have $g_{i+1} = \delta(g_i, a_i)$. Note, that this sequence is determined by the infinite sequence $a_0 a_1 \ldots \in \Sigma^\omega$ because B is deterministic.

Denote by $u \prec v$ the fact that u is a finite prefix of v.

Definition 1. *The* limit extension $\approx^{\lim} \subseteq \Sigma^\omega \times \Sigma^\omega$ *of an equivalence relation* $\approx \subseteq \Sigma^* \times \Sigma^*$ *is defined by* $w_1 \approx^{\lim} w_2$ *if and only if*

- *for every* $u \in \Sigma^*$ *such that* $u \prec w_1$ *there exist* $v, v' \in \Sigma^*$ *such that* $v \prec w_2$ *and* $uv' \approx v$, *and*
- *for every* $u \in \Sigma^*$ *such that* $u \prec w_2$ *there exist* $v, v' \in \Sigma^*$ *such that* $v \prec w_1$ *and* $uv' \approx v$.

Two infinite words w_1 and w_2 are said to be *trace equivalent* if $w_1 \equiv^{\lim} w_2$. We denote trace equivalence for both finite and infinite words by using $\equiv$. A *trace* is then defined to be such an equivalence class. We sometimes denote a trace by writing one representative of the equivalence class in square brackets, e.g., when aIb and aIc but $\neg bIc$, $[abac] = \{baac, abac, aabc, baca, abca\,bcaa\}$. The alphabet and independence relation should be clear from the context. We say that a trace $[u]$ *subsumes* $[v]$, denoted $[v] \sqsubseteq [u]$ if there exists some v' such that $u \equiv vv'$.

3   Snapshot Linear Temporal Logic

We recall the definition of Snapshot Linear Temporal Logic (SLTL) as an extension of LTL with a construct for dealing with snapshots. We call the new extension *Snapshot Linear Temporal Logic* or SLTL. Let P be the finite set of propositional formulas of a system of communicating sequential processes. Let $Bool(P)$ be the set of Boolean combinations with propositions over P.

$$\varphi ::= (\varphi) \mid \neg\varphi \mid \varphi \vee \varphi \mid \varphi \wedge \varphi \mid \bigcirc\varphi \mid \Box\varphi \mid \Diamond\varphi \mid \varphi\mathcal{U}\varphi \mid \varphi\mathcal{V}\varphi \mid q \mid [q]$$

where $q \in Bool(P)$. Note that the '[ ]' construct is applied only to a Boolean expression of local propositions, never to a formula with modalities. Note also that we use square brackets for two different (although related) notions: for trace equivalence classes, as in the previous section, and in the SLTL logic to denote that a Boolean combination holds in a subsumed snapshot.

The semantic interpretation of SLTL with respect to a system B is defined over a pair of sequences $u \in \Sigma^\star$ and $v \in \Sigma^\omega$.

- $(u, v) \models \bigcirc\varphi$ iff for some $a \in \Sigma$ such that $v = av'$ it holds that $(ua, v') \models \varphi$.
- $(u, v) \models \varphi\mathcal{U}\psi$ iff there exists w, v', where $v = wv'$, such that $(uw, v') \models \psi$ and for any decomposition $w = w_1 w_2$ where w_2 is nonempty, $(uw_1, w_2v) \models \varphi$.
- $(u, v) \models \neg\varphi$ iff it is not the case that $(u, v) \models \varphi$.
- $(u, v) \models \varphi \vee \psi$ iff either $(u, v) \models \varphi$ or $(u, v) \models \psi$.
- $(u, v) \models p$ iff $p \in \lambda(\delta(s_0, u))$.
- $(u, v) \models [q]$ iff there exist a sequence $u_1, u_2 \in \Sigma^\star$ such that $u \equiv u_1u_2$ and $(u_1, u_2v) \models q$. Note that since q is restricted to be a boolean combination of atomic propositions, this depends only on a subsumed trace $[u_1] \sqsubseteq [u]$ and the set of satisfied propositions $\lambda(\delta(s_0, u_1))$.

For the rest of the temporal operators, their semantics is implied by the following definitions as usual: $\varphi \wedge \psi = \neg((\neg\varphi) \vee (\neg\psi))$, $\varphi \to \psi = (\neg\varphi) \vee \psi$, $\varphi\mathcal{V}\psi = \neg((\neg\varphi)\mathcal{U}(\neg\psi))$, $true = p \vee \neg p$, $false = p \wedge \neg p$, $\Box\varphi = false\mathcal{V}\varphi$, and $\Diamond\varphi = true\mathcal{U}\varphi$.

We recall some properties of the snapshot operator:

$\Box([p] \to \Box[p])$ Monotonicity of the snapshot operator.
$\Box(p \to [p])$
$\Box(([p \wedge q]) \to [p] \wedge [q])$
$\Box(([p] \vee [q]) \leftrightarrow [p \vee q])$
$\Box(\neg[p] \to [\neg p])$

A formula φ holds for a system (or program) B (written $B \models \varphi$) iff $(\varepsilon, u) \models \varphi$ for every execution u of B, $u \in \Sigma^\omega$. Given B and φ, the model checking problem is to verify whether $B \models \varphi$, or, equivalently, if there exists an execution u such that $(\varepsilon, u) \models \neg\varphi$.

We refer to each state subsumed by the execution as a *snapshot*. Formally, a snapshot of an infinite execution u of a system B is any state s such that there exists a finite prefix v of u with $u = v\,w$, $[v] = [v_1 v_2]$ and $s = \delta(s_0, v_1)$. Thus, the "S" in SLTL, which stands for "snapshot" refers to the ability of the logic to refer also to subsumed states, rather than only to the states appearing on a given execution sequence.

Consider the formula $\Box\varphi \wedge \Diamond[\psi]$, where φ and ψ are Boolean combinations of local properties of the involved processes. It asserts that φ holds in every state of an execution, while ψ holds on a snapshot of at least one equivalent sequence, but not necessarily the observed one, as opposed to the usual LTL formula $\Box\varphi \wedge \Diamond\psi$. The formula $(\neg[\varphi])\mathcal{U}[\psi]$ means that φ does not hold for any snapshot subsumed by states of the execution until the first state that subsumes a snapshot satisfying ψ. This can be compared to $(\neg\varphi)U\psi$, in which φ and ψ only refer to the states on the current execution sequence. For more motivation for the SLTL logic, refer to [4].

In [4], a model checking algorithm for Snapshot LTL was given. It is in EX-PSPACE with a space complexity of $\mathcal{O}(|S| \times 2^{|\Sigma|} \times |\varphi|)$. Note, that the complexity is actually EXPSPACE in $|B|$. This is due to the fact that the algorithm remembers sets of visited states. For a sublogic with only negative occurrences of the snapshot operator $[q]$, a PSPACE algorithm was given.

3.1   Elements of the Original Snapshot Construction

In [4], the algorithm for model checking SLTL uses particular components based on remembering past global states, which is the source of its EXPSPACE complexity.

The core of that construction is a deterministic automaton that remembers subsumed states. Formally, for a sequence u we keep track of all states s such that $[u] = [u_1 u_2]$ and $s = \delta(s_0, u_1)$, even when u_1 is a proper prefix of u. In order to find these global states, more information is required. As a first attempt, we could remember all pairs (s, u_2) for this decomposition. A state of such an automaton, which keeps track of subsumed states thus, consists of a set of such pairs. It always contains the pair $(\delta(u), \epsilon)$ with the current state $\delta(u)$ obtained from the initial state s_0 after executing the sequence u. When performing a transition and appending the action a to u (thus arriving at the prefix ua), this induces the substitution of (s, u_2) by $(s, u_2 a)$. If a is independent of all of u_2, another state is subsumed, as is expressed by the pair $(\delta(s, a), u_2)$. It can be shown that this approach actually maintains all subsumed states (with the information how to go "backwards" to them). However, because of keeping sequences of actions, the set of pairs maintained in this way may be infinite.

Now observe that the only relevant aspect of u_2 (as in $[u_1 u_2]$) is whether an appended label a is fully independent of u_2 or not. Hence, instead of having a sequence component u_2 in a pair, as above, u_2 can be abstracted to information representing dependency. In [4] this is done by remembering the set of occurring labels, thus the "subsumed states tracker" contains, in addition to the current state, pairs (s, A), where $s \in S$ and $A \subseteq \Sigma$.

- The number of pairs of such a tracker is $2^{S \times 2^{\Sigma}}$, and the memory required for representation of a tracker is thus $|S| \times 2^{|\Sigma|}$ bits. Note that typically $|S|$ is already exponential in the number of concurrent components.
- The initial tracker is $\{(s_0, \emptyset)\}$.
- For a tracker M and an action a, the successor tracker is the least set M' such that if $(s, A) \in M$,
    1. $(s, A \cup \{a\}) \in M'$,
    2. $(\delta(s, a), A) \in M'$ if for all $b \in A$ we have $a \, I \, b$.

Then, given a snapshot formula $[q]$ the automaton has as accepting states those that include a pair (s, A) such that $\lambda(s)$ implies the satisfaction of q at s. It was shown in [4], that without assumptions on the properties that could be satisfied by arbitrary subsets of the set of states, no smaller deterministic automaton accepting $[q]$ prefixes exists.

In this paper, we follow a different path by looking in more detail on the structure of the properties in the snapshot operator.

4   A New Model Checking Algorithm

The construction given in this paper is based on a generic LTL model checking procedure, augmented with additional components for the snapshot formulas.

4.1   Freeze Automaton

Let $q = \bigwedge_{i \in Proc} q_i$ be a conjunction of local state properties (that is, each $q_i \in Bool(P_i)$). With respect to the full logic, this restriction excludes, for instance, disjunctions between propositions of distinct processes. We will see later how to treat the general case. For simplicity, we assume a conjunct for every process, hence this can include in particular $q_i = true$.

We present a construction of a deterministic *freeze automaton* that recognizes prefixes u of sequences uv such that $(u, v) \models [q]$.

- The *states* of the freeze automaton $freeze(\bigwedge_{i \in Proc} q_i)$ are pairs $(s, \{F_1, \ldots, F_k\})$ of a system state s and a set of *freeze sets* $F_j \subseteq Proc$. Each such set F_j represents a subset of the processes where a collection of local states that satisfy a part of the above conjunction were found. Namely $\bigwedge_{i \in F_j} q_i$. Furthermore, this collection of local states can still be potentially completed after u into a full state that satisfies q.

    We add a flag that is set to *true* when we have in the state a freeze set that contains all the processes. Subsequently, the flag remains *true* and thereafter we do not need to update the freeze sets.
- The *initial state* is the set of all subsets of $\{i \mid q_i \in \lambda(s_0)\}$.
- The *successor relation* is defined as follows. Let $a \in \Sigma$ and (s, G) with $G = \{F_1, \ldots, F_k\}$ some set of freeze sets, s a state of the system and $s' = \delta(s, a)$

the successor system state and $addproc(s, a) = \{j \mid a \in \Sigma_j \wedge q_j \in \lambda(\delta(s, a))\}$ the set of processes participating in a such that their parts of the state property q are satisfied after the transition a. Then the successor state in the freeze set automaton is (s', G') where G' is the least set such that

extension For every $F_1 \subseteq addproc(s, a)$ and every $F_2 \in G$ such that $proc(a) \cap F_2 = \emptyset$ we have $F_1 \cup F_2 \in G'$. Note that F_1, F_2 can also include here the empty set.

This is the case where we can extend (or propagate, when $F_2 = \emptyset$) a freeze set from a previous state with some processes; these processes are not in the old freeze set and have just participated in the execution of the most recent action, and furthermore their new local states satisfy the corresponding literals of the conjunction q.

propagation For every $F \in G$ with $proc(a) \subseteq F$ also $F \in G'$.

This is the case where freeze sets propagate (without extension) from a previous state to the current one when the set of processes involved in the most recent action is included in the freeze set.

The crucial aspect of the freeze automata is given in the following lemma.

Lemma 1. *Let $u \in \Sigma^*$ and let (s, G) be the state of the freeze automaton reached after u (in particular $s = \delta(s_0, u)$), and let $F \subseteq Proc$ be some set of processes. Then $F \in G$ iff there exists a decomposition $[u] = [u_1 u_2]$ such that $proc(u_2) \subseteq F$ (actions in u_2 are limited to processes in F) and $q_j \in \lambda(\delta(s_0, u_1))$ for all $j \in F$.*

Proof. The lemma states an invariant, which we prove by induction on $|u|$.

In the case of $u = \varepsilon$ the obvious decomposition is $u_1 = u_2 = \varepsilon$ with $proc(u_1) = \emptyset \subseteq F$ for any $F \subseteq Proc$. The statement of the lemma then degenerates to the fact that $F \subseteq \{x \mid q_x \in \lambda(s_0)\}$, which corresponds precisely to the definition of the initial state of the freeze automaton.

Now let $u = u'a$, (s, G) be the state of the freeze automaton reached by $u'a$, and (s', G') be the state of the freeze automaton reached by u'.

$\Rightarrow$: Let $F \in G$. The inductive definition of the sets G allows for two cases (according to the two rules used in the transition relation of the freeze set automaton):

- By using the extension rule, there is some $F' \in G'$ with $F = F' \cup F''$ with $F'' \subseteq addproc(s', a) \subseteq proc(a)$ and moreover

$$F' \cap proc(a) = \emptyset. \tag{1}$$

Then apply by induction the lemma to u', F'. Let $u_1 = u_1'$ and $u_2 = u_2'$. We obtain a decomposition $[u'] = [u_1' u_2']$ with $[u_1' u_2' a] = [u'a]$, where

$$proc(u_2') \subseteq F' \tag{2}$$

and $q_x \in \lambda(\delta(s_0, u_1'))$ for each $x \in F'$. Because of (1) and (2), all actions in u_2' are independent of a and hence $[u_1' a u_2'] = [u_1' u_2' a]$. Thus, the actions in u_2 are also invisible for q_x for each $x \in F'' \subseteq proc(a)$, and we also obtain $q_x \in \lambda(\delta(s_0, u_1' a))$ for each $x \in F''$. Hence, the decomposition $[u'a] = [(u_1' a) u_2']$ satisfies the desired consequence.

- By using the propagation rule, $F \in G'$ and $proc(a) \subseteq F$. In this case, we apply the induction hypothesis to u' thus obtaining a decomposition $[u'] = [u'_1 u'_2]$ with $q_x \in \lambda(\delta(s_0, u'_1))$ for each $x \in F$ and $proc(u'_2) \subseteq F$ and we can extend it to a desired decomposition $[u] = [u_1 u_2]$ with $u_1 = u'_1$ and $u_2 = u'_2 a$.

$\Leftarrow$: Now let $[u'a] = [u_1 u_2]$ such that $proc(u_2) \subseteq F$ and $q_x \in \lambda(\delta(s_0, u_1))$ for all $x \in F$. We have to show that $F \in G$ for the set G reached by $u = u'a$. There are three cases concerning this decomposition:

- $proc(a) \subseteq F$. Then either (1a) a decomposition as required exists already for u', i.e. $[u'] = [u'_1 u'_2]$, $proc(u'_2) \subseteq F$, $q_x \in \lambda(\delta(s_0, u'_1))$ with $x \in F$, in which case the induction hypothesis will yield $F \in G'$ where G' is the set of freeze sets reached by u', which is preserved in G due to the propagation rule for freeze sets. Or (1b) a decomposition as required does not exist for u'. In this case, the decomposition $[u'a] = [u_1 u_2]$ with $q_x \in \lambda(\delta(s_0, u_1))$ for all $x \in F$ will not have a occur in u_2 and can be assumed to have it occur as last element of $u_1 = u'_1 a$, but then the decomposition $[u'] = [u'_1 u_2]$ (we simply remove a from u_1, where a is independent of u_2, the price is that we may modify its visible properties) satisfies all the preconditions for $F' = F \setminus proc(a)$. By independence of a with u_2, all the actions of u_2 are invisible for q_x, for each $x \in proc(a)$. Therefore, $g_x \in \lambda(\delta(s_0, u))$. By induction, $F' \in G'$ reached by u'. Thus, by the extension rule we obtain $F \in G$.
- $proc(a) \cap F = \emptyset$. Then we can assume for the decomposition $[u'a] = [u_1 u_2]$ that $u_1 = u'_1 a$, where a is independent of u_2, and we obtain a decomposition $[u'] = [u'_1 u_2]$ as required by the lemma and by induction we obtain $F \in G'$ and by the extension rule we obtain $F \in G$.
- There is a non trivial intersection $proc(a) \cap F \neq \emptyset$, but $proc(a) \not\subseteq F$. This case is quite similar to (1b) above, but here we partition F into $F' := F \setminus proc(a)$ and $F'' := F \cap proc(a)$. Thus, a cannot occur in u_2 and the decomposition of $[u] = [u_1 u_2]$ must have a occurring in $[u_1]$. Without loss of generality $u_1 = u'_1 a$, where $q_x \in \lambda(\delta(s_0, u'_1 a))$ for $q_x \in F$. Then we can apply the induction hypothesis to $[u'] = [u'_1 u_2]$ and F' to find $F' \in G'$. On the other hand, due to the invisibility with respect to the propositions $\cup \{P_x | x \in F''\}$ of all of u_2 (because of independence of u_2 w.r.t. a), we also have that $q_x \in \lambda(\delta(s_0, u'a))$ for all $x \in F''$, thus by the extension rule we obtain $F \in G$. $\square$

Corollary 1. *Let uv be some infinite execution and (s, G) be a state of the freeze automaton reached by a word u. Then $(u, v) \models [\bigwedge_{i \in Proc} q_i]$ iff $Proc \in G$.*

Proof. The case of $F = Proc$ in Lemma 1 means that there exists a decomposition $[u] = [u_1 u_2]$ with $q_x \in \lambda(\delta(s_0, u_1))$ for all $x \in Proc$. This means that the decomposition $[u] = [u_1 u_2]$ corresponds to the existence of a previous snapshot satisfying the conjunction. $\square$

This completes the correctness proof of the freeze automaton. However, a naive "implementation" of the set of freeze sets would require space exponential in the number of processes. Next, we show that a polynomial memory representation with an efficient update operation is possible. The first step is a technical observation:

Lemma 2. *For any state (s, G) reachable in the freeze automaton, the set of sets G is closed under arbitrary union and intersection and thus forms a complete lattice.*

Proof. The lemma states an invariant that we prove by induction: We have to show that the property is preserved over the execution of transitions. First note that invariantly $\emptyset \in G$. Since G is finite, to show closure under arbitrary union and intersection it is sufficient to show that $F_1, F_2 \in G$ implies $F_1 \cup F_2, F_1 \cap F_2 \in G$.

Now let (s', G') satisfy the property and let (s, G) be a successor state reached from it by executing $a \in \Sigma$. Let $F_1, F_2 \in G$. For each F_i there are two cases: (1) $F_i' := F_i \setminus proc(a) \in G'$ and for all $i \in proc(a) \cap F_i$ it holds that $s \models q_i$ (this corresponds to the extension rule) and (2) $proc(a) \subseteq F_i$, where $F_i = F_i' \in G'$ (this is the case of the propagation).

By induction, we know that $F_1' \cap F_2', F_1' \cup F_2' \in G'$. Now, there are several cases of combinations for the two sets F_1, F_2:

If both F_1, F_2 satisfy (1), then $F_1' \cap F_2' = (F_1 \setminus proc(a)) \cap (F_2 \setminus proc(a)) = (F_1 \cap F_2) \setminus proc(a) \in G'$, and for all $i \in (F_1 \cap proc(a) \cap (F_2 \cap proc(a))) = (F_1 \cap F_2) \cap proc(a)$ we have $s \models q_i$. Hence, by the extension rule, we obtain $F_1 \cap F_2 \in G$. Similarly, $F_1' \cup F_2' = (F_1 \setminus proc(a)) \cup (F_2 \setminus proc(a)) = (F_1 \cup F_2) \setminus proc(a) \in G$ and for all $i \in (F_1 \cap proc(a)) \cup (F_2 \cap proc(a)) = (F_1 \cup F_2) \cap proc(a)$ we have $s \models q_i$, thus by rule extension we have $(F_1 \cup F_2) \in G$.

If both satisfy (2), then one immediately finds $(F_1 \cap F_2), (F_1 \cup F_2) \in G'$ and $proc(a) \subseteq (F_1 \cap F_2) \subseteq F_1 \cup F_2$, hence, by the propagation rule we obtain $(F_1 \cap F_2), (F_1 \cup F_2) \in G$.

Now let one (say F_1) satisfy (1) and the other (F_2) satisfy (2), then $F_1 \setminus proc(a), F_2 \in G'$. Then $(F_1 \setminus proc(a)) \cap F_2 = (F_1 \cap F_2) \setminus proc(a) \in G'$ and for all $i \in proc(a) \cap (F_1 \cap F_2) \subseteq proc(a) \cap F_1$ we have $s \models q_i$ and hence by the rule extension we obtain $F_1 \cap F_2 \in G$. On the other hand, $(F_1 \setminus proc(a)) \cup F_2 = F_1 \cup F_2 \in G'$ as $proc(a) \subseteq F_2 \subseteq F_1 \cup F_2$, hence by the propagation rule $F_1 \cup F_2 \in G$. $\qquad\square$

The closure properties of sets of freeze sets of Lemma 2 allow us to keep a compact representation, where we do not represent sets that are unions of other sets. In terms of lattice theory, we represent the sublattice of the powerset lattice by a *minimal basis*, which is very small, as expressed by the following constructive formulation of Birkhoff's theorem on distributive lattices.

Definition 2. *Let S be a finite set of elements and $\mathcal{T} \subseteq 2^S$ a set of subsets S, such that $\emptyset \in \mathcal{T}$ and for $T_1, T_2 \in \mathcal{T}$ also $T_1 \cap T_2, T_1 \cup T_2 \in \mathcal{T}$. Let $\mathcal{B} \subseteq \mathcal{T}$ be the set of nonempty elements of $\mathcal{T}$ such that each element is not a trivial (i.e., of size one) union of any subset of $\mathcal{T}$.*

Proposition 1. *For every set $T \in \mathcal{T}$, (a) $T = \bigcup\{B \in \mathcal{B} \mid B \subseteq T\}$, i.e. $\mathcal{B}$ is a basis of $\mathcal{T}$ and (b) $|\mathcal{B}| \leq |\bigcup \mathcal{B}| \leq |S|$.*

Proof. Let us first define $U_i := \bigcap\{V \in \mathcal{T} \mid i \in V\}$ and observe that $U_i \in \mathcal{T}$ because of closure under intersection. In fact $U_i \in \mathcal{B}$ because if $U_i = V_1 \cup V_2$ either $i \in V_1$ (and hence $U_i = V_1$) or $i \in V_2$ (and hence $U_i = V_2$).

For claim (a), it suffices to observe that $V = \bigcup\{U_i \mid i \in V\}$. For claim (b), we will show that for each $V \in \mathcal{B}$, there exists some $i \in V$ such that $V = U_i$. By contradiction, suppose that this is not the case. Let $\mathcal{K} = \{U_i | i \in V\}$. Then $V \notin \mathcal{K}$. But $V = \bigcup \mathcal{K}$, which contradicts the fact that $V \in \mathcal{B}$. This gives a surjective function $\bigcup \mathcal{T} \longrightarrow \mathcal{B}$ (surjective since it can be that $U_i = U_j$ for $i \neq j$) and hence $|\mathcal{B}| \leq |\bigcup \mathcal{T}| \leq |S|$ as required. $\square$

Hence, we can represent a basis for freeze sets using a $|Proc|^2$ matrix where each row represents a basis set and each column represents an element. Unused rows can be filled with the empty set.

4.2   Updating Freeze Sets Bases

Let $\mathcal{B}_s$ be a basis for the freeze sets $\mathcal{G}_s$ at a state s, with action a occurring, producing a successor state s' with set of freeze sets $\mathcal{G}_{s'}$ with basis $\mathcal{B}_{s'}$. We describe now how to update $\mathcal{B}_s$ into $\mathcal{B}_{s'}$ using a polynomial amount of space and, in fact, polynomial time.

To understand the updating, we first construct a set C which will satisfy $\mathcal{B}_{s'} \subseteq C \subseteq \mathcal{G}_{s'}$. In a second step, C can be reduced by omitting elements that are non-trivial unions of other elements in the basis, so as to obtain $\mathcal{B}_{s'}$.

C is the least set such that:

1. If $F \in \mathcal{B}_s$ with $F \cap proc(a) = \emptyset$, then $F \in C$.
2. If $F \in \mathcal{B}_s$ with $proc(a) \subseteq F$, then $F \in C$.
3. If $proc(a) \subseteq \bigcup \mathcal{B}_s$, then for each $F' \in \mathcal{B}_s$ such that neither $F' \cap proc(a) = \emptyset$ nor $proc(a) \subseteq F'$, we have $F' \cup \bigcup_{x \in proc(a)} \bigcap \{F \in \mathcal{B}_s \mid x \in F\} \in C$.
4. If $x \in proc(a)$ such that $q_x \in \lambda(s')$, then $\{x\} \in C$.

We prove that $C \subseteq \mathcal{G}_{s'}$. It is sufficient to check that for each of the for cases, the corresponding set is added to $\mathcal{G}_{s'}$ either due to the extension rule or due to the propagation rule. Case 1 is added by extension with the empty set. Case 4 is added by extending the empty set. Case 2 is an obvious consequence of the propagation rule. To understand the slightly more complicated case 3, observe that $\mathcal{B}_s \subseteq \mathcal{G}_s$ and that due to the closure properties of $\mathcal{G}_s$ (union and intersection), the constructed sets are in $\mathcal{G}_s$ also; moreover by construction $proc(a) \subseteq F' \cup \bigcup_{x \in proc(a)} \bigcap \{F \in \mathcal{B}_s \mid x \in F\}$ and hence these sets are in $\mathcal{G}_{s'}$ by propagation.

Now we prove that $\mathcal{B}_{s'} \subseteq C$. For this, it is sufficient to check that every set in $\mathcal{G}_{s'}$ is a union of elements of C. First suppose some $F \in \mathcal{G}_{s'}$ is obtained by the extension rule. Then $F = F_1 \cup F_2$ with $F_1 \in \mathcal{G}_s$, $F_1 \cap proc(a) = \emptyset$ and $F_2 \subseteq \{x \in proc(a) \mid q_x \in \lambda(s')\}$. Now, F_2 is a union of the elements added to C under case 4, and F_1 is a union of sets F' in $\mathcal{B}_s$ which are added to C according to case 1. Suppose, on the other hand, that F is obtained by the propagation rule. To find that F is a union of sets in C let us consider a set $F' \in \mathcal{B}_s$ with $F' \subseteq F$. Now, either $F' \in C$ according to case 1 or 2 or F' is incomparable with $proc(a)$, therefore not propagated. But then, the preconditions of case 3 are satisfied, and $F' \cup \bigcup_{x \in proc(a)} \bigcap \{F_1 \in \mathcal{B}_s \mid x \in F_1\} \in C$. Moreover, for each $x \in proc(a)$ it holds that $\bigcap \{F_1 \in \mathcal{B}_s \mid x \in F_1\} \subseteq F$ (because for some F_1 with $x \in F_1$ it must hold that $F_1 \subseteq F$). Thus, we can conclude that $F' \cup \bigcup_{x \in proc(a)} \bigcap \{F_1 \in \mathcal{B}_s \mid x \in F_1\} \subseteq F$. Hence, for each set $F' \in \mathcal{B}_s$ with $F' \subseteq F$ we find a set $F'' \in C$ with $F' \subseteq F'' \subseteq F$, hence F is a union of sets in C.

The size of C is limited by $|\mathcal{B}_s| + |proc(a)|$, because for each set in $\mathcal{B}_s$, at most one set is added to C according to the disjoint cases 1, 2 and 3. Additionally case 4 results in some singletons. More coarsely, $|C| \leq 2 \cdot |Proc|$ (see Proposition 1), and the update can be performed with $3 \times |Proc|$ sets, or $\mathcal{O}(|Proc|^2)$ space. The time requirement of computing C is easily seen to be equally $\mathcal{O}(|Proc|^2)$. The identification of a subset $\mathcal{B}_{s'}$ can be done on the same space by first ordering the vectors representing elements of C by set size (this can be done in $\mathcal{O}(|Proc|^2 \times \log_2(|Proc|))$ steps) and then searching for each $x \in Proc$ the first set F containing it (in $\mathcal{O}(|Proc| \times \log_2(|Proc|))$ steps), finally compressing the list by eliminating the sets that are not minimal sets of any element (in $\mathcal{O}(|Proc|^2)$ steps), all in essentially the space of memory containing C (additional $2 \times |Proc|$ bits are needed to mark elements in C).

4.3   Integration into a Model Checking Algorithm

We assume that in the negated property $\neg\varphi$, the (negative) occurrences of the snapshot operator only occur as conjunctions $[\bigwedge_{i \in Proc} q_i]$ as given in Section 4.1. In a more general setting, the observation that $[\varphi \vee \psi]$ is equivalent to $[\varphi] \vee [\psi]$ can be used to distribute the snapshot operator over disjunctions with an at most linear growth of the size of the formula (each disjunction potentially introducing an additional snapshot operator). In the case of arbitrary boolean properties, a translation to DNF has to be applied first, leading to a potentially exponential blowup of the formula.

The freeze automaton is deterministic, it thus can be used to determine both the satisfaction of positive and negative occurrences of $[q]$ provided that q is of the form indicated above. Pragmatically, the construction can be optimized using sharing of data structures on several levels (the system state space is needed just once, for instance).

In order to check that a concurrent system B satisfies a property φ, we intersect several automata components as follows. For optimizing on space complexity, we perform a binary search, hence do not fully construct the components. Instead, we only need to be able to enumerate pairs of successor states.

- The verified system B. This can be itself obtained as an asynchronous product of several subcomponents, one per each processor, as described in Section 2.
- For each snapshot formula $[\bigwedge_{i \in Proc} q_i]$ occurring in $\neg\varphi$ we construct a component $freeze(\bigwedge_{i \in Proc} q_i)$ as above (basis representation). Recall that each such component has states that include sets of subsets of processes, whereas they can share the access to B (the states S). The transition between two such states is marked by an action. If a state of $freeze(\bigwedge_{i \in Proc} q_i)$ contains a component that includes all the processes, then $[\bigwedge_{i \in Proc} q_i]$ holds thereafter. A special stable flag marks this situation.

- A component $\mathcal{A}_{\neg\varphi}$ for the Büchi translation of $\neg\varphi$. We keep the snapshot subformulas $[d]$ unprocessed as if they were special new propositions. According to the translation algorithm in [3], $\neg\varphi$ is written in a *negated normal form* first, and $[d]$ may appear negated or non-negated.

The product of these components enforces the following correspondences:

- Between a triple (s, a, s') with $\delta(s, a) = s'$ of the checked system B and a triple (t_i, b_i, t'_i) of $freeze(\bigwedge_{i \in Proc} q_i)$:
  - $a = b_i$.
  - The freeze sets of t'_i are updated from t_i according to a and the state s', as explained above. In particular, it depends on whether the components of s that belong to the processes of a satisfy the local predicates of $\bigwedge_{i \in Proc} q_i$.
- Between the collection of triples (t_i, b_i, t'_i) of $freeze(\bigwedge_{i \in Proc} q_i)$ and a triple (r, c, r') of the property automaton $\mathcal{A}_{\neg\varphi}$. The node r contains propositions and snapshot subformulas negated or non-negated, according to the case where they need to hold or not in the current state. Accordingly, if r contains $[q]$ where $q = \bigwedge_{i \in Proc} q_i$, then we will have that t_i (and thus also t'_i) indicates that $[\bigwedge_{i \in Proc} q_i]$ was detected. Conversely, if r contains $\neg[\bigwedge_{i \in Proc} q_i]$ then for each t_i we must have not yet detected $\bigwedge_{i \in Proc} q_i$.
- Between triples (s, a, s') of B and (r, c, r') of $\mathcal{A}_\varphi$ we have the usual correspondence, i.e., that r and s (and r' and s') agree on propositions.

The space needed for a single state of the constructed Büchi automaton is thus the sum of the space needed for a state of B (that is $\mathcal{O}(|B|)$), the space needed for the property automaton $\mathcal{A}_{\neg\varphi}$ which requires $\mathcal{O}(|\varphi|)$ bits, and the space required for the freeze automata (without the B component, which is shared). Each freeze automaton thus requires $|Proc|^2$ bits to store the basis of the set of freeze sets and there is one for every snapshot formula $[q]$, which we bound by $\mathcal{O}(|\varphi| \times |Proc|^2)$. A single state thus requires $\mathcal{O}(|B| + |\varphi| + |\varphi| \times |Proc|^2) = \mathcal{O}(|B| + |\varphi| \times |Proc|^2) \leq \mathcal{O}(|\varphi| \times |B|^2)$ bits, the algorithm (based on binary search) requiring $\mathcal{O}((|B| + |\varphi| \times |Proc|^2)^2)$ bits, which subsumes the $\mathcal{O}(|Proc|^2)$ space needed for the computation of successors on bases. This was based on the assumption that φ only contained occurrences of the snapshot operator with conjunctions of local properties as required in Section 4.1. To obtain them, a transformation to DNF of properties in some snapshot operators may be necessary, resulting in a potentially exponential blowup of the size of φ. Taking this step into account thus gives us $\mathcal{O}(|B| + 2^{|\varphi|} \times |Proc|^2)$ bits per state and $\mathcal{O}((|B| + 2^{|\varphi|} \times |Proc|^2)^2)$ bits for the algorithm.

4.4   Optimization for Negative Snapshots

In searching for a counter example, a negative occurrence of some $[q]$ in φ becomes a positive occurrence in $\neg\varphi$. On a given infinite sequence v, either $[q]$ never holds or there is a first prefix, i.e. a first decomposition $v = v_1 v_2$ such that $(v_1, v_2) \models [q]$, i.e. there exists a trace decomposition $[v_1] = [v'_1 v''_1]$ such that $(v'_1, v''') \models q$, where $v_1' v''' = v_1 v_2$. Then choosing $q' := \bigwedge \lambda(\delta(s_0, v'_1))$ provides a formula which implies q and such that on v the snapshot formula $[q]$ holds exactly where $[q']$ holds. Hence, a non-deterministic freeze automaton for $[q]$ first guesses a truth assignment implying q and then runs as normal. In terms of DNF, this automaton guesses a witness minterm of q transformed to DNF. On any run where this non-deterministic freeze automaton says that $[q']$ holds we know that $[q]$ holds and conversely for a sequence where $[q]$ holds there exists a guess q' such that $[q']$ is observed in the freeze automaton and this guess can be done in a coherent manner for all prefixes satisfying $[q]$.

Note that this optimization relies on a construction that does not force every state of the property automaton $\mathcal{A}_{\neg\varphi}$ to have each snapshot formula either negated or non-negated (i.e., a construction in the style of [3] rather than as in [11] needs to be used). This trick allows to enumerate the satisfying truth assignments of the different such positive subformulas separately. This may induce an exponential number of repetitions, but does not increase space. Unfortunately, this trick does not work for positive occurrences of formulas of the type $\neg[q]$ in φ. It is interesting to observe that in [4], the negated snapshots also make an easier case, treated by a separate construction called *lazy automata*.

5 Conclusion

We described in this paper a refined model checking algorithm for Snapshot Linear Temporal Logic. Due to a refined analysis we were able to obtain an algorithm with PSPACE-Complexity in terms of the system description, albeit EXPSPACE in the size of the formula - unless the use of the Snapshot operator is restricted to, essentially, disjunctive normal form. An open problem remains to prove non-trivial lower bounds for the space complexity in terms of the properties.

Moreover, our analysis was based on boolean combinations of local properties, whereas certain uses of the snapshot operator might require global properties (like the sum of integer variables of the processes, etc), where the approach applied here cannot be applied directly. However, depending on the nature of the properties, a compromise between the state storing approach of [4] and the symbolic approach here may be possible: by freezing one process, one might symbolically induce a property remaining to be satisfied for the other processes. If for example the global property is $x_1 + x_2 > 5$ and x_1 of process 1 is frozen when $x_1 = 3$, the remaining property can be factored to $x_2 > 2$ without full knowledge of the state of process 1.

We believe that our construction is of value beyond model checking: The fact that the freeze automaton is deterministic with a polynomial time computable successor function suggests use in further applications, where one might actually want to implement and execute it, for instance in the domain of testing.

Acknowledgements

This work was done while the second author was on visit as invited professor at the Université de Provence, Marseille. The authors thank Blaise Genest for useful comments on a previous version of the paper.

References

1. Rajeev Alur, Ken McMillan, Doron Peled. Deciding Global Partial-Order Properties. In *ICALP 1998*, LNCS 1443, 41–52.
2. K. M. Chandy, L. Lamport, Distributed Snapshots: determining the global state of distributed systems, ACM Transactions on Computer Systems 3 (1985), 63–75.
3. R. Gerth, D. Peled, M. Vardi, P. Wolper, Simple on-the-fly automatic verification of linear temporal logic, PSTV 1995, 3–18.
4. B. Genest, D. Kuske, A. Muscholl, D. Peled, Snaphot Verification, TACAS 2005, LNCS 3440, 510-525.
5. C. A. R. Hoare. Communicating Sequential Processes Communication of the ACM 21 (8), 1978, 666-677.
6. A. Mazurkiewicz, Trace semantics In Proceedings of Advances in Petri Nets 1986, Bad Honnef, LNCS 255, pp. 279–324, 1987.
7. D. Peled.   Specification and verification of Message Sequence Charts.   In *FORTE/PSTV 2000*, pp.139-154.
8. D. Peled, A. Pnueli.   Proving Partial Order Properties.   Theoretical Computer Science, 126:143–182, 1994.
9. S. Stoller, Y.A. Liu, Efficient Symbolic Detection of Global Properties in Distributed Systems, CAV 1998, LNCS 1427, 357–368.
10. I. Walukiewicz. Difficult Configurations – On the Complexity of LTrL. In *ICALP 1998*, LNCS 1443, 140–151.
11. M.Y. Vardi, P. Wolper. Reasoning about infinite computations. Information and Computation, 115(1994), 1–37.

A Local Shape Analysis Based on Separation Logic

Dino Distefano[1], Peter W. O'Hearn[1], and Hongseok Yang[2]

[1] Queen Mary, University of London
[2] Seoul National University

Abstract. We describe a program analysis for linked list programs where the abstract domain uses formulae from separation logic.

1 Introduction

A shape analysis attempts to discover the shapes of data structures in the heap at program points encountered during a program's execution. It is a form of pointer analysis which goes beyond the tabulation of shallow aliasing information (e.g., can these two variables be aliases?) to deeper properties of the heap (e.g., is this an acyclic linked list?).

The leading current shape analysis is that of Sagiv, Reps and Wilhelm, which uses very generic and powerful abstractions based on three-valued logic [17]. Although powerful, a problem with this shape analysis is that it behaves in a global way. For example, when one updates a single abstract heap cell this may require also the updating of properties associated with all other cells. Furthermore, each update of another cell might itself depend on the whole heap. This global nature stems from the use of certain instrumentation predicates, such as ones for reachability, to track properties of nodes in the heap: an update to a single cell might alter the value of a host of instrumentation predicates.

In contrast, separation logic provides an approach to reasoning about the heap that has a strong form of locality built in [14]. Typically, one reasons about a collection of cells in isolation, and their update does not necessitate checking or updating cells that are held in a different component of a separating conjunction. It thus seems reasonable to try to use ideas from separation logic in program analysis, with an eye towards the central problem of modularity in the analysis.

Our technical starting point is recent work of Berdine, Calcagno and O'Hearn [5], who defined a method of symbolic execution of certain separation logic formulae called symbolic heaps. Their method is not, by itself, suitable as an abstract semantics because there are infinitely many symbolic heaps and there is no immediate way to guarantee convergence of fixed-point calculations. Here, we obtain a suitable abstract domain by working with (a variation on) their method of symbolic execution, and adding to it an abstraction or widening operator which converts any symbolic heap to one in a certain "canonical form". This abstraction method is an adaptation of work in [7, 8] to the symbolic heaps of Berdine et. al. In contrast to unrestricted symbolic heaps we show that there

H. Hermanns and J. Palsberg (Eds.): TACAS 2006, LNCS 3920, pp. 287–302, 2006.
© Springer-Verlag Berlin Heidelberg 2006

are only finitely many canonical forms, resulting in termination of the fixed-point calculation used in the abstract semantics of while loops.

Our abstract domain uses linked lists only. Other abstractions based on separation logic might be considered as well.

After defining the analysis we turn to locality. We describe a sense in which the abstract semantics obeys the Frame Rule of separation logic, and we identify a notion of footprint as an input-output relation that mentions only those symbolic heap cells accessed by a program. The footprint provides a sound over-approximation of a program's entire (abstract) meaning. The results on locality give a way to automatically infer sound answers for large states from those obtained on small ones as input, suggesting further possible developments in interprocedural and concurrency analyses.

1.1   Related Work

In work on heap analysis (see [15] for discussion) much use has been made of a "storeless semantics" where the model is built from equivalence classes of paths rather than locations. The storeless semantics has the pleasant property that it is garbage collecting by its very nature, but it is also extremely complex. This makes it highly nontrivial to see that a particular analysis based on it is sound. In contrast, here we work directly with a store model, and soundness is almost immediate. The abstraction we use is defined by rewrite rules which are all true implications in separation logic, and the symbolic execution rules are derived from true Hoare triples.

Recent work on shape analysis [15, 16] might be regarded as taking some steps towards separation logic. Early on in separation logic there was an emphasis on what was referred to as "local reasoning": reasoning concentrates on the cells accessed during computation [12]. In [15, 16] an interprocedural analysis is described where a procedure summary is constructed which involves only the (abstract) cells reachable from input parameters or variables free in a procedure. The method of applying a procedure does not, however, explicitly utilize a separating conjunction operator $*$; one might say that the general idea of local reasoning is adopted (or altered), but the formal apparatus of separation logic is not.

In this paper we reciprocate by taking some steps towards shape analysis. Our intention initially was full reciprocation: to build an interprocedural analysis. But, after labouring for the better part of a year, we decided to aim lower: to define an abstract domain and abstract post operator, together with an account of its locality, for a language without procedures. In doing this we have been influenced by shape analysis, but have not adopted the formal apparatus of shape graphs or 3-valued logic. We hope that this paper can serve as a springboard for further developments in local interprocedural and modular concurrency analysis.

We want to make clear that we do not claim that our analysis is superior, in a practical sense, to existing shape analyses. Although it works well on small examples, we have not yet demonstrated that it scales to large programs. Also, from a methodological point of view, in the framework of [17] different abstractions are obtained in a uniform way, where a notion of "canonical abstraction" results once instrumentation predicates are nailed down. In contrast, here we have just one particular set of rewrite rules that have been hand-built; how this might be turned into a more general scheme is not obvious.

Nonetheless, we believe that research on how separation logic, or more particularly, the local reasoning idea, might be used in program analysis is of interest because it suggests a genuinely different approach which has promise for the central problem of obtaining modular analyses. A very good example of this is the recent work of Amtoft et. al. [2, 1] which uses local reasoning in information flow analysis (this is a more shallow form of analysis than shape analysis, but they are successful in formulating a very modular analysis).

Finally, in work carried out independently of (and virtually in parallel to) that here, Magill et. al. have defined a method of inferring invariants for linked list programs in separation logic [9]. They also utilize a symbolic execution mechanism related to [5], and give rewrite rules to attempt to find fixed points. There are many detailed differences: (i) they use a different basic list predicate than we do and, as they point out, have difficulty dealing with acyclic lists, where that is a strong point of our analysis; (ii) they do predicate abstraction of arithmetic operations, where we do not; (iii) and they use an embedding into Presburger arithmetic to help decide implications and Hoare triples, where we do not provide a method for deciding implications (or Hoare triples); (iv) their algorithm does not always terminate, where ours does. But, there is remarkable similarity.

2   Semantic Setting

We first describe the general semantic setting for this work. Following the framework of abstract interpretation [6], we will work with complete lattices D: The semantics of a command c will be given by a continuous function $[\![c]\!]: D \to D$.

If we are given a programming language with certain primitive operations p, together with conditionals, sequencing and while loops, then to define the semantics we must specify the meaning $[\![p]\!]$ of each primitive operation as well as a continuous function, filter$(b): D \to D$, for each boolean. Typically, D is built from subsets of a set of states, and the filter function removes those elements that are not consistent with b's truth. The semantics extends to the rest of the language in the usual way.

$$[\![c\,;c']\!] = [\![c]\!]\,;[\![c']\!] \qquad [\![\text{if } b \text{ then } c \text{ else } c']\!] = (\text{filter}(b)\,;[\![c]\!]) \sqcup (\text{filter}(\neg b)\,;[\![c']\!])$$
$$[\![\text{while } b \text{ do } c]\!] = \lambda d.\ \text{filter}(\neg b)\,(\text{fix } \lambda d'.\ d \sqcup (\text{filter}(b)\,;[\![c]\!])(d'))$$

One way to understand the semantics of **while** is to view d' as a loop invariant. The d in the lhs of $\sqcup$ means that the loop invariant d' should be implied by the precondition, and the rhs of $\sqcup$ means that d' is preserved by the body. (Here, the fixed-point operator has been moved inward from its usual position in semantics, so that it applies to predicates instead of two command denotations.)

Our domains D will be constructed using a powerset operation. If S is a set we denote by $\mathcal{P}(S)$ the "topped" powerset of S, that is, the set of subsets of $S \cup \{\top\}$. Here, $\top \notin S$ is a special element that corresponds to memory fault (accessing a dangling pointer). If we were to take logical implications between elements of $\mathcal{P}(S)$ into account then we would make $\{\top\}$ the top and equate all sets containing $\top$. For simplicity in this paper we just use the subset order.

Given a relation $(p \Longrightarrow) \subseteq S \times (S \cup \{\top\})$, with membership notated $\sigma, p \Longrightarrow \sigma'$, we can lift it to a function $p^\dagger : \mathcal{P}(S) \to \mathcal{P}(S)$ by

$$p^\dagger X = \{\sigma' \mid \exists \sigma \in X. \ (\sigma, p \Longrightarrow \sigma') \ \text{or} \ (\sigma = \sigma' = \top)\}.$$

The semantics of primitive commands will be given by first specifying an execution semantics $\Longrightarrow$ and then lifting it to $\mathcal{P}(S)$.

Every semantics we work with will have two additional properties: that $\{\top\}$ is mapped to $\{\top\}$ and that it preserves unions. Because of this we could in fact work with a corresponding map $[\![c]\!]_\dagger : S \to \mathcal{P}(S)$ instead of $[\![c]\!] : \mathcal{P}(S) \to \mathcal{P}(S)$.

3 Concrete and Symbolic Heaps

Throughout this paper we assume a fixed *finite* set Vars of program variables (ranged over by $x, y, \ldots$), and an infinite set Vars' of primed variables (ranged over by $x', y', \ldots$). The primed variables will not be used within programs, only within logical formulae (where they will be implicitly existentially quantified).

Definition 1. *A symbolic heap $\Pi \mid \Sigma$ consists of a finite set Π of equalities and a finite set Σ of heap predicates. The equalities $E{=}F$ are between* expressions E *and F, which are variables x, or primed variables x', or* nil. *The elements of Σ are of the form*

$$E \mapsto F \qquad \mathsf{ls}(E, F) \qquad \text{junk}.$$

We use $\mathcal{SH}$ to denote the set of consistent *symbolic heaps. (For the definition of consistency, see below.)*

The first two heap predicates are "precise" in the sense of [13]; each cuts out a unique piece of (concrete) heap. The points-to assertion $E \mapsto F$ can hold only in a singleton heap, where E is the only active cell. Similarly, when a list segment holds of a given heap, the path it traces out is unique, and goes through all the cells in the heap. This precise nature of the predicates is helpful when accounting for deallocation. For each symbolic heap $\Pi \mid \Sigma$, we call Π *pure part* of $\Pi \mid \Sigma$, and Σ *spatial part* of $\Pi \mid \Sigma$.

The junk predicate is used in the canonicalization phase of our analysis to swallow up garbage. It is crucial for termination of our analysis, and it has the useful property to reveal memory leaks.

Besides the heap formulae, symbolic heaps also keep track of equalities involving pointer variables and nil.

We often use the notation $\Sigma * P$ for the (disjoint) union of a formula P onto the spatial part of a symbolic heap, and we similarly use $\Pi \wedge P$ in the pure part.

The meaning of a symbolic heap corresponds to a formula

$$\exists x_1' x_2' \ldots x_n'. \ \left(\bigwedge_{P \in \Pi} P \right) \wedge \left(\bigstar_{Q \in \Sigma} Q \right),$$

Table 1. Semantics of Symbolic Heaps

$$C[\![x]\!]s = s(x) \qquad C[\![x']\!]s = s(x') \qquad C[\![\mathsf{nil}]\!]s = \mathsf{nil}$$

$s, h \vDash \{\}$	iff h is the empty heap $[\,]$
$s, h \vDash \{E \mapsto F\}$	iff $h = [C[\![E]\!]s \mapsto C[\![F]\!]s]$
$s, h \vDash \{\mathsf{ls}(E, F)\}$	iff there is a nonempty acyclic path from $C[\![E]\!]s$ to $C[\![F]\!]s$ in h
	and this path contains all heap cells in h
$s, h \vDash \{\mathsf{junk}\}$	iff $h \neq \emptyset$
$s, h \vDash \Sigma_0 * \Sigma_1$	iff $\exists h_0, h_1.\ h = h_0 * h_1$ and $s, h_0 \vDash \Sigma_0$ and $s, h_1 \vDash \Sigma_1$
$s \vDash \{\}$	always
$s \vDash \{E = F\}$	iff $C[\![E]\!]s = C[\![F]\!]s$
$s \vDash \Pi_0 \cup \Pi_1$	iff $s \vDash \Pi_0$ and $s \vDash \Pi_1$
$s, h \vDash \Pi \mid \Sigma$	iff $\exists v'.\ (s(x' \mapsto v') \vDash \Pi)$ and $(s(x' \mapsto v'), h \vDash \Sigma)$
	where x' is the collection of primed variables in $\Pi \mid \Sigma$

in separation logic, where $\{x_1', \ldots, x_n'\}$ is the set of all the primed variables in Σ and Π. More formally, the meaning of a symbolic heap is given by a satisfaction relation $s, h \vDash \Pi \mid \Sigma$, where s is a stack and h a (concrete) heap.

$$\mathsf{Values} = \mathsf{Locations} \cup \{\mathsf{nil}\} \qquad\qquad \mathsf{Heaps} = \mathsf{Locations} \rightharpoonup_f \mathsf{Values}$$
$$\mathsf{Stacks} = (\mathsf{Vars} \cup \mathsf{Vars}') \to \mathsf{Values} \qquad \mathsf{States} = \mathsf{Stacks} \times \mathsf{Heaps}$$

The semantics is given in Table 1. The operation $h_0 * h_1$ there is the union of heaps with disjoint domains. We give the semantics for the singleton sets in the pure and spatial parts, and then for unions. There, the clause for list segments is given informally, but corresponds to the least predicate satisfying

$$\mathsf{ls}(E, F) \iff E \neq F \wedge (E \mapsto F \vee (\exists x'.E \mapsto x' * \mathsf{ls}(x', F))).$$

Our analysis will require us to be able to answer some questions about symbolic heaps algorithmically: whether two expressions are equal, whether they are unequal, whether the heap is inconsistent, and whether a cell is allocated.

$$\Pi \vdash E = F \qquad\qquad \Pi \mid \Sigma \vdash E \neq F \ (\text{when } \mathsf{Vars}'(E, F) = \emptyset)$$
$$\Pi \mid \Sigma \vdash \mathsf{false} \qquad\qquad \Pi \mid \Sigma \vdash \mathtt{Allocated}(E) \ (\text{when } \mathsf{Vars}'(E) = \emptyset)$$

$\Pi \vdash E = F$ is easy to check. It just considers whether E and F are in the same equivalence class induced by the equalities in Π. The other operators use subroutine $\mathsf{allocated}$, which takes Σ and an expression E, and decides whether Σ implies that E points to an allocated cell, by a "nontrivial reason": $\mathsf{allocated}$ ignores the case where Σ is not satisfiable and implies all formulae.

$$\mathsf{allocated}(\Sigma, E) = \exists E'.\ (E \mapsto E' \in \Sigma) \text{ or } (\mathsf{ls}(E, E') \in \Sigma).$$

We then define the other querying operators as follows:

$$\Pi \mid \Sigma \vdash \mathsf{false} \iff (\exists E. \ \Pi \vdash E{=}\mathsf{nil} \text{ and } \mathsf{allocated}(\Sigma, E)), \text{ or}$$
$$(\exists E, F. \ \Pi \vdash E{=}F \text{ and } \mathsf{ls}(E, F) \in \Sigma), \text{ or}$$
$$\left(\begin{array}{l} \exists E, F. \ \Pi \vdash E{=}F \text{ and } \Sigma \text{ contains two distinct} \\ \text{predicates whose lhs's are, respectively, } E \text{ and } F \end{array} \right)$$

$$\Pi \mid \Sigma \vdash E{\neq}F \iff (E{=}F \wedge \Pi \mid \Sigma) \vdash \mathsf{false}$$

$$\Pi \mid \Sigma \vdash \mathtt{Allocated}(E) \iff \Pi \mid \Sigma \vdash \mathsf{false}, \text{ or } (\exists E'. \ \Pi \vdash E{=}E' \text{ and } \mathsf{allocated}(\Sigma, E'))$$

These definitions agree with what one would obtain from a definition in terms of the satisfaction relation $\vDash$, but they are simple syntactic checks that do not require calling a theorem prover.

The rules that define our analysis will preserve consistency of symbolic heaps (that $\Pi \mid \Sigma \nvdash \mathsf{false}$). In particular, inconsistent heaps introduced in branches of if statements or as a result of tests in a while loop will be filtered out.

4   Concrete and Symbolic Execution Semantics

The grammar of commands for the programming language used in this paper is given by

$$
\begin{array}{lll}
b & ::= E{=}E \mid E{\neq}E & \\
p & ::= x{:=}E \mid x{:=}[E] \mid [E]{:=}F \mid \mathbf{new}(x) \mid \mathbf{dispose}(E) & \text{Primitive Commands} \\
c & ::= p \mid c \,;\, c \mid \mathbf{while} \ b \ \mathbf{do} \ c \mid \mathbf{if} \ b \ \mathbf{then} \ c \ \mathbf{else} \ c & \text{Commands}
\end{array}
$$

We do not consider commands that contain any primed variables amongst their expressions. We include only a single heap dereferencing operator $[\cdot]$ which refers to the "next" field. In the usual way, our experimental implementation ignores commands that access fields other than "next" (say, a data field), and treats any boolean conditions other than those given as nondeterministic.

4.1   Concrete Semantics

The execution rules for the primitive commands are as follows, where in the faulting rule (the last rule) we use notation for primitive commands that access heap cell E:

$$A(E) ::= [E]{:=}F \mid x{:=}[E] \mid \mathbf{dispose}(E)$$

CONCRETE EXECUTION RULES

$$\frac{\mathcal{C}[\![E]\!]s = n}{s, h, \ x{:=}E \implies (s \mid x \mapsto n), h} \qquad \frac{\mathcal{C}[\![E]\!]s = \ell \quad h(\ell) = n}{s, h, \ x{:=}[E] \implies (s \mid x \mapsto n), h}$$

$$\frac{\mathcal{C}[\![E]\!]s = \ell \quad \mathcal{C}[\![F]\!]s = n \quad \ell \in \mathsf{dom}(h)}{s, h, \ [E]{:=}F \implies s, (h \mid \ell \mapsto n)} \qquad \frac{\ell \notin \mathsf{dom}(h)}{s, h, \ \mathbf{new}(x) \implies (s \mid x \mapsto \ell), (h \mid \ell \mapsto n)}$$

$$\frac{\mathcal{C}[\![E]\!]s = \ell}{s, h * [\ell \mapsto n], \ \mathbf{dispose}(E) \implies s, h} \qquad \frac{\mathcal{C}[\![E]\!]s \notin \mathsf{dom}(h)}{s, h, \ A(E) \implies \top}$$

Notice the tremendous amount of nondeterminism in **new**: it picks out *any* location not in the domain of the heap, and *any* value n for its contents.

The concrete semantics is given in the topped powerset $\mathcal{P}(\mathsf{States})$, where the filter map is

$$\mathsf{filter}(b)X \;=\; \{(s,h) \in X \mid \mathcal{C}[\![b]\!]s \;=\; \mathsf{true}\} \cup \{\top \mid \top \in X\}$$

where $\mathcal{C}[\![b]\!]s \in \{\mathsf{true, false}\}$ just checks equalities by looking up in the stack s.

With these definitions we may then set $\mathcal{C}[\![p]\!] \;=\; p^\dagger$ and by the recipe of Section 2 we obtain the concrete semantics, $\mathcal{C}[\![c]\!] : \mathcal{P}(\mathsf{States}) \to \mathcal{P}(\mathsf{States})$, of every command c.

4.2   Symbolic Semantics

The symbolic execution semantics $\sigma, A \Longrightarrow \sigma'$ takes a symbolic heap σ and a primitive command, and transforms it into an output symbolic heap or $\top$. In these rules we require that the primed variables x', y' be fresh.

SYMBOLIC EXECUTION RULES

$$
\begin{array}{lll}
\Pi \mid \Sigma, & x := E & \Longrightarrow x = E[x'/x] \wedge (\Pi \mid \Sigma)[x'/x] \\[4pt]
\Pi \mid \Sigma * E \mapsto F, & x := [E] & \Longrightarrow x = F[x'/x] \wedge (\Pi \mid \Sigma * E \mapsto F)[x'/x] \\[4pt]
\Pi \mid \Sigma * E \mapsto F, & [E] := G & \Longrightarrow \Pi \mid \Sigma * E \mapsto G \\[4pt]
\Pi \mid \Sigma, & \mathbf{new}(x) & \Longrightarrow (\Pi \mid \Sigma)[x'/x] * x \mapsto y' \\[4pt]
\Pi \mid \Sigma * E \mapsto F, & \mathbf{dispose}(E) & \Longrightarrow \Pi \mid \Sigma
\end{array}
$$

$$\frac{\Pi \mid \Sigma \not\vdash \mathtt{Allocated}(E)}{\Pi \mid \Sigma, \, A(E) \Longrightarrow \top}$$

REARRANGEMENT RULES

$$P(E, F) \;::=\; E \mapsto F \mid \mathsf{ls}(E, F)$$

$$\frac{\Pi_0 \mid \Sigma_0 * P(E, G), \, A(E) \Longrightarrow \Pi_1 \mid \Sigma_1}{\Pi_0 \mid \Sigma_0 * P(F, G), \, A(E) \Longrightarrow \Pi_1 \mid \Sigma_1} \quad \Pi_0 \vdash E = F$$

$$\frac{\Pi_0 \mid \Sigma_0 * E \mapsto x' * \mathsf{ls}(x', G), \, A(E) \Longrightarrow \Pi_1 \mid \Sigma_1}{\Pi_0 \mid \Sigma_0 * \mathsf{ls}(E, G), \, A(E) \Longrightarrow \Pi_1 \mid \Sigma_1} \qquad \frac{\Pi \mid \Sigma * E \mapsto F, \, A(E) \Longrightarrow \Pi' \mid \Sigma'}{\Pi \mid \Sigma * \mathsf{ls}(E, F), \, A(E) \Longrightarrow \Pi' \mid \Sigma'}$$

The execution rules that access heap cell E are stated in a way that requires their pre-states to explicitly have $E \mapsto F$. Sometimes the knowledge that E is allocated is less explicit, such as in $\{E = x\} \mid \{x \mapsto y\}$ or $\mathsf{ls}(E, F)$, and we use rearrangement rules to put the pre-state in the proper form. The first rearrangement rule simply makes use of equalities to recognize that a dereferencing step is possible, and the other two correspond to unrolling a list segment.

In contrast to the concrete semantics, the treatment of allocation is completely deterministic (up to renaming of primed variables). However, a different kind of nondeterminism results in rearrangement rules that unroll list segments.

All that is left to define the symbolic (intermediate) semantics $\mathcal{I}[\![c]\!] \colon \mathcal{P}(\mathcal{SH}) \to \mathcal{P}(\mathcal{SH})$ by the recipe before is to define the filter map. It adds the equality for the $E{=}F$ case, but does not do so for the $E{\neq}F$ case because we do not have inequalities in our symbolic domain.

$$\mathsf{filter}(E{=}F)X = \{\top \mid \top{\in}X\} \cup \{(E{=}F \wedge \Pi \mid \Sigma) \mid \Pi \mid \Sigma \in X \text{ and } \Pi \mid \Sigma \not\vdash E{\neq}F\}$$

$$\mathsf{filter}(E{\neq}F)X = \{\top \mid \top{\in}X\} \cup \{(\Pi \mid \Sigma) \in X \mid \Pi \not\vdash E{=}F \text{ and } \Pi \mid \Sigma \not\vdash \mathsf{false}\}$$

To state the sense in which the symbolic semantics is sound we define the "meaning function" $\gamma \colon \mathcal{P}(\mathcal{SH}) \to \mathcal{P}(\mathsf{States})$:

$$\gamma(X) = \text{if } (\top \in X) \text{ then } (\mathsf{States} \cup \{\top\}) \text{ else } (\{(s,h) \mid \exists \Pi \mid \Sigma \in X.\ (s,h) \models \Pi \mid \Sigma\})$$

Theorem 2. *The symbolic semantics is a sound overapproximation of the concrete semantics:* $\forall X \in \mathcal{P}(\mathcal{SH}).\ \mathcal{C}[\![c]\!](\gamma(X)) \subseteq \gamma(\mathcal{I}[\![c]\!]X).$

5   The Analysis

The domain $\mathcal{SH}$ of symbolic heaps is infinite. Even though there are finitely many program variables, primed variables can be introduced during symbolic execution. For example, in a loop that includes allocation we can generate formulae $x{\mapsto}x' * x'{\mapsto}x'' \cdots$ of arbitrary length.

In order to ensure fixed-point convergence we perform abstraction. The abstraction we consider is specified by a collection of rewrite rules which perform abstraction by gobbling up primed variables. This is done by merging lists, swallowing single cells into lists, and abstracting two cells by a list. We also remove primed variables from the pure parts of formulae, and we collect all garbage into the predicate junk.

5.1   Canonicalization Rules

The canonicalization rules are reported in Table 2. We again use the notation $P(E,F)$ to stand for an atomic formula either of the form $E{\mapsto}F$ or $\mathsf{ls}(E,F)$.

Table 2. Abstraction Rules

$$\dfrac{}{E{=}x' \wedge \Pi \mid \Sigma \rightsquigarrow (\Pi \mid \Sigma)[E/x']} \text{ (St1)} \qquad \dfrac{}{x'{=}E \wedge \Pi \mid \Sigma \rightsquigarrow (\Pi \mid \Sigma)[E/x']} \text{ (St2)}$$

$$\dfrac{x' \notin \mathsf{Vars}'(\Pi, \Sigma)}{\Pi \mid \Sigma * P(x', E) \rightsquigarrow \Pi \mid \Sigma \cup \mathsf{junk}} \text{ (Gb1)} \qquad \dfrac{x', y' \notin \mathsf{Vars}'(\Pi, \Sigma)}{\Pi \mid \Sigma * P_1(x', y') * P_2(y', x') \rightsquigarrow \Pi \mid \Sigma \cup \mathsf{junk}} \text{ (Gb2)}$$

$$\dfrac{x' \notin \mathsf{Vars}'(\Pi, \Sigma, E, F) \qquad \Pi \vdash F{=}\mathsf{nil}}{\Pi \mid \Sigma * P_1(E, x') * P_2(x', F) \rightsquigarrow \Pi \mid \Sigma * \mathsf{ls}(E, \mathsf{nil})} \text{ (Abs1)}$$

$$\dfrac{x' \notin \mathsf{Vars}'(\Pi, \Sigma, E, F, G, H) \qquad \Pi \vdash F{=}G}{\Pi \mid \Sigma * P_1(E, x') * P_2(x', F) * P_3(G, H) \rightsquigarrow \Pi \mid \Sigma * \mathsf{ls}(E, F) * P_3(G, H)} \text{ (Abs2)}$$

The most important rules are the last two. The sense of abstraction that these rules implement is that we ignore any facts that depend on a midpoint in a list segment, unless it is named by a program variable. There is a subtlety in interpreting this statement, however. One might perhaps have expected the last rule to leave out the $P_3(G, H)$ *-conjunct, but this would result in unsoundness; as Berdine and Calcagno pointed out [4, 5] (our abstraction rules are obtained from their proof rules), we must know that the end of a second list segment does not point back into the first if we are to concatenate them. We are forced, by considerations of soundness, to keep some primed midpoints, such as in the formula $\mathsf{ls}(x, x') * \mathsf{ls}(x', y)$, to which no rewrite rule applies.

Notice the use of a $\cup$ rather than a $*$ on the rhs of the (Gb1) and (Gb2) rules. This has the effect that when more than one unreachable node named by a primed variable is present, all of them get put into the unique junk node.

5.2   The Algorithm

We say that $\Pi \mid \Sigma$ is a canonical symbolic heap if it is consistent (i.e., $\Pi \mid \Sigma \not\vdash$ false) and no canonicalization rule applies to it, and we denote by $\mathcal{CSH}$ the set of all such. We can immediately observe:

Lemma 3 (Strong Normalization). $\leadsto$ *has no infinite reduction sequences.*

This, together with the results in the next section, would be enough to define a terminating analysis. But, there are many distinct reduction sequences and to try all of them in an analysis would lead to a massive increase in nondeterminism. We have not proven a result to the effect that choosing different reduction sequences matters in the final result (after applying the meaning function γ), but neither have we found examples where the difference can be detected. So, in our implementation we have chosen a specific strategy which applies the equality rules, followed by (Gb1), followed by abstraction rules, followed by (Gb2). In the theory, we just presume that we have a function (rather than relation)

$$\mathsf{can}: \mathcal{SH} \to \mathcal{CSH}$$

which takes a symbolic heap $\Pi \mid \Sigma$ and returns a canonical symbolic heap $\Pi' \mid \Sigma'$ where $\Pi \mid \Sigma \leadsto^* \Pi' \mid \Sigma'$.

[We remark that $\mathsf{can}(\Pi \mid \Sigma)$ is not the best (logically strongest) canonical heap implied by $\Pi \mid \Sigma$. A counterexample is $\{\} \mid \{x \mapsto x', x' \mapsto y, y \mapsto \mathsf{nil}\}$. This symbolic heap is reduced to $\{\} \mid \{\mathsf{ls}(x, y), y \mapsto \mathsf{nil}\}$ by the canonicalization, but implies another symbolic heap $\{\} \mid \{x \mapsto x', x' \mapsto z', y \mapsto \mathsf{nil}\}$, which is not (logically) weaker than $\{\} \mid \{\mathsf{ls}(x, y), y \mapsto \mathsf{nil}\}$. We believe that this "problem" is fixable; we conjecture that there is a preorder $\sqsubseteq$ on $\mathcal{SH}$ such that (i) $\sqsubseteq$ is a sub preorder of the logical implication and (ii) $\mathsf{can}(\Pi \mid \Sigma)$ is the smallest canonical heap greater than or equal to $\Pi \mid \Sigma$ with respect to $\sqsubseteq$. As of this writing we have not succeeded in proving this conjecture. If true, it would perhaps open the way to a study pinpointing where precision is and is not lost (as in, e.g., [3]) using Galois connections. Although valuable, such questions are secondary to our more basic aim of existence (soundness and termination) of the analysis.]

Let in: $\mathcal{P}(\mathcal{CSH}) \to \mathcal{P}(\mathcal{SH})$ denote the inclusion function. We define the abstract semantics for each primitive command p by the equation

$$\mathcal{A}[\![p]\!] \;=\; \text{in} \,;\, \mathcal{I}[\![p]\!] \,;\, (\text{can}^\dagger).$$

The filtering map in the abstract semantics is just the restriction of the symbolic one to $\mathcal{CSH}$. Then, by the recipe from Section 2 we obtain a semantics

$$\mathcal{A}[\![c]\!] : \mathcal{P}(\mathcal{CSH}) \to \mathcal{P}(\mathcal{CSH})$$

for every command.

The soundness of the abstract semantics relies on the soundness of the rewriting rules.

Lemma 4 (Soundness of $\rightsquigarrow$). *If* $\Sigma \,|\, \Pi \rightsquigarrow \Sigma' \,|\, \Pi'$ *then* $\Sigma \,|\, \Pi \vdash \Sigma' \,|\, \Pi'$.

The statement of soundness of the abstract semantics is then the same as for the symbolic semantics, except that we quantify over $\mathcal{P}(\mathcal{CSH})$ instead of $\mathcal{P}(\mathcal{SH})$.

Theorem 5. *The abstract semantics is a sound overapproximation of the concrete semantics:* $\forall X \in \mathcal{P}(\mathcal{CSH}). \; \mathcal{C}[\![c]\!](\gamma(X)) \subseteq \gamma(\mathcal{A}[\![c]\!]X)$.

Here are some examples of running the analysis on particular pre-states, taken from an implementation of it in OCaml.

Example 1. This is the usual program to reverse a list. Here 0 is used to denote nil, $x{\to}tl$ is used instead of $[x]$, and the commas in the analysis results are replaced by the corresponding logical connectives.

Program: $p{:=}0$; **while** $(c{\neq}0)$ **do** $(n{:=}c{\to}tl$; $c{\to}tl{:=}p$; $p{:=}c$; $c{:=}n)$
Pre: $\{\}\,|\,\{\mathsf{ls}(c,0)\}$ **Post:** $\{c{=}0 \wedge c{=}n \wedge n{=}0\}\,|\,\{\mathsf{ls}(p,0)\} \;\vee\; \{c{=}0 \wedge c{=}n \wedge n{=}0\}\,|\,\{p{\mapsto}0\}$
Inv: $\{p{=}0\}\,|\,\{\mathsf{ls}(c,0)\} \;\vee\; \{c{=}n \wedge n{=}0\}\,|\,\{p{\mapsto}0\} \;\vee\; \{c{=}n \wedge n{=}0\}\,|\,\{\mathsf{ls}(p,0)\} \;\vee$
$\qquad \{c{=}n\}\,|\,\{p{\mapsto}0 * \mathsf{ls}(n,0)\} \;\vee\; \{c{=}n\}\,|\,\{\mathsf{ls}(p,0) * \mathsf{ls}(n,0)\}$

Given a linked list as a precondition, the analysis calculates that the postcondition might be a linked list or a single points-to fact. The postcondition has some redundancy, in that we could remove the second disjunct without affecting the meaning; this is because we have used the subset ordering on sets of states, rather than one based on implication. The analysis also calculates the pictured loop invariant, which captures that p and c point to separated linked lists.

Running the analysis to the same program with a circular linked list as input gives the following (we omit the calculated invariant, which has 11 disjuncts).

Pre: $\{\}\,|\,\{\mathsf{ls}(c,c') * \mathsf{ls}(c',c)\}$
Post: $\{c{=}0 \wedge c{=}n \wedge n{=}0\}\,|\,\{p{\mapsto}p' * \mathsf{ls}(p',p)\} \;\vee\; \{c{=}0 \wedge c{=}n \wedge n{=}0\}\,|\,\{p{\mapsto}p' * p'{\mapsto}p\}$

Example 2. This is the program to dispose a list.

Program: while $(c{\neq}0)$ **do** $(t{:=}c$; $c{:=}c{\to}tl$; **dispose**$(t))$
Pre: $\{\}\,|\,\{\mathsf{ls}(c,0)\}$ **Post:** $\{c{=}0\}\,|\,\{\}$ **Inv:** $\{c{=}0\}\,|\,\{\} \;\vee\; \{\}\,|\,\{\mathsf{ls}(c,0)\}$

The spatial part $\{\}$ of the postcondition expresses that the heap is empty on termination. If we leave out the dispose instruction, it returns postcondition $\{c{=}\mathsf{nil}\} \mid \{t{\mapsto}\mathsf{nil} * \mathsf{junk}\}$ (showing memory leak). When we run the analysis on this program on a circular list or $\mathsf{ls}(c, d)$ it reports a memory fault.

In addition to these examples we have run the analysis on a range of other small programs, such as list append, list copy, programs to insert and delete from the middle of a list, programs to delete and filter from circular lists, and to delete a segment between two values from a sorted list. The execution times ranged from a few milliseconds for reverse, copy and append to three seconds for delete-a-segment (running on a 1.5GHz PowerBook G4), and in space requirements none of them exceeded the OCaml default initial heap size of 400kB.

In coverage of examples, and in the nature of the abstraction itself, the analysis here appears to be somewhat similar to the one reported in [10]. A careful study of this relationship could be worthwhile.

6 Termination

Although the abstract semantics exists, we have not yet established that the algorithm it determines always terminates. We do that by showing that the domain $\mathcal{CSH}$, consisting of the normal forms of the rewriting rules, is finite.

To gain some insight into the nature of the canonical symbolic heaps here are some examples, where the pure part Π is empty (and left out).

Irreducible	Reducible
$\mathsf{ls}(x, x') * \mathsf{ls}(y, x') * \mathsf{ls}(x', \mathsf{nil})$	$\mathsf{ls}(x, x') * \mathsf{ls}(x', y') * \mathsf{ls}(y', \mathsf{nil})$
$\mathsf{ls}(x, x') * \mathsf{ls}(x', x)$	$\mathsf{ls}(x, y') * \mathsf{ls}(y', x') * \mathsf{ls}(x', x)$
$\mathsf{ls}(x, x')$	$\mathsf{ls}(x', x)$
$\mathsf{ls}(x, x') * \mathsf{ls}(x', y)$	$\mathsf{ls}(x, x') * \mathsf{ls}(x', y) * \mathsf{ls}(y, z)$

In the first element of the first row, variable x' is shared (pointed to by x and y), and this blocks the application of rule (Abs1) because of its variable condition. On the other hand, the second element can be reduced, in fact twice, to end up with $\mathsf{ls}(x, \mathsf{nil})$. The second row contains two cycles, one of (syntactic) length two and the other of length three. The first of these cannot be reduced. We would need to know that $x{=}\mathsf{nil}$ to apply (Abs1) and we cannot, because x in $\mathsf{ls}(x, x')$ cannot be nil or else we would have an inconsistent formula. The second in this row can, however, be reduced, to the first. In the third row x' is a reachable variable that possibly denotes a dangling pointer and there is no way to eliminate it. In the second it is not reachable, and can be removed using the (Gb1) rule. Note that this removal is sound, because all heap predicates, including $\mathsf{ls}(x', x)$, imply junk. In the final row, first x' points to a possibly dangling variable y. We cannot remove x', because transforming $\mathsf{ls}(x, x') * \mathsf{ls}(x', y)$ to $\mathsf{ls}(x, y)$ is unsound; when $y = x = 10$, no heap can satisfy $\mathsf{ls}(x, y)$, while a cycle from location 10 of length 2 satisfies $\mathsf{ls}(x, x') * \mathsf{ls}(x', y)$. The rule (Abs2) is arranged to prevent this unsoundness. If we tack on another heap formula to ensure that y does not point to any internal cells of the list segment $\mathsf{ls}(x, x')$, then (Abs2) can apply.

Based on these ideas we can characterize the normal forms of $\leadsto^*$ using "graphical" ideas of path and reachability, as well as conditions about sharing, cycles, and dangling pointers.

Definition 6.   *1. A path in $\Pi \mid \Sigma$ is a sequence of expressions $E_0, E_1, \ldots, E_n$ such that*
$$\forall i \in \{1, \ldots, n\}.\ \exists E, E'.\ \Pi \vdash E_{i-1} = E \text{ and } \Pi \vdash E_i = E' \text{ and } P(E, E') \in \Sigma.$$

Reachability between expressions is defined in the usual way: E is reachable from E' in $\Pi \mid \Sigma$ if and only if there is a path in $\Pi \mid \Sigma$ that starts from E and ends in E'.

2. *An expression E in $\Pi \mid \Sigma$ is shared if and only if Σ contains two distinct elements $P_0(E_0, E_0')$ and $P_1(E_1, E_1')$ such that $\Pi \vdash E = E_0'$ and $\Pi \vdash E = E_1'$.*
3. *A primed variable x' in a cycle (a path from E to itself) is an internal node if and only if it is not shared.*
4. *E is called possibly dangling in $\Pi \mid \Sigma$ if and only if*
   (a) *$\Pi \nvdash E = \text{nil}$,*
   (b) *there exists some E' such that $\Pi \vdash E = E'$ and E' is the second argument of some heap predicate in Σ, and*
   (c) *there are no expressions F' such that $\Pi \vdash E = F'$ and F' is the first argument of some heap predicate in Σ.*
5. *E points to a possibly dangling expression if and only if there are E', F such that $\Pi \vdash E = E'$, $P(E', F) \in \Sigma$, and F possibly dangles.*

Definition 7 (Reduced Symbolic Heap). *A symbolic heap $\Pi \mid \Sigma$ is reduced if and only if*

1. *Π does not contain primed variables;*
2. *every primed variable x' in Σ is reachable from some unprimed variable; and*
3. *for every reachable variable x', either (a) x' is shared, or (b) x' is the internal node of a cycle of length precisely two, or (c) x' points to a possibly dangling variable, or (d) x' is possibly dangling.*

In (b) of this definition the length refers to the syntactic length of a path, not the length of a denoted cycle. For example, $\text{ls}(x, x') * \text{ls}(x', x)$ has syntactic length two, even though it denotes cycles of length two or greater.

This definition of reduced heaps is not particularly pretty; its main point is to give us a way to prove termination of our analysis.

Proposition 8 (Canonical Characterization). *When a symbolic heap $\Pi \mid \Sigma$ is consistent, $\Pi \mid \Sigma$ is reduced if and only if $\Pi \mid \Sigma \nleadsto$.*

We consider the formulae in $\mathcal{CSH}$ as being equivalent up to renaming of primed variables. With this convention, we can show $\mathcal{CSH}$ finite.

Proposition 9. $\mathcal{CSH}$ *is finite.*

The proof of this proposition proceeds by first showing a lemma that bounds the number of primed variables in any reduced form. In essence, the condition 3 of the definition of "reduced" stops there being infinitely many possible primed variables (starting from a fixed finite set of program variables). This then limits the number of atomic formulas that can appear, giving us finiteness. The overall bound one obtains is exponential (for the record, we have an argument that gives a very coarse bound of $2^{(129n^2+18n+2)}$). This the leads us to

Theorem 10. *The algorithm specified by $\mathcal{A}[\![\cdot]\!]$ always terminates.*

7 Locality

We now describe locality properties of the semantics, beginning with an example. Suppose that we have a queue, represented in memory as a list segment from c to d. An operation for getting an element is

$$x:=c \; ; \; c:=c{\rightarrow}tl \qquad /* \text{ get from left of queue, put in } x \; */$$

The list segment might not be the whole storage, of course. In particular, we might have an additional element pointed to by d which is (perhaps) used to place an element into the queue. When we run our tool on an input reflecting this state of affairs we obtain

Pre: $\{\}\,|\,\{\mathsf{ls}(c,d)*d{\mapsto}d'\}$ **Post:** $\{c{=}d\}\,|\,\{x{\mapsto}d*d{\mapsto}d'\} \vee \{\}\,|\,\{x{\mapsto}c*\mathsf{ls}(c,d)*d{\mapsto}d'\}$

However, it is clear that the $d \mapsto d'$ information is irrelevant, that a run of the tool on the smaller input gives us all the information we need.

Pre: $\{\}\,|\,\{\mathsf{ls}(c,d)\}$ **Post:** $\{c{=}d\}\,|\,\{x{\mapsto}d\} \vee \{\}\,|\,\{x{\mapsto}c*\mathsf{ls}(c,d)\}$

In fact, the behaviour of the tool in the first case follows from that in the second, using the Frame Rule of separation logic. This example is motivated by the treatment of a concurrent queue in [11]. The fact that we do not have to consider the cell d when inserting is crucial for a verification which shows that the two ends of a nonempty queue can be manipulated concurrently. To produce such results from an analysis, rather than a by-hand proof, we would similarly like to avoid the need to analyze the entire state including the cell d.

We can give a theoretical account of the locality of our analysis using the following notions. First, we define a notion of $*$ on entire symbolic heaps.

$$(\Pi_1 \mid \Sigma_1) * (\Pi_2 \mid \Sigma_2) = (\Pi_1 \cup \Pi_2 \mid \Sigma_1 * \Sigma_2).$$

This is a partial operation, which is undefined when $\Sigma_1 * \Sigma_2$ is undefined, or when $(\Pi_1 \cup \Pi_2 \mid \Sigma_1 * \Sigma_2)$ is inconsistent, or when some primed variable appears both in $\Pi_1 \mid \Sigma_1$ and in $\Pi_2 \mid \Sigma_2$. We extend this to $\mathcal{SH} \cup \{\top\}$ by stipulating $(\Pi \mid \Sigma) * \top = \top = \top * (\Pi \mid \Sigma)$. It then lifts to a total binary operation on $\mathcal{P}(\mathcal{SH})$ by

$$X * Y = \{\sigma_1 * \sigma_2 \mid \sigma_1 \in X, \sigma_2 \in Y\}.$$

To formulate the locality property we suppose a fixed set *Mod* of modified variables, that appear to the left of := or in **new**(x) in a given command c.

Theorem 11 (Frame Rule). *For all* $X, Y \in \mathcal{P}(\mathcal{CSH})$, *if* $\mathsf{Vars}(Y) \cap Mod = \emptyset$ *then* $\gamma(\mathcal{A}[\![c]\!](X * Y)) \subseteq \gamma((\mathcal{A}[\![c]\!]X) * Y)$.

There are two reasons why we get an overapproximation $\subseteq$ rather than exact match here. First, and trivially, there might be states in X where c faults, returns $\top$, while it never does for states in $X * Y$. The second reason is best understood by example. When the program $\mathbf{new}(x); (\mathbf{if}\ x{=}y\ \mathbf{then}\ z{:=}a\ \mathbf{else}\ z{:=}b); \mathbf{dispose}(x)$ is run in the empty heap, it returns two post-states, one where $z{=}a$ and the another where $z{=}b$. But when run in $y{\mapsto}y'$ the **if** branch is ruled out and we only get $z{=}b \mid y{\mapsto}y'$ as a conclusion. However, we get $z{=}a \mid y{\mapsto}y'$ as an additional possibility starting from $y{\mapsto}y'$, when we put the small output together with $y{\mapsto}y'$ using $*$. Although precision can be lost when passing to smaller states, in many examples we have considered it is an acceptable loss or none.

For a given command c and symbolic heap σ we define

1. $\mathsf{safe}(c, \sigma)$ iff $\top \notin \mathcal{A}[\![c]\!]\{\sigma\}$
2. $\sigma_1 \preceq \sigma_3$ iff $\exists \sigma_2. \sigma_3 = \sigma_1 * \sigma_2$
3. $\sigma \prec \sigma'$ iff $\sigma \preceq \sigma'$ and $\sigma \neq \sigma'$
4. $\mathsf{onlyaccesses}(c, \sigma)$ iff $\mathsf{safe}(c, \sigma)$ and $\neg \exists \sigma' \prec \sigma. \mathsf{safe}(c, \sigma')$.

The notion of accesses is coarse. For example, $\mathsf{onlyaccesses}([x]{:=}y, \mathsf{ls}(x, \mathsf{nil}))$ holds, even though a single cell can be picked out of the list segment. A stronger notion of accesses, and hence footprint, might be formulated taking implications between symbolic heaps into account as well as $\preceq$.

The footprint is partial function $\mathsf{foot}(c): \mathcal{CSH} \rightharpoonup \mathcal{P}(\mathcal{CSH})$,

$$\mathsf{foot}(c)\sigma = \text{if } (\mathsf{onlyaccesses}(c, \sigma)) \text{ then } (\mathcal{A}[\![c]\!]\{\sigma\}) \text{ else (undefined)}.$$

The point of the footprint is that, as a set of pairs, it can be compact compared to the entire meaning. For the disposelist program in Example 2, the footprint has three entries, with preconditions $\{\} \mid \{\mathsf{ls}(c, \mathsf{nil})\}$, $\{\} \mid \{c{\mapsto}\mathsf{nil}\}$ and $\{c{=}\mathsf{nil}\} \mid \{\}$. The entire meaning has 16 entries, corresponding to the number of canonical symbolic heaps over a single input variable c.

To express the sense in which the footprint is a sound representation of the semantics of c we show how any potential footprint can be "fleshed out" by applying the idea behind the Frame Rule. Again, let Mod be the set of modified variables in a given command c, and for each $\Pi \mid \Sigma$, let $\mathsf{unaffectedEqs}(\Pi \mid \Sigma)$ be the set of equalities $E{=}F$ in Π such that $\mathsf{Vars}(E{=}F) \cap Mod = \emptyset$. If $f: \mathcal{CSH} \rightharpoonup \mathcal{P}(\mathcal{CSH})$, then $\mathsf{flesh}(f): \mathcal{CSH} \to \mathcal{P}(\mathcal{CSH})$ is defined as follows:

$$\mathsf{validSplit}(\sigma_0, \sigma_1, \sigma) \iff \sigma_0 * \sigma_1 = \sigma \text{ and } \mathsf{Vars}(\sigma_1) \cap Mod = \emptyset \text{ and}$$
$$\sigma_0 \in \mathsf{dom}(f) \text{ and } \mathsf{unaffectedEqs}(\sigma_1) = \mathsf{unaffectedEqs}(\sigma)$$
$$\mathsf{flesh}(f)\sigma = \text{if } (\neg \exists \sigma_0, \sigma_1. \mathsf{validSplit}(\sigma_0, \sigma_1, \sigma)) \text{ then } \{\top\}$$
$$\text{else let } \sigma_0', \sigma_1' \text{ be symbolic heaps s.t. } \mathsf{validSplit}(\sigma_0', \sigma_1', \sigma)$$
$$\text{in } \mathcal{P}(\mathsf{can})(f(\sigma_0') * \{\sigma_1'\})$$

The fleshing out picks one access point, and adds as many $*$-separated invariants as possible to the access point.

Theorem 12. *The footprint is a sound overapproximation of the abstract semantics:* $\forall X \in \mathcal{P}(\mathcal{CSH}). \ \gamma(\mathcal{A}[\![c]\!]X) \subseteq \gamma(\mathsf{foot}(c)^\dagger X)$.

The calculation of whole footprints is, of course, not realistic. A more practical way to employ the footprint idea would be, given an input state σ, to look at substates on which a procedure or command does not produce a fault. In interprocedural analysis, we might record the input-output behaviour on as small states as possible when tabulating a procedure summary. This would be similar to [16], but would not involve entire reachable substates. In concurrency, we would look for disjoint substates of an input state on which to run parallel commands: if these input states were safe for the commands in question, then we could soundly avoid (many) interleavings during symbolic execution. We hope to report on these matters at a later time.

Acknowledgements. Thanks to Josh Berdine, Cristiano Calcagno, Ivana Mijajlovic, Anindya Banerjee, Andreas Podelski, Noam Rinetzky, Mooly Sagiv, and the anonymous referees for helpful comments on this work. Yang was supported by R08-2003-000-10370-0 from the Basic Research Program of Korea Science & Engineering Foundation. Distefano and O'Hearn were supported by the EPSRC.

References

[1] T. Amtoft, S. Bandhakavi, and A. Banerjee. A logic for information flow analysis of pointer programs. 33rd POPL, to appear, 2006.

[2] T. Amtoft and A. Banerjee. Information flow analysis in logical form. 11th Static Analysis Symposium, LNCS3184, pp100-115, 2004.

[3] T. Ball, A. Podelski, and S. K. Rajamani. Boolean and Cartesian abstraction for model checking C programs. *7th TACAS, LNCS*, 2031:268–283, 2001.

[4] J. Berdine, C. Calcagno, and P. O'Hearn. A decidable fragment of separation logic. Proceedings of FSTTCS, LNCS 3328, Chennai, December, 2004.

[5] Josh Berdine, Cristiano Calcagno, and Peter W. O'Hearn. Symbolic execution with separation logic. In K. Yi, editor, *APLAS 2005*, volume 3780 of *LNCS*, 2005.

[6] P. Cousot and R. Cousot. Abstract interpretation: A unified lattice model for static analysis of programs by construction or approximation of fixpoints. 4th ACM Symposium on Principles of Programming Languages. pages 238–252, 1977.

[7] D. Distefano. *On model checking the dynamics of object-based software: a foundational approach*. PhD thesis, University of Twente, 2003.

[8] D. Distefano, A. Rensink, and J.-P. Katoen. Who is pointing when to whom: on model-checking pointer structures. CTIT Technical Report TR-CTIT-03-12, Faculty of Informatics, University of Twente, March 2003.

[9] S. Magill, A. Nanevski, E. Clarke, and P. Lee. Inferring invariants in Separation Logic for imperative list-processing programs. Draft, July 2005, 2005.

[10] R. Manevich, E. Yahav, G. Ramalingam, and S. Sagiv. Predicate abstraction and canonical abstraction for singly-linked lists. *Proceedings of 6th VMCAI*, pp181-198, 2005.

[11] P. O'Hearn. Resources, concurrency and local reasoning. *Theoretical Computer Science*, 2006. to appear. Preliminary version appeared in CONCUR'04, LNCS 3170, 49–67.

[12] P. O'Hearn, J. Reynolds, and H. Yang. Local reasoning about programs that alter data structures. In *Proc. of 15th CSL*, LNCS, pages 1–19. Springer-Verlag, 2001.

[13] P. W. O'Hearn, H. Yang, and J. C. Reynolds. Separation and information hiding. In *31st POPL*, pages 268–280, 2004.

[14] J. C. Reynolds. Separation logic: A logic for shared mutable data structures. In *17th LICS*, pp 55-74, 2002.

[15] N. Rinetzky, J. Bauer, T. Reps, S. Sagiv, and R. Wilhelm. A semantics for procedure local heaps and its abstractions. *32nd POPL*, pp296–309, 2005.

[16] N. Rinetzky, M. Sagiv, and E. Yahav. Interprocedural shape analysis for cutpoint-free programs. In *12th International Static Analysis Symposium (SAS)*, 2005.

[17] M. Sagiv, T. Reps, and R. Wilhelm. Parametric shape analysis via 3valued logic. *ACM Trans. Program. Lang. Syst.*, 24(3):217–298, 2002.

Compositional Model Extraction for Higher-Order Concurrent Programs

D.R. Ghica[1] and A.S. Murawski[2,*]

[1] School of Computer Science, Univ. of Birmingham, Birmingham B15 2TT, UK
[2] Oxford University Computing Laboratory, Oxford OX1 3QD, UK

Abstract. The extraction of accurate finite-state models of higher-order or open programs is a difficult problem. We show how it can be addressed using newly developed game-semantic techniques and illustrate the solution with a model-checking tool based on such techniques. The approach has several important advantages over more traditional ones: precise account of inter-procedural behaviour, concise procedure summaries and economical extracted models.

1   Introduction and Background

Automated verification of software systems is one of the most urgent problems in computer science. This hardly needs to be argued for, as we are exposed to a world increasingly dominated by software. The theoretical and practical difficulty of the problem is well known. In general, the problem is undecidable but, even subject to simplifying assumptions and approximation techniques which make it decidable, the complexity poses a substantial challenge. Nevertheless, theoretical developments combined with an increase in available computational power give grounds for optimism, and automated verification of software systems is becoming increasingly feasible, to the point that it is about to become a meaningful part of industrial software development [1].

The most effective methods of automated software verification turn out to be based on *model checking* (MC) [2], in particular on *finite-state* model checking. A software system is represented as (or approximated by) a finite-state machine (FSM) and its interesting properties are expressed as *temporal* properties of the FSM. The challenges that need to be tackled include efficient extraction of models and automatic derivation of smaller but safe approximations. Some of the most advanced MC frameworks available centre around these issues [3, 4, 5, 6].

For programming languages with procedures, especially higher-order procedures, the extraction of an FSM representation or approximation is especially difficult because one needs to account for the often subtle interaction between procedures and other computational features such as state, concurrency or control. We can illustrate this point with a very simple example. Consider the following (second-order) procedure p taking as argument procedure c:

```
int p(void c(int d)) { int x=1;  c(2); return x }.
```

* Supported by the UK EPSRC (GR/R88861/01) and St John's College, Oxford.

H. Hermanns and J. Palsberg (Eds.): TACAS 2006, LNCS 3920, pp. 303–317, 2006.

In virtually any programming language if p returns a value then that value will be 1. There should be no way that the non-local procedure c, taken as an argument, can modify the value of the locally-scoped variable x. However, producing a FSM representation of this procedure, which makes it obvious that x and c cannot interact, turns out quite difficult. The same issues arise in modeling *open* programs, i.e. programs with procedures which are not defined locally. In both cases the obstacle is that operational techniques, which are ordinarily employed for model extraction, only apply for closed, ground-type terms.

Dealing with issues pertaining to *inter-procedural* interactions such as the one illustrated above is the subject of numerous lines of research: data-flow analysis, control-flow analysis, effect analysis, locality analysis and so on. Many of these analyses are syntactic or operational, and it is quite awkward to integrate them into a MC framework. However, they are essential in modeling and verifying higher-order programs. The problem of model extraction is particularly difficult in the presence of concurrency, because the naive model based on interleaved execution is very computationally expensive.

The research programme we are pursuing proposes a new kind of analysis, called *algorithmic game semantics*, which subsumes inter-procedural analysis and is compatible with FSM representation and model-checking. This analysis focuses on finding concrete representations for game-semantic models (or *game models*, for brevity) of programming languages. Having a *semantics-directed* approach to model construction has several important advantages:

Consistency. A semantics-directed approach provides a unified framework which encompasses and supersedes the techniques mentioned earlier in a uniform, substantially simplified fashion.

Correctness. The model extraction is correct (and in fact complete) by construction, relative to a specified notion of *observation*. In principle, any inter-procedural analysis compatible with the specified notion of observation can be derived from the semantics. For example, we will see that game models immediately validate the earlier observation about the interaction between local state and non-local procedures.

Concreteness. We can construct a concrete FSM representation of the behaviour of a higher-order program, which is independent of the syntax. Once the model is constructed we can apply standard model-checking methods to verify its properties efficiently.

Compositionality. Models are constructed *inductively on the structure of the program*, i.e. the model of a program P is constructed out of the models of its subprograms P_i. Most importantly, in constructing the models for subprograms P_i's we need not know the larger context in which they will be used. The beneficial consequences of a compositional method are:
- an ability to model and verify *open* programs, i.e. programs which must function in an unknown environment (for example *libraries*);
- the possibility to break up a larger system in smaller systems which can be modeled and verified independently (*scalability*);
- modeling procedures independently and incorporating their models efficiently into the model of a larger program (*procedure summaries*) [7].

Code-level specification. Program properties are described at *code-level* using assertions, rather than at *model-level* using temporal logics.

Note that a semantics-directed approach to model extraction was not feasible using the traditional styles of semantics extant before the introduction of game semantics, i.e. *operational* and *denotational*. Operational semantics is concrete enough, but has virtually no meta-theory, is not compositional and cannot model open programs. Denotational semantics, on the other hand, meets these requirements but is abstract and essentially non-finitary. Game semantics seems to combine the advantages of the two in a way that is particularly promising for automated verification.

Game semantics was introduced in order to tackle the long-standing *full abstraction* problem for the functional language PCF [8, 9]. The framework proved to be very useful for constructing semantics for a variety of programming languages involving diverse computational features such as state [10], control [11], concurrency [12] and more. The first steps in the direction of application of game semantics for program analysis were taken by Hankin and Malacaria [13]. The first application to model checking was proposed by Ghica and McCusker [14], and further developed by Ghica [15]. A model-checker based on these ideas was implemented in [16] with very positive results: it illustrates the ability to model open second-order programs by verifying invariants of abstract data type implementations (ADT) and it shows how the compositionality of the model construction allows the modeling of data-intensive programs such as sorting programs.

Contribution

The model checking technique described in [16] is for a *second-order sequential procedural language*. In this paper we substantially expand the expressivity of the programming language we model, by adding *higher-order procedures, shared-variable concurrency and semaphores*. The immediately relevant theoretical developments which led to this new model checking technique are a game model for shared-variable concurrency [12] and a type system used to identify decidable terms in the language [19].

Note that in this paper we focus almost exclusively on the problem of model extraction and representation. In order to tackle the other standard problems of MC (specification and efficient verification) we rely on the commercially-available model-checker FDR [17].

2   The Language SCC

We consider a higher-order call-by-name procedural language with parallel composition and binary semaphores. Its types are generated by the grammar given below

$$\beta ::= \mathsf{com} \mid \mathsf{int} \mid \mathsf{var} \mid \mathsf{sem} \qquad \theta ::= \beta \mid \theta \to \theta,$$

where com is the type of commands, int is a *finite* data-type of expressions which can take values from the set $\{\,0,\cdots,max\,\}$ ($max > 0$), var is the type of variables holding values from $\{\,0,\ldots,max\,\}$ and sem is the type of binary semaphores. The syntax of the language is defined by the standard λ-calculus rules ($\lambda x.M, MN$) augmented with rules for arithmetic, branching, iteration (while M do N), variable manipulation (assignment $M{:=}N$, dereferencing $!M$, variable definition with initialisation newvar $X{:=}i$ in M), parallel composition ($M_1 \,\|\, M_2$) and binary semaphore manipulation ($\mathsf{grb}(S)$, $\mathsf{release}(S)$, semaphore definition with initialisation newsem $S{:=}i$ in M, where $S{:=}0$ means that the semaphore is released initially).

The semantics of the language is defined using a (small-step) transition relation $\Sigma \vdash M, s \longrightarrow M', s'$. Σ is a set of names of variables denoting *memory cells* and names of semaphores denoting *locks*; s, s' are states, i.e. functions $s, s' : \Sigma \to \mathbb{N}$, and M, M' are terms.

We say that a term M *may* terminate from state s, written $M, s \Downarrow$, if there exists a terminating evaluation at start state s: $\exists s', \ M, s \longrightarrow^* c, s'$, with $c \in \{\,0,\cdots,max,\mathsf{skip}\,\}$. If M is closed and $M, \emptyset \Downarrow$ we write $M \Downarrow$. We consider the program *approximation* and *equivalence* relations induced by this angelic notion of termination. They are defined contextually as follows. Two terms $\Gamma \vdash M_1$ and $\Gamma \vdash M_2$ are deemed *may-equivalent* (written $\Gamma \vdash M_1 \cong M_2$) iff $\forall \mathcal{C}[-] :$ com, $\mathcal{C}[M_1] \Downarrow$ if and only if $\mathcal{C}[M_2] \Downarrow$, where $\mathcal{C}[M_i]$ are closed programs of type com. The corresponding notion of program approximation is defined by: $\Gamma \vdash M_1 \precsim M_2$ iff $\forall \mathcal{C}[-] :$ com, $\mathcal{C}[M_1] \Downarrow$ implies $\mathcal{C}[M_2] \Downarrow$ (where as before $\mathcal{C}[M_i]$ are closed programs of com type). Note that the two notions apply to terms with free identifiers (open terms) and are defined with respect to all possible uses (instantiations of the free identifiers).

Although we consider finite data-types and iteration rather than general recursion, it turns out that both $\cong$ and $\precsim$ are undecidable even for terms with free identifiers of first order. Indeed, in [19] we show that, unlike in the sequential case, it is impossible to decide the equivalence or approximation of terms of the shape $p : \mathsf{com} \to \mathsf{com} \vdash M : \mathsf{com}$. The reason is that functions of type com $\to$ com can use their argument in any number of concurrently running threads, which is powerful enough for encoding the halting problem for counter machines as an equivalence query. In order to recover decidability one needs to weaken the meaning of free identifiers and impose bounds on the number of concurrent threads of execution.

To formalise this sort of constraint specification we introduced a new type system, called *Syntactic Control of Concurrency* (SCC) [19]. Types of that system are the same as before except that they are annotated with numeric bounds. Thus an SCC typing judgment has the shape $x_1{:}\theta_1^{n_1}, \ldots, x_k{:}\theta_k^{n_k} \vdash_r M : \theta$ where θ is generated by the grammar $\theta ::= \beta \,|\, \theta^n \to \theta, \ n \in \mathbb{N}$. The numeric bounds concern the number of concurrent threads of execution that can arise during various stages of computation.

The key rules are the four rules below. Parallel composition and application increase the degree of concurrency, whereas sequential composition (and its iterated form, the **while** loop) does not affect the bounds in any way. Technically this is achieved by using disjoint contexts for $\|$ and application (unlike in the rule for sequential composition). The bounds for shared variables can then be added up using a special *contraction* rule.

$$\frac{\Gamma \vdash_r M_1 : \mathsf{com} \quad \Gamma \vdash_r M_2 : \mathsf{com}}{\Gamma \vdash_r M_1; M_2 : \mathsf{com}} \qquad \frac{\Gamma \vdash_r M_1 : \mathsf{com} \quad \Delta \vdash_r M_2 : \mathsf{com}}{\Gamma, \Delta \vdash_r M_1 \| M_2 : \mathsf{com}}$$

$$\frac{\Gamma \vdash_r M : \theta^n \to \theta' \quad \Delta \vdash_r N : \theta}{\Gamma, n\Delta \vdash_r MN : \theta'} \qquad \frac{\Gamma, x_1 : \theta^m, x_2 : \theta^n \vdash_r M : \theta'}{\Gamma, x : \theta^{m+n} \vdash_r M[x/x_1, x/x_2] : \theta'}$$

$n\Delta$ is the environment Δ in which all the outermost bounds have been multiplied by n.

Bounds have an intuitive *assume-guarantee* interpretation. A bound n is an assume (resp. guarantee) if it occurs in the left-hand scope of an even (resp. odd) number of $\to$ (the turnstile $\vdash$ is also considered an arrow for this purpose). Assumes concern the behaviour of the program context and guarantees that of the program. Intuitively, if the environment behaves according to the assumes, the program's behaviour satisfies the guarantees. For example, SCC can derive:

$$f : (\mathsf{com}^n \to \mathsf{com})^2, x : \mathsf{com}^{2n} \vdash_r f(x) \| f(x) : \mathsf{com},$$

where n (occurring in the type of f) is the only assume. SCC is made flexible by the use of subsumption: assumes can be decreased and guarantees increased.

Given an SCC typing derivation of M and a context $\mathcal{C}[-]$ such that $\mathcal{C}[M]$ is closed, we can verify whether $\mathcal{C}[-]$ is consistent with the assumes of M simply by checking if $\vdash_r \mathcal{C}[M]$ can be derived from the typing derivation of M. Given $\Gamma \vdash_r M_1$ and $\Gamma \vdash_r M_2$ sharing the same assumes, we now define new approximation and equivalence relations, denoted by $\precsim_r$ and $\cong_r$. The definitions are analogous to those of $\precsim$ and $\cong$ with the exception that the quantification ranges over all contexts $\mathcal{C}[-]$ that respect the assumes of M_1 and M_2.

Unlike $\precsim$ and $\cong$, $\precsim_r$ and $\cong_r$ are decidable, which can be proved using game semantics. $\precsim_r$ and $\cong_r$ can then be shown to correspond to containment and equality of the sets of the complete plays generated by the two terms in question. These in turn can be represented by regular languages. Thus the game model for SCC seems an ideal foundation for a model-checking tool: it is sound, complete (for $\precsim_r$ and $\cong_r$) and decidable [19].

The primary interest is, of course, to verify programs written in the original type system, without bounds on concurrency. Imposing the numerical bounds brings about two limitations. First, only terms with redexes of order less than two are guaranteed to admit an SCC typing. There exist known programs, albeit contrived, that do not admit any SCC typing and thus cannot be analysed using the technique proposed here, e.g.: $(\lambda g.g(\lambda x.g(\lambda y.x)))(\lambda f.f(f\mathsf{skip}))$. Second, bounds on concurrency in the environment (i.e. the assumes) must be imposed somewhat arbitrarily, and the resulting analysis is sound only within the assumed bounds. Fortunately, the type system SCC will (automatically) certify whether in given execution contexts free identifiers are bound to terms that satisfy the bounds.

3 CSP Representation of Strategies

Game semantics interprets programs as strategies in two-player games between O (Opponent) and P (Proponent), who represent the context and the program respectively. Strategies can be viewed simply as sequences of moves (actions) of the two players, which makes it possible to employ automata-theoretic techniques to their analysis. Strategies corresponding to SCC terms can be represented by regular languages. In this section we show how to do that using CSP [17].

CSP is a particularly convenient formalism for expressing strategies, because it features primitives for (selectively synchronised) parallel composition and hiding, the two operations on which *composition* of strategies is based. Additionally, we will take advantage of CSP channels (to indicate the source of a move), the flexibility to define new alphabets for multiple tagging (to indicate and compare membership in threads) and substitution (for re-tagging). CSP has been used before to represent strategies, but only for sequential programs [18].

First we briefly review the game-theoretic notions involved in the interpretation of terms. Due to space restrictions we omit many technical details, and only try to give the flavour of the approach. Formally, games can be regarded as triples $G = \langle M_G, \lambda_G, P_G^{\max} \rangle$ where M_G is the set of available moves, $\lambda_G : M_G \to \{O, P\}$ indicates the ownership of moves and $P_G^{\max} \subseteq M_G^*$ is the set of *complete* (maximal) positions. All other positions are simply prefixes of complete positions, so we can define the set of positions on G as $P_G = \{ s \mid \exists t \in P_G^{\max}.s \leq t \}$. Below we list the complete positions in the games corresponding to base types (the initial moves are O-moves, the final ones are P-moves; $0 \leq i \leq max$):

$[\![\mathsf{com}]\!]$	$[\![\mathsf{int}]\!]$	$[\![\mathsf{var}]\!]$	$[\![\mathsf{sem}]\!]$
$run \cdot done$	$q \cdot i$	$read \cdot i$	$grb \cdot okg$
		$write(i) \cdot ok$	$rls \cdot okr.$

SCC higher-order types have shape $\theta^n \to \theta'$, but for technical reasons it is useful to decompose such types using more elementary type constructors $\otimes$ (interleaved product), $\mathop{!}$ (iteration), and $\multimap$ (linear function space): $\theta^n \to \theta' = (\bigotimes_n \mathop{!}\theta) \multimap \theta'$. The definitions of the three game constructions are:

(M_G) $M_{\mathop{!}G} = M_G, M_{G_1 \otimes G_2} = M_{G_1 \multimap G_2} = M_{G_1} + M_{G_2}$

(λ_G) The constructions of $\mathop{!}G$ and $G_1 \otimes G_2$ preserve ownership of moves. In $G_1 \multimap G_2$ moves originating from G_2 have the same owners as in G_2, whereas O-moves (resp. P-moves) from G_1 are P-moves (resp. O-moves) in $G_1 \multimap G_2$.

$(P_G^{\max})$ $P_G^{\max}$ consists of sequences of complete positions from $P_G^{\max}$ ($P_{\mathop{!}G}^{\max} = \{ s_1 \cdots s_n \mid n > 0 \text{ and } \forall_{1 \leq i \leq n} s_i \in P_G^{\max} \}$). $P_{G_1 \otimes G_2}^{\max}$ contains interleavings of a position from $P_{G_1}^{\max}$ with a position from $P_{G_2}^{\max}$. $P_{G_1 \multimap G_2}^{\max}$ is similar except that the interleavings have to start and end with moves from G_2.

Game semantics interprets programs as strategies over games defined by the associated types (strategies are simply prefix-closed sets of positions). A term-in-context $x_1{:}\theta_1^{n_1}, \ldots, x_k{:}\theta_k^{n_k} \vdash_r M : \theta$ is then interpreted by a strategy for the game $[\![\theta_1^{n_1}]\!] \otimes \cdots \otimes [\![\theta_k^{n_k}]\!] \multimap [\![\theta]\!]$. Suppose $\theta = \alpha_l^{m_l} \to \cdots \to \alpha_1^{m_1} \to \beta$. Because the sets of moves $M_{\flat G} = M_G$ and $M_{G_1 \otimes G_2} = M_{G_1 \multimap G_2} = M_{G_1} + M_{G_2}$, the game corresponding to a type consists of disjoint copies of games for base types. Hence, $M_{[\![\theta_1^{n_1}]\!] \otimes \cdots \otimes [\![\theta_k^{n_k}]\!] \multimap [\![\theta]\!]} = \sum_{i=1,k} M_{[\![\theta_i^{n_i}]\!]} + \sum_{j=1,l} M_{[\![\alpha_j^{m_j}]\!]} + M_{[\![\beta]\!]}$.

A major design decision in employing CSP to represent strategies concerns the way all the disjoint sums $+$ are interpreted. For the instances of $+$ distinguished above we are going to use $k + l + 1$ different channels (one for each of the components). The disjoint sums involved in the construction of $\theta_i^{n_i}$ or $\alpha_j^{m_j}$ will be tackled differently by using subscripts for $\multimap$ and numeric tags for $\otimes$ (to enumerate the threads in the game $\flat G \otimes \cdots \otimes \flat G$). In general the moves will have the shape $m_{c_1,\ldots,c_v}.d_1.\ldots.d_w$ (abbreviated as $m_{\mathbf{c}}.\mathbf{d}$), where $c_i, d_j \in \mathbb{N}$ are indices identifying the type-component of a higher-order type (the c_is) and the thread-component of a nested set of threads (the d_is). To be precise, in order to represent moves of $M_{[\![\theta^n]\!]}$ we will use the alphabet $\mathcal{A}(\theta^n)$ which is defined as follows. For base types we take $\mathcal{A}(\beta) = M_{[\![\beta]\!]}$ and further:

$$\mathcal{A}(\theta^n) = \{\, m_{\mathbf{c}}.i.\mathbf{d} \mid m_{\mathbf{c}}.\mathbf{d} \in \mathcal{A}(\theta), 1 \le i \le n \,\}$$

$$\mathcal{A}(\gamma_n \to \cdots \to \gamma_1 \to \beta) = \bigcup_{i=1}^{n} \{\, m_{i,\mathbf{c}}.\mathbf{d} \mid m_{\mathbf{c}}.\mathbf{d} \in \mathcal{A}(\gamma_i) \,\} \cup \mathcal{A}(\beta).$$

Concretely, the structure of an action used to represent a move is *identifier.move$_{rank}$.thread*. The channel *identifier* represents the free identifier associated with the move, or special identifier *"main"* if the move is associated with the term type. The *rank* is a tag representing the type component (from right to left) associated with the move. Finally, the list of thread indices identify the threads and the (nested) sub-threads containing the move.

We are going to define CSP processes whose traces will coincide with strategies denoting terms in such a way that complete positions $\mathsf{comp}([\![\Gamma \vdash_r M]\!])$ will be followed by special action $\sqrt{}$. This will enable us to compare complete positions defined by terms and, by the theorem below, verify program equivalence and approximation. Because we use tags for identifying threads, in order to compare strategies we will have to introduce a canonical way of tag usage, e.g. lowest unused. The convention can be enforced by putting the processes corresponding to terms in parallel with a separate CSP process that acts as a "name server".

Theorem 1 ([19]). *Given* $\Gamma \vdash_r M_i : \theta$ *(i = 1, 2) let us write* $\mathsf{comp}([\![\Gamma \vdash_r M_i]\!])$ *for the set of complete positions in* $[\![\Gamma \vdash_r M_i]\!]$. *Then* $\Gamma \vdash M_1 \lesssim_r M_2$ *iff* $\mathsf{comp}([\![\Gamma \vdash_r M_1]\!]) \subseteq \mathsf{comp}([\![\Gamma \vdash_r M_2]\!])$ *and* $\Gamma \vdash M_1 \cong_r M_2$ *iff* $\mathsf{comp}([\![\Gamma \vdash_r M_1]\!]) = \mathsf{comp}([\![\Gamma \vdash_r M_2]\!])$.

CSP processes corresponding to terms can be defined by induction on their structure. Free identifiers $x : \theta^1 \vdash_r x : \theta$ are interpreted by the *copy-cat* strategy in which O-moves are simply copied by P between the two copies of $[\![\theta]\!]$ (possibly with a delay) subject to the exchange of moves being a position in the relevant game. The behaviour of this strategy resembles that of an unbounded buffer. Its CSP process can be defined inductively on the structure of types.

Suppose $\theta = \theta_k^{n_k} \to \cdots \to \theta_1^{n_1} \to \beta$. $ID(L, R_k, \cdots, R_0, \theta)$ returns a process representing $[\![x : \theta^1 \vdash_r x : \theta]\!]$ in such a way that the moves from $[\![\theta^1]\!]$ are

```
PLUS(A1,A2,A,b) = A.q ->A1.q ->A1?x ->A2.q ->A2?y ->A.((x+y)%b) ->SKIP
EQ(A1,A2,A,b) = A.q -> A1.q -> A1?x -> A2.q -> A2?y
                   -> A.(if x==y then 1 else 0) -> SKIP
ASSIGN(A2,A1,A) = A.run -> A2.q -> A2?y -> A1.write.y -> A1.wok
                   -> A.done -> SKIP
PAR(A1,A2,A) = A.run -> ((A1.run -> A1.done -> SKIP)
                 ||| (A2.run -> A2.done -> SKIP));(A.done -> SKIP)
SEQCOM(A1,A2,A) = A.run -> A1.run -> A1.done -> A2.run -> A2.done
                   -> A.done -> SKIP
IFCOM(A0,A1,A2,A) = A.run -> A0.q -> A0?y -> if (y==0) then
                     (A2.run -> A2.done -> A.done -> SKIP)
                    else (A1.run -> A1.done -> A.done -> SKIP)
WHILE(A1,A2,A) = A.run -> WHILE_AUX(A1,A2,A)
WHILE_AUX(A1,A2,A) = A1.q -> A1?y -> if (y==0) then (A.done -> SKIP)
                     else (A2.run -> A2.done -> WHILE_AUX(A1,A2,A))
GRAB(A1,A) = A.run -> A1.grb -> A1.gok -> A.done -> SKIP
RELEASE(A1,A) = A.run -> A1.rls -> A1.rok -> A.done -> SKIP
CELL(A,m) = (A.read?b -> A.m.b -> CELL(A,m))
            [] (A.write?v?b -> A.wok.b -> CELL(A,v)) [] SKIP
SEM(A,m) = if (m==0) then (A.grb?b -> A.gok.b -> SEM(A,1) [] SKIP)
           else (A.rls?b -> A.rok.b -> SEM(A,0) [] SKIP)
```

Fig. 1. CSP representation of some strategies

transmitted on channel L, those from $[\![\theta_i^{n_i}]\!]$ on channel R_i and those from $[\![\beta]\!]$ on R_0. Let $P_i = ID_{aux}(LL, RR, \theta_i)$ $(1 \leq i \leq k)$ for some fresh channel names LL, RR, where $ID_{aux}(LL, RR, \theta_i)$ is defined below. For $1 \leq i \leq k, 1 \leq j \leq n_i$ define $P_{i,j} = P_i[\![RR.m_c.d \leftarrow L.m_{i,c}.j.d, LL.m_c.1.d \leftarrow R_i.m_{i,c}.j.d]\!]$. Let $P' = |||_{i=1}^{k} |||_{j=1}^{n_i} STAR(P_{i,j})$, where $STAR(P) = SKIP \,[]\, (P; STAR(P))$. Then return $[]_{m_1 m_2 \in P_{[\![\beta]\!]}}(R.m_1 \rightarrow L.m_1.1 \rightarrow P'); (L.m_2.1 \rightarrow R.m_2 \rightarrow SKIP)$.

$ID_{aux}(L, R, \theta)$ returns a process representing $[\![x : \theta^1 \vdash_r x : \theta]\!]$ in such a way that the moves from $[\![\theta^1]\!]$ are transmitted on channel L and those from $[\![\theta]\!]$ on R. It can be defined recursively as follows. Suppose $\theta = \theta_k^{n_k} \rightarrow \cdots \rightarrow \theta_1^{n_1} \rightarrow \beta$. Let $P_i = ID_{aux}(LL, RR, \theta_i)$ $(1 \leq i \leq k)$ for some fresh channel names LL, RR. For $1 \leq i \leq k, 1 \leq j \leq n_i$ define $P_{i,j} = P_i[\![RR.m_c.d \leftarrow L.m_{i,c}.j.d, LL.m_c.1.d \leftarrow R.m_{i,c}.j.d]\!]$. Let $P' = |||_{i=1}^{k} |||_{j=1}^{n_i} STAR(P_{i,j})$, where $STAR(P) = SKIP \,[]\, (P; STAR(P))$. Then return $[]_{m_1 m_2 \in P_{[\![\beta]\!]}}(R.m_1 \rightarrow L.m_1.1 \rightarrow P'); (L.m_2.1 \rightarrow R.m_2 \rightarrow SKIP)$.

The CSP representation of some of the key constants of the language is given in Fig. 1. Using different channels for moves of $[\![\alpha_j^{m_j}]\!]$ makes interpreting application relatively easy, because it suffices to use the channel corresponding $\alpha_l^{m_l}$ to synchronise the process corresponding to the function term with m_l interleaved copies of that corresponding to the argument. Suppose P_1, P_2 are the CSP processes representing $[\![\Gamma \vdash_r M_1 : \theta_1]\!]$ and $[\![\Gamma \vdash_r M_2 : \theta_2]\!]$ respectively and R_0^i are the channels on which moves from the right copies of respectively $[\![\theta_i]\!]$, $i = 1, 2$ are transmitted. Then the process P representing $\Gamma \vdash_r M_1 \square M_2$ is:

$$P = ((P_1 \mid\mid\mid P_2) \; [\mid R_0^1, R_0^2 \mid] \; PROC_\square(R_0^1, R_0^1, R_0)) \setminus \{\mid R_0^1, R_0^2 \mid\},$$

where $PROC_\square(\cdots)$ is the CSP representation of the $\square$ binary operator $(+, =, ;,$ $:=,$ etc), as given in Fig. 1. Operators of different arity (if-then-else, grab, release, etc.) are treated analogously.

Application is parallel composition synchronised on the actions corresponding to the type of the argument, followed by the hiding of those actions. Contraction amounts to renumbering threads: m threads (indexed by $1, \ldots, m$) on one channel and n threads on another (with indices from $1, \ldots, n$) have to be renumbered as threads indexed $1, \cdots, m+n$ on a new channel, done by CSP substitution.

For example, the main processes generated in the representation of the strategies for $f : \mathsf{com}^2 \to \mathsf{com}, x : \mathsf{com} \vdash fx : \mathsf{com}$ are:

```
P8 = ||| j:{0..1} @ STAR(ADD(ADD(P7,j,C7,C3),j,C5,C6))
P9 = (P8[|{|C3|}|]P3)\{|C3|}
ADD(P,j,IN,OUT)=P[[IN.done.x<-OUT.done.((x+j)%(3))|x<-{0..2}]]
              [[IN.run.x<-OUT.run.((x+j)%(3))|x<-{0..2}]]
              [[IN.done_1.x<-OUT.done_1.((x+j)%(2))|x<-{0..1}]]
              [[IN.run_1.x<-OUT.run_1.((x+j)%(2))|x<-{0..1}]]
```

In the above, process P8 generates 2 interleavings of the argument (represented by P7, not shown) using auxiliary processes STAR (which iterates its argument) and ADD (which serves as the renaming server). Process P9 is the actual application (in which P3 represents the free variable f, not shown) consisting on synchronisation on channel C3 followed by the hiding of C3.

Variable and semaphore introduction can be represented by application of special (higher-order) constants newvar_m and newsem_m: $\mathsf{newvar}\, x := m$ in $M \equiv \mathsf{newvar}_m(\lambda x.M)$, and $\mathsf{newsem}\, x := m$ in $M \equiv \mathsf{newsem}_m(\lambda x.M)$. The applications are modeled by parallel composition with hiding using the CSP processes $\mathsf{CELL}(\cdots, \mathsf{m})$ and $\mathsf{SEM}(\cdots, \mathsf{m})$ respectively.

4 Tool Support and Case Studies

Using translation to CSP we can employ FDR to verify several classes of properties: program equivalences $(\cong_r)$ and inequivalences, approximation $(\sqsubseteq_r)$, assertions, invariants and other safety properties.

In our examples, the channel names associated with free identifiers will always have a name related to the identifier, $\mathsf{int\$i}$ will stand for the type $\{0, \ldots, i-1\}$. We also use n-ary semaphores $(n > 1)$, which can be easily added to SCC, writing $\mathsf{sem\$n}$ for the corresponding type ($\mathsf{sem\$1}$ is identical to the type sem of binary semaphores). In the programs below, the assumed bounds on the behaviour of the environment, e.g. $p : \mathsf{com}^2 \to \mathsf{int}$, are represented as $\mathsf{p:com\{2\}->exp}$.

We implemented a tool which takes as input SCC terms (only the assumes are actually required), infers the missing guarantee bounds then compiles the term in the CSP process algebra. The FDR model-checker is invoked to verify safety properties or to check (may) equivalence of terms.

4.1   Warm-Up Example

Let us illustrate the model with a classic example from the literature [20]:

$$p : \mathsf{com} \to \mathsf{int} \to \mathsf{com} \vdash \mathsf{newvar}\, x{:=}0 \text{ in } p(x{:=}x + 1; x{:=}x - 1)(x) \not\equiv p\,\mathsf{skip}\,0.$$

The non-local procedure p can increment then decrement the local variable x or dereference it, but has no other access to it. Therefore, in a *sequential* programming language the equivalence stands. However, in a *concurrent* language the equivalence may fail because the arguments can generate race conditions. Indeed, if we give p the SCC typing $\mathsf{com}^m \to \mathsf{int}^n \to \mathsf{com}$ for some $m, n > 0$, FDR identifies a trace which can occur in the LHS but not in the RHS (we present it along with a move-by-move interpretation):

$main.run$	start execution, first main thread
$p.run.1$	start executing p's main thread
$p.q_1.1.1$	start executing p's right argument, first thread
$p.run_2.1.1$	start executing p's left argument, first thread
$p.1_1.1.1$	p's right argument in first thread produces 1

We can see that the reason for the equivalence failing was a race condition. SCC is call-by-name, i.e. the arguments are *thunks*, so the right argument may begin to be evaluated *before* the evaluation of the left argument has completed ($p.ok_2.1.1$). In fact, the diagrammatic representation of the processes produced by FDR shows quite clearly that the two processes are not similar (Fig. 2).

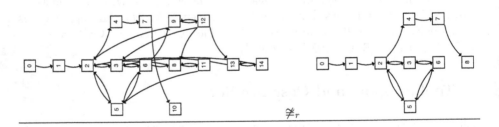

Fig. 2. Two inequivalent processes

4.2   Verifying Algorithm Implementations

Consider the code in Fig. 3, implementing the tie-breaker algorithm [21] as a procedure which takes as arguments two critical regions, two non-critical regions and two termination conditions (LHS). We can verify the algorithm by comparing it against a simpler implementation which assumes the existence of semaphores in the language and serves as a specification (RHS). By compiling the two implementations into CSP, we can use FDR to verify that, indeed, they are equivalent.

```
1   mutex1(crtc1:com, crtc2:com, nonc1:com, nonc2:com, b1:int$2, b2:int$2) =
2     int in1, in2, last;
3     while b1 do {
4         in1:=1; last:=1; while (in2 & last=1) do skip; crtc1; in1:=0; nonc1 }
5     || while b2 do {
6         in2:=1; last:=2; while (in1 & last=2) do skip; crtc2; in2:=0; nonc2 }
7   ≅ mutex2(crtc1:com, crtc2:com, nonc1:com, nonc2:com, b1:int$2, b2:int$2)=
8     sem s; while b1 do {grab(s); crtc1; release(s); nonc1}
9     || while b2 do {grab(s); crtc2; release(s); nonc2}
```

Fig. 3. The tie-breaker algorithm vs semaphores

4.3 Verifying ADT Implementations

One of the principal advantages of our approach is that we can model *open* programs, such as ADTs. For example, let us consider the stack implementation given in Fig. 4, where n is the size of the stack and *empty, overflow* are (unspecified) user-defined procedures to handle usage errors. The implementation stores the stack elements in an array and uses a semaphore to protect the changes to the array as well as the variable `crt` that indicates the top of the stack. However, it is not actually *thread-safe* and contains a non-trivial (but common) error which we will "discover" using our model-checker. In order to model and verify the ADT we consider the program *VERIFY push pop top*, where *VERIFY* : (int → com)[1] → com[1] → int[1] → com plays the role of *the most general environment*. After generating the game model with FDR we can check the stack ADT for safety properties such as buffer over-runs or assertion failures. For instance, if we introduce an additional free identifier

```
empty:com,  overflow:com,  VERIFY:(int->com){1}->com{1}->int{1}->com |-    1
  int buf[n], crt; sem s;                                                   2
  let size:int = n                                                          3
      isempty:int = (crt = 0)                                               4
      isfull:int = (crt = size)                                             5
      push:(int->com) = fun x : int.                                        6
        if isfull then overflow                                            7
        else (grab(s); buf[crt]:=x; crt:=crt+1; release(s))                8
      top:int =                                                             9
        int tmp;                                                           10
        if isempty then (empty; 0)                                         11
        else (grab(s); tmp:=buf[crt-1]; release(s); tmp)                   12
      pop:com =                                                            13
          if isempty then empty else (grab(s); crt:=crt-1; release(s))     14
  in VERIFY push pop top : com.                                            15
```

Fig. 4. A bounded-stack implementation

segf : com (segmentation fault) and arrange for *segf* to be invoked for buffer overrun errors, the FDR will identify the following safety violation:

main.run	start execution
VERIFY.*run*.1	start running *VERIFY*
VERIFY.*run*$_3$.1.1	call *push*
VERIFY.$q_{3,1}$.1.1.1	*push* requests an argument
VERIFY.q_1.1.1	call *top*
VERIFY.$0_{3,1}$.1.1.1	provide an argument to *push*
VERIFY.*run*$_2$.1.1	call *pop*
segf.*run*	a violation has occurred.

The reason for the violation is the fact that only the changes to the buffer and the top of the stack have been protected by a semaphore. As seen in the trace, a violation can still occur if *top* starts executing on a one-element stack, then *pop* is executed concurrently between the empty-stack check and the dereferencing of the buffer. A thread-safe implementation must protect with semaphores the entire scope of the stack methods, including the testing for empty and full buffer.

5   Higher-Order Procedures: Producer-Consumer

Our final example will examine a producer-consumer algorithm [21]: the procedure accepts as arguments a *producer* and a *consumer* function along with a parameter indicating when termination should occur. The value returned by the producer function is stored in a circular buffer. The consumer function takes a value from the circular buffer and performs some (unknown) action. The main procedure executes p copies of the producer process in parallel with c copies of the consumer process, each in a loop controlled by the argument $b1$ or $b2$. Information in the form of numbers from 0 to $i - 1$ is shared using an n-place buffer. The values of n, p, c, i are constants.

In the implementation shown in Fig. 5, semaphores s and t are used to prevent race conditions between the producers and, respectively, the consumers. Note that a producer and a consumer may access the buffer concurrently. N-ary semaphores *full* and *empty* make the producers and the consumers wait if the buffer is full, respectively empty.

This procedure is interesting because it is not possible to reduce it meaningfully to a first-order program. The SCC typing of the *prodcon* procedure means that the analysis requires that the consume procedure uses its argument in at most one thread of execution, which is not an unreasonable restriction. We can perform the same safety analyses as described before, and the implementation in Fig. 5 does not produce violations. We can also perform various safety tests using the FDR-specific idiom, *refinement* [17].

However, in the case of a complex program such as this, the real challenge lies in constructing the model, so we will use this example primarily to illustrate how the state space of the model is affected by the various constants occurring in

```
1   prodcon(produce:int$i, consume:int$i{1}->com, b1:int$2, b2:int$2) =
2   int$i buf[n], front, rear;
3   sem$n full=n, empty;
4   sem s, t;
5     dopar j := 1,p while b1 do {
6       int$i tmp := produce;
7       grab(empty); grab(s);
8       buf[rear] := tmp;
9       rear := (rear + 1) mod n;
10      release(s); release(full) }
11  || dopar j := 1,c while b2 do {
12      grab(full); grab(t);
13      int$i tmp := buf[front];
14      front := (front + 1) mod n;
15      release(t); release(empty);
16      consume(tmp) }
```

Fig. 5. A higher-order producer-consumer procedure

the program. We will also compare the size of the resulting model, as produced by FDR, with the size of a *naive* model generated by state exploration and interleaving of basic operational steps. (According to the operational semantics of the language each thread needs around 30 such steps.)

The results of the comparison are given in Tbl. 1. The *workspace* column indicates the largest *intermediate* model generated in the course of creating the final model. It is clear from the data above that the savings achieved using an *observational model*, which hides state changes that are not externally observable, are substantial. This is consistent with our earlier analysis of data-intensive algorithms. We can also see the importance of *compositional* model construction and *concise procedure summaries*, because a client of the prodcon procedure can now be modeled using the very compact observational model. Inlining the procedure even a couple of times would generate models of unmanageable size.

Table 1. Benchmark results

n	p	c	i	naive model	game model	FDR workspace	time (s)
3	1	1	1	40,000	114	2,554	112
4	1	1	1	62,500	143	5,168	142
3	2	1	1	1,000,000	1,684	39,758	247
3	1	2	1	1,000,000	1,735	43,206	351
3	1	1	2	5,120,000	464	4,632	223
2	2	2	1	14,062,500	6,478	495,621	1,733
3	2	2	1	25,000,000	13,813	760,389	4,889
2	2	2	2	3,600,000,000	24,489	1,763,637	54,617

Our experiments also confirm that increasing the amount of *observable* concurrency in the system has a far worse effect over model size than increasing the amount of data available to the system. The last case is perhaps the most interesting. The very large naive model state space is due to increasing the size of variable `tmp` which occurs in 4 threads. But the variable is local, hence invisible from outside its scope, so it does not contribute directly to the final model.

6   Conclusions

Game semantics provides a new technique for software model extraction which, as we have seen, has several advantages. The semantics-directed nature of the approach ensures correctness and completeness by construction and a compositional, incremental way of generating the model. What makes game models substantially different from more traditional models is a focus on *observational behaviour*, i.e. on the interaction between a program and its context, and hiding the non-observable details such as internal state changes.

Our experiments show that game semantics leads to much more compact models than those obtained by naive interleaving. We believe that further gains in efficiency are possible with the help of partial-order reduction techniques [23]. However, their incorporation into game semantics has not been investigated yet, especially the subtle relation between partial-order reduction and composition, and we leave it for future work.

Software verification using game models is still in its infancy but the initial developments are promising. However, we are some distance away from providing true competition to industrial-level tools. The following developments, which are within reach, will however bring us closer to realistic applications:

Real languages. The language we study here is realistic and expressive, but it is ultimately an academic exercise. We believe game-semantic techniques are now mature enough so that we can soon tackle a real programming language, such as a substantial subset of Java or C.

Liveness. The game model for SCC is derived from an *angelic* notion of termination which corresponds to trace equivalence. This does not account for deadlock or live-lock. Upgrading the semantic model to handle these phenomena is the subject of on-going research.

Algorithmics. So far we have used off-the-shelf model checkers which do not exploit the features of our semantics perfectly. FDR, for example lacks features which are common in modern model checkers, such as BDD representation. SPIN [6] is a powerful model-checker, but (unlike FDR) is essentially stateful. Moreover, neither of the two supports *composition*, i.e. creating a model from two independently generated models (although FDR uses compositional reductions internally).

Refinement. Our use of data abstraction in this model checker is relatively informal. The problem of automatically abstracting and refining the model is critical for software verification, and is dealt with separately [22].

References

1. Ball, T., Cook, B., Levin, V., Rajamani, S.K.: SLAM and static driver verifier: technology transfer of formal methods inside Microsoft. In: IFM 2004, LNCS **2999** 1–20
2. Clarke, E.M., Grumberg, O., Peled, P.: Model Checking. The MIT Press, Cambridge, Massachusetts (1999)
3. Robby, Dwyer, M.B., Hatcliff, J.: Bogor: an extensible and highly-modular software model checking framework. In: ESEC / SIGSOFT FSE (2003) 267–276
4. Ball, T., Rajamani, S.K.: The SLAM toolkit. In: CAV 2001, LNCS **2102** 260–264
5. Andrews, T., Qadeer, S., Rajamani, S.K., Rehof, J., Xie, Y.: Zing: A model checker for concurrent software. In: CAV 2004, LNCS **3114** 484–487
6. Holzmann, G.J.: The Spin model checker. IEEE Trans. on Soft. Eng. **23** (1997) 279–295
7. Qadeer, S., Rajamani, S.K., Rehof, J.: Summarizing procedures in concurrent programs. In: POPL (2004) 245–255
8. Abramsky, S., Jagadeesan, R., Malacaria, P.: Full abstraction for PCF. Information and Computation **163** (2000)
9. Hyland, J. M. E., Ong, C.-H. L.: On full abstraction for PCF: I, II and III. Information and Computation **163** (2000)
10. Abramsky, S., McCusker, G.: Linearity, sharing and state: a fully abstract game semantics for Idealized Algol with active expressions. ENTCS **3** (1996)
11. Laird, J.: Full abstraction for functional languages with control. In: LICS (1997) 58–67
12. Ghica, D.R., Murawski, A.S.: Angelic semantics of fine-grained concurrency. In: FOSSACS 2004, LNCS **2987** 211–225
13. Hankin, C., Malacaria, P.: Generalised flowcharts and games. In: ICALP (1998) 363–374
14. Ghica, D.R., McCusker, G.: Reasoning about Idealized ALGOL using regular languages. In: ICALP 2000, LNCS **1853** 103–116
15. Ghica, D.R.: A Games-based Foundation for Compositional Software Model Checking. PhD thesis, Queen's University, Kingston, Canada (2002)
16. Abramsky, S., Ghica, D. R., Murawski, A. S., Ong, C.-H. L.: Applying game semantics to compositional software modeling and verification. In: TACAS'04, LNCS **2988** 421–435
17. Roscoe, W.A.: Theory and Practice of Concurrency. Prentice-Hall (1998)
18. Dimovski, A., Lazic, R.: CSP Representation of Game Semantics for Second-Order Idealized Algol. In: ICFEM 2004, LNCS **3308** 146–191.
19. Ghica, D.R., Murawski, A. S., Ong, C.-H. L.: Syntactic control of concurrency. In: ICALP'04, LNCS **3142** 683–694
20. Brookes, S.: The essence of Parallel Algol. In: LICS (1996) 164–173
21. Andrews, G.: Concurrent Programming: principles and practice. Addison-Wesley Publishing Company (1991)
22. Dimovski, A., Ghica, D.R., Lazic, R.: Data-Abstraction Refinement: A Game Semantic Approach In: SAS'05, LNCS **3672** 102-117
23. Rajeev, A., et. al.: Partial-Order Reduction in Symbolic State-Space Exploration. Formal Methods in System Design **18**(2): 97-116 (2001)

A Region Graph Based Approach to Termination Proofs

Stefan Leue and Wei Wei

Department of Computer and Information Science, University of Konstanz,
D-78457 Konstanz, Germany
{Stefan.Leue, wei}@inf.uni-konstanz.de

Abstract. Automated termination proofs are indispensable in the mechanic verification of many program properties. While most of the recent work on automated termination proofs focuses on the construction of linear ranking functions, we develop an approach based on region graphs in which regions define subsets of variable values that have different effects on loop termination. In order to establish termination, we check whether (1) any region will be exited once it is entered, and (2) no region is entered an infinite number of times. We show the effectiveness of our proof method by experiments with Java code using a prototype implementation of our approach.

1 Introduction

Automated termination proofs are indispensable in the mechanic verification of many program properties. Our interest in automated termination proofs comes from the precursory work on determining communication buffer boundedness for communicating finite state machine based models such as they occur in UML RT models [6, 7, 8]. In UML RT models the action code of a transition in a state machine can contain arbitrary program code, for instance Java code. When the action code contains a program loop within which some messages are sent, we need the information of how many times the loop iterates in order to determine how many messages are sent along the transition.

Automated termination proving has recently received intensive attention [10, 12, 2, 1, 4, 3], in particular those approaches based on transition invariants [11]. Most of the recent work [10, 1] focuses on the construction of linear ranking functions. However, loops may not always possess linear ranking functions, c.f. Example 1 in Section 2.

We develop a method to prove termination for an important class of loops, *deterministic multiple-path linear numerical loops with conjunctive conditions*, whose subclasses are also studied in [10, 12]. Given a loop, we construct one or more region graphs in which regions define subsets of variable values that have different effects on loop termination. In order to establish termination, we check for some generated region graph whether (1) any region will be exited once it is entered, and (2) no region is entered an infinite number of times. We show the effectiveness of our proof method by experiments with Java code using a prototype implementation of our approach.

Related Work. [10] gives a complete and efficient linear ranking function synthesis method for loops that can be represented as a linear inequality system. It considers nondeterministic update of variable values to allow for abstraction. However, it does not

H. Hermanns and J. Palsberg (Eds.): TACAS 2006, LNCS 3920, pp. 318–333, 2006.

apply to multiple-path loops. [1] can discover linear ranking functions for any linear loops over integer variables based on building ranking function templates and checking satisfiability of template instantiations that are Presburger formulas. The method is complete but neither efficient nor terminating on some loops. [2] gives a novel solution to proving termination for polynomial loops based on finite difference trees. In fact it applies only to those polynomial loops whose behavior is also polynomial, i.e., the considered guarding function value at any time can be represented as a polynomial expression in terms of the initial guarding function value. Note that Example 1 does not have a polynomial behavior. [12] proves the decidability of termination for linear single-path loops over real variables. However, the decidability of termination for integer loops remains a conjecture. [4] suggests a constraint solving based method of synthesizing nonlinear ranking functions for linear and quadratic loops. The method is incomplete due to the Lagrangian Relaxation of verification conditions that it takes advantage of.

Outline. We define loops, regions, and region graphs in Sections 2 and 3. The region graph based termination proof methods are explained for three subclasses of loops: (1) $G^1 P^1$ in Section 4, (2) $G^1 P^*$ in Section 5, and (3) $G^* P^1$ in Section 6. We generalize these methods to handle the whole loop class that we consider in this paper in the end of Section 6. Experimental results are reported in Section 7 before a conclusion in Section 8.

2 Loops

We formalize the class of loops that we consider in this paper. We call this class *deterministic multiple-path linear numerical[1] loops with conjunctive conditions*, or $G^* P^*$ (multiple-guard-multiple-path) in short. Loops in $G^* P^*$ have the following syntactic form:

while lc **do**
$$pc^1 \rightarrow \bar{x}' = U^1 \bar{x} + \bar{u}^1$$
...
$$pc^p \rightarrow \bar{x}' = U^p \bar{x} + \bar{u}^p$$
od

where

- $\bar{x} = [x_1, ..., x_n]^T$ is a column variable vector where T is transposition of matrices. $x_1, ..., x_n$ can be either integer variables or real variables. We use $\bar{x}' = [x'_1, ..., x'_n]^T$ to denote the new variable values after one loop iteration.
- $lc = \bigwedge_{i=1}^{m} lc^i$ is the loop condition. Each conjunct lc^i is a linear inequality in the form $\bar{a}^i \bar{x} \geq b^i$ where $\bar{a}^i = [a_1^i, ..., a_n^i]$ is a constant row vector of coefficients of variables and b^i is a constant. We call $\bar{a}^i \bar{x}$ a *guard*. We know that values of $\bar{a}^i \bar{x}$ are always bounded from below during loop iterations.

---

[1] With numerical loops we will not consider the rounding and overflow problems as usually considered while analyzing programs.

- Each $pc^i \rightarrow \bar{x}' = U^i \bar{x} + \bar{u}^i$ is a path with a path condition pc^i which is a conjunction of linear inequalities. We require that $\bigvee_{i=1}^p pc^i = true$, which guarantees a complete specification of the loop body. We further require that, for any i and j such that $i \neq j$, $pc^i \wedge pc^j = false$. This means that only one path can be taken at any given point in time.
- Each U^i is a constant matrix of dimension $n \times n$. Each $\bar{u}^i$ is a constant column vector of dimension n. They together describe how values of variables are updated along the i-th path.

If a loop has only one single path, then the loop body can be written as $\bar{x}' = U^1 \bar{x} + \bar{u}^1$, in which we leave out the path condition $true$. Here are some examples of $G^* P^*$ loops.

Example 1. This loop is an example of a loop without linear ranking functions [10]:
   while $x \geq 0$ **do**
   $\qquad x' = -2x + 10$
   od

Example 2. This is a loop with two paths:
   while $x \geq -4$ **do**
   $\qquad x \geq 0 \rightarrow x' = -x - 1$
   $\qquad x < 0 \rightarrow x' = -x + 1$
   od

Example 3. This loop has more than one inequality in its loop condition:
   while $x_1 \geq 1 \wedge x_2 \geq 1$ **do**
   $$\begin{bmatrix} x_1' \\ x_2' \end{bmatrix} = \begin{bmatrix} 1 & -1 \\ 0 & 1 \end{bmatrix} \begin{bmatrix} x_1 \\ x_2 \end{bmatrix}$$
   od

The three examples above represent three interesting subclasses of $G^* P^*$ that are studied in the paper: (1) $G^1 P^1$ are single-guard-single-path loops such as Example 1; (2) $G^1 P^*$ are single-guard-multiple-path loops such as Example 2; and (3) $G^* P^1$ are multiple-guard-single-path loops such as Example 3.

We say that a loop is *terminating* if it terminates on *any* initial assignment of variable values.

3   Region Graph

We define regions, positive and negative regions, still regions, and region graphs.

Definition 1. *Given a loop, a region is a set of vectors of variable values such that*

- *all the vectors in the region satisfy the loop condition.*
- *it forms a convex polyhedron, i.e., it can be expressed as a system of linear inequalities.*

We will also call a vector of variable values a *point*. We say that the loop iteration is *at some point* when the variables have the same values as in the point.

Definition 2. *Given a loop and a guard in the loop condition, a positive (negative, still, resp.) region with respect to the guard is a region such that, starting at any point in the region, the value of the guard is decreased (increased, unchanged, resp.) after one iteration.*

For instance, a positive region of Example 1 with respect to the guard x is $\{v \mid v > 10/3\}$, a negative region with respect to x is $\{v \mid 0 \leq v < 10/3\}$, and the only still region with respect to x is $\{10/3\}$. Moreover, if x is an integer variable, then there is no still region with respect to x. In the remainder, when we mention a positive (or negative or still) region, we will omit the respective guard if it is clear from the context.

Definition 3. *Given a loop and two regions R_1 and R_2 of the loop, there is a transition from R_1 to R_2 if and only if, starting at some point p in R_1, a point p' in R_2 is reached after one iteration. R_1 is the origin of the transition. R_2 is the target of the transition.*

In the definition, if R_1 and R_2 are distinct, then we say that R_1 is *exited* at p and R_2 is *entered* at p'. A transition is a *self-transition* if it starts and ends in one same region. We define that a self-transition on a region means that the region is neither exited nor entered.

For instance, there is a transition from the positive region $\{v \mid v > 10/3\}$ to the negative region $\{v \mid 0 \leq v < 10/3\}$ of Example 1 because $-2 \times 4 + 10 = 2$ while 4 is in the positive region and 2 is in the negative region.

Definition 4. *Given a loop, a region graph is a pair $< \mathbb{R}, \mathbb{T} >$ such that*

- $\mathbb{R}$ *is a finite set of pairwisely disjoint regions such that the union of all the regions is the complete set of points satisfying the loop condition.*
- $\mathbb{T}$ *is the complete set of transitions among regions in $\mathbb{R}$.*

In general, a region graph may contain regions that are neither positive, nor negative, nor still. However, the region graphs constructed by our termination proving methods contain only positive, negative, or still regions. A loop may have infinitely many region graphs.

Definition 5. *Given a region graph, a cycle is a sequence of transitions $< T_1, ..., T_n >$, where $n \geq 2$, such that*

- *for any two successive transitions T_i and T_{i+1}, the origin of T_{i+1} is the target of T_i;*
- *the origin of T_1 is the target of T_n.*

The condition $(n \geq 2)$ in the above definition excludes self-transitions to be cycles. Cycles such as $< T_1, T_2, T_3 >$, $< T_3, T_1, T_2 >$ and $< T_2, T_3, T_1 >$ are regarded as one

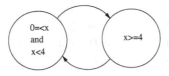

Fig. 1. A Region Graph

same cycle. A *simple cycle* is a cycle that cannot be further decomposed into smaller cycles. In the remainder, all the cycles under consideration are simple cycles.

A region graph of Example 1 is illustrated in Figure 1, assuming that x is an integer variable. There is one cycle passing the two regions.

The basic idea of our region graph based termination proofs is stated in Theorem 1.

Theorem 1. *Given a loop and one of its region graphs, the loop is terminating, if and only if, during loop iterations starting with any variable values, we have*

- *once a region is entered, it will be exited eventually.*
- *and no region is entered infinitely often.*

Proof (sketched). During loop iterations starting with some variable values, we construct a sequence of points by recording the variable values before each iteration. If the two conditions in the theorem are satisfied, then there exists no infinite sequence of points during loop iterations, and vice versa.   ∎

In the next sections we will show how to construct region graphs for proving termination.

4   Proving Termination for $G^1 P^1$

We first show how to prove termination based on region graphs for loops in the simplest class $G^1 P^1$. The concepts and methods described in this section can also apply to more general subclasses with little adaption as explained in the subsequent sections.

4.1   Constructing Region Graphs

Given a $G^1 P^1$ loop as below,

while $\bar{a}\bar{x} \geq b$ **do**
$\quad \bar{x}' = U\bar{x} + \bar{u}$
od

we construct a region graph as follows in a straightforward way:

- The only positive region is defined by the system of the linear inequalities (1–3) in Figure 2 if it has solutions. Otherwise, there is no positive region.
- The only negative region is defined by the system of the linear inequalities (4–6) if it has solutions. Otherwise, there is no negative region.
- The only still region is defined by the system of the linear inequalities (7–9) if it has solutions. Otherwise, there is no still region.

$$\bar{a}\bar{x} \geq b \quad (1) \qquad\qquad \bar{a}\bar{x} \geq b \quad (4) \qquad\qquad \bar{a}\bar{x} \geq b \quad (7)$$
$$\bar{x}' = U\bar{x} + \bar{u} \quad (2) \qquad \bar{x}' = U\bar{x} + \bar{u} \quad (5) \qquad \bar{x}' = U\bar{x} + \bar{u} \quad (8)$$
$$\bar{a}\bar{x} > \bar{a}\bar{x}' \quad (3) \qquad\qquad \bar{a}\bar{x} < \bar{a}\bar{x}' \quad (6) \qquad\qquad \bar{a}\bar{x} = \bar{a}\bar{x}' \quad (9)$$

Fig. 2. Region defining linear inequality systems

- For a region R_1 defined by an inequality system I_1 and a region R_2 defined by I_2, there is a transition from R_1 to R_2 if the following system of inequalities has solutions: $\bigwedge_{e \in I_1} e \wedge \bigwedge_{e \in I_2} e[\bar{x} \mapsto \bar{x}', \bar{x}' \mapsto \bar{x}'']$ where $e[\bar{x} \mapsto \bar{x}', \bar{x}' \mapsto \bar{x}'']$ is the same inequality as e except that $\bar{x}$ is substituted with $\bar{x}'$ and $\bar{x}'$ is substituted with $\bar{x}''$ simultaneously.

The constructed region graph for Example 1 is exactly the one in Figure 1, assuming that x is an integer variable. The right region is positive and defined by the inequalities (10–12). The left region is negative and defined by the inequalities (13–15). There is a transition from the positive region to the negative region because the system of the inequalities (16–21) has solutions.

$$
\begin{array}{rlcrl}
x \geq 0 & \text{(10)} & \qquad & x \geq 0 & \text{(16)} \\
x' = -2x + 10 & \text{(11)} & & x' = -2x + 10 & \text{(17)} \\
x > x' & \text{(12)} & & x > x' & \text{(18)} \\
x \geq 0 & \text{(13)} & & x' \geq 0 & \text{(19)} \\
x' = -2x + 10 & \text{(14)} & & x'' = -2x' + 10 & \text{(20)} \\
x < x' & \text{(15)} & & x' < x'' & \text{(21)}
\end{array}
$$

Fig. 3. The above linear inequality systems define regions and a transition in a region graph of Example 1

Construction of region graphs can be fully automated since feasibility of linear inequality systems can be checked using linear optimization tools such as a linear programming problem solver.

Next, we propose a method of proving termination by studying region graphs.

4.2 Checking Regions

One of the two termination conditions in Theorem 1 is that any region will be eventually exited once it is entered. For any region without a self-transition, after it is entered, it will be exited after one iteration. For any positive region with a self-transition, the runtime values of variables cannot stay in the region forever. This is because the respective guard value is always decreased during self-transitions and also bounded from below as imposed by the loop condition. On the contrary, negative and still regions with self-transitions introduce the potential of staying in one region forever.

Every time that the self-transition of a negative region is taken, the respective guard value is increased. However, if the guard value has an upper bound within the region, then the self-transition cannot be continuously taken forever. In such a case, we call this region a *bounded* region.

The boundedness of a negative (or positive or still, respectively) region can be checked at the same time when the region is created during region graph construction. For instance, the system of the inequalities (13–15) defines the negative region of Example 1. We can use an optimizer to determine the maximum of guard values under the constraint of the inequalities (13–15) while checking feasibility, by adding the objective function $max : x$. In this example, the negative region is bounded since x has an upper bound 3 within the region.

Having an unbounded negative region, however, does not imply that the runtime values of variables can stay in the region forever. Consider Example 4 whose negative region is unbounded and defined by the inequalities (22–25). Note that the difference of the guard values before and after one iteration is the value of x_2 before the iteration. By Inequality (24) we know that the value of x_2 is always decreased in this region and cannot remain positive forever. This implies eventual leaving of the region. We call such a region a *slowdown* region.

$$x_1 \geq 0 \qquad (22)$$
$$x_1' = x_1 + x_2 \qquad (23)$$

Example 4. This loop has an unbounded negative region.

$$x_2' = x_2 - 1 \qquad (24)$$

while $x_1 \geq 0$ **do**

$$\begin{bmatrix} x_1' \\ x_2' \end{bmatrix} = \begin{bmatrix} 1 & 1 \\ 0 & 1 \end{bmatrix} \begin{bmatrix} x_1 \\ x_2 \end{bmatrix} + \begin{bmatrix} 0 \\ -1 \end{bmatrix}$$

$$x_1' > x_1 \qquad (25)$$

od

$$x_2' \geq x_2 \qquad (26)$$

Checking whether a negative region R is a slowdown region can be done by checking the feasibility of a linear inequality system. The checked inequality system describes a subregion of R in which the difference of the respective guard value is increased or unchanged after one iteration. If no such a subregion exists, then R is a slowdown region. For instance, the negative region of Example 4 is a slowdown region because the system of the inequalities (22–26) has no solutions.

We generalize the concept of slowdown regions using an idea similar to the concept of finite difference trees [2]. For an unbounded negative region and an arbitrary natural number n, we build a finite chain $d_0, d_1, ..., d_n$ where the root d_0 is the difference of the respective guard values before and after one loop iteration within the region, and d_1 is the difference of d_0 before and after one iteration within the region, i.e, the "difference of difference", and so forth. When any d_i of the $d_0, d_1, ..., d_n$ is decreased within the region, the region is a slowdown region since d_i dominates the change of d_0, making it impossible to remain positive forever.

4.3   Checking Cycles

Eventual exiting of regions is not enough to show termination. We must make sure that no region is entered an infinite number of times.

In a region graph, if there are no cycles, then no region is entered infinitely often. The region graph in Figure 1 of Example 1 does not have this property. There is a cycle passing the positive region and the negative region. If this cycle can be taken forever, then both regions are entered infinitely often.

We observe that, for Example 1, if the negative region is entered at some point p, then it will be entered at the next time at such a point p' that the value of the guard x at p is greater than the value of x at p'. Because of the loop condition $x \geq 0$, we know that the cycle cannot be taken forever. So, no region is entered infinitely often.

We generalize the above idea by the following definition.

Definition 6. *A cycle is* progressive *on a region* R *if one of the following is satisfied:*

- *Along the cycle, every time that* R *is entered, the respective guard value is greater than the guard value at the last time that* R *is entered. In such a case, we say that the cycle is* upward progressive *if* R *is bounded.*
- *Along the cycle, every time that* R *is entered, the respective guard value is smaller than the guard value at the last time that* R *is entered. In such a case, we say that the cycle is* downward progressive.

It is easy to prove that the following cycles are progressive: (1) a cycle passing the positive region and the still region, and (2) a cycle passing the negative region and the still region if the negative region is bounded.

For other types of cycles, we can check their progressiveness by checking feasibility of a set of linear inequality systems. We have at most six choices: checking whether the cycle is upward (or downward) progressive on the positive (or negative or still) region. For the purpose of illustration, we show how to check downward progressiveness on negative regions. The idea can be easily adapted for other choices and other cases.

Given a $G^1 P^1$ loop as below,

while $\bar{a}\bar{x} \geq b$ **do**

$\quad \bar{x}' = U\bar{x} + \bar{u}$

od

we assume that there is a cycle passing the positive region and negative region in its constructed region graph. If both regions have no self-transitions, then we can use the linear inequality system in Figure 4 to describe the behavior in which the respective guard value is not decreased every time that the negative region is entered along the cycle. The inequalities (27–29) define that the negative region is entered at a point $\bar{x}$. The inequalities (30–32) define that the positive region is then entered at $\bar{x}'$. The inequalities (33–35) define that the negative region is re-entered at $\bar{x}''$. Inequality (36) imposes that the guard value at $\bar{x}''$ is no smaller than the guard value at $\bar{x}$. If the inequality system has no solutions, then the guard value is always decreased and the cycle is downward progressive on the negative region.

$$\begin{array}{llllll}
\bar{a}\bar{x} \geq b & (27) & \bar{a}\bar{x}' \geq b & (30) & \bar{a}\bar{x}'' \geq b & (33) \\
\bar{x}' = U\bar{x} + \bar{u} & (28) & \bar{x}'' = U\bar{x}' + \bar{u} & (31) & \bar{x}''' = U\bar{x}'' + \bar{u} & (34) \\
\bar{a}\bar{x}' > \bar{a}\bar{x} & (29) & \bar{a}\bar{x}' > \bar{a}\bar{x}'' & (32) & \bar{a}\bar{x}'' > \bar{a}\bar{x}''' & (35) \\
& & & & \bar{a}\bar{x} \leq \bar{a}\bar{x}'' & (36)
\end{array}$$

Fig. 4. A linear inequality system for checking progressiveness

If one of the regions above has a self-transition, then we do not know precisely at which point this region is exited after being entered. In such a case, we have to overapproximate the exit point. Assume that both regions have a self-transition. The linear inequality system to check downward progressiveness is shown in Figure 5. Note that the negative region is entered at a point $\bar{x}$ as defined by the inequalities (37–39), and it is exited at $p_{\bar{x}'}^-$ as defined by the inequalities (41–43). An additional inequality (40) guarantees that the successor $\bar{s}_{\bar{x}}^-$ of $\bar{x}$ satisfies the loop condition because loop iterations cannot continue otherwise. Inequality (44) relates the entry point and the exit point by imposing that the guard value at $\bar{x}$ is no larger than the guard value at $p_{\bar{x}'}^-$ due to the effect of self-transitions of a negative region. Note that the "equal" part cannot be dropped since it is still possible to leave the negative region immediately without taking the self-transition. The inequalities (45–52) describe the entering and the exiting of the positive region similarly.

$$\bar{a}\bar{x} \geq b \quad (37)$$
$$\bar{s}_x = U\bar{x} + \bar{u} \quad (38)$$
$$\bar{a}\bar{s}_x > \bar{a}\bar{x} \quad (39)$$
$$\bar{a}\bar{s}_x \geq b \quad (40)$$
$$\bar{a}p_{\bar{x}'}^- \geq b \quad (41)$$
$$\bar{x}' = Up_{\bar{x}'}^- + \bar{u} \quad (42)$$
$$\bar{a}\bar{x}' > \bar{a}p_{\bar{x}'}^- \quad (43)$$
$$\bar{a}p_{\bar{x}'}^- \geq \bar{a}\bar{x} \quad (44)$$

$$\bar{a}\bar{x}' \geq b \quad (45)$$
$$\bar{s}_{\bar{x}'}^- = U\bar{x}' + \bar{u} \quad (46)$$
$$\bar{a}\bar{x}' > \bar{a}\bar{s}_{\bar{x}'}^- \quad (47)$$
$$\bar{a}\bar{s}_{\bar{x}'}^- \geq b \quad (48)$$
$$\bar{a}p_{\bar{x}''}^- \geq b \quad (49)$$
$$\bar{x}'' = Up_{\bar{x}''}^- + \bar{u} \quad (50)$$
$$\bar{a}p_{\bar{x}''}^- > \bar{a}\bar{x}'' \quad (51)$$
$$\bar{a}\bar{x}' \geq \bar{a}p_{\bar{x}''}^- \quad (52)$$

$$\bar{a}\bar{x}'' \geq b \quad (53)$$
$$\bar{x}''' = U\bar{x}'' + \bar{u} \quad (54)$$
$$\bar{a}\bar{x}'' > \bar{a}\bar{x}''' \quad (55)$$
$$\bar{a}\bar{x} \leq \bar{a}\bar{x}'' \quad (56)$$

Fig. 5. A linear inequality system for checking progressiveness

The progressiveness of each individual cycle is sufficient to show no infinite number of entering of any region only if any two cycles do not pass a same region (see [9] for the proof). Otherwise, this condition is insufficient.

Definition 7. *Given a region graph, if two cycles pass one same region, then we say that these two cycles interfere with each other on this region. The region is called an interfered region of both cycles.*

Fig. 6. Two interfering cycles   **Fig. 7.** Three interfering cycles

Consider the region graph in Figure 6 where transitions are distinctly named for convenience. Two cycles $< T_1, T_2 >$ and $< T_1, T_3, T_4 >$ interfere with each other on R_1 and R_2.

We say that a cycle is *completed* when, starting from a region in the cycle, the region is re-entered along the cycle. Furthermore, a cycle C is *uninterruptedly completed* if no other cycle is completed during the completion of C. If a cycle C_1 interferes with some other cycle C_2 on a region R, then a completion of C_1 can be interrupted at R to enter C_2 and resumed from R after C_2 is completed. In such a case, even if C_1 is progressive on some region R', R' may still be entered infinitely often since the respective guard value can be arbitrary when the completion of C_1 is resumed from R after one interruption. However, the following case deserves special attention.

Definition 8. *A region R is a* base region *if the following is satisfied. For any cycle C that passes R, all the cycles that interfere with C also pass R. The set of cycles $\{C \mid C \text{ passes } R\}$ is called an* orbital cycle set.

An orbital cycle set can have more than one base region. For instance, in Figure 6 both R_1 and R_2 are base regions of the orbital set consisting of two cycles. In contrast no region in Figure 7 is a base region.

Orbital sets have an interesting property as follows. Given a base region and its corresponding orbital set, between two successive times that the base region is entered, some cycle in the orbital set is uninterruptedly completed. The proof is sketched here. It is trivial to show that a cycle is completed between two successive times that the base region is entered. Assume that this completion is interrupted at some region R and resumed after some other cycle C is completed. Because C is also in the same orbital set, the base region must be entered while completing C, which contradicts that there is no entering of the base region in-between.

Lemma 1. *Given an orbital cycle set O, any region in any cycle in O is entered only a finite number of times during loop iterations if all the cycles in O are uniformly upward or uniformly downward progressive on some base region* (see [9] for the proof).

4.4 Determining Termination

Based on the previous discussion, we suggest a termination proving algorithm for loops in $G^1 P^1$ as follows. Given a loop,

1. Check the existence of a still region[2]. If it exists, then check whether it has a self-transition. If the self-transition exists, then return "UNKNOWN".
2. Check the existence of a negative region. If neither a negative region nor a still region exists, then return "TERMINATING". In such a case, the loop has linear ranking functions (see Theorem 2).
3. If the negative region exists, then check whether it has a self-transition. If the self-transition exists and the region is unbounded, then check whether it is a slowdown region. If it cannot be determined to be a slowdown region, then return "UN-KNOWN".
4. Complete construction of the region graph by constructing the positive region and the rest of the transitions.
5. Check if there are any cycles. If no cycle exists, then return "TERMINATING".
6. Construct all the orbital cycle sets. If there is any interfering cycle that does not belong to any orbital set, then return "UNKNOWN".
7. Check if all the simple cycles are progressive. If there is one simple cycle whose progressiveness cannot be determined, then return "UNKNOWN". With presence of an orbital set, check whether all the cycles in the set are progressive on one base region and agree on the direction of progress (upward or downward). If it is satisfied, then return "TERMINATING".

---

[2] Remember that the boundedness of a region is checked at the same time that the region is created.

All the steps in this algorithm are arranged in an optimal order so that no unnecessary step is taken. Since all the constructions and checks are performed by automatic translation into linear inequality systems and and automated solving of these systems, the algorithm requires no human intervention.

Complexity. Let N be a parameter to the algorithm as the upper bound on the length of finite difference chains built to check slowdown regions. The number of the linear inequality systems constructed by the algorithm is no more than $16 + N$. Each constructed inequality system has a size linear in the number of variables. If all the variables used in the loop are real variables, then solving of a linear inequality system is polynomial. Otherwise, it is NP-complete. However, in practice constructed inequality systems are usually very small. For the class of loops that have linear ranking functions, the algorithm in [10] needs to construct only one linear inequality system to determine termination, which seems much more efficient than our method. However, we can show that, for any $G^1 P^1$ loop with linear ranking functions, its constructed region graph contains only one positive region as stated in Theorem 2 (see [9] for the proof). So, for any $G^1 P^1$ loop that has linear ranking functions, our algorithm only generates 2 inequality systems to check the existence of a negative region and a still region.

Theorem 2. *A $G^1 P^1$ loop has linear ranking functions if and only if its constructed region graph contains no negative region and no still region.*

Soundness. The algorithm is sound. The proof is sketched in [9]. The basic idea is to show that, if the algorithm returns "TERMINATING" for a loop, then the two termination conditions in Theorem 1 are satisfied by the constructed region graph.

Completeness. The algorithm is incomplete and may return "UNKNOWN". Although termination for $G^1 P^1$ loops in which all the variables are real variables is decidable, the decidability of termination for $G^1 P^1$ loops that have integer variables remains a conjecture [12]. Furthermore, our algorithm can prove termination for a large set of $G^1 P^1$ loops whose iterations change the guard value in one of the patterns as informally illustrated in Figure 8. The horizontal axes represent passage of time and the vertical axes represent change of guard values. The left pattern corresponds to existence of linear ranking functions. The middle one corresponds to existence of slowdown regions. The right one corresponds to progressiveness of cycles.

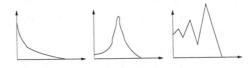

Fig. 8. Patterns in which the guard value changes

In the next two sections, we will generalize the idea of determining termination for $G^1 P^*$ and $G^* P^1$ loops.

5 Proving Termination for $G^1 P^*$

All the ideas in the previous section can be used for $G^1 P^*$ loops without too much adaption except that some concepts are generalized with path conditions.

5.1 Constructing Region Graphs

Given a $G^1 P^*$ loop as below,

> **while** $\bar{a}\bar{x} \geq b$ **do**
>> $pc^1 \rightarrow \bar{x}' = U^1\bar{x} + \bar{u}^1$
>>
>> ...
>>
>> $pc^p \rightarrow \bar{x}' = U^p\bar{x} + \bar{u}^p$
>
> **od**

the construction of region graphs is similar to the construction for $G^1 P^1$ loops as follows:

- For each i-th path, we create a positive region, a negative region and a still region if their respective defining inequality system has solutions. Let the path condition be $pc^i = \bar{c}_1\bar{x} \geq d_1 \wedge \ldots \wedge \bar{c}_q\bar{x} \geq d_q$. The system of the linear inequalities (57–60) defines the positive region. The linear inequality systems to define the negative and the still region differ only in the relational operator in Inequality (60) accordingly.
- Transitions are built in exactly the same way as for $G^1 P^1$.

$$\bar{a}\bar{x} \geq b \tag{57}$$

$$\bigwedge_{j=1}^{q} \bar{c}_j\bar{x} \geq d_j \tag{58}$$

$$\bar{x}' = U^j\bar{x} + \bar{u}^j \tag{59}$$

$$\bar{a}\bar{x} > \bar{a}\bar{x}' \tag{60}$$

5.2 Using Path Conditions

Path conditions can be used to determine eventual exiting of still regions and negative regions with self-transitions.

Consider Example 5. If the first path is taken, the guard value x_1 remains unchanged. However, the path cannot be taken forever. This is because the value of x_2 is always decreased every time that the path is taken and is bounded by 0 as imposed by the path condition.

Example 5. This is a loop with two paths.

> **while** $x_1 \geq 0$ **do**
>> $x_2 \geq 0 \rightarrow \begin{bmatrix} x_1' \\ x_2' \end{bmatrix} = \begin{bmatrix} 1 & 0 \\ 0 & 1 \end{bmatrix} \begin{bmatrix} x_1 \\ x_2 \end{bmatrix} + \begin{bmatrix} 0 \\ -1 \end{bmatrix}$
>>
>> $x_2 < 0 \rightarrow \begin{bmatrix} x_1' \\ x_2' \end{bmatrix} = \begin{bmatrix} 1 & 1 \\ 0 & 1 \end{bmatrix} \begin{bmatrix} x_1 \\ x_2 \end{bmatrix}$
>
> **od**

To generalize the idea, we define *drag regions* as follows.

Definition 9. *A negative region or a still region is a* drag region *with respect to the respective path condition* $pc = \bar{c}_1 \bar{x} \geq d_1 \wedge \ldots \wedge \bar{c}_q \bar{x} \geq d_q$ *if, for some* $\bar{c}_j \bar{x}$ *in* pc, *the value of* $\bar{c}_j \bar{x}$ *is always decreased within the region.*

Drag regions can be checked by solving a linear inequality systems. The construction is similar to the linear inequality system for checking slowdown. Due to space limitations we do not give the full detail here.

Progressiveness of cycles can also be generalized when taking path conditions into consideration. For a region R with respect to a path condition $pc = \bar{c}_1 \bar{x} \geq d_1 \wedge \ldots \wedge \bar{c}_q \bar{x} \geq d_q$, a cycle is progressive on R if, along the cycle, every time that R is entered, the value of some $\bar{c}_j \bar{x}$ in pc is smaller than the value of $\bar{c}_j \bar{x}$ at the last time that R is entered.

5.3 Determining Termination

The algorithm in Subsection 4.4 is modified for proving termination for $G^1 P^*$ loops as follows.

- Positive, negative, and still regions are created for all paths.
- When a still region has a self-transition, instead of returning "UNKNOWN", check whether it is a drag region. If not, return "UNKNOWN".
- For an unbounded negative region, check whether it is a drag region. If not, check whether it is a slowdown region. If not, return "UNKNOWN".
- Progressiveness is checked also with respect to path conditions.

Since the number of cycles is exponential in the number of loop paths, so is the number of linear inequality systems constructed by the modified algorithm. The size of each constructed inequality system is linear both in the number of loop paths and in the number of variables. The algorithm is sound and incomplete. In fact, termination of $G^1 P^*$ has been shown undecidable [12].

6   Proving Termination for $G^* P^1$

The basic idea to prove termination for a $G^* P^1$ loop (c.f. Example 3) is to check whether termination can be proved by the region graph constructed with respect to some guard in the loop condition. While analyzing the region graph with respect to a chosen guard, we also consider other guards in the loop condition as explained below.

Construction of region graphs. Choosing a guard in the loop condition, the construction of the region graph is similar to the construction for $G^1 P^1$. The linear inequality system to define the positive region contains (1) all the inequalities in the loop condition, (2) variable update equations, and (3) the inequality that expresses the decrease of the chosen guard value. The inequality systems defining the negative region and the still region are constructed similarly.

Generalization of concepts. A negative or a still region is a drag region with respect to some guard that is not chosen for constructing the region graph if the value of the considered guard is decreased within the region. For a region R and some guard g that is not chosen for constructing the region graph, a cycle is progressive on R also if, along the cycle, every time that R is entered, the value of g is smaller than the value of g at the last time that R is entered.

Determining termination. The algorithm to determine termination for a G^*P^1 loops is as follows. Given a G^*P^1 loop, a guard in the loop condition is chosen nondeterministically. The algorithm in Subsection 4.4 is then used to construct and check the region graph with respect to the chosen guard, with a slight modification which allows for checking drag regions and generalized progressiveness. If termination cannot be determined, then another guard is chosen. This procedure is repeated until termination is proved or all the guards have been checked.

Complexity, soundness and completeness. Let m be the number of guards in the loop condition and N be the parameter as the upper bound on the length of finite difference chains. In the worst case m region graphs are constructed and checked. For each region graph, the number of constructed linear inequality systems is no more than $14+2m+N$. The size of each inequality system is linear in both m and the number of variables. The algorithm is sound and incomplete. In fact it remains a conjecture that termination of G^*P^1 loops that have integer variables is decidable [12]. Furthermore, we conjecture that the algorithm can prove termination for any G^*P^1 loop that has linear ranking functions.

Proving termination for G^*P^*. In our paper we present incomplete approaches to prove termination for G^1P^* and G^*P^1. These two methods are orthogonal and can be easily combined to yield an approach to prove termination for the G^*P^* class.

7 Experimental Results

We implemented our method in a prototype tool named "PONES" (positive-negative-still). Finding a representative sample of realistic software systems that exhibit a large number of non-trivial loops that fall into our categorization is not easy, as it was also observed in [2]. Also, automated extraction of loop code and the resulting loop information has not yet been but will be implemented in the future. For the experiments described here, we manually collected program loops from the source code of Azureus[3] which is a peer-to-peer file sharing software written in Java. The software contains 3567 while- and for-loops. We analyzed the 1636 loops that fall into our categorization. There were only 3 loops in G^1P^* and 4 in G^*P^1. In fact, most of the loops were of the form "while (i<j) i++". The prevalent simplicity of the loops encountered corresponds to the desire of programmers to code loops that are easy to comprehend.

PONES failed to prove termination for 14 of the analyzed loops and proved termination within 65 milliseconds for each of all other loops on a Pentium IV 3.20GHz machine with 2GB memory. Manual inspection revealed that the 14 loops that PONES failed on are not terminating on arbitrary initial variable values but do terminate in the context of the Azureus software system which limits the range of the initial variable values.

---

[3] Available from sourceforge.net.

We propose that our analysis method can be improved by incorporating value analysis [5] to generate linear inequalities over variables as loop invariants. These inequalities are then used to shrink some regions in the constructed region graph in order to exclude those points that will never be reached during loop iterations.

As further future work we propose to generalize the concept of program loops as explicitly constructed by the *while* or *for* constructs to control flow cycles resulting from mutual and recursive function calls. These control flow cycles are usually more complex but we expect that our analysis can handle them nonetheless.

We cannot give a direct comparison with other termination proof methods because other works use different extraction and abstraction techniques than our method to collect loops from programs. It should also be noted that our method can be considered as being complementary to linear ranking function based approaches.

8   Conclusion

We propose a new termination proof method based on constructing and analyzing region graphs. The method is incomplete and efficient in practice. It can prove termination for some loops that have no linear ranking functions. We implemented the method in the PONES tool and conducted several experiments with Java programs. Future work includes: (1) the adaption of the method to approximate loop iteration times; (2) refining the method by discovering other useful information from loops; (3) analysis of loops with more general loop conditions, i.e., with the presence of disjunction; (4) abstraction of nested loops and control flow cycles into $G^* P^*$ loops.

Acknowledgment. We thank Alin Stefanescu for his beneficial and helpful comments on our work and Daniel Butnaru for his assistance in programming the PONES prototype. We also thank anonymous reviewers for their useful comments and suggestions.

References

1. Aaron R. Bradley, Zohar Manna, and Henny B. Sipma. Termination analysis of integer linear loops. In *Concurrency Theory, 16th International Conference, CONCUR 2005, Proceedings*, volume 3653 of *Lecture Notes in Computer Science*, pages 488–502. Springer, 2005.
2. Aaron R. Bradley, Zohar Manna, and Henny B. Sipma. Termination of polynomial programs. In *Verification, Model Checking, and Abstract Interpretation, 6th International Conference, VMCAI 2005, Proceedings*, volume 3385 of *Lecture Notes in Computer Science*, pages 113–129. Springer, 2005.
3. Byron Cook, Andreas Podelski, and Andrey Rybalchenko. Abstraction refinement for termination. In *Static Analysis, 12th International Symposium, SAS 2005, Proceedings*, volume 3672 of *Lecture Notes in Computer Science*, pages 87–101. Springer, 2005.
4. Patrick Cousot. Proving program invariance and termination by parametric abstraction, lagrangian relaxation and semidefinite programming. In *Verification, Model Checking, and Abstract Interpretation, 6th International Conference, VMCAI 2005, Proceedings*, volume 3385 of *Lecture Notes in Computer Science*, pages 1–24. Springer, 2005.
5. Patrick Cousot and Nicolas Halbwachs. Automatic discovery of linear restraints among variables of a program. In *5th Symposium on Principles of Programming Languages (POPL 1978), Proceedings*, pages 84–97, 1978.

6. Stefan Leue, Richard Mayr, and Wei Wei. A scalable incomplete boundedness test for UML RT models. In *Tools and Algorithms for the Construction and Analysis of Systems, 10th International Conference, TACAS 2004, Proceedings*, volume 2988 of *Lecture Notes in Computer Science*, pages 327–341. Springer, 2004.
7. Stefan Leue, Richard Mayr, and Wei Wei. A scalable incomplete test for buffer overflow of Promela models. In *Model Checking Software, 11th International SPIN Workshop, Proceedings*, volume 2989 of *Lecture Notes in Computer Science*, pages 216–233. Springer, 2004.
8. Stefan Leue and Wei Wei. Counterexample-based refinement for a boundedness test for CFSM languages. In *Model Checking Software, 12th International SPIN Workshop, Proceedings*, volume 3639 of *Lecture Notes in Computer Science*, pages 58–74. Springer, 2005.
9. Stefan Leue and Wei Wei. A region graph based approach to termination proofs. Technical report soft-06-01, University of Konstantz, 2006.
10. Andreas Podelski and Andrey Rybalchenko. A complete method for the synthesis of linear ranking functions. In *Verification, Model Checking, and Abstract Interpretation, 5th International Conference, VMCAI 2004, Proceedings*, volume 2937 of *Lecture Notes in Computer Science*, pages 239–251. Springer, 2004.
11. Andreas Podelski and Andrey Rybalchenko. Transition invariants. In *19th IEEE Symposium on Logic in Computer Science (LICS 2004), Proceedings*, pages 32–41. IEEE Computer Society, 2004.
12. Ashish Tiwari. Termination of linear programs. In *Computer Aided Verification, 16th International Conference, CAV 2004, Proceedings*, volume 3114 of *Lecture Notes in Computer Science*, pages 70–82. Springer, 2004.

Verifying Concurrent Message-Passing C Programs with Recursive Calls*

S. Chaki[1], E. Clarke[1], N. Kidd[2], T. Reps[2], and T. Touili[3]

[1] Carnegie Mellon University, Pittsburgh, USA
[2] University of Wisconsin, Madison, USA
[3] LIAFA, CNRS & University of Paris 7, Paris, France

Abstract. We consider the model-checking problem for C programs with (1) data ranging over very large domains, (2) (recursive) procedure calls, and (3) concurrent parallel components that communicate via synchronizing actions. We model such programs using *communicating pushdown systems*, and reduce the reachability problem for this model to deciding the emptiness of the intersection of two context-free languages L_1 and L_2. We tackle this undecidable problem using a CounterExample Guided Abstraction Refinement (CEGAR) scheme. We implemented our technique in the model checker MAGIC and found a previously unknown bug in a version of a Windows NT Bluetooth driver.

1 Introduction

Analysis of concurrent software represents a major challenge in the model-checking community. Concurrent programs include various complex features such as: (1) the manipulation of data ranging over unbounded domains, e.g., integers and reals (or very large domains like 32-bit ints and floats), (2) the presence of recursive procedure calls, which can lead to an unbounded number of calls, (3) concurrency and the existence of synchronization statements. Unfortunately, checking whether a given control point is reachable is undecidable, even if the program includes only recursive procedures and synchronization statements [1]. Consequently, any method for solving the reachability problem for these systems is incomplete, and all we can hope for is either an approximate technique, or a semi-decision procedure for which termination is not guaranteed. This work uses the latter approach to sidestep the undecidability issue. Though not guaranteed to terminate, such an approach can still be useful; for instance, our tool found a previously unknown bug in a version of a Windows NT Bluetooth driver.

During the last few years, several authors have addressed related issues. *Pushown systems* have been proposed as an adequate formalism to describe *pure sequential recursive programs* [2, 3]. They are able to represent the potentially infinite configurations of recursive programs in a symbolic manner using regular languages [4, 5]. Recently, compositions of *pushown systems*, called *communicating pushown systems*, have been used to model *concurrent recursive programs* [6, 7]. However, in these cases, all data were assumed to have a *small* finite domain.

On the other hand, abstract-interpretation techniques [8] have been used to deal with data ranging over unbounded (or very large) domains. More recently, automated

* Supported by ONR under contracts N00014-01-1-{0796,0708}.

H. Hermanns and J. Palsberg (Eds.): TACAS 2006, LNCS 3920, pp. 334–349, 2006.

predicate-abstraction techniques [9] have been proposed to deal with this issue. The idea of predicate abstraction is to abstract the infinite data domain into a finite one defined by a given set of predicates. The precision of the abstraction and the model-checking algorithm depend on the number and the form of the predicates. The size of the model increases with the number of predicates, which increases the cost of model checking. Hence, a central problem in predicate abstraction is the discovery of a *small* set of predicates sufficient to prove the desired property. *CounterExample Guided Abstaction Refinement* (CEGAR) techniques [10, 11] have been used to find such a small set. The idea is: (1) Start with an empty set of predicates. (2) Perform the verification procedure on the obtained model; if the property is satisfied by the model, we conclude that it is also satisfied by the real program because the program has fewer behaviors than the model; otherwise, we obtain a counterexample. (3) If the counterexample corresponds to an execution of the program, we conclude that the program does not satisfy the property. (4) Otherwise, we compute a new set of predicates that eliminate future exploration of the spurious trace, and go back to step (2).

This schema has been successfully applied to handle both pure *non-concurrent* (sequential) recursive programs in the tool SLAM [12], and concurrent *non-recursive* programs in the tools BLAST [13] and MAGIC [14].

In this work, we go one step further, and combine CEGAR predicate-abstraction techniques with pushdown-system modeling to handle *concurrency, recursion, and very large data domains* at the same time. Our approach consists of using communicating pushdown systems (CPDSs) to model concurrent programs. To do this, we (1) define CEGAR predicate-abstraction techniques to obtain successively more precise CPDSs from the C source code of a parallel program, and (2) define model-checking algorithms for CPDSs. The main contributions of this paper are:

1. Defining new *automatic* CEGAR predicate-abstraction techniques that can create a CPDS from the source code of a concurrent (recursive) C program that manipulates variables that range over very large domains, and that can refine CPDS abstractions to eliminate a given counterexample. Our techniques are defined *componentwise*, which makes them *compositional* and *scalable to large programs* (e.g., one experiment on an 18 KLOC program ran in less than 2.2 seconds).

2. Defining new model-checking techniques for CPDSs. We restrict ourselves in this work to solving reachability queries. We reduce the reachability problem for CPDSs to the undecidable problem of checking the emptiness of the intersection of two context-free languages (CFLs) L_1 and L_2. To tackle this problem, we apply a second CEGAR scheme that consists of (1) computing over-approximations A_1 and A_2 of L_1 and L_2. (2) If $A_1 \cap A_2 = \emptyset$, we conclude that $L_1 \cap L_2 = \emptyset$. (3) Otherwise, we check whether the intersection $A_1 \cap A_2$ is spurious. In this case, we refine the over-approximations A_1 and A_2, and return to step (2). This semi-decision procedure is guaranteed to terminate if the intersection $L_1 \cap L_2$ is not empty.

3. Implementing our technique in the model-checker MAGIC, and carrying out a number of non-trivial experiments. Our implementation was able to handle two non-trivial examples (a Windows NT Bluetooth driver and an algorithm for concurrent insertions in a binary search tree) that could not be handled with the previous version of MAGIC. In addition, it discovered a previously unknown bug in a second

version of the Windows NT Bluetooth driver. Moreover, the implementation provides improved performance for non-recursive examples that the previous version of MAGIC was able to handle only via in-lining. This shows that our technique represents an advance for *non-recursive* as well as recursive concurrent programs.

One of the novel features of this work is that it applies the CEGAR scheme at two levels: (1) at the model-checking level to solve reachability queries in CPDSs: the CPDS model checker uses a CEGAR scheme in its semi-decision procedure for testing emptiness of the intersection of two CFLs (see §4), and (2) at the predicate-abstraction level to deal with unbounded domain variables (see §5). As far as we know, this is the first time that CEGAR is used in the model-checker itself.

The remainder of the paper is organized as follows: §2 defines the CPDS model; §3 describes how to generate a CPDS from a C program using predicate abstraction; §4 presents the semi-decision procedure for model-checking a CPDS; §5 presents our predicate-abstraction-refinement techniques; §6 reports experimental results; §7 discusses related work.

2 Preliminary Definitions

A *pushdown system* (PDS) is a four-tuple $\mathcal{P} = (Q, Act, \Gamma, \Delta)$ where Q is a finite set of *states*, Act is a finite set of *actions*, Γ is a finite *stack alphabet*, and Δ is a finite set of *transition rules* of the form $\langle q, \gamma \rangle \overset{a}{\hookrightarrow} \langle q', w \rangle$, where $q, q' \in Q, a \in Act, \gamma \in \Gamma$, and $w \in \Gamma^*$. Without loss of generality, we assume that for all rules of Δ, $|w| \leq 2$. This is not restrictive because any PDS can be transformed into a PDS of this form [15]; moreover, the transition rules obtained from a program have this form. A *configuration* of $\mathcal{P}$ is a pair $\langle q, w \rangle$, where $q \in Q$ and $w \in \Gamma^*$ is *the contents of the stack*. A set of configurations C is *regular* if for each $q \in Q$ the language $\{w \in \Gamma^* \mid \langle q, w \rangle \in C\}$ is regular.

For every $a \in Act$, we define a transition relation $\overset{a}{\longrightarrow}$ between the configurations of $\mathcal{P}$ as follows: if $\langle q, \gamma \rangle \overset{a}{\hookrightarrow} \langle q', w \rangle \in \Delta$, then $\langle q, \gamma v \rangle \overset{a}{\longrightarrow} \langle q', wv \rangle$ for every $v \in \Gamma^*$. For $a_1 \cdots a_n \in Act^*$, the relation $\overset{a_1 \cdots a_n}{\longrightarrow}$ is defined in the obvious way. Let C be a set of configurations. $Post^*(C)$ is the set of successors of C, defined as follows:

$$Post^*(C) = \{c' \mid \exists c \in C, a_1 \cdots a_n \in Act^*, c \overset{a_1 \cdots a_n}{\longrightarrow} c'\}.$$

A *communicating pushdown system* (CPDS) [7] is a tuple $CP = (\mathcal{P}_1, \ldots, \mathcal{P}_n)$ of PDSs over the same set of actions Act such that $Act = Lab \cup \{\tau\}$, where Lab is the set of synchronization actions, and τ represents internal actions: τ has the property that for every $a \in Lab, \tau a = a\tau = a$. As we will see later, we need this to reduce the reachability problem for CPDSs to checking the emptiness of the intersection of two CFLs.

A *global configuration* of CP is a tuple $g = (c_1, \ldots, c_n)$ of configurations of $\mathcal{P}_1, \ldots \mathcal{P}_n$. The relation $\overset{a}{\longrightarrow}$ is extended to global configurations as follows:

- $(c_1, \ldots, c_n) \overset{\tau}{\longrightarrow} (c'_1, \ldots, c'_n)$ if there is an index $1 \leq i \leq n$ such that $c_i \overset{\tau}{\longrightarrow} c'_i$ and, for every $j \neq i, c'_j = c_j$.
- $(c_1, \ldots, c_n) \overset{a}{\longrightarrow} (c'_1, \ldots, c'_n)$ if there are two distinct indices $i \neq j$ such that $c_i \overset{a}{\longrightarrow} c'_i$ and $c_j \overset{a}{\longrightarrow} c'_j$, and, for every k such that $i \neq k \neq j, c'_k = c_k$.

Given a set of global configurations G, the successors of G (denoted by $Post^*(G)$) are defined as before.

3   Componentwise Predicate Abstraction

We model concurrent recursive programs using CPDSs. This section describes how to extract a CPDS from a parallel program. (A more in-depth discussion is given in [16].)

Suppose that we are given n concurrent recursive C components. For each component i, we extract a PDS $\mathcal{P}_i$. The parallel composition of the C components is represented by the CPDS corresponding to the tuple $(\mathcal{P}_1,...,\mathcal{P}_n)$. To extract each $\mathcal{P}_i$, we extend the approach originally used in MAGIC [14], which *automatically* extracts a finite-state automaton from C code, to extract a PDS. Without loss of generality, we assume there are only six kinds of statements in programs: assignments, procedure calls, if-then-else branches, gotos, synchronization statements, and returns. We use CIL [17] to transform arbitrary C programs into this form.

Each PDS is defined in terms of a current set of seed predicates (which is initially empty). Each predicate represents a set of assignments over the variables of the program. Let p be a predicate over the sets of variables X and Y, where X (resp. Y) is a set of local (resp. global) variables. Then p^{loc} (resp. p^{glob}) is the "projection" of p over the local variables X (resp. global variables Y). For example, let $p = (x > 0 \ \& \ y < 8)$ be a predicate that represents the set of values $\{x > 0, y < 8\}$. If x is a local variable, and y is a global one; p^{loc} denotes the predicate $(x > 0)$; and p^{glob} the predicate $(y < 8)$. We extend these notations to sets of predicates in the obvious manner.

3.1   Predicate Inference

The weakest precondition of a set of predicates p is defined as follows. Let s be an assignment of the form $v = e$. Then, the weakest precondition of p with respect to s (denoted by $\mathcal{W}_s(p)$) is obtained from p by replacing every occurrence of v in p by e. Assignments through pointers, i.e., statements of the form $*p = e$, are handled by the approach of Morris [18].

Let C be a set of seed predicates. To create a PDS that is an abstraction of a sequential component relative to the predicates in seed set C, we repeatedly compute weakest preconditions. That is, for every control point n, we compute a set of predicates $P[C]_n$ as follows:

Initially, $P[C]_n = \emptyset$ for every point n. We repeat the following until for every n, $P[C]_n$ is no longer modified. Let s_n be the statement that corresponds to control point n:

1. if s_n is an assignment that has n' as successor, then add $\mathcal{W}_{s_n}(P[C]_{n'})$ to $P[C]_n$.
2. if s_n is an if statement and n' is its then or else successor, then add $P[C]_{n'}$ to $P[C]_n$. Moreover, if c is the corresponding condition of s_n such that $c \in C$, then add c to $P[C]_n$.
3. if s_n is a goto or a synchronisation statement that has n' as successor, then add $P[C]_{n'}$ to $P[C]_n$.
4. if s_n is a call to a procedure π, where s_n has n' as successor, and if e_π is the initial control point of procedure π, then add $P[C]^{loc}_{n'}$ and $P[C]^{glob}_{e_\pi}$ to $P[C]_n$.

(This method might not terminate in the presence of loops and recursive procedure calls. In this case, we impose termination by bounding the number of predicates in $\mathcal{P}[C]_n$, for every control point n.)

Let us explain the intuition behind item 1. Predicate set $P[C]_n$ is only capable of making a certain set of distinctions among the concrete states that can arise at execution time at point n. Let s_n be an assignment that has n' as successor. Item 1 adds $\mathcal{W}_{s_n}(P[C]_{n'})$ to $P[C]_n$ because if $\mathcal{W}_{s_n}(\varphi)$ is true at n, then φ must be true at n'. We wish to minimize the loss of precision in characterizing the states at n': to be able to determine whether φ holds at n', we need to know whether $\mathcal{W}_{s_n}(\varphi)$ holds at n.

Finally, let $P[C] = \cup P[C]_n$, where the union is taken over all the control points n of the sequential component, be the set of all the generated predicates.

3.2 PDS Extraction

Using C, we assign to a sequential (possibly recursive) component the PDS $\mathcal{P} = (Q, Act, \Gamma, \Delta)$, defined as follows: Q is the set of valuations on $P[C]^{glob}$; Act contains the action τ, as well as the other synchronization actions of the program; Γ is the set of all pairs (n, loc), where n is a control point of the sequential component, and loc is a valuation of $P[C]_n^{loc}$; Δ is defined using the sequential component's control flow graph. For example, if s is a non-synchronizing assignment statement at control location n_1 with successor n_2, then Δ contains all the PDS rules $\langle glob, (n_1, loc) \rangle \xrightarrow{\tau} \langle glob', (n_2, loc') \rangle$, where $glob \in P[C]_{n_1}^{glob}$, $glob' \in P[C]_{n_2}^{glob'}$ (resp. $loc \in P[C]_{n_1}^{loc}$, $loc' \in P[C]_{n_2}^{loc'}$), such that they potentially satisfy $(\mathcal{W}_s(glob') \wedge glob)$ (resp. $(\mathcal{W}_s(loc') \wedge loc)$).[1] These formulas ensure that the generated PDS has more behaviors than the concrete program.

If instead s is a synchronizing statement with action a, then Δ contains all the PDS rules $\langle glob, (n_1, loc) \rangle \xrightarrow{a} \langle glob', (n_2, loc') \rangle$, where again $glob$ and $glob'$ (resp. loc and loc') potentially satisfy the conditions stated above. Further details about converting the various types of C statements to their corresponding PDS rules are given in [16].

3.3 Comparision with the Predicate-Abstraction Technique of SLAM

The SLAM tool [12] uses predicate-abstraction techniques to extract a Boolean program from C source code. One can then use Schwoon's translation [15] to obtain a PDS from a Boolean program. Compared with the techniques used in SLAM, the approach sketched in §3.2 has two main differences:

1. Our translation is more efficient because it produces directly, in one step, a PDS from C code without going through an intermediate Boolean program.
2. We close a given set of seed predicates C by computing weakest preconditions along the different possible paths of the program. In contrast, SLAM uses the seed set of predicates C as is, without computing its closure by weakest precondition. Instead, it computes largest disjunctions of predicates in C that imply the weakest preconditions. Consequently, the abstract model we obtain is more precise than SLAM's because it uses more predicates.

---

[1] Determining whether $(p_1 \wedge p_2)$ is satisfiable is in general undecidable when p_1 and p_2 are first-order formulas over the integers. To sidestep this problem, we use a sound validity checker [19] that always terminates and answers TRUE, FALSE, or UNKNOWN to the question whether a given formula $\neg(p_1 \wedge p_2)$ is valid. If the validity checker returns FALSE or UNKNOWN to the question "Is $\neg(p_1 \wedge p_2)$ valid?", then $(p_1 \wedge p_2)$ is potentially satisfiable.

4   Reachability Analysis of CPDSs

Given a program that consists of n sequential components, we usually ask the following query: "Suppose that the system starts from a configuration where each component i, for $i = 1,\ldots,n$, is at its initial control point n_0^i. Can one of the components reach an error point?" Our technique answers this kind of question by modeling the program as the CPDS $(\mathcal{P}_1,\ldots,\mathcal{P}_n)$ with initial configurations $C_1 \times \ldots \times C_n$ and error configurations $C_1' \times \ldots \times C_n'$ (where the states of configurations in some C_i' correspond to error points and the states of configurations in $C_1',\ldots,C_{i-1}',C_{i+1}',\ldots,C_n'$ are unconstrained). If the error configurations are reachable from the initial configurations, our algorithm returns a sequence of synchronization actions that yield a failing program run. We show in this section how to tackle the reachability analysis of these systems. In the remainder of the paper, we restrict ourselves to systems that consist of two components. The technique can be extended in a straightforward manner to the general case (see [7] for more details); the implementation discussed in §6 supports an arbitrary number of components.

We reduce the reachability problem for CPDSs to deciding the emptiness question for the intersection of two CFLs as follows: Let $(\mathcal{P}_1,\mathcal{P}_2)$ be a CPDS, and let $C_1 \times C_2$ and $C_1' \times C_2'$ be two sets of global configurations of the system. Because all the internal actions are represented by τ (which is a neutral element for concatenation), $C_1' \times C_2'$ is reachable from $C_1 \times C_2$ if and only if there exists at least one sequence of synchronization actions that simultaneously leads $\mathcal{P}_1$ from a configuration in C_1 to a configuration in C_1' and $\mathcal{P}_2$ from a configuration in C_2 to a configuration in C_2'. This holds iff $L(C_1,C_1') \cap L(C_2,C_2') \neq \emptyset$, where $L(C_i,C_i')$ is the CFL consisting of all the sequences of actions (or, equivalently, of synchronization actions because the internal actions are represented by τ) that lead $\mathcal{P}_i$ from C_i to C_i'.

Because deciding the emptiness of the intersection of two CFLs is undecidable, we propose a semi-decision procedure that, in case of termination, answers *exactly* whether the intersection is empty or not. Moreover, if $L(C_1,C_1') \cap L(C_2,C_2') \neq \emptyset$, the semi-decision procedure is *guaranteed to terminate* and return a witness sequence in the intersection.

The semi-decision procedure is based on a CounterExample Guided Abstraction Refinement (CEGAR) scheme as follows:

1. **Abstraction:** We compute an over-approximation A_i of each path language $L(C_i,C_i')$.
2. **Verification:** We check if $A_1 \cap A_2 = \emptyset$, and, if so, we conclude that $L(C_1,C_1') \cap L(C_2,C_2') = \emptyset$, i.e., that $C_1' \times C_2'$ is unreachable from $C_1 \times C_2$. Otherwise, we compute the "counterexample" $I = A_1 \cap A_2$.
3. **Counterexample Validation:** We check whether I contains a sequence x that is in $L(C_1,C_1') \cap L(C_2,C_2')$. In this case I is not spurious, and we conclude that $L(C_1,C_1') \cap L(C_2,C_2') \neq \emptyset$, i.e., that $C_1' \times C_2'$ is reachable from $C_1 \times C_2$. Otherwise, we proceed to the next step.
4. **Refinement:** If I is spurious, we refine the over-approximations A_1 and A_2, i.e., we compute other over-approximations A_1' and A_2' such that $L(C_i,C_i') \subseteq A_i' \subseteq A_i$. We then continue from step 2.

In the remainder of this section, we discuss these steps in detail. We fix two sets of global configurations $C_1 \times C_2$ and $C_1' \times C_2'$. For brevity, we denote $L(C_1, C_1')$ by L_1, and $L(C_2, C_2')$ by L_2.

4.1 Computing Over-Approximations of Path Languages

To compute over-approximations of PDS path languages, our technique is based on the approach presented by Bouajjani et al. [7], which is summarized below.

Consider an abstract lattice $(D, \leq, \sqcap, \sqcup, \bot, \top)$ associated with an idempotent semiring $(D, \oplus, \odot, \bar{0}, \bar{1})$ such that $\oplus = \sqcup$ is an associative, commutative, and idempotent $(a \oplus a = a)$ operation; $\odot$ is an associative operation; $\bar{0} = \bot$; $\bar{0}$ and $\bar{1}$ are neutral elements for $\oplus$ and $\odot$, respectively; $\bar{0}$ is an annihilator for $\odot$ $(a \odot \bar{0} = \bar{0} \odot a = \bar{0})$; and $\odot$ distributes over $\oplus$. Finally, $\forall a, b \in D, a \leq b \iff a \oplus b = a$.

Let D be related to the concrete domain 2^{Lab^*} as follows:

- D contains an element v_a for every letter $a \in Lab$,
- There is an abstraction function $\alpha : 2^{Lab^*} \to D$ and a concretization function $\gamma : D \to 2^{Lab^*}$ defined as follows:
$$\alpha(L) = \bigoplus_{a_1 \cdots a_n \in L} v_{a_1} \odot \cdots \odot v_{a_n} \quad \text{and} \quad \gamma(x) = \{a_1 \cdots a_n \in Lab^* \mid v_{a_1} \odot \cdots \odot v_{a_n} \leq x\},$$
such that $\gamma(\bot) = \emptyset$.

It is easy to see that for every language $L \subseteq Lab^*$; $\alpha(L) \in D$, and $\gamma(\alpha(L)) \supseteq L$. In other words, $\gamma(\alpha(L))$ is an over-approximation of L that is represented in the abstract domain D by the element $\alpha(L)$. Intuitively, the abstract operations $\odot$ and $\oplus$ correspond to concatenation and union, respectively; $\leq$ and $\sqcap$ correspond to inclusion and intersection, respectively; and the abstract elements $\bar{0}$ and $\bar{1}$ correspond to the empty language and $\{\epsilon\}$, respectively.

Therefore, to compute the over-approximation $\gamma(\alpha(L_i))$, we need to compute its representative $\alpha(L_i)$ in the abstract domain D. Let a *finite-chain abstraction* be an abstraction such that D does not contain an infinite ascending chain, and let h be the maximal height of a chain in D. Then we have:

Theorem 1. *[7, 20] Let $\mathcal{P} = (Q, Act, \Gamma, \Delta)$ be a PDS; let C, C' be two regular sets of configurations of $\mathcal{P}$; and let α be a finite-chain abstraction defined on the abstract domain D. Then $\alpha(L(C, C'))$ can be effectively computed in time $O(h|\Delta||Q|^2)$.*

Two different algorithms provide the basis of this theorem, one due to Bouajjani et al. [6, 7], the other to Reps et al. [20, 21]. The latter has been implemented in a tool called WPDS++ [22]. We use this tool to compute abstractions of path languages.

To check the emptiness of the intersection of the over-approximations $\gamma(\alpha(L_1))$ and $\gamma(\alpha(L_2))$, it suffices to check whether $\alpha(L_1) \sqcap \alpha(L_2) = \bot$. Indeed, using the fact that $\gamma(\bot) = \emptyset$, we can show that
$$\forall L_1, L_2 \in Lab^*, \alpha(L_1) \sqcap \alpha(L_2) = \bot \Leftrightarrow \gamma(\alpha(L_1)) \cap \gamma(\alpha(L_2)) = \emptyset.$$

4.2 Defining Refinable Finite-Chain Abstractions

To be able to apply our CEGAR scheme, we need to define refinable finite-chain abstractions, i.e., a series $(\alpha_i)_{i \geq 1}$ such that α_i is at least as precise as α_j if $i > j$; i.e., for every language $L \subseteq Lab^*$, if $i > j$ then $L \subseteq \gamma_i(\alpha_i(L)) \subseteq \gamma_j(\alpha_j(L))$.

For this we define the ith-*prefix abstraction* as follows: Let W_i be the set of words of Lab^* of length less than or equal to i. The abstract lattice D_i is equal to 2^{W_i}; for every $a \in Lab$, $v_a = a$; $\oplus = \cup$; $\sqcap = \cap$; $U \odot V = \{(uv)_i \mid u \in U, v \in V\}$, where $(w)_i$ is the prefix of w of length i; $\bar{0} = \emptyset$; $\bar{1} = \{\varepsilon\}$; $\leq = \subseteq$.

Let α_i and γ_i be the abstraction and concretization functions associated with this domain. It is easy to see that $\alpha_i(L)$ is the set of words of L of length less than i, union the set of prefixes of length i of L, i.e., $\alpha_i(L) = \{w \mid |w| < i \text{ and } w \in L, \text{ or } |w| = i \text{ and } \exists v \in Lab^* \text{ s.t. } wv \in L\}$. Therefore, $\gamma_i(\alpha_i(L)) = \{w \in \alpha_i(L) \mid |w| < i\} \cup \{wv \mid w \in \alpha_i(L), |w| = i, v \in Lab^*\}$.

Note that it is possible to decide whether $\alpha_i(L_1) \cap \alpha_i(L_2) = \emptyset$ because, for every $L \subseteq Lab^*$, $\alpha_i(L)$ is a finite set of words.

It is also easy to see that if $i > j$, then α_i is at least as precise as α_j. Indeed, we have $L \subseteq \gamma_i(\alpha_i(L)) \subseteq \gamma_j(\alpha_j(L))$. We have thus defined a refinable series of finite-chain abstractions $\alpha_1, \alpha_2, \alpha_3, \dots$.

Remark 1. The ith-*prefix* abstraction is only one abstraction that can be used to instantiate the framework. Others are possible, such as the ith-*suffix* or the ith-*subword* abstractions (defined in an analogous way).

4.3   Checking Whether the Counterexample Is Spurious

It remains to check whether $I = \gamma_i(\alpha_i(L_1)) \cap \gamma_i(\alpha_i(L_2))$ contains an element x such that $x \in L_1 \cap L_2$. This amounts to deciding whether $I \cap L_1 \cap L_2 = \emptyset$. Unfortunately, this problem is undecidable because I is a regular language (because for $L \subseteq Lab^*$, $\gamma_i(\alpha_i(L))$ is regular). To sidestep this problem, we check instead whether L_1 and L_2 have a common word of length at most i. This amounts to checking whether $(\alpha_i(L_1) \cap L_1) \cap (\alpha_i(L_2) \cap L_2) = \emptyset$. This is decidable because $\alpha_i(L)$ is a finite set.

4.4   The Semi-decision Procedure

Summarizing the previous discussion, we obtain the following semi-decision procedure (based on the ith-*prefix* abstraction) for the reachability problem for CPDSs:

1. Initially, $i = 1$;
2. Compute the common words of length less than i, and the common prefixes of length i of $L(C_1, C_1')$ and $L(C_2, C_2')$: $I' = \alpha_i(L(C_1, C_1')) \cap \alpha_i(L(C_2, C_2'))$.
3. If $I' = \emptyset$, conclude that $L(C_1, C_1') \cap L(C_2, C_2') = \emptyset$, and that $C_1' \times C_2'$ is unreachable from $C_1 \times C_2$. Otherwise, determine whether or not I' is spurious: Check whether $I' \cap L(C_1, C_1') \cap L(C_2, C_2') \neq \emptyset$. If this holds, conclude that $L(C_1, C_1')$ and $L(C_2, C_2')$ have a common word of length less than or equal to i, and therefore, that $L(C_1, C_1') \cap L(C_2, C_2') \neq \emptyset$, and $C_1' \times C_2'$ is reachable from $C_1 \times C_2$.
4. Otherwise, increment i and continue from step 2.

Theorem 2. *If $L(C_1, C_1') \cap L(C_2, C_2') \neq \emptyset$, then the above semi-decision procedure terminates with the exact solution.*

Proof. Let $x \in L(C_1, C_1') \cap L(C_2, C_2')$, and let k be the length of x. Then $x \in \alpha_k(L(C_1, C_1')) \cap \alpha_k(L(C_2, C_2'))$.

Remark 2. It follows from Theorem 1 that at each step i, computing $\alpha_i(L)$ necessitates $O(2^{|Lab|^i}|\Delta||Q|^2)$ time since there are at most $|Lab|^i$ words of length i, and therefore at most $2^{|Lab|^i}$ elements in D_i. This is the worst-case complexity of the algorithm. However, in practice, our implementation behaves well, as discussed in §6.

4.5 Example

Let $\mathcal{P}_1$ be the PDS that has the following rules:

$$r_1 : \langle p,n_0 \rangle \xrightarrow{a} \langle p,n_1 \rangle; \; r_2 : \langle p,n_1 \rangle \xrightarrow{\tau} \langle p,n_0 n_2 \rangle; \; r_3 : \langle p,n_2 \rangle \xrightarrow{b} \langle p,\varepsilon \rangle; \; r_4 : \langle p,n_0 \rangle \xrightarrow{b} \langle p,\varepsilon \rangle.$$

Let $\mathcal{P}_2$ be the PDS that has the following rules:

$$r'_1 : \langle q,m_0 \rangle \xrightarrow{a} \langle q,m_1 \rangle; \; r'_2 : \langle q,m_1 \rangle \xrightarrow{b} \langle q,m_2 \rangle; \; r'_3 : \langle q,m_2 \rangle \xrightarrow{\tau} \langle q,m_0 m_3 \rangle;$$

$$r'_4 : \langle q,m_3 \rangle \xrightarrow{b} \langle q,\varepsilon \rangle; \text{ and } r'_5 : \langle q,m_0 \rangle \xrightarrow{d} \langle q,\varepsilon \rangle.$$

For $\mathcal{P}_1$, let L_1 be $L(\langle p,n_0 \rangle, \langle p,\varepsilon \rangle) = \{a^k bb^k \mid k \geq 0\}$. For $\mathcal{P}_2$, let L_2 be $L(\langle q,m_0 \rangle, \langle q,\varepsilon \rangle) = \{(ab)^k db^k \mid k \geq 0\}$. Note that $L_1 \cap L_2 = \emptyset$. We use this straightforward example to illustrate our approach:

- $\alpha_1(L_1) \cap \alpha_1(L_2) = \{a\} \neq \emptyset$;
- $a \notin L_1$, therefore, we refine the abstraction and go to α_2;
- $\alpha_2(L_1) \cap \alpha_2(L_2) = \{ab\} \neq \emptyset$;
- $ab \notin L_2$, therefore, we refine the abstraction and go to α_3;
- $\alpha_3(L_1) \cap \alpha_3(L_2) = \emptyset$. Therefore, we conclude that $L_1 \cap L_2 = \emptyset$.

5   Componentwise Refinement

The construction of the CPDS model from the C program involves predicate abstraction. It is parametrized by a set of predicates. A central issue in predicate abstraction is how to find a small set of predicates that allows a property of interest to be established. In our case, the property in question is whether the system can reach an error configuration from the initial configuration, where component i (where, e.g., $i = 1, 2$) starts in configuration $\langle glob_0^i, (n_0^i, loc_0^i) \rangle$, n_0^i is the initial control point of component i, and $glob_0^i, loc_0^i$ are initial valuations of the global and local variables, respectively. Similarly, an error configuration is a configuration where at least one component i is in a configuration of the form $\langle glob, (n_e^i, loc) \rangle$, where n_e^i correponds to an error point, and $glob$ and loc are arbitrary valuations of the variables. MAGIC finds an appropriate set of predicates by applying a CEGAR approach, as described below.

We start with a model involving an empty set of seed predicates, and perform the model-checking step described in §4. If the model checker answers that the error state is unreachable in the CPDS model, we are sure that this is also the case for the concrete program, because the program has fewer behaviors than the model. Otherwise, if the model checker finds that the CPDS can reach an error state by performing a sequence of synchronization actions $a_1 \cdots a_n$ $(a_1 \cdots a_n \in I' \cap L(C_1, C'_1) \cap L(C_2, C'_2))$, we need to verify whether this behavior corresponds to a real execution of the program (in which case, we have shown that the program is not correct), or whether the apparently-erroneous behavior has been introduced by abstraction. If the latter is the case, we need to refine the CPDS model. More precisely, the model checker returns two sequences of rules $r_1^1, \ldots, r_{m_1}^1$ and $r_1^2, \ldots, r_{m_2}^2$ such that the CPDS $(\mathcal{P}_1, \mathcal{P}_2)$ reaches the error state if $\mathcal{P}_i$ performs the sequence $r_1^i, \ldots, r_{m_i}^i$ (in this case, $a_1 \cdots a_n$ is the sequence of synchronization actions corresponding to these sequences of rules). We say that the sequence $r_1^i, \ldots, r_{m_i}^i$ is a counterexample for component i. To check whether this counterexample is spurious, we need to check whether component i can perform the sequence of statements that correspond to the rule sequence $r_1^i, \ldots, r_{m_i}^i$. If either component fails to perform its corresponding sequence, we refine its corresponding PDS to eliminate the spurious rule sequence. Note that all of these steps are done *componentwise*, which makes the technique compositional and scalable to large programs.

5.1   Counterexample Validation

We present in this subsection an algorithm that takes as input a counterexample given by a sequence of rules $r_1, \ldots, r_n$ of a PDS that models a sequential component, and answers whether it is spurious. Let $s_1, \ldots, s_n$ be the sequence of statements that corresponds to $r_1, \ldots, r_n$. Intuitively, the algorithm simulates the different steps to determine whether the concrete component could possibly perform them. The algorithm starts from the initial point n_0, and the valuations $glob_0$ and loc_0 of the variables. Then, it applies successively the different statements $s_i, i = 1, \ldots, n$, updates the values of the variables, and checks whether the if-then-else conditions are satisfied in this sequence of instructions. More precisely, the algorithm works as follows:

- Initially $\varphi = glob_0 \wedge loc_0$,
- For $i = 1$ to n do
  - if s_i is an assignment, compute the strongest postcondition of φ with respect to s_i. For example, if s_i is the assignment $x := x + 5$, and φ is the valuation $(1 < x < 4) = \text{true}$; the updated valuation φ is $(6 < x < 9) = \text{true}$.
  - if s_i is an if statement with condition c, then if s_{i+1} corresponds to its then successor, $\varphi := \varphi \wedge c$. Otherwise, if s_{i+1} corresponds to its else successor, $\varphi := \varphi \wedge \neg c$.
- If φ is satisfiable, then the program can execute the sequence of statements, and the counterexample is valid; otherwise, the counterexample is spurious.

5.2   Eliminating the Counterexample

If the counterexample is spurious for component i, we need to refine the PDS model $\mathcal{P}_i$ corresponding to this component by adding new seed predicates. The predicates that we add are subsets of the set of conditions of the if-then-else branches of the program. Intuitively, it works as follows: In most cases, the counterexample is spurious because in the abstract model we have not modeled an if condition with sufficient precision, and we have allowed both of its branches to be followed (at some "moment" during an abstract execution), whereas in any concrete execution run only one branch can be followed; the counterexample corresponds to a trace that takes the "wrong" branch. So, to eliminate this trace, we need to add the condition c of this if statement as a seed predicate. More precisely, let $X = \{c_1, \ldots, c_k\}$ be the set of conditions of the if statements of the program, and let C be the current set of seed predicates, i.e., such that $\mathcal{P}_i$ is computed as described in §3 using the set of predicates $P[C]$. We proceed as follows:

1. $i := 1$,
2. if $c_i \in C$, then increment i and go to step 2,
3. $C' := C \cup \{c_i\}$,
4. Create the PDS $\mathcal{P}'_i$ that corresponds to the predicates $P[C']$ as described in §3.2. If the new model eliminates the counterexample, then let the new seed set be $C := C'$. Otherwise increment i and go to step 2.

If none of the predicates $c_1, \ldots, c_k$ succeeds in eliminating the counterexample, we try to add two predicates at each step. If we try all the possibilities, and the counterexample is still not eliminated, we try to add three predicates at each step, etc.

5.3   An Example Illustrating the CEGAR Predicate-Abstraction Technique

Consider the following two sequential components D_1 and D_2 running in parallel, where a is a synchronization action:

D_1:
```
main() {                    void proc() {
    n0: int x=10;               n3: if (x < 10)
    n1: proc();                 n4:     a;
    n2: return;                 n5: else proc();
}                               n6: return;
                            }
```

D_2:
```
main() {
    m0: a;
    m1: return;
}
```

The CPDS Model

Case #1: The set of seed predicates C is empty: Let us model first the component D_1 by a PDS $\mathcal{P}_1$. There are no local variables, so the stack alphabet is the set of the control points. Moreover, because the set of seed predicates C is empty, let p be the unique state of $\mathcal{P}_1$ (p corresponds to the valuation *empty*). $\mathcal{P}_1$ contains the following rules:

$r_1: \langle p, n_0 \rangle \overset{\tau}{\longrightarrow} \langle p, n_1 \rangle$; $r_2: \langle p, n_1 \rangle \overset{\tau}{\longrightarrow} \langle p, n_3 n_2 \rangle$; $r_3: \langle p, n_2 \rangle \overset{\tau}{\longrightarrow} \langle p, \varepsilon \rangle$; $r_4: \langle p, n_3 \rangle \overset{\tau}{\longrightarrow} \langle p, n_4 \rangle$; $r_5: \langle p, n_3 \rangle \overset{\tau}{\longrightarrow} \langle p, n_5 \rangle$; $r_6: \langle p, n_4 \rangle \overset{a}{\longrightarrow} \langle p, n_6 \rangle$; $r_7: \langle p, n_5 \rangle \overset{\tau}{\longrightarrow} \langle p, n_3 n_6 \rangle$; $r_8: \langle p, n_6 \rangle \overset{\tau}{\longrightarrow} \langle p, \varepsilon \rangle$.

Similarly, we represent the second component by a PDS $\mathcal{P}_2$ that has a unique state q, and the following rules:

$r'_1: \langle q, m_0 \rangle \overset{a}{\longrightarrow} \langle q, m_1 \rangle$; and $r'_2: \langle q, m_1 \rangle \overset{\tau}{\longrightarrow} \langle q, \varepsilon \rangle$.

Case #2: We have $C = \{(x < 10)\}$: We model the component D_1 by the following PDS $\mathcal{P}'_1$. We have: $P[C]_{n_1} = P[C]_{n_3} = P[C]_{n_5} = \{x < 10\}$, and $P[C]_n = \emptyset$ for the other points (while computing $P[C]_{n_0}$, we find the predicate $10 < 10$. Because we ignore predicates that are trivially true or false, we keep $P[C]_{n_0} = \emptyset$). The states of $\mathcal{P}'_1$ are: $p_1: (x < 10) = \text{false}$, $p_2: (x < 10) = \text{true}$, and $p_3: \text{empty}$. $\mathcal{P}'_1$ contains the following rules:

$\langle p_3, n_0 \rangle \overset{\tau}{\longrightarrow} \langle p_1, n_1 \rangle$; $\langle p_1, n_1 \rangle \overset{\tau}{\longrightarrow} \langle p_1, n_3 n_2 \rangle$; $\langle p_3, n_2 \rangle \overset{\tau}{\longrightarrow} \langle p_3, \varepsilon \rangle$; $\langle p_2, n_3 \rangle \overset{\tau}{\longrightarrow} \langle p_3, n_4 \rangle$; $\langle p_1, n_3 \rangle \overset{\tau}{\longrightarrow} \langle p_1, n_5 \rangle$; $\langle p_3, n_4 \rangle \overset{a}{\longrightarrow} \langle p_3, n_6 \rangle$; $\langle p_1, n_5 \rangle \overset{\tau}{\longrightarrow} \langle p_1, n_3 n_6 \rangle$; $\langle p_3, n_6 \rangle \overset{\tau}{\longrightarrow} \langle p_3, \varepsilon \rangle$.

Refinement. Consider the query "Can D_2 reach the point m_1 if the system starts from (n_0, m_0)?" Obviously, this is not the case, because the second component can go to m_1 only if it synchronizes with D_1 using the action a, whereas the first component can never perform a, because at n_3 we do not have $x < 10$. If we model the concurrent program using no seed predicates, i.e., if we consider the model $(\mathcal{P}_1, \mathcal{P}_2)$, the model checker answers that $(n_6 n_2, m_1)$ is reachable with the following sequences: $r_1 r_2 r_4 r_6$ for $\mathcal{P}_1$, and r_1' for $\mathcal{P}_2$. Using our method, we can check that $r_1 r_2 r_4 r_6$ is spurious because $\varphi = (x = 10) \wedge (x < 10)$ is not satisfiable. Therefore, we refine PDS $\mathcal{P}_1$ using $C = \{(x < 10)\}$ to obtain the PDS $\mathcal{P}_1'$. Then it is easy to see that in the CPDS $(\mathcal{P}_1', \mathcal{P}_2)$, $\mathcal{P}_2$ cannot reach m_1.

6 Experimental Results

We implemented our method in ComFoRT [23], a model checker built on top of MAGIC [14], and experimented with a set of non-trivial benchmarks. The implementation supports two kinds of abstractions described in §4.2: the ith-prefix and the ith-suffix abstractions.

6.1 Application to Concurrent Recursive Programs

We applied the technique to two nontrivial recursive concurrent programs that could not be handled with the original (non-recursive) version of MAGIC: a Windows NT Bluetooth driver, and an algorithm for concurrent insertions in a binary search tree. The experiments were performed on a 3.0 GHz P4 SMP with 2 GB memory, running Linux 2.4.21-27.0.1.

A New Bug in a Windows NT Bluetooth Driver. The tool found bugs in two versions of this program (BT$_1$ and BT$_2$) and verified the correctness for a two-process instantiation of a third version (BT$_3$). BT$_1$ was the version for which KISS had previously found a bug [24], and our tool identified the same bug. In contrast to KISS (as well as the work reported in [25]), our approach can also verify correctness by determining that all error configurations are unreachable. The authors of [24] sent us BT$_2$ to see if correctness could be verified. Instead, we found a bug in BT$_2$ that can arise when two concurrent processes are running. Both bugs could be detected with the ith-prefix abstraction as well as the ith-suffix abstraction. Using the coun-

Table 1. Performance for the Bluetooth driver (len. = counterexample length, except for BT$_3$, where it indicates the abstraction length; mem. = memory usage (MB))

version	# procs.	abstraction	len.	time(secs.)	mem.
BT$_1$	1	i^{th}-prefix	8	8	358
BT$_1$	1	i^{th}-suffix	8	5	334
BT$_2$	2	i^{th}-prefix	14	67	490
BT$_2$	2	i^{th}-suffix	14	20	391
BT$_3$	1	i^{th}-suffix	6	2	304
BT$_3$	2	i^{th}-suffix	7	25	441

terexample found by our tool, we modified BT$_2$ to create BT$_3$, and analyzed BT$_3$ for a two-process configuration. The tool reported that the error state is unreachable in BT$_3$.

Tab. 1 shows the running times and memory consumption for these experiments. The ith-*suffix* abstraction is more efficient because we use it to compute Pre^* from the error states. Therefore, the language will stop growing once Pre^* has traversed i actions from the error state.

Note that the Bluetooth driver is not recursive; however, we use a recursive process to model a counter. In the real program, the counter is an integer (which is a global variable). Because we needed to represent global variables by means of synchronization actions, we had to represent the counter as a process. We modeled the counter process as a PDS with stack alphabet $\{1\}$. The number of 1's on the stack corresponds to the value of the counter. Then, incrementing the counter amounts to pushing a 1 onto the stack, and decrementing it amounts to popping a 1 off the stack.

An Algorithm for Concurrent Insertions in a Binary Search Tree. We also considered an algorithm that handles a finite number of concurrent insertions in a binary search tree [26]. The algorithm can be applied to handle simultaneous insertions into a database (by several users), or to reduce the time necessary for a single insertion. The algorithm was modified so that one process does not adhere to the required lock and unlock semantics, and we then applied our tool (using the ith-prefix abstraction) to the modified version. The times needed to detect the bug (as a function of number of processes) are shown in Tab. 2.

Table 2. Times needed to detect the bug in the concurrent-insertions algorithm

# procs.	len.	time (secs.)
2	1	0.8
3	1	0.8
4	1	0.8
5	1	1.1
6	1	2.7
7	1	12.9

6.2 Application to Non-recursive Examples

We applied our implementation to several examples without recursion to which MAGIC had already been applied. The previous version of MAGIC handles *non-recursive* procedure calls by in-line expansion. The purpose of the non-recursive experiments was to test whether our technique was better than inlining.

We tested sequential programs to determine whether the implementations were of comparable speed (without the complication of concurrency). They were not: the times for the *srvr-i* and *clnt-i* examples show that the overhead introduced by our technique is substantial (cf. the times in the two columns of Tab. 3 labeled "Verif"). The reason for this difference is that MAGIC performs a reachability query over an FSM, whereas we use the full CPDS machinery (which includes the inner CEGAR loop).

Despite this handicap, when model checking concurrent programs, our technique was almost always better than the in-lining technique of the base MAGIC system (see the bold entries in the right-hand table of Tab. 3). The new technique outperforms MAGIC in these cases because it avoids the state-space explosion that can occur because of in-lining. The cost of the technique depends heavily on the length of the synchronization sequences examined by the model checker. This can be seen by comparing the times for the non-recursive examples and for the Bluetooth example. Each of the

Table 3. Abs = predicate-abstraction time (sec); Verif = model-checking time (sec); Mem = memory usage (MB); * = exceeded 2 GB memory limit; Len = abstraction length

Sequential Experiments							Concurrent Experiments						
Program	MAGIC			CPDS				Program	MAGIC			CPDS		
	Abs	Verif	Mem	Abs	Verif	Mem	Len		Abs	Verif	Mem	Abs	Verif	Mem	Len
srvr-1	25.5	0.001	24.3	25.5	1.2	31.3	2	ssl-1	46.2	**16.2**	56.3	46.8	**2.82**	58.0	2
srvr-2	25.8	0.001	22.2	25.7	1.3	31.3	2	ssl-2	46.2	**16.1**	56.3	46.4	**3.83**	68.7	2
srvr-3	25.7	0.003	23.3	25.6	1.2	31.3	2	ssl-3	46.8	**14.0**	56.2	46.8	**19.2**	450	4
srvr-4	25.5	0.025	24.3	25.6	1.2	31.3	2	ssl-4	46.7	**14.2**	56.2	46.2	**2.76**	57.1	2
srvr-5	25.4	0.034	25.4	25.7	2.2	34.4	2	ssl-5	46.7	**14.0**	56.2	46.8	**3.02**	58.3	2
srvr-6	25.7	0.038	22.3	25.7	2.3	34.1	2	ssl-6	46.1	**14.0**	53.5	46.8	**2.93**	58.3	2
srvr-7	25.5	0.024	24.3	25.9	2.1	34.0	2	ssl-7	46.3	**15.0**	56.3	46.2	**3.34**	58.3	2
srvr-8	25.4	0.035	25.4	25.8	2.1	34.0	2	**ucos**	**29.1**	**0.044**	**293**	**6.8**	**0.702**	**110**	2
clnt-1	18.9	0.001	16.1	19.3	0.881	22.1	2	**ucos-2**	**84.8**	**578**	**639**	**16.5**	**1.324**	**161**	2
clnt-2	19.2	0.001	14.1	19.0	0.950	24.9	2	**ucos-3**	**168**	*****	*****	**29.2**	**2.144**	**213**	2
clnt-3	18.9	0.002	16.1	19.2	0.856	23.2	2	**casting**	**45.7**	**0.257**	**196.1**	**40.3**	**38.2**	**2145**	3
clnt-4	19.1	0.001	14.6	18.9	0.880	24.9	2								
clnt-5	18.7	0.026	18.7	19.1	1.65	27.2	2								
clnt-6	18.9	0.027	16.1	19.3	1.78	27.2	2								
clnt-7	19.2	0.027	14.1	19.1	1.71	27.2	2								
clnt-8	19.2	0.027	14.1	19.3	1.68	27.2	2								

non-recursive examples are verifed using strings of only 2–4 synchronization actions. However, BT_1, BT_2, and BT_3 need 8, 14, and 7 actions, respectively, which causes the running times to be much larger. This is an interesting aspect of our technique, namely, the limiting factor is the length of the synchronization sequences considered, not program size. Indeed, the analysis times are encouraging for the programs ucos-2 and ucos-3, which are 12K LOC and 18K LOC, respectively (see Tab. 3).

7   Related Work

Bouajjani et al. also reduced the reachability problem for CPDSs to computing over-approximations of CFLs; however, no CEGAR techniques were presented there [6, 7]. More precisely, their work computes over-approximations A_1 and A_2 of two given CFLs L_1 and L_2, and if $A_1 \cap A_2 = \emptyset$, one concludes that $L_1 \cap L_2 = \emptyset$. However, no conclusion can be made automatically if $A_1 \cap A_2 \neq \emptyset$. In particular, one can never conclude that $L_1 \cap L_2 \neq \emptyset$. In contrast, our CEGAR-based semi-decision procedure is guaranteed to terminate in this case, with the correct answer.

CEGAR-based predicate-abstraction techniques are used in several C-program model-checking tools, such as SLAM [12], BLAST [13], ZING [27], and KISS [24]. However, as mentioned previously, SLAM cannot deal with concurrency, BLAST cannot handle recursion, and KISS cannot discover errors that appear after a number of interleavings between the parallel components greater than three. ZING is an extension of SLAM to concurrent programs. SLAM and ZING are based on procedure summarization; hence, ZING might not terminate in cases where our technique will. Indeed, in the concurrent case, one needs to keep track of the calling stack, which can be unbounded in the presence of recursive calls. The contents of the stack are explicitly represented in ZING. In contrast, in our PDS modeling framework, they are symbolically represented with regular languages. On the other hand, SLAM and ZING use predicate-abstraction techniques to extract a Boolean program from a C program with recursion. Schwoon has implemented a translation from Boolean programs to PDSs in the MOPED tool [15]. However, MOPED cannot handle concurrent programs. Our CPDS predicate-abstraction-refinement techniques are performed componentwise, and amount to performing successive sequential PDS predicate-abstractions and refinements. These successive steps could be performed using SLAM and then MOPED; however, in this paper, we present predicate-abstraction techniques that create a PDS from C source code of a sequential component directly and more efficently (i.e., without going through an intermediate Boolean program).

Finally, the techniques presented in [28, 25] also use multiple PDSs to model concurrent recursive programs. However, [28] is restricted to programs that communicate via a finite number of locks, and assumes a certain nesting condition on the locks. As for [25], it uses shared-variables for communication between threads, whereas we use synchronizing actions (these two models can simulate each other). The technique presented in [25] sidesteps the undecidability of the reachability problem for multiple PDSs by putting a bound k on the number of interleavings between different threads, whereas we sidestep undecidability by computing abstractions of CFLs (without bounding the number of interleavings). In certain cases, our technique can be more powerful than the one presented in [25]. Namely, when we find $A_1 \cap A_2 = \emptyset$, we can infer that the target configurations are not reachable, whereas the technique of [25] can never establish such a property because it computes an underapproximation. Indeed, after correcting BT_2 to create BT_3, our tool verified that BT_3 is correct for two processes. Finally, the technique of [25] has not been implemented, and no automatic techniques to translate C code to PDS are presented there.

Acknowledgments. We thank M. Sighireanu for helpful discussions about the Bluetooth driver program, S. Qadeer for providing us with BT_2, and A. Lal for his helpful insights.

References

1. Ramalingam, G.: Context-sensitive synchronization-sensitive analysis is undecidable. TOPLAS **22** (2000) 416–430
2. Esparza, J., Knoop, J.: An automata-theoretic approach to interprocedural data-flow analysis. In: FOSSACS. (1999)
3. Esparza, J., Schwoon, S.: A BDD-based model checker for recursive programs. In: CAV. (2001)
4. Bouajjani, A., Esparza, J., Maler, O.: Reachability analysis of pushdown automata: Application to model checking. In: CONCUR. (1997)
5. Finkel, A., Willems, B., Wolper, P.: A direct symbolic approach to model checking pushdown systems. In: Infinity. (1997)
6. Bouajjani, A., Esparza, J., Touili, T.: A generic approach to the static analysis of concurrent programs with procedures. In: POPL. (2003)

7. Bouajjani, A., Esparza, J., Touili, T.: A generic approach to the static analysis of concurrent programs with procedures. Int. J. Found. of Comp. Sci. (2003)
8. Cousot, P., Cousot, R.: Abstract interpretation: A unified lattice model for static analysis of programs by construction of approximation of fixed points. In: POPL. (1977)
9. Graf, S., Saidi, H.: Construction of abstract state graphs with PVS. In: CAV. (1997)
10. Kurshan, R.P.: Computer-aided verification of coordinating processes: The automata-theoretic approach. In: Princeton University Press. (1994)
11. Clarke, E.M., Grumberg, O., Jha, S., Lu, Y., Veith, H.: Counterexample-guided abstraction refinement. In: CAV. (2000)
12. Ball, T., Rajamani, S.: Automatically validating temporal safety properties of interfaces. In: SPIN. (2001)
13. Henzinger, T., Jhala, R., Majumdar, R., Sutre, G.: Lazy abstraction. In: POPL. (2002)
14. Chaki, S., Clarke, E., Groce, A., Jha, S., Veith, H.: Modular verification of software components in C. In: ICSE. (2003)
15. Schwoon, S.: Model-Checking Pushdown Systems. PhD thesis, TUM (2002)
16. Chaki, S., Clarke, E., Kidd, N., Reps, T., Touili, T.: Verifying concurrent message-passing C programs with recursive calls. Tech. Rep. 1532, Univ. of Wisconsin (2005)
17. Necula, G., McPeak, S., Weimer, W., Liblit, B., To, R., Bhargava, A.: C intermediate lang. (2001) http://manju.cs.berkeley.edu/cil.
18. Morris, J.: Assignment and linked data structures. In: Theoretical Foundations of Programming Methodology. D. Reidel Publishing Co. (1982)
19. Nelson, G.: Techniques for Program Verification. PhD thesis, Stanford University (1980)
20. Reps, T., Schwoon, S., Jha, S.: Weighted pushdown systems and their application to inter-procedural dataflow analysis. In: SAS. (2003)
21. Reps, T., Schwoon, S., Jha, S., Melski, D.: Weighted pushdown systems and their application to interprocedural dataflow analysis. SCP **58** (2005)
22. Kidd, N., Reps, T., Melski, D., Lal, A.: WPDS++: A C++ library for weighted pushdown systems (2004) http://www.cs.wisc.edu/wpis/wpds++/.
23. Chaki, S., Ivers, J., Sharygina, N., Wallnau, K.: The ComFoRT reasoning framework. In: CAV. (2005)
24. Qadeer, S., Wu, D.: KISS: Keep it simple and sequential. In: PLDI. (2004)
25. Qadeer, S., Rehof, J.: Context-bounded model checking of concurrent software. In: TACAS. (2005)
26. Kung, H., Lehman, P.: Concurrent manipulation of binary search trees. TODS **5** (1980)
27. Qadeer, S., Rajamani, S., Rehof, J.: Summarizing procedures in concurrent programs. In: POPL. (2004)
28. Kahlon, V., Ivancic, F., Gupta, A.: Reasoning about threads communicating via locks. In: CAV. (2005)

Automata-Based Verification of Programs with Tree Updates[*]

Peter Habermehl[1], Radu Iosif[2], and Tomas Vojnar[3]

[1] LIAFA/Université Paris 7, 175 rue du Chevaleret, 75013 Paris, France
haberm@liafa.jussieu.fr
[2] VERIMAG/CNRS, 2 Avenue de Vignate, 38610 Gières, France
iosif@imag.fr
[3] Brno University of Technology, Bozetechova 2, CZ-612 66 Brno, Czech Republic
vojnar@fit.vutbr.cz

Abstract. This paper describes an effective verification procedure for imperative programs that handle (balanced) tree-like data structures. Since the verification problem considered is undecidable, we appeal to a classical semi-algorithmic approach in which the user has to provide manually the loop invariants in order to check the validity of Hoare triples of the form $\{P\}C\{Q\}$, where P, Q are the sets of states corresponding to the pre- and post-conditions, and C is the program to be verified. We specify the sets of states (representing tree-like memory configurations) using a special class of tree automata named Tree Automata with Size Constraints (TASC). The main advantage of using TASC in program specifications is that they recognize non-regular sets of tree languages such as the *AVL trees*, the *red-black trees*, and in general, specifications involving arithmetic reasoning about the lengths (depths) of various (possibly all) paths in the tree. The class of TASC is closed under the operations of union, intersection and complement, and moreover, the emptiness problem is decidable, which makes it a practical verification tool. We validate our approach considering red-black trees and the insertion procedure, for which we verify that the output of the insertion algorithm is a *balanced* red-black tree, i.e. the longest path is at most twice as long as the shortest path.

1 Introduction

Verification of programs using dynamic memory primitives, such as allocation, deallocation, and pointer manipulations, is crucial for a feasible method of software verification. In this paper, we address the problem of proving correctness of programs that manipulate balanced tree-like data structures. Such structures are very often applied to implement in an efficient way lookup tables, associative arrays, sets, or similar higher-level structures, especially when they are used in critical applications like real-time systems, kernels of operating systems, etc. Therefore, there arised a number of such search tree structures like the AVL trees, red-black trees, splay trees, and so on [7].

Tree automata [6] are a powerful formalism for specifying sets of trees and reasoning about them. However, one obstacle preventing them from being used currently in

---

[*] This work was supported in part by the French Ministry of Research (ACI project Securité Informatique) and the Czech Grant Agency (projects GA CR 102/04/0780 and 102/03/D211).

H. Hermanns and J. Palsberg (Eds.): TACAS 2006, LNCS 3920, pp. 350–364, 2006.
© Springer-Verlag Berlin Heidelberg 2006

program verification is that imperative programs perform destructive updates on selector fields, by temporarily violating the fact that the shape of the dynamic memory is a tree. Another impediment is the fact that tree automata represent regular sets of trees, which is not the case when one needs to reason in terms of *balanced* trees, as in the case of AVL and red-black tree algorithms.

In order to overcome the first problem, we observe that most algorithms [7] use *tree rotations* (plus the low-level addition/removal of a node to/from a tree) as the only operations that effectively change the structure of the input tree. Such updates are usually implemented as short low-level pointer manipulations [16], which are assumed to be correct in this paper. However, their correctness can be checked separately in a different formalism, such as [17], or by using tree automata extended with additional "routing" expressions on the tree backbone as in [11].

The second inconvenience has been solved in the present paper by introducing a novel class of tree automata, called Tree Automata with Size Constraints (TASC). TASC are tree automata whose actions are triggered by arithmetic constraints involving the *sizes* of the subtrees at the current node. The size of a tree is a numerical function defined inductively on the structure, as for instance the height, or the maximum number of black nodes on all paths, etc. The main advantage of using TASC in program specifications is that they recognize non-regular sets of tree languages, such as the *AVL trees*, the *red-black trees*, and in general, specifications involving arithmetic reasoning about the lengths (depths) of various (possibly all) paths in the tree. We show that the class of TASC is closed under the operations of union, intersection and complement. Also, the emptiness problem is decidable, and the semantics of the programs performing tree updates (node recoloring, rotations, nodes appending/removal) can be effectively represented as changes on the structure of the automata.

Our approach consists in writing pre- and post-condition specifications of a (sequential) imperative program and asking the user to provide loop invariants. The verification problem consists in checking the validity of the invariants and of the Hoare triples of the form $\{P\}C\{Q\}$ where P, Q are the sets of configurations corresponding to the pre- and post-condition, and C is the program to be verified. We need to stress the fact that here P and Q are languages accepted by TASC, instead of logical formulae, as it is usually the case with Hoare logic. The validity of the triple is established by computing the set of states reachable from a state in P by executing C, i.e. $post(P,C)$, and then deciding whether $post(P,C) \subseteq Q$ holds.

We have validated our approach on an example of the insertion algorithm for the red-black trees, for which we verify that for a balanced red-black tree input, the output of the insertion algorithm is also a balanced red-black tree, i.e. the number of black nodes is the same on each path.

Related Work. Verification of programs that handle tree-like structures has attracted researchers with various backgrounds, such as static analysis [12], [16], proof theory [4], and formal language theory [11]. The approach that is the closest to ours is probably the one of PALE (Pointer Assertion Logic Engine) [11], which consists in translating the verification problem into the logic SkS [15] and using tree automata to solve it. Our approach is similar in that we also specify the pre-, post-conditions and the loop invariants, reducing the validity problem for Hoare triples to the language emptiness problem. However, the use of the novel class of tree automata with arithmetic guards allows us to encode quantitative properties such as tree balancing that are not tackled in PALE. The verification of red-black trees (with balancing) is reported also in [2] by using hyper-graph rewriting systems. Two different approaches, namely net unfoldings, and graph types, are used to check that red nodes have black children and that the tree is balanced, respectively.

The definition of TASC is the result of searching for a class of counter tree automata that combines nice closure properties (union, intersection, complementation) with decidability of the emptiness problem. Existing work on extending tree automata with counters [8, 18] concentrates mostly on *in-breadth* counting of nodes with applications on verifying consistency of XML documents. Our work gives the possibility of *in-depth* counting in order to express balancing of recursive tree structures. It is worth noticing that similar computation models, such as alternating multi-tape and counter automata, have undecidable emptiness problems in the presence of two or more 1-letter input tapes, or, equivalently, non-increasing counters [13]. This result improves on early work on alternating multi-tape automata recognizing 1-letter languages [9]. However, restricting the number of counters is problematic for obtaining closure of automata under intersection. The solution is to let the actions of the counters depend exclusively on the input tree alphabet, in other words, encode them directly in the input, as size functions. This solution can be seen as a generalization of Visibly Pushdown Languages [1] to trees, for singleton stack alphabets. The general case, with more than one stack symbol, is a subject of future work.

1.1 Running Example

In this section, we introduce our verification methodology for programs using balanced trees. Several data structures based on balanced trees are commonly used, e.g. AVL trees. Here, we will use as a running example red-black trees, which are binary search trees whose nodes are colored by red or black. They are approximately balanced by constraining the way nodes can be colored. The constraints insure that no maximal path can be more than twice as long as any other path. Formally, a node contains an element of an ordered data domain, a color, a left and right pointer and a pointer to its parent. A *red-black tree* is a binary search tree that satisfies the following properties:

1. Every node is either red or black.
2. The root is black.
3. Every leaf is black.
4. If a node is red, both its children are black.
5. Each path from the root to a leaf contains the same number of black nodes.

An example of a red-black tree is given in Figure 1 (a). Because of the last condition, it is obvious that the set of red-black trees is not regular, i.e. not recognisable by standard tree automata [6]. The main operations on balanced trees are searching, insertion, and deletion. When implementing the last two operations, one has to make sure that the trees remain balanced. This is usually done using tree rotations (Figure 1 (b)) which can change the number of black nodes on a given path. The pseudo-code of the inserting operation is the following (see [7]):

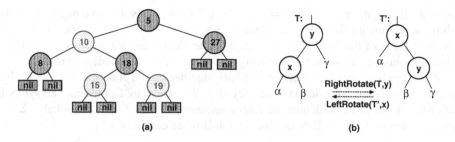

Fig. 1. (a) A red-black tree—nodes 10, 15, and 19 are red, (b) the left and right tree rotation

```
RB-Insert(T,x):
  Tree-Insert(T,x);   % Inserts a new leaf node x
  x->color = red;
  while (x != root && x->parent->color == red) {
    if (x->parent == x->parent->parent->left) {
      if (x->parent->parent->right->color == red) {
        x->parent->color = black;          % Case 1
        x->parent->parent->right->color = black;
        x->parent->parent->color = red;
        x = x->parent->parent; }
      else {
        if (x == x->parent->right) {       % Case 2
          x = x->parent;
          LeftRotate(T,x) }
        x->parent->color = black;          % Case 3
        x->parent->parent->color = red;
        RightRotate(T,x->parent->parent); }}
    else .... % same as above with right and left exchanged
  root->color = black;
```

For this program, we want to show that after an insertion of a node, a red-black tree remains a red-black tree. In this paper, we restrict ourselves to calculating the effects of program blocks which preserve the tree structure of the heap. This is not the case in general since pointer operations can temporarily break the tree structure, e.g. in the code for performing a rotation. The operations we handle are the following:

1. tests on the tree structure (like x->parent == x->parent->parent->left),
2. changing data of a node (as, e.g., recoloring of a node x->color = red),
3. left or right rotation (Figure 1 (b)),
4. moving a pointer up or down a tree structure (like x = x->parent->parent),
5. low-level insertion/deletion, i.e. the physical addition/removal of a node to/from a suitable place that is then followed by the re-balancing operations.

2   Preliminaries

In this paper, we work with the set $\mathfrak{D}$ of all boolean combinations of formulae of the form $x - y \diamond c$ or $x \diamond c$, for some $c \in \mathbb{Z}$ and $\diamond \in \{\leq, \geq\}$. We introduce the equality sign as syntactic sugar, i.e. $x - y = c \iff x - y \leq c \wedge x - y \geq c$. Notice that negation can be eliminated from any formula of $\mathcal{D}$, since $x - y \not\leq c \iff x - y \geq c + 1$, and so on. Also, any constraint of the form $x - y \geq c$ can be equivalently written as $y - x \leq -c$. For a closed formula φ, we write $\models \varphi$ meaning that it is valid, i.e. equivalent to true.

A *ranked alphabet* Σ is a set of symbols together with a function $\# : \Sigma \to \mathbb{N}$. For $f \in \Sigma$, the value $\#(f)$ is said to be the *arity* of f. We denote by Σ_n the set of all symbols of arity n from Σ. Let λ denote the empty sequence. A *tree* t over an alphabet Σ is a partial mapping $t : \mathbb{N}^* \to \Sigma$ that satisfies the following conditions:

- $dom(t)$ is a finite prefix-closed subset of $\mathbb{N}^*$, and
- for each $p \in dom(t)$, if $\#(t(p)) = n > 0$ then $\{i \mid pi \in dom(t)\} = \{1, \ldots, n\}$.

A *subtree* of t starting at position $p \in dom(t)$ is a tree $t_{|p}$ defined as $t_{|p}(q) = t(pq)$ if $pq \in dom(t)$, and undefined otherwise. Given a set of positions $P \subseteq \mathbb{N}^*$, we define the *frontier* of P as the set $fr(P) = \{p \in P \mid \forall i \in \mathbb{N} \ pi \notin P\}$. For a tree t, we use $fr(t)$ as a shortcut for $fr(dom(t))$. We denote by $T(\Sigma)$ the set of all trees over the alphabet Σ.

Definition 1. *Given two trees* $t : \mathbb{N}^* \to \Sigma$ *and* $t' : \mathbb{N}^* \to \Sigma'$, *a function* $h : dom(t) \to dom(t')$ *is said to be a* tree mapping *between* t *and* t' *if the following hold:*

- $h(\lambda) = \lambda$, *and*
- *for any* $p \in dom(t)$, *if* $\#(t(p)) = n > 0$ *then there exists a prefix-closed set* $Q \subseteq \mathbb{N}^*$ *such that* $pQ \subseteq dom(t')$ *and* $h(pi) \in fr(pQ)$ *for all* $1 \leq i \leq n$.

A *size function* (or measure) associates to every tree $t \in T(\Sigma)$ an integer $|t| \in \mathbb{Z}$. Size functions are defined inductively on the structure of the tree. For each $f \in \Sigma$, if $\#(f) = 0$ then $|f|$ is a constant c_f, otherwise, for $\#(f) = n$, we have:

$$|f(t_1, \ldots, t_n)| = \begin{cases} b_1|t_1| + c_1 \text{ if } \models \delta_1(|t_1|, \ldots, |t_n|) \\ \cdots \\ b_n|t_n| + c_n \text{ if } \models \delta_n(|t_1|, \ldots, |t_n|) \end{cases}$$

where $b_1, \ldots, b_n \in \{0, 1\}, c_1, \ldots, c_n \in \mathbb{Z}$, and $\delta_1, \ldots, \delta_n \in \mathcal{D}$, all depending on f. In order to have a consistent definition, it is required that $\delta_1, \ldots, \delta_n$ define a partition of $\mathbb{N}^n$, i.e. $\models \forall x_1 \ldots \forall x_n \ \bigvee_{1 \leq i \leq n} \delta_i \wedge \bigwedge_{1 \leq i < j \leq n} \neg(\delta_i \wedge \delta_j)$. [1] A *sized alphabet* $(\Sigma, |.|)$ is a ranked alphabet with an associated size function.

A *tree automaton with size constraints* (TASC) over a sized alphabet $(\Sigma, |.|)$ is a 3-tuple $A = (Q, \Delta, F)$ where Q is a finite set of states, $F \subseteq Q$ is a designated set of final states, and Δ is a set of transition rules of the form $f(q_1, \ldots, q_n) \xrightarrow{\varphi(|1|, \ldots, |n|)} q$, where $f \in \Sigma$, $\#(f) = n$, and $\varphi \in \mathcal{D}$ is a formula with n free variables. For constant symbols $a \in \Sigma$, $\#(a) = 0$, the automaton has unconstrained rules of the form $a \to q$.

A *run* of A over a tree $t : \mathbb{N}^* \to \Sigma$ is a mapping $\pi : dom(t) \to Q$ such that, for each position $p \in dom(t)$, where $q = \pi(p)$, we have:

---

[1] For technical reasons related to the decidability of the emptiness problem for TASC, we do not allow arbitrary linear combinations of $|t_i|$ in the definition of $|f(t_1, \ldots, t_n)|$.

- if $\#(t(p)) = n > 0$ and $q_i = \pi(pi)$, $1 \leq i \leq n$, then Δ has a rule
$t(p)(q_1, \ldots, q_n) \xrightarrow{\varphi(|1|,\ldots,|n|)} q$ and $\models \varphi(|t_{|p1}|, \ldots, |t_{|pn}|)$,
- otherwise, if $\#(t(p)) = 0$, then Δ has a rule $t(p) \to q$.

A run π is said to be *accepting*, if and only if $\pi(\lambda) \in F$. As usual, the *language* of A, denoted as $L(A)$ is the set of all trees over which A has an accepting run.

As an example, let us consider a TASC recognising the set of all balanced red-black trees. Let $\Sigma = \{red, black, nil\}$ with $\#(red) = \#(black) = 2$ and $\#(nil) = 0$. First, we define the size function to be the maximal number of black nodes from the root to a leaf: $|nil| = 1$, $|red(t_1,t_2)| = max(|t_1|, |t_2|)$, and $|black(t_1,t_2)| = max(|t_1|, |t_2|) + 1$. Let $A_{rb} = (\{q_b, q_r\}, \Delta, \{q_b\})$ with $\Delta = \{nil \to q_b, black(q_{b/r}, q_{b/r}) \xrightarrow{|1|=|2|} q_b, red(q_b, q_b) \xrightarrow{|1|=|2|} q_r\}$. By using $q_{x/y}$ within the left-hand side of a transition rule, we mean the set of rules in which either q_x or q_y take the place of $q_{x/y}$.

3 Closure Properties and Decidability of TASC

This section is devoted to the closure of the class of TASC under the operations of union, intersection and complement. The decidability of the emptiness problem is also proved.

3.1 Closure Properties

A TASC is said to be *deterministic* if, for every input tree, the automaton has at most one run. For every TASC A, we can effectively construct a deterministic TASC A_d such that $L(A) = L(A_d)$. Concretely, let $A = (Q, \Delta, F)$ and G_A be the set of all guards labelling the transitions from Δ and $G_A^n = \{\varphi \in G_A \mid \|FV(\varphi)\| = n\}$ where $n \in \mathbb{N}$ and $\|FV(\varphi)\|$ denotes the number of free variables in φ. Without loss of generality, we assume that any guard φ labelling a transition of A of the form $f(q_1, \ldots, q_n) \xrightarrow{\varphi} q$ has exactly n free variables.[2] Define B_A^n as the set of all conjunctions of formulae from G_A^n and their negations. Let $B_A = \bigcup_{n \in \mathbb{N}} B_A^n \cup \{\top\}$. With this notation, define $A_d = (Q_d, \Delta_d, F_d)$ where $Q_d = \mathcal{P}(Q) \times B_A$, $F_d = \{\langle s, \varphi \rangle \in Q_d \mid s \cap F \neq \emptyset\}$, and:

$$f(\langle s_1, \varphi_1 \rangle \ldots \langle s_n, \varphi_n \rangle) \xrightarrow{\varphi} \langle s, \varphi \rangle \in \Delta_d$$

$$\text{iff} \begin{cases} s \subseteq \{q | f(q_1, \ldots, q_n) \xrightarrow{\psi} q \in \Delta, q_i \in s_i\} \text{ and } s \neq \emptyset \\ \varphi = \bigwedge \{\psi | f(q_1, \ldots, q_n) \xrightarrow{\psi} q \in \Delta, q_i \in s_i, q \in s\} \wedge \\ \bigwedge \{\neg \psi | f(q_1, \ldots, q_n) \xrightarrow{\psi} q \in \Delta, q_i \in s_i, q \in Q \setminus s\} \end{cases}$$

$$a \to \langle s, \top \rangle \in \Delta_d \text{ iff } s = \{q | a \to q \in \Delta\}$$

Notice that A_d has no states of the form $\langle s, \bot \rangle$ since they would necessarily be unreachable. The following theorem shows that non-deterministic and deterministic TASC recognize exactly the same languages (for a proof of the theorem see [10]).

---

[2] We can add conjuncts of the form $x_i = x_i$ for all missing variables.

Theorem 1. A_d *is deterministic and* $L(A_d) = L(A)$.

Determinisation is crucial to show closure of TASC under language complementation. However, given a deterministic TASC A, the construction of a TASC recognizing the language $T(\Sigma) \setminus L(A)$ is fairly standard [6], using the fact that $\mathcal{D}$ is closed under negation. One needs to first build the *complete* TASC, i.e. in which each input leads to one state, and then switch between accepting and non-accepting states. Fairly standard is also the union of TASC, i.e. given A_1 and A_2, one can build a TASC $A_\cup$ recognizing $L(A_1) \cup L(A_2)$ by simply merging their (supposedly disjoint) sets of states and transitions. The TASC $A_\cap$ recognizing intersection of languages, i.e. $L(A_1) \cap L(A_2)$, is the automaton whose set of states is the cartesian product of the sets of states of A_1 and A_2, and the transitions are of the form $f((q_1',q_1''),\ldots,(q_n',q_n'')) \xrightarrow[A_\cap]{\varphi' \wedge \varphi''} (q',q'')$, for $f(q_1',\ldots,q_n') \xrightarrow[A_1]{\varphi'} q'$ and $f(q_1'',\ldots,q_n'') \xrightarrow[A_2]{\varphi''} q''$. For more details, we refer the reader to the full version of the paper [10].

3.2 Emptiness

In this section, we give an effective method for deciding emptiness of a TASC. In fact, we address the slightly more general problem: given a TASC $A = (Q, \Delta, F)$ we construct, for each state $q \in Q$, an arithmetic formula $\phi_q(x)$ in one variable that precisely characterizes the sizes of the trees whose roots are labelled with q by A, i.e. $\models \phi_q(n)$ iff $\exists t \; |t| = n$ and $t \xrightarrow[A]{*} q$. As it will turn out, the ϕ_q formulae are expressible in Presburger arithmetic, therefore satisfiability is decidable [14]. This entails the decidability of the emptiness problem, which can be expressed as the satisfiability of the disjunction $\bigvee_{q \in F} \phi_q$.

In order to construct ϕ_q, we shall translate our TASC into an Alternating Pushdown System (APDS) [3] whose stack encodes the value of one integer counter. An APDS is a triple $S = (Q, \Gamma, \delta, F)$ where Q is the set of control locations, Γ is the stack alphabet, F is the set of final control locations, and δ is a mapping from $Q \times \Gamma$ into $\mathcal{P}(\mathcal{P}(Q \times \Gamma^*))$. Notice that APDS do not have an input alphabet since we are interested in the behaviors they generate, rather than the accepted languages. A run of the APDS is a tree $t : \mathbb{N}^* \to (Q \times \Gamma^*)$ satisfying the following property: for any $p \in dom(t)$, if $t(p) = \langle q, \gamma w \rangle$, then $\{t(pi) \mid 1 \le i \le \#(t(p))\} = \{\langle q_1, w_1 w \rangle, \ldots, \langle q_n, w_n w \rangle\}$ where $\{\langle q_1, w_1 \rangle, \ldots, \langle q_n, w_n \rangle\} \in \delta(q, \gamma)$. The run is accepting if all control locations occurring on the frontier are final.

The idea behind the reduction is that any bottom-up run of a TASC on a given input tree can be mapped (in the sense of Definition 1) onto a top-down run of an APDS. The simulation invariant is that the size of a subtree from the run of the TASC is encoded by the corresponding stack in the run of the APDS. Next, we use the construction of [3] to calculate, for the given set of configurations σ, the set $pre_q^*(\sigma)$ of configurations with control state q that have a successor set in σ, i.e. $c = \langle q, w \rangle \xrightarrow{*} C \subseteq \sigma$. It is shown in [3] that if σ is a regular language, then so is $pre^*(\sigma)$, and the alternating finite automaton recognizing the latter can be constructed in time polynomial in the size of the APDS. Hence, the Parikh images of such $pre_q^*(\sigma)$ sets are semilinear sets definable by Presburger formulae. In our case, $\sigma = \{\langle q, \varepsilon \rangle \mid q \in F\}$ is a finite set where ε is the (encoding of the) empty stack. Using a unary encoding of the counter (as a stack), we obtain the needed formulae $\phi_q(x)$. For a detailed explanation, the reader is referred to [10].

Lemma 1. *For each TASC $A = (Q, \Delta, F)$ over a sized alphabet $(\Sigma, |.|)$ there exists an APDS $S_A = (Q_A, \Gamma, \delta, F_A)$ such that:*

1. *for any tree $t \in T(\Sigma)$ and any run $\pi : dom(t) \rightarrow Q$ of A on t, there exists an accepting run $\rho : \mathbb{N}^* \rightarrow (Q_A \times \mathbb{N})$ of S_A and a one-to-one tree mapping h between π and ρ such that:*
$$\forall p \in dom(t) \; \exists q \in Q_A \; . \; \rho(h(p)) = \langle q, |t_{|p}| \rangle \tag{1}$$

2. *for any accepting run $\rho : \mathbb{N}^* \rightarrow (Q_A \times \mathbb{N})$ of S_A there exists a tree $t \in T(\Sigma)$, a run $\pi : dom(t) \rightarrow Q$ of A on t and a one-to-one tree mapping h between π and ρ satisfying (1).*

Moreover, S_A can be effectively constructed from the description of A.

As a remark, the decidability of the emptiness problem for TASC can be also proved via a reduction to the class of *tree automata with one memory* [5] by encoding the size of a tree as a unary term, using essentially the same idea as in the reduction to APDS. The complexity of the emptiness problem can be furthermore analyzed using the double exponential bound of the emptiness problem for tree automata with one memory, and is considered as further work.

4 Semantics of Tree Updates

As explained in Section 1.1, there are three types of operations that commonly appear in procedures used for balancing binary trees after an insertion or deletion: (1) navigation in a tree, i.e. testing or changing the position a pointer variable is pointing to in the tree, (2) testing or changing certain data fields of the encountered tree nodes, such as the color of a node in a red-black tree, and (3) tree rotations. In addition, one has to consider the physical insertion or deletion to/from a suitable position in the tree as an input for the re-balancing.

It turns out that the TASC defined in Section 2 are not closed with respect to the effect of some of the above operations, in particular the ones that change the balance of subtrees (the difference between the size of the left and right subtree at a given position in the tree). Therefore, we now introduce a subclass of TASC called *restricted TASC* (rTASC) which we show to be closed with respect to all the needed operations on balanced trees. Moreover, rTASC are closed with respect to intersection and union, amenable to determinisation and minimization, though not closed with respect to complementation. The idea is to use rTASC to express loop invariants and pre- and post-conditions of programs as well as to perform the necessary reachability computations. TASC are then used in the associated language inclusion checks. Notice that, since rTASC are not closed under negation, inclusion of rTASC cannot be directly decided. Therefore we have to appeal to the more general result concerning the decidability of inclusion between TASC.

A *restricted alphabet* is a sized alphabet consisting only of nullary and binary symbols and a size function of the form $|f(t_1, t_2)| = \max(|t_1|, |t_2|) + a$ with $a \in \mathbb{Z}$ for binary symbols. A *restricted* TASC is a TASC with a restricted alphabet and with binary rules only of the form $f(q_1, q_2) \xrightarrow{|1|-|2|=b} q$ with $b \in \mathbb{Z}$. Notice that any conjunction of guards of an rTASC and their negations reduces either to false, or to only one formula of the same form, i.e. $|1| - |2| = b$. Using this fact, one can show that the intersection of two rTASC is again an rTASC, and that applying the determinisation of Section 3.1 to an rTASC yields another rTASC. Moreover, the intersection of an rTASC with a classical tree automaton is again an rTASC.[3] Clearly, rTASC are not closed under complementation, as inequality guards are not allowed.

4.1   Representing Sets of Memory Configurations

Let us consider a finite set of *pointer variables* $V = \{x, y, \ldots\}$ and a disjoint finite set of data values $\mathcal{D}$, e.g. $\mathcal{D} = \{red, black\}$. In the following, we let $\Sigma = \mathcal{P}(V \cup \mathcal{D} \cup \{nil\})$ where *nil* indicates a null pointer value. The arity function is defined as follows: $\#(f) = 2$ if $nil \notin f$, and $\#(f) = 0$ otherwise. For a tree $t \in T(\Sigma)$ and a variable $x \in V$, we say that a position $p \in dom(t)$ is *pointed to by* x if and only if $x \in t(p)$.

For the rest of this section, let $A = (Q, \Delta, F)$ be an rTASC over Σ. We say that A represents a *set of memory configurations* if and only if, for each $t \in L(A)$ and each $x \in V$, there is at most one $p \in dom(t)$ such that $x \in t(p)$. This condition can be ensured by the construction of A: let $Q = Q \times \mathcal{P}(V)$ and Δ consist only of rules of the form $f(\langle q_1, v_1 \rangle, \langle q_2, v_2 \rangle) \xrightarrow{\varphi} \langle q, v \rangle$ where (1) $v = (f \cup v_1 \cup v_2) \cap V$ and (2) $f \cap v_1 = f \cap v_2 = v_1 \cap v_2 = \emptyset$. Intuitively, a control state $\langle q, v \rangle$ "remembers" all variables encountered by condition (1), while condition (2) ensures that no variable is encountered twice.

4.2   Modelling Tree Rotations

Let $x \in V$ be a fixed variable. We shall construct an rTASC $A' = (Q', \Delta', F')$ that describes the set of trees that are the result of the *left rotation* of a tree from $L(A)$ applied at the node pointed to by x. The case of the right tree rotation is very similar.[4] In the description, we will be referring to Figure 2 illustrating the problem.

Let $R_x = \{(r_1, r_2) \in \Delta^2 \mid x \in g \wedge r_1 : f(q_1, q_2) \xrightarrow{\varphi_3} q_3 \wedge r_2 : g(q_4, q_3) \xrightarrow{\varphi_5} q_5\}$ be the set of all the pairs of automata rules that can yield a rotation, and be modified because of it. Other rules may then have to be modified to reflect the change in one of their *left hand side states*, e.g. the change of q_5 to q_3' in the *h*-rule in Figure 2, or to reflect the *change in the balance* that may result from the rotation, i.e. a change in the *difference of the sizes* of the subtrees of some node. We discuss later what changes in the balance can appear after a rotation, and Lemma 2 proves that the set D of the possible changes in the balance in the described trees is finite. The automaton A' can thus be constructed from A as follows:

1. $Q' = Q \cup R_x \cup (R_x \times D) \cup (Q \times D)$ where we add new states for the rotated parts and to reflect the changes in the balance.

---

[3] A bottom-up tree automaton can be seen as a TASC in which all guards are true.
[4] In fact, it can be implemented by temporarily swapping the child nodes in the involved rules, doing a left rotation, and then swapping the child nodes again.

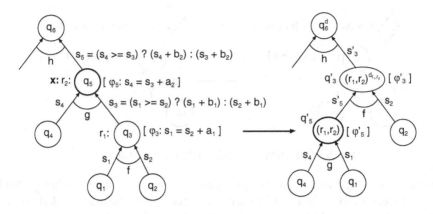

Fig. 2. Left rotation on an rTASC

2. $\Delta' = \Delta \cup \Delta_r \cup \beta(\Delta \cup \Delta_a)$ where:

   – Δ_r is the smallest set such that for all $(r_1, r_2) \in R_x$ where $r_1 : f(q_1, q_2) \xrightarrow{\varphi_3} q_3$

     and $r_2 : g(q_4, q_3) \xrightarrow{\varphi_5} q_5$, contains the rules $g(q_4, q_1) \xrightarrow{\varphi'_5} q'_5$ and $f(q'_5, q_2) \xrightarrow{\varphi'_3} q'_3$ where $q'_5 = (r_1, r_2)$ and $q'_3 = (r_1, r_2)^{d_{r_1, r_2}}$. Here, we use $(r_1, r_2)^{d_{r_1, r_2}}$ as a shorthand for $\langle (r_1, r_2), d_{r_1, r_2} \rangle$. The value $d_{r_1, r_2} \in \mathbb{Z}$ represents the change in the balance caused by the rotation based on r_1, r_2. We describe the computation of φ'_3, φ'_5, and d_{r_1, r_2} below.

   – Δ_a is the set of rules that could be applied just above the position where a rotation takes place. For each $(r_1, r_2) \in R_x$, we take all rules from Δ that have q_5 within the left hand side and add them to Δ_a, with (r_1, r_2) substituted for q_5.

   – β (described in detail in Section 4.3) is the function that implements the necessary changes in the guards and input/output states (adding the d-component) of the rules due to the changes in the balance.

3. $F' = (F \times D) \cup F_r$. Here, F_r captures the case where q'_3 becomes accepting, i.e. the right child of the node previously labelled by q_3 becomes the root of the entire tree.

Suppose that φ_3 is $|t_1| = |t_2| + a_1$ and let us denote the sizes of the sub-trees read at q_1 and q_2 before the rotation by s_1 and s_2, respectively. Let the size function associated with f be $|f(t_1, t_2)| = \max(|t_1|, |t_2|) + b_1$, and let s_3 denote the size of the subtree labelled by q_3 before the rotation. Also, suppose that φ_5 is $|t_1| = |t_2| + a_2$ and let us denote the size of the sub-tree read at q_4 before the rotation as s_4. Finally, let the size function associated with g be $|g(t_1, t_2)| = \max(|t_1|, |t_2|) + b_2$, and let s_5 denote the size of the subtree labelled by q_5 before the rotation. We denote s'_5 and s'_3 the sizes obtained at q'_5 and q'_3 after the rotation.

The key observation that allows us to compute φ'_3, φ'_5, and d_{r_1, r_2} is that due to the chosen form of guards and sizes, we can always compute any two of the sizes s_1, s_2, s_4 from the remaining one. Indeed,

   – for $a_1 \geq 0$, we have $s_3 = s_1 + b_1 = s_2 + a_1 + b_1 = s_4 - a_2$, whereas
   – for $a_1 < 0$, we have $s_3 = s_2 + b_1 = s_1 - a_1 + b_1 = s_4 - a_2$.

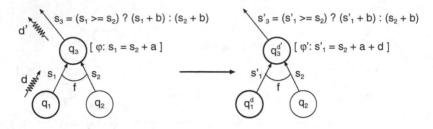

Fig. 3. Propagation of changes in the balance in an rTASC

Computing φ'_3, φ'_5, and d_{r_1, r_2} is then just a complex exercise in case splitting. Notice that all the cases can be distinguished statically according to the mutual relations of the constants a_1, b_1, a_2, and b_2. For example, in the case of φ'_5, we obtain the following (the other cases are explained in [10]):

1. For $a_1 \geq 0$, we have $s_4 = s_1 + b_1 + a_2$, and so φ'_5 relating a subtree of size s_4 and s_1 (cf. Figure 2) is $|t_1| = |t_2| + b_1 + a_2$.
2. For $a_1 < 0$, we have $s_4 = s_1 - a_1 + b_1 + a_2$, and so φ'_5 is $|t_1| = |t_2| - a_1 + b_1 + a_2$.

4.3 Propagating Changes in the Balance Through rTASC

As said, tree updates such as recoloring or rotations may introduce changes in the balance at certain points. These changes may affect the balance at all positions above the considered node. The role of the β function is to propagate a change in balance d upwards in the trees recognized by the rTASC. The way β changes a set of rules is illustrated in Figure 3. For every $d \in D$, every input rule $f(q_1, q_2) \xrightarrow{\varphi} q_3$ is changed to two rules $f(q_1^d, q_2) \xrightarrow{\varphi'} q_3^{d'}$ and $f(q_1, q_2^d) \xrightarrow{\varphi''} q_3^{d''}$ corresponding to the cases when the change in the balance originates from the left or the right. Since we consider just one rotation in every tree (at a given node pointed to by the pointer variable x), the change can never come from both sides. The new guards are $\varphi' : |t_1| = |t_2| + a + d$ and $\varphi'' : |t_1| = |t_2| + a - d$. Let us further analyse the changes in the balance propagated upwards after d comes from the bottom.

Suppose the change in balance is coming from the left as in Figure 3. We distinguish the cases of $a \geq 0$ and $a < 0$. (1) For $a \geq 0$, the original size at q_3 is $s_3 = s_1 + b$ where s_1 is the original size at q_1. After the change d happens at q_1, i.e. $s'_1 - s_1 = d$, we have the following subcases: (1.1) For $a + d \geq 0$, we have $s'_3 = s'_1 + b$, i.e. $d' = d$, and so we have the same change in the size at q_3 as at q_1. (1.2) For $a + d < 0$, we have $s'_3 = s_2 + b = s_1 - a + b$, and hence $d' = -a$. (2) For $a < 0$, $s_3 = s_2 + b$. In this case, (2.1) for $a + d \geq 0$, $s'_3 = s'_1 + b = s_1 + d + b = s_2 + a + d + b$, and so $d' = a + d$, and (2.2) for $a + d < 0$, $s'_3 = s_2 + b$, and thus $d' = 0$. The case of the change in the balance coming from the right is similar.

When a change d in the size happens at a child node, at its parent, the change is either eliminated, d' or d'' is 0, stays the same, d' or d'' equals d, becomes $-|a|$ (note that $a \geq 0$ for $d' = -a$, and $a < 0$, for $d'' = a$), or finally, becomes $-|a| + d$. We can now close our construction by showing that the set D of possible changes in the sizes is finite.

Lemma 2. *For an rTASC A over a set of variables $\mathcal{V}$ and a variable $x \in \mathcal{V}$, the set D of the possible changes in the balance generated by a left tree rotation at x is finite.*

Note that when we allow the use of two different constants b_f^1 and b_f^2 in the size function for binary nodes, the resulting class of automata will not be closed with respect to left or right rotations. It may happen that the changes in the balance could diverge, thus we would need an infinite number of compensating constants to be used for the different heights of the possible trees.

4.4   Other Operations on Sets of Trees Described by rTASC

It remains to show that in addition to tree rotations, rTASC are closed with respect to all the other needed operations on balanced trees listed in Section 1.1. Showing this fact is relatively simple, and so due to space limitations, we omit an exact description of this issue here and refer the reader to the full paper. In general, the remaining operations may be implemented by intersecting the given rTASC with a classical tree automaton encoding all the trees that fulfil a certain condition (such as x->parent->left == x or x->parent->color == red) and/or doing certain limited changes to the given rTASC. This includes changing the symbols read in certain rules (e.g., removing x from the symbol read in a certain rule and adding it to the symbol read in another rule when we move the pointer variable x in the tree) and adding, removing, and modifying certain simple rules to express the low-level insertion/deletion of nodes. Afterwards, we may possibly have to apply the function β from the previous section when the tree balance is changed.

To give an intuition on how an rTASC encoding a certain condition on pointers may look like, let us present the tree automaton describing the trees that fulfil the condition x->parent->left == x. We will have rules $f \rightarrow q_1$ and $g \rightarrow q_2$ for every $f, g \in \Sigma$ such that $x \in g \setminus f$. We recall that $\Sigma = \mathcal{P}(\mathcal{V} \cup \mathcal{D} \cup \{nil\})$. Then, we have rules $f(q_1, q_1) \rightarrow q_1$, $g(q_1, q_1) \rightarrow q_2$, $f(q_2, q_1) \rightarrow q_3$, $f(q_3, q_1) \rightarrow q_3$, and $f(q_1, q_3) \rightarrow q_3$, with q_3 being the only accepting state. Here, the pointer referencing pattern gets simply captured in the rule $f(q_2, q_1) \rightarrow q_3$. An intersection with the described tree automaton may be used to implement the if statement testing the given condition. Intersections with similar tree automata may be used to isolate rules where certain changes of data, pointer locations, or insertion/deletion of a new node should happen.

5   Case Study: Red-Black Tree Insertion

To illustrate our methodology, we show how to prove an invariant for the main loop in procedure RB-Insert. (Note that all the steps are normally to be done fully automatically.) This invariant is needed to prove the correctness of the insertion procedure given in Section 1.1 that is, given a valid red-black tree as input to the procedure, the output is also a valid red-black tree. The invariant is the conjunction of the following facts:

1. x is pointing to a non-null node in the tree.
2. If a node is red, then (i) its left son is either black or pointed to by x, and (ii) its right son is either black or pointed to by x. This condition is needed as during the

re-balancing of the tree, a red node can temporarily become a son of another red node.
3. The root is either black or x is pointing to the root.
4. If x is not pointing to the the root and points to a node whose father is red, then x points to a red node.
5. Each maximal path from the root to a leaf contains the same number of black nodes. This is the last condition from the definition of red-black trees from Section 1.1.

For presentation purposes, if no guard is specified on a binary rule, we assume it to be $|1| = |2|$. Also, we denote singleton sets by their unique element, e.g. $\{red\}$ by red, and d_x stands for $\{d, x\}$, where $d \in \{red, black, nil\}$. Let $R = \{nil \rightarrow q_b, red(q_b, q_b) \rightarrow q_r, black(q_{b/r}, q_{b/r}) \rightarrow q_b\}$. The loop invariant is given by the following rTASC A_1.

$A_1 : F = \{q_{rx}, q_{bx}, q'_{bx}\}$, $\Delta = R \cup \{black_x(q_{b/r}, q_{b/r}) \rightarrow q_{bx}\ (1), black(q_{bx/rx}, q_{b/r}) \rightarrow q'_{bx}(2),$
$black(q'_{bx/rx}, q_{b/r}) \rightarrow q'_{bx}, \qquad black(q_{b/r}, q'_{bx/rx}) \rightarrow q'_{bx}\ (3), \quad black(q_{b/r}, q'_{bx/rx}) \rightarrow q'_{bx},$
$red_x(q_b, q_b) \rightarrow q_{rx}, \qquad\qquad red(q'_{bx}, q_b) \rightarrow q'_{rx}, \qquad\qquad red(q_b, q'_{bx}) \rightarrow q'_{rx},$
$red(q_{rx}, q_b) \rightarrow q'_{rx}\ (4), \qquad red(q_b, q_{rx}) \rightarrow q'_{rx}\ (5)\}$

Intuitively, q_b labels black nodes and q_r red nodes which do not have a node pointed to by x below them. q_{bx} and q_{rx} mean the same except that they label a node which is pointed to by x. Primed versions of q_{bx} and q_{rx} are used for nodes which have a subnode pointed to by x. In the following, this intuitive meaning of states will be changed by the program steps. We refer to the pseudo-code of Section 1.1.

We choose to illustrate Case 2 of the loop (the others are similar). If the loop entrance condition x!= root && x->parent->color == red is true, we obtain a new automaton A_2 given from A_1 by setting $F = \{q'_{bx}\}$ and by removing rules (1), (2), (3). After the condition x->parent == x->parent->parent->left, we get A_3 from A_2 by changing rule (4) to $red(q_{rx}, q_b) \rightarrow q''_{rx}$, rule (5) to $red(q_b, q_{rx}) \rightarrow q''_{rx}$ and by adding $black(q''_{rx}, q_{b/r}) \rightarrow q'_{bx}$. In Case 2, x->parent->parent->right->color==red is false, i.e. x->parent->parent->right->color == black. Applying this to A_3, we get:

$A_4 : F = \{q'_{bx}\}, \Delta = R \cup \{black(q'_{bx/rx}, q_{b/r}) \rightarrow q'_{bx}, \quad black(q_{b/r}, q'_{bx/rx}) \rightarrow q'_{bx},$
$black(q''_{rx}, q_b) \rightarrow q'_{bx}, \quad red_x(q_b, q_b) \rightarrow q_{rx}\ (8), \qquad red(q'_{bx}, q_b) \rightarrow q'_{rx},$
$red(q_b, q'_{bx}) \rightarrow q'_{rx}, \qquad red(q_b, q_{rx}) \rightarrow q''_{rx}\ (9), \qquad red(q_{rx}, q_b) \rightarrow q''_{rx}\ (7)\}$

Now, q''_{rx} accepts the father of the node pointed by x and q'_{rx} its grandfather. After the condition x == x->parent->right, A_4 is changed into A_5 by removing rule (7). After x = x->parent, A_5 is changed into A_6 by changing rule (8) to $red(q_b, q_b) \rightarrow q_{rx}$ and rule (9) to $red_x(q_b, q_{rx}) \rightarrow q''_{rx}$. The operation Left-Rotate(T, x) introduces new states and transitions and we get the TASC A_7. Notice that no rebalancing is necessary.

$A_7 : F = \{q'_{bx}\}, \Delta = R \cup \{black(q'_{bx/rx}, q_{b/r}) \rightarrow q'_{bx}, \quad black(q_{b/r}, q'_{bx/rx}) \rightarrow q'_{bx},$
$black(q_{rot2}, q_b) \rightarrow q'_{bx}, \quad red_x(q_b, q_b) \rightarrow q_{rot1}, \qquad red(q'_{bx}, q_b) \rightarrow q'_{rx},$
$red(q_b, q'_{bx}) \rightarrow q'_{rx}, \qquad red(q_{rot1}, q_b) \rightarrow q_{rot2}\}$

After x->parent->color = black, and the necessary propagation of the changes in the balance through the tree, we obtain:

$$A_8 : F = \{q'_{bx}\}, \Delta = R \cup \{black(q'_{bx/rx}, q_{b/r}) \xrightarrow{|1|=|2|+1} q'_{bx}, \; red_x(q_b, q_b) \rightarrow q_{rot1},$$

$$black(q_{b/r}, q'_{bx/rx}) \xrightarrow{|1|+1=|2|} q'_{bx}, \; red(q'_{bx}, q_b) \xrightarrow{|1|=|2|+1} q'_{rx},$$

$$black(q_{rot2}, q_b) \xrightarrow{|1|=|2|+1} q'_{bx}, red(q_b, q'_{bx}) \xrightarrow{|1|+1=|2|} q'_{rx}, \; black(q_{rot1}, q_b) \rightarrow q_{rot2}\}$$

After x->parent->parent->color = red, we obtain:

$$A_9 : F = \{q'_{bx}\}, \Delta = R \cup \{black(q'_{bx/rx}, q_{b/r}) \rightarrow q'_{bx}, \; red_x(q_b, q_b) \rightarrow q_{rot1}, black(q_{b/r}, q'_{bx/rx}) \rightarrow q'_{bx},$$

$$red(q'_{bx}, q_b) \rightarrow q'_{rx}, red(q_{rot2}, q_b) \xrightarrow{|1|=|2|+1} q'_{bx}, \qquad red(q_b, q'_{bx}) \rightarrow q'_{rx}, black(q_{rot1}, q_b) \rightarrow q_{rot2} \}$$

Finally, after Right-Rotate(T,x->parent->parent), we get:

$$A_{10} : F = \{q'_{bx}\}, \Delta = R \cup \{black(q'_{bx/rx}, q_{b/r}) \rightarrow q'_{bx}, \quad black(q_{b/r}, q'_{bx/rx}) \rightarrow q'_{bx}$$

$$black(q_{b/r}, q_{rot4}) \rightarrow q'_{bx}, \quad black(q_{rot4}, q_{b/r}) \rightarrow q'_{bx}, \quad black(q_{rot1}, q_{rot3}) \rightarrow q_{rot4},$$

$$red_x(q_b, q_b) \rightarrow q_{rot1}, \quad red(q'_{bx}, q_b) \rightarrow q'_{rx}, \quad red(q_b, q'_{bx}) \rightarrow q'_{rx},$$

$$red(q_{rot4}, q_b) \rightarrow q'_{rx}, \quad red(q_b, q_b) \rightarrow q_{rot3}, \quad red(q_b, q_{rot4}) \rightarrow q'_{rx}\}$$

Now, it can be easily checked that $\mathcal{L}(A_{10}) \subseteq \mathcal{L}(A_1)$. Case 3 is then very similar to Case 2 and Case 1 is presented in [10].

6   Conclusions

We have presented a method for semi-algorithmic verification of programs that manipulate balanced trees. The approach is based on specifying program pre-conditions, post-conditions, and invariants as sets of trees recognized by a novel class of extended tree automata called TASC. TASC come with interesting closure properties and a decidable emptiness problem. Moreover, the semantics of tree-updating programs can be effectively represented as modifications on the internal structures of TASC. The framework has been validated on a case study consisting of the node insertion procedure in a red-black tree. Precisely, we verify that given a balanced red-black tree on the input to the insertion procedure, the output is again a balanced red-black tree.

In the future, we plan to implement the method to be able to perform more case studies. An interesting subject for further research is then extending the method to a fully automatic one. For this, a suitable acceleration method for the reachability computation on TASC is needed. Also, it is interesting to try to generalize the method to handle even the internals of low-level manipulations that temporarily break the tree shape of the considered structures (e.g., by lifting the technique to work over tree automata extended with routing expressions describing additional pointers over the tree backbone).

Acknowledgement. We would like to thank Eugene Asarin, Ahmed Bouajjani, Yassine Lakhnech, and Tayssir Touili for their valuable comments.

References

1. R. Alur and P. Madhusudan. Visibly Pushdown Languages. In *Proceedings of STOC'04*. ACM Press, 2004.
2. P. Baldan, A. Corradini, J. Esparza, T. Heindel, B. König, and V. Kozioura. Verifying Red-Black Trees. In *Proc. of COSMICAH'05*, 2005.
3. A. Bouajjani, J. Esparza, and O. Maler. Reachability Analysis of Pushdown Automata: Application to Model-Checking. In *Proceedings of CONCUR '97*, volume 1243 of *LNCS*. Springer, 1997.
4. C. Calcagno, P. Gardner, and U. Zarfaty. Context Logic and Tree Update. In *Proceedings of POPL'05*. ACM Press, 2005.
5. H. Comon and V. Cortier. Tree Automata with One Memory, Set Constraints and Cryptographic Protocols. *Theoretical Computer Science*, 331, 2005.
6. H. Comon, M. Dauchet, R. Gilleron, F. Jacquemard, D. Lugiez, S. Tison, and M. Tommasi. Tree Automata Techniques and Applications. Available on: http://www.grappa.univ-lille3.fr/tata, 1997. Release October 1, 2002.
7. T.H. Cormen, C.E. Leiserson, and R.L. Rivest. *Introduction to Algorithms*. The MIT Press, 1990.
8. S. Dal Zilio and D. Lugiez. Multitrees Automata, Presburger's Constraints and Tree Logics. Technical Report 08-2002, LIF, 2002.
9. D. Geidmanis. Unsolvability of the Emptiness Problem for Alternating 1-way Multi-head and Multi-tape Finite Automata over Single-letter Alphabet. In *Computers and Artificial Intelligence*, volume 10, 1991.
10. P. Habermehl, R. Iosif, and T. Vojnar. Automata-based Verification of Programs with Tree Updates. Technical Report TR-2005-16, Verimag, 2005.
11. A. Moeller and M. Schwartzbach. The Pointer Assertion Logic Engine. In *Proceeedings of PLDI'01*. ACM Press, 2001.
12. S. Parduhn. Algorithm Animation Using Shape Analysis with Special Regard to Binary Trees. Technical report, Universität des Saarlandes, 2005.
13. H. Petersen. Alternation in Simple Devices. In *Proceedings of ICALP'95*, volume 944 of *LNCS*. Springer, 1995.
14. M. Presburger. Über die Vollstandigkeit eines Gewissen Systems der Arithmetik. *Comptes Rendus du I Congrés des Pays Slaves*, Warsaw, 1929.
15. M.O. Rabin. Decidability of Second Order Theories and Automata on Infinite Trees. *Transactions of American Mathematical Society*, 141, 1969.
16. R. Rugina. Quantitative Shape Analysis. In *Proceedings of SAS'04*, volume 3148 of *LNCS*. Springer, 2004.
17. S. Sagiv, T.W. Reps, and R. Wilhelm. Parametric Shape Analysis via 3-Valued Logic. *TOPLAS*, 24(3), 2002.
18. H. Seidl, T. Schwentick, A. Muscholl, and P. Habermehl. Counting in Trees for Free. In *Proceedings of ICALP'04*, volume 3142 of *LNCS*. Springer, 2004.

An Experimental Comparison of the Effectiveness of Control Flow Based Testing Approaches on Seeded Faults

Atul Gupta and Pankaj Jalote

Dept. of Computer Science and Engineering,
Indian Institute of Technology Kanpur 208 016, India
{atulkg, jalote}@cse.iitk.ac.in

Abstract. In this paper, we describe the results of an experiment comparing the effectiveness of three structural coverage-testing methods, namely, block coverage, branch coverage and predicate coverage criteria on seeded faults. The implications of our work is two-fold: one, we describe a controlled simulation comparing the effectiveness of these criteria and two, we demonstrate a novel approach to generate minimal test suites for these coverage criteria so as to be able to predict relative performance of the three coverage-adequate test suites. Using a byte code coverage analyzer, five java programs of different sizes were tested. Faults were seeded in all five programs using a set of applicable mutation operators. Twenty-five different minimal JUnit test suites were then constructed for each coverage criteria-program pair and executed on program's mutants to compare the effectiveness. Results suggest that generally, branch coverage criterion performed consistently and was found to be most viable option for structural testing. However, in presence of composite conditions, predicate testing does better and its effectiveness increases with increase in the cardinality of the composite conditions.

Keywords: Block coverage, Branch coverage, Predicate coverage, Software testing, Test case generation, Experiment, Mutation Operator, Statistical analysis.

1 Introduction

Last two decades have seen rapid growth of research in software testing, design and analysis of experiments. Experimentation in Software Engineering supports the advancement of the field through an iterative learning process and software testing is no exception [4, 5]. In the mid 70's Goodenough and Gerhart [13] put forward perhaps the most important question in software testing: What is a test criterion for an adequate testing? Since then testing criteria has been a major research focus. A great number of criteria have been proposed and investigated [15]. E. J. Weyuker highlighted that measuring the effectiveness of testing is generally not possible, but that comparison is [23, 24]. Comparing various criteria systematically requires them to be classified and one well accepted classification of the test adequacy criteria is by underlying testing approach where there are

H. Hermanns and J. Palsberg (Eds.): TACAS 2006, LNCS 3920, pp. 365–378, 2006.

three basic approaches to software testing: structural testing, fault based testing and error based testing.

Two main groups of program based structural testing are control flow testing and data flow testing. The structural testing approaches are based on the flow graph model of program structure. A basic requirement of many coverage criteria is that all nodes and edges in the program are covered by test executions. But all nodes or edges executions cannot always be achieved because of possible existence of infeasible statements or edges. The problem to identify whether a piece of code is unreachable is undecidable [11, 12]. Because of this unreachability we cannot always attain 100% coverage of the program in terms of statements and branches and criteria like 90% coverage are used in practice.

A number of comparisons and evaluations of testing adequacy criteria using statistical methods have been studied and investigated by researchers [6, 9, 19]. Ntafos [19] compared branch coverage, random testing and required pair coverage with 14 small programs. Test cases for each program were selected from a large set of random test cases and faults are inserted artificially in the programs (mutants). The percentages of mutants killed by the test suite were considered as the fault detection ability. The experiment was identified to have invalidating factors which can influence the findings, by Hamlet [14].

To encounter potentially invalidating factors, Basily and Selby [6] used fractional factorial design methodology of replicated statistical experiments. In their comprehensive experiment, they compared code reading, functional testing and statement coverage method in three distinct phases involving 74 subjects (testers) of different background with four programs. The programs contained natural as well as artificial faults. Authors reported about fault detecting abilities of these testing strategies and efforts with respect to various classes of faults and subjects were compared. In a replicated study of effectiveness of the three testing methods, M. Wood et al. [25] have pointed out that overall effectiveness of these testing methods is similar in terms of observing failures and finding faults but their relative effectiveness depends on the nature of the program and it's faults.

E. J. Weyuker, et al [24] demonstrated that in comparing testing methods the probabilistic comparison, i.e. comparing their effectiveness based on some randomly drawn test suites satisfying desired coverage criteria, has better diagnostics than analytical comparison of testing methods. Frankl and Weiss [9] used this approach to address potential invalidating factors associated with test data. They compared branch coverage and all-uses data flow coverage criteria using 9 small programs. Instead of using one adequate test suite for each criterion, they generated a large number of adequate test suites and used proportion of the test suites that detect errors as an estimate of the probability of detecting errors.

It has been pointed out that branch coverage criterion is stronger than statement coverage because if all edges in a flow graph are covered, all nodes are necessarily covered. Therefore a test suite that satisfies the branch coverage must also satisfy statement coverage. That is branch coverage subsumes statement coverage. Interestingly, Frankl and Weyuker [11] proved that the fact that criterion C1 SUBSUMES C2 does not always guarantee that C1 is better at detecting faults.

Though a number of studies have been performed to compare and evaluate different testing strategies, various control flow structural testing approaches like block, branch, predicate coverage, etc. have not been compared experimentally [18]. As theoretically branch coverage should do better than statement coverage, one might choose this to do a more through testing. However, statement coverage analyzers are generally easier to build and results are easier to interpret. Hence, if in practice the above two are similar, then one may choose to use statement coverage only. Similarly, predicate coverage seems to require a higher number of test cases and hence more effort but at the same time may have better fault detecting abilities. It would be useful to understand the effectiveness of these different structural coverage criteria and the kinds of faults for which they are more effective. Studying this effectiveness is the main goal of our experiment. The experiment we have conducted also aims to provide some understanding about conditions under which one criterion is more effective than the other.

In our experiment, we have used five Java programs. For each program we created many mutants for detecting the testing effectiveness. To test a program, we created twenty-five different minimal test suites for each coverage criterion using an algorithm to find the minimum number of test cases from a test pool to satisfy that criterion. Performance data like number of mutants killed by the test suites for the three coverage criteria and coverage information for each test suite were obtained. Our experiment confirms that testing effectiveness of the criteria are affected by the program structure, however, in most of the cases, branch coverage performed consistently and needed more effort than block coverage but considerably less effort for predicate coverage. Our results also suggest that for testing a given program, branch coverage perform better than block coverage, irrespective of the program structure and confirmed the same at statistically significance $\alpha = 0.01$. When compared to predicate coverage, the later does better in programs with composite conditions in them, with statistical significance of 0.05. In other cases, branch and predicate coverage have shown similar effectiveness.

The rest of the paper is organized as follows. Its underlying experimental approach is presented in Section 2. Data collection and analysis methods used for comparison are explained in Section 3. Results of the experiments are presented in Section 4. Threats to validity of our results are highlighted in Section 5 and conclusions are given in Section 6.

2   Experimental Setup

Experimentation is an important method in software engineering for understanding the processes and products. To help the researchers, guidelines [4, 5, 7, 21] are laid down so as to design and conduct controlled experiments whose results can be relied upon. In our study, we have taken great care to follow the guidelines and controlling the variability that can be caused by known and unknown factors.

2.1 Goals

The goals of our experiment are to answer the following questions.

- Which coverage criterion has more fault detection ability?
- Which coverage criterion needs more testing effort?
- Are there any specific types of bugs which results in different effectiveness?
- Is there any co-relation between the parameters of the program and testing approaches.
- How one type of coverage is related with others?
- How to choose a suitable criterion for a given program?

2.2 Some Definitions

Test Case - A set of inputs, execution preconditions and expected outcomes developed for a particular objective.

Test Suite - A collection of one or more test cases for the software under test normally having some completeness criterion.

Minimal Test Suite - A test suite with minimum number of test cases to satisfy a given criterion.

Test-Pool - A collection of a large number of test cases which can be used for generation of test suites by selecting a subset of test cases from the pool.

Mutation Operator - A handle to seed faults in a program in some specific context.

Mutant - A faulty version of a correct program containing exactly one fault. It is obtained by seeding a fault by applying a mutation operator at some place in that program.

Block Coverage - A block is a set of sequential statements not having any in-between flow of control, both inward and outward. Complete block coverage requires that every such block in the program be exercised at least once.

Branch Coverage - Complete branch coverage requires that every branch be exercised at least once in both the TRUE and FALSE directions.

Predicate Coverage (or Multi-Condition Coverage) - It requires that each of the logical expressions in a logical expression must evaluate to TRUE in some test, and to FALSE in some other test.

2.3 Criteria for Comparison

To answer the questions above we need suitable metrics. To measure the fault detection effectiveness, we use the percentage of faults that are revealed. By keeping it as percentage, it helps generalize across programs. The criteria used to measure fault detection ability FDE_T of a test suite T is

$$FDE_T = \frac{\text{number of faults that are revealed}}{\text{total number of faults present in the program}} \times 100\%$$

The criteia used to measure testing effort TE_T of a test suite T is

TE_T = Number of test cases in the test suite T needed to satisfy a given coverage criterion

To understand the connection of fault detecting effectiveness with efforts required in testing, we have used a metric called performance index PI_T of a test suite T, which is obtained as

$$PI_T = \frac{\text{Number of faults revealed by test suite T}}{\text{Size of the test suite T}}.$$

2.4 Instruments Used

Test Programs. Results obtained from small programs are difficult to generalize [19]. In this study, we have considered moderately sized programs ranging 300 to 1500 lines of code. The programs are taken from diversified domains with general-purpose use to increase applicability of our results. The first program is PostalCodes, which aims at recognizing postal codes of a few countries. The second program, HotelManagement, is a simple command line hotel management application program written by the first author. CruiseControl [27] is the third program that is widely used for state based testing experiments. JavaVector is the Vector class in the Java Collection framework. Our fifth program is a game Monopoly [28], which is quite object-oriented in nature. Programs were written in Java, though we believe that the results of this experiment can be applicable to programs written in other object-oriented languages as well. Important statistics of these programs are given in table 1.

Faults and Mutants. Selecting test programs is very critical to the study and equally important issue is the bugs they contain. The number of bugs naturally committed by the developers typically much less than what is needed in such an experiment. The same is also true about the types of bugs. If bugs are introduced manually without great care, then it risks invalidating experimental findings. Most recently, Andrews et al. [1] demonstrated that mutation faults can in fact be representative of real faults, and advocated the use of mutation for effective testing experiments, although more studies are needed to generalize their conclusions.

Table 1. Subject Programs statistics

Sl. No.	Program Name	NC LOC	# of Faults/ Mutants	# of Classes/faults seeded in	# of Blocks	# of Branches	# of Predicates	Test-Pool size
1	HotelManagement	450	56	6/4	118	136	40	55
2	PostalCodes	340	93	6/4	107	134	55	105
3	CruiseControl	540	41	6/4	100	105	33	72
4	JavaVector	300	72	1/1	142	161	39	70
5	Monopoly	1600	56	34/8	270	294	55	84

A number of studies have used a controlled approach of inserting bugs in programs [2, 3], based on some set of mutation operators as proposed by [16]. We followed a similar approach in which a set of mutants of a program was obtained by seeding faults in the program using a set of applicable mutation operators. Bugs were introduced in the model part of the code and user interface part (GUI) and setter-getter methods were kept bug-free to avoid unwanted interaction between buggy code with testing code.

The mutation operators used and the kinds of faults inserted by them, in this study were:

- Literal Change Operator (LCO) - changing increment to decrement or vice versa, incorrect or missing initialization or increment, incorrect or missing state assignment.
- Language Operator Replacement (LOR) - replacing a relational or logical operator by another.
- Control Flow Disruption (CFD) - missing or incorrectly placed block markers, break, continue or return.
- Method Name Replacement (MNR) - replacing a method with other method of similar definition but different behavior.
- Statement Swap Operator (SSO) - swapping two statement in the same scope.
- Argument Order Interchange (AOI) - interchanging arguments of the same type of a method in the definition or in method-call.
- Variable Replacement Operator (VRO) - replacing a variable with other of similar type.
- Missing Condition Operator (MCO) - Missing out a condition in a composite conditional statement.
- Null Reference Operator (NRO) - Causing a null reference.

Test-Pool. It is a known fact that different test suites for the same criteria may lead to different kind of conclusions [9, 23]. To counter this, we have used a definitive procedure of generating test suites from a large test-pool, which were guided by the coverage information as to reach desired coverage early. The test-pool was constructed by writing JUnit [26] tests for each non-trivial method of the model classes in the program. It contained enough tests as to generate coverage-adequate test suites for the code under test. It was also ensured that the pool contains at least one test case for each mutant of the program to kill and hence cover the structure of the mutants under study. Constructing all the three coverage adequate test suites from the same test-pool, we ensured a fair comparison to be possible among the three coverage criteria.

Coverage Adequate Minimal Test Suites. Twenty-five test suites for each coverage criterion for each program were generated to statistically analyze the behavior of the three coverage criteria under study. For each program, test case-wise coverage information for all coverage criteria was obtained by executing the test-pool on the correct version of the program. Coverage adequate test suites then can be generated by simply picking random test cases from the test-pool but this approach will not produce minimal test suites for obvious reasons such as redundencies in elements covered by different test cases in a test suite. One of the motivation of this work is to evaluate the performance of coverage adequate test suites which is possible if we use minimal test suites. Coverage-adequate minimal test suites for a program were constructed using following steps. For constructing each minimal test suite T:

1. Select first test case randomly from the test-pool, remove it from the pool and add it to T.
2. Update the coverage information for all other remaining test cases in the test-pool so as to incorporate yet-to-cover elements in the test suite T being so constructed.
3. Select a test case which provides maximum yet-to-cover coverage (> 0)and add it to T.
4. Repeat step 2 and 3 until no more test cases can be added to T.

Monitoring Coverage and Testing. To obtain various coverage information, a locally developed tool named JavaCoverage was used [22]. This tool provides coverage information for each test case visually using different colors as to represent uncovered program elements, and therefore, effectively guides testers to design and execute further tests to meet testing objectives. The tool does program analysis at byte code level and use byte code instrumentation to obtain various coverage information from test case executions. The coverage information for each test case is recorded in a MySql database.

Each program was tested by executing all coverage-adequate test suites on all its mutants. The information regarding killed-mutants was recorded.

3   Data Collection and Analysis

Twenty-five test suites for each criterion were exercised on each of the five programs' mutants. For each program, the following data were recorded and analyzed:

- Number and type of mutants generated and killed by the coverage test suites
- All-coverage information of coverage test suites
- Number of blocks, branches, predicates, program size, test suite size.

Observations obtained for all five programs were separately analyzed to determine the effectiveness of the three coverage criteria. Subsequently, results were also compared across the programs.

3.1   Program-Wise Analysis

For each program, we graphically demonstrate (i) faults seeded as per the mutation operator used, (ii) average FDE_T of the three coverage criteria, (iii) average coverage achived by the three coverage adequate test suites and (iv) average PI_T of these coverage adequate test suites in Figure 1 at the end of this paper. We briefly discuss the program-wise results here.

Program-1: *PostalCodes*. The results showed that fault detecting effectiveness FDE_T of predicate coverage test suites were better than branch and block coverage test suites but required more testing effort TE_T. It has shown much better results in the case of missing condition bugs (seeded using MCO operator). Block coverage based test suites has shown better performance index PI_T of the test suites then the other two but shown larger variability in the results. They showed poor performance in case of control flow bugs seeded by CFD and MCO operators. Branch coverage test suites identified more bugs than block test suites and their PI_T was more stable.

Remarks: This Program has some algorithmic methods with many composite conditional statements. Hence predicate and branch coverage did perform well where as block coverage performed rather poorly and inconsistently.

Program-2: *HotelManagement*. The results showed that in this case also predicate coverage based test suites show better FDE_T but more TE_T than the other two. The box plot for PI_T shows that overall branch test suites performed better and block test suites performed poorly.

Remarks: This program also has some methods with composite conditions but of less cardinality than Postal Codes. We observed similar results here to that of Postal Code.

Program-3: *CruiseControl*. The FDE_T of the predicate coverage criterion were found to be similar to branch coverage with the fact that branch test suites were also good at MCO bugs. Block tests showed better PI_T than other two but with highest variability. Once again branch test suites were consistent and proved to be better than predicate tests. Block test suites PI_T was significantly better but having higher variance than the two other.

Remarks: This program consists of mostly small methods with states and transitions. The conditionals are simple-if statements and therefore branch test suite is somewhat larger than block test suites and consequently having considerably less PI_T. MCO bugs clearly dominate when there are conditionals of high cardinality, which wasn't the case here, and branch test suites did perform well in these conditions.

Program-4: *JavaVector*. The FDE_T of the three coverage criteria was found to be quite different than the above three programs. Branch test performed best followed by block followed by predicate tests. Their TE_T requirements were in opposite order, i.e. branch coverage test suites size was more followed by block test suites followed by predicate test suites. Three test suites demonstrated similar PI_T with predicate tests showing greatest variability.

Remarks: The reason for the diversity in results is due to the fact that there are many methods in JavaVector that do not contain any conditionals and hence predicate coverage test suites were unlikely to cover those. Also most of the conditionals were simple and hence branch and block test suites have shown similar behavior.

Program-5: *Monopoly*. This is a nicely designed object-oriented program as it has inheritance hierarchies with small method sizes and other object-oriented features. Many classes in the model part of the code are small and the methods of the controller classes are well re-factored [8] to perform single functions. Intra-method structural complexity is quite low but inter-method interaction is high. The results of this program showed similar trends as previously obtained but with lesser variability. The three coverage criteria seem to have similar FDE_T, TE_T and PI_T measures. Control flow bugs like MCO and CFD bugs were remained as the cause of difference in FDE_T of the three criteria.

Remarks: The results are interesting in the sense that the three coverage criteria show quite similarity in the results, importantly, size of the test suites and corresponding PI_T. We found comparatively fewer places to seed the kinds of faults, under study, to be inserted. This explains that object-oriented programs are to be tested with a focus on inter-method interactions rather than intra-method control flow.

3.2   Program Analysis at Method Scope

To obtain statistical evidences for coverage criteria effectiveness, we have investigated some important methods of the classes of these five programs. We collected various statistics of these methods like size, number of blocks, branches and predicates, number of faults inserted, faults identified by the coverage test suites, etc. The reason for doing analysis at method level is that it provides more data points, thereby allowing better statistical analysis of the results obtained. Since the control structure is typically represented at method level, analysis at method level is the right level of granularity for coverage analysis. Please refer to table 2 for the statistical analysis results presented in this subsection where μ denotes mean of effectiveness parameter in consideration i.e. FDE_T over twenty five test suites and subscripts Bl, Br, and Pr represent block, branch and predicate coverage criteria, respectively.

Our results show that FDE_T of branch coverage outperformed block coverage with statistical significance of $\alpha = 0.01$(row 1 table 2). When branch coverage is compared with predicate coverage, from the experiment data, we found that there is not enough evidence to reject the null hypothesis and both coverage criteria have shown similar FDE_T (row 2 table 2). However, when we drill down further, we found that predicate coverage criterion performs better then branch criterion in methods which contains composite conditional statements. This observation was confirmed statistically at a significance level of $\alpha = 0.05$(row 3 table 2).

Table 2. Method-level Analysis Results

Sl. No.	Effectiveness Parameter	Null Hypothesis	Alternate Hypothesis	t-value	t-critical	p-value	Result
1	FDE_T	$\mu_{Br} = \mu_{Bl}$	$\mu_{Br} > \mu_{Bl}$	3.612	2.079	0.001	$\mu_{Br} > \mu_{Bl}$
2	FDE_T	$\mu_{Pr} = \mu_{Br}$	$\mu_{Pr} > \mu_{Br}$	0.308	2.079	0.760	$\mu_{Pr} = \mu_{Br}$
3	FDE_T*	$\mu_{Pr} = \mu_{Br}$	$\mu_{Pr} > \mu_{Br}$	2.989	2.570	0.030	$\mu_{Pr} > \mu_{Br}$

4   Results

Our results showed that predicate tests were the best in terms of fault detecting effectiveness FDE_T under normal circumstances where programs have control flow graphs with conditionals. On the other hand they took more test cases i.e. more testing effort TE_T. Branch tests are more cost effective as the required number of tests is less and giving comparable fault detecting effectiveness to that of predicate tests. As the box-plots for PI_T demonstrated, branch tests were quite consistent in terms of their fault detecting capabilities that ensures a level of performance from testing. Block test suites were small in size but were quite inconsistent and have less FDE_T than the other two. A useful observation in this experiment is whichever criteria results into minimum number of test cases required, showed highest variability in the performance index. Table 3 shows the three idioms of effectiveness criteria for all five programs obtained as a basis of average taken over all twenty-five test suites for each coverage criteria.

Table 3. Effectiveness Criteria Results

Program Name	FDE_T			TE_T			PI_T		
	Block	Branch	Pred	Block	Branch	Pred	Block	Branch	Pred
HotelManagement	0.64	0.81	0.91	17.4	19.7	24.2	2.13	2.33	2.12
PostalCodes	0.74	0.78	0.97	33.1	35.0	48.7	2.39	2.35	1.87
CruiseControl	0.44	0.82	0.87	9.68	16.8	19.6	2.86	2.15	1.80
JavaVector	0.92	0.99	0.84	51.7	54.5	43.0	1.33	1.32	1.35
Monopoly	0.81	0.87	0.96	29.0	31.4	33.3	1.64	1.58	1.60

From the bug analysis, we found that bug of the type LCO, VRO, SSO, VRO and AOI are typically revealed by all the three coverage criteria where as LOR and CFD bugs (mainly inserted in conditionals) are poses some challenge to block coverage but likely to be identifiable by branch and predicate coverage. Predicate coverage is especially found to be much more effective in MCO bugs which might be prevalent in conditional statements with multiple conditions.

5   Validity and Generality

An important issue that greatly affects the effectiveness of writing automated tests is use of proper test oracles. Great care was taken to write automated tests with proper oracles. All the tests were written by first author and since same test pool was used in generating test suites for the coverage criteria under study, we argue that any variability, if present, should not influence our findings. Another factor that can influence the results is the interaction between code under test and test oracles. To control this effect, we did not seed any faults in the code which is used to check test oracles, i.e. JUnit assertions [26].

In terms of external validity, we believe that our results should be general enough to apply at least to other java programs in the context of the type of the faults seeded as we have considered considerable number of faults of each type. We have not considered object-oriented specific bugs such as those related with inheritance and dynamic binding as we did not find enough opportunity to seed these faults in the considered programs hence we make no claim regarding these kind of faults. It will be interesting to pursue this issue in another study.

We have considered control structure at a class's method level to obtained information of blocks and branches and hence, method calls were not treated as branches. So our results should also be viewed in this context.

6 Summary and Conclusions

The three main control-flow based coverage criteria are - block, branch and predicate coverage. The aim of this work was to study the relative effectiveness of these three criteria. In our experiment, we tested five moderately sized Java programs by generating twenty-five different minimal test suites from a large test-pool, for each program-coverage pair. To test a program, we created sufficient number of mutants using a set of applicable mutation operators and tested them with a set of generated minimal coverage test suites for each coverage criteria. The three structural coverage criteria were than compared in terms of their fault detection abilities (FDE_T, PI_T) and testing efforts (TE_T) requirements.

We found that Predicate Coverage criterion demonstrated best FDE_T but at more cost, i.e. more TE_T than the other two. On the other hand, Block coverage criterion took least testing efforts TE_T, but at lower FDE_T than the other two. Branch Coverage criterion performed in between the two in terms of FDE_T and TE_T. Performance Index PI_T of block coverage criterion found to be on higher side but with greater variability where as PI_T for branch coverage criterion found to be slightly less than that of block criterion but was quite consistent. PI_T for predicate test suites was observed to be lower than the other two. Our results show that branch test suites are likely to perform with consistent effectiveness and their effort requirements in terms of test suite size is smaller than that of predicate test suites but larger than the block test suites.

The results obtained from the analysis of PI_T for all the three coverage criteria revealed the fact that some block test suites may be more efficient, i.e. revealing faults at par with the other two criteria with smaller test suite size but other may perform worse, thereby being unreliable and in-consistent as compared to the other two criteria. Predicate coverage criterion was found to be least efficient but quite reliable whereas branch criteria demonstrated similar reliability to predicate criteria with better efficiency.

Based on our investigation for choosing a suitable criterion to test a given program, we observed that branch coverage is the best choice for getting better results with moderate testing efforts. The testing effectiveness can be improved considering predicate coverage for the methods containing composite condition-als but with increased efforts requirements.

In this work, we have used a novel approach to randomize the effect of a particular test suite. We generated twenty-five different coverage-adequate test suites from a test-pool for each coverage criterion. The test suites were algo-rithmically constructed in a manner that they contained minimum number of test cases, thereby, enabling us to do a uniform analysis. This also facilitates computation of performance indexes for the coverage test suites.

Based on our experience of testing of a well designed object-oriented program like Monopoly, we argue that such programs are more robust as we found rel-atively few places where we can insert faults related to the mutation operators considered in this study. Also because of small methods implementing single operation, the three testing approaches demonstrated similar effectiveness. It will be interesting to investigate the effectiveness of these coverage criteria and other testing approaches to test object-oriented programs with object-oriented-specific bugs like related with hierarchies, dynamic binding, method over-riding, etc. Also similar studies to be replicated to demonstrate the applicability of our results

Acknowledgement

The authors would like to thank L. Raghu, for providing enough help to use his tool JavaCoverage that he developed as part of his M Tech thesis at IIT Kanpur.

References

1. Andrews J.H., Briand L. C. and Y. Labiche *Is mutation an appropriate tool for testing experiments?* In Proc. Int'l.Conf. Softw. Eng ICSE pages 402-411, May 2005.
2. Antoniol G at al *A Case Study Using the Round-Trip Stretegy for State-Based Class Testing* In Proc of the 13th Int'l Symp. On Reliability ISSRE'02.
3. Briand L.C., Labiche Y. and Wang Y. *Using Simulation to Empirically Investigate Test Coverage Criteria Based on Statechart* In Proc of the 26th Int'l Conf. on Software Engineering ICSE 2004.
4. Barbara A. Kitchham, Shari Lawrence Pfleeger, Lesley M. Pickard, Peter W. Jones, David C. Hoaglin, Khaled El Emam, Jarrett Rosenberg *Preliminary Guidelines for Empirical Research in Software Engineering* In IEEE Trans. on Software Enginee-ing Vol.28, No.8, August 2002.
5. Basili V.R.,R.W. Silby, David H. Huchens *Experimentation in Software Engineer-ing* In IEEE Trans. on Software Engineeing Vol.SE-12, No.7, July 1986.
6. Basili V.R. and Selby R.W. *Comparing the effectiveness of software testing* In IEEE Transactions on Software Engineering Vol. SE-13, No.12, pages 1278-1296, December 1987.
7. Douglas C. Montgomery *Design and Analysis of Experiments* fifth edition, John Wiley and Sons Inc., 2001.
8. Fowler M. *Refactoring: Improving the Design of Existing Code* Addison Wesley, 1999.
9. Frankl P.G. and Weiss S.N. *An experimental comparison of the effectiveness of branch testing and data flow testing* In IEEE Transactions on Software Engineering Vol. 19, No.8, pages 774-787, August 1993.

10. Frankl P.G. and Weyuker J.E. *An applicable family of data flow testing criteria* In IEEE Transactions on Software Engineering Vol. SE-14, No.10, pages 1483-1498, October 1988.

11. Frankl P.G. and Weyuker J.E. *A formal analysis of the fault-detecting ability of testing methods* In IEEE Transactions on Software Engineering Vol 19, No.3, pages 202-213, March 1993.

12. Frankl P.G. and Weyuker J.E. *Provable improvements on branch testing* In IEEE Transactions on Software Engineering Vol 19, No.10, pages 962 - 975, 1993.

13. Goodenough J.B. and Garhart S.L. *Toward a theory of test data selection* In IEEE Transactions on Software Engineering Vol SE-3, 1975.

14. Hamlet R. *Theoretical comparison of testing methods* In Proceedings of SIGSOFT Symposium on Software Testing, Analysis and Verification pages 28-37, December 1989.

15. Hong Zhu, Patrick A.V. Hall, John H.R. May. *Software Unit Test Coverage and Adequacy* In ACM Computing Surveys Vol.29, No.4, December 1997.

16. Kim S, Clark J.A. and McDermid J.A. *The Rogorous Generation of Java Mutation Using HAZOP* In Proc. ICSSEA- 3 pages 9-10(11), 1999.

17. M. Hutchins, H. Foster, T. Goradia, and T. Ostrand. *Experiments on the effectiveness of dataflow- and controlflow-based test adequacy criteria.* In Proceedings of the 16th International Conference on Software Engineering ICSE May 1994.

18. Natalia Juristo, Ana M. Moreno and Sira Vegas *Reviewing 25 Years of Software Testing Experiments* In Jour. Empirical Software Engineering Vol 9, 1-2 pp 7-44 March 2004.

19. Ntafos, S.C. *An evaluation of required element testing strategies* In Proceedings of the Seventh International Conference on Software Engineering Pages 250-256.

20. Pankaj Jalote *An Integrated Approach to Software Engineering* second edition, Narosa Publishing House, 1999.

21. Paul D. Berger, R.E. Maurer *Experimental Design* Thomson Duxbury, 2002.

22. Raghu L. *Testing Changes made to the Code using Coverage Data*, M Tech Thesis, Dept of CSE, IIT Kanpur June 2005.

23. Weyuker E.J. *Can We Measure Software Testing Effectiveness?* In Proceedings of IEEE-CS International Software Metrics Symposium pages 100-107, May 1993.

24. Weyuker E.J., Weiss S.N., Hamlet D. *Comparison of Program Testing Strategies* In Proceedings of the Fourth Symposium on Software Testing, Analysis and Verification Pages 154-164, October 1991.

25. Wood M., Mark Roper, Andrew Brooks, James Miller *Comparing and combining software defect detection techniques: A Replicated Experimental Study* In ACM SIGSOFT Software Engineering Notes Vol. 22, No. 6, November 1997.

26. *JUnit Home Page* http://www.junit.org

27. http://www-dse.doc.ic.ac.uk/concurrency/book- applets/CruiseControl.html

28. http://open.ncsu.edu/se/monopoly/

Appendix

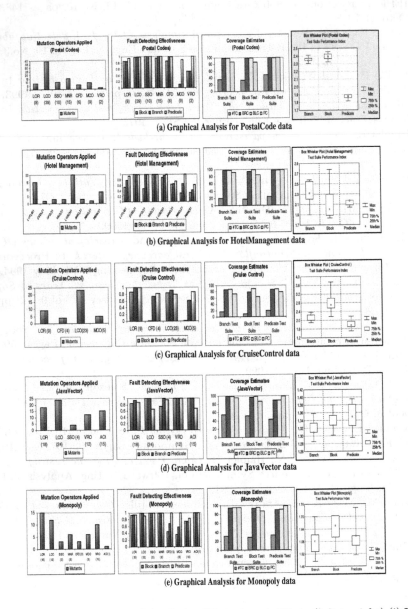

Fig. 1. Program-wise Graphical Analysis of Experimental Data (left-to-right) (i) Faults applied (ii) FDE_T of Coverage Test Suites (iii) All-Coverage information of Coverage Test Suites (iv) Performance Index PI_T

Exploiting Traces in Program Analysis*

Alex Groce and Rajeev Joshi

Laboratory for Reliable Software, Jet Propulsion Laboratory,
California Institute of Technology, Pasadena, CA 91109, USA
{Alex.D.Groce, Rajeev.Joshi}@jpl.nasa.gov
http://eis.jpl.nasa.gov/lars

Abstract. From operating systems and web browsers to spacecraft, many software systems maintain a log of events that provides a partial history of execution, supporting post-mortem (or post-reboot) analysis. Unfortunately, bandwidth, storage limitations, and privacy concerns limit the information content of logs, making it difficult to fully reconstruct execution from these traces. This paper presents a technique for modifying a program such that it can produce exactly those executions consistent with a given (partial) trace of events, enabling efficient analysis of the reduced program. Our method requires no additional history variables to track log events, and it can slice away code that does not execute in a given trace. We describe initial experiences with implementing our ideas by extending the CBMC bounded model checker for C programs. Applying our technique to a small, 400-line file system written in C, we get more than three orders of magnitude improvement in running time over a naïve approach based on adding history variables, along with fifty- to eighty-fold reductions in the sizes of the SAT problems solved.

1 Introduction

Analysis of systems that have failed after deployment is a fact of life in all engineering fields. When a bridge collapses or an engine explodes — or a computer program crashes — it is important to understand why in order to avoid future failures arising from the same causes. In the case of software, a patch may be able to correct the flaw and restore a system to working order, making tools for analyzing failure even more valuable.

The motivation for trace-based analysis of programs is straightforward: critical software systems, including file systems, web servers, and even robots exploring the surface of Mars, often produce traces of system activity that humans use to diagnose faulty behavior. Reconstructing the full state or history of a program from these traces or logs is difficult: the traces contain limited information, due to the overhead of instrumentation, privacy concerns, and (in the case of space missions) limited storage space and communication bandwidth. Almost

---

* The work described in this paper was carried out at the Jet Propulsion Laboratory, California Institute of Technology, under a contract with the National Aeronautics and Space Administration.

H. Hermanns and J. Palsberg (Eds.): TACAS 2006, LNCS 3920, pp. 379–393, 2006.

all programmers are familiar with the difficulty of this detective work: after all, "printf-debugging" is a particularly common case of trace-based analysis.

The goal of our work is to exploit failure traces in order to increase the scalability of precise program analyses. In particular, we show how restricting program behaviors given a trace can dramatically decrease the size of the SAT formulas in bounded model checking. Given the program source and a trace log, it should be possible to use bounded model checking to find detailed, concrete program executions compatible with the trace — even in cases where the full program is too large to be model checked.

Because the ultimate goal is to provide tool support for programmers dealing with anomalies in remote spacecraft, we refer to trace elements (or printfs) as EVRs, after the JPL shorthand for Event Reporting. An EVR is a command which appends information to a running log. An EVR may print a constant string and serve simply to indicate the control flow of the program, or it may contain the current values of critical variables.

A secondary benefit of our work is that program traces are useful as *specifications*. EVRs and printfs are useful for debugging *because* they provide a high-level description of program behavior. In many cases, a bug is discovered by a programmer reading a trace and noticing an event sequence that should not be possible. The techniques that allow reconstruction of concrete executions given a trace also make it possible to check properties such as: "the system must not produce trace σ" or "the system must be able to produce trace σ". We extend the language of traces to include hidden and wildcard events, producing a restrictive but convenient property language.

This paper contributes two novel techniques. First, we introduce a general method for adding assume statements to a deterministic program to restrict its behavior to exactly those executions compatible with a given trace — without introducing history variables or state. Second, we make use of the information gathered in the assume statement-generation to *slice* [20] the program, removing portions of the source code based on the information in the program trace.

The first technique is best understood by noting that EVR(a) can be seen as an operation that appends the string a to a history variable, log. Adding assume(log $= \sigma$) at the end of the program will restrict it to behaviors matching the trace σ. For deterministic programs, our analysis computes assumptions that are logically equivalent but do not mention log. This direct encoding in terms of control flow and data values aids the SAT solver in propagating constraints — and reduces the size of the state space. The value of slicing may be observed in a more concrete example: consider a program containing complex fault-handling routines. If execution of these routines always produces EVRs, and those EVRs do not appear in the trace, the fault handling component(s) can be completely eliminated during analysis, with a potential for a drastic reduction in the size of SAT instances used in model checking. Our approach addresses common variations of the basic problem, including the case where only a suffix of the full trace is known, as well as the presence of multiple, unsynchronized traces.

We implemented our approach as an extension to CBMC [13], a bounded model checker for ANSI-C programs. Analyzing a trace with known length allows us to avoid considering loops and non-terminating execution, making the problem a natural fit for bounded model checking. BMC also determinizes C programs by making all external inputs explicit. We analyzed a model of a small file system and a resource arbiter. As expected, using a trace to guide exploration improved the performance of model checking over a naïve approach based on adding history variables, providing more than three orders of magnitude improvement in running times as well as a fifty- to eighty-fold reduction in the sizes of the SAT problems produced.

2   Reducing a Program with Respect to a Trace

We now formalize the notion of reducing a statement S with respect to a trace σ. The motivation for reduction is improving the scalability of tool-based program analysis. Ideally, we would like to construct a new statement T such that T has *exactly* those executions of S matching σ — i.e., (i) all executions of S that produce σ are executions of T, (ii) all executions of T are executions of S, and (iii) all executions of T produce σ. Here, (i) ensures that we miss no executions that produce σ, (ii) ensures that the verifier produces no "false alarms", and (iii) ensures that we ignore executions that do not produce σ. Of these, (i) is critical: soundness is essential to further analysis; (ii) and (iii) are desirable but not necessary. Constructing a reduced statement T satisfying all three conditions is difficult in general, but is possible given restrictions on S. In this section, we describe these restrictions, and show how a reduced statement T may be constructed given S satisfying these restrictions.

2.1   Notation

To simplify the exposition, we describe our approach in the context of a simple do-od language with assume and EVR statements. A program is a tuple $(\mathcal{V}, \Sigma, S)$ where $\mathcal{V}$ is a set of typed program variables that contains a special variable log of type Σ^*, Σ is a finite alphabet of symbols, and S is a statement according to the syntax shown in Figure 1. In this figure, the nonterminal v denotes a variable name in $\mathcal{V}$, the nonterminal E denotes an expression (whose syntax we do not elaborate in this paper), and a denotes a symbol in Σ. A statement is said to be "well-formed" when it does not mention the variable log.

The meaning of a program is given in terms of pre- and post-condition semantics in the usual way. We expect that readers are familiar with all but the last construct of this language, and thus omit a full semantics of the language.

```
<S> ::=    v := E | IF E THEN S [ ELSE S ] FI | WHILE E DO S END
        | S ; S | SKIP | ASSUME E | ASSERT E | EVR(a)
```

Fig. 1. Language syntax

The semantics of the remaining construct, the EVR statement, is given as follows: for any symbol a in Σ, EVR(a) is equivalent to "log := log $\bullet$ a". That is, EVR(a) appends the symbol a to the variable log.

2.2   A Simple Construction

Suppose that we are given a program $(\mathcal{V}, \Sigma, S)$ and a string σ over Σ. As described above, we want to construct a reduced program $(\mathcal{V}, \Sigma, T)$ satisfying conditions (i), (ii) and (iii) above. It is not hard to show that the desired statement T satisfies the following statement equality:

$$T \;=\; \text{assume } (\log = \langle\rangle) \;;\; S \;;\; \text{assume } (\log = \sigma) \tag{1}$$

That is, T consists of exactly those executions of S that, started in a state in which the log is empty, either terminate in a state in which the log is σ, or do not terminate at all[1]. This equation suggests a simple construction: replace occurrences of EVR(a) in S with code for appending a to log, and add the two assume statements shown above.

As discussed in Section 4, experience with this simple construction for model checking C programs shows that the addition of such assume statements sometimes reduces analysis time significantly (in one instance, time to find an error improves from 17,608 seconds to 105 seconds). Unfortunately, this construction does not suffice to analyze large programs (see Table 2 in Section 4). The limitations of this construction are twofold: (a) knowledge of σ is not exploited in order to simplify the program, and (b) the introduction of log as a new program variable adds additional state, which increases the size of the state space to be explored. We now discuss how we avoid these limitations.

2.3   Pushing assume Statements Through a Program

Consider the program shown in Figure 2a, where f and g denote complex computations involving x and y. Suppose that we want to analyze this program given the singleton trace $\langle 1 \rangle$. We see that this trace is produced only if x is assigned a positive value; since the second branch of the first IF statement does not modify x, knowledge of the trace should allow us to discard the (complex) details of the computation of g in our analysis.

One way to achieve this is by pushing assume statements through a program. As illustrated in Figure 2b, we can push the final assume statement with the predicate $(\log = \langle 1 \rangle)$ backwards through the program. This allows us to add an assume statement with the predicate (x > 0) between the two IF statements; in turn, this allows us to introduce an assume(P) at the beginning of the program and thus remove the first ELSE branch.

We are therefore interested in conditions under which we can push assumes through a program. To this end, we consider the following equation: for given statement S and predicate Q, solve for P in

---

[1] Alternatively, we could require that T only have terminating executions. Since CBMC produces unrolled (hence terminating) programs, we do not explore this alternative in this paper.

$$\text{solve } P : \quad S \, ; \, \texttt{assume}(Q) \; \subseteq \; \texttt{assume}(P) \, ; \, S \qquad (2)$$

where we write $S \subseteq T$ to mean that all executions of S are executions of T. Note that this equation has many solutions in general — e.g., $P = true$. This is related to the observation that one can always push weak assumptions through a program. However, because we want T to include as few unnecessary executions as possible, we are usually interested in the *strongest* solution in P to this equation. It is not hard to show that the strongest solution to this equation exists, and can be expressed in terms of Dijkstra's weakest-precondition transformer as $\neg wp(S, \neg Q)$. Recall that $wp(S, Q)$ denotes the set of states from which all executions of S terminate in states satisfying Q, whereas $wlp(S, Q)$ denotes states from which all *terminating* executions of S end in states satisfying Q. Therefore, the dual expression $\neg wp(S, \neg Q)$ denotes the set of states from which either there is an execution of S that terminates in Q, or an execution of S that fails to terminate.

Unfortunately, although the strongest solution to equation (2) satisfies conditions (i) and (ii) above, it does not guarantee (iii), because there may be executions of the RHS that are not in the LHS. To derive assumptions guaranteeing (iii), we need to solve for P in the following equation:

$$\text{solve } P : \quad S \, ; \, \texttt{assume}(Q) \; = \; \texttt{assume}(P) \, ; \, S \qquad (3)$$

This equation is a strict equality. Thus, for any solution P, the right-hand side denotes *exactly* those computations of S that end in states satisfying Q.

The problem with this strict condition is that solutions do not exist in general. The difficulty is illustrated by the following simple example. With $\square$ denoting nondeterministic choice, consider the statement S given by

$$(\texttt{x := x+1}) \quad \square \quad (\texttt{x := x+2})$$

and let Q be the predicate $(\texttt{x=2})$. Clearly, this equation has no solution for P.

	P ∧ f(0,0)>0	P ∧ f(0,0)>0
x := 0 ; y := 0 ;	x := 0 ; y := 0 ;	x := 0 ; y := 0 ;
IF P THEN	IF P THEN	
x := f(x,y)	x := f(x,y)	x := f(x,y)
ELSE	ELSE	
y := g(x,y)	y := g(x,y)	
FI ;	FI ; x>0	
IF x>0 THEN	IF x>0 THEN	
EVR(1)	EVR(1)	SKIP
ELSE	ELSE	
EVR(2)	EVR(2)	
FI	FI	
	log = ⟨1⟩	
(a) Original program	(b) With assumes	(c) After slicing

Fig. 2. Example program for trace reduction. Shaded expressions are assumptions

It is not hard to show that for programs that are total[2] (in the sense that they can be executed from any state), equation (3) has at most one solution. The more interesting question is when the equation has at least one solution in P. This is addressed by the following result.

Lemma 1. *Let S be a total, deterministic statement. For any predicate Q, equation (3) has a unique solution in P, given by $wlp(S, Q)$, the weakest liberal precondition of Q with respect to S.*

This lemma states that for total, deterministic programs, pushing `assumes` through the program is equivalent to computing wlp.

We can also ask when it is possible to push `assumes` forward through a program. In this case, we are interested in solutions for Q in

$$\text{solve } Q : \quad \texttt{assume}(P) \;;\; S \;\subseteq\; S \;;\; \texttt{assume}(Q) \tag{4}$$

It is not hard to show that the strongest solution for Q in this equation is $sp(S, P)$, the strongest postcondition of P with respect to S. On the other hand, the strict equation (3) has a solution in Q for arbitrary P only if S is invertible[3]. In general, while determinism is not too strict a requirement (for instance, all sequential C programs are deterministic), invertibility is typically too restrictive. For instance, constant initializations, such as `x := 1`, are not invertible. (To see this, try solving for Q in equation (4) with S being `x:=1` and P being `x=0`.)

However, there are situations in which forward propagation is useful. For instance, *passive* programs which consist only of `assume` statements are trivially invertible. Such programs are often encountered in verification [7, 14]. Because CBMC generates passive programs, we use forward propagation in our implementation.

Once `assumes` have been pushed through the program (either forward or backward), they can be used to remove branches whose guards are refuted by the assumptions. Note that this requires a check to determine which guards are refuted by each assumption. In our implementation, we achieve this with a simple heuristic: for any `assume`(p) appearing before a conditional IF q THEN S_1 ELSE S_2 FI, if $p \Rightarrow q$ then we may replace the conditional with S_1 without altering the semantics of the passive program. The amount of slicing obtained depends on the amount of computational effort given to these implications. Our experience so far is that even simple syntactic tests produce effective slicing.

2.4   Removing Trace Variables

By pushing assumptions through a program, we can determine that certain guards are always false, and thus remove certain branches from the code, thereby

---

[2] Such programs are sometimes called "non-miraculous" since they satisfy Dijkstra's Law of the Excluded Miracle [4].

[3] To see this, replace S with its relational converse $\sim S$, and solve for Q instead of P in equation (3). The equation is then identical to (3) but with S replaced by $\sim S$. The condition above then states that $\sim S$ should be deterministic, which is the same as saying that S is invertible.

reducing the size of the program being analyzed. However, since the desired postcondition is ($log = \sigma$), a naive application of this method requires explicit introduction of the variable log. In general, if the alphabet Σ has k symbols, and the given trace σ has length n, addition of log adds roughly $n \cdot log_2(k)$ bits to the state space. Since this is linear in n, the length of the trace, the overhead can be considerable when σ is long. In this subsection, we discuss a technique that allows us to work with predicates that do not mention the variable log, thus avoiding any overhead.

The idea is to consider predicates in a "log-canonical" form. Let σ be a given trace of length n over Σ, and let $\sigma \uparrow i$ ("σ upto i") denote the first[4] i characters of the string σ. We say that a predicate R is in log-canonical form provided there is a vector t of predicates, such that R can be expressed as

$$(\exists i : 0 \leq i \leq n \wedge t_i \wedge log = \sigma \uparrow i) \tag{5}$$

where none of the predicates t_i mention the variable log. Because σ is fixed, this predicate is compactly represented by storing *only* the vector t (which does not mention log). For any such vector t, we write $\hat{t}$ to denote the predicate shown in (5). The usefulness of this notion is due to the following result.

Lemma 2. *Let S be a well-formed deterministic program as defined above, and let P be a predicate in log-canonical form. Then $wp(S, P)$ is also in log-canonical form.*

The proof of Lemma (2) is by induction over the grammar shown in Figure 1. Since S is deterministic, $wp(S, \_)$ distributes over the existential quantification in P. For the first five constructs, the proof is straightforward, using the assumption that none of the guards or expressions in the program mention log, since S is well-formed. For the remaining case, $\text{EVR}(a)$, we calculate

$\qquad wp(\text{EVR}(a), \hat{t})$
$\equiv \qquad \{$ definition of $\hat{t}$ $\}$
$\qquad wp(\text{EVR}(a), (\exists i : 0 \leq i \leq n \wedge t_i \wedge log = \sigma \uparrow i))$
$\equiv \qquad \{$ semantics of $\text{EVR}(a)$; the t_i don't mention log $\}$
$\qquad (\exists i : 0 \leq i \leq n \wedge t_i \wedge wp(\text{EVR}(a), log = \sigma \uparrow i))$
$\equiv \qquad \{$ meaning of $\text{EVR}(a)$ as appending to log $\}$
$\qquad (\exists i : 0 \leq i \leq n \wedge t_i \wedge log \bullet a = \sigma \uparrow i)$
$\equiv \qquad \{$ properties of $\bullet$, and using $\sigma[i-1]$ to mean the ith character in σ $\}$
$\qquad (\exists i : 0 < i \leq n \wedge t_i \wedge \sigma[i-1] = a \wedge log = \sigma \uparrow (i-1))$
$\equiv \qquad \{$ introducing u (see below) and replacing i with $j+1$ $\}$
$\qquad (\exists j : 0 \leq j \leq n \wedge u_j \wedge log = \sigma \uparrow j)$
$\equiv \qquad \{$ definition of $\hat{u}$ $\}$
$\qquad \hat{u}$

where we have introduced the vector of predicates u, defined as

$$u_j \equiv (t_{j+1} \wedge \sigma[j] = a) \quad \text{for} \quad 0 \leq j < n \quad \text{and} \quad u_n \equiv \mathit{false}$$

---

[4] Thus, $\sigma \uparrow 0$ denotes the empty string.

Since σ is a fixed string, the predicate $\sigma[j] = a$ is a constant predicate (either *true* or *false*). Furthermore, by assumption, no t_j mentions log. Thus the u_j don't mention log either, and hence $\hat{u}$ is also in log-canonical form.

Finally, recall that we are interested in constructing a statement T satisfying equation (1). Note that both the initial predicate $(\log = \langle\rangle)$ and the final predicate $(\log = \sigma)$ can be written in log-canonical form using appropriate vectors of predicates; for instance, $(\log = \langle\rangle)$ corresponds to the vector $[true, false, ...false]$. As shown in this section, we can push these predicates through the program (either backwards or forwards as appropriate). In doing so, we keep track of only vectors of predicates t_i that do not mention the variable log. Thus the assumes added to the reduced statement T do not mention log.

2.5   Extension to Suffixes

Because a trace may have a bounded length, discarding old events after a buffer fills, it is important to handle the case where σ is a *suffix* of the program's execution history. A useful benefit of handling suffixes is the potential to produce a shorter trace matching the suffix; this may be critical when the actual execution extended over a long period of time – both for reasons of analysis scalability and human understanding. In this case, the problem definition is: given a program $(\mathcal{V}, \Sigma, S)$ and a finite string σ of length n over Σ, construct a statement T such that,

$$T \ = \ \texttt{assume}(\log = \langle\rangle) \ ; \ S \ ; \ \texttt{assume}(\log \downarrow n = \sigma) \tag{6}$$

where we write $\log \downarrow i$ to mean the last i characters of log. In this case, we define $\hat{t}$ to mean the following:

$$(\exists i \ : \ 0 \le i \le n \ \wedge \ t_i \ \wedge \ \log \downarrow i = \sigma \uparrow i)$$

We leave it to the reader to check that this canonical form is preserved by wp computations as discussed above.

3   Implementation

Our analysis is implemented as an extension to CBMC [13], a bounded model checker [3] for ANSI-C programs. Given a program and a set of *unwinding depths* U (the maximum number of times each loop may be executed), CBMC produces constraints encoding all executions of the program not exceeding loop bounds. CBMC converts constraints into CNF and calls a Boolean satisfiability solver, such as zChaff [18] or LIMMAT [2]. A satisfying solution is a counterexample showing a property violation, whereas a proof of unsatisfiability indicates that the code cannot, within the given loop bounds, violate any properties. CBMC handles all ANSI C types and pointer operations, and checks safety properties such as assertion violations, null pointer dereferences, and array bound errors. CBMC supports assume statements in C source, with the expected semantics.

In order to support analysis of traces, we extended CBMC to recognize two *event reporting* functions in C source: EVR takes as argument a constant string (an identifier for the event, e.g., EVR(''timeout'')) and EVR_value takes an event identifier and an expression (typically an event-relevant program variable, e.g., EVR(''timeout'',thread_id)). A trace, for CBMC, is a sequence of event identifiers, where each identifier produced by an EVR_value call includes a value. Our trace language also allows event alphabet restrictions and the use of sets of events in the sequence.

3.1 Analyzing a Simple Program

Consider the program in Figure 3. The program is atypical in that a trace allows near-total reconstruction of the program inputs (though p and q cannot be precisely determined). For example, if the trace is $\sigma = \langle \text{foo 2, foo 1} \rangle$, we know the value of input and constraints on the values of p and q. It is this knowledge that our analysis will exploit in analyzing the program.

```
void foo () {                          void bar() {
  x--;                                   x++;
  EVR_value("foo",x);                    EVR("bar");
}                                      }

int main (int input, bool p, bool q) {
    x = input;                         x#1 == input#0
 1  if (p)                             x#2 == x#1 - 1;
      foo();   2                       x#3 == (p#0 ? x#2 : x#1)
 3  if (q)                             x#4 == x#3 - 1;
      foo();   4                       x#5 == (q#0 ? x#4 : x#3)
 5  if (p && q)
      bar();   6                       x#6 == x#5 + 1;
    else                               x#7 == x#5 - 1;
      foo();   7                       x#8 == (p#0 ∧ q#0 ? x#6 : x#7)
 8  assert ((x+1) == input);           assert ((x#8 + 1) == input#0)
}
```

Fig. 3. example.c

As discussed in Section 2.3, our implementation uses a forward analysis to compute assumptions and slices as CBMC generates the equational form of the program. This avoids a second pass over the transformed source code. The right side of Figure 3 shows the passive equational form of example.c. In the remainder, we will omit the renamings of p and q, as these inputs are never assigned.

CBMC produces predicate vectors (as described in Section 2.4) as it converts the program equations into SAT. If we restrict behavior to match σ, the vector has three elements, corresponding to the conditions under which 0, 1, or all elements of the trace have been consumed. As shown in eq. (5), the interpretation of $[t_0, t_1, t_2]$ is $(t_0 \wedge log = \langle \rangle) \vee (t_1 \wedge log = \langle \text{foo 1} \rangle) \vee (t_2 \wedge log = \langle \text{foo 2, foo 1} \rangle)$.

Table 1 shows the elements of the vectors at 8 program locations (labeled as 1-8 in Figure 3. When pushing assumptions forward, we begin with a vector

Table 1. Vectors as `example.c` is analyzed with σ. We refer to previous vector entries in a row-column format (i.e., 3B is row 3, column B: p $\wedge$ x#2 == 2).

Loc	Events Consumed		
	A $\langle\rangle$	**B** $\langle$foo 2$\rangle$	**C** $\langle$foo 2, foo 1$\rangle$
1	true	false	false
2	false	x#2 == 2	false
3	¬p	p $\wedge$ x#2 == 2	false
4	false	3A $\wedge$ x#4 == 2	3B $\wedge$ x#2 == 2 $\wedge$ x#4 == 1
5	¬q $\wedge$ ¬p	(q $\wedge$ 4B) $\vee$ (¬q $\wedge$ 3B)	q $\wedge$ 4C
6	false	false	false
7	false	5A $\wedge$ x#7 == 2	5B $\wedge$ x#7 == 1
8	false	¬(p $\wedge$ q) $\wedge$ 7B	¬(p $\wedge$ q) $\wedge$ 7C

interpreted as constraining the log to be empty: [*true, false, false*] (the first row of Table 1). At location 2 the modified vector requires that x's value at the location of the EVR_value call match the value in σ.

The vector for location 6 is *false*: if this branch is taken, the sequence of events cannot possibly match σ. When the vector for a branch is false, that branch can be sliced away. We slice the program by changing the equational form and relying on the model checker's ability to prevent un-referenced variables from appearing in the SAT constraints. The final assumption will force the program to take the ELSE-branch, which makes it safe to simplify the conditional expression for x#8 to (*false* ? x#6 : x#7), which simplifies to x#7. The equation for x#6 can then be discarded. The sliced version of the program produces a SAT problem with 696 variables and 2,312 clauses. Without slicing (leaving the irrelevant then-branch in place), the program requires 834 variables and 2,701 clauses.

3.2 Analyzing with Only a Suffix of a Trace

If we allow σ to be a suffix of the complete trace, the allowed program behaviors are the same (in this example, though not in general), but the analysis is altered. The first row of each vector is always *true*, as it is always possible to *begin* consuming events. The then-branch of the third conditional cannot be sliced away in the initial pass through the program — any events may appear before σ begins. The bar-branch can still be sliced away, as it is easy to note that the final condition (**8C**) implies ¬(p $\wedge$ q) — all allowed executions of the program will have to take the else-branch. Our analysis does not attempt to extract *all* such implications, but slices based on those that are trivially implied by the assumption (appearing on both sides of a disjunction, or either side of a conjunction, recursively), which has provided near-optimal slicing in our experience.

3.3 Using Traces as Specifications

Traces can be also be used as specifications. In order to use a trace as a specification, CBMC performs the same analysis as above, but searches for *any* execution of the program, rather than searching for property violations. We allow for multiple traces, alphabet restriction, and *sets* of events. With multiple traces, the tool maintains vectors for each trace and assumes the conjunction of all final conditions. This feature can be useful for post-mortem analysis as well, e. g., in the case of traces over different events produced by independent threads without time-stamps. Restricting which EVRs are taken into account is useful for specification: many events may be irrelevant to the property in question, although they appear in the actual code and traces. The utility of sets of events for specification should be obvious — e.g., for specifying that a file should be written to disk when either a `close` or `sync` operation occurs (see below in the experimental results). Handling alphabet restriction and event sets requires only a small modification of the mechanism for checking whether the ith event of a trace matches a particular alphabet symbol in an EVR call.

4   Experimental Results

We applied the technique to a small file system model, consisting of about 400 lines of C code. The model allows basic operations such as opening, closing, reading and writing files; it also supports reset events, which re-initialize all data structures except the disk contents (which is modeled as an array).

As written, the system is not robust across resets: a file can be opened, written to, and closed; if a reset happens at this point, the data in the file can be lost (the sync to disk in the close operation is faulty). We first consider the use of a partial

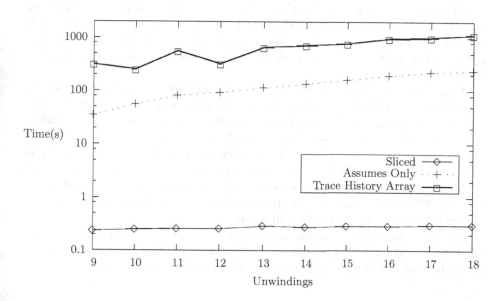

Fig. 4. Results for 8 maximum files

trace as a specification. Using a trace with an open, write, close, a sequence of wildcard actions (not allowing a delete), and an open followed by a failed read[5], we can specify that data should not be lost across any file system event sequence (of a bounded length), even if resets are present. Finding a counterexample (an execution matching this bad trace) requires 105 seconds, when using our technique and this trace as a specification. The utility of guiding the search with a trace is evident: CBMC requires 17,608 seconds to find a counterexample when checking the same property using a hand-coded monitor automaton ("blind" search) as a specification but without even a partial trace of execution. Because the wildcard actions limit the amount of slicing possible, the reduction in the size of the SAT problem is less impressive than the decrease in running time: the monitor-based approach produces a SAT instance with 613,857 variables and 2,108,934 clauses; our approach brings this down to 328,142 variables and 1,128,272 clauses.

A more significant reduction in the size of the SAT problem is seen when examining the same trace with reset in place of wildcards. Figure 4 provides a logscale graph of SAT run-times, given a complete trace for the file system in the smallest configuration we examined. Across a range of unwinding depths, full application of our approach results in a reduction of running time by several orders of magnitude. Applying our analysis to produce an assumption but using no slicing produces a smaller, but still quite significant, reduction over using a trace array semantics. Table 2 shows timing and SAT instance sizes for other configurations of the file system. Checking the property on the *largest* configuration and unwinding depth requires only 26,916 SAT variables when slicing is used; the *smallest* configuration uses 899,989 variables if slicing is not applied, and uses 3,266,123 variables in the largest configuration; running times for the sliced version are uniformly less than one second; over a thousand seconds are needed without slicing. Blind search — without a trace array — was consistently at least an order of magnitude slower than search using a trace array, and did not complete within a timeout period for larger system configurations such as those shown in Table 2.

Applying trace-based analysis to a small model of the core of the resource arbitration algorithm for the Mars Exploration Rovers also improved SAT problem sizes and running times significantly. Adding assumptions to match a failure trace the SAT instance grew slightly, but the search time decreased. Applying slicing to remove unreachable portions of the source code reduced the running time to 0.12 seconds. Scaling up to a more complex version of the same model with more properties (including some bounded liveness properties), blind search required 33 seconds, unsliced assumptions needed a little over a second, and with slicing the search time was only 0.29 seconds.

For both the resource arbiter and the file system, the additional overhead for trace-based analysis (performed while computing the passive form of the programs and unrolling loops) prior to calling the SAT solver was negligible.

---

[5] In the log, success or failure is recorded in addition to which operation is performed.

Table 2. Results for file system and arbiter. **U** indicates the unwinding depth for loops.

U	Sliced			Assumes Only			Trace Array		
	Vars	Clauses	Time	Vars	Clauses	Time	Vars	Clauses	Time
	File System Results (System Size = 10)								
11	17,884	65,816	0.29	899,989	3,085,814	91.83	952,924	3,509,042	334.04
12	18,280	67,031	0.30	998,527	3,423,893	119.28	1,067,554	3,960,332	412.91
13	18,676	68,246	0.32	1,097,065	3,762,227	146.00	1,172,149	4,370,541	550.51
14	19,072	69,461	0.32	1,195,603	4,100,816	181.05	1,276,744	4,784,989	1,152.70
15	19,468	70,676	0.32	1,294,141	4,439,660	206.25	1,381,339	5,203,676	624.28
16	19,864	71,891	0.33	1,392,727	4,778,839	248.86	1,485,982	5,626,682	806.59
17	20,260	73,106	0.34	1,491,268	5,118,198	269.77	1,590,580	6,053,852	1,495.01
18	20,656	74,321	0.34	1,589,809	5,457,812	331.40	1,695,178	6,485,261	2,115.49
	File System Results (System Size = 12)								
30	26,916	94,931	0.57	3,266,123	11,291,540	1,216.78	3,451,137	13,761,421	2,889.41
	Resource Arbiter Results (Safety)								
40	10,497	34,118	0.12	39,273	142,399	1.19	38,936	141,388	1.77
	Resource Arbiter Results (Liveness)								
40	21,311	72,142	0.29	73,244	259,308	1.30	72,099	255,639	32.96

5   Related Work

This paper presents a use of traces in program analysis — as slicing criteria and specification method — that differs in both motivation and technique from most previous work on related topics.

Assumptions and never-claims are used in many program verifiers [10, 6] to restrict explored system behavior; this kind of restriction is more general than what is described here, but does not provide any *a-priori* state-space reduction — the model checker may explore fewer states in an on-the-fly manner, but these techniques do not preclude exploration of branches that cannot match a given trace. Such methods are also less convenient than our approach for expressing the constraint that system behavior must be able (or not able) to produce a given sequence of events.

Removing code irrelevant to a given program trace is an extension of the idea of *program slicing* [20] — in particular dynamic slicing [1]. Static slicing removes the portions of a program that are not relevant to the analysis of a particular program point, under *any* set of inputs. Dynamic slicing performs the same task, for a known set of inputs. Parametric program slicing [5] makes use of a more general constraint, allowing for partial knowledge of inputs. Static slicing's utility is limited by aliasing and error handling paths, while dynamic slicing is of little utility when many program traces must be considered — for verification or bug hunting. The *path slicing* [12] of BLAST [9] removes portions of an abstract counterexample that are irrelevant to the feasibility of the path. Path slicing resembles our approach in that both are hybrids of purely static slicing and true dynamic slicing; the approaches differ in purpose (we apply slicing before model checking in order to limit system behaviors; path slicing is a step in a counterexample-refinement loop) and representation of multiple paths (a sequence of trace events vs. a fixed control flow). Millett and Teitelbaum applied more traditional program slicing to Promela models [17]. Only our approach addresses the notion of slicing based on a given event trace.

Howard et al. [11] use model checking to analyze traces produced by software, Roger and Goubault-Larrecq propose similar techniques for use in log auditing for intrusion detection [19], and Gannod and Murthy [8] describe the use of model checking to reverse engineer software architectures from a set of log files, in a largely non-automated approach.

Postmortem Symbolic Evaluation (PSE) [16] uses static analysis to *produce* possible program traces given only a failure's location and type. PSE builds on the work of Liblit and Aiken on the use of backtraces in debugging [15]. The work of Liblit and Aiken is closely related to our approach, in that they consider event traces derived from "`printf` debugging," including the suffix and multiple trace variations. Their work focuses on producing all CFL-reachable paths to a failure, rather than producing only feasible complete concrete executions. It is interesting to note that Liblit and Aiken come to similar conclusions about the advantages of backwards over forwards analysis, for largely independent reasons.

6   Summary and Future Work

We have addressed the problem of analyzing a given program given one of its traces, and demonstrated the utility of our approach for small examples such as the file system and the resource arbiter. A larger concern is how to optimize placement of EVRs in order to allow maximal slicing. The placement of EVRs is at present largely an ad-hoc process: developing a methodology for placing EVRs is critical if we are to analyze larger programs. We are pursuing these problems while applying our method to a larger, in-development, production-quality file system with over 2,000 lines of C source.

References

1. H. Agrawal and J. Horgan. Dynamic program slicing. In *Programming Language Design and Implementation*, pages 246–256, 1990.
2. A. Biere. The evolution from Limmat to Nanosat. Technical Report 444, Dept. of Computer Science, ETH Zürich, 2004.
3. A. Biere, A. Cimatti, E. Clarke, and Y. Zhu. Symbolic model checking without BDDs. In *Tools and Algorithms for the Construction and Analysis of Systems*, pages 193–207, 1999.
4. E. W. Dijkstra. *A Discipline of Programming*. Prentice-Hall, Englewood Cliffs, New Jersey, 1976.
5. J. Field, G Ramalingam, and F. Tip. Parametric program slicing. In *Principles of Programming Languages*, pages 379–392, 1995.

6. C. Flanagan, K. R. M. Leino, M. Lillibridge, G. Nelson, J. B. Saxe, and R. Stata. Extended static checking for Java. In *Proceedings of the 2002 ACM SIGPLAN Conference on Programming Language Design and Implementation (PLDI)*, pages 234–245, May 2002.

7. C. Flanagan and J. B. Saxe. Avoiding exponential explosion: Generating compact verification conditions. In *Principles of Programming Languages*, pages 193–205, 2002.

8. G. Gannod and S. Murthy. Using log files to reconstruct state-based software architectures. In *WCRE'02 Workshop on Software Architecture Reconstruction*, 2002.

9. T. A. Henzinger, R. Jhala, R. Majumdar, and G. Sutre. Lazy abstraction. In *Principles of Programming Languages*, pages 58–70, 2002.

10. G. J. Holzmann. *The SPIN Model Checker: Primer and Reference Manual*. Addison-Wesley Professional, 2003.

11. Y. Howard, S. Gruner, A. Gravell, C. Ferreira, and J. Augusto. Model-based trace-checking. In *SoftTest: UK Software Testing Research Workshop II*, 2003.

12. R. Jhala and R. Majumdar. Path slicing. In *Programming Language Design and Implementation*, pages 38–47, 2005.

13. D. Kroening, E. Clarke, and F. Lerda. A tool for checking ANSI-C programs. In *Tools and Algorithms for the Construction and Analysis of Systems*, pages 168–176, 2004.

14. K. Rustan M. Leino. Efficient weakest preconditions. *Information Processing Letters*, 93(6), 2005.

15. B. Liblit and A. Aiken. Building a better backtrace: Techniques for postmortem program analysis. Technical Report UCB CSD-02-1203, Computer Science Division, University of California at Berkeley, 2002.

16. R. Manevich, M. Sridharan, S. Adams, M. Das, and Z. Yang. PSE: explaining program failures via postmortem static analysis. In *Tools and Algorithms for the Construction and Analysis of Systems*, pages 63–72, 2004.

17. L. Millett and T. Teitelbaum. Slicing Promela and its applications to model checking, simulation, and protocol understanding. In *SPIN Workshop on Model Checking of Software*, pages 75–83, 1998.

18. M. Moskewicz, C. Madigan, Y. Zhao, L. Zhang, and S. Malik. Chaff: Engineering an Efficient SAT Solver. In *Design Automation Conference*, pages 530–535, 2001.

19. M. Roger and J. Goubault-Larrecq. Log auditing through model-checking. In *IEEE Workshop on Computer Security Foundations*, page 220, 2001.

20. F. Tip. A survey of program slicing techniques. *Journal of programming languages*, 3:121–189, 1995.

Model-Checking Markov Chains in the Presence of Uncertainties

Koushik Sen, Mahesh Viswanathan, and Gul Agha

Department of Computer Science,
University of Illinois at Urbana-Champaign
{ksen, vmahesh, agha}@uiuc.edu

Abstract. We investigate the problem of model checking Interval-valued Discrete-time Markov Chains (IDTMC). IDTMCs are discrete-time finite Markov Chains for which the exact transition probabilities are not known. Instead in IDTMCs, each transition is associated with an interval in which the actual transition probability must lie. We consider two semantic interpretations for the uncertainty in the transition probabilities of an IDTMC. In the first interpretation, we think of an IDTMC as representing a (possibly uncountable) family of (classical) discrete-time Markov Chains, where each member of the family is a Markov Chain whose transition probabilities lie within the interval range given in the IDTMC. This semantic interpretation we call Uncertain Markov Chains (UMC). In the second semantics for an IDTMC, which we call Interval Markov Decision Process (IMDP), we view the uncertainty as being resolved through non-determinism. In other words, each time a state is visited, we adversarially pick a transition distribution that respects the interval constraints, and take a probabilistic step according to the chosen distribution. We show that the PCTL model checking problem for both Uncertain Markov Chain semantics and Interval Markov Decision Process semantics is decidable in PSPACE. We also prove lower bounds for these model checking problems.

1 Introduction

Discrete time stochastic models such as *Discrete Time Markov Chains* (DTMCs) have been used to analyze the correctness, reliability, and performance of systems [8, 11, 19, 13]. In a DTMC, the system is assumed to have finitely many states, and the system's future behavior is completely determined by its current state. From each state of the system, the probability of transitioning to any other given state at the next step is fixed and is given by the transition probability matrix of the DTMC.

The assumption that the system makes transitions according to a fixed distribution at each step and that this distribution is precisely known when modeling, is a strong assumption that may often not hold in practice [12, 15, 26, 14]. If the system being modeled is an open system, i.e., interacts with an environment, then uncertainty in the transitions may arise due to imperfect information about the environment. For example, consider a system that interacts with an imperfect communication medium that may lose messages. The probability of message loss may either depend on choice of the communication medium or on a complicated, time-varying dependence on events that are not

H. Hermanns and J. Palsberg (Eds.): TACAS 2006, LNCS 3920, pp. 394–410, 2006.

precisely understood at the time of modeling the system. Another source of imprecision is that the transition probabilities in the system model are often estimated through statistical experiments, which only provide bounds on the transition probabilities.

In order to faithfully capture these system uncertainties in stochastic models, the model of *Interval-valued Discrete-time Markov Chains (IDTMC)* has been introduced [12, 14]. These are DTMC models where the exact probability of taking a state transition is not known, and instead the transition probability is assumed to lie within a range associated with the transition. Two semantic interpretations have been suggested for such models. *Uncertain Markov Chains* (UMC) [12] is an interpretation of an IDTMC as a family of (possibly uncountably many) DTMCs, where each member of the family is a DTMC whose transition probabilities lie within the interval range given in the IDTMC. In the second interpretation, called *Interval Markov Decision Process* (IMDP), we view the uncertainty as being resolved through non-determinism. In other words, each time a state is visited, we adversarially pick a transition distribution that respects the interval constraints, and take a probabilistic step according to the chosen distribution. Thus, IMDPs allow the possibility of modeling a non-deterministic choice made from a set of (possibly) uncountably many choices. An IMDP can be seen as a generalization of Markov Decision Processes (MDPs) [17, 3, 21].

We investigate the problem of model checking PCTL specifications for IDTMC. The two semantic interpretations of IDTMCs yield very different model checking results (whenever the property has at least two probabilistic operators, not necessarily nested; see example in Figure 1) and require different algorithmic techniques. For the case of UMCs, we show that PCTL model checking problem can be reduced to finding feasible solutions to inequality constraints, much like in the case of DTMC and MDP [8, 4, 3, 19, 7]. However, there is one important difference. The constraints to be solved in the case of UMCs are polynomial and not just linear (as for DTMCs and MDPs). Since the *existential theory of reals* is decidable in PSPACE [18, 6], the feasibility of the polynomial constraints arising in model checking, can be determined by making a "query" to the existential theory of reals. Thus, the PCTL model checking problem for UMCs is in PSPACE. In practice, however, this algorithm may not be the most efficient. The constraints we obtain during model checking all take a special form: the polynomials are *bilinear*[1]. Therefore, it might be more efficient to instead use algorithms for solving *bilinear matrix inequalities* (BMIs) [10, 9] or tools developed for this purpose [16]. Checking feasibility of BMIs is known to be NP-hard [24], but the exact complexity, which is lower than PSPACE, is unknown. On the other hand, in the case of IMDPs, we show that the model checking problem can be reduced to model checking an MDP of exponential size. We then use known results for MDPs to show that IMDPs can be model checked in PSPACE. We also present an iterative model checking algorithm for IMDPs which may prove to be more efficient in practice.

In addition to demonstrating the decidability of the model checking problem, we also prove lower bounds on the complexity of the model checking problem. We show that the model checking problem for UMCs is NP-hard and co-NP-hard; thus, for UMCs the problem is unlikely to be in P. A straightforward corollary of our results is that solving

---

[1] The highest power of any variable in the polynomial is 1, and any term is the product of at most two variables.

BMIs is also co-NP-hard. For IMDPs, we can only show P-hardness; in fact, even this is a consequence of the P-hardness of (classical) DTMC model checking.

The rest of the paper is organized as follows. We briefly discuss related work next. In Section 2 we formally define IDTMC and give its semantics as UMC and IMDP. PCTL and the model checking problem is introduced in Section 3. We then revisit the model checking algorithm for DTMC (Section 4) and present a modified version of the classical algorithm. The ideas in the section play a key role in our UMC model checking algorithm. Section 5 (UMC) and Section 6 (IMDP) contain our main results about the model checking problem, providing both upper and lower bounds. Finally we present our conclusions in Section 7. Due to lack of space, we do not present any proofs here; all proofs including motivating examples of UMCs and IMDPs can be found in [23].

Related Work. The model of IDTMCs has been introduced independently by Jonsson and Larsen [12] and Kozine and Utkin [14] under the names *interval specification systems* and *interval-valued finite Markov chains*, respectively. However, they consider different semantic interpretations. Jonsson and Larsen consider the UMC interpretation and study bisimulation and simulation preorders for such an interpretation. Kozine and Utkin, on the other hand, take the IMDP interpretation and present algorithms to compute the probability distribution on the states after t steps. Neither of these papers investigate the PCTL model checking problem which is the focus of this paper. We introduce new names to emphasize the subtle semantic difference in the two interpretations. A more general model called *generalized Markov processes* for describing infinite families of Markov Chains was introduced in [1]. In that paper, they showed that model checking such models with respect to PCTL* (a more general logic than PCTL) is decidable and has elementary complexity. PCTL model checking for classical DTMC and MDP models has been considered in [8, 4, 3, 19, 7].

2   Formal Models

Definition 1. A discrete-time Markov chain *(DTMC) is a 4-tuple* $\mathcal{M} = (S, s_I, \mathbf{P}, L)$, *where*

1. *S is a finite set of* states,
2. $s_I \in S$ *is the* initial *state*,
3. $\mathbf{P} \colon S \times S \to [0, 1]$ *is a* transition probability matrix, *such that* $\sum_{s' \in S} \mathbf{P}(s, s') = 1$, *and*
4. $L \colon S \to 2^{\mathrm{AP}}$ *is a* labeling *function that maps states to sets of atomic propositions from a set* AP.

A non-empty sequence $\pi = s_0 s_1 s_2 \cdots$ is called a *path* of $\mathcal{M}$, if each $s_i \in S$ and $\mathbf{P}(s_i, s_{i+1}) > 0$ for all $i \geq 0$. We denote the ith state in a path π by $\pi[i] = s_i$. We let *Path(s)* be the set of paths starting at state s. A probability measure on paths is induced by the matrix $\mathbf{P}$ as follows.

Let $s_0, s_1, \ldots, s_k \in S$ with $\mathbf{P}(s_i, s_{i+1}) > 0$ for all $0 \leq i < k$. Then $C(s_0 s_1 \ldots s_k)$ denotes a *cylinder set* consisting of all paths $\pi \in Path(s_0)$ such that $\pi[i] = s_i$ (for $0 \leq i \leq k$). Let $\mathcal{B}$ be the smallest σ-algebra on *Path(s_0)* which contains all the cylinders $C(s_0 s_1 \ldots s_k)$. The measure μ on cylinder sets can be defined as follows

$$\mu(C(s_0 s_1 \ldots s_k)) = \begin{cases} 1 & \text{if } k = 0 \\ \mathbf{P}(s_0, s_1) \cdots \mathbf{P}(s_{k-1}, s_k) & \text{otherwise} \end{cases}$$

The *probability measure* on $\mathcal{B}$ is then defined as the unique measure that agrees with μ (as defined above) on the cylinder sets.

Definition 2. An Interval-valued Discrete-time Markov chain *(IDTMC) is a 5-tuple* $\mathcal{I} = (S, s_I, \check{\mathbf{P}}, \hat{\mathbf{P}}, L)$, *where*

1. *S is a finite set of* states,
2. *$s_I \in S$ is the* initial *state,*
3. *$\check{\mathbf{P}}: S \times S \rightarrow [0, 1]$ is a* transition probability matrix, *where each $\check{\mathbf{P}}(s, s')$ gives the* lower bound *of the transition probability from the state s to the state s',*
4. *$\hat{\mathbf{P}}: S \times S \rightarrow [0, 1]$ is a* transition probability matrix, *where each $\hat{\mathbf{P}}(s, s')$ gives the* upper bound *of the transition probability from the state s to the state s',*
5. *$L: S \rightarrow 2^{\text{AP}}$ is a* labeling *function that maps states to sets of atomic propositions from a set* AP.

We consider two semantics interpretations of an IDTMC model, namely Uncertain Markov Chains (UMC) and Interval Markov Decision Processes (IMDP).

Uncertain Markov Chains. An IDTMC $\mathcal{I}$ may represent an infinite set of DTMCs, denoted by $[\mathcal{I}]$, where for each DTMC $(S, s_I, \mathbf{P}, L) \in [\mathcal{I}]$ the following is true,

– $\check{\mathbf{P}}(s, s') \leq \mathbf{P}(s, s') \leq \hat{\mathbf{P}}(s, s')$ for all pairs of states s and s' in S

In the Uncertain Markov Chains semantics, or simply, in the UMCs, we assume that the external environment non-deterministically picks a DTMC from the set $[\mathcal{I}]$ at the beginning and then all the transitions take place according to the chosen DTMC. Note that in this semantics, the external environment makes only one non-deterministic choice. Henceforth, we will use the term UMC to denote an IDTMC interpreted according to the Uncertain Markov Chains semantics.

Interval Markov Decision Processes. In the Interval Markov Decision Processes semantics, or simply, in the IMDPs, we assume that before every transition the external environment non-deterministically picks a DTMC from the set $[\mathcal{I}]$ and then takes a one-step transition according to the probability distribution of the chosen DTMC. Note that in this semantics, the external environment makes a non-deterministic choice before every transition. Henceforth, we will use the term IMDP to denote an IDTMC interpreted according to the Interval Markov Decision Processes semantics. We now formally define this semantics.

Let *Steps(s)* be the set of probability density functions over S defined as follows:

$$Steps(s) = \{\mu: S \rightarrow \mathbb{R}^{\geq 0} \mid \sum_{s' \in S} \mu(s') = 1 \text{ and } \check{\mathbf{P}}(s, s') \leq \mu(s') \leq \hat{\mathbf{P}}(s, s') \text{ for all } s' \in S\}$$

In an IMDP, at every state $s \in S$, a probability density function μ is chosen non-deterministically from the set *Steps(s)*. A successor state s' is then chosen according to the probability distribution μ over S.

A *path* π in an IMDP $\mathcal{I} = (S, s_I, \check{\mathbf{P}}, \hat{\mathbf{P}}, L)$ is a non-empty sequence of the form $s_0 \xrightarrow{\mu_1} s_1 \xrightarrow{\mu_2} \ldots$, where $s_i \in S$, $\mu_{i+1} \in Steps(s_i)$, and $\mu_{i+1}(s_{i+1}) > 0$ for all $i \geq 0$. A path can be either finite or infinite. We use π_{fin} to denote a finite path. Let $last(\pi_{\text{fin}})$ be the last state in the finite path π_{fin}. As in DTMC, we denote the ith state in a path π by $\pi[i] = s_i$. We let $Path(s)$ and $Path_{\text{fin}}(s)$ be the set of all infinite and finite paths, respectively, starting at state s. To associate a probability measure with the paths, we resolve the non-deterministic choices by an *adversary*, which is defined as follows:

Definition 3. *An adversary A of an IMDP $\mathcal{I}$ is a function mapping every finite path π_{fin} of $\mathcal{I}$ onto an element of the set $Steps(last(\pi_{\text{fin}}))$. Let $\mathcal{A}_{\mathcal{I}}$ denote the set of all possible adversaries of the IMDP $\mathcal{I}$. Let $Path^A(s)$ denote the subset of $Path(s)$ which corresponds to A.*

The behavior of an IMDP $\mathcal{I} = (S, s_I, \check{\mathbf{P}}, \hat{\mathbf{P}}, L)$ under a given adversary A is purely deterministic. The behavior of a IMDP $\mathcal{I}$ from a state s can be described by an infinite-state DTMC $\mathcal{M}^A = (S^A, s_I^A, \mathbf{P}^A, L^A)$ where

- $S^A = Path_{\text{fin}}(s)$,
- $s_I^A = s$, and
- $\mathbf{P}^A(\pi_{\text{fin}}, \pi'_{\text{fin}}) = \begin{cases} A(\pi_{\text{fin}})(s') & \text{if } \pi'_{\text{fin}} \text{ is of the form } \pi_{\text{fin}} \xrightarrow{A(\pi_{\text{fin}})} s' \\ 0 & \text{otherwise} \end{cases}$

There is a one-to-one correspondence between the paths of $\mathcal{M}^A$ and $Path^A(s)$ of $\mathcal{I}$. Therefore, we can define a probability measure $Prob_s^A$ over the set of paths $Path^A(s)$ using the probability measure of the DTMC $\mathcal{M}^A$.

3   Probabilistic Computation Tree Logic (PCTL)

In this paper we consider a sub-logic of PCTL that excludes the steady-state probabilistic operators. The formal syntax and semantics of this logic is as follows.

PCTL Syntax

$$\phi ::= true \mid a \mid \neg\phi \mid \phi \wedge \phi \mid \mathcal{P}_{\bowtie p}(\psi)$$
$$\psi ::= \phi \, \mathcal{U} \, \phi \mid \mathbf{X}\phi$$

where $a \in AP$ is an atomic propositions, $\bowtie \in \{<, \leq, >, \geq\}$, $p \in [0,1]$, and $k \in \mathbb{N}$. Here ϕ represents a *state* formula and ψ represents a *path* formula.

PCTL Semantics for DTMC

The notion that a state s (or a path π) *satisfies* a formula ϕ in a DTMC $\mathcal{M}$ is denoted by $s \models_{\mathcal{M}} \phi$ (or $\pi \models_{\mathcal{M}} \phi$), and is defined inductively as follows:

$$
\begin{aligned}
&s \models_{\mathcal{M}} true \\
&s \models_{\mathcal{M}} a && \text{iff } a \in L(s) \\
&s \models_{\mathcal{M}} \neg\phi && \text{iff } s \not\models_{\mathcal{M}} \phi \\
&s \models_{\mathcal{M}} \phi_1 \wedge \phi_2 && \text{iff } s \models_{\mathcal{M}} \phi_1 \text{ and } s \models_{\mathcal{M}} \phi_2 \\
&s \models_{\mathcal{M}} \mathcal{P}_{\bowtie p}(\psi) && \text{iff } Prob\{\pi \in Path(s) \mid \pi \models_{\mathcal{M}} \psi\} \bowtie p \\
&\pi \models_{\mathcal{M}} \mathbf{X}\phi && \text{iff } \pi[1] \models_{\mathcal{M}} \phi \\
&\pi \models_{\mathcal{M}} \phi_1 \, \mathcal{U} \, \phi_2 && \text{iff } \exists i \geq 0 \, (\pi[i] \models_{\mathcal{M}} \phi_2 \text{ and } \forall j < i. \, \pi[j] \models_{\mathcal{M}} \phi_1)
\end{aligned}
$$

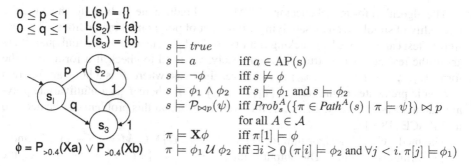

$0 \le p \le 1$ $L(s_1) = \{\}$
$0 \le q \le 1$ $L(s_2) = \{a\}$
$L(s_3) = \{b\}$

$s \models true$
$s \models a$ iff $a \in \mathrm{AP}(s)$
$s \models \neg\phi$ iff $s \not\models \phi$
$s \models \phi_1 \wedge \phi_2$ iff $s \models \phi_1$ and $s \models \phi_2$
$s \models \mathcal{P}_{\bowtie p}(\psi)$ iff $Prob_s^A(\{\pi \in Path^A(s) \mid \pi \models \psi\}) \bowtie p$
         for all $A \in \mathcal{A}$
$\pi \models \mathbf{X}\phi$ iff $\pi[1] \models \phi$
$\pi \models \phi_1 \, \mathcal{U} \, \phi_2$ iff $\exists i \ge 0 \, (\pi[i] \models \phi_2$ and $\forall j < i. \, \pi[j] \models \phi_1)$

$\phi = P_{>0.4}(\mathbf{X}a) \vee P_{>0.4}(\mathbf{X}b)$

Fig. 1. Example IDTMC and PCTL formula ϕ. The UMC interpretation of the IDTMC satisfies ϕ, whereas the IMDP interpretation of the IDTMC violates ϕ.

Fig. 2. PCTL semantics for IMDP

It can shown that for any path formula ψ and any state s, the set $\{\pi \in Path(s) \mid \pi \models_{\mathcal{M}} \psi\}$ is measurable [25]. A formula $\mathcal{P}_{\bowtie p}(\psi)$ is satisfied by a state s if $Prob$[path starting at s satisfies ψ] $\bowtie p$. The path formula $\mathbf{X}\phi$ holds over a path if ϕ holds at the second state on the path. The formula $\phi_1 \, \mathcal{U} \, \phi_2$ is true over a path π if ϕ_2 holds in some state along π, and ϕ holds along all prior states along π.

Given a DTMC $\mathcal{M}$ and a PCTL state formula ϕ, $\mathcal{M} \models \phi$ iff $s_I \models_{\mathcal{M}} \phi$.

PCTL Semantics for UMC

Given a UMC $\mathcal{I}$ and a PCTL state formula ϕ, we say $\mathcal{I} \models \phi$ iff, for all $\mathcal{M} \in [\mathcal{I}]$, $\mathcal{M} \models \phi$. Note that $\mathcal{I} \not\models \phi$ does not imply that $\mathcal{I} \models \neg\phi$. This because if $\mathcal{I} \not\models \phi$, there may exist $\mathcal{M}, \mathcal{M}' \in [\mathcal{I}]$ such that $\mathcal{M} \models \phi$ and $\mathcal{M}' \models \neg\phi$.

PCTL Semantics for IMDP

The interpretation of a state formula and a path formula of PCTL for IMDPs is same as for DTMCs except for the state formulas of the form $\mathcal{P}_{\bowtie p}(\psi)$.

The notion that a state s (or a path π) *satisfies* a formula ϕ in a IMDP $\mathcal{I}$ is denoted by $s \models \phi$ (or $\pi \models \phi$), and is defined inductively in Figure 2.

The model checking of IDTMC with respect to the two semantics can give different results. For example, consider the IDTMC in Figure 1 and the PCTL formula ϕ. The UMC semantics of this IDTMC satisfies ϕ, while the IMDP semantics violates ϕ.

4   Revisiting DTMC Model-Checking

In this section we outline the basic model checking algorithm for (classical) DTMCs. The algorithm that we outline here for DTMCs is not the most efficient (like the one presented in [8]); however the main ideas presented here will form the crux of our model checking algorithm for UMCs.

The algorithm for model checking DTMCs will reduce the problem to checking the feasibility of simultaneously satisfying a finite set of polynomial inequalities. This feasibility test can be done by checking if a first-order formula with existential quantifiers about the real numbers is true. More precisely, we need to check if a formula of the form $\exists x_1, \ldots, x_n P(x_1, \ldots, x_n)$ is valid over the reals, where P is a boolean function of atomic predicates of the form $f_i(x_1, \ldots, x_n) \bowtie 0$, where f_i is a multivariate polynomial and $\bowtie \in \{=, \neq, \leq, \geq, <, >\}$. It is well-known that this problem can be decided in PSPACE [18, 6] [2].

The model checking algorithm for DTMC takes a DTMC $\mathcal{M} = (S, s_I, \mathbf{P}, L)$ and a PCTL formula ϕ as input. The output is the set $\mathrm{Sat}(\phi) = \{s \in S \mid s \models_{\mathcal{M}} \phi\}$, i.e., the set of all states of the model that satisfy ϕ. We say $\mathcal{M} \models \phi$ iff $s_I \in \mathrm{Sat}(\phi)$.

The algorithm works by recursively computing the set $\mathrm{Sat}(\phi')$ for each sub-formula ϕ' of ϕ as follows.

$$\mathrm{Sat}(\mathit{true}) = S \qquad\qquad \mathrm{Sat}(a) = \{s \mid a \in L(S)\}$$
$$\mathrm{Sat}(\neg\phi) = S \setminus \mathrm{Sat}(\phi) \qquad \mathrm{Sat}(\phi_1 \wedge \phi_2) = \mathrm{Sat}(\phi_1) \cap \mathrm{Sat}(\phi_2)$$
$$\mathrm{Sat}(\mathcal{P}_{\bowtie p}(\psi)) = \{s \in S \mid p_s(\psi) \bowtie p\}$$

where $p_s(\psi) = \mathit{Prob}\{\pi \in \mathit{Path}(s) \mid \pi \models_{\mathcal{M}} \psi\}$. The computation of the set $\mathrm{Sat}(\mathcal{P}_{\bowtie p}(\psi))$ requires the computation of $p_s(\psi)$ at every state $s \in S$.

If $\psi = \mathbf{X}\phi$, then $p_s(\psi) = \sum_{s' \in \mathrm{Sat}(\phi)} \mathbf{P}(s, s')$.

To compute $p_s(\phi_1 \, \mathcal{U} \, \phi_2)$, we first split the set of states S into three disjoint subsets, S^{no}, S^{yes}, and $S^?$ where $S^{\mathrm{no}} = \mathrm{Sat}(\neg\phi_1 \wedge \neg\phi_2)$, $S^{\mathrm{yes}} = \mathrm{Sat}(\phi_2)$, and $S^? = S \setminus (S^{\mathrm{no}} \cup S^{\mathrm{yes}})$. Moreover, let $S^{?\mathrm{no}}$ be the set $\{s \mid p_s(\phi_1 \, \mathcal{U} \, \phi_2) = 0\} \setminus S^{\mathrm{no}}$ and $S^{>0}$ be the set $\{s \mid p_s(\phi_1 \, \mathcal{U} \, \phi_2) > 0\}$. Note that $S = S^{>0} \cup S^{?\mathrm{no}} \cup S^{\mathrm{no}}$. By [8], $\{x_s = p_s(\phi_1 \, \mathcal{U} \, \phi_2) \mid s \in S\}$ is a solution of the following linear equation system.

$$x_s = \begin{cases} 0 & \text{if } s \in S^{\mathrm{no}} \\ 1 & \text{if } s \in S^{\mathrm{yes}} \\ \sum_{s' \in S} \mathbf{P}(s, s') x_{s'} & \text{if } s \in S^? \end{cases} \tag{1}$$

Note that the equation system (1) can have infinite number of solutions. For example, consider the formula $\mathit{true} \, \mathcal{U} \, a$, where a is an atomic proposition and the DTMC $\mathcal{M} = (\{s\}, s, \mathbf{P}, L)$, where $\mathbf{P}(s, s) = 1$ and $L(s) = \emptyset$. Note that $s \in S^{?\mathrm{no}}$. The linear equation system (1) that is instantiated for computing $p_s(\mathit{true} \, \mathcal{U} \, a)$ for $\mathcal{M}$ is $x_s = x_s$. The system has infinite number of solutions.

We can ensure that $\{x_s = p_s(\phi_1 \, \mathcal{U} \, \phi_2) \mid s \in S\}$ is a unique solution of a system of equations as follows. Fix a γ such that $0 < \gamma < 1$. Consider the following linear equation system.

$$x'_s = \begin{cases} 0 & \text{if } s \in S^{\mathrm{no}} \\ 1 & \text{if } s \in S^{\mathrm{yes}} \\ \sum_{s' \in S} \gamma \mathbf{P}(s, s') x'_{s'} & \text{if } s \in S^? \end{cases} \tag{2}$$

---

[2] If one takes the computational model to be Turing machines, then this result holds when the coefficients of the polynomials are rationals. One the other hand, if one considers a model of computation that is appropriate for real number computation, like the one proposed by Blum, Shub, and Smale [5], then the algorithm can handle even real coefficients.

Lemma 1. $x'_s > 0$ iff $s \in S^{>0}$.

Lemma 2. *The system of linear equations in* (2) *has a unique solution.*

Lemma 3. $x'_s = 0$ iff $s \in S^{?no} \cup S^{no}$.

Consider the following system of constraints.

$$x'_s = 0 \text{ iff } x_s = 0 \text{ for all } s \in S \tag{3}$$

where x'_s are variables of (2) and x_s are variables of (1).

Lemma 4. *The system of linear equations in* (1) *and* (2) *has a unique solution given that the constraints in* (3) *hold. Moreover, for this unique solution* $x_s = p_s(\phi_1 \,\mathcal{U}\, \phi_2)$, *for all* $s \in S$.

Note that the set of constraints (1), (2), and (3) can be written compactly as follows.

$$x_s = \begin{cases} 0 & \text{if } s \in S^{no} \\ 1 & \text{if } s \in S^{yes} \\ \sum_{s' \in S} \mathbf{P}(s, s') x_{s'} & \text{if } s \in S^? \end{cases} \qquad x'_s = \begin{cases} 0 & \text{if } s \in S^{no} \\ 1 & \text{if } s \in S^{yes} \\ \sum_{s' \in S} \gamma \mathbf{P}(s, s') x'_{s'} & \text{if } s \in S^? \end{cases} \tag{4}$$

$$\delta_s > 0 \qquad x_s = \delta_s x'_s$$

where for each $s \in S$, we introduce the variable δ_s, such that we can impose the constraint that $x_s = 0$ iff $x'_s = 0$. The satisfiability of the set of constraints (4) can be easily reduced to checking if a formula with existential quantifiers belongs to the theory of reals. The constructed formula is linear in the size of the DTMC.

5   Model Checking UMC

In this section, we reduce the problem of model-checking a UMC to checking the feasibility of a bilinear matrix inequality. (More details about bilinear matrix inequality can found in [23].) In the non-trivial reduction, we introduce a number of auxiliary variables to achieve the goal. Note that a simpler PSPACE algorithm, which avoids the extra auxiliary variables by guessing their values non-deterministically, is possible and is easy to come up from our reduction. However, we believe that the following reduction is important from the perspective of implementation in practice using algorithms to solve bilinear matrix inequalities (BMIs).

Given a UMC $\mathcal{I}$ and a PCTL state formula ϕ, our goal is to check whether $\mathcal{I} \models \phi$. In other words, for every $\mathcal{M} \in [\mathcal{I}]$, $\mathcal{M} \models \phi$. Thus, to check whether $\mathcal{I} \models \phi$, we check if there exists some $\mathcal{M} \in [\mathcal{I}]$ such that $\mathcal{M} \models \neg\phi$. If such an $\mathcal{M}$ does not exist, we conclude that $\mathcal{I} \models \phi$. We will view the problem of discovering whether a $\mathcal{M} \in [\mathcal{I}]$ satisfies $\neg\phi$ as problem of checking the feasibility of a set of bilinear inequality constraints as follows. Each transition probability of the DTMC $\mathcal{M}$ that we are searching for, will be a variable taking a value within the bounds. We will also have variables denoting the satisfaction (or non-satisfaction) of each subformula at each state, and variables denoting the probability of a path subformula being satisfied at each state. Inequality constraints on these variables will ensure that they all have consistent values. We now describe this construction formally.

Let us fix an UMC $\mathcal{I} = (S, s_I, \check{\mathbf{P}}, \hat{\mathbf{P}}, L)$ and a PCTL formula ϕ. Let $\mathcal{M} = (S, s_I, \mathbf{P}, L)$ be an arbitrary Markov chain in $[\mathcal{I}]$.

For every pair of states $s, s' \in S$, let the variable $p_{ss'}$ denote the transition probability from s to s' in $\mathcal{M}$, i.e., $p_{ss'}$ denotes $\mathbf{P}(s, s')$. Since $\mathcal{M}$ is an arbitrary DTMC in $[\mathcal{I}]$, by the definition of UMC, the following constraints hold: For every state $s \in S$, $\sum_{s' \in S} p_{ss'} = 1$ and for every pair of states $s, s' \in S$, $\check{\mathbf{P}}(s, s') \leq p_{ss'} \leq \hat{\mathbf{P}}(s, s')$.

Given any PCTL formula ϕ, let us define the set $subfS(\phi)$ (of state sub-formulas) recursively as follows:

$$subfS(a) = \{a\} \qquad\qquad subfS(\neg\phi) = \{\neg\phi\} \cup subfS(\phi)$$
$$subfS(\phi_1 \wedge \phi_2) = \{\phi_1 \wedge \phi_2\} \cup subfS(\phi_1) \cup subfS(\phi_2) \qquad subfS(\mathcal{P}_{\bowtie p}(\psi)) = \{\mathcal{P}_{\bowtie p}(\psi)\} \cup subfS(\psi)$$
$$subfS(\phi_1 \,\mathcal{U}\, \phi_2) = subfS(\phi_1 \wedge \neg\phi_2) \qquad\qquad subfS(\mathbf{X}\phi) = subfS(\phi)$$

Given a state $s \in S$ and any formula $\phi' \in subfS(\phi)$, either $s \models_\mathcal{M} \phi'$ or $s \not\models_\mathcal{M} \phi'$. For each $s \in S$ and each $\phi' \in subfS(\phi)$, let the variable $t_s^{\phi'}$ be such that $t_s^{\phi'} = 1$ iff $s \models_\mathcal{M} \phi'$; and, $t_s^{\phi'} = 0$ iff $s \not\models_\mathcal{M} \phi'$. Following the definition of the various logical operators in PCTL, we can set up a set of constraints among these variables such that for any $\mathcal{M} \in [\mathcal{I}]$, the values taken by these variables is consistent with their intended semantic interpretation. We introduce the following additional variables to aid in setting up these constraints. For every state $s \in S$ and $\phi' \in subfS(\phi)$, let the auxiliary variables $f_s^{\phi'}$, and $u_s^{\phi'}$ be such that $t_s^{\phi'} = 1 \iff f_s^{\phi'} = 0 \iff u_s^{\phi'} = 1$ and $t_s^{\phi'} = 0 \iff f_s^{\phi'} = 1 \iff u_s^{\phi'} = -1$ Clearly, $t_s^{\phi'}$, $f_s^{\phi'}$, and $u_s^{\phi'}$ are related by the following set of constraints:

$$t_s^{\phi'} f_s^{\phi'} = 0 \qquad t_s^{\phi'} + f_s^{\phi'} = 1 \qquad 2t_s^{\phi'} = u_s^{\phi'} + 1$$

For every formula $\phi' \in subfS(\phi)$ of the form $\mathcal{P}_{\bowtie p}(\psi)$ and for every state $s \in S$, let p_s^ψ be the variable such that p_s^ψ denotes $Prob\{\pi \in Path(s) \mid \pi \models_\mathcal{M} \psi\}$ in $\mathcal{M}$.

For each state $s \in S$ and for each $\phi' \in subfS(\phi)$ exactly one of the following constraints hold depending on the form of ϕ':

$$t_s^{\phi'} = 1 \quad \text{if } \phi' = a \in L(s) \qquad\qquad t_s^{\phi'} = 0 \quad \text{if } \phi' = a \notin L(s)$$
$$t_s^{\phi'} = 1 - t_s^{\phi_1} \quad \text{if } \phi' = \neg\phi_1 \qquad\qquad t_s^{\phi_1} t_s^{\phi_2} = t_s^{\phi'} \quad \text{if } \phi' = \phi_1 \wedge \phi_2$$
$$u_s^{\phi'} p_s^\psi \geq u_s^{\phi'} p + \delta f_s^{\phi'} \quad \text{if } \phi' = \mathcal{P}_{\geq p}(\psi) \qquad u_s^{\phi'} p_s^\psi \geq u_s^{\phi'} p + \delta t_s^{\phi'} \quad \text{if } \phi' = \mathcal{P}_{> p}(\psi)$$
$$u_s^{\phi'} p_s^\psi + \delta f_s^{\phi'} \leq u_s^{\phi'} p \quad \text{if } \phi' = \mathcal{P}_{\leq p}(\psi) \qquad u_s^{\phi'} p_s^\psi + \delta t_s^{\phi'} \leq u_s^{\phi'} p \quad \text{if } \phi' = \mathcal{P}_{< p}(\psi)$$

where δ is slack variable that is required to be strictly greater than 0.

Note that the above constraints do not reflect the fact that for each $\phi' \in subfS(\phi)$ of the form $\mathcal{P}_{\bowtie p}(\psi)$, p_s^ψ denotes $Prob\{\pi \in Path(s) \mid \pi \models_\mathcal{M} \psi\}$. To set up such constraints, we introduce the set $subfP(\phi)$ (of path sub-formulas) as follows:

$$subfP(a) = \emptyset \qquad\qquad subfP(\neg\phi) = subfP(\phi)$$
$$subfP(\phi_1 \wedge \phi_2) = subfP(\phi_1) \cup subfP(\phi_2) \qquad subfP(\mathcal{P}_{\bowtie p}(\psi)) = \{\psi\} \cup subfP(\psi)$$
$$subfP(\phi_1 \,\mathcal{U}\, \phi_2) = subfP(\phi_1) \cup subfP(\phi_2) \qquad subfP(\mathbf{X}\phi) = subfP(\phi)$$

Thus for all sub-formula of ϕ of the form $\mathcal{P}_{\bowtie p}(\psi)$, $subfP(\phi)$ contains ψ.

For any $\psi \in subfP(\phi)$ of the form $\mathbf{X}\phi_1$ and for each $s \in S$ the following constraint holds:

$$p_s^\psi = \sum_{s' \in S} p_{ss'} t_{s'}^{\phi_1}$$

For each $\psi \in subfS(\phi)$ of the form $\phi_1 \, \mathcal{U} \, \phi_2$ and $s \in S$ the following constraints hold.

$$p_s^\psi = t_s^{\phi_2} + t_s^{\phi_1 \wedge \neg\phi_2} w_s^\psi \qquad w_s^\psi = \sum_{s' \in S} p_{ss'} p_s^\psi$$

As in simple DTMC, if we consider the above constraints only, then we may not have unique solution for certain p_s^ψ. Therefore, we fix a γ such that $0 < \gamma < 1$. Then, as in simple DTMC model-checking, for each $\psi \in subfP(\phi)$ of the form $\phi_1 \, \mathcal{U} \, \phi_2$ and $s \in S$, we introduce the variables $p_s'^\psi$ and $w_s'^\psi$, such that the following constraints hold.

$$p_s'^\psi = t_s^{\phi_2} + t_s^{\phi_1 \wedge \neg\phi_2} w_s'^\psi \qquad w_s'^\psi = \gamma \sum_{s' \in S} p_{ss'} p_s'^\psi$$

We want $p_s^\psi = 0$ if $p_s'^\psi = 0$. To ensure this, for each $\psi \in subfP(\phi)$ of the form $\phi_1 \, \mathcal{U} \, \phi_2$ and $s \in S$, we introduce the auxiliary variable δ_s^ψ and ensure that the following constraint hold.

$$\delta_s^\psi > 0 \qquad p_s^\psi = \delta_s^\psi p_s'^\psi$$

Let $V(\mathcal{I}, \phi) = \{\delta\} \cup \bigcup_{s,s' \in S}\{p_{ss'}\} \cup \bigcup_{s \in S, \phi' \in subfS(\phi)}\{t_s^{\phi'}, f_s^{\phi'}, u_s^{\phi'}\} \cup \bigcup_{s \in S, \psi \in subfP(\phi)}\{p_s^\psi, w_s^\psi, p_s'^\psi, w_s'^\psi, \delta_s^\psi\}$ denote the set of variables over which the above constraints are described and let $C(\mathcal{I}, \phi)$ denote the above set of constraints.

Lemma 5. *For every solution* $I : V(\mathcal{I}, \phi) \to \mathbb{R}$ *of* $C(\mathcal{I}, \phi)$, *there exists a DTMC* $\mathcal{M} = (S, s_I, \mathbf{P}, L) \in [\mathcal{I}]$ *such that the following holds:*

1. $I(p_{ss'}) = \mathbf{P}(s, s')$ *for any* $s, s' \in S$
2. $t_s^{\phi'}, f_s^{\phi'} \in \{0, 1\}$ *and* $u_s^{\phi'} \in \{-1, 1\}$ *for any* $s \in S$ *and* $\phi' \in subfS(\phi)$
3. $t_s^{\phi'} = 1 \wedge f_s^{\phi'} = 0 \wedge u_s^{\phi'} = 1$ *iff* $s \models_\mathcal{M} \phi'$ *for any* $s \in S$ *and* $\phi' \in subfS(\phi)$
4. $t_s^{\phi'} = 0 \wedge f_s^{\phi'} = 1 \wedge u_s^{\phi'} = -1$ *iff* $s \not\models_\mathcal{M} \phi'$ *for any* $s \in S$ *and* $\phi' \in subfS(\phi)$
5. $p_s^\psi = Prob\{\pi \in Path(s) \mid \pi \models_\mathcal{M} \psi\}$ *for any* $\psi \in subfP(\phi)$

The proof follows from the observations made while setting up the constraints. An immediate consequence of the Lemma 5 is the following theorem.

Theorem 1. *If there exists a solution* I *of* $C(\mathcal{I}, \phi)$ *such that* $I(t_{s_I}^\phi) = 1$, *then there exists an* $\mathcal{M} \in [\mathcal{I}]$ *such that* $\mathcal{M} \models \phi$.

In order to check if $\mathcal{I} \models \phi$, the model checking algorithm sets up the constraints $C(\mathcal{I}, \neg\phi)$ and checks its feasibility. Clearly, checking the feasibility of $C(\mathcal{I}, \neg\phi)$ is equivalent to checking if a sentence with existential quantifiers is valid for the reals; the size of the sentence is polynomial in the size of the UMC. However, the constraints $C(\mathcal{I}, \neg\phi)$ are bilinear constraints, and we need to satisfy the conjunction of all these constraints (not an arbitrary boolean function). The feasibility of such constraints can be more efficiently checked viewing them as *bilinear matrix inequalities* (BMIs) for which algorithms [10, 9] and tools [16] have been developed. (More details can seen in [23].) We also observe that to prove that the model checking problem can be solved in PSPACE, we could have constructed a simpler set of constraints by first guessing the values of the variables $t_s^{\phi'}, u_s^{\phi'}$, and $f_s^{\phi'}$ for the subformulas ϕ', and then solving the constraints resulting from those guesses; since NPSPACE = PSPACE, we can obtain a deterministic algorithm from this. However, we believe that in practice solving this single BMI presented here will be more efficient than solving the exponentially many simpler BMIs that this alternative approach would yield.

5.1   Complexity of Model-Checking UMC

We showed that the model-checking problem for UMC can be reduced to checking the validity of a formula in the existential theory of the reals. Therefore, the model-checking problem of UMC is in PSPACE.

The model checking problem for UMCs is however intractable: we can reduce both the satisfiability and validity of propositional boolean formulas to the model checking problem (details in [23]).

Theorem 2. *The model checking problem for UMC with respect to PCTL is NP-hard and co-NP-hard.*

6   Model-Checking IMDP

We consider the problem of model checking IMDPs in this section. We will solve the problem by showing that we can reduce IMDP model checking to model checking (classical) a Markov Decision Process (MDP) [4, 20]. Before presenting this reduction we recall some basic properties of the feasible solutions of a linear program and the definition of an MDP.

6.1   Linear Programming

Consider an IMDP $\mathcal{I} = (S, s_I, \check{\mathbf{P}}, \hat{\mathbf{P}}, L)$. For a given $s \in S$, let $IE(s)$ be the following set of inequalities over the variables $\{p_{ss'} \mid s' \in S\}$:

$$\sum_{s' \in S} p_{ss'} = 1 \qquad \check{\mathbf{P}}(s, s') \le p_{ss'} \le \hat{\mathbf{P}}(s, s') \text{ for all } s' \in S$$

Definition 4. *A map* $\theta^s : S \to [0, 1]$ *is called a* basic feasible solution (BFS) *to the above set of inequalities* $IE(s)$ *iff* $\{p_{ss'} = \theta^s(s') \mid s' \in S\}$ *is a solution of* $IE(s)$ *and there exists a set* $S' \subseteq S$ *such that* $|S'| \ge |S| - 1$ *and for all* $s' \in S'$ *either* $\theta^s(s') = \check{\mathbf{P}}(s, s')$ *or* $\theta^s(s') = \hat{\mathbf{P}}(s, s')$.

Let Θ^s be the set of all BFS of $IE(s)$. The set of BFS of linear program have the special property that every other feasible solution can be expressed as a linear combination of basic feasible solutions. This is the content of the next proposition.

Proposition 1. *Let* $\{p_{ss'} = \bar{p}_{ss'} \mid s' \in S\}$ *be some solution of* $IE(s)$. *There there are* $0 \le \alpha_{\theta^s} \le 1$ *for all* $\theta^s \in \Theta^s$, *such that*

$$\bar{p}_{ss'} = \sum_{\theta^s \in \Theta^s} \alpha_{\theta^s} \theta^s(s') \text{ for all } s' \in S \qquad and \qquad \sum_{s \in S} \alpha_{\theta^s} = 1$$

Lemma 6. *The number of basic feasible solutions of* $IE(s)$ *in the worst case can be* $O(|S|2^{|S|-1})$.

6.2   Markov Decision Processes (MDP)

A Markov decision process (MDP) is a Markov chain that has non-deterministic transitions, in addition to the probabilistic ones. In this section we formally introduce this model along with some well-known observations about them.

Definition 5. *If S is the set of states of a system, a* next-state probability distribution *is a function $\mu : S \to [0,1]$ such that $\sum_{s \in S} \mu(s) = 1$. For $s \in S$, $p(s)$ represents the probability of making a direct transition to s from the current state.*

Definition 6. *A Markov decision Process (MDP) is a 4-tuple $\mathcal{D} = (S, s_I, \tau, L)$, where*

1. *S is a finite set of states,*
2. *$s_I \in S$ is the initial state,*
3. *$L: S \to 2^{AP}$ is a labeling function that maps states to sets of atomic propositions from a set AP,*
4. *τ is a function which associates to each $s \in S$ a finite set $\tau(s) = \{\mu_1^s, \ldots, \mu_{k_s}^s\}$ of next-state probability distributions for transitions from s.*

A *path* π in an MDP $\mathcal{D} = (S, s_I, \tau, L)$ is a non-empty sequence of the form $s_0 \xrightarrow{\mu_1} s_1 \xrightarrow{\mu_2} \ldots$, where $s_i \in S$, $\mu_{i+1} \in \tau(s_i)$, and $\mu_{i+1}(s_{i+1}) > 0$ for all $i \geq 0$. A path can be either finite or infinite. We use π_{fin} to denote a finite path. Let $last(\pi_{\text{fin}})$ be the last state in the finite path π_{fin}. As in DTMC, we denote the ith state in a path π by $\pi[i] = s_i$. We let $Path(s)$ and $Path_{\text{fin}}(s)$ be the set of all infinite and finite paths, respectively, starting at state s. To associate a probability measure with the paths, we resolve the non-deterministic choices by a randomized *adversary*, which is defined as follows:

Definition 7. *A* randomized adversary A *of an MDP $\mathcal{D}$ is a function mapping every finite path π_{fin} of $\mathcal{D}$ and an element of the set $\tau(last(\pi_{\text{fin}}))$ to $[0,1]$, such that for a given finite path π_{fin} of $\mathcal{D}$, $\sum_{\mu \in \tau(last(\pi_{\text{fin}}))} A(\pi_{\text{fin}}, \mu) = 1$. Let $\mathcal{A}_{\mathcal{D}}$ denote the set of all possible randomized adversaries of the MDP $\mathcal{D}$. Let $Path^A(s)$ denote the subset of $Path(s)$ which corresponds to an adversary A.*

The behavior of an MDP under a given randomized adversary is purely probabilistic. If an MDP has evolved to the state s after starting from the state s_I and following the finite path π_{fin}, then it chooses the next-state distribution $\mu^s \in \tau(s)$ with probability $A(\pi_{\text{fin}}, \mu^s)$. Then it chooses the next state s' with probability $\mu^s(s')$. Thus the probability that a direct transition to s' takes place is $\sum_{\mu^s \in \tau(s)} A(\pi_{\text{fin}}, \mu^s)\mu^s(s')$. Thus as for IMDPs, one can define DTMC $\mathcal{D}^A$ that captures the probabilistic behavior of MDP $\mathcal{D}$ under adversary A and also associate a probability measure on execution paths. Given a MDP $\mathcal{D}$ and a PCTL formula φ, we can define when $\mathcal{D} \models \varphi$ in a way analogous to the IMDPs (see Figure 2).

6.3   The Reduction

We are now ready to describe the model checking algorithm for IMDPs. Consider an IMDP $\mathcal{I} = (S, s_I, \check{\mathbf{P}}, \hat{\mathbf{P}}, L)$. Recall from Section 6.1, we can describe the transition probability distributions from state s that satisfy the range constraints as the feasible solutions of the linear program $IE(s)$. Furthermore, we denote by Θ^s is the set of all BFS of $IE(s)$. Define the following MDP $\mathcal{D} = (S', s'_I, \tau, L')$ where $S' = S$, $s'_I = s_I$, $L' = L$, and for all $s \in S$, $\tau(s) = \Theta^s$. Observe that $\mathcal{D}$ is exponentially sized in $\mathcal{I}$, since $\tau(s)$ is exponential (see Lemma 6).

The main observation behind the reduction is that the MDP $\mathcal{D}$ "captures" all the possible behaviors of the IMDP $\mathcal{I}$. This is the formal content of the next proposition.

Proposition 2. *For any adversary A for $\mathcal{I}$, we can define a randomized adversary A' such that $Prob_s^{\mathcal{I}^A} = Prob_s^{\mathcal{D}^{A'}}$ for every s, where $Prob_s^{X^A}$ is measure on paths from s defined by machine X under A. Similarly for every adversary A for $\mathcal{D}$, we can find an adversary A' for $\mathcal{I}$ that defines the same probability measure on paths.*

Proof. Consider an adversary A for $\mathcal{I}$. For a path π_{fin} let $A(\pi_{\text{fin}}) = \mu \in Steps(last(\pi_{\text{fin}}))$. We know from Proposition 1, that there are α_{θ^s} for $\theta^s \in \Theta^s$ such that

$$\mu(s') = \sum_{\theta^s \in \Theta^s} \alpha_{\theta^s} \theta^s(s') \text{ for all } s' \in S \qquad \text{and} \qquad \sum_{s \in S} \alpha_{\theta^s} = 1$$

We now define $A'(\pi_{\text{fin}}, \theta^s) = \alpha_{\theta^s}$. It is straightforward to see that $Prob_s^{\mathcal{I}^A} = Prob_s^{\mathcal{D}^{A'}}$. The converse direction also can be proved similarly. □

An important consequence of the above observation is the following main theorem.

Theorem 3. *For any PCTL formula φ, $\mathcal{I} \models \varphi$ iff $\mathcal{D} \models \varphi$.*

Thus, in order to model check IMDP $\mathcal{I}$, we can model check the MDP $\mathcal{D}$ for which algorithms are known [4, 20]. The algorithms for MDP run in time (and space) which is polynomial in the size of the MDP. Thus, if we directly model check $\mathcal{D}$ we get an EXP-TIME model checking algorithm for $\mathcal{I}$. However, we can improve this to get a PSPACE algorithm. The reason for this is that it is known that as far as model checking MDPs is concerned, we can restrict our attention to *deterministic, memoryless* adversaries, i.e., adversaries that always pick the same single non-deterministic choice whenever a state is visited.

Proposition 3 ([4, 20]). *Let $\mathcal{A}_{\text{det}}$ be the set of deterministic, memoryless adversaries for MDP $\mathcal{D}$, i.e., for all $A \in \mathcal{A}_{\text{det}}$, $A(s, \mu) = 1$ for exactly one $\mu \in \tau(s)$. Consider a PCTL formula $\varphi = \mathcal{P}_{\bowtie p}(\psi)$ such that the truth or falsity of every subformula of ψ in every state of $\mathcal{D}$ is already determined. Then $\mathcal{D} \models \varphi$ iff $\mathcal{D}^A \models \varphi$ for all $A \in \mathcal{A}_{\text{det}}$.*

For every subformula of the form $\mathcal{P}_{\bowtie p}(\psi)$, our model checking algorithm, will model check each of the DTMCs $\mathcal{D}^A$, where A is a deterministic, memoryless adversary. This will give us the desired PSPACE algorithm.

Theorem 4. *The model-checking algorithm for IMDP is in PSPACE.*

Proof. From Lemma 6, we know that the total number of BFSs is $O(|S|2^{|S|-1})$. Hence the total number of DTMCs $\mathcal{D}^A$ for $A \in \mathcal{A}_{\text{det}}$ is $O(|S|^{|S|}2^{|S|^2-|S|})$. By reusing space for every subformula $\mathcal{P}_{\bowtie p}(\psi)$, all of these model checking problems can be solved in PSPACE. □

6.4   Iterative Algorithm

The above PSPACE algorithm is computationally expensive for large IMDPs. There-fore, we propose an alternative iterative algorithm motivated by a similar algorithm in [2].

The iterative model checking algorithm for PCTL over IMDPs works exactly as for DTMCs with the exception of handling of $\mathcal{P}_{\bowtie p}(\psi)$. For these, we need to check if $p_s^A(\psi) = Prob_s^A(\{\pi \in Path^A(s) \mid \pi \models \psi\})$ satisfies the bound $\bowtie p$ for all adver-saries $A \in \mathcal{A}_\mathcal{I}$. Let $p_s^{\max}(\psi)$ and $p_s^{\min}(\psi)$ be the *minimum* or *maximum* probability, respectively, for all adversaries $A \in \mathcal{A}_\mathcal{I}$, i.e.,

$$p_s^{\max}(\psi) \stackrel{\text{def}}{=} \sup_{A \in \mathcal{A}_\mathcal{I}}[p_s^A(\psi)], \quad p_s^{\min}(\psi) \stackrel{\text{def}}{=} \inf_{A \in \mathcal{A}_\mathcal{I}}[p_s^A(\psi)].$$

Then if $\bowtie \in \{<, \leq\}$,

$$Sat(\mathcal{P}_{\bowtie p}(\psi)) = \{s \in S \mid p_s^{\max}(\psi) \bowtie p\}$$

and if $\bowtie \in \{>, \geq\}$,

$$Sat(\mathcal{P}_{\bowtie p}(\psi)) = \{s \in S \mid p_s^{\min}(\psi) \bowtie p\}$$

We next describe how to compute the values $p_s^{\max}(\psi)$ and $p_s^{\min}(\psi)$ for $\psi = X\phi$ and $\psi = \phi_1 \mathcal{U} \phi_2$. Recall that Θ^s is the set of all BFS of $IE(s)$. It can be shown following [2] that $p_s^{\max} = \lim_{n \to \infty} p_s^{\max(n)}$ where:

$$p_s^{\max(n)} = \begin{cases} 1 & \text{if } s \in S^{\text{yes}} \\ 0 & \text{if } s \in S^{\text{no}} \\ 0 & \text{if } s \in S^? \text{ and } n = 0 \\ \max_{\{\bar{p}_{ss'} \mid s' \in S\} \in \Theta^s} \left\{ \sum_{s' \in S} \bar{p}_{ss'} \cdot p_{s'}^{\max(n-1)} \right\} & \\ & \text{if } s \in S^? \text{ and } n > 0 \end{cases}$$

and $p_s^{\min} = \lim_{n \to \infty} p_s^{\min(n)}$ where:

$$p_s^{\min(n)} = \begin{cases} 1 & \text{if } s \in S^{\text{yes}} \\ 0 & \text{if } s \in S^{\text{no}} \\ 0 & \text{if } s \in S^? \text{ and } n = 0 \\ \min_{\{\bar{p}_{ss'} \mid s' \in S\} \in \Theta^s} \left\{ \sum_{s' \in S} \bar{p}_{ss'} \cdot p_{s'}^{\min(n-1)} \right\} & \\ & \text{if } s \in S^? \text{ and } n > 0 \end{cases}$$

Note that although the size of Θ^s can be $O(|S|2^{|S|-1})$ (by Lemma 6), the computa-tion of the expressions

$$\max_{\{\bar{p}_{ss'} \mid s' \in S\} \in \Theta^s} \left\{ \sum_{s' \in S} \bar{p}_{ss'} \cdot p_{s'}^{\max(n-1)} \right\} \text{ or } \min_{\{\bar{p}_{ss'} \mid s' \in S\} \in \Theta^s} \left\{ \sum_{s' \in S} \bar{p}_{ss'} \cdot p_{s'}^{\min(n-1)} \right\}$$

$$(5)$$

can be done in $O(|S|)$ time as follows:

We consider the ordering $s_1, s_2, \ldots, s_{|S|}$ of the states of S such that $p_{s_1}^{\max(n-1)}, p_{s_2}^{\max(n-1)}, \ldots, p_{s_{|S|}}^{\max(n-1)}$ is in descending order. Then the following result holds.

Lemma 7.

a) *There exists an* $1 \leq i \leq |S|$ *such that* $\{\hat{\mathbf{P}}(s, s_1), \ldots, \hat{\mathbf{P}}(s, s_{i-1}), q, \check{\mathbf{P}}(s, s_{i+1}),$
$\ldots, \check{\mathbf{P}}(s, s_{|S|})\}$ *is a BFS of IE(s), where* $q = 1 - \sum_{1 \leq j \leq (i-1)} \hat{\mathbf{P}}(s, s_j) - \sum_{(i+1) \leq j \leq |S|} \check{\mathbf{P}}(s, s_j)$.

b) *and for that* i

$$\max_{\{\bar{p}_{ss'} | s' \in S\} \in \Theta^s} \left\{ \sum_{s' \in S} \bar{p}_{ss'} \cdot p_{s'}^{\max(n-1)} \right\} = p_{s_i}^{\max(n-1)} \cdot q$$

$$+ \sum_{1 \leq j \leq (i-1)} p_{s_j}^{\max(n-1)} \cdot \hat{\mathbf{P}}(s, s_j) + \sum_{(i+1) \leq j \leq |S|} p_{s_j}^{\max(n-1)} \cdot \check{\mathbf{P}}(s, s_j)$$

Proof.
a) Let i_0 be defined as follows:

$$i_0 = \min\{i \mid \sum_{j=1}^{i} \hat{\mathbf{P}}(s, s_j) + \sum_{j=i+1}^{|S|} \check{\mathbf{P}}(s, s_j) \geq 1\}$$

Observe that such an i_0 must exist if the IMDP is well-defined. Consider the solution $\{\hat{\mathbf{P}}(s, s_1), \ldots, \hat{\mathbf{P}}(s, s_{i_0-1}), q, \check{\mathbf{P}}(s, s_{i_0+1}), \ldots, \check{\mathbf{P}}(s, s_{|S|})\}$ where $q = 1 - \sum_{1 \leq j \leq (i_0-1)} \hat{\mathbf{P}}(s, s_j) - \sum_{(i_0+1) \leq j \leq |S|} \check{\mathbf{P}}(s, s_j)$. This solution is a BFS of IE(s).

b) Let $\{\bar{p}_{ss_1}, \ldots, \bar{p}_{ss_{|S|}}\}$ be any solution (it may be BFS or not) of IE(s). Then by simple algebraic simplification it can be shown that

$$\sum_{1 \leq j \leq (i-1)} p_{s_j}^{\max(n-1)} \cdot \hat{\mathbf{P}}(s, s_j) + p_{s_i}^{\max(n-1)} \cdot q + \sum_{(i+1) \leq j \leq |S|} p_{s_j}^{\max(n-1)} \cdot \check{\mathbf{P}}(s, s_j) \geq \sum_{s' \in S} \bar{p}_{ss'} \cdot p_{s'}^{\max(n-1)}$$

given the fact that $p_{s_1}^{\max(n-1)} \geq p_{s_2}^{\max(n-1)} \geq \ldots \geq p_{s_{|S|}}^{\max(n-1)}$, and $\check{\mathbf{P}}(s, s') \leq \bar{p}_{ss'} \leq \hat{\mathbf{P}}(s, s')$ for all $s' \in S$.   □

Similarly, if we consider the ordering $s_1, s_2, \ldots, s_{|S|}$ of the states of S such that $p_{s_1}^{\min(n-1)}, p_{s_2}^{\min(n-1)}, \ldots, p_{s_{|S|}}^{\min(n-1)}$ is in ascending order, then the above Lemma holds with max replaced by min.

The expressions (5) can be computed in $O(|S|)$ time by finding an i as in Lemma 7.

6.5   Lower Bound for IMDP Model-Checking

We can show that the model checking problem for IMDPs is P-hard. The result follows from observing that the problem of determining the truth value of propositional logic formula under an assignment (which is known to be P-complete) can be reduced to the PCTL model checking problem of DTMCs; since DTMCs are special IMDPs, the result follows. The details can be found in [23].

7   Conclusion

We have investigated the PCTL model checking problem for two semantic interpretations of IDTMCs, namely UMC and IMDP. We proved the upper bounds and the lower bounds on the complexity of the model checking problem for these models. Our bounds however are not tight. Finding tight lower and upper bounds for these model-checking problems is an interesting open problem.

Acknowledgment

We would like to thank anonymous referees and Timo Latvala for providing valuable comments. This work is supported in part by the ONR Grant N00014-02-1-0715, the NSF Grants NSF CNS 05-09321, NSF CCF 04-29639, NSF CCF 04-48178, and the Motorola Grant Motorola RPF #23.

References

1. A. Aziz, V. Singhal, R. K. Brayton, and A. L. Sangiovanni-Vincentelli. It usually works: The temporal logic of stochastic systems. In *Proc. of Computer Aided Verification*, volume 939, pages 155–165, 1995.
2. C. Baier. On algorithmic verification methods for probabilistic systems. Habilitation Thesis. Fakultät für Mathematik and Informatik, Universität Mannheim, 1998.
3. C. Baier and M. Z. Kwiatkowska. Model checking for a probabilistic branching time logic with fairness. *Distributed Computing*, 11(3):125–155, 1998.
4. A. Bianco and L. de Alfaro. Model checking of probabilistic and nondeterministic systems. In *Proceedings of 15th Conference on the Foundations of Software Technology and Theoretical Computer Science (FSTTCS'95)*, volume 1026 of *LNCS*.
5. L. Blum, M. Shub, and S. Smale. On a theory of computation and complexity over real numbers: NP-completeness, recursive functions and universal machines. *Bulletin of the American Mathematical Society*, 21:1–46, 1989.
6. J. Canny. Some algebraic and geometric computations in PSPACE. In *20th ACM Symposium on Theory of Computing (STOC'88)*, pages 460–467, 1988.
7. C. Courcoubetis and M. Yannakakis. Markov decision processes and regular events. In *Proceedings of the seventeenth international colloquium on Automata, languages and programming*, pages 336–349, 1990.
8. C. Courcoubetis and M. Yannakakis. The complexity of probabilistic verification. *Journal of ACM*, 42(4):857–907, 1995.
9. M. Fukuda and M. Kojima. Branch-and-cut algorithms for the bilinear matrix inequality eigenvalue problem. *Comput. Optim. Appl.*, 19(1):79–105, 2001.
10. K. C. Goh, M. G. Safonov, and G. P. Papavassilopoulos. Global optimization for the biaffine matrix inequality problem. *Journal of Global Optimization*, 7:365–380, 1995.
11. H. Hansson and B. Jonsson. A logic for reasoning about time and reliability. *Formal Aspects of Computing*, 6(5):512–535, 1994.
12. B. Jonsson and K. G. Larsen. Specification and refinement of probabilistic processes. In *Proceedings of the IEEE Symposium on Logic in Computer Science*, pages 266–277, 1991.
13. J. Kemeny, J. Snell, and A. Knapp. *Denumerable Markov chains*. Springer, 1976.
14. I. O. Kozine and L. V. Utkin. Interval-valued finite markov chains. *Reliable Computing*, 8(2):97–113, 2002.

15. V. P. Kuznetsov. Interval statistical models. *Radio and Communication*, 1991.

16. PENbmi. http://www.penopt.com/.

17. M. Puterman. *Markov decision processes: discrete stochastic dynamic programming*. Wiley, New York, 1994.

18. J. Renegar. A faster pspace algorithm for deciding the existential theory of the reals. In *29th Annual IEEE Symposium on Foundations of Computer Science*, pages 291–295, 1988.

19. J. Rutten, M. Kwiatkowska, G. Norman, and D. Parker. *Mathematical Techniques for Analyzing Concurrent and Probabilistic Systems*, volume 23 of *CRM Monograph Series*. American Mathematical Society, 2004.

20. R. Segala. *Modeling and Verification of Randomized Distributed Real-Time Systems*. PhD thesis, MIT, 1995.

21. R. Segala and N. A. Lynch. Probabilistic simulations for probabilistic processes. In *International Conference on Concurrency Theory*, pages 481–496, 1994.

22. K. Sen, M. Viswanathan, and G. Agha. Statistical model checking of black-box probabilistic systems. In *16th conference on Computer Aided Verification (CAV'04)*, volume 3114 of *LNCS*, pages 202–215, 2004.

23. K. Sen, M. Viswanathan, and G. Agha. Model-checking markov chains in the presence of uncertainties. Technical Report UIUCDCS-R-2006-2677, UIUC, 2006.

24. O. Toker and H. Özbay. On the NP-hardness of solving bilinear matrix in equalities and simultaneous stabilization with static output feedback. In *Proc. of American Control Conference*, 1995.

25. M. Y. Vardi. Automatic verification of probabilistic concurrent finite-state programs. In *26th Annual Symposium on Foundations of Computer Science*, pages 327–338. IEEE, 1985.

26. P. Walley. Measures of uncertainty in expert systems. *Artificial Intelligence*, 83:1–58, 1996.

Safety Metric Temporal Logic Is Fully Decidable

Joël Ouaknine and James Worrell

Oxford University Computing Laboratory, UK
{joel, jbw}@comlab.ox.ac.uk

Abstract. Metric Temporal Logic (MTL) is a widely-studied real-time extension of Linear Temporal Logic. In this paper we consider a fragment of MTL, called Safety MTL, capable of expressing properties such as invariance and time-bounded response. Our main result is that the satisfiability problem for Safety MTL is decidable. This is the first positive decidability result for MTL over timed ω-words that does not involve restricting the precision of the timing constraints, or the granularity of the semantics; the proof heavily uses the techniques of infinite-state verification. Combining this result with some of our previous work, we conclude that Safety MTL is *fully decidable* in that its satisfiability, model checking, and refinement problems are all decidable.

1 Introduction

Timed automata and real-time temporal logics provide the foundation for several well-known and mature tools for verifying timed and hybrid systems [21]. Despite this success in practice, certain aspects of the real-time theory are notably less well-behaved than in the untimed case. In particular, timed automata are not determinisable, and their language inclusion problem is undecidable [4]. In similar fashion, the model-checking problems for (linear-time) real-time logics such as *Metric Temporal Logic* and *Timed Propositional Temporal Logic* are also undecidable [5, 6, 17].

For this reason, much interest has focused on *fully decidable* real-time specification formalisms. We explain this term in the present context as follows. We represent a computation of a real-time system as a *timed word*: a sequence of instantaneous events, together with their associated timestamps. A specification denotes a *timed language*: a set of allowable timed words. Then a formalism (a logic or class of automata) is fully decidable if it defines a class of timed languages that is closed under finite unions and intersections and has a decidable language-inclusion problem[1]. Note that language emptiness and universality are special cases of language inclusion.

In this paper we are concerned in particular with Metric Temporal Logic (MTL), one of the most widely known real-time logics. MTL is a variant of

---

[1] This phrase was coined in [12] with a slightly more general meaning: a specification formalism closed under finite unions, finite intersections and complementation, and for which language emptiness is decidable. However, since the main use of complementation in this context is in deciding language inclusion, we feel that our definition is in the same spirit.

H. Hermanns and J. Palsberg (Eds.): TACAS 2006, LNCS 3920, pp. 411–425, 2006.

Linear Temporal Logic in which the temporal operators are replaced by time-constrained versions. For example, the formula $\Box_{[0,5]}\varphi$ expresses that φ holds for the next 5 time units. Until recently, the only positive decidability results for MTL involved placing syntactic restrictions on the precision of the timing constraints, or restricting the granularity of the semantics. For example, [5, 12, 19] ban punctual timing constraints, such as $\Diamond_{=1}\varphi$ (φ is true in exactly one time unit). Semantic restrictions include adopting an integer-time model, as in [6, 11], or a bounded-variation dense-time model, as in [22]. These restrictions guarantee that a formula has a finite tableau: in fact they yield decision procedures for model checking and satisfiability that use exponential space in the size of the formula. However, both the satisfiability and model checking problems are undecidable in the unrestricted logic, cf. [5, 17].

The main contribution of this paper is to identify a new fully decidable fragment of MTL, called *Safety MTL*. Safety MTL consists of those MTL formulas which, when expressed in negation normal form, are such that the interval I is bounded in every instance of the constrained until operator $\mathcal{U}_I$ and the constrained eventually operator $\Diamond_I$. For example, the time-bounded response formula $\Box(a \to \Diamond_{=1}b)$ (every a-event is followed after one time unit by a b-event) is in Safety MTL, but not $\Box(a \to \Diamond_{(1,\infty)}b)$. Because we place no limit on the precision of the timing constraints or the granularity of the semantics, the tableau of a Safety MTL formula may have infinitely many states. However, using techniques from infinite-state verification, we show that the restriction to safety properties facilitates an effective analysis.

In [16] we already gave a procedure for model checking Alur-Dill timed automata against Safety MTL formulas. As a special case we obtained the decidability of the *validity* problem for Safety MTL ('Is a given formula satisfied by every timed word?'). The two main contributions of the present paper complement this result, and show that Safety MTL is fully decidable. We show the decidability of the *satisfiability problem* ('Is a given Safety MTL formula satisfied by some timed word?') and, more generally, we claim decidability of the *refinement problem* ('Given two Safety MTL formulas φ_1 and φ_2, does every timed word that satisfies φ_1 also satisfy φ_2?'). Note that Safety MTL is not closed under negation, so neither of these results follow trivially from the decidability of validity.

Closely related to MTL are *timed alternating automata*, introduced in [15, 16]. Both cited works show that the language-emptiness problem for one-clock timed alternating automata over finite timed words is decidable. This result is the foundation of the above-mentioned model-checking procedure for Safety MTL. The procedure involves translating the negation of a Safety MTL formula φ into a one-clock timed alternating automaton over finite words that accepts all the *bad prefixes* of φ. (Every infinite timed word that fails to satisfy a Safety MTL formula φ has a *finite bad prefix*, that is, a finite prefix none of whose extensions satisfies φ.) In contrast, the results in the present paper involve considering timed alternating automata over infinite timed words.

Our main technical contribution is to show the decidability of language-emptiness over infinite timed words for a class of timed alternating automata rich enough to capture Safety MTL formulas. A key restriction is that we only consider automata in which every state is accepting. We have recently shown that language emptiness is undecidable for one-clock alternating automata with Büchi or even weak parity acceptance conditions [17]. Thus the restriction to safety properties is crucial.

As in [16], we make use of the notion of a *well-structured transition system (WSTS)* [9] to give our decision procedure. However, whereas the algorithm in [16] involved reduction to a reachability problem on a WSTS, here we reduce to a fair nontermination problem on a WSTS. The fairness requirement is connected to the assumption that timed words are non-Zeno. Indeed, we remark that our results provide a rare example of a decidable nontermination problem on an infinite-state system with a nontrivial fairness condition. For comparison, undecidability results for nontermination under various different fairness conditions for Lossy Channel Systems, Timed Networks, and Timed Petri Nets can be found in [2, 3].

Related Work. An important distinction among real-time models is whether one records the *state* of the system of interest at every instant in time, leading to an *interval semantics* [5, 12, 19], or whether one only sees a countable sequence of instantaneous *events*, leading to a *point-based* or *trace semantics* [4, 6, 7, 10, 11, 22]. In the interval semantics the temporal operators of MTL quantify over the whole time domain, whereas in the point-based semantics they quantify over a countable set of positions in a timed word. For this reason the interval semantics is more natural for reasoning about states, whereas the point-based semantics is more natural for reasoning about events. In this paper we adopt the latter.

MTL and Safety MTL do not differ in terms of their decidability in the interval semantics: Alur, Feder, and Henzinger [5] showed that the satisfiability problem for MTL is undecidable, and it is easy to see that their proof directly carries over to Safety MTL. We pointed out in [16] that the same proof does not apply in the point-based semantics, and we recently gave a different argument to show that MTL is undecidable in this setting. However, our proof crucially uses a 'liveness formula' of the form $\Box\Diamond p$, and it does not apply to Safety MTL. The results in this paper confirm that by excising such formulas we obtain a fully decidable logic in the point-based setting.

2   Metric Temporal Logic

In this section we define the syntax and semantics of Metric Temporal Logic (MTL). As discussed above, we adopt a point-based semantics over timed words.

A *time sequence* $\tau = \tau_0\tau_1\tau_2\ldots$ is an infinite nondecreasing sequence of time values $\tau_i \in \mathbb{R}_{\geq 0}$. Here it is helpful to adopt the convention that $\tau_{-1} = 0$. If $\{\tau_i : i \in \mathbb{N}\}$ is bounded then we say that τ is *Zeno*, otherwise we say that τ is *non-Zeno*. A *timed word* over finite alphabet Σ is a pair $\rho = (\sigma, \tau)$, where $\sigma = \sigma_0\sigma_1\ldots$ is an infinite word over Σ and τ is a time sequence. We also represent

a timed word as a sequence of *timed events* by writing $\rho = (\sigma_0, \tau_0)(\sigma_1, \tau_1) \ldots$.
Finally, we write $T\Sigma^\omega$ for the set of non-Zeno timed words over Σ.

Definition 1. *Given an alphabet Σ of atomic events, the formulas of MTL are built up from Σ by monotone Boolean connectives and time-constrained versions of the **next** operator $\bigcirc$, **until** operator $\mathcal{U}$ and the **dual until** operator $\tilde{\mathcal{U}}$ as follows:*

$$\varphi ::= \top \mid \bot \mid \varphi_1 \wedge \varphi_2 \mid \varphi_1 \vee \varphi_2 \mid a \mid \bigcirc_I \varphi \mid \varphi_1 \, \mathcal{U}_I \, \varphi_2 \mid \varphi_1 \, \tilde{\mathcal{U}}_I \, \varphi_2$$

where $a \in \Sigma$, and $I \subseteq \mathbb{R}_{\geq 0}$ is an open, closed, or half-open interval with endpoints in $\mathbb{N} \cup \{\infty\}$.

  Safety MTL is the fragment of MTL obtained by requiring that the interval I in each 'until' operator $\mathcal{U}_I$ have finite length. (Note that no restriction is placed on the dual until operators $\tilde{\mathcal{U}}_I$ or next operators $\bigcirc_I$.)

Additional temporal operators are defined using the usual conventions. We have the *constrained eventually* operator $\Diamond_I \varphi \equiv \top \, \mathcal{U}_I \, \varphi$, and the *constrained always* operator $\Box_I \varphi \equiv \bot \, \tilde{\mathcal{U}}_I \, \varphi$. We use pseudo-arithmetic expressions to denote intervals. For example, the expression '$= 1$' denotes the interval $[1,1]$. In case $I = [0, \infty)$ we simply omit the annotation I on temporal operators. Finally, given $a \in \Sigma$, we write $\neg a$ for $\bigvee_{b \in \Sigma \setminus \{a\}} b$.

Definition 2. *Given a timed word $\rho = (\sigma, \tau)$ and an MTL formula φ, the satisfaction relation $(\rho, i) \models \varphi$ (read ρ satisfies φ at position i) is defined as follows:*

- *$(\rho, i) \models a$ iff $\sigma_i = a$*
- *$(\rho, i) \models \varphi_1 \wedge \varphi_2$ iff $(\rho, i) \models \varphi_1$ and $(\rho, i) \models \varphi_2$*
- *$(\rho, i) \models \varphi_1 \vee \varphi_2$ iff $(\rho, i) \models \varphi_1$ or $(\rho, i) \models \varphi_2$*
- *$(\rho, i) \models \bigcirc_I \varphi$ iff $\tau_{i+1} - \tau_i \in I$ and $(\rho, i + 1) \models \varphi$*
- *$(\rho, i) \models \varphi_1 \, \mathcal{U}_I \, \varphi_2$ iff there exists $j \geq i$ such that $(\rho, j) \models \varphi_2$, $\tau_j - \tau_i \in I$, and $(\rho, k) \models \varphi_1$ for all k with $i \leq k < j$.*
- *$(\rho, i) \models \varphi_1 \, \tilde{\mathcal{U}}_I \, \varphi_2$ iff for all $j \geq i$ such that $\tau_j - \tau_i \in I$, either $(\rho, j) \models \varphi_2$ or there exists k with $i \leq k < j$ and $(\rho, k) \models \varphi_1$.*

We say that ρ satisfies φ, denoted $\rho \models \varphi$, if $(\rho, 0) \models \varphi$. The **language** of φ is the set $L(\varphi) = \{\rho \in T\Sigma^\omega : \rho \models \varphi\}$ of non-Zeno words that satisfy φ.

Example 1. Consider an alphabet $\Sigma = \{req_i, aq_i, rel_i : i = X, Y\}$ denoting the actions of two processes X and Y that request, acquire, and release a lock. The following formulas are all in Safety MTL.

- $\Box(aq_X \rightarrow \Box_{<3} \neg aq_Y)$ says that Y cannot acquire the lock less than 3 seconds after X acquires the lock.
- $\Box(aq_X \rightarrow rel_X \, \tilde{\mathcal{U}}_{<3} \, \neg aq_Y)$ says that Y cannot acquire the lock less than 3 seconds after X acquires the lock, unless X first releases it.
- $\Box(req_X \rightarrow \Diamond_{<2}(aq_X \wedge \Diamond_{=1} rel_X))$ says that whenever X requests the lock, it acquires the lock within 2 seconds and releases it exactly one second later.

3   Timed Alternating Automata

In this paper, following [15, 16], a timed alternating automaton is an alternating automaton augmented with a single clock variable[2].

We use x to denote the single clock variable of an automaton. A *clock constraint* is a term of the form $x \bowtie c$, where $c \in \mathbb{N}$ and $\bowtie \in \{<, \leqslant, \geqslant, >\}$. Given a set S of *locations*, $\Phi(S)$ denotes the set of formulas generated from S and the set of clock constraints by positive Boolean connectives and variable binding. Thus $\Phi(S)$ is generated by the grammar

$$\varphi ::= s \mid x \bowtie c \mid \top \mid \bot \mid \varphi_1 \wedge \varphi_2 \mid \varphi_1 \vee \varphi_2 \mid x.\varphi,$$

where $s \in S$ and $x.\varphi$ binds x to 0 in φ.

In the definition of a timed alternating automaton, below, the transition function δ maps each location $s \in S$ and event $a \in \Sigma$ to an expression in $\Phi(S)$. Thus alternating automata allow two modes of branching: existential branching, represented by disjunction, and universal branching, represented by conjunction. Variable binding corresponds to the automaton resetting x to 0. For example, $\delta(s, a) = (x < 1) \wedge s \wedge x.t$ means that when the automaton is in location s with clock value less than 1, it can make a simultaneous a-labelled transition to locations s and t, resetting the clock as it enters t.

Definition 3. *A* timed alternating automaton *is a tuple* $\mathcal{A} = (\Sigma, S, s_0, \delta)$, *where*

- Σ *is a finite alphabet*
- S *is a finite set of locations*
- $s_0 \in S$ *is the initial location*
- $\delta : S \times \Sigma \to \Phi(S)$ *is the transition function.*

We consider all locations of $\mathcal{A}$ to be accepting.

The following example illustrates how a timed alternating automaton accepts a language of timed words.

Example 2. We define an automaton $\mathcal{A}$ over the alphabet $\Sigma = \{a, b\}$ that accepts all those timed words in which every a-event is followed one time unit later by a b-event. $\mathcal{A}$ has three locations $\{s, t, u\}$, with s the initial location. The transition function δ is given by the following table:

	a	b
s	$s \wedge x.t$	s
t	$t \wedge (x \leqslant 1)$	$(t \wedge (x < 1)) \vee (u \wedge (x = 1))$
u	u	u

A run of $\mathcal{A}$ starts in location s. Every time an a-event occurs, the automaton makes a simultaneous transition to both s and t, thus opening up a new thread

---

[2] Virtually all decision problems, and in particular language emptiness, are undecidable for alternating automata with more than one clock.

of computation. The automaton resets a fresh copy of clock x when it moves from location s to t, and in location t it only performs transitions as long as the clock does not exceed one. Therefore if location t is entered at some point in a non-Zeno run, it must eventually be exited. Inspecting the transition table, we see that the only way for this to happen is if a b-event occurs exactly one time unit after the a-event that spawned the t-state.

Next we proceed to the formal definition of a run.

Define a *tree* to be a directed acyclic graph (V, E) with a distinguished *root node* such that every node is reachable by a unique finite path from the root. It is clear that every tree admits a stratification, $level : V \to \mathbb{N}$, such that $v \mathrel{E} v'$ implies $level(v') = level(v) + 1$ and the root has level 0.

Let $\mathcal{A} = (\Sigma, S, s_0, \delta)$ be an automaton. A *state* of $\mathcal{A}$ is a pair (s, ν), where $s \in S$ is a location and $\nu \in \mathbb{R}_{\geq 0}$ is the clock value. Write $Q = S \times \mathbb{R}_{\geq 0}$ for the set of all states. A finite set of states is a *configuration*. Given a clock value ν, we define a satisfaction relation $\models_\nu$ between configurations and formulas in $\Phi(S)$ according to the intuition that state (s, ν) can make an a-transition to configuration C if $C \models_\nu \delta(s, a)$. The definition of $C \models_\nu \varphi$ is given by induction on $\varphi \in \Phi(S)$ as follows: $C \models_\nu t$ if $(t, \nu) \in C$, $C \models_\nu x \bowtie c$ if $\nu \bowtie c$, $C \models_\nu x.\varphi$ if $C \models_0 \varphi$, and we handle the Boolean connectives in $\Phi(S)$ in the obvious way.

Definition 4. *A **run** Δ of $\mathcal{A}$ on a timed word (σ, τ) consists of a tree (V, E) and a labelling function $l : V \to Q$ such that if $l(v) = (s, \nu)$ for some level-n node $v \in V$, then $\{l(v') \mid v \mathrel{E} v'\} \models_{\nu'} \delta(s, \sigma_n)$, where $\nu' = \nu + (\tau_n - \tau_{n-1})$.*

*The **language** of $\mathcal{A}$, denoted $L(\mathcal{A})$, consists of all non-Zeno words over which $\mathcal{A}$ has a run whose root is labelled $(s_0, 0)$.*

Figure 1 depicts part of a run of the automaton $\mathcal{A}$ from Example 2 on the timed word $\langle (a, 0.3), (b, 0.5), (a, 0.8), (b, 1.3), (b, 1.8) \ldots \rangle$.

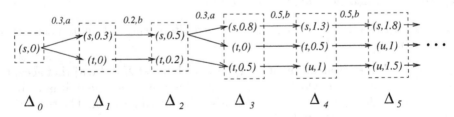

Fig. 1. Consecutive levels in a run of $\mathcal{A}$

One typically applies the acceptance condition in an alternating automaton to all paths in the run tree [20]. In the present context, since every location is accepting, the tree structure plays no role in the definition of acceptance; in this respect, a run could be viewed simply as a sequence of configurations. This motivates the following definition.

Definition 5. *Given a run $\Delta = ((V, E), l)$ of $\mathcal{A}$, for each $n \in \mathbb{N}$ the configuration $\Delta_n = \{l(v) \mid v \in V, level(v) = n\}$ consists of the states at level n in Δ (cf. the dashed boxes in Figure 1).*

The reader may wonder why we mention trees at all in Definition 4. The reason is quite subtle: the tree structure is convenient for expressing a certain fairness property (cf. Lemma 2) that allows a Zeno run to be transformed into a non-Zeno run by inserting extra time delays.

Definition 4 only allows runs that start in a single state. More generally, we allow runs that start in an arbitrary configuration $C = \{(s_i, \nu_i)\}_{i \in I}$. Such a run is a *forest* consisting of $|I|$ different run trees, where the i-th run starts at (s_i, ν_i).

3.1   Translating Safety MTL into Timed Automata

Given a Safety MTL formula φ, one can define a timed alternating automaton $\mathcal{A}_\varphi$ such that $L(\mathcal{A}_\varphi) = L(\varphi)$. Since space is restricted, and since we have already given a similar translation in [16], we refer the reader to [18] for details. However, we draw the reader's attention to two important points. First, it is the restriction to timed-bounded until operators combined with the adoption of a non-Zeno semantics that allows us to translate a Safety MTL formula into an automaton in which every location is accepting; this is illustrated in Example 2, where location t, corresponding to the response formula $\Diamond_{=1} b$, is accepting. Secondly, we point out that each automaton $\mathcal{A}_\varphi$ is *local* according to the definition below. This last observation is important because it is the class of local automata for which Section 5 shows decidability of language emptiness.

Definition 6. *An automaton $\mathcal{A} = (\Sigma, S, s_0, \delta)$ is **local** if for each $s \in S$ and $a \in \Sigma$, each location $t \neq s$ appearing in $\delta(s, a)$ lies within the scope of a reset quantifier $x.(-)$, i.e., the automaton resets the clock whenever it changes location.*

We call such automata local because the static and dynamic scope of any reset quantification agree, i.e., the scope does not 'extend' across transitions to different locations. An investigation of the different expressiveness of local and non-local temporal logics is carried out in [8].

4   The Region Automaton

Throughout this section let $\mathcal{A} = (\Sigma, S, s_0, \delta)$ be a timed alternating automaton, and let c_{max} be the maximum constant appearing in a clock constraint in $\mathcal{A}$.

4.1   Abstract Configurations

We partition the set $\mathbb{R}_{\geq 0}$ of nonnegative real numbers into the set $REG = \{r_0, r_1, \ldots, r_{2c_{max}+1}\}$ of *regions*, where $r_{2i} = \{i\}$ for $i \leq c_{max}$, $r_{2i+1} = (i, i+1)$ for $i < c_{max}$, and $r_{2c_{max}+1} = (c_{max}, \infty)$. The *successor* of each region is given by $succ(r_i) = r_{i+1}$ for $i < 2c_{max} + 1$ and $succ(r_{2c_{max}+1}) = r_{2c_{max}+1}$. Henceforth let r_{max} denote $r_{2c_{max}+1}$ and write $reg(u)$ to denote the region containing $u \in \mathbb{R}_{\geq 0}$.

The *fractional part* of a nonnegative real $x \in \mathbb{R}_{\geq 0}$ is $frac(x) = x - \lfloor x \rfloor$.

We use the regions to define a discrete representation of configurations that abstracts away from precise clock values, recording only their values to the nearest integer and the relative order of their fractional parts, cf. [4].

Definition 7. An **abstract configuration** is a finite word over the alphabet $\Lambda = \wp(S \times REG)$ of nonempty finite subsets of $S \times REG$.

Define an *abstraction function* $H : \wp(Q) \rightarrow \Lambda^*$, yielding an abstract configuration $H(C)$ for each configuration C as follows. First, lift the function *reg* to configurations by $reg(C) = \{(s, reg(\nu)) : (s, \nu) \in C\}$. Now given a configuration C, partition C into a sequence of subsets $C_1, \ldots, C_n$, such that for all $(s, \nu) \in C_i$ and $(t, \nu') \in C_j$, $frac(\nu) \leqslant frac(\nu')$ iff $i \leqslant j$ (so (s, ν) and (t, ν') are in the same block C_i iff ν and ν' have the same fractional part). Then define $H(C) = \langle reg(C_1), \ldots, reg(C_n) \rangle \in \Lambda^*$.

Example 3. Consider the automaton $\mathcal{A}$ from Example 1. The maximum clock constant appearing in $\mathcal{A}$ is 1, and the corresponding regions are $r_0 = \{0\}$, $r_1 = (0, 1)$, $r_2 = \{1\}$ and $r_3 = (1, \infty)$. Given a concrete configuration $C = \{(s, 1), (t, 0.4), (s, 1.4), (t, 0.8)\}$, the corresponding abstract configuration $H(C)$ is $\langle \{(s, r_2)\}, \{(t, r_1), (s, r_3)\}, \{(t, r_1)\} \rangle$.

The image of the function H, which is a proper subset of Λ^*, is the set of *well-formed* words according to the following definition.

Definition 8. Say that an abstract configuration $w \in \Lambda^*$ is **well-formed** if it is empty or if both of the following hold.

- The only letter of w containing a pair (s, r) with r a singular region is the first letter w_0.
- Whenever w_0 contains a singular region, the only nonsingular region that also appears in w_0 is r_{max}.

Write $W \subseteq \Lambda^*$ for the set of well formed words.

We model the progression of time by introducing the notion of the *time successor* of an abstract configuration. We first illustrate the idea informally with concrete configurations.

Example 4. Consider a configuration $C = \{(s, 1.2), (t, 2.5), (s, 0.8)\}$. Intuitively, the time successor of C is $C' = \{(s, 1.4), (t, 2.7), (s, 1)\}$, where time has advanced 0.2 units and the clock value in C with largest fractional part has moved to a new region. On the other hand, a time successor of $C = \{(s, 1), (t, 0.5)\}$ is obtained after any time evolution δ, with $0 < \delta < 0.5$, so that the clock value with zero fractional part moves to a new region, while all other clock values remain in the same region. (Different values of δ lead to different configurations, but the underlying abstract configuration is the same.)

The definition below formally introduces the time successor of an abstract configuration. The two clauses correspond to the two different cases in Example 4. The first clause models the case where a clock with zero fractional part advances to the next region, while the second clause models the case where the clock with maximum fractional part advances to the next region.

Definition 9. *Let $w = w_0 \cdots w_n \in W$ be an abstract configuration. We say that w is **transient** if w_0 contains a pair (s, r) with r singular.*

- *If $w = w_0 \cdots w_n$ is transient, then its **time successor** is $w_0' w_1 \cdots w_n$, where $w_0' = \{(s, succ(r)) : (s, r) \in w_0\}$.*
- *If $w = w_0 \cdots w_n$ is not transient, then its **time successor** is $w_n' w_0 \cdots w_{n-1}$, where $w_n' = \{(s, succ(r)) : (s, r) \in w_n\}$.*

4.2   Definition of $R(\mathcal{A})$

The *region automaton* $R(\mathcal{A})$ is a nondeterministic infinite-state untimed automaton (with ε-transitions) that mimics $\mathcal{A}$. The states of $R(\mathcal{A})$ are abstract configurations, representing levels in a run of $\mathcal{A}$, and the transition relation contains those pairs of states representing consecutive levels in a run. We partition the transitions into two classes: *conservative* and *progressive*. Intuitively, a transition is progressive if it cycles the fractional order of the clock values in a configuration. This notion will play a role in our analysis of non-Zenoness in Section 5.

The definition of $R(\mathcal{A})$ is as follows:

- **Alphabet.** The alphabet of $R(\mathcal{A})$ is Σ.
- **States.** The set of states of $R(\mathcal{A})$ is the set $W \subseteq \Lambda^*$ of well-formed words over alphabet $\Lambda = \wp(S \times REG)$. The initial state is $\{(s_0, r_0)\}$.
- **ε-transitions.** If $w \in W$ has time successor $w' \neq w$, then we include a transition $w \xrightarrow{\varepsilon} w'$ (excluding self-loops here is a technical convenience). This transition is classified as conservative if w is transient, otherwise it is progressive.
- **Labelled transitions.** Σ-labelled transitions in $R(\mathcal{A})$ represent instantaneous transitions of $\mathcal{A}$. Given $a \in \Sigma$, we include a transition $w \xrightarrow{a} w'$ in $R(\mathcal{A})$ if there exist $\mathcal{A}$-configurations C and C' with $H(C) = w$, $H(C') = w'$, $C = \{(s_i, \nu_i)\}_{i \in I}$ and

$$C' = \bigcup_{i \in I} \{M_i : M_i \models_{\nu_i} \delta(s_i, a)\}.$$

We say that this transition is progressive if $C' = \emptyset$ or

$$\max\{frac(\nu) : (s, \nu) \in C'\} < \max\{frac(\nu) : (s, \nu) \in C\}, \tag{1}$$

otherwise we say that the transition is conservative. Note that (1) says that the clocks in C with maximal fractional part get reset in the course of the transition.

The above definition of the Σ-labelled transition relation (as a quotient) is meant to be succinct and intuitive. However, it is straightforward to compute the successors of each state $w \in W$ directly from the transition function δ of $\mathcal{A}$. For example, if $\delta(s, a) = s \wedge x.t$ then we include a transition $\langle \{(s, r_1)\} \rangle \xrightarrow{a} \langle \{(t, r_0)\}, \{(s, r_1)\} \rangle$ in $R(\mathcal{A})$.

Given $a \in \Sigma$, write $w \xRightarrow{a} w'$ if w' can be reached from w by a sequence of ε-transitions, followed by a single a-transition. The following is a variant of [16, Definition 15].

Lemma 1. *Let Δ be a run of $\mathcal{A}$ on a timed word (σ, τ), and recall that $\Delta_n \subseteq Q$ is the set of states labelling the n-th level of Δ. Then $R(\mathcal{A})$ has a run*

$$[\Delta] : \; H(\Delta_0) \overset{\sigma_0}{\Longrightarrow} H(\Delta_1) \overset{\sigma_1}{\Longrightarrow} H(\Delta_2) \overset{\sigma_2}{\Longrightarrow} \cdots$$

on the untimed word $\sigma \in \Sigma^\omega$.

Conversely, if $R(\mathcal{A})$ has an infinite run r on $\sigma \in \Sigma^\omega$, then there is a time sequence τ and a run Δ of $\mathcal{A}$ on (σ, τ) such that $[\Delta] = r$.

Lemma 1 is a first step towards reducing the language-emptiness problem for $\mathcal{A}$ to the language-emptiness problem for $R(\mathcal{A})$. What is lacking is a characterisation of non-Zeno runs of $\mathcal{A}$ in terms of $R(\mathcal{A})$. Also, since $R(\mathcal{A})$ has infinitely many states, its own language-emptiness problem is nontrivial. We deal with both these issues in Section 5.

5   A Decision Procedure for Satisfiability

Let $\mathcal{A}$ be a local timed alternating automaton. We give a procedure for determining whether $\mathcal{A}$ has nonempty language. The key ideas are as follows. We define the notion of a *progressive* run of the region automaton $R(\mathcal{A})$, such that $R(\mathcal{A})$ has a progressive run iff $\mathcal{A}$ has a non-Zeno run. We then use a backward-reachability analysis to determine the set of states of $R(\mathcal{A})$ from which there is a progressive run. The effectiveness of this analysis depends on a well-quasi-order on the states of $R(\mathcal{A})$.

5.1   Background on Well-Quasi-Orders

Recall that a *quasi-order* on a set Q is a reflexive and transitive relation $\preccurlyeq \subseteq Q \times Q$. Given such an order we say that $L \subseteq Q$ is a *lower set* if $x \in Q$, $y \in L$ and $x \preccurlyeq y$ implies $x \in L$. The notion of an *upper set* is similarly defined. We define the *upward closure* of $S \subseteq Q$, denoted $\uparrow S$, to be $\{x \mid \exists y \in S : y \preccurlyeq x\}$. This is the smallest upper set that contains S. A *basis* of an upper set U is a subset $U_b \subseteq U$ such that $U = \uparrow U_b$. A *cobasis* of a lower set L is a basis of the upper set $Q \setminus L$.

Definition 10. *A **well-quasi-order** (wqo) is a quasi-order $(Q, \preccurlyeq)$ such that for any infinite sequence $q_0, q_1, q_2, \ldots$ in Q, there exist indices $i < j$ such that $q_i \preccurlyeq q_j$.*

Example 5. Let $\leqslant$ be a quasi-order on a finite alphabet Λ. Define the induced *monotone domination order* $\preccurlyeq$ on Λ^*, the set of finite words over Λ, by $a_1 \ldots a_m \preccurlyeq b_1 \ldots b_n$ if there exists a strictly increasing function $f : \{1 \ldots m\} \to \{1, \ldots, n\}$ such that $a_i \leqslant b_{f(i)}$ for all $i \in \{1, \ldots, m\}$. Higman's Lemma states that if $\leqslant$ is a wqo on Λ, then the induced monotone domination order $\preccurlyeq$ is a wqo on Λ^*.

Proposition 1. *[9, Lemma 2.4] Let $(Q, \preccurlyeq)$ be a wqo. Then*

1. *each lower set $L \subseteq Q$ has a finite cobasis;*
2. *each infinite decreasing sequence $L_0 \supseteq L_1 \supseteq L_2 \supseteq \cdots$ of lower sets eventually stabilises, i.e., there exists $k \in \mathbb{N}$ such that $L_n = L_k$ for all $n \geqslant k$.*

5.2   Progressive Runs

Definition 11. *Overloading terminology, we say that a run $r : w \longrightarrow w' \longrightarrow w'' \longrightarrow \cdots$ of $R(\mathcal{A})$ is **progressive** if it contains infinitely many progressive transitions.*

The above definition is motivated by the notion of a progressive run of an (ordinary) timed automaton [4, Definition 4.11]. However our definition is more primitive. In particular, Lemma 2, which for us is a *property* of progressive runs, is the actual analog of Alur and Dill's *definition* of a progressive run.

Lemma 2. *Suppose Δ is a run of $\mathcal{A}$ over (σ, τ) such that the corresponding run $[\Delta]$ of $R(\mathcal{A})$ is progressive. Then there exists an infinite sequence of integers $n_0 < n_1 < \cdots$ such that $\tau_{n_0} < \tau_{n_1} < \cdots$ and every path in Δ running from a level-n_i node to a level-n_{i+1} node contains a node (s, ν) in which $\nu = 0$ or $\nu > c_{max}$.*

We use Lemma 2 in the proof of Theorem 1 below, which closely follows [4, Lemma 4.13].

Theorem 1. *$\mathcal{A}$ has a non-Zeno run iff $R(\mathcal{A})$ has a progressive run.*

Proof (sketch). It is straightforward that if Δ is a non-Zeno run of $\mathcal{A}$, then $[\Delta]$ is a progressive run of $R(\mathcal{A})$. The interesting direction is the converse.

Suppose that $R(\mathcal{A})$ has a progressive run r on a word $\sigma \in \Sigma^\omega$. Then by Lemma 1 there is a time sequence τ and a run Δ of $\mathcal{A}$ over (σ, τ) such that $[\Delta] = r$. If τ is non-Zeno then there is nothing to prove. We therefore suppose that τ is Zeno, and show how to modify Δ by inserting extra time delays to obtain a non-Zeno run Δ'.

Since τ is Zeno there exists $N \in \mathbb{N}$ such that $\tau_j - \tau_i < 1/4$ for all $i, j \geqslant N$. Let $n_0 < n_1 < \cdots$ be the sequence of integers in Lemma 2 where, without loss of generality, $N < n_0$. Define a new time sequence τ' by inserting extra delays in τ as follows:

$$\tau'_{i+1} - \tau'_i = \begin{cases} \tau_{i+1} - \tau_i & \text{if } i \notin \{n_1, n_2, \ldots\} \\ 1/2 & \text{if } i \in \{n_1, n_2, \ldots\}. \end{cases}$$

Clearly τ' is non-Zeno. We claim that a run Δ' over the timed word (σ, τ') can be constructed by appropriately modifying the clock values of the states occurring in Δ to account for the extra delay. What needs to be checked here is that the modified clock values remain in the same region.

Consider a path π through Δ, and let $\pi[m, n]$ denote the segment of π from level m to level n in Δ. If the clock x does not get reset in the segment $\pi[n_0, n_i]$ for some i, then, by Lemma 2, it is continuously greater than c_{max} along the segment $\pi[n_1, n_i]$: so the extra delay in Δ' is harmless on this part of π. Now if x gets reset in the segment $\pi[n_i, n_{i+1}]$ for some i, it can thereafter never exceed $1/4$ along π. Thus, by Lemma 2, it must get reset at least once in every segment $\pi[n_j, n_{j+1}]$ for $j \geqslant i$. In this case the extra delay in Δ' is again harmless.   □

5.3   Fixed-Point Characterisation

Let $PR \subseteq W$ denote the set of states of $R(\mathcal{A})$ from which a progressive run can originate. In order to compute PR we first characterise it as a fixed-point.

Definition 12. *Let $I \subseteq W$ be a set of states of $R(\mathcal{A})$. Define $Pred_+(I)$ to consist of those $w \in W$ such that there is a (possibly empty) sequence of conservative transitions $w \longrightarrow w' \longrightarrow w'' \longrightarrow \cdots \longrightarrow w^{(n)}$, followed by a single progressive transition $w^{(n)} \longrightarrow w^{(n+1)}$, such that $w^{(n+1)} \in I$.*

It is straightforward that PR is the greatest fixed point of $Pred_+(-) : 2^W \to 2^W$ with respect to the set-inclusion order[3]. Given this characterisation, one idea to compute PR is via the following decreasing chain of approximations:

$$W \supseteq Pred_+(W) \supseteq (Pred_+)^2(W) \supseteq \cdots . \tag{2}$$

But it turns out that we have to refine this idea a little to get an effective procedure. We start by observing the existence of a well-quasi-order on W.

Definition 13. *Define the quasi-order $\preccurlyeq$ on $W \subseteq \Lambda^*$ to be the monotone domination order over Λ (cf. Example 5).*

We might hope to use Proposition 1 to show that the chain (2) stabilises after finitely many steps. However $Pred_+$ does not map lower sets to lower sets in general. This reflects a failure of the progressive-transition relation to be downwards compatible with $\preccurlyeq$ in the sense of [9]. (This is not surprising—the possibility of $w \in W$ performing a progressive transition depends on its first and last letters.)

Example 6. Consider the automaton $\mathcal{A}$ in Example 2, with associated regions including $r_0 = \{0\}$, $r_1 = (0,1)$ and $r_2 = \{1\}$. Then, in $R(\mathcal{A})$, $w = \langle \{(s, r_1)\}, \{(t, r_1)\} \rangle$ makes a progressive ε-transition to $w' = \langle \{(t, r_2)\}, \{(s, r_1)\} \rangle$. However, $\langle \{(s, r_1)\} \rangle$, which is a subword of w, does not belong to $Pred_+(\downarrow w')$. Indeed, any state reachable from $\langle \{(s, r_1)\} \rangle$ by a sequence of conservative transitions followed by a single progressive transition must contain the letter $\{(s, r_2)\}$.

Although $Pred_+$ fails to enjoy one-step compatibility with $\preccurlyeq$, it satisfies a kind of infinitary compatibility. More precisely, even though $Pred_+$ does not map lower sets to lower sets, its greatest fixed point is a lower set.

Proposition 2. *PR is a lower set.*

Proof. We exploit the correspondence between non-Zeno runs of $\mathcal{A}$ and progressive runs of $R(\mathcal{A})$, as given in Proposition 1.

Suppose $w' \in PR$ and $w \preccurlyeq w'$. Then there exist $\mathcal{A}$-configurations C, C' such that $C \subseteq C'$, $H(C) = w$ and $H(C') = w'$. Since $w' \in PR$, by Proposition 1 $\mathcal{A}$ has a run Δ' on some non-Zeno word ρ such that $\Delta'_0 = C'$. Now let Δ be the subgraph of Δ' consisting of all nodes reachable from those level-0 nodes of Δ' labelled by elements of $C \subseteq C'$. Then Δ is also a run of $\mathcal{A}$ on ρ, so $w \in PR$ by Proposition 1 again.   □

---

[3] It is not possible for w to belong to the greatest fixed point of $Pred_+$ merely by virtue of being able to perform an infinite consecutive sequence of ε-transitions that includes infinitely many progressive ε-transitions. The reason is that once all the clock values in a configuration have advanced beyond the maximum of clock constant c_{max}, then the configuration is no longer capable of performing ε-transitions (cf. Section 4.2.)

In anticipation of applying Proposition 2, we make the following definition.

Definition 14. *Define $\Psi : 2^W \to 2^W$ by $\Psi(I) = W \backslash \uparrow (W \setminus Pred_+(I))$.*

By construction, Ψ maps lower sets to lower sets. Also, being a monotone self-map of $(2^W, \subseteq)$, it has a greatest fixed point, denoted $gfp(\Psi)$.

Proposition 3. *PR is the greatest fixed point of Ψ.*

Proof. Since PR is both a fixed point of $Pred_+$ and a lower set we have:

$$\begin{aligned}
\Psi(PR) &= W \backslash \uparrow (W \setminus Pred_+(PR)) \\
&= W \backslash \uparrow (W \setminus PR) \\
&= W \setminus (W \setminus PR) \\
&= PR.
\end{aligned}$$

That is, PR is a fixed point of Ψ. It follows that $PR \subseteq gfp(\Psi)$.

The reverse inclusion, $gfp(\Psi) \subseteq PR$ follows easily from the fact that $\Psi(I) \subseteq Pred_+(I)$ for all $I \subseteq W$.   □

Next we assert that Ψ is computable.

Proposition 4. *Given a finite cobasis of a lower set $L \subseteq W$, there is a procedure to compute a finite cobasis of $\Psi(L)$.*

Proposition 4 is nontrivial since the definition of Ψ involves $Pred_+$, which refers to multi-step reachability (by conservative transitions), not just single-step reachability. We refer the reader to [18] for a detailed proof. The proof exploits the fact that conservative transitions on local automata have a very restricted ability to transform a configuration—for instance, the only way they can change the order of the fractional values of the clocks is by resetting some clocks to 0.

5.4   Main Results

Theorem 2. *The satisfiability problem for Safety MTL is decidable.*

Proof. Since every Safety MTL formula can be translated into a local automaton, it suffices to show that language emptiness is decidable for local automata.

Given a local automaton $\mathcal{A}$, let Ψ be as in Definition 14. Since Ψ is monotone and maps lower sets to lower sets, $W \supseteq \Psi(W) \supseteq \Psi^2(W) \supseteq \cdots$ is a decreasing sequence of lower sets in $(W, \preccurlyeq)$. By Proposition 1 this sequence stabilises after some finite number of iterations. By construction, the stabilising value is the greatest fixed point of Ψ, which by Proposition 3 is the set PR. Furthermore, using Proposition 4 we can compute a finite cobasis of each successive iterate $\Psi^n(W)$ until we eventually obtain a cobasis for PR. We can then decide whether the initial state of $R(\mathcal{A})$ is in PR which, by Theorem 1, holds iff $\mathcal{A}$ has nonempty language.   □

We leave the complexity of the satisfiability problem for future work. The argument used to derive the nonprimitive recursive lower bound for MTL satisfiability over finite timed words [16] does not apply here.

By combining the techniques used to prove Theorem 2 with the techniques used in [16] to show that the model-checking problem is decidable for Safety MTL, one can show the decidability of the refinement problem: 'Given two Safety MTL formulas φ_1 and φ_2, does every word satisfying φ_1 also satisfy φ_2?'

Theorem 3. *The refinement problem for Safety MTL is decidable.*

6   Conclusion

It is folklore that extending linear temporal logic in any way that enables expressing the *punctual* specification 'in one time unit φ will hold' yields an undecidable logic over a dense-time semantics. Together with [17], this paper reveals that there is an unexpected factor affecting the truth or falsity of this belief. While [17] shows that Metric Temporal Logic is undecidable over timed ω-words, the proof depends on being able to express liveness properties, such as $\Box\Diamond p$. On the other hand, this paper shows that the safety fragment of MTL remains fully decidable in the presence of punctual timing constraints. This fragment is not closed under complement, and the decision procedures for satisfiability and model checking are quite different. The algorithm for satisfiability solves a nontermination problem on a well-structured transition system by iterated backward reachability, while the algorithm for model checking, given in a previous paper [16], used forward reachability.

Acknowledgement. The authors would like to thank the anonymous referees for providing many helpful suggestions to improve the presentation of the paper.

References

1. P. A. Abdulla, J. Deneux, J. Ouaknine and J. Worrell. Decidability and complexity results for timed automata via channel systems. In *Proceedings of ICALP 05*, LNCS 3580, 2005.
2. P. A. Abdulla and B. Jonsson. Undecidable verification problems with unreliable channels. *Information and Computation*, 130:71–90, 1996.
3. P. A. Abdulla, B. Jonsson. Model checking of systems with many identical timed processes. *Theoretical Computer Science*, 290(1):241–264, 2003.
4. R. Alur and D. Dill. A theory of timed automata. *Theoretical Computer Science*, 126:183–235, 1994.
5. R. Alur, T. Feder and T. A. Henzinger. The benefits of relaxing punctuality. *Journal of the ACM*, 43:116–146, 1996.
6. R. Alur and T. A. Henzinger. Real-time logics: complexity and expressiveness. *Information and Computation*, 104:35–77, 1993.
7. R. Alur and T. A. Henzinger. A really temporal logic. *Journal of the ACM*, 41:181–204, 1994.

8. P. Bouyer, F. Chevalier and N. Markey. On the expressiveness of TPTL and MTL. *Research report LSV-2005-05*, Lab. Spécification et Vérification, May 2005.
9. A. Finkel and P. Schnoebelen. Well-structured transition systems everywhere! *Theoretical Computer Science*, 256(1-2):63–92, 2001.
10. T. A. Henzinger. It's about time: Real-time logics reviewed. In *Proceedings of CONCUR 98*, LNCS 1466, 1998.
11. T. A. Henzinger, Z. Manna and A. Pnueli. What good are digital clocks? In *Proceedings of ICALP 92*, LNCS 623, 1992.
12. T. A. Henzinger, J.-F. Raskin, and P.-Y. Schobbens. The regular real-time languages. In *Proceedings of ICALP 98*, LNCS 1443, 1998.
13. G. Higman. Ordering by divisibility in abstract algebras. *Proceedings of the London Mathematical Society*, 2:236–366, 1952.
14. R. Koymans. Specifying real-time properties with metric temporal logic. *Real-time Systems*, 2(4):255–299, 1990.
15. S. Lasota and I. Walukiewicz. Alternating timed automata. In *Proceedings of FOSSACS 05*, LNCS 3441, 2005.
16. J. Ouaknine and J. Worrell. On the decidability of Metric Temporal Logic. In *Proceedings of LICS 05*, IEEE Computer Society Press, 2005.
17. J. Ouaknine and J. Worrell. Metric temporal logic and faulty Turing machines. Proceedings of FOSSACS 06, LNCS, 2006.
18. J. Ouaknine and J. Worrell. Safety MTL is fully decidable. Oxford University Programming Research Group Research Report RR-06-02.
19. J.-F. Raskin and P.-Y. Schobbens. State-clock logic: a decidable real-time logic. In *Proceedings of HART 97*, LNCS 1201, 1997.
20. M. Vardi. Alternating automata: Unifying truth and validity checking for temporal logics. In *Proceedings of CADE 97*, LNCS 1249, 1997.
21. F. Wang. Formal Verification of Timed Systems: A Survey and Perspective. *Proceedings of the IEEE*, 92(8):1283–1307, 2004.
22. T. Wilke. Specifying timed state sequences in powerful decidable logics and timed automata. *Formal Techniques in Real-Time and Fault-Tolerant Systems*, LNCS 863, 1994.

Simulation-Based Graph Similarity*

Oleg Sokolsky, Sampath Kannan, and Insup Lee

Department of Computer and Information Science,
University of Pennsylvania
{sokolsky, kannan, lee}@cis.upenn.edu

Abstract. We present symmetric and asymmetric similarity measures for labeled directed rooted graphs that are inspired by the simulation and bisimulation relations on labeled transition systems. Computation of the similarity measures has close connections to discounted Markov decision processes in the asymmetric case and to perfect-information stochastic games in the symmetric case. For the symmetric case, we also give a polynomial-time algorithm that approximates the similarity to any desired precision.

1 Introduction

The motivation for this work comes from the need for rapid detection of new computer viruses. The proliferation of virus development kits that can be downloaded from the Internet has dramatically lowered the entry threshold for virus developers [16]. What used to require considerable skill and substantial knowledge can now be accomplished by a relatively inexperienced hacker. As a result, large numbers of new virus programs appear every week. They are different enough from known viruses that conventional signature-based techniques become ineffective. Yet, since these viruses are developed using the same development kits, they share distinctive similarities with known representatives of viruses developed using the same kit. The classification of viruses into families is an attempt to capture such similarity.

The starting point of this work was the question of how the similarity between viruses of the same family can be captured and quantified. Our approach to similarity is *behavioral*, by which we mean that similar virus programs should be able to perform similar actions, arranged in similar ways. In order to make this intuition precise, we define a similarity metric on *control flow graphs* of programs. Control flow graphs, which can be defined either at the object code level or at the level of high-level programming language, are directed graphs, whose nodes and possibly edges are labeled with code fragments. There is also a dedicated initial node. Such labeled rooted graphs are often formalized as *labeled transition systems* (LTS).

One notion commonly used for semantic comparison for LTSs is *simulation*. The simulation relation defined on pairs of LTS nodes captures whether one node

---

* Research has been supported in part by the ONR MURI N00014-04-1-0735 and ARO DAAD19-01-1-0473.

H. Hermanns and J. Palsberg (Eds.): TACAS 2006, LNCS 3920, pp. 426–440, 2006.

simulates the other, or not. Intuitively, a node s_1 in an LTS G_1 simulates a node t_1 in another LTS G_2 if any outgoing edge of $t_1 \rightarrow t_2$ labeled by, say, a can be matched by an edge $s_1 \rightarrow s_2$, also labeled by a, in such a way that s_2 simulates t_2. A symmetric version of the simulation relation is known as *bisimulation*.

For the purpose of comparing control flow graphs of similar programs, we need to generalize the simulation relation into a function that captures *how well* one control flow graph simulates another. The first step in defining such a function is to introduce *local* similarity between graph nodes and edges. Local similarity functions define how well the label of a node matches the label of another node, and how well the label of an edge matches the label of another edge. The definition of local similarity functions depends on the nature of the labels of nodes and edges of the graphs. The labels may be viewed as symbols in a given alphabet, variable-length strings over a fixed alphabet, or have a more complicated structure such as, for example, assembly-language instructions or short fragments of assembly-language code. Different local similarity functions are appropriate in each of these situations. For the purpose of this paper, we assume that local similarity functions are given to us, and abstract away the nature of the graph labels.

In designing the similarity measure, we also need to decide whether we are pursuing an *aggregate* or *extremal* measures. In extremal measures, the computed value is based on the closest (or the most distant) match between components in the graph. Aggregate measures take into consideration matches from all paths. We argue that extremal measures can lead to counterintuitive results, where a single unmatched component yields a very low similarity value for two otherwise quite similar graphs. The advantage of extremal measures, on the other hand, is that they allow us to easily obtain distance metrics that obey the triangle inequality: the distance between two graphs does not exceed the sum of distances between each of the graphs and an arbitrary third graph. In general, it is useful to work with distance metrics. In our case, however, we do not necessarily need a distance metric. Our goal is to raise an alarm when a graph of the new program is similar enough to a known malicious program to warrant a closer inspection. If the program is found to be close to two quite different malicious programs, so much the better.

Guided by this motivation, we present new aggregate similarity measures that generalize simulation and bisimulation. We call these measures *quantitative* simulation and bisimulation. The contribution of this paper is a collection of algorithms for computing quantitative simulation and bisimulation on finite graphs. The algorithms rely on techniques similar to the ones used for the analysis of Markov decision processes and perfect-information stochastic games. Of particular practical importance are polynomial-time approximation algorithms for quantitative simulation and bisimulation.

Related Work. In [6], several metrics have been proposed for *quantitative transition systems*, which are labeled with tuples of numbers instead of more conventional symbolic labels. The introduced measures are extremal and have the advantage of relatively low computational complexity. Similar metrics for labeled Markov processes have been considered in [8] as means of approximating bisimulation relations. In both cases, quantitative information is present in the transition system and serves as the basis for the metric. In our case, however, transition systems do not contain quantitative information.

Existing work on graph similarity has been applied mostly in pattern recognition and data mining contexts. In these domains, graphs can have rich structures, but little associated semantics with graphs nodes and edges. In our case, however, similarity is rooted in graph labels and the structure is less important and serves only to capture relationships between labels. The idea that similarity between two graphs can be computed as a fixed point of local similarities propagated through the transition relation has appeared in [2, 10], but was treated in an *ad hoc* fashion.

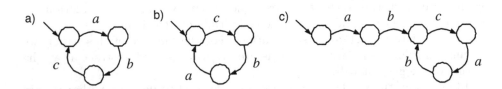

Fig. 1. Different notions of graph similarity

Most other existing graph similarity measures can be grouped into two categories [14]. Cost-based distance measures (also known as *edit distances*) are based on the number of modifications that are needed to transform one graph into the other. On the other hand, feature-based distance measures, for example [13], rely on extracting a set of structural features (such as vertex degrees) from the graphs and comparing vectors of features. For our purposes, both kinds of measures have the disadvantage that they are purely structural, while the measures we are proposing utilize significant amount of semantic information contained in the graph and its labels. To see the difference between our approach and the approach based on edit distances, consider the graphs is Figure 1. Graphs a) and b) have very small edit distance (high similarity): one needs only to swap two of the labels to make the graphs identical. However, if similarity between a and c is small, we would consider these graphs to be quite different as they admit different executions. Conversely, graphs a) and c) are quite different structurally, but they are, in fact, bisimilar and thus should be considered identical for our purposes.

Algorithmic techniques studied in this paper are similar to the approaches used in solving perfect-information quantitative stochastic games [4].

Structure of the Paper. The rest of the paper is organized as follows. In Section 2 we briefly consider an extremal simulation-like measure and discuss its disadvantages. In Sections 3 and 4, we define strong and weak versions of an aggregate measure called *quantitative simulation*, discuss its properties and introduce an approach to compute quantitative simulation that is based on linear programming. Section 5 introduces quantitative bisimulation, which is a symmetric version of quantitative simulation. Computing quantitative bisimulation turns out to be naturally related to finding the value of an appropriately defined infinite stochastic game and has a number of interesting connections to the recent work such as [4]. Finally, we offer a polynomial-time procedure to approximate quantitative bisimulation to any desired precision.

2   Extremal Quantitative Simulation

Preliminaries. A *labeled transition system* (LTS) is a labeled directed graph $G = \langle S, \mathcal{L}, T, s_0 \rangle$, where S is a set of states, $\mathcal{L}$ is a set of labels, $T \subseteq S \times \mathcal{L} \times S$ is a transition relation, and $s_0 \in S$ is the initial state. As usual, we denote $(s_1, a, s_2) \in T$ as $s_1 \xrightarrow{a} s_2$. In addition, assume two similarity functions: a *node similarity* function $N : S \times S \rightarrow [0, 1]$, and *label similarity* function $L : \mathcal{L} \times \mathcal{L} \rightarrow [0, 1]$. We assume that each node and each label is perfectly similar to itself: $N(s, s) = L(l, l) = 1$, and that the similarity functions are symmetric: $N(s_1, s_2) = N(s_2, s_1)$ and $L(a, b) = L(b, a)$.

Definition 1. Extremal quantitative simulation *(mq-simulation, for short) is a function $Q : S \times S \rightarrow [0, 1]$, such that for all states s_1, s_2, the following condition holds:*

$$Q(s_1, s_2) = \begin{cases} N(s_1, s_2) & \text{if } \forall a, s_1 \xnrightarrow{a} \\ N(s_1, s_2) \cdot \prod_{s_1 \xrightarrow{a} s_1'} \max_{s_2 \xrightarrow{b} s_2'} L(a, b) \cdot Q(s_1', s_2') & \text{otherwise} \end{cases} \quad (1)$$

If $Q(s_1, s_2) = n$, we say that s_2 simulates s_1 up to n. If we have two LTSs, G_1 and G_2 with initial states s_0^1 and s_0^2, respectively, we say that G_2 simulates G_1 up to n if $Q(s_0^1, s_0^2) = n$.

As a motivation for this definition, consider the case when the node similarity function does not distinguish nodes, that is, $\forall s_1, s_2 \in S, N(s_1, s_2) = 1$ and the label similarity function is binary, that is, $L(l_1, l_2) = 1$ if $l_1 = l_2$ and 0 otherwise. In this case, we recover the traditional definition for simulation relation $\precsim$ on labeled transition systems: $s_1 \precsim s_2$ *iff* s_2 simulates s_1 up to 1.

Example. Consider the classical example from the (bi)simulation literature, shown in Figure 2. It is well-known that t_1 simulates s_1, but not vice versa. Let us

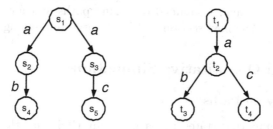

Fig. 2. Example of quantitative similarity

assume, however, that b and c are not completely dissimilar. Let $L(b,c) = 0.5$. With the definition above, we have that $Q(s_1, t_1) = 1$, which is not surprising because t_1 simulates s_1. In the reverse direction, we have that $Q(t_2, s_2) = Q(t_2, s_3) = 0.5$. This is because s_2 (and, similarly, s_3) matches one transition of t_2 perfectly and the other by 0.5, the product of this yields 0.5. Finally, $Q(t_1, s_1) = 0.5$.

Fixpoint Characterization of mq-Simulation. Consider the set of tuples $Q = \{Q_{i,j}\}$ with $i, j \in 1 \ldots |S|$ and every $Q_{i,j} \in [0,1]$. Equipped with the operations of pointwise minimum and maximum, the set forms a complete lattice.

Consider the function $f : Q \rightarrow Q$, which is the simultaneous application of Equation (1) for all i, j. The function is monotonic. By the Tarski-Knaster theorem, a fixed point of f exists, and is an mq-simulation.

Discussion. The attractive feature of mq-simulation is that it is an immediate generalization of the classical simulation relation to the domain of reals. However, it does not make a good measure for LTS similarity, because it can produce quite counterintuitive results. Consider the following two examples.

One problem of quantitative simulation is that it assigns too much importance to "eventual dissimilarity." Consider, for example, the LTSs

$$s_1 \xrightarrow{a_1} s_2 \xrightarrow{a_2} \ldots \ s_{n-1} \xrightarrow{a_{n-1}} s_n \text{ and } t_1 \xrightarrow{b_1} t_2 \xrightarrow{b_2} \ldots t_{n-1} \xrightarrow{b_{n-1}} t_n. \qquad (2)$$

Let $L(a_i, b_i) = 1$, except for the last pair, where $L(a_{n-1}, b_{n-1}) = 0$, and $N(s_i, t_i) = 1$ for all i, j. Intuitively, one would expect to see these LTSs rather similar, because the dissimilarity is far down the road. However, $Q(s_1, t_1) = 0$.

The second problem is that mq-simulation is too strict in combining alternatives. Consider two star-shaped LTSs constructed as follows: $s_0 \xrightarrow{a_i} s_i$ and $t_0 \xrightarrow{b_i} t_i$. Again, let all nodes be similar and let labels be pairwise similar $L(a_i, b_i) = 1$ for all i except $i = n$. In all other cases, that is, $i \neq j$ or $i = j = n$, $L(a_i, b_j) = 0$. Again, our intuition suggests that these LTSs should be considered similar since all but one branches are matched perfectly. Still, $Q(s_1, t_1) = 0$.

Analysis of these two problems suggest that perhaps a more useful definition would be a function, additive both in terms of different branches leaving the same state and in terms of number of states along a path. To address the first problem, this function should give more weight to close states and progressively less weight to more distant states. It is important, however, to ensure that the similarity measure remains bounded over long paths and for states with large branching factors. The next section will be devoted to defining such a function.

3   Weighted Quantitative Simulation

3.1   Similarity on Paths

We begin by comparing states in paths of an LTS, and then generalize the obtained notion of similarity to LTSs in general.

In order to overcome the problems with the mq-simulation, we introduce a parameter p that describes the relative importance of local similarity vs. "step similarity." Consider two edges in an LTS: $s_0 \xrightarrow{a} s_1$ and $t_0 \xrightarrow{b} t_1$. Similarity between s_0 and t_0 based on these two edges can be defined to be $(1-p) \cdot N(s_0, t_0) + p \cdot L(a,b) \cdot N(s_1,t_1)$. Consider now two paths of the same length, $s_0 \xrightarrow{a_1} s_1 \xrightarrow{a_2} s_2 \xrightarrow{a_3} \ldots s_n$ and $t_0 \xrightarrow{b_1} t_1 \xrightarrow{b_2} t_2 \xrightarrow{b_3} \ldots t_n$. We can extend the similarity between s_0 and t_0 to recursively consider paths instead of single edges as follows: $Q(s_0, t_0) = (1-p) \cdot N(s_0, t_0) + p \cdot L(a_1, b_1) \cdot Q(s_1, t_1)$. Unfolding the recursive expression, we obtain that, for the paths of length n, the similarity between the paths is

$$Q(s_0, t_0) = \sum_{i=0}^{n} (1-p) \cdot p^i \cdot N(s_i, t_i) \cdot \prod_{k=1}^{i} L(a_k, b_k), \tag{3}$$

with the convention that the product over an empty set is 1.

The value of the similarity between two paths is bounded from above by the similarity of two identical traces. Since all node and edge similarity functions yield 1 in this case, it is clear that the similarity between two identical infinite paths is 1.

Consider again the LTSs of (2). The effect of dissimilarity after n steps is now negligible for large n: $Q(s_1, t_1) = 1 - 2^{-n}$ for $p = 1/2$.

3.2   Graph Similarity

Definition 2. *For a parameter $0 < p < 1$, p-weighted quantitative simulation (q-simulation) is a function $Q : S \times S \to [0,1]$, such that for all states s_1, s_2, the following condition holds:*

$$Q_p(s_1, s_2) = \begin{cases} N(s_1, s_2) & \text{if } \forall a, s_1 \xrightarrow{a} \\ (1-p) \cdot N(s_1, s_2) + \frac{p}{n} \cdot \sum_{s_1 \xrightarrow{a} s_1'} \max_{s_2 \xrightarrow{b} s_2'} L(a,b) \cdot Q_p(s_1', s_2') & \text{otherwise,} \end{cases} \tag{4}$$

where n is the number of transitions leaving s_1.

Consider the same example of Figure 2. Let $p = 1/2$. Here we again have $Q_{\frac{1}{2}}(s_1, t_1) = 1$. Indeed, $Q_{\frac{1}{2}}(s_2, t_2) = (1-p) + p \cdot Q_{\frac{1}{2}}(s_4, t_3) = 1$ (as well as $Q_{\frac{1}{2}}(s_3, t_2)$), and $Q_{\frac{1}{2}}(s_1, t_1) = (1-p) + p \cdot \frac{1}{2} \cdot (Q_{\frac{1}{2}}(s_2, t_2) + Q_{\frac{1}{2}}(s_3, t_2)) = 1$. In the reverse direction, $Q_{\frac{1}{2}}(t_2, s_2) = (1-p) + p \cdot \frac{1}{2} \cdot (1 + \frac{1}{2}) = \frac{7}{8}$. Finally, $Q_{\frac{1}{2}}(t_1, s_1) = (1-p) + p \cdot Q_{\frac{1}{2}}(t_2, s_2) = \frac{15}{16}$. The number is much higher than for the mq-simulation, because here considerable weight is given to node similarity, which in this case does not make any distinction between nodes and only drives the similarity up.

We now show two important properties of q-simulation. Proofs of these properties use the functional $T(Q)(s_1, s_2)$ derived from (4). That is, let Q be the set of functions $Q : S \times S \to [0,1]$. $T : Q \to Q$ is defined as

$$T(Q(s_1, s_2)) = \begin{cases} N(s_1, s_2) & \text{if } \forall a, s_1 \xrightarrow{a} \\ (1-p) \cdot N(s_1, s_2) + \frac{p}{n} \sum_{s_1 \xrightarrow{a} s_1'} \max_{s_2 \xrightarrow{b} s_2'} L(a,b) \cdot Q(s_1', s_2') & \text{otherwise,} \end{cases}$$

The following theorem shows that q-simulation is well-defined:

Theorem 1. *Equation (4) has a unique solution.*

Proof (Sketch): We reduce the problem of computing q-simulation to the problem of optimal control in discrete event systems, studied in [1]. Given an LTS G, we construct the dynamical system

$$x_{i+1} = f(x_i, c_i, w_i),$$

where the next state x_{i+1} depends on the current state x_i, the current control input c_i, and random disturbance w_i. The state space is given by pairs of graph nodes, $x \in S \times S$. Control inputs $c_i \in C(x)$ are state-dependent. Given the current state $x_i = (s_1, s_2)$, $C(x) = \{s_2 \xrightarrow{b} s_2'\}$. That is, control inputs represent the choice of transition in the simulating state. Disturbance $w_i \in W(x) = \{s_1 \xrightarrow{a} s_1'\}$, on the other hand, represents the choice of transition in the simulated state. Fixing a control strategy, that is, the sequence of control inputs, yields a random trajectory $x_0, x_1, \ldots$. The value of a given trajectory is given according to (3). The optimal control problem for the given dynamical system is to determine the maximum expected value over the set of possible control strategies. For uniformly distributed disturbances, independently chosen in each step, this maximum expected value coincides with 4. The proof then closely follows [1], p. 182ff, which shows that the control problem – albeit for a different but also monotonic value function – has a unique solution. We show that the functional $T(Q)$ is a *contraction mapping* over the space of functions $Q : S \times S \to [0,1]$, measured by the distance function $d(Q, Q') = max_{x \in S \times S} |Q(x) - Q'(x)|$. Since T is a contraction mapping, it has a unique fixed point by the Banach's theorem, and the fixed point coincides with Q_p. □

A more direct proof in the style of Theorem 3 is also possible; however, the proof we chose here points to a clear connection with an established approach. The next theorem shows that q-simulation generalizes the simulation relation:

Theorem 2. *Let $N(s_1, s_2) = 1$ for all s_1, s_2, and $L(a, b) = 1$ iff $a = b$, and 0 otherwise. Then $s_1 \precsim s_2$ iff $Q_p(s_1, s_2) = 1$ for any $0 < p < 1$.*

Proof: ($\Rightarrow$) We proceed by contradiction. Assume that $s_1 \precsim s_2$ but $Q_p(s_1, s_2) \neq 1$. Consider the function $Q^+ : S \times S \to [0, 1]$, such that $Q^+(s_1, s_2) = 1$ if $s_1 \precsim s_2$ and $Q^+(s_1, s_2) = Q_p(s_1, s_2)$ otherwise. Clearly, $Q_p < Q^+$ in the lattice of functions $S \times S \to [0, 1]$. Consider the functional $T(Q)$ defined above. It is clear that when $s_1 \precsim s_2$, $T(Q^+)(s_1, s_2) = Q^+(s_1, s_2)$, because the maximum value over the transitions of s_2 in Equation (4) will always be 1. It is also easy to see that, for any s_1 and s_2, $T(Q^+)(s_1, s_2) \geq Q^+(s_1, s_2)$. By repeating this argument, we see that $T^n(Q^+)(s_1, s_2) \geq Q^+(s_1, s_2)$. Since T has a unique fixed point by Theorem 1, the sequence T^n converges to the fixed point of T, which is Q_p. Thus we have $Q_p < Q^+ \leq Q_p$, which is a contradiction. ($\Leftarrow$) Consider relation $R \subseteq S \times S$ such that $(s_1, s_2) \in R \Leftrightarrow Q_p(s_1, s_2) = 1$. We show that R is a simulation relation. The case when s_1 does not have outgoing transitions is obvious. Otherwise, for each transition $s_1 \xrightarrow{a} s_1'$, $\max\limits_{s_2 \xrightarrow{b} s_2'} L(a,b) \cdot Q_p(s_1', s_2') = 1$, which is possible only if $a = b$ and $Q_p(s_1', s_2') = 1$, that is, $(s_1', s_2') \in R$.   □

3.3 Computing Weighted Quantitative Simulation

Given an LTS G and functions N and L, we transform (4) into an instance of the linear programming problem in the following way. For every two states s_i, s_j, we introduce a variable $Q_{i,j}$. For every edge $e = s_i \xrightarrow{a} s_k$ and state s_j, we introduce a variable $X_{e,j}$. The objective function minimizes the sum of all variables:

$$min \sum_{i,j \in S} Q_{i,j} + \sum_{e \in T, s_j \in S} X_{e,j}.$$

We represent the relationship between variables using the following constraints: $0 \leq Q_{i,j} \leq 1$, $0 \leq X_{e,j} \leq 1$ for all i, j, and e. For m such that $s_j \xrightarrow{b} s_m$, $X_{e,j} \geq L(a,b) \cdot Q_{k,m}$. Finally, for all i, j,

$$Q_{i,j} = (1-p) \cdot N(s_i, s_j) + \sum_{e \in s_i \xrightarrow{a} s_k} \frac{p}{n} X_{e,j}$$

By Theorem 1, this linear programming problem has a unique solution, so that $Q_{i,j} = Q_p(s_i, s_j)$.

4 Weak Weighted Quantitative Simulation

A deficiency of q-simulation as defined by Equation 4 is that it requires the graphs to unfold synchronously - that is, every step of one graph has to be matched by a similar step of another graph. Consider two paths $s_1 \xrightarrow{a} s_2 \xrightarrow{b} s_3 \xrightarrow{c} \ldots$ and $t_1 \xrightarrow{a} t_2 \xrightarrow{a'} t_3 \xrightarrow{b} t_4 \xrightarrow{c} \ldots$.... The paths are identical, except for the insertion of an a'-step in the second path. If $L(a', b) = 0$, the similarity of the two paths will be very low, despite the fact that almost every step in the paths can be matched to a step in the other path in the same order. Intuitively, the role of the inserted step should be heavily discounted.

We can compare graph similarity to the well-known notion of string similarity, known as the *string alignment problem*, widely used in biological sequence analysis. We consider a particular dynamic-programming formulation of this problem that serves as the basis for the Needleman-Wunsch alignment algorithm [12]. We assume a similarity score between elements of the alphabets of the two strings. Consider strings $s_1 = as_1'$ and $s_2 = bs_2'$. The optimal alignment score of s_1 and s_2, denoted $F(s_1, s_2)$, is computed as the maximum of $F(s_1', s_2') + s(a, b)$, $F(as_1', s_2') - d$, and $F(s_1', bs_2') - d$. Here, $s(a, b)$ is the similarity score of a and b, and d is the *gap penalty*.

We want to introduce a similar notion – that "skipping a step" is permissible but carries a penalty – into the q-simulation framework and define *weak q-simulation.* We remind the reader, that the classical definition of the weak simulation relation, a transition of the simulated state labeled with the action a can be matched by a finite sequence of transitions from the simulating state, exactly one of which is labeled with a and the rest are labeled with a special internal action τ[1]. The intuition for our definition comes from the fact that, in the binary world, classical weak (bi)simulation is strong (bi)simulation applied to the τ-*closed* transition system, in which every such sequence of transitions is represented by a single transition.

It is tempting to use this intuition directly. Consider a special "skip" action $\epsilon \notin \mathcal{L}$. Suppose we construct the ϵ-closure of G. Since ϵ is a new action, the closure amounts to adding a self-loop transition labeled ϵ to every state in G. The edge similarity function $L(a, \epsilon) = L(\epsilon, a)$ serves as the label-sensitive "gap penalty". Treating ϵ differently than any other action, we require that $L(\epsilon, \epsilon) = 0$. This precludes the pathological case when both states stutter and yet similarity increases. We can then use the same equation (4) to define weak q-simulation using the extended transition relation instead of T.

Although such simple solution gives a very intuitive definition, it is easy to see that this is not the definition we want. We lose a desirable property that q-simulation reduces to classical simulation in the binary case. Indeed, according to the definition above, a state will not be weakly q-similar to itself! To see this, consider a deadlocked state. Its weak q-similarity to itself would be $1 - p$ instead of 1. The source of this problem is that equation (4) is including the stuttering step in computing the average of matches. To fix this problem, we use the following definition.

Definition 3. *A (weighted) weak quantitative simulation is a function* $Q^W :$ $S \times S \to [0, 1]$, *such that for all* s_1, s_2, *the following condition holds:*

$$Q^W(s_1, s_2) = \begin{cases} N(s_1, s_2) & \text{if } \forall a, s_1 \overset{a}{\not\to} \\ (1 - p) \cdot N(s_1, s_2) + \max(W_1, W_2) & \text{otherwise,} \end{cases} \quad (5)$$

where
$$W_1 = \max_{s_2 \overset{b}{\to} s_2'} L(b, \epsilon) \cdot Q^W(s_1, s_2')$$
$$W_2 = \frac{p}{n} \cdot \sum_{s_1 \overset{a}{\to} s_1'} \max(\max_{s_2 \overset{b}{\to} s_2'} (L(a, b) \cdot Q^W(s_1', s_2')), L(a, \epsilon) \cdot Q^W(s_1', s_2)),$$
and n is the number of transitions leaving s_1.

Weak q-simulation can be computed using a slightly modified linear programming problem from the previous section.

5   Quantitative Bisimulation

A natural extension of the q-simulation idea is to define a symmetric similarity function. That is, for all states s_1 and s_2, $B(s_1, s_2) = B(s_2, s_1)$. It is natural to

---

[1] Note that "skipping a step" is more similar to stuttering than to executing an internal step. Therefore, our weak q-simulation is closer in spirit to stuttering (bi)simulation [3, 11] than to classical weak (bi)simulation.

think of this function as quantitative bisimulation (q-bisimulation). We construct such a function by taking the minimum of the asymmetric one-step similarities between two states.

Definition 4. *Given the graph* $G = \langle S, \mathcal{L}, T \rangle$, *the (p-weighted) quantitative bisimulation is the function* $B_p : S \times S \to [0,1]$, *defined as*

$$B_p(s_1, s_2) = \min(B_p^l(s_1, s_2), B_p^r(s_1, s_2)),$$

where B_p^l, B_p^r *are left and right similarities, respectively, are defined as*

$$B_p^l(s_1, s_2) = \begin{cases} N(s_1, s_2) & \text{if } \forall a, s_1 \overset{a}{\not\to} \\ (1-p) \cdot N(s_1, s_2) + W(s_1, s_2) & \text{otherwise} \end{cases}$$

$$B_p^r(s_1, s_2) = \begin{cases} N(s_2, s_1) & \text{if } \forall b, s_2 \overset{b}{\not\to} \\ (1-p) \cdot N(s_2, s_1) + W(s_2, s_1) & \text{otherwise,} \end{cases}$$

where $W(s,t) = \frac{p}{n} \cdot \sum_{s \overset{a}{\to} s'} \max_{t \overset{b}{\to} t'} L(a,b) \cdot B_p(s', t')$

Similarly to q-simulation, q-bisimulation can be considered in the strong as well as the weak form by constructing a symmetric version of Definition 3.

5.1   Computing Quantitative Bisimulation

We can reduce the problem of computing strong quantitative bisimulation to the problem of computing the value of a *stochastic game with extended payoffs and Büchi winning condition*. Such games are extensions of simple stochastic games [9, 5] to include value derived from infinite runs.

A stochastic game with payoffs is a graph $\mathcal{B} = \langle V, E, N, L \rangle$, where V is a set of vertices partitioned into three subsets V_{min}, V_{max}, and V_{avg}, $E \subseteq V \times V$ is the transition relation, $N : V \to [0,1]$ is the node payoff function, and $L : E \to [0,1]$ is the edge payoff function. We use $v_1 \overset{l}{\to} v_2$ to denote $L(v_1 \to v_2) = l$.

Given a graph $G = \langle S, \mathcal{L}, T \rangle$, we construct $\mathcal{B}(G)$ as follows. We introduce two parameters, $\lambda, \delta \in (0,1)$, to define edge payoffs and game values to match the discounting structure of q-bisimulation. We set $\lambda = \sqrt[3]{p}$ and $\delta = 1 - p$. For each pair of states $s_i, s_j \in S$, we introduce vertices $v_{ij}^b, v_{ij}^t \in V_{min}$, $v_{ij}^s \in V_{avg}$, and, for each edge $e : s_i \to s_k$, $v_{ej}^m \in V_{max}$. The edges in $\mathcal{B}$ are introduced according to the following rules:

- $v_{ij}^b \overset{1}{\to} v_{ij}^s$, $v_{ij}^b \overset{1}{\to} v_{ji}^s$;
- $v_{ij}^t \overset{\lambda^2}{\to} v_{ij}^t$;
- for each edge $e : s_i \overset{a}{\to} s_k$, $v_{ij}^s \overset{1}{\to} v_{ej}^m$;
- for each s_n such that $s_j \overset{b}{\to} s_n$, $v_{ej}^m \overset{L(a,b)}{\to} v_{kn}^b$.
- if s_i does not have outgoing transitions, then $v_{ij}^s \overset{\lambda}{\to} v_{ij}^t$ for every s_j.
- if s_j does not have outgoing transitions, then $v_{ej}^m \overset{0}{\to} v_{ij}^t$ for every $e : s_i \overset{a}{\to} s_k$.

For every $s_i, s_j \in S$ and $e \in T$, $N(v_{ij}^b) = N(v_{ij}^t) = N(s_i, s_j)$, $N(v_{ij}^s) = N(v_{ej}^m) = 0$.

The game has two players, one of which selects the transitions at the *max* vertices, while the other selects the transitions at the *min* vertices. The choice of a transition by a player is given by a *strategy* of the player. We consider only *pure memoryless strategies*, in which the choice depends only on the current vertex and not on the history of the game. Such a strategy for the *max* player is represented by a function $\sigma : V_{max} \to V$ (respectively, $\pi : V_{min} \to V$ for the *min* player). The choices at a vertex $v \in V_{avg}$ are made randomly according to a uniform distribution over the successors of v.

Given strategies σ, π and a starting vertex v, a play $w_v^{\sigma,\pi}$ is an infinite random path through the game graph, in which steps from the *min* and *max* vertices comply with the strategies.

The Büchi winning condition for this game is defined as follows. A play is a winning play for player *min* if it contains an infinite number of the vertices from V_{min}. It is easy to see from the construction of the game graph that every play is a winning play for player *min*.

The *discounted payoff* of a play $w_{v_0} = v_0 \xrightarrow{l_1} v_1 \xrightarrow{l_2} \ldots$ for a discount factor λ and a scaling factor δ is defined as

$$Q(w_v) = \delta \cdot \sum_{i=0}^{\infty} \lambda^i \cdot N(v_i) \cdot \prod_{k=1}^{i} l_k. \tag{6}$$

The value of the game for an initial state v and given strategies σ, π is given as the expected payoff of $w_v^{\sigma,\pi}$. Strategies σ_o, π_o are called optimal for v if $w_v^{\sigma_o,\pi_o} = \min_\pi \max_\sigma w_v^{\sigma,\pi}$ The optimal value of the game $\mathcal{B}(G)$ for a node v, denoted $B(v)$, is the value of the play $w_v^{\sigma_o,\pi_o}$ yielded by the optimal strategies.

Considering the structure of the game graph, we conclude that relations between optimal values of the nodes are as shown in Figure 3. Putting these equations together, we can see that the value of a node $v_{i,j}^b$ is the q-bisimulation $B_p(s_i, s_j)$.

$$
\begin{array}{ll}
B(v_{ij}^t) = \delta \cdot N(v_{ij}^t) \cdot \sum_{i=0}^{\infty} \lambda^i \cdot (\lambda^2)^i = \delta \cdot N(v_{ij}^t) \cdot \frac{1}{1-\lambda^3} = N(v_{ij}^t) & \\
B(v_{ej}^m) = 0 & \text{if } v_{ej}^m \to v_{ij}^t \\
B(v_{ej}^m) = \lambda \cdot \max_{v_{ijk}^m \xrightarrow{l_n} v_{nk}^b} (l_k \cdot B(v_k^b)) & \text{otherwise} \\
B(v_{ij}^s) = \lambda^2 \cdot B(v_{ij}^t) & \text{if } v_{ij}^s \to v_{ij}^t \\
B(v_{ij}^s) = \lambda \cdot \text{avg}_{v_{ij}^s \to v_{ej}^m} Q(v_{ej}^m) & \text{otherwise} \\
B(v_{ij}^b) = \delta \cdot N(v_{ij}^s) + \lambda \cdot \min_{v_{ij}^b \to v_k^s} B(v_k^s) &
\end{array}
$$

Fig. 3. Relationships between optimal values in graph nodes

It is well known that there exist optimal pure memoryless strategies for both players for similar payoffs. By using techniques similar to [4], we can show that there are optimal pure memoryless strategies in our case as well. Thus the value of the game can be computed, since there are finitely many pure memoryless strategies. Several approaches for computing game values exist [7, 4], with complexity no more than exponential in the size of the game graph. Since, in our

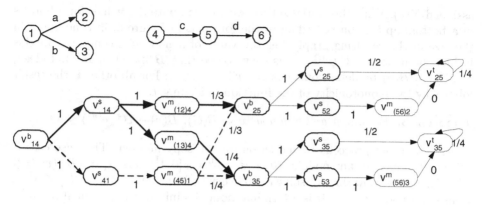

Fig. 4. Game graph construction

case, the game graph $\mathcal{B}(G)$ is polynomial in the size of G ($O(|G|^3)$, to be precise), the complexity of computing q-bisimulation is also no worse than exponential in the size of G.

To illustrate how the game graph construction works, consider the example in Figure 4. Let $L(a, c) = 1/3$, $L(b, c) = 1/4$, and $p = 1/8$. Let $N(s, t) = 1$ for all nodes s, t. Consider, for example, nodes 2 and 5. $B^l(2, 5) = 1$ since node 2 is deadlocked, while $B^r(2, 5) = 7/8$ since node 2 cannot match the transition of node 5, and $B(2, 5) = 7/8$. Accordingly, $B(v_{25}^b) = \delta + \lambda \cdot \min(\lambda^2, 0) = 7/8$. Similarly, $B^l(1, 4) = (1 - p) + p \cdot 1/2 \cdot (L(a, c) \cdot B(2, 5) + L(b, c) \cdot B(3, 5))$ and $B^r(1, 4) = (1 - p) + p \cdot \max(L(c, a) \cdot B(2, 5), L(c, b) \cdot B(3, 5))$. Game steps that correspond to the computation of $B^l(1, 4)$ and $B^r(1, 4)$ shown as block and dashed arrows, respectively. Note that a path from v_{ij}^b to $v_{i'j'}^b$ is always three steps long. Thus, discounting during a game is applied three times, where it is applied once in the definition of q-bisimulation. This observation explains the relationship between p and λ.

5.2   Approximating Quantitative Bisimulation

In many cases, it is not necessary to compute the precise value of q-bisimulation, especially considering that the node and edge similarity functions are likely to be heuristic estimates. It may be sufficient to know whether it exceeds a certain threshold value. It is therefore useful to have a polynomial algorithm to compute an approximation of q-bisimulation up to a required degree of accuracy.

Given the game $\mathcal{B}(G)$, we compute an approximation of q-bisimulation for all states of G as follows. For a chosen n, we make n copies of $\mathcal{B}(G)$, $\mathcal{B}^{(0)}, \ldots, \mathcal{B}^{(n-1)}$. The copy of a node v in $\mathcal{B}^{(i)}$ is denoted $v^{(i)}$. We connect these copies into a single graph by replacing every edge $v^{m(i)} \xrightarrow{l} v^{b(i)}$ ($i > 0$) with $v^{m(i)} \xrightarrow{l} v^{b(i-1)}$. All nodes $v^{t(i)}$ and all incident edges are removed. In $\mathcal{B}^{(0)}$, we keep only the nodes $v_{ij}^{b(0)}$ and remove all other nodes and edges. As a result, we have an acyclic graph $\mathcal{B}^+$. We assign initial values to terminal nodes of $\mathcal{B}^+$ as follows: (1) every node $v^{(0)}$ is assigned $\delta \cdot N(v)$; (2) every node $v^{m(i)}$ is assigned 0; (3) every node $v^{s(i)}$ is assigned $N(v)$. With this initialization, we can compute the values for all nodes in a bottom-up fashion according to the formulas in Figure 3, in time linear in the size of the resulting graph. Let the value of a node $v^{(i)}$ computed in this fashion be denoted $B^+(v^{(i)})$. It is easy to see that $B^+(v^{(i)}) \leq B(v)$. Indeed, $q \cdot N(v) \leq B(v)$ by definition, thus $B^+(v^{(0)}) \leq B(v)$. For all other i, the result follows by the monotonicity of the functional defining B.

Theorem 3. *For any n and any node v in $\mathcal{B}(G)$, $B(v) - B^+(v^{(n)}) \leq \lambda^n$.*

Proof: The proof proceeds by induction on the copy number. The base case is immediate, since for any node v, $B(v), B^+(v^{(0)}) \in [0, 1]$, thus $B(v) - B^+(v^{(0)}) \leq \lambda^0 = 1$. Suppose now that for some i and every node v, $B(v) - B^+(v^{(i-1)}) \leq \lambda^{i-1}$. Consider a node $v^{m(i)}$. If it is a terminal node, its initial value is equal to $B(v)$. Otherwise,

$$B(v^s) - B^+(v^{s(i)}) = \max_{v^s \xrightarrow{l_m} v_m^b} \lambda \cdot l_m \cdot B(v_m^b) - \max_{v^s \xrightarrow{l_k} v_k^b} \lambda \cdot l_k \cdot B^+(v_k^{b(i-1)}).$$

Here, we have to consider two cases. Either $k = m$, that is, the same strategy is chosen by the original and the approximated computation. In that case, clearly,

$$B(v^s) - B^+(v^{s(i)}) = \lambda \cdot l_m \cdot (B(v_m^b) - B^+(v_m^{b(i-1)})) \leq$$
$$\lambda \cdot (B(v_m^b) - B^+(v_m^{b(i-1)})) \leq \lambda \cdot \lambda^{(i-1)} = \lambda^i.$$

Otherwise,

$$l_m \cdot B(v_m^b) - l_k \cdot B^+(v_k^{b(i-1)}) \leq l_m \cdot B(v_m^b) - l_m \cdot B^+(v_m^{b(i-1)}),$$

since $B^+(v_k^{b(i-1)}) \geq B^+(v_m^{b(i-1)})$, and the result follows by the same argument as above. For a node $v^{s(i)}$ the result is immediate, since the calculation computes the average of the values in $v^{m(i)}$, covered by the case above. Finally, for a node $v^{b(i)}$, the argument is similar to the first case. The node has two successor nodes, and the computed value is based on the minimum value of the two successors. As above, the interesting case is the one where the exact and the approximate values come from different successors. Let the successors of v^b be v_1^s and v_2^s, considered in the previous case. Without loss of generality, let us assume that $B(v_1^s) \leq B(v_2^s)$ and $B^+(v_1^{s(i)}) \geq B^+(v_2^{s(i)})$. We then have

$$B(v^b) - B^+(v^{b(i)}) = \lambda \cdot (B(v_1^s) - B^+(v_2^{s(i)})) \leq \lambda \cdot (B(v_2^s) - B^+(v_2^{s(i)})) \leq \lambda^i. \quad \square$$

6   Conclusions and Future Work

We have presented aggregate similarity measures for labeled transition systems. The asymmetric similarity measure, called q-simulation, is well aligned with our original motivation for this work, which involved asymmetric comparisons: a control-flow graph of a new program would compared to well-known representatives of virus families. In general, a symmetric similarity measure may be more useful. Such a symmetric measure, called q-bisimulation, is also more complex to compute. However, for both measures, the more practical approach is to compute an approximate value. Such value, which can be made arbitrarily close to the exact value, can be obtained in time polynomial in the graph size.

A prototype tool for computing q-simulation using the approach of Section 3.3, has been implemented using the lp_solve tool as a back-end, and applied to the samples from the Virus Source Code Database [18]. The tool operates on control-flow graphs in the VCG format produced by the GCC compiler. Our initial experiments demonstrated the need for the weak q-simulation, which is currently being implemented. Out current work concentrates on further experimental evaluation. A matter of practical importance is the choice of the parameters of the function: the weight p and, for weak similarity, the gap penalty. We are considering machine learning approaches for determining parameter values.

An interesting direction of future work is to identify areas of very high similarity within graphs, instead of trying to compare the graphs in their entirety. This would allow us to draw the user's attention to programs that have common parts along with substantially different parts. An example of such programs would be viruses that exploit different vulnerabilities but have the same payload. The relationship between these two graph similarity approaches would be reminiscent of the relationship between global [12] and local [15] string alignment in bioinformatics. Another important direction is to modify the definition of q-simulation to obtain a distance metric, which will make it appealing in various applications, particularly, in bioinformatics.

Although the original motivation for this work comes from the goal to identify potential virus programs from their similarity to known virus family representatives, quantitative simulation and bisimulation have many other potential applications. Work on such applications in the domains of bioinformatics and literature citation databases is already under way [17].

Acknowledgments. We are grateful to Lyle Ungar and Ted Sandler for many fruitful discussions on further applications of q-simulation.

References

1. D. Bertsekas. *Dynamic Programming: Deterministic and Stochastic Models.* Prentice-Hall, Inc., 1987.
2. V. D. Blondel, A. Gajardo, M. Heymans, P. Senellart, and P. Van Dooren. A measure of similarity between graph vertices: Applications to synonym extraction and web searching. *SIAM Review*, 46(4):647–666, 2004.
3. M. C. Browne, E. M. Clarke, and O. Grümberg. Characterizing finite Kripke structures in propositional temporal logic. *Theoretical Computer Science*, 59(1–2):115–131, 1988.
4. K. Chatterjee, M. Jurdziński, and T. Henzinger. Quantitative stochastic parity games. In *SODA '04: Proceedings of the 15th annual ACM-SIAM Symposium on Discrete Algorithms*, pages 121–130, 2004.

5. A. Condon. The complexity of stochastic games. *Information and Computation*, 96(2):203–224, 1992.
6. L. de Alfaro, M. Faella, and M. Stoelinga. Linear and branching metrics for quantitative transition systems. In *ICALP '04: 31st International Colloquium on Automata, Languages, and Programming*, volume 3142 of *LNCS*, pages 97–109, 2004.
7. L. de Alfaro and R. Majumdar. Quantitative solution of omega-regular games. *Journal of Computer and System Sciences*, 68:374–397, 2004.
8. J. Desharnais, V. Gupta, R. Jagadeesan, and P. Panangaden. Metrics for labelled Markov processes. *Theoretical Computer Science*, 318(3):323–354, 2004.
9. J. A. Filar. Ordered field property for stochastic games when the player who controls transitions changes from state to state. *Journal of Optiraization Theory and Applications*, 34:503–515, 1981.
10. S. Melnik, H. Garcia-Molina, and E. Rahm. Similarity flooding: A versatile graph matching algorithm and its application to schema matching. In *Proceedings of 18th ICDE*, 2002.
11. K. Namjoshi. A simple characterization of stuttering bisimulation. In *Proceedings of the 17th Conference on Foundations of Software Technology and Theoretical Computer Science*, pages 284–296, 1997.
12. S. Needleman and C. Wunsch. A general method applicable to the search for similarities in the amino acid sequence of two proteins. *Journal of Molecular Biology*, 48:443–453, 1970.
13. A. Papadopoulos and Y. Manolopoulos. Structure-based similarity search with graph histograms. In *Proceedings International DEXA Workshop on Similarity Search (IWOSS), Florence, Italy*, pages 174–178, 1999.
14. A. Sanfeliu and K. Fu. A distance measure between attributed relational graphs for pattern recognition. *IEEE Transactions on Systems, Man and Cybernetics*, SMC-13(3):353–362, 1983.
15. T. F. Smith and M. S. Waterman. Identification of common molecular subsequences. *Journal of Molecular Biology*, 147:195–197, 1981.
16. P. Szor. *The Art of Computer Virus Research and Defense*. Addison Wesley Professional, 2005.
17. L. Ungar and T. Sandler, Sept. 2005. Personal communication.
18. Virus source code database. `http://www.totallygeek.com/vscdb/`.

PRISM: A Tool for Automatic Verification of Probabilistic Systems[*]

Andrew Hinton, Marta Kwiatkowska, Gethin Norman, and David Parker

School of Computer Science, University of Birmingham,
Birmingham B15 2TT, United Kingdom
{ug60axh, mzk, gxn, dxp}@cs.bham.ac.uk

Abstract. Probabilistic model checking is an automatic formal verification technique for analysing quantitative properties of systems which exhibit stochastic behaviour. PRISM is a probabilistic model checking tool which has already been successfully deployed in a wide range of application domains, from real-time communication protocols to biological signalling pathways. The tool has recently undergone a significant amount of development. Major additions include facilities to manually explore models, Monte-Carlo discrete-event simulation techniques for approximate model analysis (including support for distributed simulation) and the ability to compute cost- and reward-based measures, e.g. "the expected energy consumption of the system before the first failure occurs". This paper presents an overview of all the main features of PRISM. More information can be found on the website: www.cs.bham.ac.uk/~dxp/prism.

1 Overview

Probabilistic model checking is an automatic formal verification technique for the analysis of systems which exhibit stochastic behaviour. Examples of such systems include well-known communication protocols such as FireWire and Bluetooth, which employ randomisation, and a wide range of computer and communication systems, unpredictable characteristics of which, such as message delays or times to failure, are best represented in a probabilistic fashion. Like traditional model checking, this technique involves constructing, from a description in some high-level formalism, a finite-state model of a real-life system, but additionally including information about the likelihood and timing of transitions between states occurring. From this model, a wide range of quantitative measures of the original system can be automatically computed.

PRISM is a probabilistic model checking tool which has already been used to apply these techniques to a large and diverse set of case studies. In the following sections we describe the types of probabilistic model supported by PRISM and the properties of these models which can be analysed. We then give an overview of the main features of the tool. Finally, we summarise the case studies to which the tool has already been applied and the various resources which are available.

[*] Supported in part by EPSRC grants GR/S11107 and GR/S46727 and Microsoft Research Cambridge contract MRL 2005-44.

H. Hermanns and J. Palsberg (Eds.): TACAS 2006, LNCS 3920, pp. 441–444, 2006.

2   PRISM Model Specification

PRISM has direct support for three types of probabilistic models: *discrete-time Markov chains* (DTMCs), *Markov decision processes* (MDPs) and *continuous-time Markov chains* (CTMCs). In DTMCs, time is modelled as discrete time-steps and the probabilities of transitions occurring are also discrete. They are suitable for analysing systems with simple probabilistic behaviour and no concurrency e.g. synchronous randomised distributed algorithms. MDPs extend DTMCs by permitting a combination of nondeterminism and probability, making them well suited to modelling multiple probabilistic processes executing in parallel or to cases where some parameters of the system or the behaviour of the environment in which it is operating are unknown. CTMCs do not support nondeterminism but model time in a continuous fashion, through the use of the negative exponential distributions, allowing accurate representation of the timing characteristics of e.g. component failures and job arrivals.

PRISM now also allows models to be augmented with *costs* and *rewards*, real values assigned to states and transitions of the model. This permits reasoning about a much wider range of quantitative measures of a system, e.g. "completion time", "energy consumption" or "number of messages lost".

Models are specified using the PRISM modelling language, a simple, state-based language based on the Reactive Modules formalism. Systems are described as the parallel composition of a set of modules. Each module's state is given by a set of finite-ranging variables and its behaviour by a set of probabilistic guarded commands. The language also supports global variables, synchronisation and various process algebraic operations. See the PRISM documentation and example repository at [1] for more information.

3   PRISM Property Specification

The specification language for properties of the probabilistic models to be analysed in PRISM is based on temporal logic, in particular PCTL and CSL, probabilistic extensions of the logic CTL. The principal operators are P, S and R which refer, respectively, to the probability of an event occurring, the long-run probability of some condition being satisfied and the expected value of the model's costs or rewards. For precise details of the specification language, see the PRISM documentation [1]. For the theoretical background and further references, see [2]. For illustrative purposes, a selection of example properties is shown below:

- P $\geq$ 0.9 [!*repair* U $\leq$ 200 *done*] - "with probability 0.9 or more, the process will successfully complete within 200 hours and without requiring repairs"
- P =? [F $\leq$ *T error* {init}{max}] - "what is the worst-case probability, over all possible initial configurations, that an error has occurred by time T"
- S =? [*num_sensors* $\geq$ *min_sensors*] - "what is the long-run probability that an acceptable number of sensors are operational?"
- R < 3 [C $\leq$ *T*] - "the expected number of messages lost during the first T minutes of execution of the communication protocol is less than 3"

- R =? [F *shutdown* {*error_ detected*}{max}] - "from all situations where an error has been detected, what is the worst-case expected power consumption before the system shuts itself down?"

Note that is possible to either determine whether a probability or expected quantity satisfies a given bound or obtain the actual value. In the latter case, it is often beneficial to compute a range of values in order to identify trends or anomalies. The ability to examine worst-case (or best-case) scenarios, as illustrated in the examples above, is also very powerful.

4 The PRISM Tool

The core functionality of PRISM, namely constructing a probabilistic model, and then evaluating the result of one or more corresponding properties, is available from either a command-line or a graphical user interface. The latter includes editors for the PRISM modelling and property specification languages. It also facilitates generation of series of quantitative results and plotting of graphs to visualise them. A recent addition is the ability to view specific traces of model execution for the purposes of debugging or sanity checks. These are generated either by manual exploration or automatically in probabilistic fashion. Figure 1 shows screenshots of some of this functionality in operation.

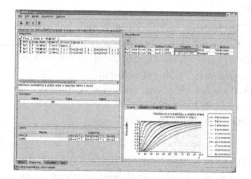 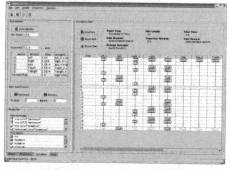

Fig. 1. Screenshots of PRISM running. Left: graphical visualisation of quantitative model checking results. Right: manual exploration of model traces.

PRISM incorporates a range of model analysis techniques. These include qualitative methods, such as graph-based algorithms for reachability, and quantitative methods for numerical computation of probabilities and expected cost or reward values. For the latter, multiple implementations are provided. In particular, this includes state-of-the-art symbolic approaches which use data structures based on binary decision diagrams (BDDs) to exploit model structure and regularity.

The most recent addition is support for approximate numerical computation using Monte-Carlo methods and discrete event simulation. PRISM can generate multiple executions through a model based on a faithful simulation of its probabilistic and timing characteristics. These samples are then used to compute approximate quantitative results. Since this approach avoids the (costly) construction of the full probabilistic model, working instead with the PRISM language description, it is potentially applicable to much larger models than the alternative numerical solution approach. Furthermore, samples can be generated independently, so it is possible to distribute the simulation process over multiple computers. The PRISM user interface includes a tool to manage this process.

Connections to other tools and formalisms. To allow connections with external tools, PRISM allows the export of a model's transition matrix and state space in a variety of formats: either plain text or tailored for specific tools, including Matlab, ETMCC and MRMC. Models specified in alternative formalisms can also be imported via translation. PRISM already has native support for a subset of the stochastic process algebra PEPA and others are underway. It is now also possible to import the transition matrix and state space of a model directly in a simple textual format.

Examples and case studies. PRISM has been successfully applied to a large number of case studies from a wide array of application areas, on several occasions resulting in the identification of interesting or anomalous behaviour. The website [1] provides details of over thirty case studies, developed both by members of the PRISM team and external research groups, including links to the corresponding publications and source code. Examples include analysis of the performance, reliability or correctness of:

- real-time communication protocols, including IEEE 1394 FireWire, Bluetooth, Zeroconf, IEEE 802.3 CSMA/CD and IEEE 802.11 wireless LANs;
- probabilistic security protocols for anonymity (Crowds protocol, synchronous batching), contract signing, fair exchange and non-repudiation;
- randomised distributed algorithms for leader election, consensus, Byzantine agreement, self-stabilisation and mutual exclusion;
- dynamic power management and voltage scaling schemes;
- biological signalling pathways.

Tool availability and resources. PRISM is a free and open source tool, distributed under the GNU General Public License (GPL), and now supports most major operating systems: Linux, Solaris, Windows and Mac OS X. Ports have also been developed for 64-bit architectures. The PRISM website [1] contains a wealth of further information and resources, including related publications, the tool source code and binaries, user manual and a large repository of illustrative example models.

References

[1] PRISM web site. www.cs.bham.ac.uk/~dxp/prism.
[2] J. Rutten, M. Kwiatkowska, G. Norman, and D. Parker. *Mathematical Techniques for Analyzing Concurrent and Probabilistic Systems*, P. Panangaden and F. van Breugel (eds.), volume 23 of *CRM Monograph Series*. AMS, 2004.

DISTRIBUTOR and BCG_MERGE: Tools for Distributed Explicit State Space Generation

Hubert Garavel, Radu Mateescu, Damien Bergamini, Adrian Curic,
Nicolas Descoubes, Christophe Joubert,
Irina Smarandache-Sturm, and Gilles Stragier

INRIA Rhône-Alpes / VASY,
655, avenue de l'Europe, F-38330 Montbonnot St Martin, France

1 Introduction

The explicit-state verification of complex concurrent systems, whose underlying state spaces may be prohibitively large, requires an important amount of memory and computation time. Although explicit state space generation is known to be exponential as the number of concurrent processes in the system increases, it is tempting to push forward the capabilities of verification tools by exploiting the computing resources (memory and processors) of massively parallel machines, such as clusters and grids.

Several distributed algorithms have been proposed for analyzing stochastic Petri nets and Markov chains (e.g., by Nicol and Ciardo, by Haverkort, Bell, and Bohnenkamp, etc.), as well as for model checking (e.g., by Stern and Dill, by Lerda and Sisto, etc.). Our own distributed algorithms [3] allow the construction of Labelled Transition Systems (LTSs) using several machines connected by a network. These algorithms are implemented in the DISTRIBUTOR and BCG_MERGE tools using the facilities of the CADP [2] verification toolbox. In a nutshell, each machine used by DISTRIBUTOR is responsible for generating and storing a fragment of the entire LTS. Upon termination of the distributed state space generation, all these fragments are combined together using BCG_MERGE to obtain the entire LTS.

Between 2000 and 2005, we developed three successive versions (1.0, 2.0, and 3.0) of DISTRIBUTOR and BCG_MERGE. This led to significant functionality improvements. For instance, version 3.0 of DISTRIBUTOR can also reduce LTSs on-the-fly, by applying τ-compression (elimination of τ-cycles denoting divergence) or τ-confluence (a form of partial order reduction preserving branching equivalence) [4] using the algorithms proposed in [6]. However, besides the distributed algorithms themselves, we realized that it was also essential to pay attention to often-neglected practical issues, such as software architecture concepts and user-oriented features pertaining to ergonomy, and this is what the present paper is about.

2 Software Architecture and User-Oriented Features

Source language independence. Developing verification tools for sequential machines is a demanding, long-term effort. But the development effort is

H. Hermanns and J. Palsberg (Eds.): TACAS 2006, LNCS 3920, pp. 445–449, 2006.

even higher for verification tools intended to work on parallel machines. Therefore, it is desirable to design tools that can support multiple input languages instead of a single one. For this reason, DISTRIBUTOR is implemented using the OPEN/CÆSAR generic environment [1], which is the basis for all on-the-fly verification algorithms implemented within CADP. OPEN/CÆSAR offers an *implicit* representation for LTSs to be explored on-the-fly by providing a language-independent API that basically defines the states, labels, and transitions of the LTS, together with functions for comparing, hashing, accessing the initial state, and computing the successors of a given state. It also provides C libraries containing a rich set of LTS exploration primitives (transition lists, stacks, tables, etc.). Thus, DISTRIBUTOR can be used for any input language equipped with a compiler supporting the OPEN/CÆSAR API.

Platform independence. A key design goal of DISTRIBUTOR and BCG_MERGE is to allow them to run on the largest possible number of computing platforms (networks of workstations, clusters of PCs, or even laptops, etc.) For this reason, DISTRIBUTOR and BCG_MERGE only use the features present in mainstream operating systems and do not to rely on any dedicated middleware (such as MPI, etc.) that is not installed by default. Similarly, they do not assume the existence of a common file system (e.g., NFS, SAMBA, etc.) shared between machines.

Separation between algorithms and communications. Starting from version 2.0 of DISTRIBUTOR and BCG_MERGE, a clear separation was established between, on the one hand, the distributed algorithms themselves and, on the other hand, the primitives used for communication between machines. Such primitives are encapsulated into a dedicated library (named CÆSAR_NETWORK), which provides functionalities such as blocking and non-blocking buffered send/receive. Following the "platform independence" requirement, CÆSAR_NETWORK only requires ordinary TCP sockets and standard remote connection protocols (e.g., rsh/rcp, ssh/scp, etc.) to be available. CÆSAR_NETWORK is also used by other VASY tools for distributed equivalence checking [5] and distributed model checking.

Instances on local and remote machines. The machine on which DISTRIBUTOR and BCG_MERGE are launched by the end-user is called the *local* machine, all the other ones being called *remote* machines. DISTRIBUTOR and BCG_MERGE work by launching distributed processes, called *instances*. Each instance corresponds to a pair (M, D), indicating that a distributed process will be launched on machine M and will store its files in directory D (the *working directory* of the instance) located on some filesystem of M. Several instances with different working directories may execute on the same machine. A working directory may be either local to its machine, or shared between several machines.

Description of network resources. To specify the list of machines and instances involved in the distributed computation, the CÆSAR_NETWORK library uses a dedicated file named *Grid Configuration File* (GCF), whose format is defined in [8]. This file also specifies the various configuration parameters to be used for launching instances and connecting machines: TCP port number(s)

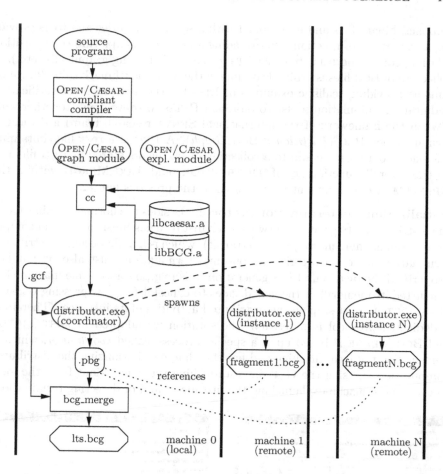

used by sockets, remote connection protocol (rsh, ssh, etc.), remote copy protocol (rcp, scp, etc.), login name(s) used for remote authentication, size of communication buffers, pathname of the CADP installation directory, connection timeout, pathname of the working directory, and list of files to be copied in the working directories upon launching.

Partitioned Labelled Transition Systems. The result of the distributed LTS generation performed by DISTRIBUTOR is a theoretical model defined in [3] and called *Partitioned* LTS (PLTS for short). A PLTS is a collection of *fragments* (one per instance), each fragment containing a subset of the states and transitions of the entire LTS to be generated. Taken altogether, the fragments form a partition of the entire LTS. Taken individually, each fragment can be seen as an LTS, with the important difference that it may be a disconnected graph, which is never the case with an LTS generated from a "meaningful" specification. The role of BCG_MERGE is to take a PLTS and merge all its fragments into one single LTS.

To represent LTSs, as well as fragments, we use the BCG (*Binary-Coded Graphs*) format of CADP. This format provides an *explicit* representation for LTSs given by their states, labels, and transitions. It allows to store LTSs in compact, binary files and is equipped with a set of C libraries and tools providing a wide range of functionalities (reading and writing, exploring the transition relation, converting from/to other LTS formats, visualizing graphically, etc.). A collection of BCG files is available on-line in the VLTS benchmark suite [9], which aims at providing realistic examples of LTSs for the assessment of verification and graph manipulation tools. To represent PLTSs, we developed (together with CWI in the framework of the international SENVA research team) a dedicated format named PBG (*Partitioned* BCG *Graph*). A PBG is a text file containing references to a GCF file and to a collection of fragments stored as BCG files.

The overall functioning of DISTRIBUTOR and BCG_MERGE within the OPEN/CÆSAR environment is illustrated in the previous figure.

Initialization and termination protocols. Besides the normal termination of the distributed LTS generation (when each instance has finished its local computations and no more messages are in transit), which is handled using a distributed termination detection algorithm, abnormal termination must also be handled properly. If the distributed LTS generation fails (e.g., because some machine has exhausted its memory) or the user decides to cancel it (e.g., by pressing Ctrl-C), DISTRIBUTOR must stop all the distributed activities of its instances. Therefore, a dedicated protocol is necessary. The solution we adopted in DISTRIBUTOR and BCG_MERGE is based upon a special process, called *coordinator*, which is launched on the local machine and has the charge of initializing the distributed computation (parsing the GCF file, establishing the connections from the local to the remote machines, launching the instances) and of detecting termination.

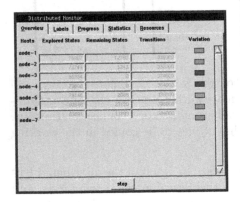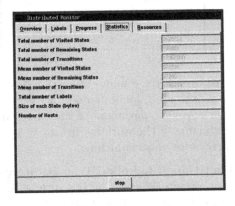

Real-time monitoring. Because end-users naturally want to observe the progression of distributed computations, DISTRIBUTOR and BCG_MERGE are equipped with (optional) graphical monitors providing information in real-time about computation status (when generating or merging of the PBG) and resource usage (processors and memories). The monitor of DISTRIBUTOR (see the figure above) is driven by the coordinator process, which periodically inspects the status of each instance. The monitor window has five panels, each giving a different view of the distributed computation. The "Overview" panel (on the left) shows, for each instance, the number of explored states (whose successors have been visited), the number of remaining states (visited, but not explored yet), and the number of transitions in the corresponding fragment; the variation of remaining states (increasing, decreasing, steady) is represented as a coloured box (green, orange, red). The "Statistics" panel (on the right) shows various global data, such as the total and average number of visited and remaining states, of transitions, of labels, etc.

3   Conclusion and Future Work

Versions 3.0 of DISTRIBUTOR and BCG_MERGE are documented [8, 7] and distributed as part of the CADP toolbox. They run on several platforms (Linux, MacOS, Solaris, Windows). Experiments performed on various case-studies and different computing platforms have shown quasi-linear speedups and a good load balancing between machines.

We plan to continue our work along two directions. Using DISTRIBUTOR, generating very large LTSs becomes easier and one is now confronted to the limits of standard 32-bit machines, especially when state numbers become larger than 2^{32} and/or when BCG files become larger than 4 Gbytes. Shifting to 64-bit machines should solve these issues and overcome the current size limitations.

BCG_MERGE is valuable as it allows (at least for small or medium-sized models) to verify that the LTSs generated by DISTRIBUTOR are identical to those generated on a single machine. For large models however, BCG_MERGE may be a bottleneck because of the aforementioned 4 Gbytes limit. This can be avoided by performing verification directly on the PBG file, without invoking BCG_MERGE first. We seek to develop a PBG_OPEN tool connecting the PBG model to the API defined by OPEN/CÆSAR, thus allowing the model checking and equivalence checking tools of CADP to be applied on PBG models directly.

References

1. H. Garavel. OPEN/CÆSAR: An Open Software Architecture for Verification, Simulation, and Testing. In *Proc. of TACAS'98*, LNCS vol. 1384, pp. 68–84.
2. H. Garavel, F. Lang, and R. Mateescu. An Overview of CADP 2001. *European Association for Software Science and Technology (EASST) Newsletter*, 4:13–24, 2002.
3. H. Garavel, R. Mateescu, and I. Smarandache. Parallel State Space Construction for Model-Checking. In *Proc. SPIN'2001*, LNCS vol. 2057, pp. 217–234.
4. J.F. Groote and J. van de Pol. State Space Reduction using Partial τ-Confluence. In *Proc. of MFCS'2000*, LNCS vol. 1893, pp. 383–393.
5. Ch. Joubert and R. Mateescu. Distributed On-the-Fly Equivalence Checking. In *Proc. of PDMC'2004*, ENTCS vol. 128.
6. R. Mateescu. On-the-fly State Space Reductions for Weak Equivalences. In *Proc. of FMICS'05*, ACM, pp. 80–89.
7. Vasy. BCG_MERGE Manual Page. http://www.inrialpes.fr/vasy/cadp/man/bcg_merge.html, December 2004.
8. Vasy. DISTRIBUTOR Manual Page. http://www.inrialpes.fr/vasy/cadp/man/distributor.html, December 2004.
9. Vasy and Sen2. The VLTS benchmark suite. http://www.inrialpes.fr/vasy/cadp/resources/benchmark_bcg.html, March 2003.

MCMAS: A Model Checker for Multi-agent Systems

Alessio Lomuscio and Franco Raimondi*

Department of Computer Science,
University College London, London, UK
{a.lomuscio, f.raimondi}@cs.ucl.ac.uk

1 Overview

This paper presents MCMAS, a model checker for Multi-Agent Systems (MAS). Differently from traditional model checkers, MCMAS permits the automatic verification of specifications that use epistemic, correctness, and cooperation modalities, in addition to the standard temporal modalities. These additional modalities are used to capture properties of various scenarios (including communication and security protocols, games, etc.) that may be difficult or unnatural to express with temporal operators only; a small number of applications are presented in Section 4. Agents are described in MCMAS by means of the dedicated programming language ISPL (Interpreted Systems Programming Language). The approach is symbolic and uses ordered binary decision diagrams (OBDDs), thereby extending standard techniques for temporal logic to other modalities distinctive of agents. MCMAS and all the examples presented in this paper are available for download [14] under the terms of the GPL license.

2 Theoretical Background

Interpreted systems [5] provide the formal semantics for MCMAS programs. In the formalism of interpreted systems, each agent is characterised by a set of *local states* and by a set of local *actions* that are performed following a local *protocol*. Given a set of initial states, the system evolves in compliance with an evolution function that determines how the local state of an agent changes as a function of its local state and of the other agents' actions. The evolution of all the agents' local states describes a set of *runs* and a set of *reachable states*. These can be used to interpret formulae involving temporal operators, epistemic operators to reason about what agents *know*, operators to reason about the *correct behaviour* of the agents, and ATL operators expressing states of affairs that agents can enforce. Due to space limitations, we refer to [5, 13, 10, 1, 7] for a detailed presentation of this formalism, and for theoretical results on completeness, decidability, complexity, etc.

Interpreted systems' specifications can be given by means of ISPL programs: a simple example is depicted in Figure 1 (a). We refer to the files available online for the full syntax of ISPL.

Given an interpreted system and a formula in the syntax of ISPL, MCMAS computes the set of states in which the formula holds and compares it to the set of reachable states. The methodology used to calculate this set extends the standard fix-point boolean

---

* Corresponding author. The authors acknowledge EPSRC grants CN04/04 and GR/S49353/01.

H. Hermanns and J. Palsberg (Eds.): TACAS 2006, LNCS 3920, pp. 450–454, 2006.

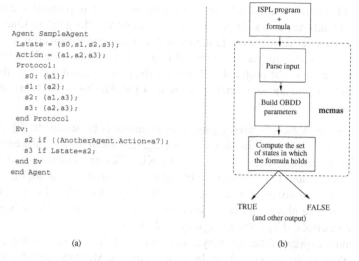

```
Agent SampleAgent
  Lstate = {s0,s1,s2,s3};
  Action = {a1,a2,a3};
  Protocol:
    s0: {a1};
    s1: {a2};
    s2: {a1,a3};
    s3: {a2,a3};
  end Protocol
  Ev:
    s2 if ((AnotherAgent.Action=a7);
    s3 if Lstate=s2;
  end Ev
end Agent
```

ISPL program
+
formula

Parse input

Build OBDD
parameters   mcmas

Compute the set
of states in which
the formula holds

TRUE   FALSE
(and other output)

(a)   (b)

Fig. 1. Implementation structure and ISPL example

characterisation for temporal operators [4] to epistemic, correctness, and cooperation operators. We refer to [15] for more details.

3   Implementation

Figure 1 (b) shows the structure of the implementation of MCMAS. The tool can be run from the command line and accepts various options to modify verbosity, to inspect OBDDs statistics [16] and memory usage, and to enable variable reordering in the OBDDs. The tool is written in C/C++ and it has been compiled on various platforms, including PowerPC (Mac OS X 10.2 and 10.3), x86 (various CPUs running Linux 2.4 and 2.6), SPARC (SunOS 5.8 and 5.9), and Windows using Cygwin. The source code has been compiled with gcc/g++ from version 2.95 until version 3.4.

4   Examples and Experimental Results

Various ISPL programs are available for download from [14]. We consider here three of them to illustrate different verification scenarios.

Communication protocol: The bit transmission protocol with faults. In this example from [5], an agent (the Sender) wants to communicate the value of a bit to another agent (the Receiver) using a faulty line that may drop messages. To achieve this, the Sender starts sending messages to the Receiver; when the Receiver receives the bit, it starts sending acknowledgements back to the Sender. The protocol terminates when the Sender receives the acknowledgement. This scenario can be described in terms of interpreted systems, and it is easy to verify with MCMAS the key specification of the protocol: $\mathbf{recack} \rightarrow AG(K_S(K_R(\mathbf{bit})).$

This formula expresses formally that, upon receipt of an acknowledgement, the Sender will forever know that the Receiver knows the value of the bit. This scenario is extended in [11] to include faulty behaviours of the Receiver. In particular, it is possible to model two faulty scenarios. In the first one, the Receiver "forgets" to send acknowledgements when it receives the bit. In the second scenario, the Receiver may send faulty acknowledgements without receiving the bit first. It is possible to verify with MCMAS the key specification of the protocol still holds in the first case, but it fails in the second. More complex specifications, referring explicitly to violations in the local behaviours, can also be verified.

Strategic games: A simple card game. This example is presented in [8] and in [9]: an agent (the player) plays a simple card game against another agent, the environment. There are just three cards in the deck: Ace (A), King (K), and Queen (Q); A wins over K, K wins over Q, and Q wins over A. In the initial state no cards are distributed; in the first step, the environment gives a card to the player and takes a card for itself. In the second step, the player can either keep its card, or change it. The following ATL formula can be checked by MCMAS: $\langle\langle player \rangle\rangle F(\mathbf{win})$.

The formula expresses that the player may *always* bring about a winning state, by randomly selecting the correct action. In addition to this, MCMAS supports an operator that considers only *feasible strategies* in the sense of [9, 8]. These are strategies that cannot be "guessed". MCMAS correctly verifies that in this example the player *does not* have a feasible strategy to win.

Anonymity example: The protocol of the dining cryptographers. The protocol of the dining cryptographers is introduced in [3] to describe a scenario in which information is exchanged anonymously. The scenario consists of three cryptographers having dinner at a restaurant. When the waiter informs them that the charge has been covered already, they would like to find out whether it is one of them, or the company they work for who paid for it. In order to guarantee the anonymity of the payer (in case it is one of them), they proceed as follows: each of them flips a coin behind a menu on the right hand side of his dish and observes this coin and the coin at his left (flipped by another cryptographer). If the cryptographer did not pay for the dinner, then he announces whether the two coins he can see are equal or different. However, if the cryptographer paid for the dinner, he says the opposite of what he sees. It is possible to check that, if a cryptographer did not pay for the dinner and he hears an odd number of "different" utterances, then he knows that one of the remaining cryptographers paid for the dinner, but he cannot say who. This property is captured by the following formula:

$$(\neg\mathbf{paid_1} \wedge \mathbf{odd}) \rightarrow AX(K_{C_1}(\mathbf{paid_2} \vee \mathbf{paid_3}) \wedge \neg K_{C_1}(\mathbf{paid_2}) \wedge \neg K_{C_1}(\mathbf{paid_3}))$$

Notice that the same protocol works for any number of cryptographers greater or equal than three, thereby allowing for an evaluation of the scalability of MCMAS. The ISPL code for various instances of the protocol, including some in which cheating cryptographers are introduced, is available form [14].

5   Discussion

Differently from previous approaches [2], MCMAS does not involve the translation nor the reduction of the model checking problem for MAS to other available model checkers. Our technique is based on OBDDs but, differently from [6], we consider various

Table 1. Experimental results

N.Crypt.	States (n. bool var)	OBDDs nodes	Memory (MBytes)	Time (sec)
3	$\approx 7 \cdot 10^{13} (47)$	$\approx 10^4$	≈ 4.4	0.37
4	$\approx 2 \cdot 10^{18} (63)$	$\approx 6 \cdot 10^4$	≈ 5.2	3.9
5	$\approx 2 \cdot 7.5^{22} (77)$	$\approx 8 \cdot 10^4$	≈ 5.6	12.6
6	$\approx 1.2 \cdot 10^{27} (91)$	$\approx 1.6 \cdot 10^5$	≈ 7.1	64.5
7	$\approx 2 \cdot 10^{31} (105)$	$\approx 1.7 \cdot 10^5$	≈ 7.5	168.8
8	$\approx 1.3 \cdot 10^{36} (121)$	$\approx 1.2 \cdot 10^7$	≈ 450	28788

modalities on top of the epistemic and the temporal ones, and our semantics does not assume perfect recall. The tool presented in [12] allows for the verification of temporal, epistemic, and correct behaviour operators but, differently form MCMAS, it uses bounded and un-bounded techniques, and it has a different input language.

Average experimental results for the example of the dining cryptographers on a 2.8 GHz Pentium 4 running Linux 2.4.20 with 1 Gbytes of RAM are presented in Table 1. We see these results as encouraging, considering that optimisation techniques have not been included in MCMAS yet, and that the code is currently under active development. In particular, we aim at including *fairness constraints* in the verification process, and counter-example generation for false formulae.

References

1. R. Alur, T. A. Henzinger, and O. Kupferman. Alternating-time temporal logic. *Journal of the ACM*, 49(5):672–713, 2002.
2. R. Bordini, M. Fisher, C. Pardavila, W. Visser, and M. Wooldridge. Model checking multi-agent programs with CASP. In *Proceedings of the 15th International Conference on Computer Aided Verification (CAV'03)*, volume 2725 of *LNCS*, pages 110–113. Springer-Verlag, 2003.
3. D. Chaum. The dining cryptographers problem: Unconditional sender and recipient untraceability. *Journal of Cryptology*, 1(1):65–75, 1988.
4. E. M. Clarke, O. Grumberg, and D. A. Peled. *Model Checking*. The MIT Press, Cambridge, Massachusetts, 1999.
5. R. Fagin, J. Y. Halpern, Y. Moses, and M. Y. Vardi. *Reasoning about Knowledge*. MIT Press, Cambridge, 1995.
6. P. Gammie and R. van der Meyden. MCK: Model checking the logic of knowledge. In *Proceedings of 16th International Conference on Computer Aided Verification (CAV'04)*, volume 3114 of *LNCS*, pages 479–483. Springer-Verlag, 2004.
7. W. van der Hoek and M. Wooldridge. Tractable multiagent planning for epistemic goals. In M. Gini, T. Ishida, C. Castelfranchi, and W. L. Johnson, editors, *Proceedings of the First International Joint Conference on Autonomous Agents and Multiagent Systems (AAMAS'02)*, pages 1167–1174. ACM Press, 2002.
8. W. Jamroga and W. van der Hoek. Agents that know how to play. *Fundamenta Informaticae*, 62:1–35, 2004.
9. G. Jonker. Feasible strategies in alternating-time temporal epistemic logic. Master's thesis, University of Utrech, The Netherlands, 2003.
10. A. Lomuscio and M. Sergot. Deontic interpreted systems. *Studia Logica*, 75(1):63–92, 2003.
11. A. Lomuscio and M. Sergot. A formalisation of violation, error recovery, and enforcement in the bit transmission problem. *Journal of Applied Logic*, 2(1):93–116, March 2004.

12. W. Nabialek, A. Niewiadomski, W. Penczek, A. Pólrola, and M. Szreter. VerICS 2004: A model checker for real time and multi-agent systems. In *Proceedings of the International Workshop on Concurrency, Specification and Programming (CS&P'04)*, volume 170 of *Informatik-Berichte*, pages 88–99. Humboldt University, 2004.
13. W. Penczek and A. Lomuscio. Verifying epistemic properties of multi-agent systems via bounded model checking. *Fundamenta Informaticae*, 55(2):167–185.
14. F. Raimondi and A. Lomuscio. MCMAS - A tool for verification of multi-agent systems. http://www.cs.ucl.ac.uk/staff/f.raimondi/MCMAS/.
15. F. Raimondi and A. Lomuscio. Automatic verification of multi-agent systems by model checking via OBDDs. *Journal of Applied Logic*, 2005. To appear in Special issue on Logic-based agent verification.
16. F. Somenzi. CUDD: CU decision diagram package - release 2.4.0. http://vlsi.colorado.edu/~fabio/CUDD/cuddIntro.html.

MSCan – A Tool for Analyzing MSC Specifications

Benedikt Bollig[1], Carsten Kern[2], Markus Schlütter[3], and Volker Stolz[2]

[1] LSV, CNRS UMR 8643 & ENS de Cachan, France
bollig@lsv.ens-cachan.fr
[2] Software Modeling and Verification Group, RWTH Aachen University, Germany
{kern, stolz}@informatik.rwth-aachen.de
[3] Department of Process Control Engineering, RWTH Aachen University, Germany
schluetter@plt.rwth-aachen.de

Abstract. We present the tool MSCan, which supports MSC-based system development. In particular, it automatically checks high-level MSC specifications for implementability.

1 Introduction

Message Sequence Charts (MSCs) constitute a prominent notion for describing protocols in the early stages of system development [8]. An MSC depicts a collection of processes, which, in their visual representation, are drawn as vertical lines and interpreted as time axes. An arrow from one line to a second corresponds to sending and receiving a message. Not only does the MSC standard allow to specify single scenarios; to make MSCs a flexible specification language, it also supports *choice*, *concatenation*, and *iteration*, which give rise to *high-level MSCs*. Consider Fig. 1: the MSCs M_1, M_2, and M_3 are the building blocks of the high-level MSC G, which generates scenarios such as the MSC M.

A high-level MSC specification permits a *global* view of a distributed system, whereas the future implementation thereof will usually be controlled *locally* by rather autonomous processes. Due to this inherent discrepancy, a preliminary high-level MSC specification might not be suitable for an implementation and often requires further refinement and adjustment steps. If, for example, the specification admits some global system behavior where the choice of two alternatives can be triggered by independent processes, inconsistent (local) decisions might lead the system into a deadlock. This phenomenon is known as *non-local choice* [2]. Otherwise, the high-level MSC from Fig. 1 has the local-choice property: the only choice point is entirely under the control of process 2.

A system specification with the local-choice property can always be realized by a deadlock-free distributed implementation. Other requirements ensuring implementability with various characteristics are *local cooperativity*, *global cooperativity*, and *regularity* [5, 7]. Last but not least, high-level MSCs with above-mentioned properties come along with decidable model-checking problems for further analyses that, in general, are undecidable [1, 5].

H. Hermanns and J. Palsberg (Eds.): TACAS 2006, LNCS 3920, pp. 455–458, 2006.

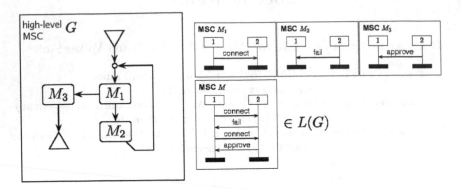

Fig. 1. A (local-choice) high-level MSC

2   The Tool MSCAN

MSCAN supports the system development based on high-level MSCs. It automatically checks a high-level MSC specification for (several variants of) local choice, local and global cooperativity, as well as regularity and many other reasonable requirements to draw conclusions about implementability, consistency, and decidable model-checking problems. Moreover, MSCAN offers numerous features for editing, displaying, and debugging high-level MSCs. It converts an ITU Z.120 textual description of a high-level MSC specification into a graph structure that naturally reflects choice, concatenation, and iteration. Based on the internal graph representation, MSCAN applies graph algorithms to explore the specification and to detect global control structures that do not allow an embedding into a locally controlled implementation.

Note that high-level MSCs, in their basic form, are only capable of specifying *finitely generated* behavior [7]. To overcome those drawbacks and to be able to specify *non* finitely generated behavior such as the alternating-bit protocol, *compositional* high-level MSCs have been introduced by Gunter et al. [6]. We would like to stress that, in all aspects, our tool supports this extension, which enjoys many nice properties and increasing popularity [4].

2.1   Graphical User Interface

To grant the user a maximum degree of comfort, the graphical user interface is partitioned into four main components (cf. Fig. 2). The upper part of the GUI is taken by the menu component of the tool (1). It offers facilities to *create*, *load*, and *save* MSC documents and to change the level of detail and the mode of analysis (e.g., lazy evaluation). Moreover, the menu allows to select a single high-level MSC property as well as grouping several properties together.

Further features that are controlled via the menu component of MSCAN are: (i) processing the MSC document and displaying its graph structure in the graph component of the GUI, (ii) displaying the properties of the currently

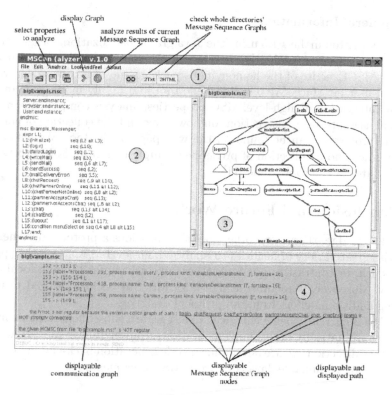

Fig. 2. An MSCAN Session

selected high-level MSC that have been detected so far, and (iii) checking directories recursively for high-level MSCs, executing all tests currently supported by
the tool, and creating a text or HTML output containing the results of the
analysis. The left component (2) may be used for editing MSC documents.
Herein, the user can specify the system behavior to be analyzed as well as
alter faulty specifications to eventually converge to a protocol that exhibits
exactly the desired properties. Label (3) is associated with the graph component of MSCAN, in which the high-level MSC under consideration can be
displayed. It allows the user to zoom in and out partial behavior as well as
clicking onto nodes to depict the associated MSCs. The fourth component (4)
is addressed to the analysis output of a test execution providing the user with
counter examples, which may be used for debugging and system refinement.
It displays test results and calls the user's attention to potential conflicts or
inconsistencies in the protocol specification. Additionally, it eases the protocol
designer's task of ruling out errors by visualizing high-level MSC components
like nodes, edges, paths and all kinds of graphs (e.g., channel and communication graphs). This guides the user and substantially reduces her effort to detect
faulty or inconsistent system behavior. For further screenshots and a more elaborate feature description, the reader may visit the web page of MSCAN located
at [11].

2.2   General Information

MSCAN is written in Java 1.5 using the Java graph visualization package *Grappa*
[10] and the parser *MSC2000* [9]. It consists of a console application started by
the class MSCExecute of the homonymous package and of a concise, interactive
graphical user interface. We developed the tool in a highly modular manner to
ease the integration of high-level MSC properties, analysis components, and the
graphical user interface. Instructions on how to extend the collection of currently
available properties can be found on the web page of the tool. We also offer a
web interface and a collection of predefined sample high-level MSCs to test the
basic features of the tool online [11].

3   Conclusion and Future Work

To our knowledge, there is no other tool that provides a protocol designer with
a likewise great variety of facilities to analyze high-level MSCs. Another project
is [3], which, in contrast to our tool, checks exclusively for the non-local choice
property. Moreover, it requires a high-level MSC to be in a normal form, demanding additional effort from the protocol designer.

MSCAN is currently being enhanced to integrate a subsequent implementation
phase to automatically derive implementations from high-level MSCs. As a first
step in that direction, we are developing a code generation back-end, which emits
out-of-the-box compilable Java code from MSC documents [12].

References

1. R. Alur and M. Yannakakis. Model checking of message sequence charts. In
   CONCUR 1999, volume 1664 of *LNCS*. Springer, 1999.
2. H. Ben-Abdallah and S. Leue. Syntactic detection of process divergence and non-
   local choice in message sequence charts. In *TACAS 1997*, volume 1217 of *LNCS*.
   Springer, 1997.
3. H. Ben-Abdallah and S. Leue. Mesa: Support for scenario-based design of concurrent systems. In *TACAS 1998*, volume 1384 of *LNCS*. Springer, 1998.
4. B. Genest. Compositional message sequence charts (CMSCs) are better to implement than MSCs. In *TACAS 2005*, volume 3340 of *LNCS*. Springer, 2005.
5. B. Genest, A. Muscholl, H. Seidl, and M. Zeitoun. Infinite-state high-level MSCs:
   Model-checking and realizability. In *ICALP 2002*, volume 2380 of *LNCS*. Springer,
   2002.
6. E. Gunter, A. Muscholl, and D. Peled. Compositional message sequence charts. In
   TACAS 2001, volume 2031 of *LNCS*. Springer, 2001.
7. J. G. Henriksen, M. Mukund, K. Narayan Kumar, and P. S. Thiagarajan. On
   message sequence graphs and finitely generated regular MSC languages. In *ICALP
   2000*, volume 1853 of *LNCS*. Springer, 2000.
8. ITU-TS Recommendation Z.120: Message Sequence Chart 1999 (MSC99), 1999.
9. H. Neukirchen. *MSC2000 Parser*. CS Dept., University of Göttingen.
10. *Grappa (Version 1.2)*. http://www.research.att.com/~john/Grappa/.
11. MSCAN. http://www-i2.informatik.rwth-aachen.de/MSCan/.
12. MSC EXECUTE. http://www-i2.informatik.rwth-aachen.de/MSCExecute/.

A Practical and Complete Approach to Predicate Refinement

Ranjit Jhala and K.L. McMillan

[1] University of California, San Diego
[2] Cadence Berkeley Labs

Abstract. Predicate abstraction is a method of synthesizing the strongest inductive invariant of a system expressible as a Boolean combination of a given set of atomic predicates. A predicate selection method can be said to be complete for a given theory if it is guaranteed to eventually find atomic predicates sufficient to prove a given property, when such exist. Current heuristics are incomplete, and often diverge on simple examples. We present a practical method of predicate selection that is complete in the above sense. The method is based on interpolation and uses a "split prover", somewhat in the style of structure-based provers used in artificial intelligence. We show that it allows the verification of a variety of simple programs that cannot be verified by existing software model checkers.

1 Introduction

Predicate abstraction [14] is a technique commonly used in software model checking in which an infinite-state system is represented abstractly by a finite-state system whose states are the truth valuations of a chosen set of atomic predicates. The reachable state set of the abstract system corresponds to the strongest inductive invariant of the infinite-state system expressible as a Boolean combination of the given predicates.

Given a decision procedure for the underlying theory, predicate abstraction can prove a property of a system exactly when the property is implied by a quantifier-free inductive invariant of that system. That is, suppose that a system has a quantifier-free inductive invariant ψ that implies some condition that we wish to prove invariant and suppose we can supply the atomic predicates occurring in ψ. Since predicate abstraction synthesizes the strongest inductive invariant expressible as a Boolean combination of these predicates, it is guaranteed to generate an invariant as strong as ψ, and hence to prove the property. There remains only the question of how to guess these atomic predicates. We will say that a predicate selection heuristic is *complete* if it is guaranteed eventually to choose enough predicates to prove any given property ϕ, as long as there is some quantifier-free inductive invariant of the system that implies ϕ. This definition of completeness is strictly stronger than that of [1], which restricts invariants to atomic predicates generated by the "pre" operator.

There is, of course, a trivial complete heuristic. Since the atomic predicates are countable, one has only to enumerate them in a complete way. Each time we

H. Hermanns and J. Palsberg (Eds.): TACAS 2006, LNCS 3920, pp. 459–473, 2006.

generate a new predicate, we add it to our set, and try predicate abstraction. Eventually our set of predicates will contain all the atomic predicates in ψ, and we will prove the property.

Obviously, this approach is not practical. Since predicate abstraction is exponential (or worse!) in the number of predicates, a practical approach must generate a sufficient set of predicates that is as small as possible. A number of heuristic approaches based on computing weakest preconditions have been suggested [8, 2, 3]. The approaches of [15, 7] derive predicates from proofs. None of these is complete in the above sense (though [8] includes an acceleration heuristic that may prevent divergence).

As an example of divergence of a predicate heuristic, consider the following simple C program fragment:[1]

```
x = i; y = j;
while (x!=0) {x--; y--;}
if (i == j) assert (y == 0);
```

A typical predicate heuristic will examine counterexamples produced by model checking the abstraction. A counterexample is a program execution path that reaches an error state, and cannot be refuted using the available predicates (a notion we will formally define later). Suppose our first counterexample passes through the loop zero times (which means $i = 0$ initially). We might obtain new predicates by computing the weakest precondition of the assertion in a backward manner along the path. From this we obtain formulas containing the atomic predicates $i = j$, $x = 0$, $y = 0$, $i = 0$ and $j = 0$. Using these predicates, we obtain a counterexample in which the loop is executed once. Computing weakest preconditions, we obtain the additional predicates $x = 1$, $y = 1$, $i = 1$, $j = 1$, and so on. Thus, by analyzing counterexamples, we obtain a diverging sequence of predicates in which the integer constants tend to infinity. On the other hand, the predicates $i = j$, $x = 0$ and $x = y$ are sufficient to prove the assertion (at the level of basic blocks). The loop invariant is $i = j \Rightarrow x = y$. Thus, predicate heuristics based on weakest precondition over counterexamples are incomplete, essentially due to a failure to generalize.

Heuristics based on interpolation [7] are potentially more effective in focusing on relevant predicates, but suffer from the same problem of divergence. In this paper, we propose a method that is both heuristically useful and complete (in the above limited sense). Like the method of [7], it is based on the computation of interpolants from the refutation of counterexamples. However, in this case the use of a specialized "split" prover allows us to restrict the language of the interpolants in a way that prevents the atomic predicates from diverging as the counterexamples become longer.

In the next section of the paper, we discuss the method of deriving predicates from interpolants, which are in turn derived from the refutation of counterexamples. We then show that by restricting the interpolants to a finite language L, and gradually expanding this language, we can guarantee convergence of predi-

---

[1] Thanks to Anubhav Gupta for this example.

cate abstraction (when the property is provable). In section 3 we introduce the notion of a *split prover*, and show that such a prover can be used to generate interpolants in a restricted language, and thus can be used as a complete predicate heuristic. In section 4, we describe an implementation of such a prover for a particular theory. In section 5, we show that this method is capable in practice of verifying programs that cannot be verified by existing heuristic methods because of predicate divergence.

2   Predicates from Interpolants

Throughout this paper, we will use standard first-order logic (FOL) and we will use the notation $\mathcal{L}(\Sigma)$ to denote the set of well-formed formulas (*wff*'s) of FOL over a vocabulary Σ of non-logical symbols. For a given formula or set of formulas ϕ, we will use $\mathcal{L}(\phi)$ to denote the *wff*'s over the vocabulary of ϕ.

For every non-logical symbol s, we presume the existence of a unique symbol s' (that is, s with one prime added). We think of s with n primes added as representing the value of s at n time units in the future. For any formula or term ϕ, we will use the notation $\phi^{\langle n \rangle}$ to denote the addition of n primes to every symbol in ϕ (meaning ϕ at n time units in the future). For any set Σ of symbols, let Σ' denote $\{s' \mid s \in \Sigma\}$ and $\Sigma^{\langle n \rangle}$ denote $\{s^{\langle n \rangle} \mid s \in \Sigma\}$.

Modeling Programs. We will use first-order formulas to characterize programs. To this end, let S, the state vocabulary, be a set of individual variables and uninterpreted n-ary functional and propositional constants. A *state formula* is a formula in $\mathcal{L}(S)$ (which may also include various interpreted symbols, such as = and +). A *transition formula* is a formula in $\mathcal{L}(S \cup S')$. We require a technical condition: a transition formula must contain an occurrence of every symbol in S and S'. This condition can easily be made to hold by adding tautologies, such as $a = a$.

A *program* will be represented (somewhat abstractly) by a pair $(\mathcal{T}, \Pi)$ where $\mathcal{T}$ is a set of *transition formulas* (representing program statements) and $\Pi \subset \mathcal{T}^*$ is a regular language representing the possible execution paths of the program. For any sequence of transitions $\pi = T_1, \ldots, T_n$ in $\mathcal{T}^*$, we will say the *unfolding* $\mathcal{U}(\pi)$ is the sequence $T_1^{\langle 0 \rangle}, \ldots, T_n^{\langle n-1 \rangle}$. For example, the unfolding of the error path of our example program that executes the loop once is:

$$x^{\langle 1 \rangle} = i^{\langle 0 \rangle} \wedge y^{\langle 1 \rangle} = j^{\langle 0 \rangle} \wedge i^{\langle 1 \rangle} = i^{\langle 0 \rangle} \wedge i^{\langle 1 \rangle} = j^{\langle 0 \rangle},$$

$$x^{\langle 1 \rangle} \neq 0 \wedge x^{\langle 2 \rangle} = x^{\langle 1 \rangle} - 1 \wedge y^{\langle 2 \rangle} = y^{\langle 1 \rangle} - 1 \wedge i^{\langle 2 \rangle} = i^{\langle 1 \rangle} \wedge j^{\langle 2 \rangle} = j^{\langle 1 \rangle},$$

$$x^{\langle 2 \rangle} = 0 \wedge i^{\langle 2 \rangle} = j^{\langle 2 \rangle} \wedge y^{\langle 2 \rangle} \neq 0$$

We will say that π is *feasible* when $\bigwedge \mathcal{U}(\pi)$ is consistent. We can think of a model of $\bigwedge \mathcal{U}(\pi)$ as a concrete program execution, assigning a value to every program variable at every time $0 \ldots n$. A program $(\mathcal{T}, \Pi)$ is said to be *infeasible* when every path in Π is infeasible. The problem of safety verification can be reduced to infeasibility by intersecting Π with the language of paths leading to "error" states.

Predicate Abstraction. Given a set of predicates β, we will say that *strongest β-postcondition* of a state formula ϕ with respect to transition T, denoted $\text{sp}_T^\beta(\phi)$, is the strongest Boolean combination ψ over β such that $\phi \wedge T$ implies $\psi^{\langle 1 \rangle}$. That is, $\text{sp}_T^\beta(\phi)$ is the strongest Boolean formula expressible over β that must be true after executing T from a state satisfying ϕ. We define the notion of strongest β-postcondition over sequences of transitions by induction over the sequence:

$$\text{sp}_\epsilon^\beta(\phi) = \phi$$
$$\text{sp}_{\pi \cdot t}^\beta(\phi) = \text{sp}_t^\beta(\text{sp}_\pi^\beta(\phi))$$

A sequence π of transitions is *β-refutable* when $\text{sp}_\pi^\beta(\text{TRUE}) \equiv \text{FALSE}$. Further, a program (T, Π) is β-refutable when every path in Π is β-refutable. This is exactly the condition tested by predicate abstraction. That is, predicate abstraction can verify a program to be infeasible using predicates β exactly when the program is β-refutable. We will say that a *verifier* is a procedure that takes a program as input and returns TRUE or FALSE, or diverges. It is *sound* if it returns TRUE only when the program is infeasible. Moreover:

Definition 1. *A verifier $\mathcal{V}$ is complete for predicate abstraction if, for every program $\mathcal{A} = (T, \Pi)$ that is β-refutable for some set β of atomic predicates, $\mathcal{V}$ converges on $\mathcal{A}$ and returns TRUE.*

Interpolants from Proofs. Given a pair of formulas (A, B), such that $A \wedge B$ is inconsistent, an *interpolant* for (A, B) is a formula $\hat{A}$ with the following properties:

- A implies $\hat{A}$,
- $\hat{A} \wedge B$ is unsatisfiable, and
- $\hat{A} \subseteq \mathcal{L}(A) \cap \mathcal{L}(B)$.

The Craig interpolation lemma [5] states that an interpolant always exists for inconsistent formulas in FOL. To allow us to speak of interpolants of program paths, we generalize this idea to sequences of formulas. That is, given a sequence of formulas $\Gamma = A_1, \ldots, A_n$, we say that $\hat{A}_0, \ldots \hat{A}_n$ is an *interpolant* for Γ when

- $\hat{A}_0 = \text{TRUE}$ and $\hat{A}_n = \text{FALSE}$ and,
- for all $1 \leq i \leq n$, $\hat{A}_{i-1} \wedge A_i$ implies $\hat{A}_i$ and
- for all $1 \leq i < n$, $\hat{A}_i \in \mathcal{L}(A_i) \cap \mathcal{L}(A_{i+1})$.

That is, the i-th element of the interpolant is a formula in the common language of A_i and A_{i+1}, and is provable from the first i elements of Γ.

If Γ is quantifier-free, we can derive a quantifier-free interpolant for Γ from a refutation of Γ, in certain interpreted theories [11]. This fact was exploited in [7] to derive predicates for predicate abstraction. This is based on the following result, where $AP(\phi)$ denotes the set of atomic predicates in ϕ:

Theorem 1. *Given a set of atomic predicates β, a program path $\pi = A_1, \ldots, A_n$ is β-refutable iff $\mathcal{U}(\pi)$ has a quantifier-free interpolant $\hat{A}_0, \ldots, \hat{A}_n$ such that for all $1 \leq i < n$, $AP(\hat{A}_i) \subseteq \beta^{\langle i \rangle}$.*

Proof. For the *only if* direction, we observe that the sequence $\hat{P}_0, \ldots, \hat{P}_n$, where $\hat{P}_i = \mathrm{sp}^\beta_{A_1, \ldots, A_i}(\mathrm{TRUE})^{\langle i \rangle}$, is a suitable interpolant (guaranteeing that $\hat{P}_i \in \mathcal{L}(A_{i-1}) \cap \mathcal{L}(A_i)$ requires our technical condition on transition formulas). For the *if* direction, we show by induction that P_i (as defined above) implies $\hat{A}_i$, hence $\mathrm{sp}^\beta_\pi(\mathrm{TRUE}) \equiv \mathrm{FALSE}$. □

If a counterexample path π is not β-refutable for the current set of predicates β we can compute an interpolant for π, and augment β by adding the atomic predicates occurring in the interpolant (dropping the primes). Thus, π is now β-refutable (for the new β). For example, a possible interpolant for the error path example above is

$$\mathrm{TRUE}, (x^{\langle 1 \rangle} = i^{\langle 1 \rangle} \wedge y^{\langle 1 \rangle} = j^{\langle 1 \rangle}), (x^{\langle 2 \rangle} = i^{\langle 2 \rangle} - 1 \wedge y^{\langle 2 \rangle} = j^{\langle 2 \rangle} - 1), \mathrm{FALSE}$$

From this we derive the predicates $x = i, y = j, x = i - 1$ and $y = j - 1$. This gives us a predicate heuristic (used in [7]) that is guaranteed to rule out any given counterexample path, but may produce predicates that diverge as the number of loop iterations increases. To prevent this divergence, we propose in this work to restrict the interpolants to some finite language L. For example, we could restrict L to contain numeric constants only in some fixed range, and thus prevent constants in the predicates from tending to infinity.

Definition 2. *Given a language L, an L-restricted interpolant for $\Gamma = A_1, \ldots, A_n$ is an interpolant $\hat{A}_0, \ldots \hat{A}_n$ for Γ, such that each $\hat{A}_i \in L$.*

By gradually enlarging the restriction language L, we obtain a complete procedure. That is, let us define a chain of finite, quantifier-free, propositionally closed languages $L_0 \subseteq L_1 \subseteq \cdots$ such that every atomic predicate is contained in some L_i. We can then use the following procedure for program verification:

procedure RELAX($\mathcal{A}$)
    let $k = 0$ and $\beta = \emptyset$
    repeat
        if $\mathcal{A}$ is β-refutable return TRUE
        else let π be a non-β-refutable path of $\mathcal{A}$ in
            if π has an L_k-restricted interpolant $\hat{A}_0, \ldots \hat{A}_n$
            then let $\beta = \beta \cup \{p \mid p^{\langle i \rangle} \in AP(\hat{A}_i)$, for some $1 \le i < n\}$
            else let $k = k + 1$

That is, as long as the counterexamples produced by predicate abstraction are refutable using predicates in language L_k we continue using L_k-restricted interpolants to generate predicates. When we obtain a counterexample not refutable in L_k, we move on to L_{k+1}.

Theorem 2. *Procedure RELAX is complete for predicate abstraction.*

Proof. Theorem 1 tells us that each interpolant must contain some atomic predicate not in β. Thus in every iteration of the loop, either β increases, or k increases. Since $\beta \subseteq L_k$, it cannot increase unboundedly without increasing k.

Thus either the procedure terminates, or k increases unboundedly. Now suppose program $\mathcal{A}$ is β-refutable. β must be contained in some L_m. We know k cannot increase beyond m, since by Theorem 1, every path of $\mathcal{A}$ has an L_m-restricted interpolant. Thus the procedure terminates (and returns TRUE).   □

Of course, the choice of restriction languages L_k is a heuristic one, and we would like to make that choice in a way that will lead to rapid convergence. One observation we can make in this area is that invariants of loops rarely contain large numeric constants. Thus, we might define L_k so as to contain numeric constants no larger in absolute value than k. This heuristic is effective for our example program. Note that L_0 does not contain the interpolant we obtained above for our example path (since it contains the constant 1). Thus, it forces us to choose an interpolant like this: TRUE,$(x^{\langle 1 \rangle} = i^{\langle 1 \rangle} \wedge y^{\langle 1 \rangle} = j^{\langle 1 \rangle})$, $(i^{\langle 2 \rangle} = j^{\langle 2 \rangle} \Rightarrow x^{\langle 2 \rangle} = y^{\langle 2 \rangle})$, FALSE. This yields predicates $x = i, y = i, x = j$ and $x = y$, which are adequate to prove the program. One way to view this is that the inability to use the specific constant 1 forces us to generalize. Thus, the verification terminates at L_0.

3   The Split Prover

The problem of predicate selection has now been reduced to finding an L-restricted interpolant for a given sequence of formulas $A_1, \ldots, A_n$. As in [11] we derive interpolants from proofs. However, we restrict the interpolants to formulas in L by placing a restriction on allowable proofs. We define a notion of *split proof* in which all reasoning is local. That is, each deduction step is labeled by some A_i, such that both its antecedents and consequent are contained in $\mathcal{L}(A_i)$, and the deduction depends only on A_i. This is as if we have n communicating provers, each of which knows one A_i, and can see the results of other provers only if they are over the vocabulary of A_i. To be more precise:

Definition 3. *A split proof over a set of hypotheses Γ is a triple (V, E, P), such that V is a set of formulas, (V, E) is a directed acyclic graph, and P is a labeling function $V \to \Gamma$, and*

- *for all edges $(g, f) \in E$, we have $g, f \in \mathcal{L}(P(f))$, and*
- *$preds(f), P(f) \models f$.*

where $preds(f) = \{g \mid (g, f) \in E\}$. A split refutation of Γ is a split proof over Γ whose unique leaf is the formula FALSE.

In order to restrict the interpolants to a given language L, we have only to restrict the set of formulas that can be communicated between provers:

Definition 4. *An L-restricted split proof over a set of hypotheses Γ is a split proof (V, E, P) over Γ, such that, for all edges $(f, g) \in E$, if $P(f) \neq P(g)$, then $f \in L$.*

We will say that a sequence of hypotheses $\Gamma = \{A_1, \ldots, A_n\}$ is *strict* if the vocabularies of A_i and A_j only intersect when $i-1 \leq j \leq i+1$ (*i.e.*, if only nearest neighbors share non-logical symbols). This condition is satisfied by program path unfoldings. We can now show the following:

Theorem 3. *Given a strict sequence of hypotheses $\Gamma = \{A_1, \ldots, A_n\}$, and a propositionally closed language L, Γ has an L-restricted interpolant if and only if it has an L-restricted split refutation.*

Proof. The *only if* is straightforward, since the interpolant itself acts as the refutation. That is, each formula in the interpolant proves the next, given the next hypothesis, and each is over the common language of neighboring hypotheses. For the *if* direction, we construct an interpolant from the proof as follows. First, we rewrite the proof so that every edge is between vertices with distinct labels. If an edge (f, g) is such that $P(f) = P(g)$, we eliminate it by adding preds(f) to preds(g). Now we transform each vertex f into the formula $f' = \bigwedge \text{preds}(f) \Rightarrow f$. We then create new strict hypotheses $\Gamma' = \{A'_1, \ldots, A'_n\}$ where $A'_i = \{f' \mid P(f) = A_i\}$. Note that A_i implies A'_i and $A'_i \in \mathcal{L}(A_i)$, by Definition 3, and $A'_i \in L$, by Definition 4. This set of formulas is propositionally unsatisfiable (*i.e.*, no truth assignment to the atoms makes it true). Therefore, we can construct a propositional interpolant for it, without introducing new atoms, by the method of [10] (this step requires strictness). Since each A_i implies A'_i, it follows that this is also an interpolant for $A_1, \ldots, A_n$, and moreover it is L-restricted.   □

The proof of this theorem also gives us a procedure for constructing an L-restricted interpolant from an L-restricted split proof. We transform the proof into a sequence of formulas, refute this sequence propositionally, and then derive the interpolant from the propositional refutation. This is actually a polynomial-time operation, since the refutation can be done by unit resolution (*i.e.*, BCP).

The key question is how to find a suitable split proof. Proofs generated by an arbitrary prover will not in general fit our restrictions. Interestingly, this question has been studied in the artificial intelligence community, for the purpose not of generating interpolants, but of creating more efficient provers by localizing the proof effort. The method is based on the notion of *consequence finding*.

A consequence finder is a function that takes a set of hypotheses Γ in its input language and generates a set of consequences of Γ. For a given language L, we will say that a consequence finder $\mathcal{R}$ is *complete for L-generation* when every consequence of Γ in L is implied by $\mathcal{R}(\Gamma)$. That is, to be complete $\mathcal{R}$ need not generate *every* consequence of Γ in L, but it must preserve all consequences of Γ expressible in L. To be more formal:

Definition 5. *A consequence finder $\mathcal{R}$, with input language $\mathcal{L}(\mathcal{R})$ is a function $\mathcal{P}(\mathcal{L}(\mathcal{R})) \to \mathcal{P}(\text{wff})$ that is monotone, $\cup$-continuous, and such that, for every $\phi \in \mathcal{R}(\Gamma)$, $\Gamma \models \phi$.*

Definition 6. *Given a language L, a consequence finder $\mathcal{R}$ is complete for L-generation iff, for every formula $f \in L$, if $\Gamma \models f$, then $\mathcal{R}(\Gamma) \cap L \models f$.*

We now use this notion of consequence finding to build a prover that constructs split proofs. For each partition A_i, we construct a consequence finder $\mathcal{R}_i$ that is complete for $\mathcal{L}(A_{i-1})$-generation and for $\mathcal{L}(A_{i+1})$-generation. In other words, each prover can generate all consequences in the languages of its neighbors. The initial input of $\mathcal{R}_i$ is just A_i. Each time a consequence ϕ is generated by some $\mathcal{R}_i$, it is added to the input of every $\mathcal{R}_j$ such that $\phi \in \mathcal{L}(A_j)$. We can formalize this notion of a combination of local consequence finders as follows:

Definition 7. *Let $\mathcal{R}$ be an indexed set of consequence finders $\{\mathcal{R}_1, \dots, \mathcal{R}_n\}$. The composition of $\mathcal{R}$, denoted $\otimes \mathcal{R}$, is a function that takes an indexed set of hypotheses $\Gamma = \{A_1, \dots, A_n\}$, such that $\mathcal{L}(A_i) \subseteq \mathcal{L}(\mathcal{R}_i)$, and returns the least fixed point of function $\mathcal{F}$, where*

$$\mathcal{F}(Q) = \bigcup_i \mathcal{R}_i(A_i \cup (Q \cap \mathcal{L}(\mathcal{R}_i)))$$

Note that the monotonicity of consequence finders guarantees the existence of the least fixed point of $\mathcal{F}$ in the above definition. In [9] it is shown (in a somewhat more general setting) that such a split prover is complete for refutation in FOL:

Theorem 4 ([9]). *Let $\Gamma = \{A_1, \dots, A_n\}$ be a strict sequence of hypotheses in FOL, and let $\mathcal{R} = \mathcal{R}_1, \dots, \mathcal{R}_n$ be an indexed set of consequence finders, such that $\mathcal{L}(\mathcal{R}_i) = \mathcal{L}(A_i)$. If for every $1 \leq i < n$, $\mathcal{R}_i$ is complete for $\mathcal{L}(A_{i+1})$-generation, then FALSE $\in (\otimes \mathcal{R})(\Gamma)$ iff Γ is inconsistent.*

This is a simple consequence of Craig's interpolation lemma. That is, assuming $\mathcal{R}_i$ receives enough facts to prove component $\hat{A}_i$ of the interpolant, it produces enough facts to imply $\hat{A}_{i+1}$. Thus we must derive $\hat{A}_n$, which is false.

In [9], various resolution strategies are discussed which are complete for $\mathcal{L}(\Sigma)$-generation in FOL, where Σ is an arbitrary vocabulary of non-logical symbols. This makes it possible to construct a complete split prover for FOL. Our concern, however, is not to implement a complete prover, but rather a prover that is "complete" for generation of L-restricted split proofs, for a particular language L. Our approach to this is to restrict communication between consequence finders to just sentences in the restriction language L:

Definition 8. *Let $\mathcal{R}$ be an indexed set of consequence finders $\mathcal{R}_1, \dots, \mathcal{R}_n$, and let L be a language. The L-restricted composition of $\mathcal{R}$, denoted $\otimes^L \mathcal{R}$, is a function that takes an indexed set of hypotheses $\Gamma = \{A_1, \dots, A_n\}$, such that $\mathcal{L}(A_i) \subseteq \mathcal{L}(\mathcal{R}_i)$, and returns the least fixed point of function $\mathcal{F}$, where*

$$\mathcal{F}(Q) = \bigcup_i \mathcal{R}_i(A_i \cup (Q \cap \mathcal{L}(\mathcal{R}_i) \cap L))$$

We can show that the L-restricted split prover defined above is complete for generation of L-restricted split refutations, provided the consequence finders are complete for L-generation:

Theorem 5. *Let $\Gamma = \{A_1, \dots, A_n\}$ be a strict sequence of hypotheses in FOL, and let $\mathcal{R} = \{\mathcal{R}_1, \dots, \mathcal{R}_n\}$ be an indexed set of consequence finders, such that $\mathcal{L}(\mathcal{R}_i) = \mathcal{L}(A_i)$, and let L be an arbitrary language. If for each $1 \leq i < n$, $\mathcal{R}_i$ is complete for $(\mathcal{L}(A_{i+1}) \cap L)$-generation, then FALSE $\in (\otimes^L \mathcal{R})(\Gamma)$ iff Γ has an L-restricted split refutation.*

Proof. For the *if* direction, if Γ has an L-restricted split refutation, it has an L-restricted interpolant $\hat{A}_0, \ldots, \hat{A}_n$ (by Theorem 3). By induction on i, each $\mathcal{R}_i$ must generate facts implying $\hat{A}_i$, since it is complete for $(\mathcal{L}(A_{i+1}) \cap L)$-generation. Thus $\mathcal{R}_n$ generates FALSE. For the *only if* direction, we show by induction that each fact $f \in (\otimes \mathcal{R})(\Gamma)$ has an L-restricted split proof. The function $\mathcal{F}$ is a finite union of $\cup$-continuous functions and so is $\cup$-continuous. Therefore, by the Tarski-Knaster theorem f must occur in some fixed point iteration $\mathcal{F}^j(\emptyset)$. Thus f is a consequence of some facts $\Theta \subseteq \mathcal{F}^{j-1}(\emptyset)$, generated by some $\mathcal{R}_i$. By inductive hypothesis, these facts have L-restricted split proofs. Thus f has an L-restricted split proof.   □

An immediate consequence is, of course, that the L-restricted split prover generates a proof exactly when Γ has an L-restricted interpolant, and moreover this proof can be translated directly into an interpolant (Theorem 3).

Note that for completeness the fixed point of Definition 8 need not converge finitely – the prover may generate consequences infinitely if no L-restricted refutation exists. One could still obtain a complete verifier by trying all the restriction languages L_k in parallel. In practice, of course, we want to obtain a negative result quickly so we can advance to the next L_k.

4   Implementing a Split Prover

In this section we describe an attempt to implement an efficient split prover for a limited theory. Our *wff*'s are limited to quantifier-free first-order sentences, with equality, separation predicates (difference bounds), and restricted use of the array operators "select" and "store". The only arithmetic predicates allowed in the theory are of the form $x - y \leq c$, $x \leq c$ and $c \leq x$, where c is an integer constant. This simple theory appears to be sufficient to handle many properties of programs that manipulate arrays. The prover is complete for split proof generation for rational models, but not (yet) for integer models. The prover generates interpolants in a restriction language L. This language is defined by a finite set C_D of constants that may occur in difference bounds of the form $x - y \leq c$, and a finite set C_B of constants that may occur in absolute bounds of the form $x \leq c$ or $x \geq c$. To make L finite, we also require a bound b_f on the nesting depth of uninterpreted function symbols.

There is not space here to discuss all of the issues involved in constructing an efficient prover. Rather, we will give an informal overview of the main features of the prover, with emphasis on the issues that differentiate a split prover from a non-split prover. For efficiency, we separate the propositional reasoning from the theory reasoning. Propositional reasoning is handled by an efficient Boolean satisfiability (SAT) solver, similar to Chaff [12]. We construct complete consequence finders for the several theories, and combine them using the Nelson Oppen approach [13]. As in that method, we rely on convexity of the theories to avoid generating disjunctions, and we split cases when necessary to eliminate non-convexities.

Coupling of propositional and theory reasoning is done in the "lazy" manner, as in [6]. The SAT solver tests whether the entire set of hypotheses $\Gamma = \{A_1, \ldots, A_n\}$ is propositionally consistent. If so, it produces a propositional satisfying assignment as a set of literals $\mathcal{W}$. This set is partitioned into subsets $\{W_1, \ldots, W_n\}$, such that each atom of W_i occurs in A_i. This set of hypotheses is then passed to the split theory prover for refutation. The hypotheses used in the generated refutation are collected, and their dual is passed to the SAT solver as a "blocking clause" – a tautology that rules out the given satisfying assignment. The process continues until either the system becomes propositionally unsatisfiable (and thus Γ is refuted) or until some propositional satisfying assignment cannot be refuted. The propositional decision procedure need not be "split". Rather the propositional proof and the split proofs of the blocking clauses can be combined as in [11]. The interpolant derived from this combined proof is still guaranteed to be L-restricted, since the propositional interpolation rules do not generate new atoms.

By separating propositional and theory reasoning in this way, we limit the hypotheses of the split prover to just sets of literals. This greatly simplifies consequence generation. In particular, it allows us to take advantage of the *convexity* of a given theory, as in [13]. We will say that a complete consequence finder is convex if it generates only Horn clauses (clauses with at most one positive literal). If our consequence finders are convex, then we can further restrict the language L by which the provers communicate to contain only positive literals. This is because unit resolution is complete for Horn clause refutation (and is exploited in the Nelson Oppen method).

Difference Bounds. The problem is thus reduced (in the convex case) to one of "unit" consequence finding in the given theory, in the given language L. We will begin with the theory of difference bounds (considering rational models first). For this theory, we use the linear combination rule to generate consequences. This derivation rule takes as antecedents two inequalities $0 \leq x$ and $0 \leq y$ (where x and y are arbitrary terms) and derives an inequality $0 \leq c_1 x + c_2 y$, where c_1 and c_2 are positive constants. We restrict use of the rule to just cases where the consequent is a difference bound. For example, from $x \leq y + 2$ and $y \leq z + 3$, we can derive $x \leq z + 5$. We can discard consequences that are subsumed by previously generated consequences, and we terminate if a contradiction (say, $0 \leq -1$) is derived. This rule is complete for consequence generation over a given vocabulary (applying it exhaustively amounts to an all-pairs shortest path computation on a graph whose vertices are terms and whose edges are labeled with difference bounds).

The rule is not complete, however, for consequence generation in our restriction language L. Consider the case, for example, where we can derive $x \leq y - 1$, but the set C_D of allowed difference constants is just $\{0\}$. Thus $x \leq y - 1$ is not in L, but its consequence $x \leq y$ *is* in L. Unfortunately, $x \leq y$ cannot be derived by the linear combination rule. To remedy this, we add a weakening rule, that derives from an inequality $0 \leq x$ a weaker inequality $0 \leq x + c$, where c is a positive constant. This rule is used to derive the strongest consequence of any inequality that is contained in L. With this rule, and similar rules for strict inequalities, our system is complete for L-generation over the rationals.

Equality and Uninterpreted Functions. Next, we consider equality and uninterpreted function symbols. For this theory, we use the usual derivation rules for equality: symmetry, reflexivity, transitivity and congruence, along with the contradiction rule (any literal and its negation imply FALSE). These rules are complete for unit consequence finding. They are not, however, finitely terminating, because of the congruence rule. For example, given $a = b$, we will derive $f(a) = f(b)$, $f(f(a)) = f(f(b))$, and so on. Though termination is not necessary for completeness, it is, of course, desirable in practice. For purposes of refutation, we can force termination by restricting the congruence rule to generate only terms that occur in the hypotheses. This is done in the usual congruence closure approach (completeness of this approach is another consequence of Craig's interpolation lemma). However, this method is not complete for consequence finding. Suppose, for example, we have the hypotheses $a = b$ and $f(a) = c$, and $L = \mathcal{L}(\{b, c, f\})$. There are no consequences in this language over just the terms $a, b, c, f(a)$. However, $f(b) = c$ is derivable. We can remedy this deficit by allowing the congruence rule to derive equalities over any terms occurring in the hypotheses *or* having function nesting depth within our bound b_f on function nesting. Since this is a finite set of terms, our rules are now terminating, and complete for L-consequence generation.

We combine difference bound and equality reasoning in the manner of Nelson and Oppen [13]. That is, we compose two consequence finders, one for difference bounds and one for equality. For difference bounds, complete consequence generation in the language of equality is achieved by a rule that derives $a = b$ from $a \leq b$ and $b \leq a$. For equality, complete consequence generation in the language of difference bounds is obtained by a rule that derives $a \leq b$ and $b \leq a$ from $a = b$.

The Theory of Arrays. The first-order theory of arrays provides two interpreted functions select and store. The term $\text{select}(a, n)$ represents the n-th element of array a, while $\text{store}(a, n, b)$ is the array resulting from setting the n-th element of array a to value b. These functions obey the following axioms:

$$\text{select}(\text{store}(a, n, b), n) = b$$

$$n \neq n' \Rightarrow \text{select}(\text{store}(a, n, b), n') = \text{select}(a, n')$$

The second axiom is problematic on two counts. First, it generates an infinite set of quantifier-free consequences. For example, if we have the hypothesis $a' = \text{store}(a, n, b)$, then we can derive $\text{select}(a', n+1) = \text{select}(a, n+1), \text{select}(a', n+2) = \text{select}(a, n+2), \ldots$. There is one such consequence for every term provably not equal to n. Although there is a finite number of such terms occurring in L, enumerating them all would still be extremely inefficient. However, we can avoid this difficulty by restricting the use of arrays. That is, we allow array-valued terms to occur in A_i only as the first argument of select and in expressions of the following form:

$$a' = \text{store}(\text{store}(\ldots \text{store}(a, n_1, b_1), n_2, b_2) \ldots, n_k, b_k)$$

where a' does not occur in A_{i-1} and a does not occur in A_{i+1}. This corresponds to the way in which arrays are used in imperative programs (that is, once the array is modified, the old value of the array is no longer accessible). In this case, it suffices to instantiate the second array axiom only for terms n' that occur as array indices in some select or store term (as no consequences are possible for other array indices in $\mathcal{L}(A_{i-1})$ or $\mathcal{L}(A_{i+1})$).

The second problem is the non-convexity of the array theory. That is, the second axiom is in effect a disjunction of positive literals. In the case where we cannot infer the truth value of either literal in the disjunction, and we cannot otherwise obtain a refutation, we simply abandon the proof and introduce the clause $(n = n' \vee n \neq n')$ into the SAT solver, causing it to decide the value $n = n'$, and thus eliminate the non-convexity. This tactic is also used in various "lazy" decision procedures.

Integer Models. For program verification, we need to interpret formulas over integer models. This is problematic, since integer difference-bound arithmetic is non-convex when L includes equality formulas. In fact, deciding consistency of a set of literals in this theory is already NP-complete. Moreover, our additional restrictions on L introduce additional non-convexity. For example, suppose that $C_D = \{0\}$ and we have $x \leq j$ and $y \leq x + 1$. The disjunction $x \geq y \vee y \leq j$ is a consequence, but is not implied by any unit consequence in L. At this point we have not attempted to tackle the problem of a complete and heuristically efficient split prover for integers. Rather, we have added two simple rules that seem to be adequate in most practical cases for programs manipulating arrays. The first derives $a \geq b + 1$ from $\neg(a \leq b)$ and the second derives $a \geq b + 1$ from $a \geq b$ and $a \neq b$.

Unfoldings in SSA Form. A common optimization used, *e.g.*, in [7] is to write the unfolding of a program path in the more compact "static single-assignment" form (SSA). This can also be done with the split prover, if we relax our requirement of strictness in the unfolding (*i.e.*, that each time frame shares symbols only with its nearest neighbors). This complicates the above theory, but does not present any difficulty in practice. Further, since in this scheme a fact may be deduced by many consequence finders, we adopt an approach in which such a fact is deduced only once, and its derivation labeled with the range of time frames in which it is deducible. Thus, we can more efficiently handle long unfoldings.

5   Experiments

To test the split prover as a predicate heuristic, we wrote a collection of small C programs containing loops and decorated with assertions.[2] The assertions are all provable by quantifier-free invariants, and thus by predicate abstraction.

---

[2] Available at http://www-cad.eecs.berkeley.edu/~kenmcmil

Table 1. Outcomes on test programs

Outcome	SATABS	MAGIC	BLAST (old)	BLAST (new)
Verified	0	0	8	12
Refinement failed	13	13	0	0
Did not finish	0	0	5	1

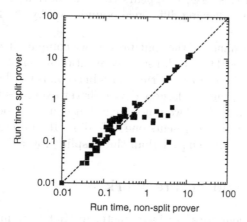

Fig. 1. Run time comparison of split and unsplit provers

All require non-trivial invariants, in the sense that the loop index variable(s) must occur in the invariants. Most of the programs perform operations on arrays or zero-terminated C strings, such as filling, copying, concatenating and substring extraction. We tested four predicate abstraction tools on these programs: SATABS [4], MAGIC [3], BLAST [7] without the split prover (old), and BLAST with the split prover (new). The outcomes are tabulated in Table 1. SATABS and MAGIC, whose predicate heuristics are based on weakest preconditions, are unable to verify any of the 13 programs.[3] In all cases, the predicate refinement step fails to produce new predicates at some point (except for three cases in which MAGIC incorrectly produces counterexamples). BLAST, whose predicate heuristic is based on interpolation, verifies 8 of the 13 examples without using the split prover. On the remaining 5, the constants in the predicates diverge to infinity (or toward some intractably large upper bound).

For the split prover version of BLAST, we define the restriction language L_k by $C_D = \{-k, \ldots, k\}$ and $C_B = \{c + d \mid c \in C_P, \ d \in C_D\}$, where C_P is the set of numeric constants occurring in the program. That is, we allow difference bounds nearby to zero, and absolute bounds (such as $x \leq c$) nearby to some constant occurring in the program. The latter are useful for loops whose upper or lower bounds are fixed constants. As we increase k, we gradually expand

---

[3] For SATABS, we used version 1.1 with default settings. For MAGIC, we used version 1.0 with `--optPred --predLoop 2`.

the set of available constants until an inductive invariant can be expressed. For these programs, we do not require a limit b_f on function symbol nesting, since no functions are iterated (we might require a limit, for example, if the programs traversed linked lists). Using this heuristic, we find that 12 of the 13 programs can be verified. All successful runs complete in under 30 seconds. In one case, we time out because a loop requires the invariant $i \leq j <= 200$, which does not occur until L_{200}. In this case, it appears that our notion of C_D requires some adjustment – perhaps allowing difference bounds nearby the large constants in the program.

To test the performance of the split prover, we compare it with the non-split interpolating prover of [11], which uses a conventional Nelson Oppen procedure for theory reasoning. Figure 1 plots run times in seconds for the set of unfoldings generated in verifying the two largest device driver examples from [7], with the split prover restricted to L_0. Two unfoldings that could not be refuted using L_0 were removed. Each point represents one unfolding. It can be seen that the split prover is only slightly less efficient than the unsplit prover.

6   Conclusion and Future Work

Existing predicate heuristics are incomplete, in that they may fail to find an adequate set of predicates when one exists. However, by restricting the predicates to a finite set, and progressively relaxing this restriction, we can obtain a complete method. In an interpolant-based approach, this can be done using a "split prover" that restricts the language of communication between time frames. We have shown that a practical split prover can be built, at least for difference bound arithmetic over the rationals. Moreover, a suitable choice of restriction language allows us to verify programs for which existing methods fail in practice. Thus, we have a predicate heuristic that is both theoretically complete and practically useful. For future work, it would be useful to expand the prover beyond difference bound arithmetic (though it is not clear what a suitable restriction language would be in this case) and to handle additional theories, such as the theory of bit vectors.

The main limitation of the method is a limitation of predicate abstraction itself, which cannot synthesize quantified invariants. For example, consider the following simple C program:

```
for(i = 0; i < n; i++) x[i] = 0;
for(i = 0; i < n; i++) assert(x[i] == 0);
```

An invariant for this program requires a quantifier. Though in principle predicate abstraction can use quantified predicates, they must be provided by the predicate heuristic – predicate abstraction cannot synthesize them from atomic formulas. The next step in this work is to produce quantified predicates. Some preliminary results have been obtained in this area. For example, by removing the restriction that interpolants be quantifier-free, we can obtain sufficient quantified predicates to verify the above program (including the invariant for the first loop $\forall j$.

$(0 \leq j < i) \Rightarrow x[j] = 0)$.[4] Ultimately the goal is to extend the range of predicate abstraction to a richer class of programs and properties.

Acknowledgment. The authors thank Tal Lev-Ami for pointing out related work in Artificial Intelligence.

References

1. T. Ball, A. Podelski, and S. K. Rajamani. Relative completeness of abstraction refinement for software model checking. In *TACAS*, pages 158–172, 2002.
2. T. Ball and S. K. Rajamani. Generating abstract explanations of spurious counterexamples in c programs. Technical Report MSR-TR-2002-09, Microsoft, 2002.
3. S. Chaki, E. M. Clarke, A. Groce, and O. Strichman. Predicate abstraction with minimum predicates. In *CHARME*, pages 19–34, 2003.
4. E. Clarke, D. Kroening, N. Sharygina, and K. Yorav. Predicate abstraction of ANSI–C programs using SAT. *Formal Methods in System Design (FMSD)*, 25:105–127, September–November 2004.
5. W. Craig. Three uses of the Herbrand-Gentzen theorem in relating model theory and proof theory. *J. Symbolic Logic*, 22(3):269–285, 1957.
6. L. de Moura, H. Rueß, and M. Sorea. Lazy theorem proving for bounded model checking over infinite domains. In *CADE*, pages 438–455, 2002.
7. T. A. Henzinger, R. Jhala, R. Majumdar, and K. L. McMillan. Abstractions from proofs. In *POPL*, pages 232–244, 2004.
8. Y. Lakhnech, S. Bensalem, S. Berezin, and S. Owre. Incremental verification by abstraction. In *TACAS*, pages 98–112, 2001.
9. S. McIlraith and E. Amir. Theorem proving in structured theories (full report). Technical Report KSL-01-04, Stanford, 2001.
10. K. L. McMillan. Interpolation and sat-based model checking. In *CAV*, pages 1–13, 2003.
11. K. L. McMillan. An interpolating theorem prover. In *TACAS*, pages 16–30, 2004.
12. M. W. Moskewicz, C. F. Madigan, Y. Zhao, L. Zhang, and S. Malik. Chaff: Engineering an efficient SAT solver. In *Design Automation Conference*, pages 530–535, 2001.
13. G. Nelson and D. C. Oppen. Simplification by cooperating decision procedures. *ACM Trans. on Prog. Lang. and Sys.*, 1(2):245–257, 1979.
14. H. Saïdi and S. Graf. Construction of abstract state graphs with PVS. In *CAV*, pages 72–83, 1997.
15. R. Majumdar T. A. Henzinger, R. Jhala and G. Sutre. Lazy abstraction. In *POPL*, pages 58–70, 2002.

---

[4] Thanks to Daniel Kröning for integrating this in SATABS.

Counterexample Driven Refinement
for Abstract Interpretation

Bhargav S. Gulavani[1] and Sriram K. Rajamani[2]

[1] IIT Bombay
[2] Microsoft Research India

Abstract. Abstract interpretation techniques prove properties of programs by computing abstract fixpoints. All such analyses suffer from the possibility of false errors. We present a new counterexample driven refinement technique to reduce false errors in abstract interpretations. Our technique keeps track of the precision losses during forward fixpoint computation, and does a precise backward propagation from the error to either confirm the error as a true error, or identify a refinement so as to avoid the false error.

Our technique is quite simple, and is independent of the specific abstract domain used. An implementation of our technique for affine transition systems is able to prove invariants generated by the StInG tool [19] without doing any specialized analysis for linear relations. Thus, we hope that the technique can work for other abstract domains as well. We sketch how our technique can be used to perform shape analysis by simply defining an appropriate widening operator over shape graphs.

1 Introduction

Abstract interpretation [8] is a generic technique to compute sound fixpoints for programs. Suppose we are interested in checking if a program satisfies invariant φ. If the fixpoint computed by an abstract interpretation of the program P satisfies φ, then we know that all concrete behaviors of the program satisfy φ. However, if such a fixpoint does not satisfy the property φ, then there are two possibilities: (1) the program does not satisfy φ (we have found a "true error" in the program), or (2) the program indeed satisfies the property φ, but the abstract interpretation was not precise enough to verify it (we have found a "false error" in the program). Losing precision while computing fixpoints is inevitable if we want to analyze programs with infinite domains, or scale the analysis to large programs. However, losing too much precision leads to too many false errors and reduces usability of the analysis tool.

Predicate abstraction [10] is a particular form of abstract interpretation. Tools based on predicate abstraction to verify finite state interface protocols on programs have become popular over the past few years [4, 12, 6]. In order to reduce false errors, these tools analyze an abstract counterexample to check if the counterexample is feasible in the concrete program. If the counterexample is infeasible they add more predicates to improve precision of predicate abstraction. This process, called *counterexample driven refinement* continues iteratively until (1) the

H. Hermanns and J. Palsberg (Eds.): TACAS 2006, LNCS 3920, pp. 474–488, 2006.

property is proved, or (2) a true error is found, or (3) either time or memory is exhausted [14, 7].

Abstract interpretations operate over lattices, and compute overapproximations to semantics of programs as fixpoints. Such fixpoint computations may not converge if the lattice has infinite ascending chains. Widening is a technique used to ensure convergence of fixpoint computations. The widening operator ∇ has the property that for all x and y the result $x \nabla y$ is greater than both x and y. Furthermore, widening guarantees convergence of fixpoint computation in the following sense. Given any infinite increasing sequence $x_0, x_1, x_2, \ldots$, the sequence $y_0, y_1, y_2, \ldots$ given by $y_0 = x_0$ and $y_{i+1} = y_i \nabla (y_i \cup x_{i+1})$ is guaranteed to converge. Examples of widening operators on polyhedral domains can be found in [9, 3].

In this paper, we present a new counterexample driven refinement that can be used to reduce false errors in any abstract interpretation. Precision loss in abstract interpretation occurs primarily due to widen operators. We parameterize the abstract interpreter with a set of hints, which specify the steps in the fixpoint computation where more precise operators should be used in place of widen. Initially the set of hints is empty. We analyze spurious counterexamples and make additions to the set of hints, thereby guiding the fixpoint to be as precise as necessary to prove the property of interest. Furthermore, powerset domains can add further precision to abstract interpretation. However, powerset domains do not scale to large programs without aggressive use of widening. We describe how counterexample driven refinement can be applied to powerset domains. The key idea here is a new connector that allows lifting a widening operator from a base domain to the corresponding widen operator in a powerset domain. We explain our technique informally using two examples below. A formal description is given in Section 2.

Consider the example program shown in Figure 1(a). For this example, we use the abstract domain of convex polyhedra. First, we perform a symbolic fixpoint computation applying widening every time along the back edge of the while-loop to ensure termination. When the loop head is first encountered, we have the symbolic state $S_0 \triangleq 0 \leq x \leq 2 \land 0 \leq y \leq 2$. After executing the loop body once, we get a new set of states $2 \leq x \leq 4 \land 2 \leq y \leq 4$. We perform widening to obtain the set $S_1 \triangleq 0 \leq x \land 0 \leq y$. It turns out that S_1 is a fixpoint for the loop. However, this loop invariant is not sufficient to ensure that $x \neq 4 \lor y \neq 0$, and the analysis reports that the assertion may fail.

The error state reached by the analysis is $x = 4 \land y = 0$, which is a false error that resulted due to the imprecision in the widening operator. Inspired by approaches to perform counterexample driven refinement for predicate abstraction [7], we propagate this error state backwards, using pre-image computations, and determine that the first application of widening is responsible for the false error, and that using least upper bound (LUB) instead of widening in the first iteration avoids the error. Thus, we add iteration count 1 to the set of hints.

Using the updated hints, we recompute the abstract fixpoint, using the LUB operator (convex hull for convex polyhedral domain) in the first iteration. This

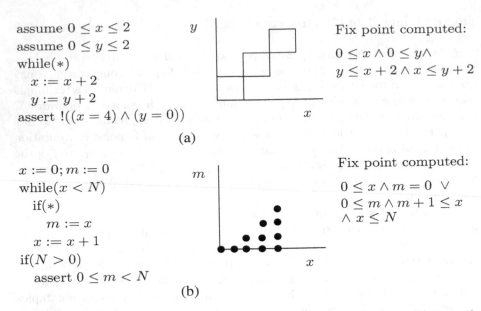

(a)

(b)

Fig. 1. (a) Example program that has a stair-case like reachable region (b) Example program that finds the index of the minimum element in an array

results in the set of states $S_1' \overset{\Delta}{=} 0 \leq x \leq 4 \wedge 0 \leq y \leq 4 \wedge y \leq x + 2 \wedge x \leq y + 2$. Applying widening after second iteration we get the set of states $S_2' \overset{\Delta}{=} 0 \leq x \wedge 0 \leq y \wedge y \leq x + 2 \wedge x \leq y + 2$. This turns out to be the fixpoint for the loop as well and is strong enough to prove the assertion.

Next, consider the example program shown in Figure 1(b). The program searches for the index m of the minimum element in an array of size N. The array contents and the minimum element have been abstracted out, and only the updates to the index variables m and x have been retained. No loop invariant expressed as a single convex polyhedron is strong enough to prove the assertion. Thus, we need to use sets of convex polyhedra as our abstract domain. As we describe below, our technique discovers a disjunctive loop invariant that is strong enough to prove the assertion.

We start by performing symbolic fixpoint computation, applying widening every time along the back edge of the while-loop to ensure termination. When the loop-head is first encountered, we have the set of states $S_0 \overset{\Delta}{=} x = 0 \wedge m = 0$. After executing the loop body once, we get a new set of states $x = 1 \wedge m = 0 \wedge x \leq N$. We perform widening to obtain the set $S_1 \overset{\Delta}{=} x \geq 0 \wedge m = 0$. The second iteration of the loop produces different states depending on whether the if branch is taken inside the loop: $(x \geq 1 \wedge x \leq N \wedge m = 0) \vee (x \leq N \wedge x = m+1 \wedge m \geq 0)$. Applying widening again, we obtain the set $S_2 \overset{\Delta}{=} x \geq 0 \wedge m \geq 0$. It turns out that S_2 is a fixpoint for the loop. However, this loop invariant is not sufficient to ensure that $m < N$, and the analysis reports that the assertion may fail.

The error state reached by the analysis is $m \geq N \wedge x \geq 0 \wedge x \geq N \wedge N > 0$. This is a false error that resulted due to imprecision in the widening operator. Here again we propagate this error state backwards using pre-image computations, and determine that the second application of widening is responsible for the false error, and that using LUB operation instead of widening in the second iteration avoids the error. Thus, we add iteration count 2 to the set of hints.

Using the updated hints, we recompute the abstract fixpoint, taking care to use LUB operator after the second iteration. This results in the set of states $S_2' \triangleq (x \geq 0 \wedge m = 0) \vee (x \leq N \wedge x = m+1 \wedge m \geq 0)$ after the second iteration. Continuing the fixpoint computation, we apply widening after the third iteration resulting in a set of states $S_3' \triangleq (x \geq 0 \wedge m = 0) \vee (x \geq m+1 \wedge x \leq N \wedge m \geq 0)$. It turns out that S_3' is a fixpoint for the loop. Further, it is strong enough to prove the assertion. Note that the computed loop invariant has a disjunction, and our refinement algorithm was necessary to prove the assertion.

The above description of our technique is informal and simplistic. We give a precise description in Section 2. In our second example, we have assumed the existence of widening operators that operate over finite powerset domains. Section 3 shows how to lift widening operators over base domains to widening operators over power-set domains, using the theory developed in [1]. In particular, we define a new connector ⊞, which provides a lifted widening operator over the powerset domain with appropriate precision necessary for our purposes.

Widening is non-monotonic, and thus refining the widening operator in the earlier stages of fixpoint computation, could result in a larger set of states in a later iteration! We present a simple technique to avoid this problem in Section 4, using reachable states computed from the previous iteration.

We have implemented our technique for affine transition systems. Our implementation is able to prove invariants generated by the StInG tool [19] without doing any specialized analysis for linear relations. Section 5 presents empirical results from running our implementation. Our technique is independent of the specific abstract domain used. To illustrate this, Section 6 defines LUB and widen operators for an abstract domain of shape graphs, and enables our counterexample driven refinement to do shape analysis. Section 7 surveys related work and Section 8 concludes the paper.

2   Algorithm

We first present the algorithm in a very simple setting. Assume that we have a possibly infinite domain called **States**. We assume that the domain **States** has a precise LUB operator $\cup$, and a widening operator ∇. A transition system Θ is a pair $\langle I, \theta \rangle$. $I \subseteq$ **States** and $\theta : 2^{\textbf{States}} \rightarrow 2^{\textbf{States}}$. Informally, θ is referred to as the "image" operator, which takes a set of current states as input, gives the set of possible next states as output. We use θ^{-1} to denote the "pre-image" operator, which takes the set of current states as input, and gives the set of previous states as output.

Transition systems are generated by *programs*. We describe the link between programs and transition systems below. A program P is a triple $\langle V, I, T \rangle$ where

- V is a finite set of variables, each of which takes valuations from a potentially infinite domain. A *state* is a valuation to all the variables in V. The set of all possible valuations to V is the domain **States**.
- I is a set of initial valuations to variables in V.
- $T \subseteq$ **States** $\times$ **States** is a binary relation such that $T(s, s')$ holds whenever it is possible for the program to transition from state s to state s' in one step.

A program $P = \langle V, I, T \rangle$ gives rise to a transition system $\Theta = \langle I, \theta \rangle$, where $\theta(S) = \{s' \mid \exists s \in S.T(s, s')\}$, and $\theta^{-1}(S) = \{s \mid \exists s' \in S.T(s, s')\}$

A specification $\psi \subseteq$ **States** is a set of bad states that we do not want the system to reach. To check if a system $\Theta = \langle I, \theta \rangle$ satisfies a specification ψ, we first compute an over-approximation to the set of reachable states of the system, and check if the over-approximation intersects ψ. The least fixpoint **PreciseReach**$(\Theta) = \mu X.I \cup X \cup \theta(X)$ precisely represents the set of all reachable states of the system, though the fixpoint computation may not terminate. The system Θ satisfies specification ψ iff **PreciseReach**$(\Theta) \cap \psi = \emptyset$.

Widening operators from the abstract-interpretation community can help ensure termination of the fixpoint computation, at the cost of losing precision. If S_1 and S_2 are two sets such that $S_1 \subseteq S_2$, then $S_3 = S_1 \nabla S_2$ is a set such that $S_1 \subseteq S_3$ and $S_2 \subseteq S_3$. Further, there is some metric (such as the number of conjuncts in the formula representing the set) that decreases from S_1 to S_3. Thus, if we consider the least fixpoint **WidenReach**$(\Theta) = \mu X.(I \cup X) \nabla (I \cup X \cup \theta(X))$, it is guaranteed that (1) the computation of **WidenReach**(Θ) will terminate, and (2) **WidenReach**$(\Theta) \supseteq$ **PreciseReach**(Θ). Thus, we can conclude that Θ satisfies specification ψ if **WidenReach**$(\Theta) \cap \psi = \emptyset$. On the other hand, if **WidenReach**$(\Theta) \cap \psi \neq \emptyset$, we cannot distinguish between the possibilities that either the system Θ does not satisfy ψ or the computation of **WidenReach** lost too much precision.

If we can keep track of the intermediate states in the fixpoint computation, then we can generate an *abstract counterexample* that can be automatically analyzed to classify if the error found is a false error or true error. If it is a false error, the analysis can also identify the precise point at which the abstract counterexample needs to be refined to avoid the recurrence of this specific false error.

More formally, let us consider the stages of the fixpoint computation **WidenReach**$(\Theta) = \mu X.(I \cup X) \nabla (I \cup X \cup \theta(X))$. Let $R_0 = I$, and let $R_i = R_{i-1} \nabla (R_{i-1} \cup \theta(R_{i-1}))$. Suppose n is the smallest index such that $R_n \cap \psi \neq \emptyset$. Let $\psi_n = \psi$. If $(R_{n-1} \cup \theta(R_{n-1})) \cap \psi_n = \emptyset$, then we note that step n is the exact index where the precision loss for the false error happened, and replace the widening operator with the LUB operator in that particular step of the fixpoint computation. Otherwise, if $(R_{n-1} \cup \theta(R_{n-1})) \cap \psi_n \neq \emptyset$, then we compute $\psi_{n-1} = \theta^{-1}(R_n \cap \psi_n)$, and check if $(R_{n-2} \cup \theta(R_{n-2})) \cap \psi_{n-1} = \emptyset$. This process continues until either an index is found where the widening operator needs to be refined into a LUB operator ($\cup$) to avoid the false error, or we find

AbsRefine($\Theta = \langle I, \theta \rangle$, ψ)
  $hints := \emptyset$
  while true **do**
    ($R,i,result$) := AbstractFixPoint(Θ, ψ, $hints$)
    if $result$ = true **then**
      return true
    else
      $newHints$:= Refine(Θ, ψ, i, R)
      $hints := hints \cup \{newHints\}$
    end if
  end while

Refine($\Theta = \langle I, \theta \rangle$, ψ, $count$, R)
Requires $count \geq 0 \;\wedge\; R[count] \cap \psi \neq \emptyset$
Returns step i where ∇ is replaced by $\cup$
  $i := count$
  while $i > 0$ **do**
    $\psi := R[i] \cap \psi$
    if $(R[i-1] \cup \theta(R[i-1])) \cap \psi = \emptyset$ **then**
      return i
    else
      $i := i - 1$; $\psi := \theta^{-1}(\psi)$
    end if
  end while
  assert $i = 0 \;\wedge\; R[i] \cap \psi \neq \emptyset$
  print error trace and exit

AbstractFixPoint($\Theta = \langle I, \theta \rangle$, ψ, $hints$)
Returns $(R, i, result)$, where array R is
an array of set of states, $result$ is boolean
and i is integer
  $i := 1$; $R[0] := I$
  if $I \cap \psi \neq \emptyset$ **then**
    return $(R, 0, \text{false})$
  end if
  while true **do**
    if $i \in hints$ **then**
      {precise next set of states}
      $R[i] := R[i-1] \cup \theta(R[i-1])$
    else
      {next set of states using widen}
      $R[i] := R[i-1] \nabla (R[i-1] \cup \theta(R[i-1]))$
    end if
    if $R[i] \cap \psi \neq \emptyset$ **then**
      {We are not sure if System Θ satisfies ψ}
      return (R, i, false)
    end if
    if $R[i] = R[i-1]$ **then**
      {fixpoint, System Θ satisfies ψ}
      return (R, i, true)
    end if
    $i := i + 1$
  endwhile

Fig. 2. Iterative Refinement

that the repeated backward propagation of the error state intersects with the initial states $R_0 = I$, in which case we have evidence of a true error.

The procedure AbsRefine in Figure 2, together with the procedures Abstract-FixPoint and Refine give a complete description of our iterative refinement procedure.

3   A Widening Operator for Finite Powerset Domains

In procedure AbstractFixPoint, we use a widening operator ∇ which takes as operands two arbitrary sets of states. The widening operator for convex polyhedral domain is studied at length in [9, 3]. The original widening operator as defined by Cousot and Halbwachs [9] did not allow for disjunctions in the first operand. If our abstraction refinement procedures are to be applied to powerset domains, a widening operator needs to be defined for that domain. In this section we show how to lift a widening operator over a base domain to a widening operator over its powerset domain. We follow the framework provided by Bagnara, Hill and Zaf-fanella [1], but define a new connector to provide the appropriate precision.

An abstract domain $\hat{D} = \langle D, \vdash, \mathbf{0}, \oplus \rangle$ is a join-semilattice where $\vdash$ is the partial order, $\mathbf{0}$ is the bottom element of the lattice and the LUB $d_1 \oplus d_2$ exists for all $d_1, d_2 \in D$. For example, convex hull is such an operator for convex polyhedra. For all $d_1, d_2 \in D$, we will use the notation $d_1 \Vdash d_2$ to mean that $d_1 \vdash d_2$ and $d_1 \neq d_2$.

Let $d_1 = \wedge_i c_i$. Then, the standard widening operator [9] is defined as

$$d_1 \nabla d_2 \overset{\Delta}{=} \wedge \{c_j \mid d_2 \vdash c_j\}$$

For a set S, let $\wp(S)$ be the powerset of S, and let $\wp_f(S)$ be the set of all finite subsets of S. The operator $\oplus$ is overloaded so that, for each $S \in \wp_f(D)$, $\oplus S$ denotes the LUB of S. A set $S \in \wp(D)$ is *non-redundant* if and only if $\mathbf{0} \notin S$ and $\forall d_1, d_2 \in S : d_1 \vdash d_2 \Rightarrow d_1 = d_2$. The set of finite non-redundant subsets of D is denoted by $\wp_{fn}(D, \vdash)$. The reduction function $\Omega_D^{\vdash} : \wp_f(D) \rightarrow \wp_{fn}(D)$ maps each finite set into its non-redundant counterpart as follows:

$$\Omega_D^{\vdash}(S) \overset{\Delta}{=} S \setminus \{d \in S \mid d = \mathbf{0} \vee \exists d' \in S.d \Vdash d'\}$$

The finite powerset domain over $\hat{D}$ is the join-semilattice

$$\hat{D}_P = \langle \wp_{fn}(D, \vdash), \vdash_P, \mathbf{0}_P, \oplus_P \rangle$$

where $\mathbf{0}_P = \emptyset$ and $\forall S_1, S_2 \in \wp_{fn}(D, \vdash)$, $S_1 \oplus_P S_2 \overset{\Delta}{=} \Omega_D^{\vdash}(S_1 \cup S_2)$, and $S_1 \vdash_P S_2$ if and only if $\forall d_1 \in S_1 : \exists d_2 \in S_2.d_1 \vdash d_2$.

We say that $S_1 \preceq S_2$ if and only if either $S_1 = \mathbf{0}_P$ or $S_1 \vdash_P S_2$ and $\forall d_2 \in S_2 : \exists d_1 \in S_1.d_1 \vdash d_2$. Our goal is to define a *connector* operator $\boxplus$, such that for all $S_1, S_2 \in \wp_{fn}(D, \vdash)$, if $S_1 \vdash_P S_2$, then $S_1 \preceq (S_1 \boxplus S_2)$. Intuitively, $S_1 \boxplus S_2$ is obtained by minimally combining the elements of S_2 so as to obtain an S_2' such that $S_1 \preceq S_2'$. More precisely, let $\hat{S}_2$ be a maximal subset of S_2 such that $\forall \hat{d} \in \hat{S}_2 : \exists d_1 \in S_1. d_1 \vdash \hat{d}$. and let $\tilde{S}_2 \overset{\Delta}{=} \oplus \{d \mid d \in S_2 \setminus \hat{S}_2\}$. For any $\hat{d} \in \hat{S}_2$, let $J_{\hat{d}} \overset{\Delta}{=} (S_2 \setminus \{\hat{d}\}) \cup (\hat{d} \oplus \tilde{S}_2)$. We define $S_1 \boxplus S_2$ to be a minimal element(with respect to $\vdash_P$) from the set $\{J_{\hat{d}} \mid \hat{d} \in \hat{S}_2\}$. We find that this particular definition of the connector yields very good results in our abstraction refinement algorithm. It is easily checked that if $S_1 \vdash_p S_2$, then $S_1 \preceq S_1 \boxplus S_2$. Let $S_1, S_2 \in \wp_{fn}(D, \vdash)$, where $S_1 \Vdash S_2$. Then, $S_1 \nabla_P S_2$ is defined as follows:

$$
\begin{aligned}
S_1 \nabla_P S_2 \overset{\Delta}{=} \ &let \ \ S_2' = \ if \ (S_1 \preceq S_2) \ then \ S_2 \ else \ S_1 \boxplus S_2 \ \ in \\
&S_2' \oplus_P \Omega_D^{\vdash}(\{d_1 \nabla d_2 \in D \mid d_1 \in S_1, d_2 \in S_2', d_1 \Vdash d_2\})
\end{aligned}
$$

To illustrate the need for the connector operator, recall the example from Figure 1(b) from Section 1. Recall that during the second iteration of the refinement loop, the symbolic state after second iteration of the fixpoint is $S_2' \overset{\Delta}{=} (x \geq 0 \ \wedge \ m = 0) \vee (x \leq N \ \wedge \ x = m+1 \ \wedge \ m \geq 0)$. The new symbolic state that is generated after one more execution of the loop body is $S_{new} = (x \leq N \wedge x = m+2 \wedge m \geq 0)$. Here $S_2'' \overset{\Delta}{=} S_2' \oplus_P S_{new} \overset{\Delta}{=} (x \geq 0 \wedge m = 0) \vee (x \leq N \ \wedge \ x = m+1 \ \wedge \ m \geq 0) \vee (x \leq N \ \wedge \ x = m+2 \ \wedge \ m \geq 0)$. Our goal is to compute $S_3' \overset{\Delta}{=} S_2' \nabla_P S_2''$. Since $S_2' \preceq S_2''$ does not hold, we need to compute $S_2' \boxplus S_2''$ by merging some of the elements of S_2''. Here

$\hat{S}_2'' \triangleq (x \geq 0 \ \wedge \ m = 0) \vee (x \leq N \ \wedge \ x = m + 1 \ \wedge \ m \geq 0)$ and $\tilde{S}_2'' \triangleq (x \leq N \ \wedge \ x = m + 2 \ \wedge \ m \geq 0)$. If we merge $\hat{S}_2''$ with first element of $\hat{S}_2''$ then the result is $S_2' \boxplus S_2'' \triangleq (x \geq 0 \ \wedge \ m \geq 0 \ \wedge \ x \geq m)$ whereas if we merge $\tilde{S}_2''$ with second element of $\hat{S}_2''$ then the result is $S_2' \boxplus S_2'' \triangleq (x \geq 0 \ \wedge \ m = 0) \vee (x \leq N \ \wedge \ m \geq 0 \ \wedge \ x \geq m + 1 \ \wedge \ x \leq m + 2)$. The result of widening in the first case is $x \geq 0 \ \wedge \ m \geq 0$ which is less precise than the widening result of second case $(x \geq 0 \ \wedge \ m = 0) \vee (x \leq N \ \wedge \ x \geq m + 1 \ \wedge \ m \geq 0)$ when using the widening operator defined in [9] for the base domain of convex polyhedra. Thus, it is seen that choosing the minimal result (second case) is necessary to obtain a fixpoint that is strong enough to prove the assertion. Our definition of connector is necessary to prove this example, and most of the other examples we have encountered.

Using the theory developed in [1], it can be shown that ∇_P satisfies the convergence properties of a widening operator. Without transforming S_2 to S_2' using the $\boxplus$ connector, such convergence guarantees cannot be given (see [1]). In Section 2, when we discuss the algorithm, we did not explicitly mention the difficulties of dealing with powerset domains. The operator $\cup$ used in Section 2 corresponds to $\oplus_P$ operator defined in this Section.

4   Dealing with Non-monotonicity

One technical issue with widening is its non-monotonicity. That is, if $S_1 \subseteq S_1'$ and $S_2 \subseteq S_2'$, then it is not necessarily the case that $(S_1 \nabla S_2) \subseteq (S_1' \nabla S_2')$. Thus, refining the widening operator to a least upper bound operation in step i of the abstract fixpoint computation, could result in a larger set of states in a later iteration! However, this problem can be easily avoided since we already keep track of the intermediate set of states reached at each iteration of the abstract fixpoint computation. At every iteration of the abstract fixpoint computation, we can intersect the states reached at step i with the set of states reached at step i during the previous iteration of the abstract fixpoint computation. If the step count i is greater than the number of steps required in the previous iteration, then we can intersect with the fixpoint computed in previous iteration. The modified algorithm is shown in [11].

Progress guarantee. With the monotonic abstraction refinement procedure, it is clear that in the successive abstraction iterations we compute more precise abstract fixpoint as compared to the previous iteration. We can make a stronger statement about progress by defining an ordering between counterexamples. An abstract counterexample C is a sequence of set of states $R_0, R_1, \ldots, R_n$ such that (1) R_i is the set of states computed in step i of the abstract fixpoint computation, and (2) $R_n \cap \psi \neq \emptyset \ \wedge \ \forall i < n.R_i \cap \psi = \emptyset$. The length of counterexample C is denoted by $|C|$. We define a binary relation $\prec_c$ on abstract counterexamples as $C_1 \prec_c C_2$ iff either (1) $|C_1| < |C_2|$, or (2) $|C_1| = |C_2|$ and $\forall i.0 \leq i < |C_1| : R_i(C_2) \subseteq R_i(C_1) \ \wedge \ \exists i.0 \leq i < |C_1| : R_i(C_2) \subset R_i(C_1)$. We state our progress guarantees below.

Theorem 1. *Let C_i be the abstract counterexample generated during the iteration i of abstraction computation. Then, we have for all $i \geq 0$, $C_i \prec_c C_{i+1}$.*

Lemma 1. *Let C_i be the counterexample of length n generated during the ith iteration of abstraction, then after at most n iterations of refinement and abstraction, counter examples generated, if any, will be of length greater than n.*

The proof of Theorem 1 is given in [11]. Lemma 1 follows from Theorem 1 and the fact that the set of hints monotonically increases in successive iterations of refinement. All these results make use of our assumption from Section 2 that the LUB operator $\cup$ in algorithm MAFixpoint is precise. Lemma 1 guarantees that if an abstract counterexample is a false error, then it will necessarily get refined in bounded number of refinement iterations and will never reappear as an abstract counterexample at subsequent iterations of iterative refinement. However, there is no guarantee that the iterative refinement loop will ever terminate. In practice, we terminate the outer iterative refinement loop after a certain time or memory limit is exhausted and return the answer "don't know".

Systematic abstraction refinement. For powerset abstract domains like the sets of convex polyhedra, the least upper bound operator $\oplus$ is the non-redundant union as defined in Section 3. Thus the refinement will add more and more disjuncts to the reachable set of states. It is possible that this increase in the number of disjuncts will continue infinitely even though the assertion can be satisfied by an abstract fixpoint computed by merging some intermediate disjuncts and doing widening later on. Thus intermediate merging may provide convergence. We use the *connector* $\boxplus$ operator described in Section 3 as an operator to merge some disjuncts into one convex polyhedra. The refinement algorithm now checks whether using the merging operation instead of widening avoids error. If it does then widening operator is replaced by the merge operation. Thus we have three upper bound operators $\cup$, $\boxplus$ and ∇ of decreasing precision. The refinement algorithm can now refine a widening operator to either $\boxplus$ operator or a $\cup$ operator. It can also refine the $\boxplus$ operator to $\cup$ operator. The hints that are generated by the refinement algorithm now are of the form $\langle i, op \rangle$, where i is the step number and $op \in \{\cup, \boxplus\}$ is the operator to be applied after that step. The procedure $MAFixPoint$ in [11] gives the abstraction procedure which ensures monotonicity and uses the new hints just described.

If the refinement algorithm returns $\langle i, \cup \rangle$ then, it is clear that refining the widening operator in step i to LUB will remove the abstract counterexample. However, if the refinement algorithm returns $\langle i, \boxplus \rangle$, then the widening operator in step i could be replaced either by a $\cup$ or by $\boxplus$. It is not clear whether it is provident to convert the widening operation to $\cup$ or $\boxplus$ in this case. It is possible that exactly one choice results in computation of the abstract fixpoint necessary to prove the property, whereas the other choice leads to non-termination of the abstraction refinement cycle. Thus, it is more advantageous to try both possibilities. The procedure SARefinement in [11] systematically tries both possibilities if the refinement returns $\langle i, \boxplus \rangle$.

5   Implementation and Empirical Results

Our implementation is for an imperative language with integer variables, and usual control structures including sequencing, conditionals and loops. The implementation is based on the algorithm SARefinement from [11], but it differs in three ways: (1) While the algorithm SARefinement from [11] is fully symbolic, the implementation does a mixture of explicit and symbolic state exploration. In particular, the control (program counter) is kept explicit, and we never merge symbolic constraints from two different program counters. (2) Widening is performed in our implementation only along the back edges of loops. Thus, at join points such as the end of if-then-else statements, the states from the two branches are kept separate unless they turn out to be identical. (3) We use two heuristics to prune the space of refinements explored by the algorithm. The first heuristic disallows conversion of widening to $\boxplus$ in consecutive iterations of refinement. In such a case, we convert widening to $\cup$ in the latter iteration. The second heuristic restricts the size of set H in procedure SARefinement to 3. Any successive refinement does not increase size of H, but converts the widening to one of $\boxplus$ or $\cup$ depending on the first heuristic.

Our prototype implementation uses the library PPL [2] for polyhedral operations. We have run our program on a machine with Intel Pentium 3.0GHz processor, 512 KB cache and 512 MB RAM.

We have experimented with two widening operators for polyhedral domain: (1) the original widening operator defined by Cousot and Halbwachs [9] (we refer to this as "CH78"), and (2) the widening operator defined by Bagnara, Hill, Ricci and Zaffanella [3] (we refer to this as "BHRZ03"). Both these widening operators are defined for convex polyhedra. Since our abstract domain is the set of convex polyhedra, we use Section 3 to lift these widening operators to the powerset domain.

We evaluated the implementation on two sets of examples. The results show that our technique is robust, regardless of the widening operator used.

The first set of examples were obtained from Rustan Leino [15], and are part of his test suite for the tool Boogie. All these programs have embedded assertions in the program and our goal is to discover loop invariants strong enough to prove the assertions. Two of these programs (Prog 7 and Prog 9) are incorrect, in that the assertions fail. Table 1 shows for each of the two different widening operators, the time taken, and the number of widenings that were converted to $\cup$ and $\boxplus$ respectively, to either prove the assertion or find the error. Our implementation is able to successfully prove the assertions in all the 11 correct programs, and it is able to find the error in the two erroneous programs. Out of the 11 correct programs, 5 programs require non-trivial iterative refinement. Prog0 is the example from Figure 1(b). Prog8 is very similar to Prog0, except that the assertion after the while loop is stronger. It asserts that $(0 \leq m < N \land x = N)$. Our iterative refinement computes the more precise invariant $(x - m = 1 \land 0 \leq m \leq 1 \land 1 + m \leq N) \lor (m = 0 \land 0 \leq x \leq 1) \lor (m = 0 \land 1 \leq x \leq N) \lor (2 \leq x \leq N \land m \geq 0 \land x \geq m + 1)$ needed to prove the property. The choice of the widening operator (CH78 or BHRZ03) influences only the number of refinement steps, but not the ability of our technique to prove the property.

Table 1. Experimental results, Programs on left are from Rustan Leino [15], Programs on right are from the StInG web page [18]. The column head (I) indicates the time (in sec) taken for example program to be verified and column head (II). indicates the number of refinement steps ($\cup$, $\boxplus$). * programs are incorrect(i.e., assertion fails).

Program	CH78		BHRZ03		Program	CH78		BHRZ03	
Name	I	II	I	II	Name	I	II	I	II
Prog0	0.055	(1, 1)	0.054	(1, 1)	See-Saw	0.816	(3, 3)	0.811	(3, 3)
Prog1	0.01	(0, 0)	0.011	(0, 0)	Robot-HH96	0.01	(0, 0)	0.01	(0, 0)
Prog2	0.012	(0, 0)	0.014	(0, 0)	Berkeley	0.098	(1, 1)	0.085	(0, 1)
Prog3	0.014	(0, 0)	0.01	(0, 0)	Berkeley-nat	0.432	(2, 1)	3.44	(2, 1)
Prog4	0.047	(2, 0)	0.138	(2, 2)	Heapsort	0.719	(2, 1)	0.162	(0, 1)
Prog5	0.058	(2, 0)	0.093	(2, 1)	Train-RM03	0.022	(0, 0)	0.02	(0, 0)
Prog6	0.035	(1, 0)	0.021	(0, 0)	EFM	0.06	(0, 0)	0.06	(0, 0)
Prog7*	0.01	(0, 0)	0.009	(0, 0)	EFM1	0.06	(0, 0)	0.06	(0, 0)
Prog8	0.097	(2, 1)	0.268	(3, 2)	LIFO	3.325	(3, 3)	1.29	(2, 1)
Prog9*	0.01	(0, 0)	0.008	(0, 0)	LIFO-NAT	29.55	(7, 5)	2.537	(2, 2)
Prog10	0.015	(0, 0)	0.011	(0, 0)	cars-midpt	≥10000	(≥3, ≥3)	≥10000	(≥3, ≥3)
Prog11	0.029	(0, 0)	0.032	(0, 0)	barber	10.48	(3, 3)	17.12	(3, 3)
Prog12	0.01	(1, 0)	0.014	(1, 0)	Swim-pool	11.13	(3, 3)	18.029	(3, 3)
					Swim-pool-1	11.24	(3, 3)	18.50	(3, 3)

The second set of examples are available at the StInG website [18]. The StInG tool [18, 19] uses Farkas' Lemma to synthesize the strongest linear invariant. We requested Sriram Sankaranarayanan to provide the exact invariants that StInG computes. Then, we modified the examples to assert the invariant computed by StInG (the invariants are also now available at [18]). Then, we used our iterative refinement algorithm to prove these assertions. Our implementation is able to prove the invariants in all examples with the exception of the program 'cars-midpt'. This run took more than 10000 seconds but had done only 6 refinement steps. Thus, we are unsure if the algorithm will converge if more refinement steps can be executed. We find that the polyhedral operations are very time consuming in this example. The last powerset widening call to the PPL library took 6910 seconds, where both arguments to this widening operation had 4 disjuncts with an average of 125 constraints per disjunct.

Though the invariants generated by StInG itself do not contain disjunctions, our iterative refinement algorithm used disjunctions in some cases to prove these invariants. Again, the choice of the widening operator (CH78 or BHRZ03) influences only the number of refinement steps, but not the ability of our technique to prove the property.

6   Shape Analysis

We briefly sketch an abstract domain for representing heap configurations, with LUB and widen operators. This immediately enables application of our iterative refinement algorithm to do shape analysis [17]. Our approach does not capture reachability information in the heap, and only certain programs with unbounded state spaces can be verified using our approach. Our approach currently does not have all the sophistications of [17].

A *Boolean Linked List Program* (BLL Program for short) is a single-procedure program with a finite number of variables, where every variable has the following datatype:

```
class Node {
  bool data;
  Node next;
}
```

BLL programs allow dynamic creation of objects, so they have potentially infinite state spaces. Our abstract domain is the domain of abstract heap graphs $\hat{\mathcal{G}} = \langle \mathcal{G}, \vdash, \mathbf{0}_{\mathcal{G}}, \oplus \rangle$. Let $V = \{v_1, v_2, \ldots, v_n\}$ be the variables in a BLL Program P. An abstract heap graph A of program P is a 5-tuple $\langle \mathbf{U^A}, \mathbf{V^A}, \mathbf{Data^A}, \mathbf{Next^A}, \mathbf{Z^A} \rangle$, where (1) $\mathbf{U^A}$ is a finite set of nodes $\{U_0, U_1, \ldots, U_k\}$, (2) $\mathbf{V^A}: V \rightarrow 2^{\mathbf{U^A}}$, maps every variable to a set of nodes, (3) $\mathbf{Data^A} : \mathbf{U^A} \rightarrow \{0, 1, \top\}$ maps the data field of each node to boolean values or $\top$, and (4) $\mathbf{Next^A}: \mathbf{U^A} \rightarrow 2^{\mathbf{U^A}}$, maps the next field of each node to a set of nodes, and (5) $\mathbf{Z^A} \subseteq \mathbf{U^A}$ is the subset of nodes that are designated as summary nodes. An abstract heap graph represents a set of concrete heap graphs. A concrete heap graph represents a state of a BLL Program, which is a set of heap addresses, with variables pointing to specific addresses, and specific concrete values to objects in each of these addresses. The concretization function γ maps every abstract heap graph to a set of concrete heap graphs. The LUB of two abstract heap graphs A and B such that $\mathbf{U^A} \cap \mathbf{U^B} = \emptyset$, is intuitively just the disjoint union of the two heap graphs. The widen of two abstract heap graphs A and B, given by $C = A \nabla B$ is intuitively obtained by fixing the nodes of the result to $\mathbf{U^A}$ and adding more edges representing B into A, and updating to coarser data values representing nodes of B into nodes of A. A precise description of the concretization function γ, the LUB operator, and the widening operator can be found in [11].

The intuition is that the application of the LUB operator can add more nodes to the abstract heap graph, but the application of the widening operator cannot. Thus, if the LUB operator is used only a finite number of times during the fixpoint, the number of nodes in the abstract heap graph stops growing after a finite number of iterations. Thereafter, the fixpoint converges after sufficient applications of widening.

Using this abstract domain, we are able to prove some programs that allocate unbounded number of nodes by using our refinement algorithm. Consider the program shown in Figure 3. First, our abstract fixpoint computation uses widening along the back edge of every while loop. Intuitively, repeated applications of the widening operator allow only one summary node, which results in the second abstract heap graph in Figure 3. This invariant is not strong enough to prove the assertion. Then, our refinement algorithm detects that the second widening in the second while loop is the reason for the loss of precision and

```
head := null; p := null;
while (*) {
    p := new node;
    p.data := 0;
    p.next := head;
    head := p;
}
p := head;
while (p != null) {
    assume (p != null);
    p.data = 1;
    p := p.next;
}
assume (p = null);
p := head;
while (*) {
    assume (p != null);
    assert (p.data = 1);
    p := p.next;
}
```

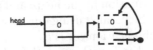

Abstract heap graph after first while loop

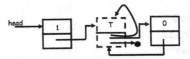

Imprecise heap graph obtained using widening in the
second while loop (not sufficient to prove assertion)

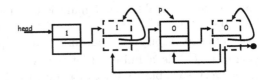

Heap graph obtained after doing one refinement,
where widening in the second iteration of the second
while loop is converted to LUB (sufficient to prove
assertion)

Fig. 3. Example program that creates an unbounded linked list

converts this widen to LUB. After this refinement, subsequent applications of the
widening operator are now able to allow two summary nodes as shown in the
third abstract heap graph in Figure 3. In this domain, converting widen to LUB
results in allowing more nodes in the the resulting fixpoint. This is analogous
to adding more disjuncts by converting widen to LUB in the powerset domain of
convex polyhedra.

7   Related Work

Counterexample driven refinement [14], has gained popularity in recent
years [7, 4], as a technique to prove properties of systems, while reducing false
errors. Several tools based on counterexample driven refinement have appeared
in the past few years [4, 12, 6]. All these efforts use predicate abstraction [10],
which is a particular case of abstract interpretation [8]. In contrast to these efforts, we present a technique to refine any abstract interpretation automatically
using counterexamples. Thus, our work has the potential to make counterexample driven refinement more broadly applicable to a variety of abstract domains,
in order to reduce false errors.

Techniques to reduce precision loss due to widening have been studied in
the abstract interpretation community. We compare our work with (1) generic

approaches that work for any abstract domain, and (2) specific approaches for particular abstract domains. In the category of generic approaches, Jeannet, Halbwachs and Raymond partition the abstract domain with predicates on the control state [13] to improve precision. They first perform a combination of forward and backward analysis, and use predicates present in the conditionals in the program to do such partitioning. Unlike their approach we use a backward propagation of the abstract counterexample in the spirit of [7] to generate refinement hints. Bourdouncle has noted that more precise abstract domains can be obtained by applying widening only in certain equations (cutting of dependence loops) [5]. Bourdouncle also defines new widening operators together with disjunctive completion by representing sets of abstract elements. This approach does not use counterexamples to refine the abstract domain. In the category of approaches that are specific to particular domains, the StInG tool [18, 19] uses Farkas' Lemma to synthesize linear invariants by extracting non-linear constraints on the coefficients of a target invariant from an affine program. Unlike StInG, our technique uses fixpoints, and is independent of the abstract domain.

Leino and Logozzo use counterexample contexts obtained from the theorem prover to re-run the abstract interpreter restricted to the counterexample context, with the hope of obtaining more precise loop invariants [16]. This approach has philosophical similarities to our approach, but there are several technical differences. Their approach is implemented entirely inside the theorem prover, unlike ours. Unlike the technique presented here, there is no progress guarantee with their approach, and their technique does not stop the iterative refinement if there is a true error.

8   Conclusion

We presented a new counterexample driven refinement technique that can refine any abstract interpretation, and tune the precision depending on the property of interest. Our technique is independent of the abstract domain used. We instantiated the technique for affine programs and our implementation is able to prove invariants generated by the StInG tool. We also sketched how the technique can be applied to do shape analysis.

Acknowledgment. We thank Rustan Leino for providing his example programs from the Boogie project, and Sriram Sankaranarayanan for providing us the invariants generated by StInG. We thank Supratik Chakraborty, Prasad Naldurg and Mooly Sagiv for insightful discussions.

References

1. R. Bagnara, P. Hill, and E. Zaffanella. Widening operators for powerset domains. In *VMCAI 04: Verification, Model Checking and Abstract Interpretation*. Springer-Verlag, 2004.
2. R. Bagnara, P. M. Hill, and E. Zaffanella. PPL: The Parma Polyhedral Library — http://www.cs.unipr.it/ppl/.

3. R. Bagnara, P.M. Hill, E. Ricci, and E. Zaffanella. Precise widening opertors for convex polyhedra. In *SAS 03: Static Analysis*. Springer-Verlag, 2003.
4. T. Ball and S. K. Rajamani. Automatically validating temporal safety properties of interfaces. In *SPIN 01: SPIN Workshop*, LNCS 2057. Springer-Verlag, 2001.
5. F. Bourdoncle. Abstract interpretation by dynamic partitioning. *Journal of Functional Programming*, 2(4):407–423, 1992.
6. S. Chaki, E. M. Clarke, A. Groce, S. Jha, and H. Veith. Modular verification of software components in C. *IEEE Transactions on Software Engineering*, 30(6):388–402, 2004.
7. E. M. Clarke, O. Grumberg, S. Jha, Y. Lu, and H. Veith. Counterexample-guided abstraction refinement. In *CAV 00: Computer-Aided Verification*, LNCS 1855, pages 154–169. Springer-Verlag, 2000.
8. P. Cousot and R. Cousot. Abstract interpretation: a unified lattice model for the static analysis of programs by construction or approximation of fixpoints. In *POPL 77: Principles of Programming Languages*, pages 238–252. ACM, 1977.
9. P. Cousot and N. Halbwachs. Automatic discovery of linear restraints among variables of a program. In *POPL 78: Principles of Programming Languages*, pages 84–97. ACM Press, 1978.
10. S. Graf and H. Saïdi. Construction of abstract state graphs with PVS. In *CAV 97: Computer-aided Verification*, LNCS 1254, pages 72–83. Springer-Verlag, 1997.
11. B. S. Gulavani and S. K. Rajamani. Counterexample driven refinement for abstract interpretation. Technical Report MSR-TR-2006-02, Microsoft Research, 2006.
12. T. A. Henzinger, R. Jhala, R. Majumdar, and G. Sutre. Lazy abstraction. In *POPL '02*, pages 58–70. ACM, January 2002.
13. B. Jeannet, N. Halbwachs, and P. Raymond. Dynamic partitioning in analyses of numerical properties. In *SAS 99: Static Analysis*, LNCS 1694, pages 39–50. Springer-Verlag, 1999.
14. R.P. Kurshan. *Computer-aided Verification of Coordinating Processes*. Princeton University Press, 1994.
15. K. Rustan M. Leino. Personal communication, September 2005.
16. K. Rustan M. Leino and Francesco Logozzo. Loop invariants on demand. In *APLAS 2005: Asian Symposium on Programming Languages and Systems*, 2005. To appear.
17. M. Sagiv, T. Reps, and R. Wilhelm. Parametric shape analysis via 3-valued logic. In *POPL 99: Principles of Programming Languages*, pages 105–118. ACM, 1999.
18. S. Sankaranarayanan. StInG: The Stanford Invarint Generator — http://theory.stanford.edu/ srirams/software/sting.html.
19. S. Sankaranarayanan, H. Sipma, and Z. Manna. Constraint based linear-relations analysis. In *SAS 04: Static Analysis*. Springer-Verlag, 2004.

Abstraction Refinement with Craig Interpolation and Symbolic Pushdown Systems*

Javier Esparza, Stefan Kiefer, and Stefan Schwoon

Institute for Formal Methods in Computer Science, University of Stuttgart
{esparza, kiefersn, schwoosn}@informatik.uni-stuttgart.de

Abstract. Counterexample-guided abstraction refinement (CEGAR) has proven to be a powerful method for software model-checking. In this paper, we investigate this concept in the context of sequential (possibly recursive) programs whose statements are given as BDDs. We examine how Craig interpolants can be computed efficiently in this case and propose a new, special type of interpolants. Moreover, we show how to treat multiple counterexamples in one refinement cycle. We have implemented this approach within the model-checker Moped and report on experiments.

1 Introduction

CEGAR is a powerful tool for automated abstraction of hardware and software systems. Originally designed for verification of hardware designs, this technique has been successfully utilized for software verification as well. Particularly, the SLAM project [1] has gained attention and has demonstrated the effectiveness of software verification for device drivers. The BLAST tool [2] and the MAGIC tool [3] have been applied successfully in domains of security protocols and real-time operating-system kernels.

The CEGAR paradigm was introduced in [4]. The goal is to check if a given concrete program can reach a certain *error label*. Since the data space of the concrete program is too large, it is abstracted with a predicate abstraction method. Initially, there are no predicates, therefore the initial abstraction is very coarse (no data, only control flow). This abstract program is then model-checked.

Since the abstract program is, by construction, an overapproximation of the concrete one, model-checking it can have two possible outcomes: Either the error label is not reachable, then we know that it is not reachable in the concrete program either and the CEGAR process terminates. Or it is reachable in the abstract program, illustrated by means of a counterexample, i.e., a path leading to the error label. Due to the overapproximation, this path may be *spurious*, i.e., not realizable in the concrete system. If it is not spurious (*real* counterexample), it can be reported to the user and the process terminates. If it is spurious, then suitable new predicates have to be introduced to refine the abstraction such that this counterexample is excluded in future predicate abstractions.

---

* This work was partially supported by the DFG project *Algorithms for Software Model Checking*.

H. Hermanns and J. Palsberg (Eds.): TACAS 2006, LNCS 3920, pp. 489–503, 2006.

This process continues in cycles, until the abstraction is fine enough to either conclude that the error label is unreachable or that a real counterexample exists.

1.1   Our Work and Related Work

We develop a CEGAR scheme for the BDD-based model-checker Moped, a combined reachability and LTL model-checker for symbolic pushdown systems [5].

From a high-level perspective, our approach can be characterized as follows: We first translate a program with integer variables to a program with finitely many variable bits (e.g. 8 or 16 bits per variable), as it is also done by compilers. Thus, we reduce an infinite data space to a finite, but possibly still large data space. Then we use CEGAR to reduce the state space even further. Whereas, in the first step, we might lose some bugs that occur only with large numbers, no precision is lost in the second step, because the abstraction is appropriately refined during the process. Since we do not change the procedural structure in both steps, recursion may always induce an infinite state space.

The input for our CEGAR scheme is essentially a sequential program with procedures (potentially recursive) whose variables are represented by a finite number of bits. BDDs capture the modification of the variables through the program statements. The problem is whether this program can reach a specific error label or not.

Moped could be directly used for this problem, but we use a CEGAR scheme to reduce its resource consumption. Our abstract programs are other boolean programs whose variables are previously introduced predicates. The statements of the abstract programs modify the truth values of the predicates. This is again captured by BDDs. Those abstract programs are checked using Moped.

The consequent use of BDDs throughout the CEGAR process distinguishes our work from related work about CEGAR in software. For instance, in the SLAM project [1], a BDD-based model-checker is employed on the abstract level, but symbolic expression representations together with theorem provers are applied on the concrete level. [3] does not use BDDs at all, but relies on SAT solvers and theorem provers. Also [2, 6] make use of theorem provers, whereas we use BDD technology for the concrete program, the abstract programs, and for the predicates in our abstraction mechanism. We therefore avoid theorem provers, which assume infinite ranges of integer variables and often form bottlenecks in related projects, e.g. in [1].

Another feature of our work is the use of multiple counterexamples in a single refinement step. Moped constructs a "witness graph" (see [7]) which, in the model-checking phase, records information about which program states can be reached via which previously reached program states. When viewed from the perspective of the error label, this graph is a DAG containing possible (abstract) error traces. We use this DAG for abstraction refinement, not only a single counterexample. If the counterexample DAG contains a real (non-spurious) counterexample, it is reported. Otherwise we compute predicates that ensure that none of the counterexamples in the DAG will occur again in future abstractions. In [8], multiple counterexamples are also used in a CEGAR scheme, but not for software and not in a DAG structure.

For the predicate generation we use Craig interpolation (see [6,9]). In contrast to [6], we consider Craig interpolation for pure propositional logics. We show that the computation of Craig interpolants works well with BDDs and that their use gives us flexibility for heuristics about *which* interpolants to use, since Craig interpolants are, in general, not unique.

Organization of the Paper. This paper proceeds as follows. In Sect. 2 we investigate Craig interpolation for propositional logics and derive computation schemes that are suitable for BDDs. In Sect. 3, symbolic pushdown systems, a model for sequential programs, are reviewed. In Sect. 4, the techniques of Sect. 2 are applied to the computation of predicates that rule out DAGs of abstract counterexamples. Section 5 sketches our predicate abstraction scheme. We give evidence for the usefulness of our concepts in Sect. 6 and conclude in Sect. 7. In [10], we give further details and proofs.

2   Craig Interpolation

In [11,6], Craig interpolation was used to automatize abstraction refinement. As in [11] (and in contrast to [6], where a specialized arithmetic proof system is used) we are interested in Craig interpolants for pure propositional logic. We write $Occ(F)$ for the set of variables that occur (syntactically) in a formula F.

Definition 1. *Let (F, G) be a pair of formulas with $F \wedge G$ unsatisfiable. A (syntactic) interpolant for (F, G) is a formula I s.t. F implies I (written: $F \models I$), $I \wedge G$ is unsatisfiable and $Occ(I) \subseteq Occ(F) \cap Occ(G)$.*

Craig's Interpolation Theorem [12] states that interpolants always exist, but they are not unique. In [11], interpolants are obtained from a resolution proof of the unsatisfiability of $F \wedge G$, which is, in turn, constructed by a SAT solver. However, in our BDD-based setting this result is no longer useful, because we do not prove unsatisfiability of $F \wedge G$ by means of a SAT solver. We show that there exist interpolants that do not depend on the internal strategies of a SAT solver or a theorem prover, and can be naturally computed by standard BDD operations.

2.1   Strongest and Weakest Interpolants

It is easy to see that if I and I' are interpolants for (F, G), then so are $I \vee I'$ and $I \wedge I'$ (see also [13]). It follows that "the strongest interpolant" and "the weakest interpolant", as defined below, exist and are unique.

Definition 2. *The strongest interpolant for (F, G), denoted $SI(F, G)$, is the unique interpolant for (F, G) that implies any other interpolant. The weakest interpolant for (F, G), denoted $WI(F, G)$, is the unique interpolant implied by any other interpolant.*

Clearly, $SI(F, G) \models WI(F, G)$ holds. Proposition 1 below shows that $SI(F, G)$ and $WI(F, G)$ can be obtained by standard BDD operations (quantification over variables). If F and G are any formulas, we define the notation $F \uparrow G :=$ $\exists(Occ(F) \setminus Occ(G)).F$ and $F \downarrow G := \forall(Occ(F) \setminus Occ(G)).F$. Notice that $F \downarrow G$ $\models F \models F \uparrow G$ always holds.

Proposition 1 (Strongest and Weakest Interpolants). *Let (F, G) be a formula pair with $F \wedge G$ unsatisfiable. Then $SI(F, G) \equiv F \uparrow G$ and $WI(F, G) \equiv (\neg G) \downarrow F$.*

In the next sections, we consider the following problem: Given a formula $F = F_1 \wedge \ldots \wedge F_n$, determine if F is unsatisfiable, and if so, find interpolants for the pairs (G^i, G_i), $i \in \{1, \ldots, n\}$, where $G^i := F_1 \wedge \ldots \wedge F_i$ and $G_i := F_{i+1} \wedge \ldots \wedge F_n$. We show that strongest and weakest interpolants for (G^i, G_i) can be computed iteratively.

Proposition 2. *Let $F = F_1 \wedge F_2 \wedge \ldots \wedge F_n$ be a formula and let G^i and G_i be defined as above. Let $\{I_i\}$ and $\{J_i\}$ be families of predicates defined according to the following procedures:*
$I_0 := \textbf{true}, I_{i+1} := (I_i \wedge F_{i+1}) \uparrow G_{i+1}$ *and* $J_n := \textbf{false}, J_{i-1} := (F_i \rightarrow J_i) \downarrow G^{i-1}$.

(i) F is unsatisfiable iff $I_n \equiv \textbf{false}$ iff $J_0 \equiv \textbf{true}$.
(ii) If F is unsatisfiable, then $I_i \equiv SI(G^i, G_i)$ and $J_i \equiv WI(G^i, G_i)$.

Now, given $F = F_1 \wedge \ldots \wedge F_n$, we can iteratively compute BDDs for the sequence I_i or J_i with the above procedure. We can decide if F is satisfiable using (i). If F is unsatisfiable, then, by (ii), we have computed $SI(G^i, G_i)$ or $WI(G^i, G_i)$.
For our CEGAR purposes, we will need the following property:

Definition 3 (Tracking Property). *Let $F_1 \wedge \ldots \wedge F_n$ be unsatisfiable, and let K_i be interpolants for (G^i, G_i). We say that the family $\{K_i\}$ satisfies the tracking property if $K_i \wedge F_{i+1} \models K_{i+1}$.*

Proposition 3. *Let $F_1 \wedge F_2 \wedge \ldots \wedge F_n$ be unsatisfiable. Let $\{I_i\}$ and $\{J_i\}$ be families of predicates defined according to the following procedures:*

$I_0 := \textbf{true}, I_{i+1} :=$ *any interpolant for* $(I_i \wedge F_{i+1}, G_{i+1})$,
$J_n := \textbf{false}, J_{i-1} :=$ *any interpolant for* $(G^{i-1}, \neg(F_i \rightarrow J_i))$.

Then $\{I_i\}$ and $\{J_i\}$ are interpolants for (G^i, G_i) and satisfy the tracking property.

Corollary 1. *$\{SI(G^i, G_i)\}$ and $\{WI(G^i, G_i)\}$ satisfy the tracking property.*

Finally, Prop. 4 shows the interplay between interpolants and disjunction:

Proposition 4.

(i) If $(F \vee G) \wedge H$ is unsatisfiable, then $SI(F \vee G, H) \equiv SI(F, H) \vee SI(G, H)$.
(ii) If $F \wedge (G \vee H)$ is unsatisfiable, then $WI(F, G \vee H) \equiv WI(F, G) \wedge WI(F, H)$.

2.2   Conciliated Interpolants

Interpolants can be seen as explanations indicating why counterexamples are spurious. It makes sense to look for "simple" explanations. It seems reasonable to consider an interpolant "simple" if few variables occur in it. Since we work with BDD libraries, it is natural to strengthen the notion of occurrence semantically:

Definition 4. *A variable v occurs semantically in F if $\exists v.F \not\equiv F$. The set of variables that occur semantically in F is denoted by $OccSem(F)$.*

One could strengthen the notion of interpolants accordingly (by replacing Occ by $OccSem$ in Def. 1). Such *semantic* interpolants are also *syntactic* interpolants. We now show that one can find simpler interpolants than the weakest and strongest ones, still using only quantifications. If I and J are strongest and weakest (syntactic or semantic) interpolants for (F, G), respectively, then we have $F \models I \models J \models \neg G$, but not necessarily $OccSem(I) = OccSem(J)$. Now we can compute the strongest and weakest *semantic* interpolants I_1, J_1 for the pair $(I, \neg J)$. Since $F \models I \models I_1 \models J_1 \models J \models \neg G$, we have that I_1 and J_1 are also interpolants for (F, G). If $OccSem(I) \neq OccSem(J)$, then at least one of I_1 and J_1 will be simpler than I and J, since the variables in the symmetric difference are quantified out. This simplification procedure can be iterated until a pair I_n, J_n is reached such that $OccSem(I_n) = OccSem(J_n)$.

Definition 5. *Let (F, G) be formulas over a set V of variables s.t. $F \wedge G$ is unsatisfiable, and let $Z \subseteq V$ s.t. $\exists Z.F$ and $\forall Z.\neg G$ are interpolants for (F, G). We say that $\exists Z.F, \forall Z.\neg G$ are conciliated interpolants if $OccSem(\exists Z.F) = OccSem(\forall Z.\neg G)$. We call $OccSem(\exists Z.F)$ a conciliating set in this case.*

The algorithm in Fig. 1 computes a pair of conciliated interpolants.

```
function conciliate(formulas F, G) returns (Z, ∃(V \ Z).F, ∀(V \ Z).¬G)
/* F ∧ G unsatisfiable is an input requirement */
/* Z is the maximal conciliating set */
I := F;  J := ¬G;  Z := OccSem(F) ∪ OccSem(G)
repeat  X := OccSem(I) \ OccSem(J);   I := ∃X.I;   Z := Z \ X
        Y := OccSem(J) \ OccSem(I);   J := ∀Y.J;   Z := Z \ Y
until Y = ∅
return (Z, I, J)
```

Fig. 1. Computation of conciliated interpolants

Given a pair of formulas, the pair of conciliated interpolants is not unique. Proposition 5 characterizes the pair computed by the algorithm.

Proposition 5.

(i) Let C_1, C_2 be the conciliating sets of the pairs I_1, J_1 and I_2, J_2 of conciliated interpolants. Then $C_1 = C_2$ if and only if $I_1 \equiv I_2$ and $J_1 \equiv J_2$.

(ii) Conciliating sets are closed under union, but not under intersection.
(iii) There is a unique maximal conciliating set.
(iv) The algorithm of Fig. 1 computes the unique maximal conciliating set.

One may argue that, since we are interested in simple interpolants, we would like to compute a *minimal* conciliating set. Unfortunately, there may be several. We can compute one by means of a greedy algorithm that tries to quantify out more and more variables. The interpolants produced by such a procedure might be "simpler", but could strongly depend on the arbitrarily chosen variable order.

In the context of abstraction refinement, one can use the algorithm from Fig. 1 as interpolation (and simplification) method when computing a family of interpolants according to Prop. 3. Thus, the tracking property is satisfied.

3   Symbolic Pushdown Systems

As our program model, we use symbolic pushdown systems (SPDSs) [5].

Definition 6 (SPDS[1]). *An SPDS is a quadruple $(G, \Gamma_0 \times L, \Delta, \gamma_0)$, where*

- *$G = \{\text{true}, \text{false}\}^{n_G}, n_G \geq 0$, is the set of global variable valuations,*
- *Γ_0 is a set of control points,*
- *$L = \{\text{true}, \text{false}\}^{n_L}, n_L \geq 0$, is the set of local variable valuations,*
- *Δ is a set of symbolic transition rules, where each rule is of the form $\langle \gamma \rangle \hookrightarrow \langle \gamma_1 \ldots \gamma_n \rangle$ (R) with $0 \leq n \leq 2, \gamma, \gamma_1, \ldots, \gamma_n \in \Gamma_0$ and $R \subseteq (G \times L) \times (G \times L^n)$,*
- *$\gamma_0 \in \Gamma_0$ is the start address.*

SPDSs model (possibly recursive) programs with procedures. The rules model statements in a programming language. The relation R of a rule describes the relation between the variables before and after execution of the rule. In our setting, they are given as BDDs.

The right side of the rules can consist of zero, one or two control points. Whereas a rule with one control point on the right side describes an intraprocedural statement, a rule with two control points on the right side describes a procedure call, a *push*: γ_1 is the start address of the newly called procedure, and γ_2 the return address of the calling procedure. Parameter passing can be encoded in the relation R of the rule by initializing the local variables of the called procedure. A rule with zero statements is the termination of a procedure, a *pop*. Return values can be encoded in the relation R of the rule by restricting the global variables. SPDSs are discussed in greater detail in [5] and [13].

Example 1. Consider the procedures in Fig. 2. The procedure m calls the procedure f. Procedure f returns a value using the global variable G. Procedure m has a local variable L, procedure f has a local variable A. The transition rules of a corresponding SPDS are shown on the right side. The start address is $m0$.

Moped can model-check such a concrete SPDS. However, in our CEGAR scheme we use Moped only to model-check boolean SPDSs that have the same control flow structure, but overapproximate the given concrete SPDS.

---

[1] This definition is slightly more restrictive than in [5].

```
procedure m
m0:  L := L · (L + 1)
m1:  call f(L)
m2:  if G ≠ 0 then goto error


procedure f(A)
f0:  if A even then
f1:        A := 0
f2:  else A := 561
f3:  G := A
```

$$\langle m0 \rangle \hookrightarrow \langle m1 \rangle \quad (L' = L \cdot (L+1) \ \wedge \ G' = G)$$
$$\langle m1 \rangle \hookrightarrow \langle f0, m2 \rangle \ (L'' = A' = L \ \wedge \ G' = G)$$
$$\langle m2 \rangle \hookrightarrow \langle error \rangle \quad (G \neq 0 \ \wedge \ G' = G)$$

$$\langle f0 \rangle \hookrightarrow \langle f1 \rangle \quad (A \text{ even} \ \wedge \ G' = G)$$
$$\langle f1 \rangle \hookrightarrow \langle f3 \rangle \quad (A' = 0 \ \wedge \ G' = G)$$
$$\langle f0 \rangle \hookrightarrow \langle f2 \rangle \quad (A \text{ odd} \ \wedge \ G' = G)$$
$$\langle f2 \rangle \hookrightarrow \langle f3 \rangle \quad (A' = 561 \ \wedge \ G' = G)$$
$$\langle f3 \rangle \hookrightarrow \langle \rangle \quad (G' = A)$$

Fig. 2. Two simple procedures along with an equivalent SPDS

4   Computing Predicates for a DAG of Counterexamples

We use Moped to model-check the (abstract) SPDSs generated in our refinement cycle. If Moped finds that the error label is reachable in a given SPDS, it constructs a DAG that illustrates the abstract paths leading to the error (see [7] for details on this construction). In brief, the nodes of the DAG are the configurations of the SPDS, the arcs are labeled by symbolic transition rules. There is a single "sink" node with no outgoing arcs, the error configuration.

For instance, consider the program in Fig. 3. In the initial abstraction, all data is discarded, therefore Moped finds two counterexamples, one that does not enter the loop body, and one that enters it exactly once. The resulting counterexample DAG produced by Moped is shown on the right side of Fig. 3. (For the time being, ignore the predicates in curly brackets.)

Once we have the DAG, we discard the information about the abstract variable values and replace the abstract rules by their concrete counterparts. We then need to decide if all counterexamples in the DAG are spurious or not. We call the DAG spurious in the first case.

Let D be a DAG for the rest of the section. We describe our predicate generation method in three steps: for single counterexamples without procedures, for counterexample DAGs without procedures, and finally for counterexamples DAGs with a procedural structure. In all cases, we proceed as follows:

- We construct a so-called *characteristic formula* F_D that is unsatisfiable if and only if the DAG is spurious.
- For each node n in D, we compute a predicate P_n in such a way that, for every edge (n_1, R, n_2) in D, $\{P_{n_1}\} \ R \ \{P_{n_2}\}$ is a valid Hoare triple (recall that a SPDS rule R corresponds to a program instruction).
- We show that unsatisfiability of F_D can be decided by computing and examining these predicates P_n. If F_D is unsatisfiable, i.e., if D is spurious, then the predicates explain the infeasibility of the traces of D, and adding them in future abstractions excludes those traces.

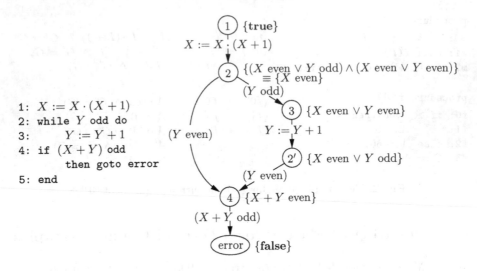

Fig. 3. Program and counterexample DAG with weakest interpolants

4.1   Single Counterexamples

We first consider the case where D contains a single path. Since we do not consider procedures yet, the nodes in D correspond to control points in the program (without any calling context). In this case, we can equivalently view D as a sequence of (intraprocedural) statements.

Consider the following SPDS with its equivalent program formulation:

$$\langle 0 \rangle \hookrightarrow \langle 1 \rangle \; (x' \wedge (y' \leftrightarrow y) \wedge (z' \leftrightarrow z))$$
$$\langle 1 \rangle \hookrightarrow \langle 2 \rangle \; ((x' \leftrightarrow x) \wedge (y' \leftrightarrow x) \wedge (z' \leftrightarrow z))$$
$$\langle 2 \rangle \hookrightarrow \langle 3 \rangle \; ((\neg y \wedge z) \wedge (x' \leftrightarrow x) \wedge (y' \leftrightarrow y) \wedge (z' \leftrightarrow z))$$

```
0:  x := true
1:  y := x
2:  if (¬y ∧ z) then
3:      error
```

Clearly, **error** is not reachable. However, if we check the initial abstraction that ignores data, we obtain the (unique) abstract counterexample trace $x :=$ **true**; $y := x$; $\texttt{assume}(\neg y \wedge z)$. We demonstrate how by computing interpolants we can simultaneously show that the trace is spurious and find an explanation of why it is so. Renaming the variables in the trace yields the following formulas:

$$F_1 \equiv x_1 \wedge (y_1 \leftrightarrow y_0) \wedge (z_1 \leftrightarrow z_0) \qquad\qquad // \; x := \textbf{true}$$
$$F_2 \equiv (x_2 \leftrightarrow x_1) \wedge (y_2 \leftrightarrow x_1) \wedge (z_2 \leftrightarrow z_1) \qquad // \; y := x$$
$$F_3 \equiv (\neg y_2 \wedge z_2) \wedge (x_3 \leftrightarrow x_2) \wedge (y_3 \leftrightarrow y_2) \wedge (z_3 \leftrightarrow z_2) \; // \; \texttt{assume}(\neg y \wedge z)$$

For instance, the variables with index 2 (x_2, y_2 and z_2) refer to the values of x, y and z after $x :=$ **true**; $y := x$ has been executed, and before $\texttt{assume}(\neg y \wedge z)$ has been executed. The characteristic formula of the trace is $F_D \equiv F_1 \wedge F_2 \wedge F_3$. It is unsatisfiable if and only if the trace is spurious.

The procedures derived from Prop. 2 show that F_D is indeed unsatisfiable and yield the following strongest and weakest interpolants:

$$I_1 = SI(G^1, G_1) \equiv \exists\{y_0, z_0, y_1\}.F_1 \qquad\qquad \equiv x_1$$
$$I_2 = SI(G^2, G_2) \equiv \exists\{x_1, z_1\}.(SI(G^1, G_1) \wedge F_2) \quad \equiv (x_2 \wedge y_2)$$
$$J_2 = WI(G^2, G_2) \equiv \forall\{x_3, y_3, z_3\}.\neg F_3 \qquad\qquad \equiv (y_2 \vee \neg z_2)$$
$$J_1 = WI(G^1, G_1) \equiv \forall\{x_2, y_2, z_2\}.(F_2 \rightarrow WI(G^2, G_2)) \equiv (x_1 \vee \neg z_1)$$

Thus, the predicate P_n we are interested in at node n (where $n = 0, 1, 2, 3$), is an interpolant for the formula pair (G^n, G_n), which is in fact a predicate over variable values at n. For instance, the interpolants $SI(G^2, G_2)$ and $WI(G^2, G_2)$, or any other interpolant for this pair, can only contain logical variables common to G^2 and G_2, which must necessarily have index 2. These logical variables refer to the values of the program variables after the execution of $x := \mathbf{true}; y := x$ and before the execution of $\mathtt{assume}(\neg y \wedge z)$.

Fact 1. *Let $F_1 \wedge \ldots \wedge F_k$ be the (unsatisfiable) characteristic formula of a spurious trace consisting of statements $c_1; c_2; \ldots; c_k$, let $\{K_i\}$ be a family of interpolants satisfying the tracking property, and let P_i be the predicate over program variables obtained by removing the index i from all logical variables in K_i.*
Then $\{\mathbf{true}\}c_1\{P_1\}c_2\{P_2\}\ldots\{P_{k-1}\}c_k\{\mathbf{false}\}$ is a valid Hoare annotation.

Hence, interpolants satisfying the tracking property "explain" the infeasibility of a trace by providing Hoare annotations. In our example we obtain

$$\{\mathbf{true}\}\ x := \mathbf{true} \quad \{x\} \quad y := x \ \{x \wedge y\}\ \mathtt{assume}(\neg y \wedge z)\ \{\mathbf{false}\} \qquad (I_i),$$
$$\{\mathbf{true}\}\ x := \mathbf{true}\ \{x \vee \neg z\}\ y := x\ \{y \vee \neg z\}\ \mathtt{assume}(\neg y \wedge z)\ \{\mathbf{false}\} \qquad (J_i).$$

Notice that, by definition, we have $I_i \models J_i$; for instance, $x \wedge y \models y \vee \neg z$. In this example, conciliated interpolants provide a better explanation of infeasibility. The procedures of Prop. 3 guarantee the tracking property and lead to the Hoare annotation $\{\mathbf{true}\}\ x := \mathbf{true}\ \{x\}\ y := x\ \{y\}\ \mathtt{assume}(\neg y \wedge z)\ \{\mathbf{false}\}$.

4.2 Multiple Counterexamples

We now extend the techniques from Sect. 4.1 to the more general case where D contains multiple paths to the error. First, we adapt the construction of F_D. This is illustrated by the following formula, which represents the DAG in Fig. 3. The main addition to the technique from Sect. 4.1 is the disjunction at control point 4, where two branches of the DAG merge:

$$(X_2 = X_1 \cdot (X_1 + 1)) \wedge (Y_2 = Y_1)$$
$$\wedge (X_3 = X_2) \qquad\qquad \wedge (Y_3 = Y_2\ odd)$$
$$\wedge (X_{2'} = X_3) \qquad\qquad \wedge (Y_{2'} = Y_3 + 1)$$
$$\wedge (((X_4 = X_2) \qquad\quad \wedge (Y_4 = Y_2\ even)) \vee ((X_4 = X_{2'}) \wedge (Y_4 = Y_{2'}\ even)))$$
$$\wedge (X_{error} = X_4) \qquad\quad \wedge (Y_{error} = Y_4) \wedge (X_4 + Y_4\ odd).$$

As before, D is spurious if and only if F_D is unsatisfiable [13]. For a node n, let us define the *formula pair of n* as (F, G), where F is the formula corresponding to the DAG "above n" and G is the formula corresponding to the DAG "below n".

Then, our predicate P_n is an interpolant for its formula pair (F, G). In the example above, P_3 is an interpolant for the formula pair (F_3, G_3), where

$$F_3 \equiv (X_2 = X_1 \cdot (X_1 + 1)) \wedge (Y_2 = Y_1) \wedge (X_3 = X_2) \wedge (Y_3 = Y_2 \text{ odd}),$$
$$G_3 \equiv (X_{2'} = X_3) \wedge (Y_{2'} = Y_3 + 1) \wedge (X_4 = X_{2'}) \wedge (Y_4 = Y_{2'} \text{ even})$$
$$\wedge (X_{error} = X_4) \wedge (Y_{error} = Y_4) \wedge (X_4 + Y_4 \text{ odd}).$$

It is easy to see that, in spurious DAGs, such formula pairs are unsatisfiable. By definition, only current variable values can occur in interpolants for those pairs, in above example, variable values with index 3.

Strongest and weakest interpolants at each control point in D can be computed in a stepwise way as sketched in Props. 2 and 4.

In the example, the predicates in curly brackets in Fig. 3 are weakest interpolants. Proposition 4 (ii) is used to compute the interpolant at point 2, as sketched in the figure. Since the predicate computed at 1 turns out to be **true**, one can infer (cf. Prop. 2) that the DAG is spurious and the computed predicates are indeed interpolants. Strongest interpolants could be computed similarly. In that case, the DAG is spurious if the predicate at $error$ is indeed **false**.

Thanks to the tracking property, the interpolants computed in this manner explain the infeasibility of the traces in the DAG. For instance, we have the valid Hoare triple $\{X \text{ even} \vee Y \text{ even}\}$ $Y := Y + 1$ $\{X \text{ even} \vee Y \text{ odd}\}$. Combined, we have for the whole DAG D the Hoare triple $\{\textbf{true}\}$ D $\{\textbf{false}\}$, which is an alternative way to state the spuriousness of D.

In [10], we provide an example where exponentially (in the size of the DAG) many counterexamples are excluded in only one refinement cycle.

4.3   Programs with Procedures

We now show how to handle the case where the underlying SPDS represents a program with (possibly recursive) procedures. The nodes of D now represent control points of the program *plus calling context*, i.e., a stack of return addresses.

The construction of the characteristic formula F_D is the same as in Sect. 4.2. However, F_D now contains global and local variables. Local variables are saved during procedure calls and restored upon completion of a procedure. Thus, if we consider the formula pair (F, G) at a node n, where n is inside a callee, the local variables of the callers become part of the common variables of F and G and could occur in P_n. However, we believe that P_n should be independent of the calling context, for two reasons:

- To generate the abstract transition rules in a simple and efficient way (see Sect. 5), the predicate P_n should depend only on the data that is available in the concrete transition rules that lead into or out of n.
- Allowing local data from the callers to 'pollute' the abstract data space of the callee would severely impair the usefulness of the SPDS model, effectively 'flattening' the system into one that resembles a version where all procedures have been inlined.

In the following, we sketch the modifications that arise in this case. Our goals are to ensure that the predicates P_n at each node n are independent of the calling context and still satisfy the tracking property. More details, in particular concerning the computation of strongest and weakest interpolants, are given in [10, 13].

- For all nodes n, we generate a predicate $P_n(g_{in}, l_{in}, g, l)$ recording a relation between the global/local data g, l at n and the data g_{in}, l_{in} that was valid when entering the procedure that n belongs to. If n_0 corresponds to the entry point of a procedure, we ensure $(g_{in} \leftrightarrow g) \wedge (l_{in} \leftrightarrow l) \models P_{n_0}$.
- If an edge from node n is labeled by a transition rule $Push(g, l, g', l', l'')$ (modeling a call), we generate an interpolant $P_{>n}(g_{in}, l_{in}, g', l', l'')$ s.t. $P_n \wedge Push \models P_{>n}$. Thus, $P_{>n}$ contains information about the arguments given to the callee and the saved local data.
- If an edge from node n' is labeled by transition rule $Pop(g, l, g')$ (a return statement) and n is the node at which the corresponding call took place, we first generate an interpolant $P_{<n}(g_{in}, l_{in}, g')$, effectively a predicate that argues about the effect of the callee, s.t. $P_{n'} \wedge Pop \models P_{<n}$. Then, if n'' is the target node of the edge, we ensure that $P_{>n} \wedge P_{<n} \models P_{n''}$.
- If an edge from n to n' is labeled by an intraprocedural rule R, we ensure $P_n \wedge R \models P_{n'}$, preserving the tracking property.

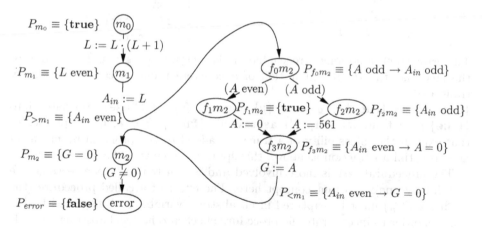

Fig. 4. An example for counterexample DAG with procedure call

Figure 4 gives an example for a (spurious) counterexample DAG to the SPDS in Fig. 2, which contains a procedure call. The left-hand side shows the control flow in the procedure m, which is interrupted by a call to a function f, whose control flow is shown on the right. The predicates associated with the nodes are the weakest interpolants for our example.

5 Computing the Abstract SPDS

In each CEGAR cycle, we derive predicates to refine our abstraction. By the methods of Sect. 4, each predicate naturally belongs to a control point. Thus, as in [6], we maintain for each control point a list of predicates that are useful there. In this section we sketch how to compute an (overapproximating) abstract SPDS given a concrete one along with the predicate lists.

Consider the example SPDS of Sect. 4.1. We derived conciliated interpolants that explain the infeasibility of the error trace. At each control point, we now associate each predicate (except for **true** and **false**) with a boolean variable that reflects the truth of the predicate: $[1] := l_1 \leftrightarrow x$ and $[2] := l_2 \leftrightarrow y$. A *concretization* $[i]$ would be a conjunction of more than one equivalence if the predicate list of control point i consists of more than one predicate.

For the computation of the abstract rules, we use existential abstraction. For instance, the concrete BDD $R \equiv (x' = x) \wedge (y' = x) \wedge (z' = z)$ of the SPDS rule $\langle 1 \rangle \hookrightarrow \langle 2 \rangle$ (R) is replaced by an "abstract" BDD

$$\exists \{x,y,z,x',y',z'\}.((l_2 \leftrightarrow x) \wedge ((x' \leftrightarrow x) \wedge (y' \leftrightarrow x) \wedge (z' \leftrightarrow z)) \wedge (l'_3 \leftrightarrow y')) \equiv l'_2 \leftrightarrow l_1.$$

We can save variables, because we track the predicates only at the control points where they were derived. In our example, we have only one predicate per control point. Therefore, one abstract boolean variable suffices for the abstract SPDS:

$$\langle 0 \rangle \hookrightarrow \langle 1 \rangle \ (l')$$
$$\langle 1 \rangle \hookrightarrow \langle 2 \rangle \ (l' \leftrightarrow l)$$
$$\langle 2 \rangle \hookrightarrow \langle 3 \rangle \ (\neg l)$$

```
0:  l := true
1:  skip
2:  if ¬l then
3:      error
```

The error label is no longer reachable in the abstract program. This is due to the fact that the Hoare annotation of a concrete program can be abstractly translated:
{**true**} $x :=$ **true** $\{x\}$ $y := x$ $\{y\}$ assume($\neg y \wedge z$) {**false**} translates into {**true**} $l :=$ **true** $\{l\}$ skip $\{l\}$ assume($\neg l$) {**false**}. Hence, if the predicates that explain the infeasibility of a trace are added to the program by means of an existential abstraction as above, this spurious trace is excluded.

The procedural case is more involved and is omitted for space reasons. We sketch only one important concept here: The effect of a called procedure (the predicate $P_{<n}$) must be captured in an abstract variable and inspected by the caller in order to incorporate the procedure effect into its local abstract variable values. The details can be found in [13].

6 Case Studies

We have implemented the ideas of this paper in an extension of Moped, in order to decrease resources needed for model-checking SPDSs. Moped accepts multiple input languages including a subset of Java [14]. We did not compare our program with existing CEGAR tools, since the assumptions of tools like BLAST and SLAM (infinite variable ranges, theorem provers) differ significantly from ours (finite variable ranges).

6.1   Locking Example

Figure 5 shows an example of a program where CEGAR clearly pays off, especially when the number of bits for the integer variables ("bit width") is increased. We want to model-check the fact that the assertions in the program always hold. This property is actually independent of the integer variables. Table 1 shows performance results (on an Intel Xeon CPU 2.40GHz and using 8 bits of bit width).

```
struct file {                    rw(file f) {
    bool locked;                     assert(f.locked ∨ f.pos==0);
    int pos;                         f.pos = f.pos + 1;
};                               }
open(file f) {                   main() {
    assert(¬f.locked);               file f1,f2;
    f.locked = true;                 f1.locked = f2.locked = false;
    f.pos = 0;                       open(f1);
}                                    while(*) { open(f2);
close(file f) {                          while(*) { rw(f2); rw(f1); }
    assert(f.locked ∨                    close(f2);
           f.pos==0);                }
    f.locked = false;                close(f1);
}                                }
```

Fig. 5. Locking example (pseudo code)

Table 1. Results of different Moped versions applied on the locking example

	time/s	memory/BDD nodes	# cycles	# gl. var.	# loc. var.
w/o abstraction	460	440482	n/a	n/a	n/a
weakest interp.	0.43	89936	14	13	6
concil. interp.	0.29	80738	10	10	7

Moped without abstraction needs exponential time in the bit width. On the other hand, using weakest or conciliated interpolants, our CEGAR scheme automatically abstracts from the integers and proves the assertions in constantly many refinement cycles. The number of global and local variables in the final abstract program (containing no spurious error traces anymore) is also shown in the table and is also independent of the bit width. Time and memory consumption of the abstract versions grows modestly with the bit width. Conciliated interpolants have the best performance, because the predicate simplification allows them to "discover" that the f.pos fields are irrelevant to the property.

6.2   LinkedList Example

Abstraction can also be useful in positive instances (where the error label is reachable) and in larger programs. As an example, we took Java code for the class LinkedList from a textbook on data structures [15] and modified only the main method simulating a user who accesses class methods randomly:

```
public class LinkedList { ...
    private ListNode header;
    public static void main (String[] args) {
        LinkedList l = new LinkedList();
        while (NONDET()) if (NONDET()) l.insert(null, l.zeroth());
                         else l.remove(null);
        assert(l.header == null);
} }
```

The assertion to be checked is not valid in the class implementation. (This is not a bug though.) Using 4 bits of bit width and 64 bits for Moped's heap representation, Moped without abstraction needs 143 seconds to find an error trace, whereas with CEGAR, only 7.4 seconds are needed (memory consumption: about 2.5 Mio. BDD nodes in both cases). A refinement is not necessary. Moped's performance without abstraction quickly degrades with growing heap size, whereas with abstraction, the influence of the heap size is small.

We also discovered cases where with our predicate generation heuristics, abstraction did not pay off, particularly if complicated properties are checked.

7   Conclusions

Whereas Craig interpolation has been used for CEGAR in SAT solver and theorem prover contexts, we found that it is useful as well to enhance a BDD-based model-checker. Strongest and weakest interpolants, which are defined independently from other tools, form a frame inside which heuristics can be applied to find *good* predicates, e.g. conciliated interpolants. The number of refinement cycles often depends crucially on the quality of the derived predicates.

BDD-based model-checkers record how program states can be reached, to be able to report possible counterexamples. This information can be exploited by a CEGAR scheme to exclude multiple counterexamples at the same time. This can save exponentially (in the size of the DAG) many refinement cycles.

Our CEGAR scheme can achieve large savings, especially if the property to be checked is much simpler than the full functionality of the program. For future research, we plan to further improve predicate generation heuristics. Possibilities include an adapted form of lazy abstraction [2, 13] and the incorporation of dataflow information to detect relevant counterexample parts [16].

Acknowledgement. We thank Dejvuth Suwimonteerabuth for his great support with jMoped.

References

1. Ball, T., Rajamani, S.: Automatically validating temporal safety properties of interfaces. In: SPIN 01. LNCS 2057 (2001) 103–122
2. Henzinger, T., Jhala, R., Majumdar, R., Sutre, G.: Lazy abstraction. In: Proc. POPL'02, ACM Press (2002) 58–70

3. Chaki, S., Clarke, E., Groce, A., Jha, S., Veith, H.: Modular verification of software components in C. In: Proc. 25th International Conference on Software Engineering (ICSE), IEEE Computer Society Press (2003) 385–395

4. Clarke, E., Grumberg, O., Jha, S., Lu, Y., Veith, H.: Counterexample-guided abstraction refinement. In: Proc. CAV'00. LNCS 1855, Springer (2000) 154–169

5. Schwoon, S.: Model-Checking Pushdown Systems. PhD thesis, TU München (2002)

6. Henzinger, T., Jhala, R., Majumdar, R., McMillan, K.: Abstractions from proofs. In: Proc. POPL'04, ACM Press (2004) 232–244

7. Reps, T., Schwoon, S., Jha, S., Melski, D.: Weighted pushdown systems and their application to interprocedural dataflow analysis. Science of Computer Programming **58** (2005) 206–263 Special Issue on the Static Analysis Symposium 2003.

8. Glusman, M., Kamhi, G., Mador-Haim, S., Fraer, R., Vardi, M.: Multiple-counterexample guided iterative abstraction refinement: An industrial evaluation. In: Proceedings of TACAS 2003. LNCS 2619, Springer (2003) 176–191

9. McMillan, K.: Applications of Craig interpolants in model checking. [17] 1–12

10. Esparza, J., Kiefer, S., Schwoon, S.: Abstraction refinement with Craig interpolation and symbolic pushdown systems. Technical Report 2006/02, University of Stuttgart (2006)

11. McMillan, K.: Interpolation and SAT-based Model Checking. In: Proc. CAV'03. LNCS 2725, Springer (2003) 1–13

12. Craig, W.: Linear reasoning. A new form of the Herbrand-Genzen theorem. Journal of Symbolic Logic **22** (1957) 250–268

13. Kiefer, S.: Abstraction refinement for pushdown systems. Master's thesis, University of Stuttgart (2005)

14. Suwimonteerabuth, D., Schwoon, S., Esparza, J.: jMoped: A Java bytecode checker based on Moped. [17] 541–545

15. Weiss, M.: Data Structures and Algorithm Analysis in Java. Addison-W. (1998)

16. Jhala, R., Majumdar, R.: Path slicing. In: Proc. of PLDI '05, ACM (2005) 38–47

17. Proceedings of TACAS 2005. LNCS 3440, Springer (2005)

Author Index

Lecture Notes in Computer Science

For information about Vols. 1–3811

please contact your bookseller or Springer

Vol. 3855: E. A. Emerson, K.S. Namjoshi (Eds.), Verification, Model Checking, and Abstract Interpretation. XI, 443 pages. 2005.

Vol. 3854: I. Stavrakakis, M. Smirnov (Eds.), Autonomic Communication. XIII, 303 pages. 2006.

Vol. 3853: A.J. Ijspeert, T. Masuzawa, S. Kusumoto (Eds.), Biologically Inspired Approaches to Advanced Information Technology. XIV, 388 pages. 2006.

Vol. 3852: P.J. Narayanan, S.K. Nayar, H.-Y. Shum (Eds.), Computer Vision – ACCV 2006, Part II. XXXI, 977 pages. 2006.

Vol. 3851: P.J. Narayanan, S.K. Nayar, H.-Y. Shum (Eds.), Computer Vision – ACCV 2006, Part I. XXXI, 973 pages. 2006.

Vol. 3850: R. Freund, G. Păun, G. Rozenberg, A. Salomaa (Eds.), Membrane Computing. IX, 371 pages. 2006.

Vol. 3849: I. Bloch, A. Petrosino, A.G.B. Tettamanzi (Eds.), Fuzzy Logic and Applications. XIV, 438 pages. 2006. (Sublibrary LNAI).

Vol. 3848: J.-F. Boulicaut, L. De Raedt, H. Mannila (Eds.), Constraint-Based Mining and Inductive Databases. X, 401 pages. 2006. (Sublibrary LNAI).

Vol. 3847: K.P. Jantke, A. Lunzer, N. Spyratos, Y. Tanaka (Eds.), Federation over the Web. X, 215 pages. 2006. (Sublibrary LNAI).

Vol. 3846: H. J. van den Herik, Y. Björnsson, N.S. Netanyahu (Eds.), Computers and Games. XIV, 333 pages. 2006.

Vol. 3845: J. Farré, I. Litovsky, S. Schmitz (Eds.), Implementation and Application of Automata. XIII, 360 pages. 2006.

Vol. 3844: J.-M. Bruel (Ed.), Satellite Events at the MoD-ELS 2005 Conference. XIII, 360 pages. 2006.

Vol. 3843: P. Healy, N.S. Nikolov (Eds.), Graph Drawing. XVII, 536 pages. 2006.

Vol. 3842: H.T. Shen, J. Li, M. Li, J. Ni, W. Wang (Eds.), Advanced Web and Network Technologies, and Applications. XXVII, 1057 pages. 2006.

Vol. 3841: X. Zhou, J. Li, H.T. Shen, M. Kitsuregawa, Y. Zhang (Eds.), Frontiers of WWW Research and Development - APWeb 2006. XXIV, 1223 pages. 2006.

Vol. 3840: M. Li, B. Boehm, L.J. Osterweil (Eds.), Unifying the Software Process Spectrum. XVI, 522 pages. 2006.

Vol. 3839: J.-C. Filliâtre, C. Paulin-Mohring, B. Werner (Eds.), Types for Proofs and Programs. VIII, 275 pages. 2006.

Vol. 3838: A. Middeldorp, V. van Oostrom, F. van Raamsdonk, R. de Vrijer (Eds.), Processes, Terms and Cycles: Steps on the Road to Infinity. XVIII, 639 pages. 2005.

Vol. 3837: K. Cho, P. Jacquet (Eds.), Technologies for Advanced Heterogeneous Networks. IX, 307 pages. 2005.

Vol. 3836: J.-M. Pierson (Ed.), Data Management in Grids. X, 143 pages. 2006.

Vol. 3835: G. Sutcliffe, A. Voronkov (Eds.), Logic for Programming, Artificial Intelligence, and Reasoning. XIV, 744 pages. 2005. (Sublibrary LNAI).

Vol. 3834: D.G. Feitelson, E. Frachtenberg, L. Rudolph, U. Schwiegelshohn (Eds.), Job Scheduling Strategies for Parallel Processing. VIII, 283 pages. 2005.

Vol. 3833: K.-J. Li, C. Vangenot (Eds.), Web and Wireless Geographical Information Systems. XI, 309 pages. 2005.

Vol. 3832: D. Zhang, A.K. Jain (Eds.), Advances in Biometrics. XX, 796 pages. 2005.

Vol. 3831: J. Wiedermann, G. Tel, J. Pokorný, M. Bieliková, J. Štuller (Eds.), SOFSEM 2006: Theory and Practice of Computer Science. XV, 576 pages. 2006.

Vol. 3830: D. Weyns, H. V.D. Parunak, F. Michel (Eds.), Environments for Multi-Agent Systems II. VIII, 291 pages. 2006. (Sublibrary LNAI).

Vol. 3829: P. Pettersson, W. Yi (Eds.), Formal Modeling and Analysis of Timed Systems. IX, 305 pages. 2005.

Vol. 3828: X. Deng, Y. Ye (Eds.), Internet and Network Economics. XVII, 1106 pages. 2005.

Vol. 3827: X. Deng, D.-Z. Du (Eds.), Algorithms and Computation. XX, 1190 pages. 2005.

Vol. 3826: B. Benatallah, F. Casati, P. Traverso (Eds.), Service-Oriented Computing - ICSOC 2005. XVIII, 597 pages. 2005.

Vol. 3824: L.T. Yang, M. Amamiya, Z. Liu, M. Guo, F.J. Rammig (Eds.), Embedded and Ubiquitous Computing – EUC 2005. XXIII, 1204 pages. 2005.

Vol. 3823: T. Enokido, L. Yan, B. Xiao, D. Kim, Y. Dai, L.T. Yang (Eds.), Embedded and Ubiquitous Computing – EUC 2005 Workshops. XXXII, 1317 pages. 2005.

Vol. 3822: D. Feng, D. Lin, M. Yung (Eds.), Information Security and Cryptology. XII, 420 pages. 2005.

Vol. 3821: R. Ramanujam, S. Sen (Eds.), FSTTCS 2005: Foundations of Software Technology and Theoretical Computer Science. XIV, 566 pages. 2005.

Vol. 3820: L.T. Yang, X.-s. Zhou, W. Zhao, Z. Wu, Y. Zhu, M. Lin (Eds.), Embedded Software and Systems. XXVIII, 779 pages. 2005.

Vol. 3819: P. Van Hentenryck (Ed.), Practical Aspects of Declarative Languages. X, 231 pages. 2005.

Vol. 3818: S. Grumbach, L. Sui, V. Vianu (Eds.), Advances in Computer Science – ASIAN 2005. XIII, 294 pages. 2005.

Vol. 3817: M. Faundez-Zanuy, L. Janer, A. Esposito, A. Satue-Villar, J. Roure, V. Espinosa-Duro (Eds.), Nonlinear Analyses and Algorithms for Speech Processing. XII, 380 pages. 2006. (Sublibrary LNAI).

Vol. 3816: G. Chakraborty (Ed.), Distributed Computing and Internet Technology. XXI, 606 pages. 2005.

Vol. 3815: E.A. Fox, E.J. Neuhold, P. Premsmit, V. Wuwongse (Eds.), Digital Libraries: Implementing Strategies and Sharing Experiences. XVII, 529 pages. 2005.

Vol. 3814: M. Maybury, O. Stock, W. Wahlster (Eds.), Intelligent Technologies for Interactive Entertainment. XV, 342 pages. 2005. (Sublibrary LNAI).

Vol. 3813: R. Molva, G. Tsudik, D. Westhoff (Eds.), Security and Privacy in Ad-hoc and Sensor Networks. VIII, 219 pages. 2005.

Vol. 3812: C. Bussler, A. Haller (Eds.), Business Process Management Workshops. XIII, 520 pages. 2006.